Data Compression

Springer
New York
Berlin
Heidelberg
Barcelona
Budapest
Hong Kong
London
Milan
Paris
Santa Clara
Singapore
Tokyo

David Salomon

Data Compression

The Complete Reference

Springer

David Salomon
Department of Computer Science
California State University
Northridge, CA 91330-8281
USA

Library of Congress Cataloging-in-Publication Data
Salomon, D. (David), 1938-
    Data compression / David Salomon.
        p.   cm.
    Includes bibliographical references and index.
    ISBN 0-387-98280-9 (softcover : alk. paper)
    1. Data compression (Computer science)   I. Title.
QA76.9.D33S25   1997
005.74´6—dc21   97-22855

Printed on acid-free paper.

Production managed by Steven Pisano; manufacturing supervised by Jeffrey Taub.
Photocomposed pages prepared from the authors' TeX files.
Printed and bound by Hamilton Printing Co., Rensselaer, NY.
Printed in the United States of America.

9 8 7 6 5 4 3 2 1

ISBN 0-387-98280-9 Springer-Verlag New York Berlin Heidelberg   SPIN 10633122

Preface

Giambattista della Porta, a Renaissance scientist, was the author in 1558 of *Magia Naturalis* (Natural Magic), a book where he discusses many subjects, including demonology, magnetism, and the camera obscura. The book mentions an imaginary device that has since become known as the "sympathetic telegraph." This device was to have consisted of two circular boxes, similar to compasses, each with a magnetic needle. Each box was to be labeled with the 26 letters, instead of the usual directions, and the main point was that the two needles were supposed to be magnetized by the *same lodestone*. Porta assumed that this would somehow coordinate the needles such that when a letter was dialed in one box, the needle in the other box would swing to point to the same letter.

Needless to say, such a device does not work (this, after all, was about 300 years before Samuel Morse), but in 1711 a worried wife wrote to the *Spectator*, a London periodical, asking for advice on how to bear the long absences of her beloved husband. The adviser, Joseph Addison, offered some practical ideas, then mentioned Porta's device, adding that a pair of such boxes might enable her and her husband to communicate with each other even when they "were guarded by spies and watches, or separated by castles and adventures." Mr. Addison then added that, in addition to the 26 letters, the sympathetic telegraph dials should contain, when used by lovers, "several entire words which always have a place in passionate epistlcs." The message "1 love you," for example, would, in such a case, require sending just three symbols instead of ten.

This advice is an early example of *text compression* achieved by using short codes for common messages and longer codes for other messages. Even more importantly, this shows how the concept of data compression comes naturally to people who are interested in communications.

Data compression is the process of converting an input data stream (the source stream or the original raw data) into another data stream (the output, or the compressed, stream) that has a smaller size. A stream is either a file or a buffer in memory. Data compression is popular because of two reasons: (1) People like to accumulate data and hate to throw anything away. No matter how big a storage device one has, sooner or later it is going to overflow. Data compression seems useful because it delays this inevitability. (2) People hate to wait a long time for data transfers. When sitting at the computer, waiting for a Web page to come in, or for a file to download, we naturally feel that anything longer than a few seconds is a long time to wait.

Data compression has come of age in the last 10–15 years. Both the quantity and the quality of the body of literature in this field provides ample proof of this. However, the need for compressing data has been felt in the past, even before the advent of computers, as the following quote suggests:

> I have made this letter longer than usual because I lack the time to make it shorter.
>
>   —Blaise Pascal (1623–1662).

There are many known methods for data compression. They are based on different ideas, are suitable for different types of data, and produce different results, but they are all based on the same principle, namely, they compress data by removing *redundancy* from the original data in the source file. In typical English text, for example, the letter "E" appears very often, while "Z" is rare (Tables 1 and 2). This suggests assigning variable-size codes to the letters, with "E" getting the shortest code and "Z", the longest one. Section 2.1 discusses the theory of information and presents a definition of redundancy. However, even if we don't have a precise definition for this term, it is intuitively clear that a variable-size code has less redundancy than a fixed-size code (or no redundancy at all). Fixed-size codes make it easier to work with text, so they are useful, but they are redundant.

The idea of compression by reducing redundancy suggests the *general law* of data compression, which is to "assign short codes to common events (symbols or phrases) and long codes to rare events." There are many ways to implement this law, and an analysis of any compression method shows that, deep inside, it works by obeying the general law.

The principle of compressing by removing redundancy also answers the following question: "Why is it that an already-compressed file cannot be compressed further?" The answer, of course, is that such a file has little or no redundancy, so there is nothing to remove. An example of such a file is random text. In such text, each letter occurs with equal probability, so assigning them fixed-size codes does not add any redundancy. When such a file is compressed, there is no redundancy to remove. (Another answer is that, if it were possible to compress an already-compressed file, then successive compressions would reduce the size of the file until it becomes a single byte, or even a single bit. This, of course, is ridiculous since a single byte cannot contain the information present in an arbitrarily large file.) The reader should also consult page 283 for an interesting twist on the topic of compressing random data.

Since random data has been mentioned, let's say a few more words about it. Normally it is rare to have a file with random data, but there is one good example— an already-compressed file. Someone owning a compressed file normally knows that it is already compressed and would not try to further compress it but there is one exception—data transmission by modems. Modern modems contain hardware to

A Word to the Wise...

The main aim of the field of data compression is, of course, to develop methods for better and better compression. However, one of the main dilemmas of the *art* of data compression is when to stop looking for better compression. Experience shows that fine-tuning an algorithm to squeeze out the last remaining bits of redundancy from the data gives diminishing returns. Modifying an algorithm to improve compression by 1% may increase the run time by 10%. A good way out of this dilemma was taken by Fiala and Greene (Section 3.6). After developing their main algorithms A1 and A2, they modified them to produce less compression at a higher speed, resulting in algorithms B1 and B2. They then modified A1 and A2 again, but in the opposite direction, sacrificing speed to get a little more compression.

automatically compress the data they send and, if that data is already compressed, there will not be further compression. There may even be expansion. This is why a modem should monitor the compression ratio "on the fly" and, if it is low, should stop compressing and should send the rest of the data uncompressed. The V.42bis protocol (Section 3.17) is a good example of this technique. Section 2.7 dicusses "techniques" for compressing random data.

> The fairest order in the world is a heap of random sweepings.
> —Heraclitus of Ephesus (ca. 550–475 B.C.)

This book discusses many compression methods, some suitable for text and others for graphical data (images). Most methods are classified into three categories: run length encoding (RLE), statistical methods, and dictionary-based (sometimes called LZ) methods. Chapters 1 and 5 describe methods based on other principles.

Before delving into the details, we discuss some commonly used data compression terms.

■ The *compressor* or *encoder* is the program that compresses the raw data in the input stream and creates an output stream with compressed (low-redundancy) data. The *decompressor* or *decoder* converts in the opposite direction. Notice that the term *encoding* is very general and has wide meaning but, since we only discuss data compression, we use the name *encoder* to mean data compressor. The term *codec* is sometimes used to describe both the encoder and decoder. Similarly, the term *companding* is short for "compressing/expanding."

■ For the original input stream we use the terms *unencoded*, *raw*, or *original* data. The contents of the final, compressed stream is the *encoded* or *compressed* data.

Letter	Freq.	Prob.	Letter	Freq.	Prob.
A	51060	0.0721	E	86744	0.1224
B	17023	0.0240	T	64364	0.0908
C	27937	0.0394	I	55187	0.0779
D	26336	0.0372	S	51576	0.0728
E	86744	0.1224	A	51060	0.0721
F	19302	0.0272	O	48277	0.0681
G	12640	0.0178	N	45212	0.0638
H	31853	0.0449	R	45204	0.0638
I	55187	0.0779	H	31853	0.0449
J	923	0.0013	L	30201	0.0426
K	3812	0.0054	C	27937	0.0394
L	30201	0.0426	D	26336	0.0372
M	20002	0.0282	P	20572	0.0290
N	45212	0.0638	M	20002	0.0282
O	48277	0.0681	F	19302	0.0272
P	20572	0.0290	B	17023	0.0240
Q	1611	0.0023	U	16687	0.0235
R	45204	0.0638	G	12640	0.0178
S	51576	0.0728	W	9244	0.0130
T	64364	0.0908	Y	8953	0.0126
U	16687	0.0235	V	6640	0.0094
V	6640	0.0094	X	5465	0.0077
W	9244	0.0130	K	3812	0.0054
X	5465	0.0077	Z	1847	0.0026
Y	8953	0.0126	Q	1611	0.0023
Z	1847	0.0026			
Total	708672	1.0000			

Frequencies and probabilities of the 26 letters in a prepublication version of this book, containing 708,672 letters (upper- and lower case) comprising approximately 145,000 words.

Most, but not all, experts agree that the most common letters in English, in order, are ETAOINSHRDLU (normally written as two separate words ETAOIN SHRDLU). However, see [Fang 66] for a different viewpoint. The most common digrams (2-letter combinations) are TH, TA, RE, IA, AK, EJ, EK, ER, GJ, AD, YU, RX, and KT. The most frequently appearing letters *beginning* words are "spc", and the most frequent final letters are "eys".

Table 1: Probabilities of English Letters.

Char.	Freq.	Prob.	Char.	Freq.	Prob.	Char.	Freq.	Prob.
e	85537	0.099293	x	5238	0.006080	F	1192	0.001384
t	60636	0.070387	|	4328	0.005024	H	993	0.001153
i	53012	0.061537	-	4029	0.004677	B	974	0.001131
s	49705	0.057698	)	3936	0.004569	W	971	0.001127
a	49008	0.056889	(	3894	0.004520	+	923	0.001071
o	47874	0.055573	T	3728	0.004328	!	895	0.001039
n	44527	0.051688	k	3637	0.004222	#	856	0.000994
r	44387	0.051525	3	2907	0.003374	D	836	0.000970
h	30860	0.035823	4	2582	0.002997	R	817	0.000948
l	28710	0.033327	5	2501	0.002903	M	805	0.000934
c	26041	0.030229	6	2190	0.002542	;	761	0.000883
d	25500	0.029601	I	2175	0.002525	/	698	0.000810
m	19197	0.022284	^	2143	0.002488	N	685	0.000795
\	19140	0.022218	:	2132	0.002475	G	566	0.000657
p	19055	0.022119	A	2052	0.002382	j	508	0.000590
f	18110	0.021022	9	1953	0.002267	@	460	0.000534
u	16463	0.019111	[	1921	0.002230	Z	417	0.000484
b	16049	0.018630	C	1896	0.002201	J	415	0.000482
.	12864	0.014933	]	1881	0.002183	O	403	0.000468
1	12335	0.014319	'	1876	0.002178	V	261	0.000303
g	12074	0.014016	S	1871	0.002172	X	227	0.000264
0	10866	0.012613	_	1808	0.002099	U	224	0.000260
,	9919	0.011514	7	1780	0.002066	?	177	0.000205
&	8969	0.010411	8	1717	0.001993	K	175	0.000203
y	8796	0.010211	'	1577	0.001831	%	160	0.000186
w	8273	0.009603	=	1566	0.001818	Y	157	0.000182
$	7659	0.008891	P	1517	0.001761	Q	141	0.000164
}	6676	0.007750	L	1491	0.001731	>	137	0.000159
{	6676	0.007750	q	1470	0.001706	*	120	0.000139
v	6379	0.007405	z	1430	0.001660	<	99	0.000115
2	5671	0.006583	E	1207	0.001401	"	8	0.000009

Frequencies and probabilities of the 93 characters in a prepublication version of this book, containing 861,462 characters.

Table 2: Frequencies and Probabilities of Characters.

■ A *nonadaptive* compression method is rigid and does not modify its operations, its parameters, or its tables in response to the particular data being compressed. Such a method is best used to compress the same type of data. An example is the Group 3 and Group 4 methods for facsimile compression (Section 2.13). They are specifically designed for facsimile compression and would do a poor job compressing any other data. In contrast, an *adaptive* method examines the raw data and modifies its operations and/or its parameters accordingly. An example is the adaptive Huffman method of Section 2.9. Some compression methods use a 2-pass algorithm, where the first pass reads the input stream to collect statistics on the data to be compressed, and the second pass does the actual compressing. Such a method may be called *semi-adaptive*. A data compression method can also be *locally adaptive*, meaning it adapts itself to local conditions in the input stream and varies this adaptation as it moves from area to area in the input. An example of such a method is the move-to-front method (Section 1.5).

The Gold Bug

Here, then, we have, in the very beginning, the groundwork for something more than a mere guess. The general use which may be made of the table is obvious—but, in this particular cipher, we shall only very partially require its aid. As our predominant character is 8, we will commence by assuming it as the "e" of the natural alphabet. To verify the supposition, let us observe if the 8 be seen often in couples—for "e" is doubled with great frequency in English—in such words, for example, as "meet," "fleet," "speed," "seen," "been," "agree," etc. In the present instance we see it doubled no less than five times, although the cryptograph is brief.

—Edgar Allen Poe

■ *Lossy/lossless compression:* Certain compression methods are lossy. They achieve better compression by losing some information. When the compressed stream is decompressed, the result is not identical to the original data stream. Such a method makes sense especially when compressing images or sounds. If the loss of data is small, we may not be able to tell the difference. In contrast, text files, especially files containing computer programs, may become worthless if even one bit gets modified. Such files should only be compressed by a lossless compression method. [Two points should be mentioned regarding text files: (1) If a text file contains the source code of a program, many blank spaces can normally be eliminated, since they are disregarded by the compiler anyway. (2) When the output of a word processor is saved in a text file, the file may contain information about the different fonts used in the text. Such information may be discarded if the user wants to save just the text.]

■ *Symmetrical compression* is the case where the compressor and decompressor use basically the same algorithm but work in "opposite" directions. Such a method makes sense for general work, where the same number of files are compressed as are decompressed. In an asymmetric compression method either the compressor or the decompressor may have to work significantly harder. Such methods have their uses and are not necessarily bad. A compression method where the compressor executes a slow, complex algorithm and the decompressor is simple is a natural choice when files are compressed into an archive, where they will be decompressed and used very often. The opposite case is useful in environments where files are updated all the time and backups made. There is a small chance that a backup file will be used, so the decompressor isn't used very often.

> Like the ski resort full of girls hunting for husbands and husbands hunting for girls, the situation is not as symmetrical as it might seem.
> —Alan Lindsay Mackay, lecture, Birckbeck college, 1964.

▷ **Exercise 1:** Show an example of a compressed file where good compression is important but the speed of both compressor and decompressor isn't important.

■ Most compression methods operate in the *streaming mode* where the codec inputs a byte or several bytes, processes them, and continues until an end-of-file is sensed. Some methods, such as Burrows-Wheeler (Section 5.1), work in *block mode*, where the input stream is read block by block and each block is encoded separately.

■ Most compression methods are *physical*. They only look at the bits in the input stream and ignore the meaning of the data items in the input (e.g., the data items may be words, pixels, or sounds). Such a method translates one bit stream into another, shorter one. The only way to make sense of the output stream (to decode it) is by knowing how it was encoded. Some compression methods are *logical*. They look at individual data items in the source stream and replace common items with short codes. Such a method is normally special-purpose and can be used successfully on certain types of data only. The Pattern Substitution method described on page 10 is an example of a logical compression method.

■ *Compression performance*: Several quantities are commonly used to express the performance of a compression method.

1. The *compression ratio* is defined as

$$\text{Compression ratio} = \frac{\text{size of the output stream}}{\text{size of the input stream}}.$$

A value of 0.6 means that the data occupies 60% of its original size after compression. Values > 1 mean an output stream bigger than the input stream (negative compression). The compression ratio can also be called bpb (bit per bit), since it equals the number of bits in the compressed stream needed, on average, to compress one bit in the input stream. In modern, efficient text compression methods, it makes sense to talk about bpc (bits per character), the number of bits it takes, on average, to compress one character in the input stream.

2. The inverse of the compression ratio is called the *compression factor*:

$$\text{Compression factor} = \frac{\text{size of the input stream}}{\text{size of the output stream}}.$$

In this case values > 1 mean compression and values < 1, mean expansion. This measure seems natural to many people since the bigger the factor, the better the compression.

3. The expression

$$100 \times (1 - \text{compression ratio})$$

is also a reasonable measure of compression performance. A value of 60 means that the output stream occupies 40% of its original size (or that the compression has resulted in savings of 60%).

4. In image compression, the quantity bpp (bits per pixel) is commonly used. It equals the number of bits needed, on average, to compress one pixel of the image.

5. The *compression gain* is defined by

$$100 \log_e \frac{\text{reference size}}{\text{compressed size}},$$

where the reference size is either the size of the input stream or the size of the compressed stream produced by some standard lossless compression method. For small x it is true that $\log_e(1 + x) \approx x$, so a small change in a small compression gain is very similar to the same change in the compression ratio. Because of the use of the log function, two compression gains can be compared simply by subtracting them. The unit of the compression gain is called *percent log ratio* and is denoted $\overset{\circ}{\circ}$.

6. The speed of compression can be measured in *cycles per byte* (CPB). This is the average number of machine cycles it takes to compress one byte. This measure is important when compression is done by special hardware.

■ The *Calgary Corpus* is a set of 18 files traditionally used to test data compression programs. They include text, image, and object files, for a total of more than 3.2 million bytes (Table 3). The corpus can be downloaded by anonymous FTP from `ftp://ftp.cpsc.ucalgary.ca/pub/projects/text.compression.corpus`.

Name	Size	Description	Type
bib	111,261	A bibliography in UNIX *refer* format	Text
book1	768,771	Text of T. Hardy's *Far From the Madding Crowd*	Text
book2	610,856	Ian Witten's *Principles of Computer Speech*	Text
geo	102,400	Geological seismic data	Data
news	377,109	A Usenet news file	Text
obj1	21,504	VAX object program	Obj
obj2	246,814	Macintosh object code	Obj
paper1	53,161	A technical paper in *troff* format	Text
paper2	82,199	Same	Text
pic	513,216	Fax image (a bitmap)	Image
progc	39,611	A source program in C	Source
progl	71,646	A source program in LISP	Source
progp	49,379	A source program in Pascal	Source
trans	93,695	Document teaching how to use a terminal	Text

Table 3: The Calgary Corpus.

■ The *Canterbury Corpus* is another collection of files, introduced in 1997 to provide an alternative to the Calgary corpus for evaluating lossless compression methods. The concerns leading to the new corpus were:

a. The Calgary corpus has been used by many researchers to develop, test and compare many compression methods, and there is a chance that new methods would unintentionally be fine-tuned to that corpus. They may do well on the Calgary corpus documents but poorly on other documents.

b. The Calgary corpus was collected in 1987 and is getting old. "Typical" documents change during a decade (e.g., html documents did not exist until very recently) and any body of documents used for evaluation purposes should be examined from time to time.

c. The Calgary corpus is more or less an arbitrary collection of documents, whereas a good corpus for algorithm evaluation should be selected carefully.

The Canterbury corpus started with about 800 candidate documents, all in the public domain. They were divided into 11 classes, representing different types of documents. A representative "average" document was selected from each class by compressing every file in the class using different methods and selecting the file whose compression was closest to the average (as determined by regression). The corpus is summarized in Table 4 and can be freely obtained by anonymous ftp from `http://www.cosc.canterbury.ac.nz/~tim/corpus/index.html`.

Description	File name	Size (bytes)
English text (*Alice in Wonderland*)	alice29.txt	152,089
Fax images	ptt5	513,216
C source code	fields.c	11,150
Spreadsheet files	kennedy.xls	1,029,744
SPARC executables	sum	38,666
Technical document	lcet10.txt	426,754
English poetry ("Paradise Lost")	plrabn12.txt	481,861
HTML document	cp.html	24,603
LISP source code	grammar.lsp	3,721
GNU manual pages	xargs.1	4,227
English play (*As You Like It*)	asyoulik.txt	125,179
Complete genome of the *E. coli* bacterium	E.Coli	4,638,690
The King James version of the Bible	bible.txt	4,047,392
The CIA World Fact Book	world192.txt	2,473,400

Table 4: The Canterbury Corpus.

The last 3 files constitute the beginning of a random collection of larger files. More files are likely to be added to it.

■ The *probability model*. This concept is important in statistical data compression methods. When such a method is used, a model for the data has to be constructed before compression can begin. A typical model is built by reading the entire input stream, counting the number of times each symbol appears (its frequency of occurrence), and computing the probability of occurrence of each symbol. The data stream is then input again, symbol by symbol, and is compressed using the information in the probability model. A typical model is shown in Table 2.34, page 71.

> In a symbol there is concealment and yet revelation: here therefore, by Silence and by Speech acting together, comes a double significance.
> —Thomas Carlyle (1795–1881)

Reading the entire input stream twice is slow, so practical compression methods use estimates, or adapt themselves to the data as it is being input and compressed. It is easy to input large quantities of, say, English text and calculate the frequencies and probabilities of every character. This information can serve as an approximate model for English text, and can be used by text compression methods to compress any English text. It is also possible to start by assigning equal probabilities to all the symbols in an alphabet, then reading symbols and compressing them, and, while doing that, also count frequencies and change the model as compression goes along. This is the principle behind adaptive compression methods.

The concept of *data reliability* (page 62) is in some sense the opposite of data compression. Nevertheless the two concepts are very often related since any good data compression program should generate reliable code and so should be able to use error-detecting and error-correcting codes. Appendix E is a simple introduction to these codes.

The intended readership of this book is people who have a basic knowledge of computer science; who know something about programming and data structures; who feel comfortable with terms such as *bit, mega, ASCII, file, I/O,* and *binary search*; and who want to understand how data is compressed. The necessary mathematical background is minimal, and is limited to logarithms, matrices, polynomials, differentiation/integration, and the concept of probability. This book is not intended to be a guide to software implementors and contains few programs.

Appendix B is a bibliography of general works on data compression, followed by all the references. In addition, there are short, specialized bibliographies following many sections. The following URLs contain useful lists of data compression pointers:

http://www.sr3.t.u-tokyo.ac.jp/~arimura/compression_links.html and
http://www.internz.com/compression-pointers.html.

The attention symbol on the left is used to draw the reader's attention when important concepts or definitions are introduced.

The notation "␣" is used to indicate a blank space in places where spaces may lead to ambiguity.

The author would like to thank Peter D. Smith for his help. He has read the entire manuscript, corrected many errors, and provided many helpful suggestions and comments. In addition, J. Robert Henderson should be thanked for his mathematical help, and John M. Motil for helpful ideas and comments.

Readers who would like to get an idea of the effort it took to write this book should consult the colophon.

The author welcomes any comments, suggestions and corrections. They should be emailed to `dxs@ecs.csun.edu`.

Bibliography

Fang I. (1966) "It Isn't ETAOIN SHRDLU; It's ETAONI RSHDLC," *Journalism Quarterly* **43**:761–762.

> Some said "John, print it," others said, "Not so;"
> some said, "It might do good," others said, "no."
>
> John Bunyan (1628–1688)

> In the classroom, Grant had tried different comparisons. If you imagined the human lifespan of sixty years was compressed to a day, then eighty million years would still be 3,652 years—older than the pyramids. The velociraptor had been dead a long time.
>
> Michael Crichton, *Jurassic Park*

Contents

Contents

Contents

> I hoped that the contents of his pockets
> might help me to form a conclusion.
>
> Arthur Conan Doyle, *Memoirs of Sherlock Holmes*

1
Basic Techniques

1.1 Intuitive Compression

Data compression is achieved by reducing redundancy but this also makes the data less reliable, more prone to errors. Making data more reliable, on the other hand, is done by adding check bits and parity bits (Appendix E), a process that increases the size of the codes, thereby increasing redundancy. Data compression and data reliability are thus opposites, and it is interesting to note that the latter is a relatively recent field, whereas the former existed even before the advent of computers. The sympathetic telegraph, discussed in the Preface, the Braille code of 1820 (Section 1.1.1), and the Morse code of 1838 (Table 2.1) use simple forms of compression. It therefore seems that reducing redundancy comes naturally to anyone who works on codes, but increasing it is something that "goes against the grain" in humans. This section discusses simple, intuitive compression methods that have been used in the past. Today these methods are mostly of historical interest, since they are generally inefficient and cannot compete with the modern compression methods developed during the last 15–20 years.

1.1.1 Braille

This well-known code, which enables the blind to read, was developed by Louis Braille in the 1820s and is still in common use today, after being modified several times. The Braille code consists of groups (or cells) of 3×2 dots each, embossed on thick paper. Each of the 6 dots in a group may be flat or raised, so the information content of a group is equivalent to 6 bits, resulting in 64 possible groups. Since the letters (Table 1.1), digits, and punctuations don't require all 64 codes, the remaining groups are used to code common words—such as and, for, and of—and common strings of letters—such as ound, ation and th (Table 1.2).

A   B   C   D   E   F   G   H   I   J   K   L   M

N   O   P   Q   R   S   T   U   V   W   X   Y   Z

Table 1.1: The 26 Braille Letters.

and for of the with ch gh sh th

Table 1.2: Some Words and Strings in Braille.

Redundancy in Everyday Situations

Even though we don't increase redundancy in our data unnecessarily, we use redundant data all the time, mostly without noticing it. Here are some examples:

All natural languages are redundant. A portuguese who does not speak Italian may read an Italian newspaper and still understand most of the news because he recognizes the basic form of many Italian verbs and nouns and because most of the text he does not understand is superfluous (i.e., redundant).

PIN is an acronym for "Personal Identification Number," but banks always ask you for your "PIN number." SALT is an acronym for "Strategic Arms Limitations Talks" but TV announcers in the 1970s kept talking about the "SALT Talks." These are just two examples illustrating how natural it is to be redundant in everyday situations. More examples can be found at URL: `http://www.wolfram.com/~lou/puzzles/r.p.answers/languageA13.html`

The amount of compression achieved by Braille is small but important since books in Braille tend to be very large (a single group covers the area of about ten printed letters). Even this modest compression comes with a price. If a Braille book is mishandled or gets old and some dots become flat, serious reading errors may result since every possible group is used. (Brailler, a Macintosh shareware program by Mark Pilgrim, is a good choice for anyone wanting to experiment with Braille.)

1.1.2 Irreversible Text Compression

Sometimes it is acceptable to "compress" text by simply throwing away some information. This is called *irreversible text compression* or *compaction*. The decompressed text will not be identical to the original, so such methods are not general purpose; they can only be used in special cases.

A run of consecutive blank spaces may be replaced by a single space. This may be acceptable in literary texts and in most computer programs, but it should not be used when the data is in tabular form.

In extreme cases all text characters except letters and spaces may be thrown away, and the letters may be case flattened (converted to all lower- or all upper-case). This will leave just 27 symbols, so a symbol can be encoded in 5, instead of the usual 8 bits. The compression ratio is $5/8 = .625$, not bad, but the loss may normally be too great. (An interesting example of similar text is the last chapter of *Ulysses* by James Joyce. In addition to letters, digits, and spaces, it contains only a few punctuation marks.)

▶ **Exercise 1.1:** A character set including the 26 upper-case letters and the space can be coded with 5-bit codes but that would leave five unused codes. Suggest a way to use them.

1.1.3 Ad Hoc Text Compression

Here are some simple, intuitive ideas for cases where the compression must be reversible (lossless).

■ If the text contains many spaces but they are not clustered, they may be removed and their positions indicated by a bit-string that contains a 0 for each text character that's not a space and a 1, for each space. Thus the text

Here are some ideas,

is encoded as the bit-string "00001000100000100000" followed by the text

Herearesomeideas.

If the number of blank spaces is small, the bit-string will be sparse, and the methods of Section 5.4 can be used to compress it considerably.

■ Since ASCII codes are essentially 7 bits long, the text may be compressed by writing 7 bits per character instead of 8 on the output stream. This may be called *packing*. The compression ratio is, of course, $7/8 = 0.875$.

■ If the text includes just upper-case letters, digits, and some punctuations, the old 6-bit CDC display code (Table 1.3) may be used. This code was commonly used in second-generation computers (and even a few third-generation ones). These computers did not need more than 64 characters because they did not have any CRT screens and they sent their output to printers that could only print a limited set of characters.

Bits	Bit positions 210							
543	0	1	2	3	4	5	6	7
0		A	B	C	D	E	F	G
1	H	I	J	K	L	M	N	O
2	P	Q	R	S	T	U	V	W
3	X	Y	Z	0	1	2	3	4
4	5	6	7	8	9	+	-	*
5	/	(	)	$	=	sp	,	.
6	≡	[	]	:	≠	_	∨	∧
7	↑	↓	<	>	≤	≥	¬	;

Table 1.3: The CDC Display Code.

■ Another old code worth mentioning is the Baudot code (Table 1.4). This was a 5-bit code developed by J. M. E. Baudot in about 1880 for telegraph communication. It became popular and, by 1950, was designated as the International Telegraph Code No. 1. It was used in many first- and second-generation computers. The code uses 5 bits per character but encodes more than 32 characters. Each 5-bit code can be the code of two characters, a letter and a figure. To shift between letters and figures the "letter shift" and "figure shift" codes are used.

Using this technique, the Baudot code can represent $32 \times 2 - 2 = 62$ characters (each code can have two meanings except the LS and FS codes). The actual number of characters is, however, less than that since 5 of the codes have one meaning each, and some codes are not assigned.

The Baudot code is not reliable because no parity bit is used. A bad bit can transform a character into another. In particular, a corrupted bit in a shift character causes a wrong interpretation of all the characters following, up to the next shift character.

Letters	Code	Figures	Letters	Code	Figures
A	10000	1	Q	10111	/
B	00110	8	R	00111	-
C	10110	9	S	00101	SP
D	11110	0	T	10101	na
E	01000	2	U	10100	4
F	01110	na	V	11101	'
G	01010	7	W	01101	?
H	11010	+	X	01001	,
I	01100	na	Y	00100	3
J	10010	6	Z	11001	:
K	10011	(	LS	00001	LS
L	11011	=	FS	00010	FS
M	01011	)	CR	11000	CR
N	01111	na	LF	10001	LF
O	11100	5	ER	00011	ER
P	11111	%	na	00000	na

LS, Letter Shift; FS, Figure Shift.
CR, Carriage Return; LF, Line Feed.
ER, Error; na, Not Assigned; SP, Space.

Table 1.4: The Baudot Code.

■ If the data includes just integers, each decimal digit may be represented in 4 bits, with 2 digits packed in a byte. Data consisting of dates may be represented as the number of days since January 1, 1900 (or some other convenient start date). Each date may be stored as a 16- or 24-bit number (2 or 3 bytes). If the data consists of date/time pairs, a possible compressed representation is the number of

---

The 9/19/89 Syndrome

How can a date, such as 11/12/71, be represented inside a computer? One way to do this is to store the number of days since January 1, 1900 in an integer variable. If the variable is 16 bits long (including 15 magnitude bits and one sign bit), it will overflow after $2^{15} = 32k = 32,768$ days, which is September 19, 1989. This is precisely what happened on that day in several computers (see the Jan. 1991 issue of the *Communications of the ACM*). Notice that doubling the size of such a variable to 32 bits would have delayed the problem until after $2^{31} = 2$ giga days have passed, which would occur sometimes in the fall of year 5,885,416.

---

seconds since a convenient start date. If stored as a 32-bit number (4 bytes) it can be sufficient for about 136 years.

■ Dictionary data (or any list sorted lexicographically) can be compressed using the concept of *front compression*. This is based on the observation that adjacent words in such a list tend to share some of the their initial characters. A word can thus be compressed by dropping the n characters it shares with its predecessor in the list and replacing them with n.

a	a
aardvark	1ardvark
aback	1back
abaft	3ft
abandon	3ndon
abandoning	3ndoning
abasement	3sement
abandonment	3ndonment
abash	3sh
abated	3ted
abate	3te
abbot	2bot
abbey	3ey
abbreviating	3reviating
abbreviate	9e
abbreviation	9ion

Table 1.5: Front Compression.

Table 1.5 shows a short example taken from a word list used to create anagrams. It is clear that it is easy to get significant compression with this simple method (see also [Robinson 81] and [Nix 81]).

■ The MacWrite word processor [Young 85] uses a special 4-bit code to code the most common 15 characters "⌴etnroaisdlhcfp" plus an escape code. Any of these 15 characters is encoded by 4 bits. Any other character is encoded as the escape code followed by the 8 bits ASCII code of the character; a total of 12 bits. Each paragraph is coded separately and, if this results in expansion, the paragraph is stored as plain ASCII. One more bit is added to each paragraph to indicate whether or not it uses compression.

1.2 Run Length Encoding

The idea behind this approach to data compression is: If a data item d occurs n consecutive times in the input stream, replace the n occurrences with the single pair nd. n consecutive occurrences of a data item are called a *run length* of n, and this approach to data compression is called *run length encoding* or RLE. We apply this idea first to text compression and then to image compression.

1.3 RLE Text Compression

Just replacing "2.⌴all⌴is⌴too⌴well" with "2.⌴a2⌴is⌴t2⌴we2" will not work. Clearly the decompressor should have a way to tell that the first "2" is part of the text while the other ones are repetition factors for the letters "o" and "l". Even the string "2.⌴a2l⌴is⌴t2o⌴we2l" does not solve this problem (and also does not provide any compression). One way to solve this problem is to precede each repetition with a special escape character. If we use the character "@" as the escape character, then the string "2.⌴a@2l⌴is⌴t@2o⌴we@2l" can be decompressed unambiguously. However, it is longer than the original string, since it replaces two consecutive letters with three characters. We have to adopt the convention that only three or more repetitions of the same character will be replaced with a repetition factor. Figure 1.6a is a flow-chart for such a simple run-length text compressor.

After reading the first character, the character count is 1 and the character is saved. Subsequent characters are compared with the one already saved and, if they are identical to it, the repeat-count is incremented. When a different character is read, the operation depends on the value of the repeat count. If it is small, the saved character is written on the compressed file and the newly read character is saved. Otherwise, an "@" is written, followed by the repeat-count and by the saved character.

Decompression is also straightforward. It is shown in Figure 1.6b. When an "@" is read, the repetition count n and the actual character are immediately read, and the character is written n times on the output stream.

The main problems with this method are the following:

1. In plain English text there are not many repetitions. There are many "doubles" but a "triple" is rare. The most repetitive character is the space. Dashes or asterisks may also repeat sometimes. In mathematical texts, some digits may repeat. The following "paragraph" is a contrived example.

> The abbott from Abruzzi accedes to the demands of all abbesses from Narragansett and Abbevilles from Abyssinia. He will accommodate them, abbreviate his sabbatical, and be an accomplished accessory.

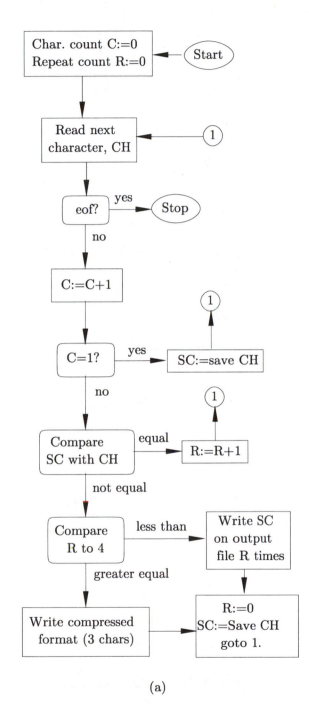

(a)

Figure 1.6: RLE. Part I: Compression.

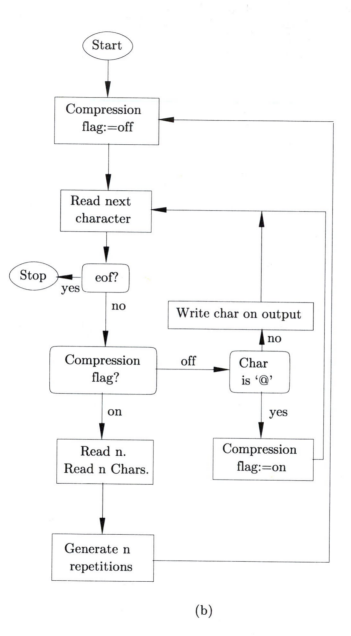

(b)

Figure 1.6: RLE. Part II: Decompression.

2. The character "@" may be part of the text in the input stream, in which case a different escape character must be chosen. Sometimes the input stream may contain every possible character in the alphabet. An example is an object file, the result of compiling a program. Such a file contains machine instructions and can be thought of as a string of bytes that can have any values. The MNP5 method described below and in Section 2.10 provides a solution.

3. Since the repetition count is written on the output stream as a byte, it is limited to counts of up to 255. This limitation can be softened somewhat when we realize that the existence of a repetition count means that there is a repetition (at least three identical consecutive characters). We may adopt the convention that a repeat count of 0 means three repeat characters. This implies that a repeat count of 255 means a run of 258 identical characters.

> There are three kinds of lies: lies, damned lies, and statistics.
> —Mark Twain.

The MNP class 5 method is commonly used for data compression by modems. It has been developed by Microcom, Inc., a maker of modems (MNP stands for Microcom Network Protocol) and it uses a combination of run length and adaptive frequency encoding. The latter technique is described in Section 2.10 but here is how MNP5 solves problem 2 above.

When three or more identical consecutive bytes are found in the input stream, the compressor writes three copies of the byte on the output stream, followed by a repetition count. When the decompressor reads three identical consecutive bytes, it knows that the next byte is a repetition count (which may be 0, indicating just three repetitions). A disadvantage of the method is that a run of three characters in the input stream results in four characters written to the output stream; expansion! A run of four characters results in no compression. Only runs longer than 4 characters get compressed. Another, slight problem is that the maximum count is artificially limited, in MNP5, to 250 instead of 255.

To get an idea of the compression ratios produced by RLE, we assume a string of N characters that needs to be compressed. We assume that the string contains M repetitions of average length L each. Each of the M repetitions is replaced by 3 characters (escape, count, and data), so the size of the compressed string is $N - M \times L + M \times 3 = N - M(L-3)$ and the compression factor is

$$\frac{N}{N - M(L-3)}.$$

(For MNP5 just substitute 4 for 3.) Examples: $N = 1000, M = 10, L = 3$ yield a compression factor of $1000/[1000 - 10(4-3)] = 1.01$. A better result is obtained in the case $N = 1000, M = 50, L = 10$, where the factor is $1000/[1000 - 50(10-3)] = 1.538$.

A variant of run length encoding for text is *Digram Encoding*. This method is suitable for cases where the data to be compressed consists only of certain characters, e.g., just letters, digits, and punctuations. The idea is to identify commonly occurring pairs of characters and to replace a pair with one of the characters that cannot occur in the data (e.g., one of the ASCII control characters). Good results can be obtained if the data can be analyzed beforehand. We know that in plain English certain pairs of characters, such as "E␣", "␣T", "TH", and "␣A", occur often. Other types of data may have different common digrams.

A similar variant is *Pattern Substitution*. This is suitable for compressing computer programs, where certain words, such as `for`, `repeat`, and `print` occur often. Each such word is replaced with a control character or, if there are many such words, with an escape character followed by a code character. Assuming that code "a" is assigned to the word `print`, the text "`m:␣print,b,a;`" will be compressed to "`m:␣@a,b,a;`".

1.3.1 Relative Encoding

This is another variant, sometimes called *differencing* (see [Gottlieb 75]). It is used in cases where the data to be compressed consists of a string of numbers that don't differ by much, or in cases where it consists of strings that are similar to each other. An example of the former is telemetry. The latter case is used in facsimile data compression described in Section 2.13 and also in LZW compression (section 3.9.4).

In telemetry, a sensing device is used to collect data at certain intervals and transmit it to a central location for further processing. An example is temperature values collected every hour. Successive temperatures normally do not differ by much, so the sensor needs to send only the first temperature, followed by differences. Thus the sequence of temperatures $70, 71, 72.5, 73.1, \ldots$ can be compressed to $70, 1, 1.5, 0.6, \ldots$. This compresses the data since the differences are small and can be expressed in fewer bits.

Notice that the differences can be negative and may sometimes be large. When a large difference is found, the compressor sends the actual value of the next measurement instead of the difference. Thus the sequence $110, 115, 121, 119, 200, 202, \ldots$ can be compressed to $110, 5, 6, -2, 200, 2, \ldots$. Unfortunately, we now need to distinguish between a difference and an actual value. This can be done by the compressor creating an extra bit (a flag) for each number sent, accumulating those bits, and sending them to the decompressor from time to time, as part of the transmission. Assuming that each difference is sent as a byte, the compressor should follow (or precede) a group of 8 bytes with a byte consisting of their 8 flags.

Another practical way to send differences mixed with actual values is to send pairs of bytes. Each pair is either an actual 16-bit measurement (positive or negative) or two 8-bit signed differences. Thus actual measurements can be between 0 and $\pm 32K$ and differences can be between 0 and ± 255. For each pair, the compressor creates a flag; 0—if the pair is an actual value, 1—if it is a pair of differences. After 16 pairs are sent, the compressor sends the 16 flags.

Example: The sequence of measurements $110, 115, 121, 119, 200, 202, \ldots$ is sent as $(110), (5, 6), (-2, -1), (200), (2, \ldots)$, where each pair of parentheses indicates a pair of bytes. The -1 has value 11111111_2, which is ignored by the decompressor (it indicates that there is only one difference in this pair). While sending this information, the compressor prepares the flags $01101\ldots$, which are sent after the first 16 pairs.

1.4 RLE Image Compression

RLE is a natural candidate for compressing graphical data. A digital image is made up of small dots called *pixels*. Each pixel can be either one bit, indicating a black or a white dot, or several bits, indicating one of several colors or shades of gray. We assume that the pixels are stored in an array called a *bitmap* in memory, so the bitmap is the input stream for the image. Pixels are normally arranged in the bitmap in scan lines, so the first bitmap pixel is the dot at the top left corner of the image, and the last pixel is the one at the bottom right corner.

Compressing an image using RLE is based on the observation that if we select a pixel in the image at random, there is a good chance that its neighbors will have the same color (see also Sections 4.12 and 4.13). The compressor thus scans the bitmap, row by row, looking for runs of pixels of the same color. If the bitmap starts, e.g., with 17 white pixels, followed by 1 black one, followed by 55 white ones, etc., then only the numbers 17, 1, 55... need be written on the output stream.

The compressor assumes that the bitmap starts with a white pixel. If this is not true, then the bitmap starts with zero white pixels, and the output stream should start with 0. The resolution of the bitmap should also be saved at the start of the output stream.

The size of the compressed stream depends on the complexity of the image. The more detail, the worse the compression. However, Figure 1.7 shows how scan lines go through a uniform area. A line enters through one point on the perimeter of the area and exits through another point, and these two points are not "used" by any other scan lines. It is now clear that the number of scan lines traversing a uniform area is roughly equal to half the length (measured in pixels) of its perimeter. Since the area is uniform, each scan line contributes one number to the output stream. The compression ratio of a uniform area thus roughly equals the ratio

$$\frac{\text{half the length of the perimeter}}{\text{total number of pixels in the area}}.$$

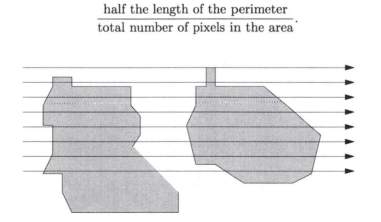

Figure 1.7: Uniform Areas and Scan Lines.

▶ **Exercise 1.2:** What would be the compressed file in the case of the following 6×8 bitmap?

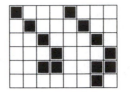

RLE can also be used to compress grayscale images. Each run of pixels of the same intensity (gray level) is encoded as a pair (run length, pixel value). The run length usually occupies one byte, allowing for runs of up to 255 pixels. The pixel value occupies several bits, depending on the number of gray levels (typically between 4 and 8 bits).

Example: An 8-bit deep grayscale bitmap that starts with

$$12, 12, 12, 12, 12, 12, 12, 12, 12, 35, 76, 112, 67, 87, 87, 87, 5, 5, 5, 5, 5, 5, 1 \ldots$$

is compressed into $\boxed{9}$,12,35,76,112,67,$\boxed{3}$,87,$\boxed{6}$,5,1..., where the boxed numbers indicate counts. The problem is to distinguish between a byte containing a grayscale value (such as 12) and one containing a count (such as $\boxed{9}$). Here are some solutions:

1. If the image is limited to just 128 grayscales, we can devote one bit in each byte to indicate whether the byte contains a grayscale value or a count.

2. If the number of grayscale is 256, it can be reduced to 255 with one value reserved as a flag to precede every byte with a count. If the flag is, say, 255, then the sequence above becomes

$$255, 9, 12, 35, 76, 112, 67, 255, 3, 87, 255, 6, 5, 1 \ldots.$$

3. Again, one bit is devoted to each byte to indicate whether the byte contains a grayscale value or a count. This time, however, these extra bits are accumulated in groups of 8, and each group is written on the output stream preceding (or following) the 8 bytes it "belongs to."

Example: the sequence $\boxed{9}$,12,35,76,112,67,$\boxed{3}$,87,$\boxed{6}$,5,1... becomes

$$\boxed{10000010},9,12,35,76,112,67,3,87,\boxed{100\ldots\ldots},6,5,1\ldots.$$

The total size of the extra bytes is, of course, 1/8 the size of the output stream (they contain one bit for each byte of the output stream) so they increase the size of that stream by 12.5%.

4. A group of m pixels that are all different is preceded by a byte with the negative value $-m$. The sequence above is encoded by
$9, 12, -4, 35, 76, 112, 67, 3, 87, 6, 5, ?, 1 \ldots$ (the value of the byte with ? is positive or negative depending on what follows the pixel of 1). The worst case is a sequence of pixels (p_1, p_2, p_2) repeated n times throughout the bitmap. It is encoded as $(-1, p_1, 2, p_2)$, four numbers instead of the original three. If each pixel requires one byte, then the original three bytes are expanded into four bytes. If each pixel requires three bytes, then the original three pixels (comprising 9 bytes) are compressed into $1 + 3 + 1 + 3 = 8$ bytes.

Three more points should be mentioned:

1. Since the run length cannot be 0, it makes sense to write the [run length minus one] on the output stream. Thus the pair $(3, 87)$ means a run of *four* pixels with intensity 87. This way, a run can be up to 256 pixels long.

2. In color images it is common to have each pixel stored as three bytes, representing the intensities of the red, green, and blue components of the pixel. In such a case, runs of each color should be encoded separately. Thus the pixels (171, 85,34), (172, 85, 35) (172, 85, 30), and (173, 85, 33) should be separated into the three sequences (171, 172, 172, 173,...), (85, 85, 85, 85,...), and (34, 35, 30, 33,...). Each sequence should be run-length encoded separately. This means that any method for compressing grayscale images can be applied to color images as well.

3. It is preferable to encode each row of the bitmap individually. Thus if a row ends with four pixels of intensity 87 and the following row starts with 9 such pixels, it is better to write ... 4, 87, 9, 87 ... on the output stream rather than ... 13, 87 .... It is even better to write the sequence ... 4, 87, eol, 9, 87, ..., where "eol" is a special end-of-line code. The reason is that sometimes the user may decide to accept or reject an image just by examining its general shape, without any details. If each line is encoded individually, the decoding algorithm can start by decoding and displaying lines 1, 6, 11, ..., repeat with lines 2, 7, 12, ..., etc. The individual rows of the image are interlaced, and the image is built on the screen gradually, in several steps. This way, it is possible to get an idea of what's in the image at an early stage. Figure 1.8c shows an example of such a scan.

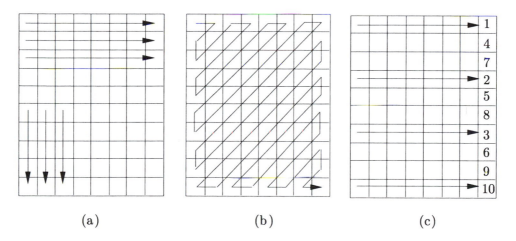

(a)	(b)	(c)

Figure 1.8: RLE Scanning.

Another advantage of this method is to make it possible to extract just part of an encoded image (rows k to l, say). Yet another application is to merge two compressed images without having to decompress them first.

If this idea (encoding each bitmap row individually) is adopted, then the compressed stream must contain information on where each bitmap row starts in the stream. This can be done by writing a header at the start of the stream, that contains a group of 4 bytes (32 bits) for each bitmap row. The kth such group contains the offset (in bytes) from the start of the stream to the start of the information for row k. This increases the size of the compressed stream but may still offer a good trade-off between space (size of compressed stream) and time (time to decide whether to accept or reject the image).

▶ **Exercise 1.3:** There is another, obvious, reason why each bitmap row should be coded individually. What is it?

Disadvantage of image RLE: When the image is modified, the run lengths usually have to be completely redone. The RLE output can sometimes be bigger than pixel-by-pixel storage (i.e., an uncompressed image, a raw dump of the bitmap) for complex pictures. Imagine a picture with many vertical lines. When it is scanned horizontally, it produces very short runs, resulting in very bad compression, or even expansion. A good, practical RLE image compressor should be able to scan the bitmap by rows, columns, or in zig-zag (Figure 1.8a and b) and it may automatically try all three ways on every bitmap compressed to achieve the best compression.

▶ **Exercise 1.4:** Given the following 8×8 bitmap, use RLE to compress it, first row by row, then column by column. Describe the results in detail.

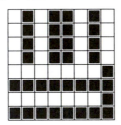

1.4.1 Lossy Image Compression

It is possible to get even better compression ratios if short runs are ignored. Such a method loses information when compressing an image but, sometimes, this is acceptable to the user. (Notable examples where no loss is acceptable are X-ray images and astronomical images taken by large telescopes, where the price of an image is astronomical.)

A lossy run-length encoding algorithm should start by asking the user for the longest run that should still be ignored. If the user says, e.g., 3, then the program merges all runs of 1, 2, or 3 identical pixels with their neighbors. The compressed data "6,8,1,2,4,3,11,2" would be saved, in this case, as "6,8,7 (1+2+4),16 (3+11+2)." This makes sense for large, high-resolution images where the loss of some detail may be invisible to the eye, yet may significantly reduce the size of the output stream (see also Chapter 4).

1.4.2 The BinHex 4.0 Format

BinHex 4.0 is a file format for safe file transfers, designed by Yves Lempereur for use on the Macintosh computer. Before delving into the details of the format, the reader should try to understand why such a format is useful. ASCII is a 7-bit code. Each character is coded into a 7-bit number, which allows for 128 characters in the

ASCII table (Appendix A). The ASCII standard recommends adding an eighth bit as parity to every character for increased reliability. However, the standard does not specify odd or even parity, and many computers simply ignore the extra bit or even set it to 0. As a result, when files are transferred in a computer network, some transfer programs may ignore the eighth bit and transfer just seven bits per character. This isn't so bad when a text file is being transferred but when the file is binary, no bits should be ignored. This is why it is safer to transfer text files, rather than binary files, over computer networks.

The idea of BinHex is to translate any file to a text file. The BinHex program reads an input file (text or binary) and produces an output file with the following format:

1. The comment:

$$(\text{This}_{\sqcup}\text{file}_{\sqcup}\text{must}_{\sqcup}\text{be}_{\sqcup}\text{converted}_{\sqcup}\text{with}_{\sqcup}\text{BinHex}_{\sqcup}\text{4.0})$$

2. A header including the following:

Field	Size
Length of FileName (1–63)	byte
FileName	("Length" bytes)
Version	byte
Type	long
Creator	long
Flags (And $F800)	word
Length of Data Fork	long
Length of Resource Fork	long
CRC	word
Data Fork	("Data Length" bytes)
CRC	word
Resource Fork	("Rsrc Length" bytes)
CRC	word

3. The input file is then read and RLE is used as the first step. Character 90_{16} is used as the RLE marker, and the following examples speak for themselves:

Source string	Packed string
00 11 22 33 44 55 66 77	00 11 22 33 44 55 66 77
11 22 22 22 22 22 22 33	11 22 90 06 33
11 22 90 33 44	11 22 90 00 33 44

(The character 00 indicates no run.) Runs of lengths 3–255 characters are encoded this way.

▶ **Exercise 1.5:** How is the string "11 22 90 00 33 44" encoded?

4. Encoding into 7-bit ASCII characters. The input file is considered a stream of bits. As the file is being read, it is divided into blocks of 6 bits, and each block

is used as a pointer to the BinHex table below. The character that's pointed at in this table is written on the output file. The table is

```
!"#$%&'()*+,-012345689@ABCDEFGHIJKLMNPQRSTUVXYZ['abcdefhijklmpqr
```

The output file is organized in "lines" of 64 characters each (except, perhaps, the last line). Each line is preceded and followed by a pair of colons ":". The following is a quotation from the designer:

"The characters in this table have been chosen for maximum noise protection."

▶ **Exercise 1.6:** Manually convert the string "123ABC" to BinHex. Ignore the comment and the file header.

1.5 Move-to-Front Coding

The basic idea of this method [Bentley 86] is to maintain the alphabet A of symbols as a list where frequently occurring symbols are located near the front. A symbol "s" is encoded as the number of symbols that precede it in this list. Thus if A=("t", "h", "e", "s",...) and the next symbol in the input stream to be encoded is "e", it will be encoded as 2, since it is preceded by two symbols. There are several possible variants to this method, the most basic of them adds one more step: after symbol "s" is encoded, it is moved to the front of list A. Thus after encoding "e", The alphabet is modified to A=("e", "t", "h", "s",...) . This move-to-front step reflects the hope that once "e" has been read from the input stream, it will be read many more times and will, at least for a while, be a common symbol. The move-to-front method is *locally adaptive* since it adapts itself to the frequencies of symbols in local areas of the input stream.

The method thus produces good results if the input stream satisfies this hope, i.e., if it contains concentrations of identical symbols (if the local frequency of symbols changes significantly from area to area in the input stream). We call this "the concentration property." Here are two examples that illustrate the move-to-front idea. Both assume the alphabet A=("a", "b", "c", "d", "m", "n", "o", "p").

1. The input stream "abcddcbamnopponm" is encoded as C=(0,1,2,3,0,1,2,3,4,5,6,7,0,1,2,3) (Table 1.9a). Without the move-to-front step it is encoded as C'=(0,1,2,3,3,2,1,0,4,5,6,7,7,6,5,4) (Table 1.9b). Both C and C' contain codes in the same range [0,7] but the elements of C are smaller on the average, since the input starts with a concentration of "abcd" and continues with a concentration of "mnop". (The average value of C is 2.5, while that of C' is 3.5.)

2. The input stream "abcdmnopabcdmnop" is encoded as C=(0,1,2,3,4,5,6,7,7,7,7,7,7,7,7,7) (Table 1.9c). Without the move-to-front step it is encoded as C'=(0,1,2,3,4,5,6,7,0,1,2,3,4,5,6,7) (Table 1.9d). The average of C is now 5.25, greater than that of C' which is 3.5. The move-to-front rule creates a worse result in this case, since the input does not contain concentrations of identical symbols (it does not satisfy the concentration property).

Before getting into further details, it's important to understand the advantage of having small numbers in C. This feature makes it possible to efficiently encode C with either Huffman or arithmetic coding (Chapter 2). Here are four ways to do this:

a	abcdmnop	0	a	abcdmnop	0	a	abcdmnop	0	a	abcdmnop	0
b	abcdmnop	1	b	abcdmnop	1	b	abcdmnop	1	b	abcdmnop	1
c	bacdmnop	2	c	abcdmnop	2	c	bacdmnop	2	c	abcdmnop	2
d	cbadmnop	3	d	abcdmnop	3	d	cbadmnop	3	d	abcdmnop	3
d	dcbamnop	0	d	abcdmnop	3	m	dcbamnop	4	m	abcdmnop	4
c	dcbamnop	1	c	abcdmnop	2	n	mdcbanop	5	n	abcdmnop	5
b	cdbamnop	2	b	abcdmnop	1	o	nmdcbaop	6	o	abcdmnop	6
a	bcdamnop	3	a	abcdmnop	0	p	onmdcbap	7	p	abcdmnop	7
m	abcdmnop	4	m	abcdmnop	4	a	ponmdcba	7	a	abcdmnop	0
n	mabcdnop	5	n	abcdmnop	5	b	aponmdcb	7	b	abcdmnop	1
o	nmabcdop	6	o	abcdmnop	6	c	baponmdc	7	c	abcdmnop	2
p	onmabcdp	7	p	abcdmnop	7	d	cbaponmd	7	d	abcdmnop	3
p	ponmabcd	0	p	abcdmnop	7	m	dcbaponm	7	m	abcdmnop	4
o	ponmabcd	1	o	abcdmnop	6	n	mdcbapon	7	n	abcdmnop	5
n	opnmabcd	2	n	abcdmnop	5	o	nmdcbapo	7	o	abcdmnop	6
m	nopmabcd	3	m	abcdmnop	4	p	onmdcbap	7	p	abcdmnop	7
	mnopabcd						ponmdcba				
	(a)			(b)			(c)			(d)	

Table 1.9: Encoding With and Without Move-to-Front.

1. Assign Huffman codes to the integers in the range $[0, n]$ such that the smaller integers get the shorter codes. Here is an example of such a code for the integers 0 through 7:

0—0, 1—10, 2—110, 3—1110, 4—11110, 5—111110, 6—1111110, 7—1111111.

2. Assign codes to the integers such that the code of integer $i \geq 1$ is its binary code preceded by $\lfloor \log_2 i \rfloor$ zeros. Table 1.10 shows some examples.

i	Code	Size
1	1	1
2	010	3
3	011	3
4	00100	5
5	00101	5
6	00110	5
7	00111	5
8	0001000	7
9	0001001	7
⋮	⋮	⋮
15	0001111	7
16	000010000	9

Table 1.10: Examples of Variable-Size Codes.

▶ **Exercise 1.7:** What is the total size of the code of i in this case?

3. Use adaptive Huffman coding (Section 2.9).

4. For maximum compression, perform two passes over C, the first pass counting frequencies of codes and the second one doing the actual encoding. The frequencies computed in pass 1 are used to assign Huffman codes to be used later by pass 2.

It can be shown that the move-to-front method performs, in the worst case, slightly worse than Huffman coding. At best, it performs significantly better.

As has been mentioned earlier, it is easy to come up with variations of the basic idea of move-to-front. Here are some of them.

1. Move-ahead-k. The element of A matched by the current symbol is moved ahead k positions instead of all the way to the front of A. The parameter k can be specified by the user, with a default value of either n or 1. This tends to reduce performance (i.e., to increase the average size of the elements of C) for inputs that satisfy the concentration property but works better for other inputs. Notice that assigning $k = n$ is identical to move-to-front. The case $k = 1$ is especially simple since it only requires swapping an element of A with the one preceding it.

▶ **Exercise 1.8:** Use move-ahead-k to encode each of the strings "abcddcbamnop-ponm" and "abcdmnopabcdmnop" twice, with $k = 1$ and $k = 2$.

2. Wait-c-and-move. An element of A is moved to the front only after it has been matched c times to symbols from the input stream (not necessarily c consecutive times). Each element of A should have a counter associated with it, to count the number of matches. This method makes sense in implementations where moving and rearranging elements of A is slow.

3. Normally, a symbol read from the input is a byte. If the input stream consists of text, however, it may make sense to treat each **word**, not each character, as a symbol. Consider the simple case where the input consists of just lower-case letters, spaces, and one end-of-text marker at the end. We can define a word as a string of letters followed by a space or by the end-of-text marker. The number of words in this case can be huge, so the alphabet list A should start empty, and words should be added as they are being input and encoded. We use the text

the␣boy␣on␣my␣right␣is␣the␣right␣boy

as an example.

The first word input is "the". It is not found in A since A is empty, so it is added to A. The encoder emits 0 (the number of words preceding "the" in A) followed by "the". The decoder also starts with an empty A. The 0 tells it to select the first word in A but, since A is empty, the decoder knows to expect the 0 to be followed by a word. It adds this word to A.

The next word is "boy". It is added to A, so A=("the", "boy") and the encoder emits "1boy". The word "boy" is moved to the front of A, so A=("boy", "the"). The decoder reads the 1, which refers to the second word of A, but the decoder's A has only one word in it so far. The decoder thus knows that a new word must follow the 1. It reads this word and adds it to the front of A. Table 1.11 summarizes the encoding steps for this example.

Word	A (before adding)	A (after adding)	Code emitted
the	()	(the)	0the
boy	(the)	(the, boy)	1boy
on	(boy, the)	(boy, the, on)	2on
my	(on, boy, the)	(on, boy, the, my)	3my
right	(my, on, boy, the)	(my, on, boy, the, right)	4right
is	(right, my, on, boy, the)	(right, my, on, boy, the, is)	5is
the	(is, right, my, on, boy, the)	(is, right, my, on, boy, the)	5
right	(the, is, right, my, on, boy)	(the, is, right, my, on, boy)	2
boy	(right, the, is, my, on, boy)	(right, the, is, my, on, boy)	5
	(boy, right, the, is, my, on)		

Table 1.11: Encoding Multiple-Letter Words.

List A may grow very large in this variant but any practical implementation has to limit its size. This is why the last item of A (the least recently used item) has to be deleted when A exceeds its size limit. This is another difference between this variant and the basic move-to-front method.

▶ **Exercise 1.9:** Decode "the␣boy␣on␣my␣right␣is␣the␣right␣boy" and summarize the steps in a table.

> "Why," said the Dodo, "the best way to explain it is to do it."
> —Lewis Carroll (1832–1898)

Bibliography

Bentley, J. L. et al. (1986) "A Locally Adaptive Data Compression Algorithm," *Communications of the ACM* **29**(4):320–330, April.

Gottlieb, D., et al (1975) *A Classification of Compression Methods and their Usefulness for a Large Data Processing Center*, Procedings of National Computer Conference 44:453–458.

Nix, R. (1981) "Experience With a Space Efficient Way to Store a Dictionary," *Communications of the ACM* **24**(5):297–298.

Robinson, P., and D. Singer (1981) "Another Spelling Correction Program," *Communications of the ACM* **24**(5):296–297.

Young, D. M. (1985) "MacWrite File Format," *Wheels for the Mind* 1:34, Fall.

> Compression algorithms are often described as squeezing, squashing, crunching or imploding data, but these are not very good descriptions of what is actually happening.
>
> James D. Murray and William Vanryper (1994)

2
Statistical Methods

The different RLE variants have one common feature, they assign fixed-size codes to the symbols (characters or pixels) they operate on. In contrast, statistical methods use variable-size codes, with the shorter codes assigned to symbols or groups of symbols that appear more often in the data (have a higher probability of occurrence). Samuel Morse used this property when he designed his well-known telegraph code (Table 2.1). The two main problems with variable-size codes are (1) assigning codes that can be decoded unambiguously and (2) assigning codes with the minimum average size.

It is interesting to note that the first version of the telegraph, developed by Morse during a transatlanic voyage in 1832, was more complex than the version he settled on in 1843. The first version sent short and long dashes that were received and drawn on a strip of paper, where sequences of those dashes represented numbers. Each word (not each letter) was assigned a code number, and Morse produced a code book (or dictionary) of those codes in 1837. This first version was thus a primitive form of compression. Morse later abandoned this version in favor of his famous dots and dashes, developed together with Alfred Vail.

Most of this chapter is devoted to the different algorithms (Shannon-Fano, Huffman, arithmetic coding, and others). However, we start with a short presentation of important concepts from *information theory*. These lead to a definition of redundancy, so that later we can clearly see and calculate how redundancy is reduced, or eliminated, by the different methods.

2.1 Information Theory Concepts

We intuitively know what information is. We constantly receive and send information in the form of text, speech, and images. We also feel that information is an elusive, non-mathematical quantity that cannot be precisely defined and measured. The standard dictionary definitions of information are: (1) Knowledge derived from study, experience, or instruction. (2) Knowledge of a specific event or situation; in-

A	.-	N	-.	1	.----	Period	.-.-.-
B	-...	O	---	2	..---	Comma	--..--
C	-.-.	P	.--.	3	...--	Colon	---...
Ch	----	Q	--.-	4	....-	Question mark	..--..
D	-..	R	.-.	5	.....	Apostrophe	.----.
E	.	S	...	6	-....	Hyphen	-....-
F	..-.	T	-	7	--...	Dash	-..-.
G	--.	U	..-	8	---..	Parentheses	-.--.-
H	....	V	...-	9	----.	Quotation marks	.-..-.
I	..	W	.--	0	-----		
J	.---	X	-..-				
K	-.-	Y	-.--				
L	.-..	Z	--..				
M	--						

If the duration of a dot is taken to be one unit, then that of a dash is three units. The space between the dots and dashes of one character is one unit, between characters is three units, and between words six units (five for automatic transmission). To indicate that a mistake has been made and for the receiver to delete the last word, send "........" (eight dots).

The first message Morse sent with his new code was "What hath God wrought!" (between Washington and Baltimore, in 1844).

Table 2.1: The Morse Code for English.

telligence. (3) A collection of facts or data. (4) The act of informing or the condition of being informed; communication of knowledge.

Imagine a person who does not know what information is. Would those definitions make it clear to them? Probably not.

The importance of information theory is that it quantifies information. It shows how to measure information, so that we can answer the question "how much information is included in this piece of data?" with a precise number! Quantifying information is based on the observation that the information contents of a message is equivalent to the amount of *surprise* in the message. If I tell you something that you already know (e.g., "you and I work here"), I haven't given you any information. If I tell you something new (e.g., "we both have got an increase"), I have given you some information. If I tell you something that really surprises you (e.g., "only I have got an increase"), I have given you more information, regardless of the number of words I have used, and of how you feel about my information.

We start with a simple, familiar event that's easy to analyze namely, the toss of a coin. There are two results, so the result of any toss is initially uncertain. We have to actually throw the coin in order to resolve the uncertainty. The result of the toss is heads or tails, which can also be expressed as a yes or no, or as a 0 or 1; a bit.

A single bit resolves the uncertainty in the toss of a coin. What's important in this example is that it can easily be generalized. Many real-life problems can be resolved, and their solutions expressed, by means of several bits. The principle of doing so is to find the minimum number of yes/no questions that must be answered in order to arrive at the result. Since the answer to a yes/no question can be expressed with 1 bit, the number of questions will be the number of bits it takes to express the information contained in the result.

A slightly more complex example is a deck of 64 cards. For simplicity let's ignore their traditional names and simply number them 1 to 64. Consider the event of **A** drawing one card and **B** having to guess what it was. The guess is a number between 1 and 64. What is the minimum number of yes/no questions that are necessary? Those who are familiar with the technique of binary search know the answer. Using this technique, **B** should divide the range 1–64 in two, and should start by asking "is the result between 1 and 32?" If the answer is No, then the result is in the range 33 to 64. This range is then divided by two and **B**'s next question should be "is the result between 33 and 48?" This process continues until the range used by **B** reduces to a single number.

It does not take much to see that exactly six questions are necessary to get at the result. This is because 6 is the number of times 64 can be divided in half. Mathematically, this is equivalent to writing $6 = \log_2 64$. This is why the **logarithm** is the mathematical function that expresses information.

Another approach to the same problem is to ask the question "given a non-negative integer N, how many digits does it take to express it?" The answer, of course, depends on N. The greater N, the more digits are necessary. The first 100 non-negative integers (0 to 99) can be expressed by two decimal digits. The first 1000 such integers can be expressed by three digits. Again it does not take long to see the connection. The number of digits required to represent N equals approximately $\log N$. The base of the logarithm is the same as the base of the digits. For decimal digits, use base 10; for binary ones (bits) use base 2. If we agree that the number of digits it takes to express N equals the information contents of N, then again the logarithm is the function that gives us a measure of the information.

▸ **Exercise 2.1:** What is the precise size, in bits, of the binary integer i?

Here is another approach to quantifying information. We are all familiar with the ten decimal digits. We know that the value of a digit in a number depends on its position. Thus the value of the digit 4 in the number 14708 is 4×10^3 or 4000 since it is in position 3 (positions are numbered from right to left, starting from 0). We are also familiar with the two binary digits (bits) 0 and 1. The value of a bit in a binary number similarly depends on its position, except that powers of 2 are used. Mathematically there is nothing special about 2 or 10. We can use the number 3 as the basis of our arithmetic. This would require the three digits, 0, 1, and 2 (we might call them *trits*). A trit t at position i would have a value of $t \times 3^i$.

▸ **Exercise 2.2:** Actually, there is something special about 10. We use base-10 numbers since we have ten fingers. There is also something special about the use of 2 as the basis for a number system. What is it?

Given a decimal (base 10) or a ternary (base 3) number with k digits, a natural question is: how much information is included in this k-digit number? We answer this by calculating how many bits it takes to express the same number. Assuming that the answer is x, then $10^k - 1 = 2^x - 1$. This is because $10^k - 1$ is the largest

k-digit decimal number and $2^x - 1$ is the largest x-bit binary number. Solving the equation above for x as the unknown is easily done using logarithms and yields

$$x = k \frac{\log 10}{\log 2}.$$

We can use any base for the logarithm, as long as we use the same base for log 10 and log 2. Selecting base 2 simplifies the result, which becomes $x = k \log_2 10 \approx 3.32k$. This shows that the information included in one decimal digit equals that contained in about 3.32 bits. In general, given numbers in base-n, we can write $x = k \log_2 n$, which expresses the fact that the information included in one base-n digit equals that included in $\log_2 n$ bits.

▸ **Exercise 2.3:** How many bits does it take to express the information included in one trit?

We now turn to a transmitter, a piece of hardware that can transmit data over a communications line (a channel). In practice, such a transmitter sends binary data (a modem is a good example). However, in order to obtain general results, we assume that the data is a string made up of occurrences of the n symbols a_1 through a_n. Such a set is an n-symbol alphabet. Since there are n symbols, we can think of each as a base-n digit, which means that it is equivalent to $\log_2 n$ bits. As far as the hardware is concerned, this means that it must be able to transmit at n discrete levels.

If the transmitter takes $1/s$ time units to transmit a single symbol, then the speed of the transmission is s symbols per time unit. A common example is $s = 28,800$ baud (*baud* is the term for "bits per second"), which translates to $1/s \approx 34.7 \mu\text{sec}$ (where the Greek letter μ stands for "micro" and $1\mu\text{sec} = 10^{-6}\text{sec}$). In one time unit the transmitter can send s symbols which, as far as information contents is concerned, is equivalent to $s \log_2 n$ bits. We denote by $H = s \log_2 n$ the amount of information transmitted each time unit.

The next step is to express H in terms of the probabilities of occurrence of the n symbols. We assume that symbol a_i occurs in the data with probability P_i. The sum of the probabilities equals, of course, unity: $P_1 + P_2 + \cdots + P_n = 1$. In the special case where all n probabilities are equal $P_i = P$, we get $1 = \sum P_i = nP$, implying that $P = 1/n$, and resulting in $H = s \log_2 n = s \log_2(1/P) = -s \log_2 P$. In general, the probabilities are different and we want to express H in terms of all of them. Since symbol a_i occurs P_i percent of the time in the data, it occurs on the average sP_i times each time unit, so its contribution to H is $-sP_i \log_2 P_i$. The sum of the contributions of all n symbols to H is thus $H = -s \sum_1^n P_i \log_2 P_i$.

As a reminder, H is the amount of information, in bits, sent by the transmitter in one time unit. The amount of information contained in one, base-n symbol is thus H/s (because it takes time $1/s$ to transmit one symbol) or $-\sum_1^n P_i \log_2 P_i$. This quantity is called the *entropy* of the data being transmitted. In analogy we can define the entropy of a single symbol a_i as $-P_i \log_2 P_i$. This is the smallest number of bits needed, on the average, to represent the symbol.

(Information theory was developed, in the late 1940s, by Claude Shannon, of Bell labs, and he selected the term *entropy* since this term is used in thermodynamics to indicate the amount of disorder in a physical system.)

The entropy of the data depends on the individual probabilities P_i, and is smallest when all n probabilities are equal. This fact is used to define the redundancy R in the data. It is defined as the difference between the entropy and the smallest entropy. Thus

$$R = \left(-\sum_1^n P_i \log_2 P_i \right) - \log_2(1/P) = -\sum_1^n P_i \log_2 P_i + \log_2 n.$$

The test for fully compressed data (no redundancy) is thus $\sum_1^n P_i \log_2 P_i = \log_2 n$.

▶ **Exercise 2.4:** Analyze the entropy of a two-symbol set.

2.2 Variable-Size Codes

Consider the four symbols a_1, a_2, a_3, and a_4. If they appear in our data strings with equal probability ($= 0.25$), then the entropy of the data is $-4(0.25 \log_2 0.25) = 2$. Two is the smallest number of bits needed, on the average, to represent each symbol in this case. We can simply assign our symbols the four 2-bit codes 00, 01, 10, and 11.

Next, consider the case where the four symbols occur with different probabilities as shown in Table 2.2, where a_1 appears in the data (on the average) about half the time, a_2 and a_3 have equal probabilities, and a_4 is rare. In this case, the data has entropy $-(0.49 \log_2 0.49 + 0.25 \log_2 0.25 + 0.25 \log_2 0.25 + 0.01 \log_2 0.01) \approx -(-0.050 - 0.5 - 0.5 - 0.066) = 1.57$. The smallest number of bits needed, on average, to represent each symbol is thus 1.57.

Symbol	Prob.	Code1	Code2
a_1	.49	1	1
a_2	.25	01	01
a_3	.25	010	000
a_4	.01	001	001

Table 2.2: Variable-Size Codes.

If we again assign our symbols the four 2-bit codes 00, 01, 10 and 11, the redundancy would be $R = -1.57 + \log_2 4 = 0.43$. This suggests assigning *variable-size codes* to the symbols. Code1 of Table 2.2 is designed such that the most common symbol, a_1, is assigned the shortest code. When long data strings are transmitted using Code1, the average size (the number of bits per symbol) is $1 \times 0.49 + 2 \times 0.25 + 3 \times 0.25 + 3 \times 0.01 = 1.77$, which is very close to the minimum. The redundancy in this case is $R = 1.77 - 1.57 = 0.2$ bits per symbol. An interesting example is the 20-symbol string $a_1 a_3 a_2 a_1 a_3 a_3 a_4 a_2 a_1 a_1 a_2 a_2 a_1 a_1 a_3 a_1 a_1 a_2 a_3 a_1$, where the four symbols occur with (approximately) the right frequencies. Encoding this string with Code1 yields the 37 bits:

1|010|01|1|010|010|001|01|1|1|01|01|1|1|010|1|1|01|010|1

(without the vertical bars). Using 37 bits to encode 20 symbols yields an average size of 1.85 bits/symbol, not far from the calculated average size. (The reader should bear in mind that our examples are short. To get results close to the best that's theoretically possible, an input stream with at least thousands of symbols is needed.)

However, when we try to decode the binary string above, it becomes obvious that Code1 is bad. The first bit is 1 and, since only a_1 has this code, it must be the first symbol. The next bit is 0, but the codes of a_2, a_3, and a_4 all start with a 0, so the decoder has to read the next bit. It is 1, but the codes of both a_2 and a_3 start with 01. The decoder does not know whether to decode the string as $1|010|01\ldots$ which is $a_1 a_3 a_2 \ldots$ or as $1|01|001\ldots$ which is $a_1 a_2 a_4 \ldots$. Code1 is thus *ambiguous*. In contrast Code2, which has the same average size as code1, can be decoded unambiguously.

The property of Code2 that makes it so much better than Code1 is called the *prefix property*. This property requires that once a certain bit pattern has been assigned as the code of a symbol, no other codes should start with that pattern (the pattern cannot be the *prefix* of any other code). Once the string "1" was assigned as the code of a_1, no other codes could start with 1 (i.e., they all had to start with 0). Once "01" was assigned as the code of a_2, no other codes could start with 01 (they all had to start with 00). This is why the codes of a_3 and a_4 had to start with 00. Naturally they became 000 and 001.

Designing variable-size codes is thus done by following two principles: (1) assign short codes to the more frequent symbols and (2) obey the prefix property. Following these principles produces short, unambiguous codes, but not necessarily the best (i.e., shortest) ones. In addition to these principles, an algorithm is needed that always produces the shortest code (the one with minimum redundancy). The only input to such an algorithm is the frequencies (or the probabilities) of the symbols in the alphabet. Two such algorithms, the Shannon-Fano method and the Huffman method, are discussed in Sections 2.6 and 2.8.

(It should be noted that not all statistical compression methods assign variable-size codes to the individual symbols of the alphabet. A notable exception is arithmetic coding, Section 2.14.)

> He uses statistics as a drunken man uses lamp-posts—for support rather than illumination.
>
>   —Andrew Lang (1844–1912), *Treasury of Humorous Quotations*

2.3 Prefix Codes

A prefix code is a variable-size code that satisfies the prefix property. The binary representation of the integers does not satisfy the prefix property. Another disadvantage of this representation is that the size n of the set of integers has to be known in advance since it determines the code size, which is $\lfloor 1 + \log_2 n \rfloor$. In some applications, a prefix code is required to code a set of integers whose size is not known in advance. Several such codes, most of which are due to P. Elias [Elias 75], are presented here.

2.3.1 The Unary Code

The *unary code* of the non-negative integer n is defined as $n - 1$ ones followed by one 0 (Table 2.3) or, alternatively, as $n - 1$ zeros followed by a single one. The length of the unary code for the integer n is $\lfloor \log_2 n \rfloor + 1$ bits.

n	Code	Alt. Code
1	0	1
2	10	01
3	110	001
4	1110	0001
5	11110	00001

Table 2.3: Some Unary Codes.

▶ **Exercise 2.5:** Discuss the use of the unary code as a variable-size code.

It is also possible to define general unary codes, also known as start-step-stop codes. Such a code depends on a triplet (start, step, stop) of integer parameters and is defined by: codewords are created to code symbols used in the data, such that the nth codeword consists of n ones, followed by one 0, followed by all the combinations of a bits where $a = \text{start} + n \times \text{step}$. If $a = \text{stop}$ then the single 0 preceding the a bits is dropped. The number of codes for a given triplet is finite and depends on the choice of parameters. Tables 2.4 and 2.5 show the 680 codes of (3,2,9) and the 2044 codes of (2,1,10). These codes are discussed in Section 3.6 in connection with the LZFG compression method.

The number of different general unary codes is

$$\frac{2^{\text{stop}+\text{step}} - 2^{\text{start}}}{2^{\text{step}} - 1}.$$

Notice that this expression increases exponentially with parameter "stop," so large sets of these codes can be generated with small values of the three parameters.

▶ **Exercise 2.6:** What codes are defined by the parameters $(n, 1, n)$ and what by $(0, 0, \infty)$?

▶ **Exercise 2.7:** How many codes are produced by the triplet $(1, 1, 30)$?

▶ **Exercise 2.8:** Develop the general unary code for (10,2,14).

2.3.2 Other Prefix Codes

Four more prefix codes are described in this section. We use B(n) to denote the binary representation of integer n. Thus $|\text{B(n)}|$ is the length, in bits, of this representation. We also use $\bar{\text{B}}(n)$ to denote B(n) without its most significant bit (which is always 1).

Code C_1 is made of two parts. To code the positive integer n we first generate the unary code of $|\text{B(n)}|$ (the size of the binary representation of n), then append $\bar{\text{B}}(n)$ to it. An example is $n = 16 = 10000_2$. The size of B(16) is 5, so we start with the unary code 11110 (or 00001) and append $\bar{\text{B}}(16)$=0000. The complete code is

n	$a =$ $3 + n \cdot 2$	nth codeword	Number of codewords	Range of integers
0	3	$0xxx$	$2^3 = 8$	0–7
1	5	$10xxxxx$	$2^5 = 32$	8–39
2	7	$110xxxxxxx$	$2^7 = 128$	40–167
3	9	$111xxxxxxxxx$	$2^9 = 512$	168–679
		Total	680	

Table 2.4: The General Unary Code (3,2,9).

n	$a =$ $2 + n \cdot 1$	nth codeword	Number of codewords	Range of integers
0	2	$0xx$	4	0–3
1	3	$10xxx$	8	4–11
2	4	$110xxxx$	16	12–27
3	5	$1110xxxxx$	32	28–59
		$\cdots$		$\cdots$
8	10	$\underbrace{11...1}_{8}\underbrace{xx...x}_{10}$	1024	1020–2043
		Total	2044	

Table 2.5: The General Unary Code (2,1,10).

thus 11110|0000 (or 00001|0000). Another example is $n = 5 = 101_2$ whose code is 110|01. The length of $C_1(n)$ is $2\lfloor \log_2 n \rfloor + 1$ bits. Notice that this code is identical to the general unary code $(0, 1, \infty)$.

Code C_2 is a rearrangement of C_1 where each of the $\lfloor \log_2 n \rfloor$ bits of the first part (the unary code) is followed by one of the bits of the second part. Thus code $C_2(16) = 101010100$ and $C_2(5) = 10110$.

Code C_3 starts with $|B(n)|$ coded in C_2, followed by $\bar{B}(n)$. Thus 16 is coded as $C_2(5) = 11101$ followed by $\bar{B}(16)=0000$, and 5 is coded as code $C_2(3) = 110$ followed by $\bar{B}(5)=01$. The size of $C_3(n)$ is $1 + \lfloor \log_2 n \rfloor + 2\lfloor \log_2(1 + \lfloor \log_2 n \rfloor) \rfloor$.

Code C_4 is multi-part. We start with $B(n)$. To the left of this we write the binary representation of $|B(n)| - 1$ (the length of n, minus 1). This continues recursively, until a 2-bit number is written. A zero is then added to the right of the entire number, to make it decodable. To encode 16, we start with 10000, add $|B(16)| - 1 = 4 = 100_2$ to the left, then $|B(4)| - 1 = 2 = 10_2$ to the left of that and finally, a zero on the right. The result is 10|100|10000|0. To encode 5, we start with 101, add $|B(5)| - 1 = 2 = 10_2$ to the left, and a zero on the right. The result is 10|101|0.

▶ **Exercise 2.9:** How does the zero on the right make the code decodable?

Table 2.6 shows examples of the four codes above as well as B(n) and $\bar{B}$(n). The lengths of the four codes shown in the table increases as $\log_2 n$, in contrast to the length of the unary code, which increases as n. These codes are therefore a good choice in cases where the data consists of integers n satisfying $P(n) \approx 1/n$.

n	Unary	$B(n)$	$\overline{B}(n)$	C_1	C_2	C_3	C_4
1	0	1		1|	1	1|	0
2	10	10	0	10|0	100	100|0	10|0
3	110	11	1	10|1	110	100|1	11|0
4	1110	100	00	110|00	10100	110|00	10|100|0
5	11110	101	01	110|01	10110	110|01	10|101|0
6	111110	110	10	110|10	11100	110|10	10|110|0
7	...	111	11	110|11	11110	110|11	10|111|0
8		1000	000	1110|000	1010100	10100|000	11|1000|0
9		1001	001	1110|001	1010110	10100|001	11|1001|0
10		1010	010	1110|010	1011100	10100|010	11|1010|0
11		1011	011	1110|011	1011110	10100|011	11|1011|0
12		1100	100	1110|100	1110100	10100|100	11|1100|0
13		1101	101	1110|101	1110110	10100|101	11|1101|0
14		1110	110	1110|110	1111100	10100|110	11|1110|0
15		1111	111	1110|111	1111110	10100|111	11|1111|0
16		10000	0000	11110|0000	101010100	10110|0000	10|100|10000|0
31		11111	1111	11110|1111	111111110	10110|1111	10|100|11111|0
32		100000	00000	111110|00000	10101010100	11100|00000	10|101|100000|0
63		111111	11111	111110|11111	11111111110	11100|11111	10|101|111111|0
64		1000000	000000	1111110|000000	1010101010100	11110|000000	10|110|1000000|0
127		1111111	111111	1111110|111111	1111111111110	11110|111111	10|110|1111111|0
128		10000000	0000000	11111110|0000000	101010101010100	1010100|0000000	10|111|10000000|0
255		11111111	1111111	11111110|1111111	111111111111110	1010100|1111111	10|111|11111111|0

Table 2.6: Some Prefix Codes.

n	Unary	C_1	C_3
1	0.5	0.5000000	
2	0.25	0.1250000	0.2500000
3	0.125	0.0555556	0.0663454
4	0.0625	0.0312500	0.0312500
5	0.03125	0.0200000	0.0185482
6	0.015625	0.0138889	0.0124713
7	0.0078125	0.0102041	0.0090631
8	0.00390625	0.0078125	0.0069444

Table 2.7: Ideal Probabilities of Eight Integers for Three Codes.

Specifically, the length L of the unary code of n is $L = n = \log_2 2^n$, so it is ideal for the case where $P(n) = 2^{-L} = 2^{-n}$. The length of code $C_1(n)$ is $L = 1 + 2\lfloor \log_2 n \rfloor = \log_2 2 + \log_2 n^2 = \log_2(2n^2)$, so it is ideal for the case where

$$P(n) = 2^{-L} = \frac{1}{2n^2}.$$

The length of code $C_3(n)$ is

$$L = 1 + \lfloor \log_2 n \rfloor + 2\lfloor \log_2(1 + \lfloor \log_2 n \rfloor) \rfloor = \log_2 2 + 2\lfloor \log \log_2 2n \rfloor + \lfloor \log_2 n \rfloor,$$

so it is ideal for the case where

$$P(n) = 2^{-L} = \frac{1}{2n(\log_2 n)^2}.$$

Table 2.7 shows the ideal probabilities that the first eight positive integers should have for the three codes above to be used.

More prefix codes for the positive integers, appropriate for special applications, may be designed by the following general approach. Select positive integers v_i and combine them in a list V (which may be finite or infinite according to needs). The code of the positive integer n is prepared in the three steps:

1. Find k such that

$$\sum_{i=1}^{k-1} v_i < n \le \sum_{i=1}^{k} v_i.$$

2. Compute the difference

$$d = n - \sum_{i=1}^{k-1} v_i - 1.$$

The largest value of n is $\sum_1^k v_i$, so the largest value of d is $\sum_i^k v_i - \sum_1^{k-1} v_i - 1 = v_k - 1$, a number that can be written in $\lceil \log_2 v_k \rceil$ bits. d is encoded, using the standard binary code, either in this number of bits or, if $d < 2^{\lceil \log_2 v_k \rceil} - v_k$, it is encoded in $\lfloor \log_2 v_k \rfloor$ bits.

3. Encode n in two parts. Start with k encoded in some prefix code, and concatenate the binary code of d. Since k is coded in a prefix code, any decoder would know how many bits to read for k. After reading and decoding k, the decoder can compute the value $2^{\lceil \log_2 v_k \rceil} - v_k$ and thus knows how many bits to read for d.

A simple example is the infinite sequence $V = (1, 2, 4, 8, \ldots, 2^{i-1}, \ldots)$ with k coded in unary. The integer $n = 10$ satisfies

$$\sum_{i=1}^{3} v_i < 10 \le \sum_{i=1}^{4} v_i,$$

so $k = 4$ (with unary code 1110) and $d = 10 - \sum_{i=1}^{3} v_i - 1 = 2$. The code of 10 is thus 1110|010.

See also the Golomb code, Section 2.4, the phased-in binary codes of Section 2.9.1, and the subexponential code of Section 4.7.1.

Bibliography

Elias, P. (1975) "Universal Codeword Sets and Representations of the Integers," *IEEE Transactions on Information Theory* IT-21(2):194–203, March.

Number Bases (Part I)

Decimal numbers use base 10. The number 2037_{10}, e.g., has a value of $2 \times 10^3 + 0 \times 10^2 + 3 \times 10^1 + 7 \times 10^0$. We can say that 2037 is the sum of the digits 2, 0, 3, and 7, each weighted by a power of 10. Fractions are represented in the same way, using negative powers of 10. Thus $0.82 = 8 \times 10^{-1} + 2 \times 10^{-2}$ and $300.7 = 3 \times 10^2 + 7 \times 10^{-1}$.

Binary numbers use base 2. Such a number is represented as a sum of its digits, each weighted by a power of 2. Thus $101.11_2 = 1 \times 2^2 + 0 \times 2^1 + 1 \times 2^0 + 1 \times 2^{-1} + 1 \times 2^{-2}$.

Since there is nothing special about 10 or 2*, it should be easy to convince yourself that any positive integer $n > 1$ can serve as the basis for representing numbers. Such a representation requires n "digits" (if $n > 10$, we use the ten digits and the letters "A", "B", "C"...) and represents the number $d_3 d_2 d_1 d_0.d_{-1}$ as the sum of the "digits" d_i, each multiplied by a power of n, thus $d_3 n^3 + d_2 n^2 + d_1 n^1 + d_0 n^0 + d_{-1} n^{-1}$. The base for a number system does not have to consist of powers of an integer but can be any *superadditive* sequence that starts with 1.

Definition: A superadditive sequence $a_0, a_1, a_2, \ldots$ is one where any element a_i is greater than the sum of all its predecessors. An example is 1, 2, 4, 8, 16, 32, 64,... where each element equals one plus the sum of all its predecessors. This sequence consists of the familiar powers of 2, so we know that any integer can be expressed by it using just the digits 0 and 1 (the two bits). Another example is 1, 3, 6, 12, 24, 50,..., where each element equals 2 plus the sum of all its predecessors. It is easy to see that any integer can be expressed by it using just the digits 0, 1, and 2 (the 3 trits).

Given a positive integer k, the sequence $1, 1+k, 2+2k, 4+4k, \ldots, 2^i(1+k)$ is superadditive since each element equals the sum of all its predecessors plus k. Any non-negative integer can be *uniquely* represented in such a system as a number $x \ldots xxy$, where x are bits and y is in the range $[0, k]$.

In contrast, a general superadditive sequence, such as 1, 8, 50, 3102 can be used to represent integers, but not uniquely. The number 50, e.g., equals $8 \times 6 + 1 + 1$, so it can be represented as $0062 = 0 \times 3102 + 0 \times 50 + 6 \times 8 + 2 \times 1$, but also as $0100 = 0 \times 3102 + 1 \times 50 + 0 \times 8 + 0 \times 1$.

It can be shown that $1 + r + r^2 + \cdots + r^k < r^{k+1}$ for any real number $r > 1$, which implies that the powers of any real number $r > 1$ can serve as the base of a number system using the digits 0, 1, 2,..., d for some d.

The number $\phi = \frac{1}{2}(1 + \sqrt{5}) \approx 1.618$ is the well known golden-ratio. It can serve as the base of a number system using the two binary digits. Thus, e.g., $100.1_\phi = \phi^2 + \phi^{-1} \approx 3.23_{10}$.

Continues...

Number Bases (Part II)

Some real bases have special properties. For example, any positive integer R can be expressed as $R = b_1 F_1 + b_2 F_2 + b_3 F_3 + b_4 F_5 + \cdots$ (that's $b_4 F_5$, not $b_4 F_4$), where b_i are either 0 or 1, and the F_i are the Fibonacci numbers $1, 2, 3, 5, 8, 13, \ldots$. This representation has the interesting property that the string $b_1 b_2 \ldots$ does not contain any adjacent 1's (this property is used by certain data compression methods; see Section 5.4.4). As an example, the integer 33 equals the sum $1 + 3 + 8 + 21$, so it is expressed in the Fibonacci base as the 7-bit number 1010101.

A non-negative integer can be represented as a finite sum of binomials

$$n = \binom{a}{1} + \binom{b}{2} + \binom{c}{3} + \binom{d}{4} + \cdots; \quad \text{where } 0 \le a < b < c < d \ldots$$

are integers and $\binom{i}{n}$ is the binomial $\frac{i!}{n!(i-n)!}$. This is the *binomial number system*.

---

*Actually, there is. Two is the smallest integer that can be a base for a number system. Ten is the number of our fingers.

2.4 The Golomb Code

The *Golomb code* for non-negative integers n [Golomb 66] can be an effective Huffman code. The code depends on the choice of a parameter b. The first step is to compute the two quantities

$$q = \left\lfloor \frac{n-1}{b} \right\rfloor, \qquad r = n - qb - 1,$$

following which, the code is constructed of two parts; the first is the value of $q + 1$, coded in unary (exercise 2.5), and the second, the binary value of r coded in either $\lfloor \log_2 b \rfloor$ bits (for the small remainders) or in $\lceil \log_2 b \rceil$ bits (for the large ones). Choosing $b = 3$, e.g., produces three possible remainders 0, 1, and 2. They are coded 0, 10, and 11, respectively. Choosing $b = 5$ produces the five remainders 0 through 4, which are coded 00, 01, 100, 101, and 110. Table 2.8 shows some examples of the Golomb code for $b = 3$ and $b = 5$.

n:	1	2	3	4	5	6	7	8	9	10
$b = 3$:	0|0	0|10	0|11	10|0	10|10	10|11	110|0	110|10	110|11	1110|0
$b = 5$:	0|00	0|01	0|100	0|101	10|110	10|00	10|01	10|100	10|101	110|110

Table 2.8: Some Golomb Codes for $b = 3$ and $b = 5$.

Imagine an input data stream consisting of positive integers where the probability of integer n appearing in the data is $P(n) = (1 - p)^{n-1}p$, for some $0 \leq p \leq 1$. It can be shown that the Golomb code is an optimal code for this data if b is chosen such that

$$(1 - p)^b + (1 - p)^{b+1} \leq 1 < (1 - p)^{b-1} + (1 - p)^b.$$

Given the right data, it is easy to generate the best variable-size codes without going through the Huffman algorithm.

> In addition to the codes, Solomon W. Golomb has his "own" Golomb constant
> 0.62432998854355087099293638310083724417964262020180529286

Bibliography

Golomb, S. W. (1966) "Run-Length Encodings," *IEEE Transactions on Information Theory* IT-12(3):399–401.

2.5 The Kraft-MacMillan Inequality

This is a relation that says something about unambiguous variable-size codes. Its first part states that given an unambiguous variable-size code, with n codes of sizes L_i, then

$$\sum_{i=1}^{n} 2^{-L_i} \leq 1. \qquad (2.1)$$

The second part states the opposite, namely, given a set of n positive integers $(L_1, L_2, \ldots, L_n)$ that satisfy equation (2.1), there exists an unambiguous variable-size code such that L_i are the sizes of its individual codes. Together, both parts say that a code is unambiguous if and only if it satisfies relation (2.1).

This inequality can be related to the entropy by observing that the lengths L_i can always be written as $L_i = -\log_2 P_i + E_i$, where E_i is simply the amount by which L_i is greater than the entropy (the extra length of code i).

This implies that $2^{-L_i} = 2^{(\log_2 P_i - E_i)} = 2^{\log_2 P_i}/2^{E_i} = P_i/2^{E_i}$. In the special case where all the extra lengths are the same ($E_i = E$), the Kraft inequality says

$$1 \geq \sum_{i=1}^{n} P_i/2^E = \left(\sum_{i=1}^{n} P_i\right)/2^E = 1/2^E \implies 2^E \geq 1 \implies E \geq 0.$$

An unambiguous code has non-negative extra length, meaning its length is greater than or equal to the length determined by its entropy.

Here is a simple example of the use of this inequality. Consider the simple case of n equal-length binary codes. The size of each code is $L_i = \log_2 n$ and the Kraft-MacMillan sum is

$$\sum_{1}^{n} 2^{-L_i} = \sum_{1}^{n} 2^{-\log_2 n} = \sum_{1}^{n} \frac{1}{\log_2 n} = 1.$$

The inequality is satisfied, so such a code is unambiguous (uniquely decodable).

A more interesting example is the case of n codes where the first one is compressed and the second one expanded. We denote $L_1 = \log_2 n - a$, $L_2 = \log_2 n + e$, and $L_3 = L_4 = \ldots = L_n = \log_2 n$, where a and e are positive. We show that $e > a$, which means that compressing a symbol by a factor a requires expanding another symbol by a larger factor. We can benefit from this only if the probability of the compressed symbol is greater than the one of the expanded symbol.

$$\sum_1^n 2^{-L_i} = 2^{-L_1} + 2^{-L_2} + \sum_3^n 2^{-\log_2 n}$$

$$= 2^{-\log_2 n + a} + 2^{-\log_2 n - e} + \sum_1^n 2^{-\log_2 n} - 2 \times 2^{-\log_2 n}$$

$$= \frac{2^a}{n} + \frac{2^{-e}}{n} + 1 - \frac{2}{n}.$$

The Kraft-MacMillan inequality requires that

$$\frac{2^a}{n} + \frac{2^{-e}}{n} + 1 - \frac{2}{n} \leq 1; \quad \text{or} \quad \frac{2^a}{n} + \frac{2^{-e}}{n} - \frac{2}{n} \leq 0$$

or $2^{-e} \leq 2 - 2^a$, implying $-e \leq \log_2(2 - 2^a)$, or $e \geq -\log_2(2 - 2^a)$.

The inequality above implies $a \leq 1$ (otherwise $2 - 2^a$ is negative) but a is also positive (since we assumed compression of symbol 1). The possible range of values of a is thus $(0, 1]$ and in this range $e > a$, proving the statement above. (It is easy to see that $a = 1 \rightarrow e \geq -\log_2 0 = \infty$, and $a = 0.1 \rightarrow e \geq -\log_2(2 - 2^{0.1}) \approx 0.10745$.)

It can be shown that this is just a special case of a general result that says: if you have an alphabet of n symbols, and you compress some of them by a certain factor, then the others must be expanded by a greater factor.

2.6 Shannon-Fano Coding

This was the first method developed for finding good, variable-size codes. We start with a set of n symbols with known probabilities (or frequencies) of occurrence. The symbols are first arranged in descending order of their probabilities. The set of symbols is then divided into two subsets that have the same (or almost the same) probabilities. All symbols in one subset get assigned codes that start with a 0, while the codes of the symbols in the other subset start with a 1. Each subset is then recursively divided into two, and the second bit of all the codes is determined in a similar way. When a subset contains just two symbols, their codes are distinguished by adding one more bit to each. The process continues until no more subsets remain. Table 2.9 illustrates the Shannon-Fano code for a seven-symbol alphabet. Notice that the symbols themselves are not shown, only their probabilities.

The first step splits the set of seven symbols into two subsets. The first one with two symbols and a total probability of 0.45. The second one with the remaining five symbols and a total probability of 0.55. The two symbols in the first subset are assigned codes that start with 1, so their final codes are 11 and 10. The second subset is divided, in the second step, into two symbols (with total probability 0.3

Prob.			Steps				Final
1. 0.25	1	1					:11
2. 0.20	1	0					:10
3. 0.15	0		1	1			:011
4. 0.15	0		1	0			:010
5. 0.10	0		0		1		:001
6. 0.10	0		0		0	1	:0001
7. 0.05	0		0		0	0	:0000

Table 2.9: Shannon-Fano Example.

and codes that start with 01) and three symbols (with total probability 0.25 and codes that start with 00). Step three divides the last three symbols into 1 (with probability 0.1 and code 001) and 2 (with total probability 0.15 and codes that start with 000).

The average size of this code is $0.25 \times 2 + 0.20 \times 2 + 0.15 \times 3 + 0.15 \times 3 + 0.10 \times 3 + 0.10 \times 4 + 0.05 \times 4 = 2.7$ bits/symbol. This is a good result because the entropy (the smallest number of bits needed, on average, to represent each symbol) is

$$-(0.25 \log_2 0.25 + 0.20 \log_2 0.20 + 0.15 \log_2 0.15 + 0.15 \log_2 0.15$$
$$+ 0.10 \log_2 0.10 + 0.10 \log_2 0.10 + 0.05 \log_2 0.05) \approx 2.67.$$

▸ **Exercise 2.10:** Repeat the above calculation but place the first split between the third and fourth symbols. Calculate the average size of the code and show that it is greater than 2.67 bits/symbol.

The reason the code of Table Ans.5 has longer average size is that the splits, in this case, were not as good as those of Table 2.9. This suggests that the Shannon-Fano method produces better code when the splits are better, i.e., when the two subsets in every split have very close total probabilities. Carrying this argument to its limit suggests that perfect splits yield the best code. Table 2.10 illustrates such a case. The two subsets in every split have identical total probabilities, yielding a code with the minimum average size (zero redundancy). Its average size is $0.25 \times 2 + 0.25 \times 2 + 0.125 \times 3 + 0.125 \times 3 + 0.125 \times 3 + 0.125 \times 3 = 2.5$ bits/symbols, which is identical to its entropy. This means that it is the theoretical minimum average size.

The conclusion is that this method produces best results when the symbols have probabilities of occurrence that are (negative) powers of 2.

▸ **Exercise 2.11:** Calculate the entropy of the codes of Table 2.10.

The Shannon-Fano method is easy to implement (see page 153 for its use in the Implode algorithm) but the code it produces is generally not as good as that produced by the Huffman method, which is described next.

	Prob.	Steps			Final
1.	0.25	1	1		:11
2.	0.25	1	0		:10
3.	0.125	0	1	1	:011
4.	0.125	0	1	0	:010
5.	0.125	0	0	1	:001
6.	0.125	0	0	0	:000

Table 2.10: Shannon-Fano Balanced Example.

2.7 The Counting Argument

Any compression method is limited. It cannot losslessly compress *all* files of size N since some of these files are random.

Let's assume that an algorithm exists that can compress losslessly all files of size N bits (or larger, but we'll concentrate on N). There are 2^N files of size N bits, and compressing them with our algorithm must produce 2^N files of sizes $< N$. How many files are there of sizes $< N$? There are 2^{N-1} files of size $N - 1$, 2^{N-2} files of size $N - 2$, and so on, down to $2^{N-N} = 1$ file of size $N - N = 0$. The total number of all these files is

$$2^{N-1} + 2^{N-2} + \cdots + 1 = 2^N - 1,$$

instead of 2^N, so there must be at least two size-N different files compressed to the same smaller size file, which means the algorithm is lossy.

Notice that this argument does not assume anything about the way the algorithm works.

So how do people develop "algorithms" for compressing random files? Here are some ways:

1. It is possible to place all the data of any file P (even random) in the filename, creation date, author, version, and resources of another file Q. The actual data of file Q may be a single byte. It is possible to recreate file P from Q since Q contains (hidden) all the data of P, yet the size of Q (just the data, ignoring "technical" details such as the filename) is one byte.

2. Use variable-size codes that don't satisfy the prefix property (page 26). Such codes can be short and may be able to compress a random file. However, the decoder won't be able to tell how long each code is, making the compressed file undecodable and thus useless.

3. Find a pseudo-random number generator that uses a seed to generate a sequence of numbers whose concatenation will be the original, decompressed file. The seed would thus be the compressed file. The counting argument (or other equivalent proofs) should discourage anyone from trying this, but some people persist.

4. Split the original file into blocks and treat each block as a large integer. Factorize each large integer, hoping that the total number of bits of all the factors will be less than that of the original large number. Again, this does not work.

The following case studies illustrate these points.

2.7.1 Case Study A: David James

Patent 5,533,051 "Method for Data Compression" was filed on March 12, 1993 and granted on July 2, 1996 to David C. James.

The patent abstract says: "Methods for compressing data including methods for compressing highly randomized data are disclosed."

The patent description says: "A second aspect of the present invention which further enhances its ability to achieve high compression percentages, is its ability to be applied to data recursively. Specifically, the methods of the present invention are able to make multiple passes over a file, each time further compressing the file. Thus, a series of recursions are repeated until the desired compression level is achieved.

The direct bit encode method of the present invention is effective for reducing an input string by one bit regardless of the bit pattern of the input string."

Notice the evasive argument: "Of course, this does not take into account any overhead registers or other "house-keeping" type information which must be tracked. However such overhead tends to be negligible when processing the large quantities of data typically encountered in data compression applications."

And later: "Thus, one skilled in the art can see that by keeping the appropriate counters, the direct bit encode method of the present invention is effective for reducing an input string by one bit regardless of the bit pattern of the input string. Although a certain amount of "loss" is necessary in keeping and maintaining various counters and registers, for files which are sufficiently large, this overhead is insignificant compared to the savings obtained by the direct bit encode method."

It took the patent office three years to examine and grant this patent, which is similar in concept to a patent on a perpetual machine. Alas, the days when Einstein was a patent examiner are over.

2.7.2 Case Study B: Michael L. Cole

Patent 5,488,364 "Recursive data compression" was filed on February 28, 1994 and granted on January 30, 1996 to Michael L. Cole.

This is another recursive lossless compression algorithm that claims to compress random data. The patent summary states: "Averaged over a statistically significant sample of random input data, the first block will have a percentage of adjacent bits of the "1" state that is high relative to that of the original input data, and the second block will have a percentage of adjacent bits of the "0" state that is high relative to that of the original input data."

A careful examination of the method shows that the small compression achieved by these percentages is more than cancelled out by the extra bits needed for the patented "bit-reversal key" and "keyword."

2.7.3 Case Study C: DataFiles/16

In 1992, WEB Technologies advertised DataFiles/16, a recursive lossless compression algorithm. Here is a short quote from their flier:

"DataFiles/16 will compress all types of binary files to approximately one-sixteenth of their original size... regardless of the type of file (word processing document, spreadsheet file, image file, executable file, etc.), NO DATA WILL BE LOST by DataFiles/16." (16:1 compression only promised for files $> 64K$ bytes in length.)

Performed on a 386/25 machine, the program can complete a compression-decompression cycle on one Mbyte of data in less than thirty seconds."

The compressed output file created by DataFiles/16 can be used as the input file to subsequent executions of the program. This feature of the utility is known as *recursive* or *iterative* compression, and will enable you to compress your data files to a tiny fraction of their original size. In fact, virtually any amount of computer data can be compressed to under 1024 bytes using DataFiles/16 to compress its own output files multiple times. Then, by repeating in reverse the steps taken to perform the recursive compression, all original data can be decompressed to its original form without the loss of a single bit."

Constant levels of compression across ALL TYPES of FILES... Convenient, single floppy DATA TRANSPORTATION..."

Needless to say, after about a year of heavy advertising, no product has been released.

2.8 Huffman Coding

This is a commonly used method for data compression. It serves as the basis for several popular programs used on personal computers. Some of them use just the Huffman method while others use it as one step in a multi-step compression process. The Huffman method [Huffman 52] is somewhat similar to the Shannon-Fano method. It generally produces better codes and, like the Shannon-Fano method, it produces best code when the probabilities of the symbols are negative powers of 2. The main difference between the two methods is that Shannon-Fano constructs its codes top to bottom (from the leftmost to the rightmost bits), while Huffman constructs a code tree from the bottom up (builds the codes from right to left). Since its development, in 1952, by D. Huffman, this method has been the subject of intensive research into data compression.

The method starts by building a list of all the alphabet symbols in descending order of their probabilities. It then constructs a tree, with a symbol at every leaf, from the bottom up. This is done in steps where, at each step, the two symbols with smallest probabilities are selected, added to the top of the partial tree, deleted from the list, and replaced with an auxiliary symbol representing both of them. When the list is reduced to just one auxiliary symbol (representing the entire alphabet) the tree is complete. The tree is then traversed to determine the codes of the symbols.

This is best illustrated by an example. Given five symbols with probabilities as shown in Figure 2.11a, they are paired in the following order:

1. a_4 is combined with a_5 and both are replaced by the combined symbol a_{45} whose probability is 0.2.

2. There are now four symbols left, a_1, with probability 0.4, and a_2, a_3 and a_{45}, with probabilities 0.2 each. We arbitrarily select a_3 and a_{45}, combine them and replace them with the auxiliary symbol a_{345} whose probability is 0.4.

3. Three symbols are now left, a_1, a_2, and a_{345}, with probabilities 0.4, 0.2 and 0.4, respectively. We arbitrarily select a_2 and a_{345}, combine them and replace them with the auxiliary symbol a_{2345} whose probability is 0.6.

4. Finally, we combine the two remaining symbols, a_1 and a_{2345}, and replace them with a_{12345} with probability 1.

The tree is now complete. It is shown "lying on its side" with the root on the right and the five leaves on the left. To assign the codes, we arbitrarily assign a bit of 1 to the top edge, and a bit of 0 to the bottom edge, of every pair of edges. This results in the codes 0, 10, 111, 1101, and 1100. The assignments of bits to the edges is arbitrary but must be consistent.

The average size of this code is $0.4 \times 1 + 0.2 \times 2 + 0.2 \times 3 + 0.1 \times 4 + 0.1 \times 4 = 2.2$ bits/symbol, but even more importantly, the Huffman code is not unique. Some of the steps above were selected arbitrarily, since there were more than two symbols with smallest probabilities. Figure 2.11b shows how the same five symbols can be combined differently to obtain a different Huffman code (11, 01, 00, 101, and 100). The average size of this code is $0.4 \times 2 + 0.2 \times 2 + 0.2 \times 2 + 0.1 \times 3 + 0.1 \times 3 = 2.2$ bits/symbol, the same as the previous code.

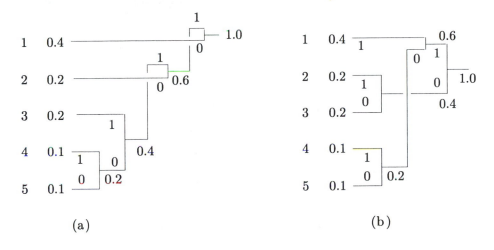

(a)

(b)

Figure 2.11: Huffman Codes.

It turns out that the arbitrary decisions made when constructing the Huffman tree affect the individual codes but not the average size of the code. Still, we have to answer the obvious question "which code is better?" The answer, while not obvious, is simple: the code with the smallest variance. The variance of a code measures how much the sizes of the individual codes deviate from the average size (see page 206 for the definition of variance). The variance of code 2.11a is

$$0.4(1 - 2.2)^2 + 0.2(2 - 2.2)^2 + 0.2(3 - 2.2)^2 + 0.1(4 - 2.2)^2 + 0.1(4 - 2.2)^2 = 1.36,$$

while that of code 2.11b is

$$0.4(2 - 2.2)^2 + 0.2(2 - 2.2)^2 + 0.2(2 - 2.2)^2 + 0.1(3 - 2.2)^2 + 0.1(3 - 2.2)^2 = 0.16.$$

Code 2.11b is thus preferable (see below). A careful look at the two trees shows how to select the one we want. In the tree of Figure 2.11a, symbol a_{45} is combined with a_3, whereas in the tree of 2.11b it is combined with a_1. The rule is: when there are more than two smallest-probability nodes, select the ones that are lowest and highest in the tree and combine them. This will combine symbols of low probability with ones of high probability, thereby reducing the total variance of the code.

If the encoder simply writes the compressed stream on a file, the variance of the code makes no difference. A small-variance Huffman code is preferable in cases where the encoder transmits the compressed stream, as it is being generated, on a communications line. In such a case, a code with large variance causes the encoder to generate bits at a rate that changes all the time. Since the bits have to be transmitted at a constant rate, the encoder has to use a buffer. Bits of the compressed stream are entered into the buffer as they are being generated and are moved out of it at a constant rate, to be transmitted. It is easy to see intuitively that a Huffman code with zero variance will enter bits into the buffer at a constant rate, so only a short buffer will be necessary. The larger the code variance, the less constant is the rate at which bits enter the buffer, requiring the encoder to use a larger buffer.

It can be shown that the size of the Huffman code for symbol a_i is less than or equal $\lceil -\log_2 P_i \rceil$. The probability of symbol a_1 in Figure 2.11 is 0.4, and $\log_2 0.4 \approx -1.32$, so two bits or fewer are required to code it. Similarly the probability of symbol a_5 is 0.1, and $\log_2 0.1 \approx -3.32$, so its code will be at most four bits long.

▶ **Exercise 2.12:** It seems that the size of a code must also depend on the number n of symbols (the size of the alphabet). A small alphabet requires just a few codes, so they can all be short; a large alphabet requires many codes, so some must be long. This being so, how can we say that the size of the code of symbol a_i depends just on its probability P_i?

Figure 2.12 shows a Huffman code for the 26 letters.

▶ **Exercise 2.13:** Calculate the average size, entropy, and variance of this code.

▶ **Exercise 2.14:** Discuss the Huffman codes in the case where all the probabilities are equal.

Exercise 2.14 shows that symbols with equal probabilities don't compress under the Huffman method. This is understandable since strings of such symbols normally make random text, and random text does not compress. There may be special cases where strings of symbols with equal probabilities are not random and can be compressed. A good example is the string $a_1a_1 \ldots a_1a_2a_2 \ldots a_2a_3a_3 \ldots$ in which each symbol appears in a long run. This string can be compressed with RLE but not with Huffman codes.

Notice that the Huffman method cannot be applied to a two-symbol alphabet. In such an alphabet one symbol can be assigned the code 0 and the other code 1. The Huffman method cannot assign to any symbol a code shorter than one bit, so it cannot improve on this simple code. If the original data (the source) consists of individual bits, such as in the case of a monochromatic image, it is possible to combine several bits (perhaps four or eight) into a new symbol, and pretend that the alphabet consists of these (16 or 256) symbols. The problem with this approach is that the original binary data may have certain statistical correlations between the bits, and some of these correlations would be lost when the bits are combined into

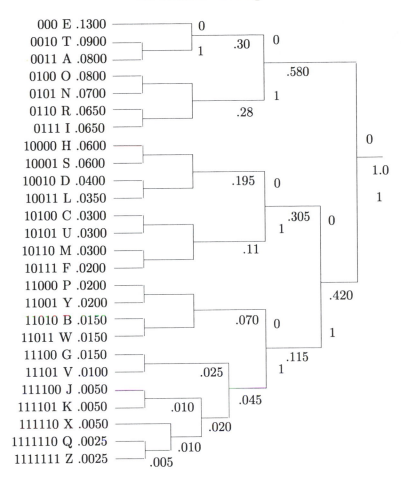

Figure 2.12: A Huffman Code for the 26-Letter Alphabet.

symbols. When a typical image (a painting or a diagram) is digitized by scan lines, a pixel is more likely to be followed by an identical pixel than by the opposite one. We thus have a file that can start with either a 0 or a 1 (each has 0.5 probability of being the first bit), a zero is more likely to be followed by another 0 and a 1 by another 1. Figure 5.28c is a finite-state machine illustrating this situation. If these bits are combined into, say groups of eight, the bits inside a group will still be correlated but the groups themselves will not be correlated by the original pixel probabilities. If the input stream contains, e.g., the two adjacent groups 00011100 and 00001110, they will be encoded independently, ignoring the correlation between the last 0 of the first group and the first 0 of the next group. Selecting larger groups improves this situation but increases the number of groups, which implies more storage for the code table and also longer time to calculate the table.

▸ **Exercise 2.15:** How does the number of groups increase when the group size increases from s bits to $s + n$ bits?

A more complex approach to image compression by Huffman coding is to create several complete sets of Huffman codes. If the group size is, e.g., eight bits, then several sets of 256 codes are generated. When a symbol S is to be encoded, one of the sets is selected, and S is encoded using its code in that set. The choice of set depends on the symbol preceding S.

2.8.1 Huffman Decoding

Before starting the compression of a data stream, the compressor (encoder) has to determine the codes. It does that based on the probabilities (or frequencies of occurrence) of the symbols. The probabilities or frequencies have to appear on the compressed stream, so that any Huffman decompressor (decoder) will be able to decompress the stream. This is easy since the frequencies are integers and the probabilities can be written as scaled integers. It normally adds just a few hundred bytes to the compressed stream. It is also possible to write the variable-size codes themselves on the stream, but this may be awkward since the codes have different sizes. It is also possible to write the Huffman tree on the stream, but this may be longer than just the frequencies.

> Truth is stranger than fiction, but this is because fiction is obliged to stick to probability; truth is not.
>
> —Anonymous

In any case, the decoder must know what's at the start of the stream, read it, and construct the Huffman tree for the alphabet. Only then can it read and decode the rest of the stream. The algorithm for decoding is simple. Start at the root and read the first bit off the compressed stream. If it is zero, follow the bottom edge; if it is one, follow the top edge. Read the next bit and move another edge toward the leaves of the tree. When the decoder gets to a leaf, it finds the original, uncompressed code of the symbol (normally, its ASCII code), and that code is emitted by the decoder. The process starts again at the root with the next bit.

This process is illustrated for the five-symbol alphabet of Figure Ans.6a. The four-symbol input string "$a_4a_2a_5a_1$" is encoded into "1001100111." The decoder starts at the root, reads the first bit "1," and goes up. The second bit "0" sends it down, as does the third bit. This brings the decoder to leaf a_4, which it emits. It again returns to the root, reads 110, moves up, up, and down, to reach leaf a_2, and so on.

Bibliography

Huffman, David (1952) "A Method for the Construction of Minimum Redundancy Codes," *Proceedings of the IRE* **40**(9):1098–1101.

2.8.2 Average Code Size

Figure 2.15a shows a set of five symbols with their probabilities and a typical Huffman tree. Symbol A appears 55% of the time and is assigned a 1-bit code, so it contributes 0.55×1 bits to the average code size. Symbol E appears only 2% of the time and is assigned a 4-bit Huffman code so it contributes $0.02 \cdot 4 = 0.08$ bits to the code size. The average code size is therefore calculated to be

$$0.55 \cdot 1 + 0.25 \cdot 2 + 0.15 \cdot 3 + 0.03 \cdot 4 + 0.02 \cdot 4 = 1.7 \text{ bits per symbol.}$$

Surprisingly, the same result is obtained by adding the values of the four internal nodes of the Huffman code-tree $0.05 + 0.2 + 0.45 + 1 = 1.7$. This provides a way to calculate the average code size of a set of Huffman codes without any multiplications. Simply add the values of all the internal nodes of the tree. Table 2.13 illustrates why this works.

$$
\begin{aligned}
.05 &= && .02 + .03 \\
.20 &= .05 + .15 && = .02 + .03 + .15 \\
.45 &= .2 + \ .25 && = .02 + .03 + .15 + .25 \\
1.0 &= .45 + .55 && = .02 + .03 + .15 + .25 + .55
\end{aligned}
$$

Table 2.13: Composition of Nodes.

$$
\begin{aligned}
0.05 &= && = 0.02 + 0.03 + \ldots \\
a_1 &= 0.05 + \ldots && = 0.02 + 0.03 + \ldots \\
a_2 &= a_1 \ + \ \ldots && = 0.02 + 0.03 + \ldots \\
&\ \ \vdots && = \\
a_{d-2} &= a_{d-3} + \ldots && = 0.02 + 0.03 + \ldots \\
1.0 &= a_{d-2} + \ldots && = 0.02 + 0.03 + \ldots
\end{aligned}
$$

Table 2.14: Composition of Nodes.

(Internal nodes are shown in italics in this table.) The left column consists of the values of all the internal nodes. The right columns show how each internal node is the sum of some of the leaf nodes. Summing the values in the left column yields 1.7, and summing the other columns shows that this 1.7 is the sum of the four values 0.02, the four values 0.03, the three values 0.15, the two values 0.25, and the single value 0.55.

This argument can be generalized for the general case. It is easy to show that, in a Huffman-like tree (a tree where each node is the sum of its children) the weighted sum of the leaves, where the weights are the distances of the leaves from the root, equals the sum of the internal nodes. Figure 2.15b shows such a tree where we assume that the two leaves 0.02 and 0.03 have d-bit Huffman codes. Inside the tree, these leaves become the children of internal node 0.05 which, in turn, is connected to the root by means of the $d-2$ internal nodes a_1 through a_{d-2}. Table 2.14 has d rows and shows that the two values 0.02 and 0.03 are included in the various internal nodes exactly d times. Adding the values of all the internal nodes produces a sum that includes the contributions $0.02 \cdot d + 0.03 \cdot d$ from the 2 leaves. Since these leaves are arbitrary, it is clear that this sum includes similar contributions from all the other leaves, so this sum is the average code size. Since this sum also equals the sum of the left column, which is the sum of the internal nodes, it is clear that the sum of the internal nodes equals the average code size.

Notice that this proof does not assume that the tree is binary. The property illustrated here exists for any tree where a node contains the sum of its children. This property has been communicated to the author by John M. Motil.

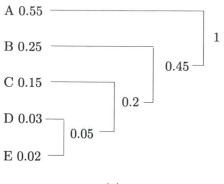

$$A\ 0.55$$
$$B\ 0.25$$
$$0.45$$
$$1$$
$$C\ 0.15$$
$$0.2$$
$$D\ 0.03$$
$$0.05$$
$$E\ 0.02$$

(a)

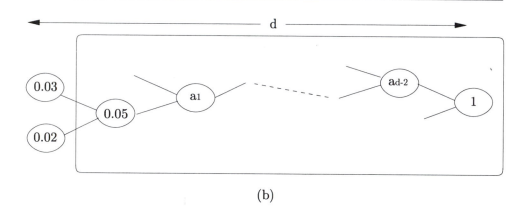

(b)

Figure 2.15: Huffman Code Trees.

2.8.3 Number of Codes

Since the Huffman code is not unique, the natural question is: How many different codes are there? Figure 2.16a shows a Huffman code-tree for six symbols, from which we can answer this question in two different ways.

Answer 1. The tree of 2.16a has five interior nodes and, in general, a Huffman code-tree for n symbols has $n-1$ interior nodes. Each interior node has two edges coming out of it, labeled 0 and 1. Swapping the two labels produces a different Huffman code-tree, so the total number of different Huffman code-trees is 2^{n-1} (in our example, 2^5 or 32). The tree of Figure 2.16b, for example, shows the result of swapping the labels of the two edges of the root. Table 2.17a,b show the codes generated by the two trees.

Answer 2. The six codes of Table 2.17a can be divided into the four classes $00x$, $10y$, 01, and 11, where x and y are 1-bit each. It is possible to create different Huffman codes by changing the first two bits of each class. Since there are four classes, this is the same as creating all the permutations of four objects, something

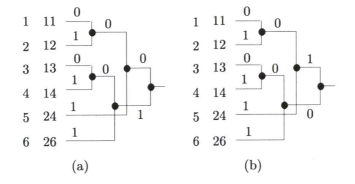

Figure 2.16: Two Huffman Code-Trees.

000	100	000
001	101	001
100	000	010
101	001	011
01	11	10
11	01	11
(a)	(b)	(c)

Table 2.17.

that can be done in $4! = 24$ ways. In each of the 24 permutations it is also possible to change the values of x and y in four different ways (since they are bits) so the total number of different Huffman codes in our six-symbol example is $24 \times 4 = 96$.

The two answers are different because they count different things. Answer 1 counts the number of different Huffman code-trees, while answer 2 counts the number of different Huffman codes. It turns out that our example can generate 32 different code-trees but 94 different codes. This shows that there are Huffman codes that cannot be generated by the Huffman method! Table 2.17c shows such an example. A look at the trees of Figure 2.16 should convince the reader that the codes of symbols 5 and 6 must start with different bits, but in the code of Table 2.17c they both start with 1. This code is therefore impossible to generate by any relabeling of the nodes of the trees of Figure 2.16.

2.8.4 Canonical Huffman Codes

Code 2.17c has a simple interpretation. It assigns the first four symbols the 3-bit codes 0, 1, 2, 3, and the last two symbols the 2-bit codes 2 and 3. This is an example of a *canonical Huffman code*. Table 2.18 shows a slightly bigger example of such a code. We assume 16 symbols (whose probabilities are irrelevant and are not shown) such that four symbols are assigned 3-bit codes, five symbols are assigned 5-bit codes, and the remaining seven symbols, 6-bit codes. Table 2.18a shows a set of possible Huffman codes, while Table 2.18b shows a set of canonical Huffman codes. It is easy to see that the seven 6-bit canonical codes are simply the 6-bit integers 0 through 6. The five codes are the 5-bit integers 4 through 8, and the four codes are the 3-bit integers 3 through 6. We first show how these codes are generated and then how they are used.

```
1:    000    011        9:  10100   01000
2:    001    100       10: 101010  000000
3:    010    101       11: 101011  000001
4:    011    110       12: 101100  000010
5:  10000  00100       13: 101101  000011
6:  10001  00101       14: 101110  000100
7:  10010  00110       15: 101111  000101
8:  10011  00111       16: 110000  000110
      (a)    (b)            (a)      (b)
```

Table 2.18.

```
length: 1 2 3 4 5 6
numl:   0 0 4 0 5 7
first:    2 4 3 5 4 0
```

Table 2.19.

The top row (length) of Table 2.19 lists the possible code lengths, from 1 to 6 bits. The second row (numl) lists the number of codes of each length, and the bottom row (first) lists the first code in each group. This is why the three groups of codes start with values 3, 4, and 0. To obtain the top two rows we need to compute the lengths of all the Huffman codes for the given alphabet (see below). The third row is computed by setting "first[6]:=0;" and iterating

   for l:=5 downto 1 do first[l]:=⌈(first[l+1]+numl[l+1])/2⌉;

this guarantees that all the 3-bit prefixes of codes longer than 3 bits will be less than first[3] (which is 3), all the 5-bit prefixes of codes longer than 5 bits will be less than first[5] (which is 4), and so on.

Now for the use of these unusual codes. Canonical Huffman codes are useful in cases where the alphabet is large and where fast decoding is mandatory. Because of the way the codes are constructed, it is easy for the decoder to identify the length of a code by reading and examining input bits one by one. Once the length is known, the symbol can be found in one step. The pseudo-code below shows the rules for decoding:

```
l:=1; input v;
while v<first[l]
append next input bit to v; l:=l+1;
endwhile
```

As an example, suppose the next code is 00110. As bits are input and appended to v, it goes through the values 0, 00=0, 001=1, 0011=3, 00110=6, while l is incremented from 1 to 5. All steps except the last satisfy v<first[l], so the last step determines the value of l (the code length) as 5. The symbol itself is found by subtracting v−first[5]=6−4=2, so it is the third symbol (numbering starts at 0) in group l=5 (symbol 7 of the 16 symbols).

It has been mentioned that canonical Huffman codes are useful in cases were the alphabet is large and fast decoding is important. A practical example is a collection of documents archived and compressed by a *word-based* adaptive Huffman (Section 5.5.1). In an archive a slow encoder is acceptable but the decoder should be fast. When the individual symbols are words, the alphabet may be huge, making it impractical, or even impossible, to construct the Huffman code-tree. However, even with a huge alphabet, the number of different code lengths is small, rarely exceeding 20 bits (just the number of 20-bit codes is about a million). If canonical Huffman codes are used, and the maximum code length is L, then the code length l of a symbol is found by the decoder in at most L steps, and the symbol itself is identified in one more step.

The last point to be discussed is the encoder. In order to calculate the canonical Huffman code, the encoder needs to know the length of the Huffman code of every symbol. The main problem is the large size of the alphabet, which may make it impractical or even impossible to build the entire Huffman code-tree in memory. The algorithm described here (see [Hirschberg 90] and [Sieminski 88]) solves this problem. It calculates the code sizes for an alphabet of n symbols using just one array of size $2n$. One half of this array is used as a *heap*, so we start with a short description of this useful data structure.

A *binary tree* is a tree where every node has at most two children (i.e., it may have 0, 1, or 2 children). A *complete binary tree* is a binary tree where every node except the leaves has exactly two children. A *balanced binary tree* is a complete binary tree where some of the bottom-right nodes may be missing (see also page 81 for another application of those trees). A heap is a balanced binary tree where every leaf contains a data item and the items are ordered such that every path from a leaf to the root traverses nodes that are in sorted order, either nondecreasing (a max-heap) or nonincreasing (a min-heap). Figure 2.20 shows examples of min-heaps.

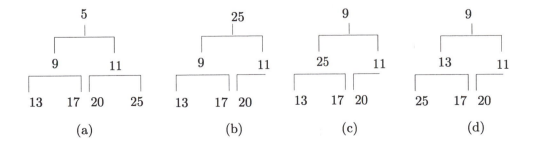

Figure 2.20: Min-Heaps.

A common operation on a heap is to remove the root and rearrange the remaining nodes to get back a heap. This is called *sifting* the heap. Figure 2.20a–d shows how a heap is sifted after the root (with data item 5) has been removed. Sifting starts by moving the bottom-right node to become the new root. This guarantees that the heap will remain a balanced binary tree. The root is then compared with its children and may have to be swapped with one of them in order to preserve the ordering of a heap. Several more swaps may be necessary to completely restore heap ordering. It is easy to see that the maximum number of swaps equals the height of the tree, which is $\lceil \log_2 n \rceil$.

The reason a heap must always remain balanced is that this makes it possible to store it in memory without using any pointers. The heap is said to be "housed" in an array. To house a heap in an array, the root is placed in the first array location (with index 1), the two children of the node at array location i are placed at locations $2i$ and $2i + 1$, and the parent of the node at array location j is placed at location $\lfloor j/2 \rfloor$. Thus the heap of Figure 2.20a is housed in an array by placing the nodes 5, 9, 11, 13, 17, 20, and 25 in the first seven locations of the array.

The algorithm uses a single array A of size $2n$. The frequencies of occurrence of the n symbols are placed in the top half of A (locations $n + 1$ through $2n$) and the bottom half of A (locations 1 through n) becomes a min-heap whose data items are pointers to the frequencies in the top half (Figure 2.21a). The algorithm then goes into a loop where, in each iteration the heap is used to identify the 2 smallest frequencies and replace them with their sum. The sum is stored in the last heap position A[h], and the heap shrinks by one position (Figure 2.21c). The loop repeats until the heap is reduced to just one pointer (Figure 2.21c).

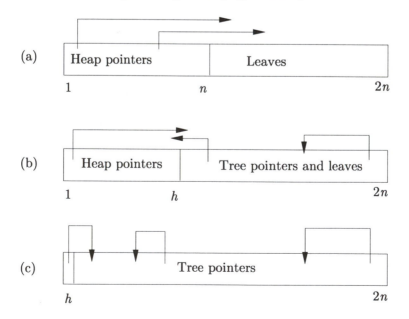

Figure 2.21: Huffman Heaps and Leaves in an Array.

We now illustrate this part of the algorithm using seven frequencies. The table below shows how the frequencies and the heap are initially housed in an array of size 14. Pointers are shown in italics and the heap is delimited by square brackets.

1	2	3	4	5	6	7	8	9	10	11	12	13	14
[*14*	*12*	*13*	*10*	*11*	*9*	*8*]	25	20	13	17	9	11	5

The first iteration selects the smallest frequency (5), removes the root of the heap (pointer 14), and leaves A[7] empty.

1	2	3	4	5	6	7	8	9	10	11	12	13	14
[*12*	*10*	*13*	*8*	*11*	*9*]		25	20	13	17	9	11	5

The heap is sifted and its new root (12) points to the second smallest frequency (9) in A[12]. The sum $5 + 9$ is stored in the empty location 7, and the three array locations A[1], A[12], and A[14], are set to point to that location.

1	2	3	4	5	6	7	8	9	10	11	12	13	14
[*7*	*10*	*13*	*8*	*11*	*9*]	5+9	25	20	13	17	*7*	11	*7*

The heap is now sifted.

1	2	3	4	5	6	7	8	9	10	11	12	13	14
[*13*	*10*	*7*	*8*	*11*	*9*]	14	25	20	13	17	*7*	11	*7*

The new root is 13, meaning that the smallest frequency (11) is stored at A[13]. The root is removed and the heap shrinks to just five positions, leaving location 6 empty.

1	2	3	4	5	6	7	8	9	10	11	12	13	14
[*10*	*11*	*7*	*8*	*9*]		14	25	20	13	17	*7*	11	*7*

The heap is now sifted. The new root is 10, so the second smallest frequency, 13, is stored at A[10]. The sum $11 + 13$ is stored at the empty location 6, and the three locations A[1], A[13], and A[10], are set to point to 6.

1	2	3	4	5	6	7	8	9	10	11	12	13	14
[*6*	*11*	*7*	*8*	*9*]	11+13	14	25	20	*6*	17	*7*	*6*	*7*

▸ **Exercise 2.16:** Complete this loop.

The final result of the loop is

1	2	3	4	5	6	7	8	9	10	11	12	13	14
[*2*]	100	*2*	*2*	*3*	*4*	*5*	*3*	*4*	*6*	*5*	*7*	*6*	*7*

from which it is easy to figure out the code lengths of all seven symbols. To find the length of the code of symbol 14, e.g., we follow the pointers 7, 5, 3, 2 from A[14] to the root. Four steps are necessary, so the code length is 4.

▸ **Exercise 2.17:** Find the lengths of all the other codes.

Bibliography

Hirschberg, D., and D. Lelewer (1990) "Efficient Decoding of Prefix Codes," *Communications of the ACM* **33**(4):449–459.

Sieminski, A. (1988) "Fast Decoding of the Huffman Codes," *Information Processing Letters* **26**(5):237–241.

2.9 Adaptive Huffman Coding

The Huffman method assumes that the frequencies of occurrence of all the symbols in the alphabet are known to the compressor. In practice, the frequencies are rarely, if ever, known in advance. One solution is for the compressor to read the original data twice. The first time it just calculates the frequencies. The second time it compresses the data. Between the two passes, the compressor constructs the Huffman tree. Such a method is called semi-adaptive (page x), and is too slow to be practical. The method used in practice is called adaptive (or dynamic) Huffman coding. This method is the basis of the UNIX `compact` program. (See also Section 5.5.1 for a word-based version of adaptive Huffman coding.)

The main idea is for the compressor and the decompressor to start with an empty Huffman tree, and to modify it as symbols are being read and processed (in the case of the compressor the word "processed" means compressed; in the case of the decompressor, it means decompressed). The compressor and decompressor should modify the tree in the same way, so at any point in the process they should use the same codes, although those codes may change from step to step. We may say that the compressor and decompressor are synchronized, or that they work in *lockstep* (although they don't necessarily work together; compression and decompression usually happen at different times). The term *mirroring* is perhaps a better choice. The decoder mirrors the operations of the encoder.

Initially, the compressor starts with an empty Huffman tree. No symbols have been assigned codes. The first symbol being input is simply written on the output stream in its uncompressed form. The symbol is then added to the tree, and a code assigned to it. The next time this symbol is encountered, its current code is written on the stream, and its frequency incremented by one. Since the tree has been modified, it is examined to see if it is still a Huffman tree (best codes). If not, it is rearranged, which entails changing the codes (Section 2.9.2).

The decompressor mirrors the same steps. When it reads the uncompressed form of a symbol, it adds it to the tree and assigns it a code. When it reads a compressed (variable-size) code, it uses the current tree to determine what symbol the code belongs to, and it updates the tree in the same way as the compressor.

The only subtle point is that the decompressor needs to know if the item it has just input is an uncompressed symbol (normally an 8-bit ASCII code, but see Section 2.9.1) or a variable-size code. To remove any ambiguity, each uncompressed symbol is preceded by a special, variable-size *escape code*. When the decompressor reads this code, it knows that the next 8 bits are the ASCII code of a symbol that appears in the compressed stream for the first time.

Trouble is, the escape code should not be any of the variable-size codes used for the symbols. Since these codes are being modified every time the tree is rearranged, the escape code should also be modified. A natural way to do this is to add an empty leaf to the tree, a leaf with a zero frequency of occurrence, that's always assigned to the 0-branch of the tree. Since the leaf is in the tree, it gets a variable-size code assigned. This code is the escape code preceding every uncompressed symbol. As the tree is being rearranged, the position of the empty leaf—and thus its code—change, but the code is always used to identify uncompressed symbols in the compressed stream. Figure 2.22 shows how the escape code moves as the tree grows.

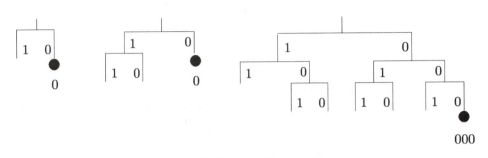

Figure 2.22: The Escape Code.

This method is used to compress/decompress data in the V.32 protocol for 14,400 baud modems.

2.9.1 Uncompressed Codes

If the symbols being compressed are ASCII characters, they may simply be assigned their ASCII codes as uncompressed codes. In the general case where there can be any symbols, uncompressed codes of two different sizes can be assigned by a simple method. Here is an example for the case $n = 24$. The first 16 symbols can be assigned the numbers 0 through 15 as their codes. These numbers require only 4 bits, but we encode them in 5 bits. Symbols 17 through 24 can be assigned the numbers $17 - 16 - 1 = 0$, $18 - 16 - 1 = 1$ through $24 - 16 - 1 = 7$ as 4-bit numbers. We end up with the sixteen 5-bit codes 00000, 00001,..., 01111, followed by the eight 4-bit codes 0000, 0001,..., 0111.

In general we assume an alphabet that consists of the n symbols a_1, a_2 through a_n. We select integers m and r such that $2^m \le n < 2^{m+1}$ and $r = n - 2^m$. The first 2^m symbols are encoded as the $(m+1)$-bit numbers 0 through $2^m - 1$. The remaining symbols are encoded as m-bit numbers such that the code of a_k is $k - 2^m - 1$. This code is also called a *phased-in binary code* (see page 147 for an application of these codes).

2.9.2 Modifying the Tree

The main idea is to check the tree each time a symbol is input. If the tree is no longer a Huffman tree, it should be updated. A glance at Figure 2.23a shows what it means for a binary tree to be a Huffman tree. The tree in the figure contains five symbols: A, B, C, D, and E. It is shown with the symbols and their frequencies (in parentheses) after 16 symbols have been input and processed. The property that makes it a Huffman tree is that if we scan it level by level, scanning each level from left to right, and going from the bottom (the leaves) to the top (the root), the frequencies will be in sorted, non-descending order. Thus the bottom left node (A) has the lowest frequency and the top right one (the root) has the highest frequency. This is called the *sibling property*.

▸ **Exercise 2.18:** Why is this the criterion for a Huffman tree?

▮▶   Here is a summary of the operations necessary to update the tree. The loop starts at the current node (the one corresponding to the symbol just input). This node is a leaf that we denote X, with frequency of occurrence F. Each iteration of the loop involves three steps:

1. Compare X to its successors in the tree (from left to right and bottom to top). If the immediate successor has frequency $F + 1$ or greater, the nodes are still in sorted order and there is no need to change anything. Otherwise, some successors of X have identical frequencies of F or smaller. In this case, X should be swapped with the last node in this group (except that X should not be swapped with its parent).

2. Increment the frequency of X from F to $F + 1$.

3. If X is the root, the loop stops; otherwise the loop repeats with the parent of node X.

Figure 2.23b shows the tree after the frequency of node A has been incremented from 1 to 2. It is easy to follow the three rules above to see how incrementing the frequency of A results in incrementing the frequencies of all its parents. No swaps are needed in this simple case because the frequency of A hasn't exceeded the frequency of its immediate successor B. Figure 2.23c shows what happens when A's frequency has been incremented again, from 2 to 3. The three nodes following A, namely, B, C, and D, have frequencies of 2, so A is swapped with the last of them D. The frequencies of the new parents of A are then incremented, each is compared to its successor, but no more swaps are needed.

Figure 2.23d shows the tree after the frequency of A has been incremented to 4. Once we decide that A is the current node, its frequency (which is still 3) is compared to that of its successor (4), and the decision is not to swap. A's frequency is incremented, followed by incrementing the frequencies of its parents.

In Figure 2.23e, A is again the current node. Its frequency (4) equals that of its successor, so they should be swapped. This is shown in Figure 2.23f, where A's frequency is 5. The next loop iteration examines the parent of A, with frequency 10. It should be swapped with its successor E (with frequency 9), which leads to the final tree of Figure 2.23g.

2.9.3 Counter Overflow

The frequency counts are accumulated in fixed-size fields that can overflow. A 16-bit unsigned field can accomodate counts of up to $2^{16} - 1 = 65,535$. A simple solution is to watch the count field of the root each time it is incremented and, when it reaches its maximum value, to *rescale* all frequency counts by dividing them by 2 (integer division). In practice this is done by dividing the count fields of the leaves, then updating the counts of the interior nodes. Each interior node gets the sum of

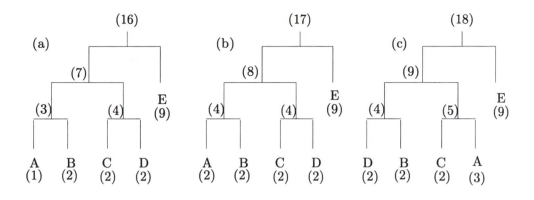

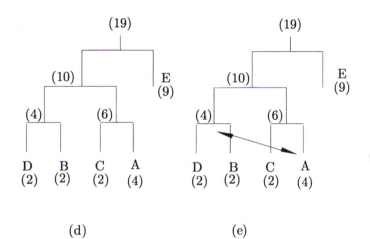

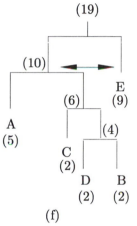

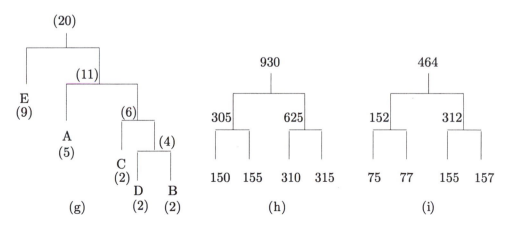

Figure 2.23: Updating the Huffman Tree.

the counts of its children. The problem is that the counts are integers, and integer division reduces precision. This may change a Huffman tree to one that does not satisfy the sibling property.

A simple example is shown in Figure 2.23h. After the counts of the leaves are halved, the three interior nodes are updated as shown in Figure 2.23i. The latter tree, however, is no longer a Huffman tree since the counts are no longer in sorted order. The solution is to rebuild the tree each time the counts are rescaled, which does not happen very often. A Huffman data compression program intended for general use should thus have large count fields that would not overflow very often. A 4-byte count field overflows at $2^{32} - 1 \approx 4.3 \times 10^9$.

It should be noted that after rescaling the counts, the new symbols being read and compressed have more effect on the counts than the old symbols (those counted before the rescaling). This turns out to be fortuitous since it is known from experience that the probability of appearance of a symbol depends more on the symbols immediately preceding it than on symbols that appeared in the distant past.

2.9.4 Code Overflow

An even more serious problem is code overflow. This may happen when more and more symbols are added to the tree, and it becomes high. The codes themselves are not stored in the tree since they change all the time, and the compressor has to figure out the code of a symbol X each time X is input. Here are the details of this operation:

1. The encoder has to locate symbol X in the tree. The tree has to be implemented as an array of structures, each a node, and the array is searched linearly.

2. If X is not found, the escape code is emitted, followed by the uncompressed code of X. X is then added to the tree.

3. If X is found, the compressor moves from node X back to the root, building the code bit by bit as it goes along. Each time it goes from a left child to a parent, a "1" is appended to the code. Going from a right child to a parent appends a "0" bit to the code (or vice versa, but this should be consistent). Those bits have to be accumulated someplace, since they have to be emitted in the *reverse order* in which they are created. When the tree gets taller, the codes get longer. If they are accumulated in a 16-bit integer, then codes longer than 16 bits would cause a malfunction.

One solution is to accumulate the bits of a code in a linked list, where new nodes can be created, limited in number only by the amount of available memory. This is general but slow. Another solution is to accumulate the codes in a large integer variable (perhaps 50 bits wide) and document a maximum code size of 50 bits as one of the limitations of the program.

Fortunately, this problem does not affect the decoding process. The decoder reads the compressed code bit by bit and uses each bit to go one step left or right down the tree until it reaches a leaf node. If the leaf is the escape code, the decoder reads the uncompressed code of the symbol off the compressed stream (and adds the symbol to the tree). Otherwise, the uncompressed code is found in the leaf node.

▶ **Exercise 2.19:** Apply the adaptive Huffman method to the following 11-symbol string "sir␣sid␣is␣...". For each symbol input, show the output, the tree after the symbol has beed added to it, the tree after being rearranged (if necessary), and the list of nodes traversed left to right and bottom up.

2.9.5 A Variant

This variant of the adaptive Huffman method is simpler but less efficient. The idea is to calculate a set of n variable-size codes based on equal probabilities, to assign those codes to the n symbols at random, and to change the assignments "on the fly," as symbols are being read and compressed. The method is not efficient since the codes are not based on the actual probabilities of the symbols in the input stream. However, it is simpler to implement and also faster than the adaptive method described above, because it has to swap rows in a table, rather than update a tree, when updating the frequencies of the symbols.

Name	Count	Code	Name	Count	Code	Name	Count	Code	Name	Count	Code
a_1	0	00	a_2	1	00	a_2	1	00	a_4	2	00
a_2	0	01	a_1	0	01	a_4	1	01	a_2	1	01
a_3	0	10	a_3	0	10	a_3	0	10	a_3	0	10
a_4	0	11	a_4	0	11	a_1	0	11	a_1	0	11
(a)			(b)			(c)			(d)		

Figure 2.24: Four Steps in a Huffman Variant.

The main data structure is an $n \times 3$ table where the three columns store the names of the n symbols, their frequencies of occurrence so far, and their codes. The table is always kept sorted by the second column. When the frequency counts in the second column change, rows are swapped but only columns 1 and 2 are moved. The codes in column 3 never change. Figure 2.24 shows an example of four symbols and the behavior of the method when the string "a_2, a_4, a_4" is compressed.

Figure 2.24a shows the initial situation. After the first symbol a_2 is read, its count is incremented and, since it is now the largest count, rows 1 and 2 are swapped (Figure 2.24b). After the second symbol a_4 is read, its count is incremented and rows 2 and 4 are swapped (Figure 2.24c). Finally, after reading the last symbol a_4, its count is the largest, so rows 1 and 2 are swapped (Figure 2.24d).

The only point that can cause a problem with this method is overflow of the count fields. If such a field is k bits wide, its maximum value is $2^k - 1$, so it will overflow when incremented for the 2^kth time. This may happen if the size of the input stream is not known in advance, which is very common. Fortunately, we do not really need to know the counts, we just need them in sorted order, making it easy to solve this problem.

One solution is to count the input symbols and, after $2^k - 1$ symbols are input and compressed, to (integer) divide all the count fields by 2 (or shift them one position to the right, if this is easier).

Another, similar solution is to check each count field every time it is incremented and, if it has reached its maximum value (if it consists of all ones), to integer divide all the count fields by 2 as above. This approach requires fewer divisions but more complex tests.

Whatever solution is adopted should be used by both the compressor and decompressor.

Bibliography

Knuth, D. E. (1985) "Dynamic Huffman Coding," *Journal of Algorithms* **6**:163–180.

Vitter, Jeffrey S. (1987) "Design and Analysis of Dynamic Huffman Codes," *Journal of the ACM* **34**(4):825-845, October.

2.10 MNP5

Microcom, Inc., a maker of modems, has developed a protocol (called MNP, for Microcom Networking Protocol) for use in its modems. Among other things, the MNP protocol specifies how to unpack bytes into individual bits before they are sent by the modem, how to transmit bits serially in the synchronous and asynchronous modes, and what modulation techniques to use. Each specification is called a *class*, and classes 5 and 7 specify methods for data compression. These methods (especially MNP5) have become very popular and are currently used by most modern modems.

The MNP5 method is a two-stage process that starts with run-length encoding, followed by adaptive frequency encoding.

The first stage has been described on page 9 and is repeated below. When three or more identical consecutive bytes are found in the source stream, the compressor emits three copies of the byte onto its output stream, followed by a repetition count. When the decompressor reads three identical consecutive bytes, it knows that the next byte is a repetition count (which may be zero, indicating just three repetitions). A disadvantage of the method is that a run of three characters in the input stream results in four characters written to the output stream (expansion). A run of four characters results in no compression. Only runs longer than four characters do actually get compressed. Another, slight problem is that the maximum count is artificially limited to 250 instead of 255.

The second stage operates on the bytes in the partially compressed stream generated by the first stage. Stage 2 is similar to the method of Section 2.9.5. It starts with a table of 256×2 entries, where each entry corresponds to one of the 256 possible 8-bit bytes "00000000" to "11111111". The first column, the frequency counts, is initialized to all zeros. Column 2 is initialized to variable-size codes, called *tokens*, that vary from a short "000|0" to a long "111|11111110". Column 2 with the tokens is shown in Table 2.25 (which shows column 1 with frequencies of zero). Each token starts with a 3-bit header, followed by some code bits.

The code bits (with three exceptions) are: The two 1-bit codes 0 and 1, the four 2-bit codes 0 through 3, the eight 3-bit codes 0 through 7, the sixteen 4-bit codes, the thirty-two 5-bit codes, the sixty-four 6-bit codes, and the one hundred and twenty-eight 7-bit codes. This provides for a total of $2 + 4 + 8 + 16 + 32 + 64 + 128 = 254$ codes. The three exceptions are the first two codes "000|0" and "000|1", and the last code, which is "111|11111110" instead of the expected "111|11111111".

Byte	Freq.	Token	Byte	Freq.	Token	Byte	Freq.	Token	Byte	Freq.	Token
0	0	000|0	9	0	011|001	26	0	111|1010	247	0	111|1110111
1	0	000|1	10	0	011|010	27	0	111|1011	248	0	111|1111000
2	0	001|0	11	0	011|011	28	0	111|1100	249	0	111|1111001
3	0	001|1	12	0	011|100	29	0	111|1101	250	0	111|1111010
4	0	010|00	13	0	011|101	30	0	111|1110	251	0	111|1111011
5	0	010|01	14	0	011|110	31	0	111|1111	252	0	111|1111100
6	0	010|10	15	0	011|111	32	0	101|00000	253	0	111|1111101
7	0	010|11	16	0	111|0000	33	0	101|00001	254	0	111|1111110
8	0	011|000	17	0	111|0001	34	0	101|00010	255	0	111|11111110

18–25 and 35–246 continue in the same pattern.

Table 2.25: The MNP5 Tokens.

When stage 2 starts, all 256 entries of column 1 are assigned frequency counts of zero. When the next byte B is read from the input stream (actually, from the output of the first stage), the corresponding token is written to the output stream, and the frequency of entry B is incremented by 1. Following this, tokens may be swapped to ensure that table entries with large frequencies always have the shortest tokens (see next section for details). Notice that only the tokens are swapped, not the frequency counts. Thus the first entry always corresponds to byte "00000000" and contains its frequency count. The token of this byte, however, may change from the original "000|0" to something longer if other bytes achieve higher frequency counts.

The frequency counts are stored in 8-bit fields. Each time a count is incremented, the algorithm checks to see if it has reached its maximum value. If yes, all the counts are scaled down by (integer) dividing them by 2.

Another, subtle point has to do with interaction between the two compression stages. Recall that each repetition of three or more characters is replaced, in stage 1, by three repetitions, followed by a byte with the repetition count. When these four bytes arrive at stage 2, they are replaced by tokens, but the fourth one does not cause an increment of a frequency count.

Example: Suppose that the character with ASCII code 52 repeats six times. Stage 1 will generate the four bytes "52, 52, 52, 6," and stage 2 will replace each with a token, will increment the entry for "52" (entry 53 in the table) by 3, but will not increment the entry for "6" (which is entry 7 in the table). (The three tokens for the three bytes of "52" may all be different, since tokens may be swapped after each "52" is read and processed.)

The output of stage 2 consists of tokens of different sizes, from 4 to 11 bits. This output is packed in groups of 8 bits, which get written into the output stream. At the end, a special code consisting of eleven bits of "1" (the flush token) is written, followed by as many "1" bits as necessary, to complete the last group of 8 bits.

The efficiency of MNP5 is a result of both stages. The efficiency of stage 1 depends heavily on the original data. Stage 2 also depends on the original data, but to a smaller extent. Stage 2 tends to identify the most frequent characters in the data and assign them the short codes. A look at Table 2.25 shows that 32 of the 256 characters have tokens that are 7 bits or fewer in length, thus resulting in compression. The other 224 characters have tokens that are 8 bits or longer. When one of these characters is replaced by a long token, the result is no compression, or even expansion.

The efficiency of MNP5 thus depends on how many characters dominate the original data. If all characters occur at the same frequency, expansion will result. In the other extreme case, if only four characters appear in the data, each will be assigned a 4-bit token, and the compression factor will be 2.

▸ **Exercise 2.20:** Assuming that all 256 characters appear in the original data with the same probability (1/256 each), what will the expansion factor in stage 2 be?

2.10.1 Updating the Table

The process of updating the table of MNP5 codes by swapping rows can be done in two ways:

1. Sorting the entire table every time a frequency is incremented. This is simple in concept but too slow in practice since the table is 256 entries long.

2. Using pointers in the table, and swapping pointers such that items with large frequencies will point to short codes. This approach is illustrated in Figure 2.26. The figure shows the code table organized in four columns labeled F, P, Q, and C. Columns F and C contain the frequencies and codes; columns P and Q contain pointers that always point to each other, so if P[i] contains index j (i.e., points to Q[j]) then Q[j] points to P[i]. The following paragraphs correspond to the nine different parts of the figure.

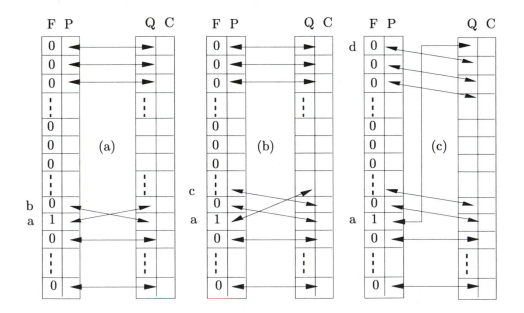

Figure 2.26: Swapping Pointers in the MNP5 Code Table (Part I).

(a). The first data item a is read and F[a] is incremented from 0 to 1. The algorithm starts with pointer P[a], which contains, say, j. The algorithm examines pointer Q[j-1], which initially points to entry F[b], the one right above F[a]. Since

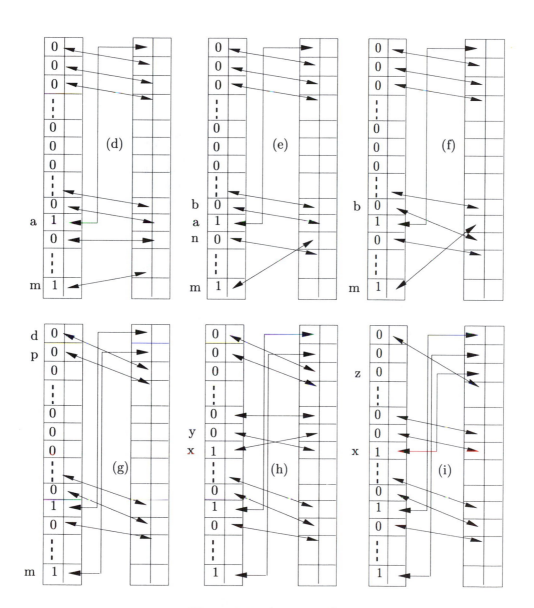

Figure 2.26 (Continued)

F[a]>F[b], entry a has to be assigned a short code, and this is done by swapping pointers P[a] and P[b] (and also the corresponding Q pointers).

(b). The same process is repeated. The algorithm again starts with pointer P[a], which now points higher, to entry b. Assuming that P[a] contains the index k, the algorithm examines pointer Q[k-1], which points to entry c. Since F[a]>F[c], entry a should be assigned a code shorter than that of c. This again is done by swapping pointers, this time P[a] and P[c].

(c). This process is repeated and since F[a] is greater than all the frequencies above it, pointers are swapped until P[a] points to the top entry d. At this point entry a has been asigned the shortest code.

(d). We now assume that the next data item has been input, and F[m] incremented to 1. Pointers P[m] and the one above it are swapped as in (a) above.

(e). After a few more swaps, P[m] is now pointing to entry n (the one just below a). The next step performs j:=P[m]; b:=Q[j-1], and the algorithm compares F[m] to F[b]. Since F[m]>F[b], pointers are swapped as shown in Figure 2.26f.

(g). After some more swaps, pointer P[m] points to the second entry p, which is how entry m is assigned the second shortest code. Pointer P[m] is not swapped with P[a] since they have the same frequencies.

(h). We now assume that the third data item has been input and F[x] incremented. Pointers P[x] and P[y] are swapped.

(i). After some more swaps, pointer P[x] points to the third table entry z. This is how entry x is assigned the third shortest code.

Assuming that F[x] is incremented next, try to figure out how P[x] is swapped, first with P[m] and then with P[a], so that entry x is assigned the shortest code.

The pseudo-code of Figure 2.27 summarizes the pointer swapping process.

```
F[i]:=F[i]+1;
repeat forever
 j:=P[i];
 if j=1 then exit;
 j:=Q[j-1];
 if F[i]<=F[j] then exit
  else
    tmp:=P[i]; P[i]:=P[j]; P[j]:=tmp;
    tmp:=Q[P[i]]; Q[P[i]]:=Q[P[j]]; Q[P[j]]:=tmp
  endif;
end repeat
```

Figure 2.27: Swapping Pointers in MNP5.

Are no probabilities to be accepted, merely because they are not certainties?
—Jane Austen, *Sense and Sensibility*

2.11 MNP7

More complex and sophisticated than MNP5, MNP7 combines run-length encoding with a two-dimensional variant of adaptive Huffman coding. Stage 1 identifies runs and emits three copies of the run character, followed by a 4-bit count of the remaining characters in the run. A count of zero implies a run of length 3, and a count of 15 (the largest possible in a 4-bit nibble), a run of length 18. Stage 2 starts by assigning to each character a complete table with many variable-size codes. When a character C is read, one of the codes in its table is selected and output, depending on the *character preceding* C in the input stream. If this character is say P, then the frequency count of the pair (digram) PC is incremented by 1, and table rows may be swapped, using the same algorithm as for MNP5, to move the pair to a position in the table that has a shorter code.

MNP7 is thus based on a first-order Markov model, where each item is processed depending on the item and its predecessor. In a k-order Markov model, an item is processed depending on itself and its k predecessors.

Here are the details. Each of the 256 8-bit bytes gets a table of codes assigned, of size 256×2, where each row corresponds to one of the 256 possible bytes. Column 1 of the table is initialized to the integers 0 through 255, and column 2 (the frequency counts) is initialized to all zeros. The result is 256 tables, each a double column of 256 rows (Table 2.28a). Variable-size codes are assigned to the rows, such that the first code is 1-bit long, and the others get longer towards the bottom of the table. The codes are stored in an additional code table that never changes.

	Current character					
	0	1	2	...	254	255
	0 0	0 0	0 0	...	0 0	0 0
	1 0	1 0	1 0	...	1 0	1 0
	2 0	2 0	2 0	...	2 0	2 0
	3 0	3 0	3 0	...	3 0	3 0
Preced.	⋮	⋮	⋮		⋮	⋮
Char.	254 0	254 0	254 0	...	254 0	254 0
	255 0	255 0	255 0	...	255 0	255 0

```
...a  b  c  d  c...
   t  l  h  o  d
   h  e  o  a  r
   c  u  r  e  s
   ⋮  ⋮  ⋮  ⋮  ⋮
```

(a)   (b)

Table 2.28: The MNP7 Code Tables.

When a character C is read (the current character to be compressed), its value is used as a pointer, to select one of the 256 tables. The first column of the table is searched, to find the row with the 8-bit value of the preceding character P. Once the row is found, the code from the same row in the code table is emitted and the count in the second column incremented by 1. Rows in the table may be swapped if the new count of the digram PC is large enough.

After enough characters have been input and rows swapped, the tables start reflecting the true digram frequencies of the data. Table 2.28b shows a possible state assuming that the digrams "ta", "ha", "ca", "lb", "eb", "ub", "hc", etc., are common. Since the top digram is encoded into 1 bit, MNP7 can be very efficient. If the original data consists of text in a natural language, where certain digrams are very common, MNP7 normally produces a high compression ratio.

2.12 Reliability

The most obvious disadvantage of variable-size codes is their vulnerability to errors. The prefix property is used to decode those codes, so an error in a single bit can cause the decompressor to lose synchronization and be unable to decode the rest of the compressed stream. (See page 340 for the meaning of the word "error" in data transmissions.) In the worst case, the decompressor may even read, decode, and interpret the rest of the compressed data wrong, without realizing that a problem has occurred.

Example: Using the code of Figure 2.12 the string "CARE" is coded into "10100 0011 0110 000" (without the spaces). Assuming the following error: "10$\boxed{0}$00 0011 0110 000", the decompressor will not notice any problem but will decode the string as "HARE".

▶ **Exercise 2.21:** What will happen in the case "11$\boxed{1}$11 0011 0110 000..." (the string "WARE..." with one bad bit)?

A simple way of adding reliability to variable-size codes is to break a long compressed stream, as it is being transmitted, into groups of 7 bits and add a parity bit to each group. This way the decompressor will at least be able to detect a problem and output an error message or ask for a retransmission. It is, of course, possible to add more than one parity bit to a group of data bits, thus making it more reliable. However, reliability is, in a sense, the opposite of compression. Compression is done by decreasing redundancy, while reliability is achieved by increasing it. The more reliable a piece of data is, the less compressed it is, so care should be taken when the two operations are going to be used together. For completeness, Appendix E discusses error-detecting and correcting codes.

2.13 Facsimile Compression

Data compression is especially important when images are transmitted over a communications line because the user is typically waiting at the receiver, eager to see the result fast. Images are commonly transmitted between fax machines, so a standard data compression method was needed when those machine became popular. Several methods were developed and proposed by the ITU-T.

The ITU-T is one of four permanent parts of the International Telecommunications Union (ITU), based in Geneva, Switzerland (http://www.itu.ch/). It issues recommendations for standards applying to modems, packet switched interfaces, V.24 connectors, etc. Although it has no power of enforcement, the standards it recommends are generally accepted and adopted by industry. Until March 1993, the ITU-T was known as the Consultative Committee for International Telephone and Telegraph (Comité Consultatif International de télégraphie et Téléphonie, or CCITT).

The first data compression standards developed by the ITU-T were T2 (also known as Group 1) and T3 (Group 2). These are now obsolete and have been replaced by T4 (Group 3) and T6 (Group 4). Group 3 is currently used by all fax machines designed to operate with the Public Switched Telephone Network (PSTN). These are the machines we have at home, and, at the time of writing, they operate at maximum speeds of 9,600 baud. Group 4 is used by fax machines designed to operate on a digital network, such as ISDN. They have typical speeds of 64K baud. Both methods can produce compression ratios of 10:1 or better, reducing the transmission time of a typical page to about a minute with the former, and a few seconds with the latter.

2.13.1 One-Dimensional Coding

A fax machine scans a document line by line, converting each line to small black and white dots called *pels* (from Picture ELement). The horizontal resolution is always 8.05 pels per millimeter (about 205 pels per inch). An 8.5-inch-wide scan line is thus converted to 1728 pels. The T4 standard, though, recommends to scan only about 8.2 inches, thus producing 1664 pels per scan line (these numbers, as well as the ones in the next paragraph, are all to within ±1% accuracy).

The vertical resolution is either 3.85 scan lines per millimeter (standard mode) or 7.7 lines/mm (fine mode). Many fax machines have also a very-fine mode, where they scan 15.4 lines/mm. Table 2.29 assumes a 10-inch-high page (254 mm), and shows the total number of pels per page, and typical transmission times for the three modes without compression. The times are long, which shows how important data compression is in fax transmissions.

Scan lines	Pels per line	Pels per page	Time (sec.)	Time (min.)
978	1664	1.670M	170	2.82
1956	1664	3.255M	339	5.65
3912	1664	6.510M	678	11.3

Ten inches equal 254 mm. The number of pels is in the millions and the transmission times, at 9600 baud without compression, are between 3 and 11 minutes, depending on the mode. However, if the page is shorter than 10 inches, or if most of it is white, the compression ratio can be 10:1 or better, resulting in transmission times of between 17 and 68 seconds.

Table 2.29: Fax Transmission Times.

To develop the Group 3 code, the ITU-T analyzed run lengths of white and black pels on many documents, and used the Huffman algorithm to assign a variable-size code to each run length. The most common run lengths were found to be 2, 3, and 4 black pixels, so they were assigned the shortest codes (Table 2.30). Next come run lengths of 2–7 white pixels, which were assigned slightly longer codes. Most run lengths were rare and were assigned long, 12-bit codes. Group 3 thus uses a combination of RLE and Huffman coding.

▶ **Exercise 2.22:** A run length of 1664 white pels was assigned the short code 011000. Why is this length so common?

Since run lengths can be long, the Huffman algorithm was modified. Codes were assigned to run lengths of 1 to 63 pels (they are the termination codes in Table 2.30a) and to run lengths that are multiples of 64 pels (the make-up codes in Table 2.30b). Group 3 is thus a *modified Huffman code* (also called MH). The code of a run length is either a single termination code (if the run length is short) or one or more make-up codes, followed by one termination code (if it is long). Here are some examples:

1. A run length of 12 white pels is coded as 001000.
2. A run length of 76 white pels (=64+12) is coded as 11011|001000 (without the vertical bar).
3. A run length of 140 white pels (=128+12) is coded as 10010|001000.
4. A run length of 64 black pels (=64+0) is coded as 0000001111|0000110111.
5. A run length of 2561 black pels (2560+1) is coded as 000000011111|010.

▶ **Exercise 2.23:** An 8.5-inch wide scan line results in 1728 pels, so how can there be a run of 2561 consecutive pels?

Each scan line is coded separately, and its code is terminated with the special EOL code 00000000001. Each line also gets one white pel appended to it on the left when it is scanned. This is done to remove any ambiguity when the line is decoded on the receiving side. After reading the EOL for the previous line, the receiver assumes that the new line starts with a run of white pels, and it ignores the first of them. Examples:

1. The 14-pel line ■■■ □ ■■ □□□□□□□ is coded as the run lengths 1w 3b 2w 2b 7w EOL, which become "000111|10|0111|11|1111|0000000001". The decoder ignores the single white pel at the start.

2. The line □□ ■■■■■ □□□□ ■■ is coded as the run lengths 3w 5b 5w 2b EOL, which becomes the binary string "1000|0011|1100|11|0000000001".

The Group 3 code has no error correction, but many errors can be detected. Because of the nature of the Huffman code, even one bad bit in the transmission can cause the receiver to get out of synchronization, and to produce a string of wrong pels. This is why each scan line is encoded separately. If the receiver detects an error, it skips bits, looking for an EOL. This way, one error can cause at most one scan line to be received incorrectly. If the receiver does not see an EOL after a certain number of lines, it assumes a high error rate, and it aborts the process, notifying the transmitter. Since the codes are between 2 and 12 bits long, the receiver detects an error if it cannot decode a valid code after reading 12 bits.

Each page of the coded document is preceded by one EOL and is followed by six EOL codes. Because each line is coded separately, this method is a *one-dimensional coding* scheme. The compression ratio depends on the image. Images with large contiguous black or white areas (text or black and white images) can be highly compressed. Images with many short runs can sometimes produce negative compression. This is especially true in the case of images with shades of gray (such as scanned photographs). Such shades are produced by halftoning, which covers areas with alternating black and white pels (runs of length one).

Run length	White code-word	Black code-word	Run length	White code-word	Black code-word
0	00110101	0000110111	32	00011011	000001101010
1	000111	010	33	00010010	000001101011
2	0111	11	34	00010011	000011010010
3	1000	10	35	00010100	000011010011
4	1011	011	36	00010101	000011010100
5	1100	0011	37	00010110	000011010101
6	1110	0010	38	00010111	000011010110
7	1111	00011	39	00101000	000011010111
8	10011	000101	40	00101001	000001101100
9	10100	000100	41	00101010	000001101101
10	00111	0000100	42	00101011	000011011010
11	01000	0000101	43	00101100	000011011011
12	001000	0000111	44	00101101	000001010100
13	000011	00000100	45	00000100	000001010101
14	110100	00000111	46	00000101	000001010110
15	110101	000011000	47	00001010	000001010111
16	101010	0000010111	48	00001011	000001100100
17	101011	0000011000	49	01010010	000001100101
18	0100111	0000001000	50	01010011	000001010010
19	0001100	00001100111	51	01010100	000001010011
20	0001000	00001101000	52	01010101	000000100100
21	0010111	00001101100	53	00100100	000000110111
22	0000011	00000110111	54	00100101	000000111000
23	0000100	00000101000	55	01011000	000000100111
24	0101000	00000010111	56	01011001	000000101000
25	0101011	00000011000	57	01011010	000001011000
26	0010011	000011001010	58	01011011	000001011001
27	0100100	000011001011	59	01001010	000000101011
28	0011000	000011001100	60	01001011	000000101100
29	00000010	000011001101	61	00110010	000001011010
30	00000011	000001101000	62	00110011	000001100110
31	00011010	000001101001	63	00110100	000001100111

(a)

Run length	White code-word	Black code-word	Run length	White code-word	Black code-word
64	11011	0000001111	1344	011011010	0000001010011
128	10010	000011001000	1408	011011011	0000001010100
192	010111	000011001001	1472	010011000	0000001010101
256	0110111	000001011011	1536	010011001	0000001011010
320	00110110	000000110011	1600	010011010	0000001011011
384	00110111	000000110100	1664	011000	0000001100100
448	01100100	000000110101	1728	010011011	0000001100101
512	01100101	0000001101100	1792	00000001000	same as
576	01101000	0000001101101	1856	00000001100	white
640	01100111	0000001001010	1920	00000001101	from this
704	011001100	0000001001011	1984	000000010010	point
768	011001101	0000001001100	2048	000000010011	
832	011010010	0000001001101	2112	000000010100	
896	011010011	0000001110010	2176	000000010101	
960	011010100	0000001110011	2240	000000010110	
1024	011010101	0000001110100	2304	000000010111	
1088	011010110	0000001110101	2368	000000011100	
1152	011010111	0000001110110	2432	000000011101	
1216	011011000	0000001110111	2496	000000011110	
1280	011011001	0000001010010	2560	000000011111	

(b)

Table 2.30: Group 3 and 4 Fax Codes: (a) Termination Codes. (b) Make-Up Codes.

▶ **Exercise 2.24:** What is the compression ratio for runs of length one (many alternating pels)?

The T4 standard also allows for fill bits to be inserted between the data bits and the EOL. This is done in cases where a pause is necessary, or where the total number of bits transmitted for a scan line must be a multiple of 8. The fill bits are zeros.

Example: The binary string "000111|10|0111|11|1111|0000000001" becomes "000111|10|0111|11|1111|0000|0000000001" after four zeros are added as fill bits, bringing the total length of the string to 32 bits (= 8 × 4). The decoder sees the four zeros of the fill, followed by the nine zeros of the EOL, followed by the single 1, so it knows that it has encountered a fill followed by an EOL.

See URL `http://www.cis.ohio-state.edu/htbin/rfc/rfc804.html` for a description of the Group 3 method.

At the time of writing, the T.4 and T.6 recommendations can also be found at ftp site `src.doc.ic.ac.uk/computing/ccitt/ccitt-standards/1988/`, as files `7_3_01.ps.gz` and `7_3_02.ps.gz`.

2.13.2 Two-Dimensional Coding

This method was developed because one-dimensional coding does not produce good results for images with gray areas. Two-dimensional coding is optional on fax machines that use Group 3 but is the only method used by machines intended to work on a digital network. When a fax machine using Group 3 supports two-dimensional coding as an option, each EOL is followed by one extra bit, to indicate the compression method used for the next scan line. That bit is 1 if the next line is encoded with one-dimensional coding, and 0, if it is encoded with two-dimensional coding.

The two-dimensional coding method is also called MMR, for *modified-modified READ*, where READ stands for *relative element address designate*. The term "modified-modified" is used since this is a modification of one-dimensional coding, which itself is a modification of the original Huffman method. The two-dimensional coding method works by comparing the current scan line (called the *coding line*) to its predecessor (which is called the *reference line*) and recording the differences between them. The assumption being that two consecutive lines in a document will normally differ by just a few pels. The method assumes that there is an all-white line above the page, which is used as the reference line for the first scan line of the page. After coding the first line, it becomes the reference line, and the second scan line is coded. Similarly to one-dimensional coding, each line is assumed to start with a white pel, which is ignored by the receiver.

The two-dimensional coding method is less reliable than one-dimensional coding since an error in decoding a line will cause errors in decoding all its successors and will propagate through the entire document. This is why the T.4 (Group 3) standard includes a requirement that says that after a line is encoded with the one-dimensional method, at most $K - 1$ lines will be encoded with the two-dimensional coding method. For standard resolution $K = 2$, and for fine resolution $K = 4$. The T.6 standard (Group 4) does not have this requirement, and uses two-dimensional coding exclusively.

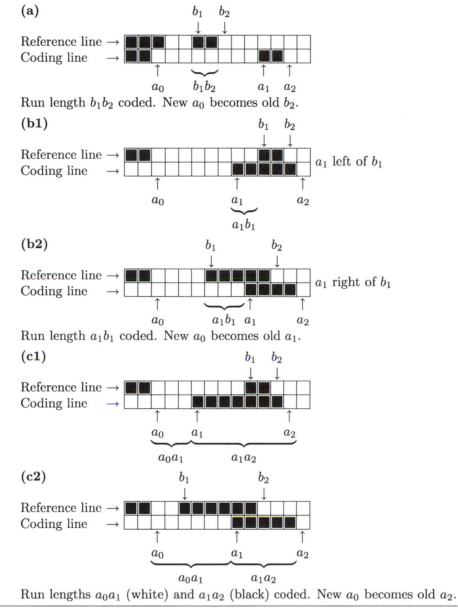

Run length b_1b_2 coded. New a_0 becomes old b_2.

a_1 left of b_1

a_1 right of b_1

Run length a_1b_1 coded. New a_0 becomes old a_1.

Run lengths a_0a_1 (white) and a_1a_2 (black) coded. New a_0 becomes old a_2.

Notes:

1. a_0 is the first pel of a new codeword and can be black or white.
2. a_1 is the first pel to the right of a_0 with a different color.
3. b_1 is the first pel on the reference line to the right of a_0 with a different color.
4. b_2 is the first pel on the reference line to the right of b_1 with a different color.

Figure 2.31: Five Run Length Configurations: (a) Pass Mode; (b) Vertical Mode; and (c) Horizontal Mode.

Scanning the coding line and comparing it to the reference line results in three cases or modes. The mode is identified by comparing the next run length on the reference line [(b_1b_2) in Figure 2.31] with the current run length (a_0a_1) and the next one (a_1a_2) on the coding line. Each of these three runs can be black or white. The three modes are (see also flow chart of Figure 2.33):

1. **Pass mode.** This is the case where (b_1b_2) is to the left of (a_1a_2). b_2 is to the left of a_1 (Figure 2.31a). This mode does not include the case where b_2 is on top of a_1. When this mode is identified, the length of run (b_1b_2) is coded using the codes of Table 2.32 and is transmitted. Pointer a_0 is moved below b_2, and b_1, b_2, a_1, and a_2 are updated.

2. **Vertical mode.** (b_1b_2) overlaps (a_1a_2) by not more than three pels (Figure 2.31b1, b2). Assuming that consecutive lines do not differ by much, this is the normal case. When this mode is identified, one of seven codes is produced (Table 2.32) and is transmitted. Pointers are updated as in case 1 above. The performance of the two-dimensional coding method depends on this case being common.

3. **Horizontal mode.** (b_1b_2) overlaps (a_1a_2) by more than three pels (Figure 2.31c1, c2). When this mode is identified, the lengths of runs (a_0a_1) and (a_1a_2) are coded using the codes of Table 2.32 and are transmitted. Pointers are updated as in cases 1 and 2 above.

Mode	Run length to be encoded	Abbreviation	Codeword
Pass	b_1b_2	P	0001+coded length of b_1b_2
Horizontal	a_0a_1, a_1a_2	H	001+coded length of a_0a_1 and a_1a_2
Vertical	$a_1b_1 = 0$	V(0)	1
	$a_1b_1 = -1$	VR(1)	011
	$a_1b_1 = -2$	VR(2)	000011
	$a_1b_1 = -3$	VR(3)	0000011
	$a_1b_1 = +1$	VL(1)	010
	$a_1b_1 = +2$	VL(2)	000010
	$a_1b_1 = +3$	VL(3)	0000010
Extension			0000001000

Table 2.32: 2D Codes for the Group 4 Method.

When scanning starts, pointer a_0 is set to an imaginary white pel on the left of the coding line. a_1 is set to point to the first black pel on the coding line. (Since a_0 corresponds to an imaginary pel, the first run length is $|a_0a_1| - 1$.) a_2 is set to the first white pel following that. Pointers b_1b_2 are set to point to the start of the first and second runs on the reference line, respectively.

After identifying the current mode and transmitting codes according to Table 2.32, a_0 is updated as shown in the flow chart, and the other four pointers are updated relative to the new a_0. The process continues until the end of the coding line is reached. The encoder assumes an extra pel on the right of the line, with a color opposite that of the last pel.

The extension code in Table 2.32 is used to abort the encoding process prematurely, before reaching the end of the page. This is necessary if the rest of the page is transmitted in a different code or even in uncompressed form.

▸ **Exercise 2.25:** Manually figure out the code generated from the two lines below.

Bibliography

Anderson, K. L., et al., (1987) "Binary-Image-Manipulation Algorithm in the Image View Facility," *IBM Journal of Research and Development* **31**(1):16–31, January.

Hunter, R., and A. H. Robinson (1980) "International Digital Facsimile Coding Standards," *Proceedings of the IEEE* **68**(7):854–867, July.

Marking, Michael P. (1990) "Decoding Group 3 Images," *The C Users Journal* pp. 45–54, June.

McConnell, Kenneth R. (1992) *FAX: Digital Facsimile Technology and Applications*, Norwood, MA, Artech House.

2.14 Arithmetic Coding

The Huffman method is more efficient than the Shannon-Fano method, but either method rarely produces the best variable-size code. Section 2.8 shows that these methods produce best results (codes whose average size equals the entropy) only when the symbols have probabilities of occurrence that are negative powers of 2. This is because these methods assign a code with an integral number of bits to each symbol in the alphabet. It has been mentioned on page 40 that a symbol with probability 0.4 is assigned a Huffman code of 1 or 2 bits since $-\log_2 0.4 \approx 1.32$. Ideally, such a symbol should be assigned a 1.32-bit code but this is impossible in the above-mentioned codes since they assign a code to each individual symbol.

Arithmetic coding overcomes this problem by assigning one (normally long) code to the entire input stream, instead of assigning codes to the individual symbols. The method reads the input stream symbol by symbol and appends more bits to the code each time a symbol is input and processed. To understand the method, it is useful to imagine the resulting code as a number in the range $[0, 1)$. [The notation $[a, b)$ means the range of real numbers from a to b, not including b. The range is "closed" at a and "open" at b.] Thus the code "9746509" should be interpreted as "0.9746509" although the "0." part will not be included in the output stream.

The first step is to calculate, or at least to estimate, the frequencies of occurrence of each symbol. For best results, the exact frequencies are calculated by reading the entire input stream in the first pass of a two-pass compression job. If the program has good estimates of the frequencies from a different source, the first pass may be omitted.

The first example involves three symbols a_1, a_2, and a_3, with probabilities $P_1 = 0.4$, $P_2 = 0.5$, and $P_3 = 0.1$, respectively. The interval $[0, 1)$ is divided among the three symbols by assigning each a subinterval proportional in size to its probability. The order of the subintervals is immaterial. In our example, the three symbols are assigned the subintervals $[0, 0.4)$, $[0.4, 0.9)$, and $[0.9, 1.0)$. To

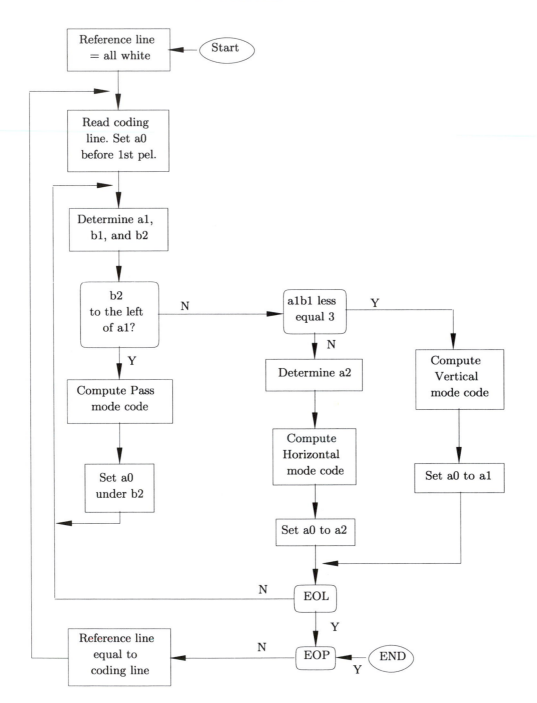

Figure 2.33: MMR Flow Chart.

encode the string "$a_2a_2a_2a_3$", we start with the interval $[0, 1)$. The first symbol a_2 reduces this interval to the subinterval from its 40% point to its 90% point. The result is $[0.4, 0.9)$. The second a_2 reduces $[0.4, 0.9)$ in the same way (see note below) to $[0.6, 0.85)$, the third a_2 reduces this to $[0.7, 0.825)$, and the a_3 reduces this to the stretch from the 90% point of $[0.7, 0.825)$ to its 100% point, producing $[0.8125, 0.8250)$. The final code our method produces can be any number in this final range.

(Note: The subinterval $[0.6, 0.85)$ is obtained from the interval $[0.4, 0.9)$ by $0.4 + (0.9 - 0.4) \times 0.4 = 0.6$ and $0.4 + (0.9 - 0.4) \times 0.9 = 0.85$.)

With this example in mind, it should be easy to understand the following rules, which summarize the main steps of arithmetic coding:

1. Start by defining the "current interval" as $[0, 1)$.

2. Repeat the following two steps for each symbol s in the input stream:

2.1. Divide the current interval into subintervals whose sizes are proportional to the symbols' probabilities.

2.2. Select the subinterval for s and define it as the new current interval.

3. When the entire input stream has been processed in this way, the output should be any number that uniquely identify the current interval.

For each symbol processed, the current interval gets smaller, so it takes more bits to express it, but the point is that the final output is a single number and does not consist of codes for the individual symbols. The average code size can be obtained by dividing the size of the output (in bits) by the size of the input (in symbols). Notice also that the probabilities used in step 2.1 may change all the time since they may be supplied by an adaptive model (Section 2.15).

The next example is a little more involved. We show the compression steps for the short string "SWISS␣MISS". Table 2.34 shows the information prepared in the first step (the *statistical model* of the data). The five symbols appearing in the input may be arranged in any order. For each symbol, its frequency is first counted, followed by its probability of occurrence (the frequency divided by the string size, 10). The range $[0, 1)$ is then divided among the symbols, in any order, with each symbol getting a chunk, or a subrange, equal in size to its probability. Thus "S" gets the subrange $[0.5, 1.0)$ (of size 0.5), whereas the subrange of "I" is of size 0.2 $[0.2, 0.4)$. The cumulative frequencies column is used by the decoding algorithm on page 76.

Char	Freq	Prob.	Range	CumFreq
		Total CumFreq=		10
S	5	$5/10 = 0.5$	$[0.5, 1.0)$	5
W	1	$1/10 = 0.1$	$[0.4, 0.5)$	4
I	2	$2/10 = 0.2$	$[0.2, 0.4)$	2
M	1	$1/10 = 0.1$	$[0.1, 0.2)$	1
␣	1	$1/10 = 0.1$	$[0.0, 0.1)$	0

Table 2.34: Frequencies and Probabilities of Five Symbols.

The symbols and frequencies in Table 2.34 are written on the output stream before any of the bits of the compressed code. This table will be the first thing input by the decoder.

The encoding process starts by defining two variables, Low and High, and setting them to 0 and 1, respectively. They define an interval [Low, High). As symbols are being input and processed, the values of Low and High are moved closer together, to narrow the interval.

After processing the first symbol "S", Low and High are updated to 0.5 and 1, respectively. The resulting code for the entire input stream will be a number in this range $(0.5 \leq \text{Code} < 1.0)$. The rest of the input stream will determine precisely where, in the interval $[0.5, 1)$, the final code will lie. A good way to understand the process is to imagine that the new interval $[0.5, 1)$ is divided among the five symbols of our alphabet using the same proportions as for the original interval $[0, 1)$. The result is the five subintervals $[0.5, 0.55)$, $[0.55, 0.60)$, $[0.60, 0.70)$, $[0.70, 0.75)$, and $[0.75, 1.0)$. When the next symbol "W" is input, the third of those subintervals is selected, and is again divided into five subsubintervals.

As more symbols are being input and processed, Low and High are being updated according to

```
NewHigh:=OldLow+Range*HighRange(X);
NewLow:=OldLow+Range*LowRange(X);
```

where Range=OldHigh−OldLow and LowRange(X), HighRange(X) indicate the low and high limits of the range of symbol X, respectively. In the example above, the second input symbol is "W", so we update Low $:= 0.5 + (1.0 - 0.5) \times 0.4 = 0.70$, High $:= 0.5 + (1.0 - 0.5) \times 0.5 = 0.75$. The new interval $[0.70, 0.75)$ covers the stretch $[40\%, 50\%)$ of the subrange of "S". Table 2.35 shows all the steps involved in coding the string "SWISS⎵MISS". The final code is the final value of Low, 0.71753375, of which only the eight digits "71753375" need be written on the output stream (but see later for a modification of this statement).

The decoder works in the opposite way. It starts by inputting the symbols and their ranges, and reconstructing Table 2.34. It then inputs the rest of the code. The first digit is "7", so the decoder immediately knows that the entire code is a number of the form 0.7.... This number is inside the subrange $[0.5, 1)$ of "S", so the first symbol is "S". The decoder then eliminates the effect of symbol "S" from the code by subtracting the lower limit 0.5 of "S" and dividing by the width of the subrange of "S" (0.5). The result is 0.4350675, which tells the decoder that the next symbol is "W" (since the subrange of "W" is $[0.4, 0.5)$). To eliminate the effect of symbol X from the code, the decoder performs Code:=(Code−LowRange(X))/Range, where Range is the width of the subrange of X. Table 2.36 summarizes the steps for decoding our example string.

The next example is of three symbols with probabilities as shown in Table 2.37(a). Notice that the probabilities are very different. One is large (97.5%) and the others much smaller. This is a case of *skewed probabilities*.

Encoding the string $a_2 a_2 a_1 a_3 a_3$ produces the strange numbers (accurate to 16 digits) in Table 2.38, where the two rows for each symbol correspond to the Low and High values, respectively.

Char.		The calculation of low and high
S	L	$0.0 + (1.0 - 0.0) \times 0.5 = 0.5$
	H	$0.0 + (1.0 - 0.0) \times 1.0 = 1.0$
W	L	$0.5 + (1.0 - 0.5) \times 0.4 = 0.70$
	H	$0.5 + (1.0 - 0.5) \times 0.5 = 0.75$
I	L	$0.7 + (0.75 - 0.70) \times 0.2 = 0.71$
	H	$0.7 + (0.75 - 0.70) \times 0.4 = 0.72$
S	L	$0.71 + (0.72 - 0.71) \times 0.5 = 0.715$
	H	$0.71 + (0.72 - 0.71) \times 1.0 = 0.72$
S	L	$0.715 + (0.72 - 0.715) \times 0.5 = 0.7175$
	H	$0.715 + (0.72 - 0.715) \times 1.0 = 0.72$
␣	L	$0.7175 + (0.72 - 0.7175) \times 0.0 = 0.7175$
	H	$0.7175 + (0.72 - 0.7175) \times 0.1 = 0.71775$
M	L	$0.7175 + (0.71775 - 0.7175) \times 0.1 = 0.717525$
	H	$0.7175 + (0.71775 - 0.7175) \times 0.2 = 0.717550$
I	L	$0.717525 + (0.71755 - 0.717525) \times 0.2 = 0.717530$
	H	$0.717525 + (0.71755 - 0.717525) \times 0.4 = 0.717535$
S	L	$0.717530 + (0.717535 - 0.717530) \times 0.5 = 0.7175325$
	H	$0.717530 + (0.717535 - 0.717530) \times 1.0 = 0.717535$
S	L	$0.7175325 + (0.717535 - 0.7175325) \times 0.5 = 0.71753375$
	H	$0.7175325 + (0.717535 - 0.7175325) \times 1.0 = 0.717535$

Table 2.35: The Process of Arithmetic Encoding.

At first glance, it seems that the resulting code is longer than the original string, but Section 2.14.3 shows how to figure out the true compression achieved by arithmetic coding.

Decoding this string is shown in Table 2.39 and involves a special problem. After eliminating the effect of a_1, on line 3, the result is 0. Earlier we implicitly assumed that this means the end of the decoding process, but now we know that there are two more occurrences of a_3 that should be decoded. These are shown on lines 4, 5 of the table. This problem always occurs when the last symbol in the input stream is the one whose subrange starts at zero. In order to distinguish between such a symbol and the end of the input stream, we need to define an additional symbol, the end-of-input (or end-of-file, eof). This symbol should be added, with a small probability, to the frequency table (see Table 2.37b), and it should be encoded at the end of the input stream.

Tables 2.40 and 2.41 show how the string $a_3a_3a_3a_3$eof is encoded into the number 0.0000002878086184764172, and then decoded properly. Without the eof symbol, a string of all a_3s would have been encoded into a 0.

Notice how the low value is 0 until the eof is input and processed, and how the

Char.	Code−low	Range
S	$0.71753375 - 0.5 = 0.21753375$	$/0.5 = 0.4350675$
W	$0.4350675 - 0.4\ =0.0350675$	$/0.1 = 0.350675$
I	$0.350675 - 0.2\ =0.150675$	$/0.2 = 0.753375$
S	$0.753375 - 0.5\ =0.253375$	$/0.5 = 0.50675$
S	$0.50675 - 0.5\ =0.00675$	$/0.5 = 0.0135$
␣	$0.0135 - 0\ =0.0135$	$/0.1 = 0.135$
M	$0.135 - 0.1\ =0.035$	$/0.1 = 0.35$
I	$0.35 - 0.2\ =0.15$	$/0.2 = 0.75$
S	$0.75 - 0.5\ =0.25$	$/0.5 = 0.5$
S	$0.5 - 0.5\ =0$	$/0.5 = 0$

Table 2.36: The Process of Arithmetic Decoding.

Char	Prob.	Range	Char	Prob.	Range
a_1	0.001838	[0.998162, 1.0)	eof	0.000001	[0.999999, 1.0)
a_2	0.975	[0.023162, 0.998162)	a_1	0.001837	[0.998162, 0.999999)
a_3	0.023162	[0.0, 0.023162)	a_2	0.975	[0.023162, 0.998162)
			a_3	0.023162	[0.0, 0.023162)
	(a)			(b)	

Table 2.37: (Skewed) Probabilities of Three Symbols.

a_2	$0.0 + (1.0 - 0.0) \times 0.023162 = 0.023162$
	$0.0 + (1.0 - 0.0) \times 0.998162 = 0.998162$
a_2	$0.023162 + .975 \times 0.023162 = 0.04574495$
	$0.023162 + .975 \times 0.998162 = 0.99636995$
a_1	$0.04574495 + 0.950625 \times 0.998162 = 0.99462270125$
	$0.04574495 + 0.950625 \times 1.0 = 0.99636995$
a_3	$0.99462270125 + 0.00174724875 \times 0.0 = 0.99462270125$
	$0.99462270125 + 0.00174724875 \times 0.023162 = 0.994663171025547$
a_3	$0.99462270125 + 0.00004046977554749998 \times 0.0 = 0.99462270125$
	$0.99462270125 + 0.00004046977554749998 \times 0.023162 = 0.994623638610941$

Table 2.38: Encoding the String $a_2 a_2 a_1 a_3 a_3$.

Char.	Code−low		Range	
a_2	$0.99462270125 - 0.023162$	$=0.97146170125$	$/0.975$	$=0.99636995$
a_2	$0.99636995 - 0.023162$	$=0.97320795$	$/0.975$	$=0.998162$
a_1	$0.998162 - 0.998162$	$=0.0$	$/0.00138$	$=0.0$
a_3	$0.0 - 0.0$	$=0.0$	$/0.023162$	$=0.0$
a_3	$0.0 - 0.0$	$=0.0$	$/0.023162$	$=0.0$

Table 2.39: Decoding the String $a_2a_2a_1a_3a_3$.

a_3	$0.0 + (1.0 - 0.0) \times 0.0 = 0.0$
	$0.0 + (1.0 - 0.0) \times 0.023162 = 0.023162$
a_3	$0.0 + .023162 \times 0.0 = 0.0$
	$0.0 + .023162 \times 0.023162 = 0.000536478244$
a_3	$0.0 + 0.000536478244 \times 0.0 = 0.0$
	$0.0 + 0.000536478244 \times 0.023162 = 0.000012425909087528$
a_3	$0.0 + 0.000012425909087528 \times 0.0 = 0.0$
	$0.0 + 0.000012425909087528 \times 0.023162 = 0.000000287808 9062853235$
eof	$0.0 + 0.000000287808 9062853235 \times 0.999999 = 0.000000287808 6184764172$
	$0.0 + 0.000000287808 9062853235 \times 1.0 = 0.000000287808 9062853235$

Table 2.40: Encoding the String $a_3a_3a_3a_3$eof.

Char.	Code−low		Range	
a_3	$0.000000287808 6184764172-0$	$=0.000000287808 6184764172$	$/0.023162$	$=0.000012425896 66161891247$
a_3	$0.000012425896 66161891247-0$	$=0.000012425896 66161891247$	$/0.023162$	$=0.000536477707521756$
a_3	$0.000536477707521756-0$	$=0.000536477707521756$	$/0.023162$	$=0.023161976838$
a_3	$0.023161976838-0.0$	$=0.023161976838$	$/0.023162$	$=0.999999$
eof	$0.999999\ 0.999999$	$=0.0$	$/0.000001$	$=0.0$

Table 2.41: Decoding the String $a_3a_3a_3a_3$eof.

high value quickly approaches 0. Now is the time to mention that the final code does not have to be the final low value but can be any number between the final low and high values. In the example of $a_3a_3a_3a_3$eof, the final code can be the much shorter number 0.0000002878086 (or 0.0000002878087 or even 0.0000002878088).

▶ **Exercise 2.26:** Encode the string $a_2a_2a_2a_2$ and summarize the results in a table similar to Table 2.40. How do the results differ from those of the string $a_3a_3a_3a_3$?

If the size of the input stream is known, it is possible to do without an eof symbol. The encoder can start by writing this size (unencoded) on the output stream. The decoder reads the size, starts decoding, and stops when the decoded stream reaches this size. If the decoder reads the compressed stream byte by byte, the encoder may have to add some zeros at the end, to make sure the compressed stream can be read in groups of 8 bits.

2.14.1 Implementation Details

The encoding process described earlier is not practical, since it assumes that numbers of unlimited precision can be stored in `Low` and `High`. The decoding process described on page 72 ("The decoder then eliminates the effect of the "S" from the code by subtracting...and dividing ... .") is simple in principle but also impractical. The code, which is a single number, is normally long and may also be very long. A 1Mbyte file may be encoded into, say, a 500Kbyte one, that's a single number. Dividing a 500Kbyte-long number is complex and slow.

Any practical implementation of arithmetic coding should use just integers (because floating-point arithmetic is slow and precision is lost), and they should not be very long (preferably just single precision). We describe such an implementation here, using two integer variables `Low` and `High`. In our example they are four decimal digits long, but in practice they might be 16 or 32 bits long. These variables hold the low and high limits of the current subinterval, but we don't let them grow too much. A glance at Table 2.35 shows that, once the leftmost digits of `Low` and `High` become identical, they never change. We therefore shift such digits out of the two variables and write one digit on the output stream. This way, the two variables don't have to hold the entire code, just the most recent part of it. As digits are shifted out of the two variables, a zero is shifted into the right end of `Low` and a 9, into the right end of `High`. A good way to understand this is to think of each of the two variables as the left end of an infinitely long number. `Low` contains $xxxx00...$, and `High`= $yyyy99....$.

One problem is that `High` should be initialized to 1, but the contents of `Low` and `High` should be interpreted as fractions less than 1. The solution is to initialize `High` to 9999...since the infinite fraction 0.999... equals 1.

▶ **Exercise 2.27:** Prove this!

▶ **Exercise 2.28:** Write the number 0.5 in binary.

Table 2.42 describes the encoding process of the string "SWISS⊔MISS". Column 1 shows the next input symbol. Column 2 shows the new values of `Low` and `High`. Column 3 shows these values as scaled integers, after `High` has been decremented by 1. Column 4 shows the next digit sent to the output stream. Column 5 shows the new values of `Low` and `High` after being shifted to the left. Notice how the last step sends the four digits 3750 to the output stream. The final output is 717533750.

Decoding is the opposite of encoding. We start with `Low`=0000, `High`=9999, and `Code`=7175 (the first four digits of the compressed stream). These are updated at each step of the decoding loop. `Low` and `High` approach each other (and both approach `Code`) until their most significant digits are the same. They are then shifted to the left, which separates them again, and `Code` is also shifted at that time. An index is calculated at each step and is used to search the cumulative frequencies column of Table 2.34 to figure out the current symbol.

1	2	3	4	5
S	L= 0+(1 − 0)×0.5= 0.5	5000		5000
	H= 0+(1 − 0)×1.0= 1.0	9999		9999
W	L=0.5+(1 − .5)×0.4= 0.7	7000	7	0000
	H=0.5+(1 − .5)×0.5= 0.75	7499	7	4999
I	L= 0 +(0.5 − 0)×0.2= 0.1	1000	1	0000
	H= 0 +(0.5 − 0)×0.4= 0.2	1999	1	9999
S	L= 0+(1 − 0)×0.5= 0.5	5000		5000
	H= 0+(1 − 0)×1.0= 1.0	9999		9999
S	L=0.5+(1 − 0.5)×0.5= 0.75	7500		7500
	H=0.5+(1 − 0.5)×1.0= 1.0	9999		9999
␣	L=.75+(1 − .75)×0.0= 0.75	7500	7	5000
	H=.75+(1 − .75)×0.1= .775	7749	7	7499
M	L=0.5+(.75 − .5)×0.1= .525	5250	5	2500
	H=0.5+(.75 − .5)×0.2= 0.55	5499	5	4999
I	L=.25+(.5 − .25)×0.2= 0.3	3000	3	0000
	H=.25+(.5 − .25)×0.4= .35	3499	3	4999
S	L=0.0+(0.5 − 0)×0.5= .25	2500		2500
	H=0.0+(0.5 − 0)×1.0= 0.5	4999		4999
S	L=.25+(.5 − .25)×0.5= .375	3750	3750	
	H=.25+(.5 − .25)×1.0= 0.5	4999		4999

Table 2.42: Encoding "SWISS␣MISS" by Shifting.

Each iteration of the loop consists of the following steps:

1. Calculate `index:=((Code-Low+1)x10-1)/(High-Low+1)` and truncate it to the nearest integer. (The number 10 is the total cumulative frequency in our example.)

2. Use `index` to find the next symbol by comparing it to the cumulative frequencies column in Table 2.34. In the example below, the first value of `index` is 7.1759, truncated to 7. Seven is between the 5 and the 10 in the table, so it selects the "S".

3. Update `Low` and `High` according to

```
Low:=Low+(High-Low+1)LowCumFreq[X]/10;
High:=Low+(High-Low+1)HighCumFreq[X]/10-1;
```

where `LowCumFreq[X]` and `HighCumFreq[X]` are the cumulative frequencies of symbol X and of the symbol above it in Table 2.34.

4. If the leftmost digits of `Low` and `High` are identical, shift `Low`, `High` and `Code` one position to the left. `Low` gets a 0 entered on the right, `High` gets a 9 and `Code` gets the next input digit from the compressed stream.

Here are all the decoding steps for our example:

0. Initialize `Low=0000`, `High=9999`, and `Code=7175`.

1. index= $[(7175 - 0 + 1) \times 10 - 1]/(9999 - 0 + 1) = 7.1759 \rightarrow 7$. Symbol "S" is selected.
Low $= 0 + (9999 - 0 + 1) \times 5/10 = 5000$. High $= 0 + (9999 - 0 + 1) \times 10/10 - 1 = 9999$.

2. index= $[(7175 - 5000 + 1) \times 10 - 1]/(9999 - 5000 + 1) = 4.3518 \rightarrow 4$. Symbol "W" is selected.
Low $= 5000 + (9999 - 5000 + 1) \times 4/10 = 7000$. High $= 5000 + (9999 - 5000 + 1) \times 5/10 - 1 = 7499$.
After the 7 is shifted out, we have Low=0000, High=4999, and Code=1753.

3. index= $[(1753 - 0 + 1) \times 10 - 1]/(4999 - 0 + 1) = 3.5078 \rightarrow 3$. Symbol "I" is selected.
Low $= 0 + (4999 - 0 + 1) \times 2/10 = 1000$. High $= 0 + (4999 - 0 + 1) \times 4/10 - 1 = 1999$.
After the 1 is shifted out, we have Low=0000, High=9999, and Code=7533.

4. index= $[(7533 - 0 + 1) \times 10 - 1]/(9999 - 0 + 1) = 7.5339 \rightarrow 7$. Symbol "S" is selected.
Low $= 0 + (9999 - 0 + 1) \times 5/10 = 5000$. High $= 0 + (9999 - 0 + 1) \times 10/10 - 1 = 9999$.

5. index= $[(7533 - 5000 + 1) \times 10 - 1]/(9999 - 5000 + 1) = 5.0678 \rightarrow 5$. Symbol "S" is selected.
Low $= 5000 + (9999 - 5000 + 1) \times 5/10 = 7500$. High $= 5000 + (9999 - 5000 + 1) \times 10/10 - 1 = 9999$.

6. index= $[(7533 - 7500 + 1) \times 10 - 1]/(9999 - 7500 + 1) = 0.1356 \rightarrow 0$. Symbol "␣" is selected.
Low $= 7500 + (9999 - 7500 + 1) \times 0/10 = 7500$. High $= 7500 + (9999 - 7500 + 1) \times 1/10 - 1 = 7749$.
After the 7 is shifted out, we have Low=5000, High=7499, and Code=5337.

7. index= $[(5337 - 5000 + 1) \times 10 - 1]/(7499 - 5000 + 1) = 1.3516 \rightarrow 1$. Symbol "M" is selected.
Low $= 5000 + (7499 - 5000 + 1) \times 1/10 = 5250$. High $= 5000 + (7499 - 5000 + 1) \times 2/10 - 1 = 5499$.
After the 5 is shifted out we have Low=2500, High=4999, and Code=3375.

8. index= $[(3375 - 2500 + 1) \times 10 - 1]/(4999 - 2500 + 1) = 3.5036 \rightarrow 3$. Symbol "I" is selected.
Low $= 2500 + (4999 - 2500 + 1) \times 2/10 = 3000$. High $= 2500 + (4999 - 2500 + 1) \times 4/10 - 1 = 3499$.
After the 3 is shifted out we have Low=0000, High=4999, and Code=3750.

9. index= $[(3750 - 0 + 1) \times 10 - 1]/(4999 - 0 + 1) = 7.5018 \rightarrow 7$. Symbol "S" is selected.
Low $= 0 + (4999 - 0 + 1) \times 5/10 = 2500$. High $= 0 + (4999 - 0 + 1) \times 10/10 - 1 = 4999$.

10. index= $[(3750 - 2500 + 1) \times 10 - 1]/(4999 - 2500 + 1) = 5.0036 \rightarrow 5$. Symbol "S" is selected.
Low $= 2500 + (4999 - 2500 + 1) \times 5/10 = 3750$. High $= 2500 + (4999 - 2500 + 1) \times 10/10 - 1 = 4999$.

▶ **Exercise 2.29:** How does the decoder know to stop the loop at this point?

1	2	3	4	5
1 L=0+(1 – 0)×0.0 = 0.0		000000	0	000000
H=0+(1 – 0)×0.023162= 0.023162		023162	0	231629
2 L=0+(0.231629 − 0)×0.0 = 0.0		000000	0	000000
H=0+(0.231629 − 0)×0.023162= 0.00536478244		005364	0	053649
3 L=0+(0.053649 − 0)×0.0 = 0.0		000000	0	000000
H=0+(0.053649 − 0)×0.023162= 0.00124261813		001242	0	012429
4 L=0+(0.012429 − 0)×0.0 = 0.0		000000	0	000000
H=0+(0.012429 − 0)×0.023162= 0.00028788049		000287	0	002879
5 L=0+(0.002879 − 0)×0.0 = 0.0		000000	0	000000
H=0+(0.002879 − 0)×0.023162= 0.00006668339		000066	0	000669

Table 2.43: Encoding $a_3a_3a_3a_3a_3$ by Shifting.

2.14.2 Underflow

Table 2.43 shows the steps in encoding the string $a_3a_3a_3a_3a_3$ by shifting. This table is similar to Table 2.42 and it illustrates the problem of underflow. Low and High approach each other and, since Low is always 0 in this example, High loses its significant digits as it approaches Low.

Underflow may happen not just in this case but in any case where Low and High need to converge very closely. Because of the finite size of the Low and High variables, they may reach values of, say, 499996 and 500003 and from there, instead of reaching values where their most significant digits are identical, they reach the values 499999 and 500000. Since the most significant digits are different, the algorithm will not output anything, there will not be any shifts, and the next iteration will only add digits beyond the first six ones. Those digits will be lost, and the first six digits will not change. The algorithm will iterate without generating any output until it reaches the eof.

The solution is to detect such a case early and *rescale* both variables. In the example above, rescaling should be done when the two variables reach values of 49xxxx and 50yyyy. Rescaling should squeeze out the second most significant digits, end up with 4xxxx0 and 5yyyy9, and increment a counter cntr. The algorithm may have to rescale several times before the most significant digits become equal. At that point, the most significant digit (which can be either 4 or 5) should be output, followed by cntr zeros (if the two variables converged to 4) or nines (if they converged to 5).

2.14.3 Final Remarks

All the examples so far have been in decimal since the computations involved are easier to understand in this number base. It turns out that all the algorithms and rules described above apply to the binary case as well and can be used with only one change: every occurrence of 9 (the largest decimal digit) should be replaced by 1 (the largest binary digit).

The examples above don't seem to show any compression at all. It seems that the three example strings "SWISS⊔MISS", "$a_2a_2a_1a_3a_3$", and "$a_3a_3a_3a_3$eof" are encoded into very long numbers. In fact it seems that the length of the final code depends on the probabilities involved. The long probabilities of Table 2.37a generate long numbers in the encoding process, whereas the shorter probabilities of Table 2.34 result in the more reasonable Low and High values of Table 2.35. This behavior demands an explanation.

To figure out the kind of compression achieved by arithmetic coding, we have to consider two facts: (1) in practice, all the operations are performed on binary numbers, so we have to translate the final results to binary before we can estimate the efficiency of the compression; and (2) since the last symbol encoded is the eof, the final code does not have to be the final value of Low; it can be any value between Low and High. This makes it possible to select a shorter number as the final code that's being output.

Table 2.35 encodes the string "SWISS⊔MISS" into the final Low and High values 0.71753375 and 0.717535. The approximate binary values of these numbers are 0.10110111101100000100101010111 and 0.10110111101100000101111111011, so we can select the number "10110111101100000100" as our final, compressed output. The ten-symbol string has thus been encoded into a 20-bit number. Does this represent good compression?

The answer is Yes. Using the probabilities of Table 2.34, it is easy to calculate the probability of the string "SWISS⊔MISS". It is $P = 0.5^5 \times 0.1 \times 0.2^2 \times 0.1 \times 0.1 = 1.25 \times 10^{-6}$. The entropy of this string is therefore $-\log_2 P = 19.6096$. Twenty bits is thus the minimum needed in practice to encode the string.

The symbols in Table 2.37a have probabilities 0.975, 0.001838, and 0.023162. These numbers require quite a few decimal digits and, as a result, the final Low and High values in Table 2.38 are the numbers 0.99462270125 and 0.994623638610941. Again it seems that there is no compression, but an analysis similar to the above shows compression that's very close to the entropy.

The probability of the string "$a_2a_2a_1a_3a_3$" is $0.975^2 \times 0.001838 \times 0.023162^2 \approx 9.37361 \times 10^{-7}$, and $-\log_2 9.37361 \times 10^{-7} \approx 20.0249$

The binary representations of the final values of Low and High in Table 2.38 are 0.11111110100111111001011111001 and 0.11111110100111111010100111101. We can select any number between these two, so we select 1111111010011111100, a 19-bit number.

▸ **Exercise 2.30:** Given the three symbols a_1, a_2, and eof, with probabilities $P_1 = 0.4$, $P_2 = 0.5$, and $P_{eof} = 0.1$, encode the string "$a_2a_2a_2$eof" and show that the size of the final code equals the (practical) minimum.

2.15 Adaptive Arithmetic Coding

Two features of arithmetic coding make it easy to extend:

1. The main encoding step is

```
Low:=Low+(High-Low+1)LowCumFreq[X]/10;
High:=Low+(High-Low+1)HighCumFreq[X]/10-1;
```

This means that, in order to encode symbol X, the encoder should be given the cumulative frequencies of the symbol and of the one above it (see Table 2.34 for an example of cumulative frequencies). This also implies that the frequency of X (or, equivalently, its probability) could be changed each time it is encoded, provided that the encoder and the decoder agree on how to do this.

2. The order of the symbols in Table 2.34 is unimportant. They can even be swapped in the table during the encoding process as long as the encoder and decoder do it in the same way.

With this in mind, it is easy to understand how adaptive arithmetic coding works. The encoding algorithm has two parts: the model and the arithmetic encoder. The model reads the next symbol from the input stream and invokes the encoder, sending it the symbol and the two required cumulative frequencies. The model then increments the count of the symbol and updates the cumulative frequencies. The point is that the symbol's probability is determined by the model from its *old* count, and the count is incremented only after the symbol has been encoded. This makes it possible for the decoder to mirror the encoder's operations. The encoder knows what the symbol is even before it is encoded, but the decoder has to decode the symbol in order to find out what it is. The decoder can therefore use only the old counts when decoding a symbol. Once the symbol has been decoded, the decoder increments its count and updates the cumulative frequencies in exactly the same way as the encoder.

The model should keep the symbols, their counts (frequencies of occurrence), and their cumulative frequencies in an array. This array should be kept in sorted order of the counts. Each time a symbol is read and its count incremented, the model updates the cumulative frequencies, then checks to see whether the symbol should be swapped with another one, to keep the counts in sorted order.

It turns out that there is a simple data structure that allows for both easy search and update. This structure is a balanced binary tree housed in an array. (A balanced binary tree is a complete binary tree where some of the bottom-right nodes may be missing.) The tree should have a node for every symbol in the alphabet and, since it is balanced, its height is $\lceil \log_2 n \rceil$, where n is the size of the alphabet. For $n = 256$ the height of the balanced binary tree is 8, so starting at the root and searching for a node takes at most eight steps. The tree is arranged such that the most probable symbols (the ones with high counts) are located near the root, which speeds up searches. Table 2.44a shows an example of a ten-symbol alphabet with counts. Table 2.44b shows the same symbols sorted by count.

The sorted array "houses" the balanced binary tree of Figure 2.46a. This is a simple, elegant way to build a tree. A balanced binary tree can be housed in an array without the use of any pointers. The rule is that the first array location (with index 1) houses the root, the two children of the node at array location i are housed at locations $2i$ and $2i + 1$, and the parent of the node at array location j is housed at location $\lfloor j/2 \rfloor$. It is easy to see how sorting the array has placed the symbols with largest counts at and near the root.

In addition to a symbol and its count, another value is now added to each tree node, the total counts of its left subtree. This will be used to compute cumulative frequencies. The corresponding array is shown in Table 2.45a.

a_1	a_2	a_3	a_4	a_5	a_6	a_7	a_8	a_9	a_{10}
11	12	12	2	5	1	2	19	12	8

(a)

a_8	a_2	a_3	a_9	a_1	a_{10}	a_5	a_4	a_7	a_6
19	12	12	12	11	8	5	2	2	1

(b)

Table 2.44: A Ten-Symbol Alphabet With Counts.

Assume that the next symbol read from the input stream is a_9. Its count is incremented from 12 to 13. The model keeps the array in sorted order by searching for the farthest array element left of a_9 that has a count smaller than that of a_9. This search can be a straight linear search if the array is short enough, or a binary search if the array is long. In our case, symbols a_9 and a_2 should be swapped (Table 2.45b). Figure 2.46b shows the tree after the swap. Notice how the left-subtree counts have been updated.

a_8	a_2	a_3	a_9	a_1	a_{10}	a_5	a_4	a_7	a_6
19	12	12	12	11	8	5	2	2	1
40	16	8	2	1	0	0	0	0	0

(a)

a_8	a_9	a_3	a_2	a_1	a_{10}	a_5	a_4	a_7	a_6
19	13	12	12	11	8	5	2	2	1
41	16	8	2	1	0	0	0	0	0

(b)

Tables 2.45: A Ten-Symbol Alphabet With Counts.

Finally, here is how the cumulative frequencies are computed from this tree. When the cumulative frequency for a symbol X is needed, the model follows the tree branches from the root to the node containing X while adding numbers into an integer `af`. Each time a right branch is taken from an interior node N, `af` is incremented by the two numbers (the count and the left-subtree count) found in that node. When a left branch is taken, `af` is not modified. When the node containing X is reached, the left-subtree count of X is added to `af`, and `af` then contains the quantity `LowCumFreq[X]`.

As an example, we trace the tree of Figure 2.46a from the root to symbol a_6 whose cumulative frequency is 28. A right branch is taken at node a_2, adding 12 and 16 to `af`. A left branch is taken at node a_1, adding nothing to `af`. When reaching a_6, its left-subtree count, 0, is added to `af`. The result in `af` is $12 + 16 = 28$, as can

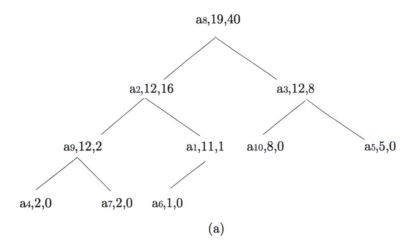

(a)

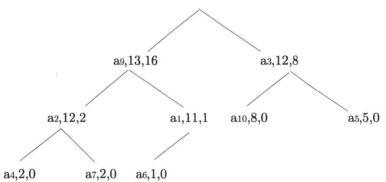

(b)

a_4	2	0—1
a_9	12	2—13
a_7	2	14—15
a_2	12	16—27
a_6	1	28—28
a_1	11	29—39
a_8	19	40—58
a_{10}	8	59—66
a_3	12	67—78
a_5	5	79—83

(c)

Figure 2.46: Adaptive Arithmetic Coding.

be verified from Figure 2.46c. The quantity `HighCumFreq[X]` is obtained by adding the count of a_6 (which is 1) to `LowCumFreq[X]`.

To trace the tree and find the path from the root to a_6, the algorithm performs the following steps:

1. Find a_6 in the array housing the tree by means of a binary search. In our example the node with a_6 is found at array location 10.

2. Integer-divide 10 by 2. The remainder is 0, which means that a_6 is the left child of its parent. The quotient is 5, which is the array location of the parent.

3. Location 5 of the array contains a_1. Integer-divide 5 by 2. The remainder is 1, which means that a_1 is the right child of its parent. The quotient is 2, which is the array location of a_1's parent.

4. Location 2 of the array contains a_2. Integer-divide 2 by 2. The remainder is 0, which means that a_2 is the left child of its parent. The quotient is 1, the array location of the root, so the process stops.

The PPM compression method, Section 2.17, is a good example of a statistical model that invokes an arithmetic encoder in the way described here.

2.16 Text Compression

Before delving into the details of the next method, here is a general discussion of text compression. Most text compression methods are either statistical or dictionary based. The latter class breaks the text into fragments that are saved in a data structure called a dictionary. When a fragment of new text is found to be identical to one of the dictionary entries, a pointer to that entry is written on the compressed stream, to become the compression of the new fragment. The former class, on the other hand, consists of methods that develop statistical *models* of the text.

A common statistical method consists of a modeling stage followed by a coding stage. The model assigns probabilities to the input symbols, and the coding stage then actually codes the symbols based on those probabilities. The model can be static or dynamic (adaptive). Most models are based on one of the following two approaches.

Frequency: The model assigns probabilities to the text symbols based on their frequencies of occurrence, such that commonly occurring symbols are assigned short codes. A static model uses fixed probabilites, while a dynamic model modifies the probabilities "on the fly" while text is being input and compressed.

Context: The model considers the context of a symbol when assigning it a probability. Since the decoder does not have access to future text, both encoder and decoder must limit the context to past text, i.e., to symbols that have already been input and processed. In practice, the context of a symbol is the N symbols preceding it. We thus say that a context-based text compression method uses the context of a symbol to "predict" it (i.e., to assign it a probability). Technically such a method is said to use an "order-N" Markov model. The PPM method, Section 2.17, is an excellent example of a context-based compression method, although the concept of context can also be used to compress images.

Some modern context-based text compression methods perform a transformation on the input data and then apply a statistical model to assign probabilities to the transformed symbols. Good examples of such methods are the Burrows-Wheeler method, Section 5.1, also known as the Burrows-Wheeler transform, or *Block Sorting*; the technique of symbol ranking, Section 5.2; and the ACB method, Section 5.3, that uses an associative dictionary.

2.17 PPM

This is a sophisticated, state of the art compression method originally developed by J. Cleary and I. Witten [Cleary 84], with extensions and an implementation by A. Moffat [Moffat 90]. The method is based on an encoder that maintains a statistical model of the text. The encoder inputs the next symbol S, assigns it a probability P, and sends S to an adaptive arithmetic encoder, to be encoded with probability P.

The simplest *statistical model* counts the number of times each symbol has occurred in the past and assigns the symbol a probability based on that. Assume that 1217 symbols have been input and encoded so far, and 34 of them were the letter "q". If the next symbol is a "q", it is assigned a probability of 34/1217 and its count is incremented by 1. Next time "q" is seen, it will be assigned a probability of $35/t$ where t is the total number of symbols input up to that point (not including the last "q").

The next model up is a *context-based* statistical model. The idea is to assign a probability to symbol S depending not just on the frequency of the symbol but on the contexts in which it has occurred so far. The letter "h" for example, occurs in "typical" English text (Table 1) with a probability of about 5%. On the average, we expect to see an "h" about 5% of the time. However, if the current symbol is "t", there is a high probability (about 30%) that the next symbol will be "h" since the digram "th" is common in English. We say that the model of typical English **predicts** an "h" in such a case. If the next symbol is in fact "h", it is assigned a large probability. In cases where an "h" is the second letter of an unlikely digram, say "xh", the "h" is assigned a smaller probability. Notice that the word "predicts" is used here to mean "estimate the probability of." A similar example is the letter "u", which has a probability of about 2%. When a "q" is encountered, however, there is a probability of more than 99% that the next letter will be a "u".

▶ **Exercise 2.31:** We know that in English, a "q" must be followed by a "u". Why not just say that the probability of the digram "qu" is 100%?

A *static* context-based modeler always uses the same probabilities. It contains static tables with the probabilities of all the possible digrams (or trigrams) of the alphabet and uses the tables to assign a probability to the next symbol S depending on the symbol (or, in general, on the context) C preceding it. We can imagine S and C being used as indexes for a row and a column of a static frequency table. The table itself can be constructed by accumulating digram or trigram frequencies from large quantities of text. Such a modeler is simple, produces good results on the average, but has two problems. The first is that some input streams may be statistically very different from the data originally used to prepare the table. A static encoder may create considerable expansion in such a case. The second problem is zero probabilities.

What if after reading and analysing huge amounts of English text, we still have never encountered the trigram "qqz"? The cell corresponding to "qqz" in the trigram frequency table will contain zero. The arithmetic encoder, Sections 2.14 and 2.15, requires all symbols to have nonzero probabilities. Even if a different encoder, such as Huffman, is used, all the probabilities involved must be nonzero. (Recall that the Huffman method works by combining two low-probability symbols into one, high-probability one. If two zero-probability symbols are combined, the resulting symbol will have the same zero probability.) Another reason why a symbol must have nonzero probability is that its entropy (the smallest number of bits into which it can be encoded) depends on $\log_2 P$, which is undefined for $P = 0$ (but gets very large when $P \to 0$). This *zero-probability problem* faces any model, static or adaptive, that uses probabilities of occurrence of symbols to achieve compression. Two simple solutions are traditionally adopted for this problem, but neither has any theoretical justification.

1. After analysing a large quantity of data and counting frequencies, go over the frequency table, looking for empty cells. Each empty cell is assigned a frequency count of 1, and the total count is also incremented by 1. This method pretends that every digram and trigram has been seen at least once.

2. Add 1 to the total count and divide this single 1 among all the empty cells. Each will get a count that's less than 1 and, as a result, a very small probability. This assigns a very small probability to anything that hasn't been seen in the data used for the analysis.

An *adaptive* context-based modeler also maintains tables with the probabilities of all the possible digrams (or trigrams or even longer contexts) of the alphabet, and uses the tables to assign a probability to the next symbol S depending on the few symbols preceding it (its context C). The tables are updated all the time as more data is being input, which adapts the probabilities to the particular data being compressed. Such a model is slower and more complex than the static one but produces better compression since it uses the correct probabilities even when the input stream contains data with probabilities much different from the average.

A text that skews letter probabilities is called a *lipogram*. (Would a computer program without any "goto" statements be considered a lipogram?) There are just a few examples of literary works that are lipograms:

1. Perhaps the best known lipogram in English is *Gadsby*, a full length novel [Wright 39], by Ernest Vincent Wright (1872–1939) that does not contain any occurrences of the letter "E".

2. *Alphabetical Africa* by Walter Abish (W. W. Norton, 1974) is a readable lipogram where the reader is supposed to discover the unusual writing style while reading. This style has to do with the initial letters of words. The book consists of 52 chapters. In the first, all words begin with "a"; in the second, all words start with either "a" or "b" etc., until, in chapter 26, all letters are allowed at the start of a word. In the remaining 26 chapters, the letters are taken away one by one. Various readers have commented on how little or how much they have missed the word "the" and how they felt on finally seeing it (in chapter 20).

3. The novel *La Disparition* is a 1969 French lipogram by Georges Perec (1936–

⚲   A Quote from the Preface to *Gadsby*

People as a rule will not stop to realize what a task such an attempt actually is. As I wrote along, in long-hand at first, a whole army of little E's gathered around my desk, all eagerly expecting to be called upon. But gradually as they saw me writing on and on, without even noticing them, they grew uneasy; and, with excited whisperings among themselves, began hopping up and riding on my pen, looking down constantly for a chance to drop off into some word; for all the world like sea birds perched, watching for a passing fish! But when they saw that I had covered 138 pages of typewriter size paper, they slid off unto the floor, walking sadly away, arm in arm; but shouting back: "You certainly must have a hodge-podge of a yarn there without Us! Why, man! We are in every story ever written, *hundreds and thousands of times!* This is the first time we ever were shut out!"
    —Ernest Vincent Wright

1982) that does not contain the letter "E" (this letter actually appears several times, outside the main text, in words that the publisher had to include, and these are all printed in red). *La Disparition* has been translated to English, where it is called *A Void*, by Gilbert Adair (Harper Collins, 1994).

La Disparition grew out of Perec's involvement with the experimental writers' group Oulipo (l'Ouvroir de Litterature Potentielle); the main character of the novel is called Anton Voyl (voyelle = French for vowel).

Perec's work is unusually varied. It seems that he tried to produce examples of every genre of literature without repeating himself. He wrote straight narrative, radio plays, detective novels, an autobiography, poetry, puzzles, filmscripts, a book on the game of GO, essays, palindromes, crosswords, and several literary tricks (e.g., a novel in which "E" is the only vowel.). His master work is *Life, a User's Manual*.

4. Gottlob Burmann, a German poet (1737–1805), created our next example of a lipogram. He wrote 130 poems, consisting of about 20,000 words, without the use of the letter "R". It is also believed that during the last 17 years of his life he even omitted this letter from his daily conversation.

5. A Portuguese lipogram is found in five stories written by Alonso Alcala y Herrera, a Portuguese writer, in 1641, each suppressing one vowel.

6. Other examples, in Spanish, are found in the writings of Francisco Navarrete y Ribera (1659), Fernando Jacinto de Zurita y Haro (1654), and Manuel Lorenzo de Lizarazu y Berbuizana (also 1654).

An order-N adaptive context-based modeler reads the next symbol S from the input stream and considers the N symbols preceding S the current order-N context C of S. The model then estimates the probability P that S appears in the input data following the particular context C. Theoretically, the larger N, the better the probability estimate (the *prediction*). To get an intuitive feeling, let's imagine a case where N=20,000. It is hard to imagine a situation where a group of 20,000 symbols in the input stream is followed by a symbol S, but another group of the same 20,000 symbols, found later in the same input stream, is followed by something other than S. We can thus say that N=20,000 allows the model to predict the next symbol (i.e., to estimate its probability) with high reliability. In practice, however, large values of N have three disadvantages:

1. If we encode a symbol based on the 20,000 symbols preceding it, how do we encode the first 20,000 symbols in the input stream? They may have to be written on the output stream as raw ASCII codes, thereby reducing the overall compression.

2. For large values of N, there may be too many possible contexts. If our symbols are the 7-bit ASCII codes, the alphabet size is $2^7 = 128$ symbols. There are therefore $128^2 = 16,384$ order-2 contexts, $128^3 = 2,097,152$ order-3 contexts, and so on. The number of contexts grows exponentially since it is 128^N or, in general, A^N where A is the alphabet size.

▶ **Exercise 2.32:** What is the number of order-2 and -3 contexts for an alphabet of size $2^8 = 256$?

For a small alphabet, larger values of N can be used. For a 16-symbol alphabet there are $16^4 = 65,536$ order-4 contexts and and $16^6 = 16,777,216$ order-6 contexts.

▶ **Exercise 2.33:** What could be a practical example of such an alphabet?

3. A very long context retains information about the nature of old data. Experience shows that large data files contain different distributions of symbols in different parts (a good example is a history book, where one chapter may commonly use words such as "Greek," "Athens," and "Troy," while the following chapter may use "Roman," "empire," and "legion"). Better compression can therefore be achieved if the model assigns less importance to information collected from old data and more weight to fresh, recent data. Such an effect is achieved by a short context.

▶ **Exercise 2.34:** Show an example of a common binary file where different parts may have different bit distributions.

As a result, relatively short contexts, in the range of 2 to 10, are used in practice. Any practical algorithm requires a carefully designed data structure that provides fast search and easy update, while holding many thousands of symbols and strings (Section 2.17.5).

We now turn to the next point in the discussion. Assume a context-based encoder that uses order-3 contexts. Early in the compression process the word **here** was seen several times but the word **there** is now seen for the first time. Assume that the next symbol is the **r** of **there**. The encoder will not find any instances of the order-3 context **the** followed by **r** (the **r** has 0 probability in this context). The encoder may simply write **r** on the compressed stream as a literal, resulting in no compression, but we know that **r** was seen several times in the past following the order-2 context **he** (**r** has nonzero probability in this context). The PPM method takes advantage of this knowledge.

2.17.1 PPM Principles

The central idea of PPM is to use this knowledge. The PPM encoder switches to a shorter context when a longer one has resulted in 0 probability. PPM thus starts with an order-N context. It searches its data structure for a previous occurrence of the current context C followed by the next symbol S. If it finds no such occurrence (i.e., if the probability of this particular C followed by this S is 0), it switches to order $N-1$, and tries the same thing. Let C' be the string consisting of the rightmost $N-1$ symbols of C. The PPM encoder searches its data structure for a previous occurrence current context C' followed by symbol S. PPM thus tries to use smaller and smaller parts of the context C, which is the reason for its name. The name PPM stands for Prediction with Partial String Matching. Here is the process in some detail.

The encoder reads the next symbol S from the input stream, looks at the current order-N context C (the last N symbols read), and, based on input data that has been seen in the past, determines the probability P that S will appear following the particular context C. The encoder then invokes an adaptive arithmetic coding algorithm to encode symbol S with probability P. In practice the adaptive arithmetic encoder is a procedure that receives the quantities `HighCumFreq[X]` and `LowCumFreq[X]` (Section 2.15) as parameters from the PPM encoder.

As an example, suppose that the current order-3 context is the string **the**, which has already been seen 27 times in the past, and was followed by the letters **r** (11 times), **s** (9 times), **n** (6 times) and **m** (just once). The encoder assigns these cases the probabilities $11/27$, $9/27$, $6/27$, and $1/27$, respectively. If the next symbol read is **r**, it is sent to the arithmetic encoder with a probability of $11/27$, and the probabilities are updated to $12/28$, $9/28$, $6/28$, and $1/28$.

What if the next symbol read is **a**? The context **the** was never seen followed by an **a**, so the probability of this case is 0. This zero-probability problem is solved in PPM by switching to a shorter context. The PPM encoder asks itself: How many times was the order-2 context **he** seen in the past, and by what symbols was it followed? The answer may be: Seen 54 times, followed by **a** (26 times), by **r** (12 times), etc. The PPM encoder now sends the **a** to the arithmetic encoder with a probability of $26/54$.

If the next symbol S was never seen before following the order-2 context **he**, the PPM encoder switches to order-1 context. Was S seen before following the string **e**? If yes, a nonzero probability is assigned to S depending on how many times it (and other symbols) were seen following **e**. Otherwise, the PPM encoder switches to order-0 context. It asks itself how many times symbol S was seen in the past, regardless of any contexts. If it was seen 87 times out of 574 symbols read, it is assigned a probability of $87/574$. If symbol S has never been seen before (a common situation at the start of any compression process), the PPM encoder switches to a mode called order -1 context, where S is assigned the fixed probability $1/($size of the alphabet$)$.

Table 2.47 shows contexts and frequency counts for orders 4 through 0 after the 11-symbol string **xyzzxyxyzzx** has been input and encoded. To understand the operation of the PPM encoder, let's assume that the 12th symbol is **z**. The order-4 context is now **yzzx** which earlier was seen followed by **y** but never by **z**. The encoder therefore switches to the order-3 context which is **zzx**, but even this hasn't been seen earlier followed by **z**. The next lower context, **zx**, is order-2, and it also fails. The encoder then switches to order-1, where it checks context **x**. Symbol **x** was found three times in the past but was always followed by **y**. Order-0 is checked next, where **z** has a frequency count of 4 (out of a total count of 11). Symbol **z** is thus sent to the adaptive arithmetic encoder, to be encoded with probability 4/11 (the PPM encoder "predicts" that it will appear 4/11 of the time).

Order-4	Order-3	Order-2	Order-1	Order-0
xyzz→x 2	xyz→z 2	xy→z 2	x→y 3	x 4
yzzx→y 1	yzz→x 2	→x 1	y→z 2	y 3
zzxy→x 1	zzx→y 1	yz→z 2	→x 1	z 4
zxyx→y 1	zxy→x 1	zz→x 2	z→z 2	
xyxy→z 1	xyx→y 1	zx→y 1	→x 2	
yxyz→z 1	yxy→z 1	yx→y 1		

(a)

Order-4	Order-3	Order-2	Order-1	Order-0
xyzz→x 2	xyz→z 2	xy→z 2	x→y 3	x 4
yzzx→y 1	yzz→x 2	xy→x 1	→z 1	y 3
→z 1	zzx→y 1	yz→z 2	y→z 2	z 5
zzxy→x 1	→z 1	zz→x 2	→x 1	
zxyx→y 1	zxy→x 1	zx→y 1	z→z 2	
xyxy→z 1	xyx→y 1	→z 1	→x 2	
yxyz→z 1	yxy→z 1	yx→y 1		

(b)

Table 2.47: (a). Contexts and Counts for "**xyzzxyxyzz**". (b). Updated After Another **z** is Input.

Next we consider the PPM decoder. There is a fundamental difference between the way the PPM encoder and decoder work. The encoder can always look at the next symbol and base its next step on what that symbol is. The job of the decoder is to find out what the next symbol is. The encoder decides to switch to a shorter context based on what the next symbol is. The decoder cannot mirror this since it does not know what the next symbol is. The algorithm needs an additional feature that will make it possible for the decoder to stay in lockstep with the encoder. The feature used by PPM is to reserve one symbol of the alphabet as an *escape symbol*. When the encoder decides to switch to a shorter context, it first writes the escape symbol (arithmetically encoded) on the output stream. The decoder can decode the escape symbol since it is encoded in the present context. After decoding an escape, the decoder also switches to a shorter context.

The worst that can happen with an order-N encoder is to encounter a symbol S for the first time (this happens mostly at the start of the compression process). The symbol hasn't been seen before in any context, not even in order-0 context (i.e., by itself). In such a case the encoder ends up sending $N+1$ consecutive escapes to be arithmetically encoded and output, switching all the way down to order -1, followed by the symbol S encoded with the fixed probability 1/(size of the alphabet). Since the escape symbol may be output many times by the encoder, it is important to assign it a reasonable probability. Initially the escape probability should be high, but it should drop as more symbols are input and decoded, and more information is collected by the modeler about contexts in the particular data being compressed.

▶ **Exercise 2.35:** The escape is just a symbol of the alphabet, reserved to indicate a context switch. What if the data uses every symbol in the alphabet and none can be reserved? A common example is image compression where a pixel is represented by a byte (256 gray scales or colors). Since pixels can have any values between 0 and 255, what value can be reserved for the escape symbol in this case?

Table 2.48 shows one way of assigning probabilities to the escape symbol (this is called variant PPMC of PPM). The table shows the contexts (up to order-2) collected while reading and encoding the 14-symbol string `assanissimassa`. (In the movie "8 1/2," Italian children use this string as a magic spell. They pronounce it `assa-neesee-massa`.) We assume that the alphabet consists of the 26 letters, the blank space, and the escape symbol, a total of 28 symbols. The probability of a symbol in order -1 is thus 1/28. Notice that it takes 5 bits to encode 1 of 28 symbols without compression.

Each context seen in the past is placed in the table in a separate group together with the escape symbol. The order-2 context `as`, e.g., was seen twice in the past and was followed by `s` both times. It is assigned a frequency of 2 and is placed in a group together with the escape symbol, which is assigned frequency 1. The probabilities of `as` and the escape in this group are thus 2/3 and 1/3, respectively. Context `ss` was seen three times, twice followed by `a` and once by `i`. These two occurrences are assigned frequencies 2 and 1, and are placed in a group together with the escape which is now assigned frequency 2 (because it is in a group of 2 members). The probabilities of the three members of this group are thus 2/5, 1/5, and 2/5, respectively.

The justification for this method of assigning escape probabilities goes like this: suppose that context `abc` was seen ten times in the past and was always followed by `x`. This suggests that the same context will be followed by the same `x` in the future, so the encoder will only rarely have to switch down to a lower context. The escape symbol can thus be assigned the small probability 1/11. However, if every occurrence of context `abc` in the past was followed by a different symbol (suggesting that the data varies a lot), then there is a good chance that the next occurrence will also be followed by a different symbol, forcing the encoder to switch to a lower context (and thus to emit an escape) more often. The escape is thus assigned the higher probability 10/20.

▶ **Exercise 2.36:** Explain the numbers 1/11 and 10/20.

Order-0 consists of the five different symbols `asnim` seen in the input string, followed by an escape, which is assigned frequency 5. Probabilities thus range from 4/19 (for `a`) to 5/19 (for the escape symbol).

2.17.2 Examples

We are now ready to look at actual examples of new symbols being read and en-

Order-2			Order-1				Order-0		
Context	f	p	Context	f		p	Symbol	f	p
as→s	2	2/3	a→	s		2 2/5	a	4	4/19
esc	1	1/3	a→	n		1 1/5	s	6	6/19
			esc→			2 2/5	n	1	1/19
ss→a	2	2/5					i	2	2/19
ss→i	1	1/5	s→	s		3 3/9	m	1	1/19
esc	2	2/5	s→	a		2 2/9	esc	5	5/19
			s→	i		1 1/9			
sa→n	1	1/2	esc			3 3/9			
esc	1	1/2							
			n→	i		1 1/2			
an→i	1	1/2	esc			1 1/2			
esc	1	1/2							
			i→	s		1 1/4			
ni→s	1	1/2	i→	m		1 1/4			
esc	1	1/2	esc			2 2/4			
is→s	1	1/2	m→	a		1 1/2			
esc	1	1/2	esc			1 1/2			
si→m	1	1/2							
esc	1	1/2							
im→a	1	1/2							
esc	1	1/2							
ma→s	1	1/2							
esc	1	1/2							

Table 2.48: Contexts, Counts (f), and Probabilities (p) for
"assanissimassa".

coded. We assume that the 14-symbol string assanissimassa has been completely
input and encoded, so the current order-2 context is "sa". Here are four typical
cases:

1. The next symbol is "n". The PPM encoder finds that "sa" followed by
"n" has been seen before and has probability 1/2. The "n" is encoded by the
arithmetic encoder with this probability which takes, since arithmetic encoding
normally compresses at or close to the entropy, $-\log_2(1/2) = 1$ bit.

2. The next symbol is "s". The PPM encoder finds that "sa" was not seen
before followed by an "s". The encoder thus sends the escape symbol to the arithmetic encoder, together with the probability (1/2) predicted by the order-2 context
of "sa". It thus takes 1 bit to encode this escape. Switching down to order-1, the
current context becomes "a" and the PPM encoder finds that an "a" followed by
an "s" was seen before and currently has probability 2/5 assigned. The "s" is then

sent to the arithmetic encoder to be encoded with probability 2/5, which produces another 1.32 bits. In total $1 + 1.32 = 2.32$ bits are generated to encode the "s".

3. The next symbol is "m". The PPM encoder finds that "sa" was never seen before followed by an "m". It therefore sends the escape symbol to the arithmetic encoder, as in 2 above, generating 1 bit so far. It then switches to order-1, finds that "a" has never been seen followed by an "m", so it sends another escape symbol, this time using the escape probability for the order-1 "a", which is 2/5. This is encoded in 1.32 bits. Switching to order-0, the PPM encoder finds "m", which has probability 1/19 and sends it to be encoded in $-\log_2(1/19) = 4.25$ bits. The total number of bits produced is thus $1 + 1.32 + 4.25 = 6.57$.

4. The next symbol is "d". The PPM encoder switches from order-2 to order-1 to order-0 sending two escapes as in 3 above. Since "d" hasn't been seen before, it is not found in order-0, and the PPM encoder switches to order -1 after sending a third escape with the escape probability of order-0, 5/19 (this produces $-\log_2(5/19) = 1.93$ bits). The "d" itself is sent to the arithmetic encoder with its order -1 probability which is 1/28, so it gets encoded in 4.8 bits. The total number of bits necessary to encode this first "d" is $1 + 1.32 + 1.93 + 4.8 = 9.05$, more than the 5 bits that would have been necessary without any compression.

▶ **Exercise 2.37:** Suppose that case 4 above has actually occurred (i.e., the 15th symbol to be input was a "d"). Show the new state of the order-0 contexts.

▶ **Exercise 2.38:** Suppose that case 4 above has actually occurred and the 16th symbol is also a "d". How many bits would it take to encode this second "d"?

▶ **Exercise 2.39:** Show how the results of the four cases above are affected if we assume an alphabet size of 256 symbols.

2.17.3 Exclusion

When switching down from order-2 to order-1, the PPM encoder can use the information found in order-2 in order to exclude certain order-1 cases that are now known to be impossible. This increases the order-1 probabilites and thus improves compression. The same thing can be done when switching down from any order. Here are two detailed examples.

In case 2 above, the next symbol is "s". The PPM encoder finds that "sa" was seen before followed by "n" but not by "s". The encoder sends an escape and switches to order-1. The current context becomes "a" and the encoder checks to see if an "a" followed by an "s" was seen before. The answer is Yes (with frequency 2), but the fact that "sa" was seen before followed by "n" implies that the current symbol cannot be "n" (if it were, it would be encoded in order-2). The encoder can thus *exclude* the case of an "a" followed by "n" in order-1 contexts (we can say that there is no need to reserve "room" (or "space") for the probability of this case since it is impossible). This reduces the total frequency of the order-1 group "a→" from 5 to 4, which increases the probability assigned to "s" from 2/5 to 2/4. Based on our knowledge from order-2, the "s" can now be encoded in $-\log_2(2/4) = 1$ bit instead of 1.32 (a total of two bits is produced, since the escape also requires 1 bit).

Another example is case 4 above, modified for exclusions. When switching from order-2 to order-1, the probability of the escape is, as before, 1/2. When in order-1, the case of "a" followed by "n" is excluded, increasing the probability of the escape from 2/5 to 2/4. After switching to order-0, both "s" and "n" represent impossible cases and can be excluded. This leaves the order-0 with the 4 symbols "a", "i", "m", and escape, with frequencies 4, 2, 1, and 5, respectively. The total frequency is 12, so the escape is assigned probability 5/12 (1.26 bits) instead of the original 5/19 (1.93 bits). This escape is sent to the arithmetic encoder, and the PPM encoder switches to order -1. Here it excludes all five symbols asnim that have already been seen in order-1 and are therefore impossible in order -1. The "d" can now be encoded with probability $1/(28 - 5) \approx 0.043$ (4.52 bits instead of 4.8) or $1/(256-5) \approx 0.004$ (7.97 bits instead of 8), depending on the alphabet size.

> Exact and careful model building should embody constraints that the final an-
> swer had in any case to satisfy.
> —Francis Harry Compton Crick, *What Mad Pursuit*

2.17.4 PPMA and PPMB

The particular method described above for assigning escape probabilities is called PPMC. Two more methods, named PPMA and PPMB, have traditionally been used to assign escape probabilities in PPM. All three methods have been selected based on the vast experience that the developers had with data compression. None of the three is supported by any theory.

Suppose that a group of contexts in Table 2.48 has total frequencies n (excluding the escape symbol). PPMA assigns the escape symbol a probability of $1/(n+1)$. This is equivalent to always assigning it a count of 1. The other members of the group are still assigned their original probabilities of x/n, and these probabilities add up to 1 (not including the escape probability).

PPMB is similar to PPMC with one difference. It assigns a probability to symbol S following context C only after S has been seen **twice** in context C. This is done by subtracting 1 from the frequency counts. If context "abc", e.g., was seen three times, twice followed by "x" and once, by "y", then "x" is assigned probability $(2-1)/3$ and "y" (which should be assigned probability $(1-1)/3 = 0$) is not assigned any probability (i.e., does not get included in Table 2.48 or its equivalent). Instead, the escape symbol "gets" the two counts subtracted from "x" and "y", and ends up being assigned probability 2/3. This method is based on the belief that "seeing twice is believing."

It should again be noted that the way escape probabilities are assigned in the three methods is based on experience and intuition, not on any underlying theory. Experience with the three variants of PPM shows that none is preferable. They produce compression ratios that normally differ by just a few percent. This is an encouraging result since it shows that the basic PPM algorithm is robust and is not affected much by the precise way of assigning escape probabilities.

2.17.5 Implementation Details

The main problem in any practical implementation of PPM is to maintain a data structure where all contexts (orders 0 through N) of every symbol read from the input stream are stored and can be located fast. The structure described here is a special type of tree, called a *trie*. This is a tree in which the branching structure at any level is determined by just part of a data item, not by the entire item. In the case of PPM, an order-N context is a string that includes all the shorter contexts of orders $N - 1$ through 0, so each context effectively adds just one symbol to the trie.

Figure 2.49 shows how such a trie is constructed for the string "zxzyzxxyzx" assuming N=2. A quick glance shows that the tree grows in width but not in depth. Its depth remains $N + 1 = 3$ regardless of how much input data has been read. Its width grows as more and more symbols are input, but not at a constant rate. Sometimes no new nodes are added, such as in case 10, when the last "x" is read. At other times up to three nodes are added, such as in cases 3 and 4, when the second "z" and the first "y" are added.

Level 1 of the trie (just below the root) contains one node for each symbol read so far. These are the order-1 contexts. Level 2 contains all the order-2 contexts, and so on. Every context can be found by starting at the root and sliding down to one of the leaves. In case 3, e.g., the two contexts are "xz" (symbol "z" preceded by the order-1 context "x") and "zxz" (symbol "z" preceded by the order-2 context "zx"). In case 10, there are seven contexts ranging from "xxy" and "xyz" on the left to "zxz" and "zyz" on the right.

The numbers in the nodes are context counts. The "z,4" on the right branch of case 10 implies that "z" has been seen 4 times. The "x,3" and "y,1" below it mean that these four occurrences were followed by "x" three times and by "y" once. The circled nodes show the different orders of the context of the last symbol added to the trie. In case 3, e.g., the second "z" has just been read and added to the trie. It was added twice, below the "x" of the left branch and the "x" of the right branch (the latter is indicated by the thick arrow). Also, the count of the original "z" has been incremented to 2. This shows that the new "z" follows the two contexts "x" (of order-1) and "zx" (order-2).

It should now be easy for the reader to follow the ten steps of constructing the tree and understand intuitively how nodes are added and counts updated. Notice that three nodes (or, in general, $N + 1$ nodes, one at each level of the trie) are involved in each step (except the first few steps when the trie hasn't reached its final height yet). Some of the three are new nodes added to the trie; the others have their counts incremented. The next point that should be discussed is how the algorithm decides which nodes to update and which to add. To simplify the algorithm, one more pointer is added to each node, pointing backward to the node representing the next shorter context. A pointer that points backwards in a tree is called a *vine pointer*. Figure 2.50 shows the first ten steps of constructing the PPM trie for the 14-symbol string "assanissimassa". Each of the ten steps shows the new vine pointers (dashed lines) constructed by the trie updating algorithm while that step was handled. Notice that old vine pointers are not deleted; they are just not shown in later diagrams. In general, a vine pointer points from a node X on level n to a node with the same symbol X on level $n - 1$. All nodes on level 1 point to the root.

A node in the PPM trie thus contains the following fields:

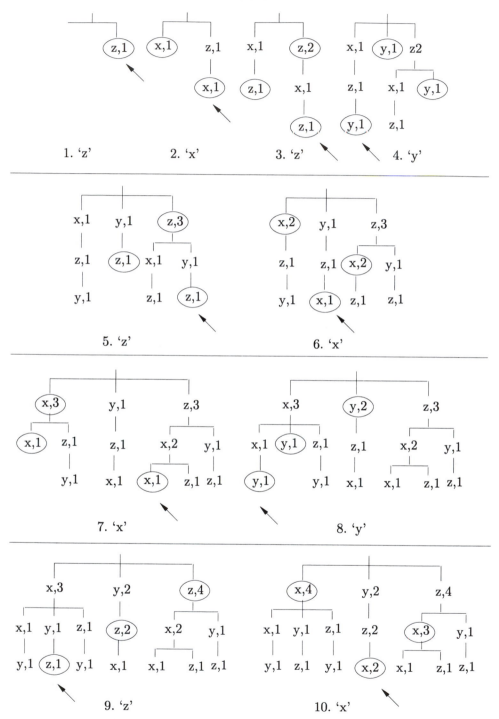

Figure 2.49: Ten Tries of "zxzyzxxyzx".

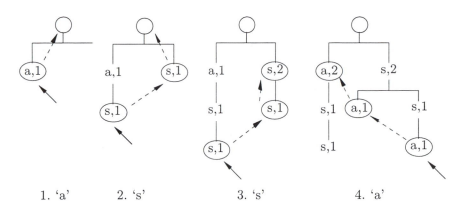

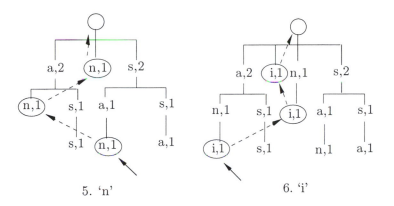

Figure 2.50: Part I. First Six Tries of "assanissimassa".

1. The code (ASCII or other) of the symbol.

2. The count.

3. A down pointer, pointing to the leftmost child of the node. In Figure 2.50.10, e.g., the leftmost son of the root is "a,2". That of "a,2" is "n,1", and that of "s,4" is "a,1".

4. A right pointer, pointing to the next sibling of the node. The root has no right sibling. The next sibling of node "a,2" is "i,2" and that of "i,2" is "m,1".

5. A vine pointer. These are shown as dashed lines in Figure 2.50.

▶ **Exercise 2.40:** Complete the construction of this trie and show it after all 14 characters have been input.

At any step during the trie construction, one pointer, called the *base*, is maintained, that points to the last node added or updated in the previous step. This is shown as a thick arrow in the figure. Suppose that symbol S has been input and the trie should now be updated. The algorithm for adding and/or updating nodes is:

1. Follow the base pointer to node X. Follow the vine pointer from X to Y

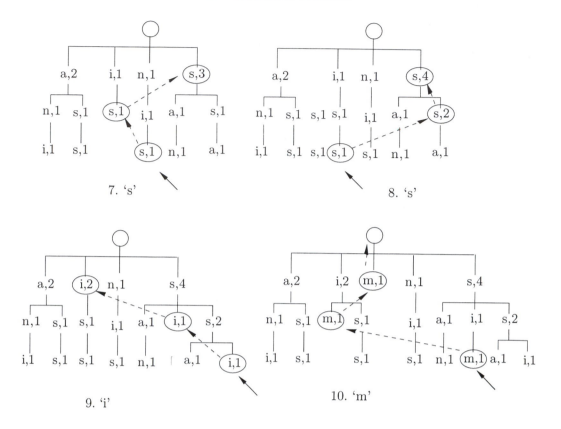

Figure 2.50: (Continued) Next Four Tries of "`assanissimassa`".

(notice that Y can be the root). Add S as a new child node of Y and set the base to point to it. However, if Y already has a child node with S, increment the count of that node by 1 (and also set the base to point to it). Call this node A.

2. Repeat the same step but without updating the base. Follow the vine pointer from Y to Z, add S as a new child node of Z, or update an existing child. Call this node B. If there is no vine pointer from A to B, install one. (If both A and B are old nodes, there will already be a vine pointer from A to B.)

3. Repeat until you have added (or incremented) a node at level 1.

During these steps the PPM encoder also collects the counts that are necessary to compute the probability of the new symbol S. Figure 2.50 shows the trie after the last two symbols "s" and "a" were added. In 2.50.13 a vine pointer was followed from node "s,2" to node "s,3", which already had the two children "a,1" and "i,1". The first child was incremented to "a,2". In 2.50.14, the subtree with the three nodes "s,3", "a,2" and "i,1" tells the encoder that "a" was seen following context "ss" twice, and "i" was seen following the same context once. Since the tree has two children, the escape symbol gets a count of 2, bringing the total count to 5. The probability of "a" is thus 2/5 (compare with Table 2.48).

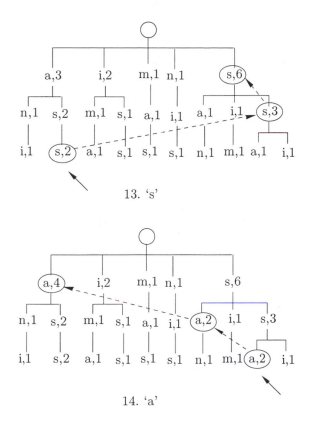

13. 's'

14. 'a'

Figure 2.50: (Continued) Final Two Tries of "assanissimassa".

It is now easy to see the reason why this particular trie is so useful. Each time a symbol is input, it takes the algorithm at most $N + 1$ steps to update the trie and collect the necessary counts by going from the base pointer toward the root. Adding a symbol to the trie and encoding it thus takes $O(N)$ steps regardless of the size of the trie. Since N is small (typically 4 or 5), an implementation can be made fast enough for practical use even if the trie is very large. If the user specifies that the algorithm should use exclusions, it becomes more complex since it has to maintain, at each step, a list of symbols to be excluded.

As has been noted, between 0 and 3 nodes are added to the trie for each input symbol encoded (in general, between 0 and $N + 1$ nodes). The trie can thus grow very large and fill up any available memory space. One elegant solution, adopted by [Moffat 90], is to discard the trie when it gets full and start constructing a new one. In order to bring the new trie "up to speed" fast, the last 2048 input symbols are always saved in a circular buffer in memory and are used to construct the new trie. This reduces the amount of inefficient code generated when tries are replaced.

Bibliography

Cleary, J. G. and I. H. Witten (1984) "Data Compression Using Adaptive Coding and

Partial String Matching," *IEEE Transactions on Communications* COM-32(4):396–402, April.

Moffat, A. (1990) "Implementing the PPM Data Compression Scheme," *IEEE Transactions on Communications* COM-38(11):1917–1921, November.

Wright, E. V. (1939) *Gadsby*, Los Angeles, Wetzel. Reprinted by University Microfilms, Ann Arbor, 1991.

I think so from the frequency of their occurrence,
and from the general correspondence in
position with that of the tip of a pointed ear.

Charles Darwin, *The Descent of Man*

The excitement that a gambler feels when making a bet is equal to
the amount he might win times the probability of winning it.

Blaise Pascal (1623–1662)

3
Dictionary Methods

Statistical compression methods use a statistical model of the data, and the quality of compression they achieve depends on how good that model is. Dictionary-based compression methods do not use a statistical model, nor do they use variable-size codes. Instead they select strings of symbols and encode each string as a *token* using a dictionary. The dictionary holds strings of symbols and it may be static or dynamic (adaptive). The former is permanent, sometimes allowing the addition of strings but no deletions, whereas the latter holds strings previously found in the input stream, allowing for additions and deletions of strings as new input is being read.

The simplest example of a static dictionary is a dictionary of the English language used to compress English text. Imagine a dictionary containing perhaps half a million words (without their definitions). A word (a string of symbols terminated by a space or a punctuation mark) is read from the input stream and the dictionary is searched. If a match is found, an index to the dictionary is written into the output stream. Otherwise, the uncompressed word itself is written. (This is an example of *logical compression.*)

The output stream thus contains indexes and raw words, and we need to distinguish between them. One way to do this is to use an extra bit in every item written. In principle, a 19-bit index is sufficient to specify an item in a $2^{19} = 524,288$-word dictionary. When a match is found, we can thus write a 20-bit token consisting of a flag bit (perhaps a zero) followed by a 19-bit index. When no match is found, a flag of 1 is written, followed by the size of the unmatched word, followed by the word itself.

Example: Assuming that the word **bet** is found in dictionary entry 1025, it is encoded as the 20-bit number 0|0000000010000000001. Assuming that the word **xet** is not found, it is encoded as 1|0000011|01111000|01100101|01110100. This is a 4-byte number where the 7-bit field 0000011 indicates that three more bytes follow.

Assuming that the size is written as a 7-bit number, and that an average word size is five characters, an uncompressed word occupies, on the average, 6 bytes (=48 bits) in the output stream. Compressing 48 bits into 20 is excellent, provided that it happens often enough. We thus have to answer the question: how many matches are needed in order to have overall compression? We denote the probability of a match (the case where the word is found in the dictionary) by P. After reading and compressing N words, the size of the output stream will be $N[20P+48(1-P)] = N[48-28P]$ bits. The size of the input stream is (assuming five characters per word) $40N$ bits. Compression is achieved when $N[48 - 28P] < 40N$, which implies $P > 0.29$. We need a matching rate of 29% or better to achieve compression.

▶ **Exercise 3.1:** What compression factor do we get with $P = 0.9$?

As long as the input stream consists of English text, most words would be found in a 500,000-word dictionary. Other types of data, however, may not do that well. A file containing the source code of a computer program may contain "words" such as "cout", "xor", and "malloc" that may not be found in an English dictionary. A binary file normally contains gibberish when viewed in ASCII, so very few matches may be found, resulting in considerable expansion instead of compression.

This shows that a static dictionary is not a good choice for a general-purpose compressor. It may, however, be a good choice for a special-purpose one. Consider a chain of hardware stores, for example. Their files may contain words such as "nut", "bolt", and "paint" many times, but words such as "philosophy", "painting", and "politics" will be rare. A special-purpose compression program for such a company may benefit from a small, specialized dictionary containing, perhaps, just a few hundred words. The computers in each branch store would have a copy of the dictionary, making it easy to compress files and send them between stores and offices in the chain.

In general, an adaptive dictionary-based method is preferable. Such a method can start with an empty dictionary or with a small, default dictionary, add words to it as they are found in the input stream, and delete old words since a big dictionary means slow search. Such a method consists of a loop where each iteration starts by reading the input stream and breaking it up (parsing it) into words or phrases. It then should search the dictionary for each word and, if a match is found, write a token on the output stream. Otherwise, the uncompressed word should be written and also added to the dictionary. The last step in each iteration checks to see whether an old word should be deleted from the dictionary. This may sound complicated but it has two advantages:

1. It involves string search and match operations, rather than numerical computations. Many programmers prefer that.

2. The decoder is simple (this is an asymmetric compression method). In statistical compression methods, the decoder is normally the exact opposite of the encoder (symmetric compression). In an adaptive dictionary-based method, however, the decoder has to read its input stream, determine whether the current item is a token or uncompressed data, use tokens to obtain data from the dictionary, and output the final, uncompressed data. It does not have to parse the input stream

in a complex way, and it does not have to search the dictionary to find matches. Many programmers like that, too.

Having one's name attached to a scientific discovery, techinque or phenomenon is considered special honor in science. Having one's name associated with an entire field of science is even more so. This is what happened to Jacob Ziv and Abraham Lempel. In the 1970s these two researchers have developed the first methods, LZ77 and LZ78, for dictionary-based compression. Their ideas have been a source of inspiration to many researchers who generalized, improved, and combined them with RLE and statistical methods to form many commonly used, lossless compression methods, for text, images, and sound. This chapter describes the most common LZ compression methods used today and shows how they were developed from the basic ideas of Ziv and Lempel.

3.1 String Compression

In general, compression methods based on strings of symbols can be more efficient than methods that compress individual symbols. To understand this, the reader should first review exercise 2.4. This exercise shows that, in principle, better compression is possible if the symbols of the alphabet have very different probabilities of occurrence. We use a simple example to show that the probabilities of strings of symbols vary more than the probabilities of the individual symbols comprising the strings.

We start with a 2-symbol alphabet a_1 and a_2, with probabilities $P_1 = 0.8$ and $P_2 = 0.2$, respectively. The average probability is 0.5, and we can get an idea of the variance (how much the individual probabilities deviate from the average) by calculating the sum of absolute differences $|0.8 - 0.5| + |0.2 - 0.5| = 0.6$. Any variable-size code would assign 1-bit codes to the two symbols, so the average size of the code is 1 bit per symbol.

We now generate all the strings of two symbols. There are four of them, shown in Table 3.1a, together with their probabilities and a set of Huffman codes. The average probability is 0.25, so a sum of absolute differences similar to the one above yields

$$|0.64 - 0.25| + |0.16 - 0.25| + |0.16 - 0.25| + |0.04 - 0.25| = 0.78.$$

The average size of the Huffman code is $1 \times 0.64 + 2 \times 0.16 + 3 \times 0.16 + 3 \times 0.04 = 1.56$ bits per string, which is 0.78 bits per symbol.

In the next step we similarly create all eight strings of three symbols. They are shown in Table 3.1b, together with their probabilities and a set of Huffman codes. The average probability is 0.125, so a sum of absolute differences similar to the ones above yields

$$|0.512 - 0.125| + 3|0.128 - 0.125| + 3|0.032 - 0.125| + |0.008 - 0.125| = 0.792.$$

The average size of the Huffman code in this case is $1 \times 0.512 + 3 \times 3 \times 0.128 + 3 \times 5 \times 0.032 + 5 \times 0.008 = 2.184$ bits per string, which equals 0.728 bits per symbol.

As we keep generating longer and longer strings, the probabilities of the strings differ more and more from their average, and the average code size gets better

String	Probability	Code
a_1a_1	$0.8 \times 0.8 = 0.64$	0
a_1a_2	$0.8 \times 0.2 = 0.16$	11
a_2a_1	$0.2 \times 0.8 = 0.16$	100
a_2a_2	$0.2 \times 0.2 = 0.04$	101

(a)

Str. size	Variance of prob.	Avg. size of code
1	0.6	1
2	0.78	0.78
3	0.792	0.728

(c)

String	Probability	Code
$a_1a_1a_1$	$0.8 \times 0.8 \times 0.8 = 0.512$	0
$a_1a_1a_2$	$0.8 \times 0.8 \times 0.2 = 0.128$	100
$a_1a_2a_1$	$0.8 \times 0.2 \times 0.8 = 0.128$	101
$a_1a_2a_2$	$0.8 \times 0.2 \times 0.2 = 0.032$	11100
$a_2a_1a_1$	$0.2 \times 0.8 \times 0.8 = 0.128$	110
$a_2a_1a_2$	$0.2 \times 0.8 \times 0.2 = 0.032$	11101
$a_2a_2a_1$	$0.2 \times 0.2 \times 0.8 = 0.032$	11110
$a_2a_2a_2$	$0.2 \times 0.2 \times 0.2 = 0.008$	11111

(b)

Table 3.1: Probabilities and Huffman Codes for a Two-Symbol Alphabet.

(Table 3.1c). This is why a compression method that compresses strings, rather than individual symbols can, in principle, yield better results. This is also the reason why the various dictionary-based methods are in general better, and more popular than the Huffman method and its variants.

3.2 LZ77 (Sliding Window)

The main idea of this method [Ziv 77] is to use part of the previously seen input stream as the dictionary. The encoder maintains a window to the input stream and shifts the input in that window from right to left as strings of symbols are being encoded. The method is thus based on a *sliding window*. The window below is divided into two parts. The part on the left is called the *search buffer*. This is the current dictionary, and it always includes symbols that have recently been input and encoded. The part on the right is the *look-ahead buffer*, containing text yet to be encoded. In practical implementations the search buffer is some thousands of bytes long, while the look-ahead buffer is only tens of bytes long. The vertical bar between the "t" and the "e" below represents the current dividing line between the two buffers.

← coded text... ⌐sir␣sid␣eastman␣easily␣t⌐eases␣sea␣sick␣seals⌐ ...← text to be read

The encoder scans the search buffer backwards (from right to left) looking for a match to the first symbol "e" in the look-ahead buffer. It finds it at the "e" of the word "easily". This "e" is at a distance (offset) of 8 from the end of the search buffer. The encoder then matches as many symbols following the two "e"s as possible. Three symbols "eas" match in this case, so the length of the match is 3. The encoder then continues the backward scan, trying to find longer matches. In our case, there is one more match, at the word "eastman", with offset 16, and it has the same length. The encoder selects the longest match or, if they are all the same length, the last one found and prepares the token (16, 3, "e").

Selecting the last match, rather than the first one, simplifies the program since it only has to keep track of the last match found. It is interesting to note that selecting the first match, while making the program somewhat more complex, also has an advantage. It selects the smallest offset. It would seem that this is not an advantage since a token should have room for the largest possible offset. However, it is possibe to follow LZ77 with Huffman, or some other statistical coding of the tokens, where small offsets are assigned shorter codes. This method, proposed by Bernd Herd, is called LZH. Having many small offsets implies better compression in LZH.

In general, an LZ77 token has three parts, offset, length, and next symbol in the look-ahead buffer (which, in our case, is the **second** "e" of the word "**teases**"). This token is written on the output stream, and the window is shifted to the right (or, alternatively, the input stream is moved to the left) four positions; three positions for the matched string, and one position for the next symbol.

$$\ldots\texttt{sir}\ \boxed{\texttt{sid}_\sqcup\texttt{eastman}_\sqcup\texttt{easily}_\sqcup\texttt{tease}\,|\,\texttt{s}_\sqcup\texttt{sea}_\sqcup\texttt{sick}_\sqcup\texttt{seals}\ldots}\ldots$$

If the backward search yields no match, an LZ77 token with zero offset and length, and with the unmatched symbol is written. This is also the reason a token has to have a third component. Tokens with zero offset and length are common at the beginning of any compression job, when the search buffer is empty or almost empty. The first five steps in encoding our example are the following:

$\boxed{\texttt{sir}_\sqcup\texttt{sid}_\sqcup\texttt{eastman}_\sqcup}$	$\Rightarrow$ $(0,0,\text{"s"})$
$\texttt{s}\,|\,\texttt{ir}_\sqcup\texttt{sid}_\sqcup\texttt{eastman}_\sqcup\texttt{e}$	$\Rightarrow$ $(0,0,\text{"i"})$
$\texttt{si}\,|\,\texttt{r}_\sqcup\texttt{sid}_\sqcup\texttt{eastman}_\sqcup\texttt{ea}$	$\Rightarrow$ $(0,0,\text{"r"})$
$\texttt{sir}\,|\,{}_\sqcup\texttt{sid}_\sqcup\texttt{eastman}_\sqcup\texttt{eas}$	$\Rightarrow$ $(0,0,\text{"}_\sqcup\text{"})$
$\texttt{sir}_\sqcup\,|\,\texttt{sid}_\sqcup\texttt{eastman}_\sqcup\texttt{easi}$	$\Rightarrow$ $(4,2,\text{"d"})$

▸ **Exercise 3.2:** What are the next two steps?

Clearly, a token of the form $(0,0,\ldots)$, which encodes a single symbol, does not provide good compression. It is easy to estimate its length. The size of the offset is $\lceil\log_2 S\rceil$ where S is the length of the search buffer. In practice the search buffer may be a few thousand bytes long, so the offset size is typically 10–12 bits. The size of the "length" field is similarly $\lceil\log_2(L-1)\rceil$ where L is the length of the look-ahead buffer (see below for the -1). In practice, the look-ahead buffer is only a few tens of bytes long, so the size of the "length" field is just a few bits. The size of the "symbol" field is typically 8 bits but, in general, it is $\lceil\log_2 A\rceil$ where A is the alphabet size. The total size of the 1-symbol token $(0,0,\ldots)$ may typically be $11+5+8=24$ bits, much longer than the raw 8-bit size of the (single) symbol it encodes.

Here is an example showing why the "length" field may be longer than the size of the look-ahead buffer:

$$\ldots\texttt{Mr.}_\sqcup\boxed{\texttt{alf}_\sqcup\texttt{eastman}_\sqcup\texttt{easily}_\sqcup\texttt{grows}_\sqcup\texttt{alf}\,|\,\texttt{alfa}_\sqcup\texttt{in}_\sqcup\texttt{his}_\sqcup\texttt{garden}}\ldots$$

The first symbol "a" in the look-ahead buffer matches the 5 a's in the search buffer. It seems that the two extreme a's match with a length of 3 and the encoder should select the last (leftmost) of them and create the token (28,3,"a"). In fact it creates the token (3,4,"␣"). The four-symbol string "`alfa`" in the look-ahead buffer is matched to the last three symbols "`alf`" in the search buffer **and** the first symbol "`a`" in the look-ahead buffer. The reason for this is that the decoder can handle such a token naturally, without any modifications. It starts at position 3 of its search buffer and copies the next four symbols, one by one, extending its buffer to the right. The first three symbols are copies of the old buffer contents, and the fourth one is a copy of the first of those three. The next example is even more convincing (and only somewhat contrived):

$$\cdots \boxed{\texttt{alf␣eastman␣easily␣yells␣A}\big|\texttt{AAAAAAAAAA}}\texttt{AAAAAH}\ldots$$

The encoder creates the token (1,9,"`A`"), matching the first nine copies of "`A`" in the look-ahead buffer and including the tenth "`A`". This is why, in principle, the length of a match could be up to the size of the look-ahead buffer minus 1.

The decoder is much simpler than the encoder (LZ77 is thus an asymmetric compression method). It has to maintain a buffer, equal in size to the encoder's window. The decoder inputs a token, finds the match in its buffer, writes the match and the third token field on the output stream, and shifts the matched string and the third field into the buffer. This implies that LZ77, or any of its variants, are useful in cases where a file is compressed once (or just a few times) and is decompressed many times. A rarely used archive of compressed files is a good example.

At first it seems that this method does not make any assumptions about the input data. Specifically, it does not pay attention to any symbol frequencies. A little thinking, however, shows that, because of the nature of the sliding window, the LZ77 method always compares the look-ahead buffer to the recently input text in the search buffer and never to text that was input long ago (and has thus been flushed out of the search buffer). The method thus implicitly assumes that patterns in the input data occur close together. Data that satisfies this assumption will compress well.

The basic LZ77 method has been improved in several ways by researchers and programmers during the 80s and 90s. One way to improve it is to use variable-size "offset" and "length" fields in the tokens. Another way is to increase the sizes of both buffers. Increasing the size of the search buffer makes it possible to find better matches, but the tradeoff is an increased search time. A large search buffer thus requires a more sophisticated data structure that allows for fast search (Section 3.9.2). A third improvement has to do with sliding the window. The simplest approach is to move all the text in the window to the left after each match. A faster method is to replace the linear window with a *circular queue*, where sliding the window is done by resetting two pointers (Section 3.2.1). Yet another improvement is adding an extra bit (a flag) to each token, thereby eliminating the third field (Section 3.3).

3.2.1 A Circular Queue

The circular queue is a basic data structure. Physically it is an array, but it is used differently. Figure 3.2 illustrates a simple example. It shows a 16-byte array with characters being appended at the "end" and others being deleted from the "start." Both the start and end positions move, and two pointers, "`s`" and "`e`" point to them all the time. In (a) there are the 8 characters "sid␣east" with the rest of the buffer empty. In (b) all 16 bytes are occupied, and "e" points to the end of the buffer. In (c), the first letter "s" has been deleted and the "l" of "easily" inserted. Notice how pointer "e" is now located *to the left* of "s". In (d), the two letters "id" have been deleted just by moving the "s" pointer; the characters themselves are still present in the array but have been effectively deleted. In (e), the two characters "y␣" have been appended and the "e" pointer moved. In (f), the pointers show that the buffer ends at "teas" and starts at "tman". Inserting new symbols into the circular queue and moving the pointers is thus equivalent to shifting the contents of the queue. No actual shifting or moving is necessary, though.

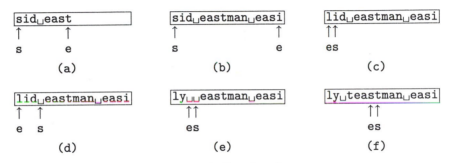

Figure 3.2: A Circular Queue.

More information on circular queues can be found in most texts on data structures.

Bibliography

Ziv, J. and A. Lempel (1977) "A Universal Algorithm for Sequential Data Compression," *IEEE Transactions on Information Theory* IT-23(3):337–343.

3.3 LZSS

This version of LZ77 was developed by Storer and Szymanski in 1982 [Storer 82]. It improves LZ77 in three ways: (1) it holds the look-ahead buffer in a circular queue, (2) it holds the search buffer (the dictionary) in a binary search tree, and (3) it creates tokens with two fields instead of three.

A binary search tree is a binary tree where the left subtree of every node A contains nodes smaller than A, and the right subtree contains nodes greater than A. Since the nodes of our binary search trees contain strings, we first need to know how to compare two strings and decide which one is "bigger." This is easily understood by imagining that the strings appear in a dictionary or a lexicon, where they are sorted alphabetically. Clearly the string "rote" precedes the string "said" since "r" precedes "s" (even though "o" follows "a"), so we consider "rote" smaller than "said". This is called *lexicographic order* (ordering strings lexicographically).

What about the string "␣abc"? All modern computers use the ASCII codes to represent characters and in ASCII the code of a blank space precedes those of the letters, so a string that starts with a space will be smaller than any string that starts with a letter. In general, the *collating sequence* of the computer determines the sequence of characters arranged from small to big. Figure 3.3 shows two examples of binary search trees.

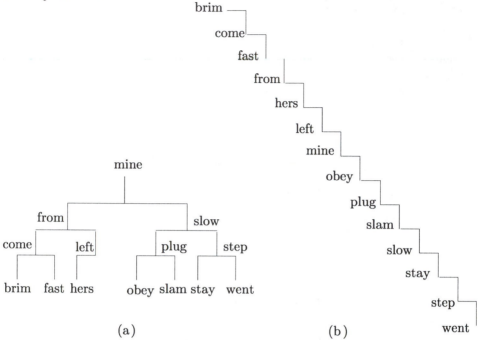

Figure 3.3: Two Binary Search Trees.

Notice the difference between the (almost) balanced tree in Figure 3.3a and the skewed one in Figure 3.3b. They contain the same 14 nodes but they look and behave very differently. In the balanced tree any node can be found in at most four steps. In the skewed tree up to 14 steps may be needed. In either case, the maximum number of steps necessary to locate a node equals the height of the tree. For a skewed tree (which is really the same as a linked list), the height is the number of elements n; for a balanced tree, the height is $\lceil \log_2 n \rceil$, a much smaller number. More information on the properties of binary search trees may be found in any text on data structures.

Here is an example showing how a binary search tree can be used to speed up the search of the dictionary. We assume an input stream with the short sentence "sid␣eastman␣clumsily␣teases␣sea␣sick␣seals". To keep the example simple, we assume a window consisting of a 16-byte search buffer followed by a 5-byte look-ahead buffer. After the first $16 + 5$ characters have been input, the sliding window looks like

$$\boxed{\text{sid␣eastman␣clum}}\boxed{\text{sily␣}}\text{teases␣sea␣sick␣seals}$$

with the string "teases␣sea␣sick␣seals" still waiting to be input.

The encoder scans the search buffer, creating the twelve five-character strings of Table 3.4 (twelve since $16 - 5 + 1 = 12$), which are inserted into the binary search tree, each with its offset.

sid␣e	16
id␣ea	15
d␣eas	14
␣east	13
eastm	12
astma	11
stman	10
tman␣	09
man␣c	08
an␣cl	07
n␣clu	06
␣clum	05

Table 3.4: Five-Character Strings.

The first symbol in the look-ahead buffer is "s", so the encoder searches the tree for strings that start with an "s". Two are found, at offsets 16 and 10, and the first of them, "sid␣e" (at offset 16) provides a longer match.

(We now have to sidetrack and discuss the case where a string in the tree completely matches that in the look-ahead buffer. In that case the encoder should go back to the search buffer, to try and match longer strings. In principle, the maximum length of a match can be $L - 1$.)

In our example, the match is of length 2, and the 2-field token (16,2) is emitted. The encoder now has to slide the window two positions to the right, and update the tree. The new window is

si$\boxed{\text{d␣eastman␣clumsi}}$$\boxed{\text{ly␣te}}$ases␣sea␣sick␣seals

The tree should be updated by deleting strings "sid␣e" and "id␣ea", and inserting the new strings "clums" and "lumsi". If a longer, k-letter string is matched, the window has to be shifted k positions and the tree should be updated by deleting k strings and adding k new strings, but which ones?

A little thinking shows that the k strings to be deleted are the first ones in the search buffer before the shift, and the k strings to be added are the last ones in it after the shift. A simple procedure for updating the tree is to prepare a string consisting of the first five letters in the search buffer, find it in the tree, and delete it. Then slide the buffer one position to the right (or shift the data to the left), prepare a string consisting of the last five letters in the search buffer, and append it to the tree. This should be repeated k times.

Since each update deletes and adds the same number of strings, the tree size never changes. It always contains T nodes, where T is the length of the search buffer minus the length of the look-ahead buffer plus 1 $T = S - L + 1$. The shape of the tree, however, may change significantly. As nodes are being added and deleted, the tree may change its shape between a completely skewed tree (the worst case for searching) and a balanced one, the ideal shape for searching.

The third improvement of LZSS over LZ77 is in the tokens created by the encoder. An LZSS token contains just an offset and a length. If no match was found, the encoder emits the uncompressed code of the next symbol instead of the wasteful three-field token $(0,0,\dots)$. To distinguish between tokens and uncompressed codes, each is preceded by a single bit (a flag).

In practice the search buffer may be a few thousand bytes long, so the offset field would typically be 11–13 bits. The size of the look-ahead buffer should be selected such that the total size of a token would be 16 bits (2 bytes). For example, if the search buffer size is 2 Kbyte ($= 2^{11}$), then the look-ahead buffer should be 32 bytes long ($= 2^5$). The offset field would be 11 bits long and the length field, 5 bits (the size of the look-ahead buffer). With this choice of buffer sizes the encoder will emit either 2-byte tokens or 1-byte uncompressed ASCII codes. But what about the flag bits? A good practical idea is to collect eight output items (tokens and ASCII codes) in a small buffer, then output one byte consisting of the eight flags, followed by the eight items (which are 1 or 2 bytes long each).

3.3.1 Deficiencies

Before we discuss LZ78, let's summarize the deficiencies of LZ77 and its variants. It has already been mentioned that LZ77 uses the built-in implicit assumption that patterns in the input data occur close together. Data streams that don't satisfy this assumption compress poorly. A common example is text where a certain word, say "`economy`", occurs many times but is uniformly distributed throughout the text. When this word is shifted into the look-ahead buffer, its previous occurrence may have already been shifted out of the search buffer. A better compression method would save commonly occurring strings in the dictionary and not simply slide it all the time.

Another disadvantage of LZ77 is the limited size L of the look-ahead buffer. The size of matched strings is limited to $L-1$ but L must be kept small, since the process of matching strings involves comparing individual symbols. If L is doubled in size, compression would improve, since longer matches would be possible, but the encoder would be much slower when searching for long matches. The size S of the search buffer is also limited. A large search buffer produces better compression but slows down the encoder since searching takes longer (even with a binary search tree). Increasing the sizes of the two buffers also means creating longer tokens, thereby reducing the compression efficiency. With 2-byte tokens, compressing a 2-character string into one token results in 2 bytes plus 1 flag. Writing the two characters as two raw ASCII codes results in 2 bytes plus 2 flags, a very small difference in size. The encoder should, in such a case, use the latter choice and write the two characters in uncompressed form, saving time and wasting just one bit. We say that the encoder has a 2-byte *break even* point. With longer tokens, the break even point increases to 3 bytes.

Bibliography

Storer, J. A. and T. G. Szymanski (1982) "Data Compression via Textual Substitution," *Journal of the ACM* **29**:928–951.

3.4 QIC-122

QIC is an international trade association, incorporated in 1987, whose mission is to encourage and promote the widespread use of quarter-inch tape cartridge technology (hence the acronym QIC, see also "`http://www.qic.org/html`").

The QIC-122 compression standard is an LZ77 variant that has been developed by QIC for text compression on 1/4-inch data cartridge tape drives. Data is read and shifted into a 2048-byte ($= 2^{11}$) input buffer from right to left, such that the first character is the leftmost one. When the buffer is full, or when all the data has been read into it, the algorithm searches from left to right for repeated strings. The output consists of raw characters and of tokens that represent strings already seen in the buffer. As an example, suppose that the following data have been read and shifted into the buffer:

ABAAAAAACABABABA.............

The first character "A" is obviously not a repetition of any previous string, so it is encoded as a raw (ASCII) character (see below). The next character "B" is also encoded as raw. The third character "A" is identical to the first character but is also encoded as raw since repeated strings should be at least two characters long. Only with the fourth character "A" we do have a repeated string. The string of five A's from position 4 to position 8 is identical to the one from position 3 to position 7. It is thus encoded as a string of length 5 at offset 1. The offset, in this method, is the distance between the start of the repeated string and the start of the original one.

The next character "C" at position 9 is encoded as raw. The string "ABA" at positions 10–12 is a repeat of the string at positions 1–3, so it is encoded as a string of length 3 at offset $10 - 1 = 9$. Finally, the string "BABA" at positions 13–16 is encoded with length 4 at offset 2 since it is a reptition of the string at positions 10–13.

▶ **Exercise 3.3:** Suppose that the next four characters of data are "CAAC"

ABAAAAAACABABABACAAC...........

How will they be encoded?

A raw character is encoded as 0 followed by the 8 ASCII bits of the character. A string is encoded as a token that starts with 1 followed by the encoded offset, followed by the encoded length. Small offsets are encoded as 1, followed by 7 offset bits; large offsets are encoded as 0 followed by 11 offset bits (recall that the buffer size is 2^{11}). The length is encoded according to Table 3.6. The 9-bit string 110000000 is written, as an end-marker, at the end of the output stream.

▶ **Exercise 3.4:** How can the decoder identify the end marker?

When the search algorithm arrives at the right end of the buffer, it shifts the buffer to the left and inputs the next character into the rightmost position of the buffer. The decoder is the reverse of the encoder (symmetric compression).

Figure 3.5 is a precise description of the compression process, expressed in BNF, which is a meta-language used to unambiguously describe processes and formal languages. BNF uses the following *meta-symbols*:

::=   The symbol on the left is defined by the expression on the right.
<expr>   An expression still to be defined.
| A logical OR.
[]   Optional. The expression in the brackets may occur zero or more times.
()   A comment.
0,1   The bits 0 and 1.

Table 3.6 shows the results of encoding "ABAAAAAACABABABA" (a 16-symbol string). The reader can easily verify that the output stream consists of the 10 bytes

$$20\ 90\ 88\ 38\ 1C\ 21\ E2\ 5C\ 15\ 80.$$

3.5 LZ78

This method [Ziv 78] does not use any search buffer, look-ahead buffer, or sliding window. Instead there is a dictionary of previously encountered strings. This dictionary starts empty (or almost empty) and its size is limited only by the amount of available memory. The encoder outputs two-field tokens. The first field is a pointer to the dictionary; the second is the code of a symbol. Tokens do not contain the length of a string since this is implied in the dictionary. Each token corresponds to a string of input symbols, and that string is added to the dictionary after the token is written on the compressed stream. Nothing is ever deleted from the dictionary, which is both an advantage over LZ77 (since future strings can be compressed by strings seen in the past) and a liability (since the dictionary tends to grow fast and to fill up the entire available memory).

The dictionary starts with the null string at position zero. As symbols are input and encoded, strings are added to the dictionary at positions 1, 2, and so on. When the next symbol "x" is read from the input stream, the dictionary is searched for an entry with the one-symbol string "x". If none are found, "x" is added to the next available position in the dictionary, and the token (0,"x") is output. This token indicates the string "null x" (a concatenation of the null string and "x"). If an entry with "x" is found (at position 37, say), the next symbol "y" is read, and the dictionary is searched for an entry containing the two-symbol string "xy". If none are found, then string "xy" is added to the next available position in the dictionary, and the token (37,"y") is output. This token indicates the string "xy" since 37 is the dictionary position of string "x". The process continues until the end of the input stream is reached.

In general, the first symbol is read and becomes a one-symbol string. The encoder then tries to find it in the dictionary. If the symbol is found in the dictionary, the next symbol is read and concatenated with the first to form a two-symbol string that the encoder then tries to locate in the dictionary. As long as those strings are found in the dictionary, more symbols are read and concatenated to the string. At a certain point the string is not found in the dictionary, so the encoder adds it to the dictionary and outputs a token with the last dictionary match as its first field, and the last symbol of the string (the one that caused the search to fail) as its second field. Table 3.8 shows the first 14 steps in encoding the string

"sir␣sid␣eastman␣easily␣teases␣sea␣sick␣seals".

▶ **Exercise 3.5:** Complete this table.

```
(QIC-122 BNF Description)
<Compressed-Stream>::=[<Compressed-String>] <End-Marker>
<Compressed-String>::= 0<Raw-Byte> | 1<Compressed-Bytes>
<Raw-Byte>           ::=<b><b><b><b><b><b><b><b> (8-bit byte)
<Compressed-Bytes> ::=<offset><length>
<offset>             ::= 1<b><b><b><b><b><b><b> (a 7-bit offset)
                         |
          0<b><b><b><b><b><b><b><b><b><b><b> (an 11-bit offset)
<length>             ::= (as per length table)
<End-Marker>         ::=110000000 (Compressed bytes with offset=0)
<b>                  ::=0|1
```

Figure 3.5: BNF Definition of QIC-122.

Bytes	Length				Bytes	Length				
2	00				17	11	11	1001		
3	01				18	11	11	1010		
4	10				19	11	11	1011		
5	11	00			20	11	11	1100		
6	11	01			21	11	11	1101		
7	11	10			22	11	11	1110		
8	11	11	0000		23	11	11	1111	0000	
9	11	11	0001		24	11	11	1111	0001	
10	11	11	0010		25	11	11	1111	0010	
11	11	11	0011		⋮					
12	11	11	0100		37	11	11	1111	1110	
13	11	11	0101		38	11	11	1111	1111	0000
14	11	11	0110		39	11	11	1111	1111	0001
15	11	11	0111		etc.					
16	11	11	1000							

Table 3.6: Values of the <length> Field.

Raw byte "A"	0 01000001
Raw byte "B"	0 01000010
Raw byte "A"	0 01000001
String "AAAAA" offset=1	1 1 0000001 1100
Raw byte "C"	0 01000011
String "ABA" offset=9	1 1 0001001 01
String "BABA" offset=2	1 1 0000010 10
End-Marker	1 1 0000000

Table 3.7: Encoding the Example.

Dictionary	Token	Dictionary	Token
0 null		8 "a"	(0,"a")
1 "s"	(0,"s")	9 "st"	(1,"t")
2 "i"	(0,"i")	10 "m"	(0,"m")
3 "r"	(0,"r")	11 "an"	(8,"n")
4 "␣"	(0,"␣")	12 "␣ea"	(7,"a")
5 "si"	(1,"i")	13 "sil"	(5,"l")
6 "d"	(0,"d")	14 "y"	(0,"y")
7 "␣e"	(4,"e")		

Table 3.8: First 14 Encoding Steps in LZ78.

In each step, the string added to the dictionary is the one being encoded, minus its last symbol. In a typical compression run, the dictionary starts with short strings but, as more text is being input and processed, longer and longer strings are added to it. The size of the dictionary can either be fixed or may be determined by the size of the available memory each time the LZ78 compression program is executed. A large dictionary may contain more strings and thus allow for longer matches but the tradeoff is longer pointers (and thus bigger tokens) and slower dictionary search.

A good data structure for the dictionary is a tree, but not a binary one. The tree starts with the null string as the root. All the strings that start with the null string (strings for which the token pointer is zero) are added to the tree as children of the root. In the above example those are "s", "i", "r", "␣", "d", "a", "m", "y", "e", "c", and "k". Each of these becomes the root of a subtree as shown in Figure 3.9. For example, all the strings that start with "s" ("si", "sil", "st", and "s(eof)") constitute the subtree of node "s".

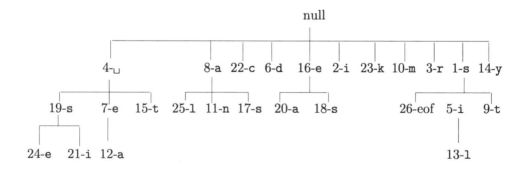

Figure 3.9: An LZ78 Dictionary Tree.

Assuming an alphabet with 8-bit symbols, there are 256 different symbols so, in principle, each node in the tree could have up to 256 children. The process of adding a child to a tree node should thus be dynamic. When the node is first created, it has no children and it should not reserve any memory space for them.

As a child is added to the node, memory space should be claimed for it. Since no nodes are ever deleted, there is no need to reclaim memory space, which simplifies the memory management task somewhat.

Such a tree makes it easy to search for a string and to add strings. To search for "sil" e.g., the program looks for the child "s" of the root, then for the child "i" of "s", and so on, going down the tree. Here are some examples:

1. When the "s" of "sid" is input in step 5, the encoder finds node "1-s" in the tree as a child of "null". It then inputs the next symbol "i", but node "s" does not have a child "i" (in fact, it has no children at all at this point), so the encoder adds node "5-i" as a child of "1-s", which effectively adds the string "si" to the tree.

2. When the blank space between "eastman" and "easily" is input in step 12, a similar situation happens. The encoder finds node "4-␣", inputs "e", finds "7-e", inputs "a", but "7-e" does not have "a" as a child, so the encoder adds node "12-a", which effectively adds the string "␣ea" to the tree.

A tree of the type described here is called a *trie*. In general a trie is a tree in which the branching structure at any level is determined by just part of a data item, not the entire item. In the case of LZ78, each string added to the tree effectively adds just one symbol, and does that by adding a branch.

Since the total size of the tree is limited, it may fill up during compression. This, in fact, happens all the time except when the input stream is unusually small. The original LZ78 method does not specify what to do in such a case, so here are some possible solutions.

1. The simplest solution is to freeze the dictionary at that point. No new nodes should be added, the tree becomes a static dictionary, but it can still be used to encode strings.

2. Delete the entire tree once it gets full and start with a new, empty tree. This solution effectively breaks the input into blocks, each with its own dictionary. If the contents of the input varies from block to block, this solution will produce good compression, since it will eliminate a dictionary with strings that are unlikely to be used in the future. We can say that this solution implicitly assumes that future symbols will benefit more from new data than from old one (the same implicit assumption used by LZ77).

3. The UNIX `compress` utility (Section 3.15) uses a more complex solution.

4. When the dictionary is full, delete some of the least recently used entries, to make room for new ones. Unfortunately there is no good algorithm to decide which entries to delete, and how many (but see the *reuse* procedure in Section 3.17).

The LZ78 decoder works by building and maintaining the dictionary in the same way as the encoder. It is thus more complex than the LZ77 decoder.

Bibliography

Ziv, J. and A. Lempel (1978) "Compression of Individual Sequences via Variable-Rate Coding," *IEEE Transactions on Information Theory* IT-24(5):530–536.

> The Red Queen shook her head, "You may call it 'nonsense' if you like," she said, "but I've heard nonsense, compared with which that would be as sensible as a dictionary!"
> —Lewis Carroll (1832–1898), *Through the Looking Glass*

3.6 LZFG

Edward Fiala and Daniel Greene have developed several related compression methods [Fiala 89] that are hybrids of LZ77 and LZ78. All their methods are based on the following scheme. The encoder generates a compressed file with tokens and literals (raw ASCII codes) intermixed. There are two types of tokens: a *literal* and a *copy*. A literal token indicates that a string of literals follow; a copy token points to a string previously seen in the data. For example, the string "the␣boy␣on␣my␣right␣is␣the␣right␣boy" produces, when encoded,

(literal 23)the␣boy␣on␣my␣right␣is␣(copy 4 23)(copy 6 13)(copy 3 29)

where the three copy tokens refer to the strings "the␣", "right␣" and "boy", respectively. The LZFG methods are best understood by considering how the decoder operates. The decoder starts with a large, empty buffer in which it generates and shifts the decompressed stream. When the decoder inputs a (literal 23) token, it inputs the next 23 bytes as raw ASCII codes into the buffer, shifting the buffer such that the last byte input will be the rightmost one. When the decoder inputs (copy 4 23) it copies the string of length 4 that starts 23 positions from the right end of the buffer. The string is then appended to the buffer, while shifting it. Two LZFG methods, denoted A1 and A2, are described here.

The A1 scheme employs 8-bit literal tokens and 16-bit copy tokens. A literal token has the format "0000nnnn" where "nnnn" indicates the number of ASCII bytes following the token. Since the 4-bit "nnnn" field can have values between 0 and 15, they are interpreted as meaning 1 to 16. The longest possible string of literals is thus 16 bytes. The format of a copy token is "sssspp...p" where the 4-bit non-zero "ssss" field indicates the length of the string to be copied, and the 12-bit "pp...p" field is a displacement showing where the string starts in the buffer. Since the "ssss" field cannot be zero, it can only have values between 1 and 15, and they are interpreted as string lengths between 2 and 16. Displacement values are in the range [0,4095] and are interpreted as [1,4096].

The encoder starts with an empty search buffer, 4,096 bytes long, and fills up the look-ahead buffer with input data. At each subsequent step it tries to create a copy token. If nothing matches in that step, the encoder creates a literal token. Suppose that at a certain point the buffer contains

←text already encoded..｜.. ⸬ ..xyz｜abcd.. ⸬ ..｜..← text yet to be input

The encoder tries to match the string "abc..." in the look-ahead buffer to various strings in the search buffer. If a match is found (of at least two symbols) a copy token is written on the compressed stream and the data in the buffers is shifted to the left by the size of the match. If a match is not found, the encoder starts a literal with the "a" and left-shifts the data one position. It then tries to match "bcd..." to the search buffer. If it finds a match, a literal token is output, followed by a byte with the "a", followed by a match token. Otherwise, the "b" is appended to the literal and the encoder tries to match from "cd..". Literals can be up to 16 bytes long, so the string "the␣boy␣on␣my..." above is encoded as

(literal 16)(literal 7)the␣boy␣on␣my␣right␣is␣(copy 4 23)(copy 6 13)(copy 3 29).

The A1 method borrows the idea of the sliding buffer from LZ77 but also behaves like LZ78 since it creates two-field tokens. This is why it can be considered a hybrid of the two original LZ methods. When A1 starts, it creates mostly literals, but when it gets up to speed (fills up its search buffer) it features strong adaptation, so more and more copy tokens appear in the compressed stream.

The A2 method uses a larger search buffer (up to 21K bytes long). This improves compression since longer copies can be found but raises the problem of token size. A large search buffer implies large displacements in copy tokens; long copies imply large "length" fields in those tokens. At the same time we expect both the displacement and "length" fields of a typical copy token to be small, since most matches are found close to the beginning of the search buffer. The solution is to use a variable-size code for those fields, and A2 uses the general unary codes of Section 2.3.1. The "length" field of a copy token is encoded with a (2,1,10) code (Table 2.5), making it possible to match strings up to 2,044 symbols long. Notice that the (2,1,10) code is between 3 and 18 bits long.

The first four codes of the (2,1,10) code are 000, 001, 010, and 011. The last three of these codes indicate match lengths of two, three and four, respectively (recall that the minimum match length is 2). The first one (code 000) is reserved to indicate a literal. The length of the literal then follows and is encoded with code (0,1,5). A literal can thus be up to 63 bytes long and the literal-length field in the token is encoded by between 1 and 10 bits. In case of a match, the "length" field is not 000 and is followed by the displacement field, which is encoded with the (10,2,14) code (Table Ans.4). This code has 21K values, and the maximum code size is 16 bits (but see points 2 and 3 below).

Three more refinements are used by the A2 method, to achieve slightly better (1% or 2%) compression.

1. A literal of maximum length (63 bytes) can immediately be followed by another literal or by a copy token of any length, but a literal of fewer than 63 bytes must be followed by a copy token matching *at least three symbols* (or by the end-of-file). This fact is used to shift down the (2,1,10) codes used to indicate the match length. Normally, codes 000, 001, 010, and 011 indicate no match, and matches of length 2, 3, and 4, respectively. However, a copy token following a literal token of fewer than 63 bytes uses codes 000, 001, 010, and 011 to indicate matches of length 3, 4, 5, and 6, respectively. This way the maximum match length can be 2046 symbols instead of 2044.

2. The displacement field is encoded with the (10,2,14) code which has 21K values and whose individual codes range in size from 11 to 16 bits. For smaller files, such large displacements may not be necessary, and other general unary codes

may be used, with shorter individual codes. Method A2 thus uses codes of the form $(10 - d, 2, 14 - d)$ for $d = 10, 9, 8, \ldots, 0$. For $d = 1$, code (9,2,13) has $2^9 + 2^{11} + 2^{13} = 10,752$ values, and individual codes range in size from 9 to 15 bits. For $d = 10$ code (0,2,4) contains $2^0 + 2^2 + 2^4 = 21$ values, and codes are between 1 and 6 bits long. Method A2 starts with $d = 10$ [meaning it initially uses code (0,2,4)] and a search buffer of size 21 bytes. When the buffer fills up (indicating an input stream longer than 21 bytes), the A2 algorithm switches to $d = 9$ [code (1,2,5)] and increases the search buffer size to 42 bytes. This process continues until the entire input stream has been encoded or until $d = 0$ is reached [at which point code (10,2,14) is used to the end]. A lot of work for a small gain in compression.

3. Each of the codes $(10 - d, 2, 14 - d)$ requires a search buffer of a certain size, from 21 up to 21K=21,504 bytes, according to the number of codes it contains. If the user wants, for some reason, to assign the search buffer a different size, then some of the longer codes may never be used, which makes it possible to cut down a little the size of the individual codes. For example, if the user decides to use a search buffer of size 16K=16,384 bytes, then code (10,2,14) has to be used [because the next code (9,2,13) contains just 10,752 values]. Code (10,2,14) contains 21K=21,504 individual codes, so the 5120 longest codes will never be used. The last group of codes ("11" followed by 14 bits) in (10,2,14) contains $2^{14} = 16,384$ different individual codes, of which only 11,264 will be used. Of the 11,264 codes the first 8,192 can be represented as "11" followed by $\lfloor \log_2 11,264 \rfloor = 13$ bits, and only the remaining 3,072 codes require $\lceil \log_2 11,264 \rceil = 14$ bits to follow the first "11". We thus end up with 8,192 15-bit codes and 3,072 16-bit codes, instead of 11,264 16-bit codes, a very small improvement.

These three improvements illustrate the great lengths that researchers are willing to go to in order to improve their algorithms ever so slightly.

Experience shows that fine-tuning an algorithm to squeeze out the last remaining bits of redundancy from the data gives diminishing returns. Modifying an algorithm to improve compression by 1% may increase the run time by 10%. (From the Preface.)

The LZFG "corpus" of algorithms contains four more methods. B1 and B2 are similar to A1 and A2 but faster because of the way they compute displacements. However, some compression ratio is sacrificed. C1 and C2 go in the opposite direction. They achieve slightly better compression than A1 and A2 at the price of slower operation.

Bibliography

Fiala, E. R., and D. H. Greene (1989), "Data Compression with Finite Windows," *Communications of the ACM* **32**(4):490–505.

3.7 LZRW1

Developed by Ross Williams [Williams 91] as a simple, fast LZ77 variant, LZRW1 is also related to method A1 of LZFG (Section 3.6). The main idea is to find a match in one step, using a hash table (Appendix H). This is fast but not very efficient since the match found is not always the longest. We start with a description of the algorithm, follow with the format of the compressed stream, and conclude with an example.

The method uses the entire available memory as a buffer and encodes the input stream in blocks. A block is read into the buffer and is completely encoded, and then the next block is read and encoded, and so on. The length of the search buffer is 4K and that of the look-ahead buffer is 16 bytes. These two buffers slide along the input block in memory from left to right. It is only necessary to maintain one pointer, p_src, pointing to the start of the look-ahead buffer. p_src is initialized to 1 and is incremented after each phrase is encoded, thereby moving both buffers to the right by the length of the phrase. Figure 3.10 shows how the search buffer starts empty, and then grows to 4K, then starts sliding to the right, following the look-ahead buffer.

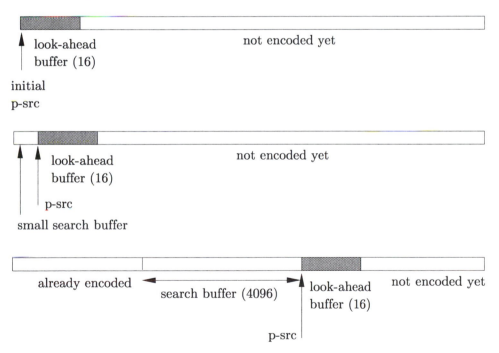

Figure 3.10: Sliding the LZRW1 Search- and Look-Ahead Buffers.

The leftmost three characters of the look-ahead buffer are hashed into a 12-bit number I, which is used to index an array of $2^{12} = 4,096$ pointers. A pointer P is retrieved and is immediately replaced in the array by I. If P points outside the search buffer, there is no match; the first character in the look-ahead buffer is output as a literal, and `p_src` is advanced by 1. The same thing is done if P points inside the search buffer but to a string that does not match the one in the look-ahead buffer. If P points to a match of at least three characters, the encoder finds the longest match (at most 16 characters), outputs a match item, and advances `p_src` by the length of the match. This process is depicted in Figure 3.12. An interesting point to note is that the array of pointers does not have to be initialized when the encoder starts since the encoder checks every pointer. Initially all pointers are random, but as they are replaced, more and more of them point to real matches.

The output of the LZRW1 encoder (Figure 3.13) consists of groups, each starting with a 16-bit *control word*, followed by 16 items. Each item is either an 8-bit literal or a 16-bit copy item (a match) made of a 4-bit length field b (where the length is $b + 1$) and a 12-bit offset (the a and c fields). The length field indicates lengths between 3 and 16. The 16 bits of the control word flag each of the 16 items that follow (a 0 flag indicates a literal and a flag of 1, a match item). The last group may contain fewer than 16 items.

The decoder is even simpler than the encoder since it does not need the array of pointers. It maintains a large buffer using a `p_src` pointer in the same way as the encoder. The decoder reads a control word from the compressed stream and uses its 16 bits to read 16 items. A literal item is decoded by appending it to the buffer and incrementing `p_src` by 1. A copy item is decoded by subtracting the offset from `p_src`, fetching a string from the search buffer, of length indicated by the length field, and appending it to the buffer. `p_src` is then incremented by the length.

Table 3.11 illustrates the first seven steps of encoding "that␣thatch␣thaws". The values produced by the hash function are arbitrary. Initially all pointers are random (indicated by "any") but they are replaced by useful ones very quickly.

▶ **Exercise 3.6:** Summarize the last steps in a table similar to Table 3.11 and write the final compressed stream in binary.

p_src	3 chars	Hash index	P	Output	Binary output
1	"tha"	4	any→4	t	01110100
2	"hat"	6	any→6	h	01101000
3	"at␣"	2	any→2	a	01100001
4	"t␣t"	1	any→1	t	01110100
5	"␣th"	5	any→5	␣	00100000
6	"tha"	4	4→4	4,5	0000|0011|00000101
10	"ch␣"	3	any→3	c	01100011

Table 3.11: First Seven Steps of Encoding "that thatch thaws".

Tests done by the original developer indicate that LZRW1 performs about 10% worse than LZC (the UNIX `compress` utility) but is four times faster. Also, it

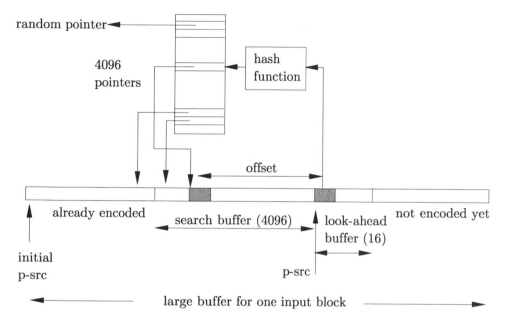

Figure 3.12: The LZRW1 Encoder.

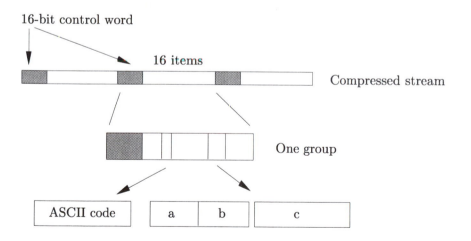

Figure 3.13: Format of the Output.

performs about 4% worse than LZFG (the A1 method) but runs ten times faster. It is therefore suited for cases where speed is more important than compression performance. A 68000 assembly language implementation has required, on average, the execution of only 13 machine instructions to compress, and four instructions to decompress, 1 byte.

Bibliography

Williams, Ross (1991), "An Extremely Fast Ziv-Lempel Data Compression Algorithm," in *Proceedings of the 1991 Data Compression Conference*, J. Storer ed., Los Alamitos, CA, IEEE Computer Society Press, pp. 362–371.

Williams, Ross N., *Adaptive Data Compression*, Boston, Kluwer Academic Publishers, 1991.

3.8 LZRW4

LZRW4 is a variant of LZ77, based on ideas of Ross Williams about possible ways to combine a dictionary method with prediction (Section 3.23.1). LZRW4 also borrows some ideas from LZRW1. It uses a 1Mbyte buffer where both the search- and look-ahead buffers slide from left to right. At any point in the encoding process, the order-2 context of the current symbol (the two most recent symbols in the search buffer) is used to predict the current symbol. The two symbols constituting the context are hashed to a 12-bit number I, which is used as an index to a $2^{12} = 4,096$-entry array A of partitions. Each partition contains 32 pointers to the input data in the 1Mbyte buffer (each pointer is thus 20 bits long).

The 32 pointers in partition A[I] are checked to find the longest match between the look-ahead buffer and the input data seen so far. The longest match is selected and coded in 8 bits. The first 3 bits code the match length according to Table 3.14; the remaining 5 bits identify the pointer in the partition. Such an 8-bit number is called a *copy item*. If no match is found, a literal is encoded in 8 bits. For each item, an extra bit is prepared, a 0 for a literal and a 1, for a copy item. The extra bits are accumulated in groups of 16, and each group is output, as in LZRW1, preceding the 16 items it refers to.

3 bits:	000	001	010	011	100	101	110	111
length:	2	3	4	5	6	7	8	16

Table 3.14: Encoding the Length in LZRW4.

The partitions are updated all the time by moving "good" pointers toward the start of their partition. When a match is found, the encoder swaps the selected pointer with the pointer halfway toward the partition (Figure 3.15a,b). If no match is found, the entire 32-pointer partition is shifted to the left and the new pointer is entered on the right, pointing to the current symbol (Figure 3.15c).

3.9 LZW   123

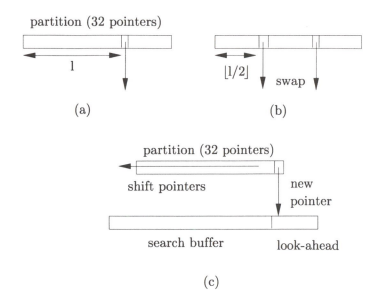

Figure 3.15: Updating An LZRW4 Partition.

3.9 LZW

This is a popular variant of LZ78, developed by T. Welch in 1984 [Welch 84]. Its main feature is eliminating the second field of a token. An LZW token consists of just a pointer to the dictionary. As a result, such a token always encodes a string of more than one symbol. To best understand LZW, we will temporarily forget that the dictionary is a tree, and will think of it as an array of variable-size strings. The LZW method starts by initializing the dictionary to all the symbols in the alphabet. In the common case of 8-bit symbols, the first 256 entries of the dictionary (entries 0 through 255) are occupied before any data is input.

⟶ The principle of LZW is: The encoder inputs symbols one by one and accumulates them in a string I. After each symbol is input and is concatenated to I, the dictionary is searched for string I. As long as I is found in the dictionary, the process continues. At a certain point, adding the next symbol x causes the search to fail; string I is in the dictionary but string Ix (symbol x concatenated to I) is not. At this point the encoder (1) outputs the dictionary pointer that points to string I, (2) saves string Ix (which is now called a *phrase*) in the next available dictionary entry, and (3) initializes string I to symbol x. To illustrate this process, we again use the text "sir␣sid␣eastman␣easily␣teases␣sea␣sick␣seals". The steps are:

0. Initialize entries 0–255 of the dictionary to all 256 8-bit bytes.

1. The first symbol "s" is input and is found in the dictionary (in entry 115, since this is the ASCII code of "s"). The next symbol "i" is input but "si" is not found in the dictionary. The encoder (1) outputs 115, (2) saves string "si" in the next available dictionary entry (entry 256), and (3) initializes I to the symbol "i".

2. The "r" of "sir" is input but string "ir" is not in the dictionary. The

In the first decoding step, the decoder inputs the first pointer and uses it to retrieve a dictionary item I. This is a string of symbols, and it is written on the decoder's output stream. String Ix needs to be saved in the dictionary, but symbol x is still unknown; it will be the first symbol in the next string retrieved from the dictionary.

In each decoding step after the first, the decoder inputs the next pointer, retrieves the next string J from the dictionary, writes it on the output stream, isolates its first symbol x, and saves string Ix in the next available dictionary entry (after checking to make sure string Ix is not already in the dictionary). The decoder then moves J to I and is ready for the next step.

In our "sir␣sid..." example, the first pointer that's input by the decoder is 115. This corresponds to the string "s", which is retrieved from the dictionary, gets stored in I and becomes the first thing written on the decoder's output stream. The next pointer is 105, so string "i" is retrieved into J and is also written on the output stream. J's first symbol is concatenated with I, to form string "si", which does not exist in the dictionary, and is therefore added to it as entry 256. Variable J is moved to I, so I is now the string "i". The next pointer is 114, so string "r" is retrieved from the dictionary into J and is also written on the output stream. J's first symbol is concatenated with I, to form string "ir", which does not exist in the dictionary, and is added to it as entry 257. Variable J is moved to I, so I is now the string "r". The next step reads pointer 32, writes "␣" on the output stream, and saves string "r␣".

▸ **Exercise 3.9:** Decode the string "alf␣eats␣alfalfa" by using the encoding results from exercise 3.7.

▸ **Exercise 3.10:** Assume a two-symbol alphabet with the symbols "a" and "b". Show the first few steps for encoding and decoding the string "ababab...".

3.9.2 LZW Dictionary Structure

Up until now, we have assumed that the LZW dictionary is an array of variable-size strings. To understand why a trie is a better data structure for the dictionary we need to recall how the encoder works. It inputs symbols and concatenates them into a variable I as long as the string in I is found in the dictionary. At a certain point the encoder inputs the first symbol x, which causes the search to fail (string Ix is not in the dictionary). It then adds Ix to the dictionary. This means that each string added to the dictionary effectively adds just one new symbol, x. (Phrased another way: for each dictionary string of more than one symbol, there exists a "parent" string in the dictionary that's one symbol shorter.)

A tree similar to the one used by LZ78 is thus a good data structure, since adding string Ix to such a tree is done by adding one node with x. The main problem is that each node in the LZW tree may have many children (the tree is multiway, not binary). Imagine the node for the letter "a" in entry 97. Initially it has no children but, if the string "ab" is added to the tree, node 97 gets one child. Later when, say, the string "ae" is added, node 97 gets a second child, and so on. The data structure for the tree should therefore be designed such that a node could have any number of children, but without having to reserve any memory for them in advance.

One way of designing such a data structure is to house the tree in an array of nodes, each a structure with two fields; a symbol and a pointer to the parent node. A node has no pointers to any child nodes. Moving down the tree, from a node to one of its children is done by a *hashing process* in which the pointer to the node and the symbol of the child are hashed to create a new pointer. Appendix H discusses hash tables in some detail.

Suppose that string "abc" has already been input, symbol by symbol and has been stored in the tree in the three nodes at locations 97, 266, and 284. Following that, the encoder has just input the next symbol "d". The encoder now searches for string "abcd" or, more specifically, for a node containing the symbol "d" whose parent is at location 284. The encoder hashes the 284 (the pointer to string "abc") and the 100 (ASCII code of "d") to create a pointer to some node say, 299. The encoder then examines node 299. There are three possibilities:

1. The node is unused. This means that "abcd" is not yet in the dictionary and should be added to it. The encoder adds it to the tree by storing the parent pointer 284 and ASCII code 100 in the node. The result is the following:

Node				
Address	:	97	266	284	299
Contents	:	(-:"a")	(97:"b")	(266:"c")	(284:"d")
Represents:		"a"	"ab"	"abc"	"abcd"

2. The node contains a parent pointer of 284 and the ASCII code of "d". This means that string "abcd" is already in the tree. The encoder inputs the next symbol, say "e", and searches the dictionary tree for string "abcde".

3. The node contains something else. This means that another hashing of a pointer and an ASCII code has resulted in 299, and node 299 already contains information from another string. This is called a *collision* and it can be dealt with in several ways. The simplest way to deal with a collision is to increment pointer 299 and examine nodes 300, 301,... until an unused node is found, or until a node with (284:"d") is found.

In practice, we build nodes that are structures with three fields, a pointer to the parent node, the pointer (or index) created by the hashing process, and the code (normally ASCII) of the symbol contained in the node. The second field is necessary because of collisions. A node can thus be illustrated by

parent
index
symbol

We illustrate this data structure using string "ababab..." of exercise 3.10. The dictionary is an array `dict` where each entry is a structure with the 3 fields `parent`, `index` and `symbol`. We refer to a field by, e.g., `dict[pointer].parent`, where `pointer` is an index to the array. The dictionary is initialized to the two entries "a" and "b". (To keep the example simple we use no ASCII codes. We assume that "a" has code 1 and "b", code 2.) The first few steps of the encoder are

Step 0. Mark all dictionary locations from 3 on as unused.

/	/	/	/	/
1	2	-	-	-
a	b			

...

Step 1. The first symbol "a" is input into variable I. What is actually input is the code of "a", which in our example is 1, so I=1. Since this is the first symbol, the encoder assumes that it is in the dictionary and so does not perform any search.

Step 2. The second symbol "b" is input into J, so J=2. The encoder has to search for string "ab" in the dictionary. It executes `pointer:=hash(I,J)`. Let's assume that the result is 5. Field `dict[pointer].index` contains "unused" since location 5 is still empty, so string "ab" is not in the dictionary. It is added by executing

```
dict[pointer].parent:=I;
dict[pointer].index:=pointer;
dict[pointer].symbol:=J;
```

with `pointer`=5. J is moved into I, so I=2.

/	/	/	/	1
1	2	-	-	5
a	b			b

...

Step 3. The third symbol "a" is input into J, so J=1. The encoder has to search for string "ba" in the dictionary. It executes `pointer:=hash(I,J);`. Let's assume that the result is 8. Field `dict[pointer].index` contains "unused", so string "ba" is not in the dictionary. It is added as before by executing

```
dict[pointer].parent:=I;
dict[pointer].index:=pointer;
dict[pointer].symbol:=J;
```

with `pointer`=8. J is moved into I, so I=1.

/	/	/	/	1	/	/	2	/
1	2	-	-	5	-	-	8	-
a	b			b			a	

...

Step 4. The fourth symbol "b" is input into J, so J=2. The encoder has to search for string "ab" in the dictionary. It executes `pointer:=hash(I,J)`. We know from step 2 that the result is 5. Field `dict[pointer].index` contains "5", so string "ab" is in the dictionary. The value of `pointer` is moved into I, so I=5.

Step 5. The fifth symbol "a" is input into J, so J=1. The encoder has to search for string "aba" in the dictionary. It executes as usual `pointer:=hash(I,J)`. Let's assume that the result is 8 (a collision). Field `dict[pointer].index` contains 8, which looks good, but field `dict[pointer].parent` contains 1 instead of the expected 5 so the hash function knows that this is a collision and string "aba" is not in dictionary entry 8. It increments `pointer` as many times as necessary until it finds a dictionary entry with `index`=8 and `parent`=5 or until it finds an unused entry. In the former case, string "aba" is in the dictionary, and `pointer` is moved to I. In the latter case "aba" is not in the dictionary, and the encoder saves it in the entry pointed at by `pointer`, and moves J to I.

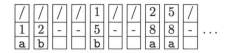

Readers who get up to this point will be happy to learn that the LZW decoder's use of the dictionary tree-array is simple and no hashing is needed. The decoder starts, like the encoder, by initializing the first 256 array locations. It then reads pointers from its input stream, and uses each to locate a symbol in the dictionary.

In the first decoding step, the decoder inputs the first pointer and uses it to retrieve a dictionary item I. This is a symbol that is now written by the decoder on its output stream. String Ix needs to be saved in the dictionary, but symbol x is still unknown; it will be the first symbol in the next string retrieved from the dictionary.

In each decoding step after the first, the decoder inputs the next pointer and uses it to retrieve the next string J from the dictionary and write it on the output stream. If the pointer is, say 8, the decoder examines field `dict[8].index`. If this field equals 8, then this is the right node. Otherwise, the decoder examines consecutive array locations until it finds the right one.

Once the right tree node is found, the **parent** field is used to go back up the tree and retrieve the individual symbols of the string *in reverse order*. The symbols are then placed in J in the right order (see below), the decoder isolates the first symbol x of J, and saves string Ix in the next available array location. (String I was found in the previous step, so only one node, with symbol x, needs be added.) The decoder then moves J to I, and is ready for the next step.

Retrieving a complete string from the LZW tree thus involves following the pointers in the **parent** fields. This is equivalent to moving up the tree, which is why the hash function is no longer needed.

The last point to discuss is string reversal. Two commonly used approaches are outlined below:

1. Use a stack. A stack is a common data structure in modern computers. It is an array in memory that is accessed at one end only. At any time, the item that was last pushed into the stack will be the first one to be popped out (last-in-first-out, or LIFO). Symbols retrieved from the dictionary are pushed into the stack. When the last one has been retrieved and pushed, the stack is popped, symbol by symbol, into variable J. When the stack is empty, the entire string has been reversed. This is a common way to reverse a string.

2. Retrieve symbols from the dictionary and concatenate them into J *from right to left*. When done, the string will be stored in J in the right order. Variable J must be long enough to accomodate the longest possible string, but then it has to be long enough even when a stack is used.

▶ **Exercise 3.11:** What is the longest string that can be retrieved from the LZW dictionary during decoding?

3.9.3 LZW in Practice

The publication of the LZW algorithm, in 1984, has strongly affected the data compression community and has influenced many people to come up with implementations and variants of this method. Some of the most important LZW "spin-offs" are described below.

Bibliography

Phillips, Dwayne (1992) "LZW Data Compression," *The Computer Application Journal* Circuit Cellar Inc., **27**:36–48, June/July.

Welch, T. A. (1984) "A Technique for High-Performance Data Compression," *IEEE Computer* **17**(6):8–19, June.

3.9.4 Differencing

The idea of differencing, or relative encoding, has already been mentioned in Section 1.3.1. It turns out to be useful in LZW image compression, since most adjacent pixels don't differ by much. It is possible to implement an LZW encoder that computes the value of a pixel relative to its predecessor and then encodes this difference. The decoder should, of course, be compatible and should compute the absolute value of a pixel after decoding its relative value.

3.9.5 LZW Variants

A word-based LZW variant is described in Section 5.5.2.

LZW is an adaptive data compression method, but it is slow to adapt to its input since strings in the dictionary only get one character longer at a time. Exercise 3.8 shows that a string of a million a's (which, of course, is highly redundant) produces dictionary phrases the longest of which contains only 1,414 a's.

The LZMW method, Section 3.10, is a variant of LZW that overcomes this problem. Its main principle is: instead of adding I plus one character of the next phrase to the dictionary, add I plus the entire next phrase to the dictionary.

The LZAP method, Section 3.11, is yet another variant based on the idea: instead of just concatenating the last two phrases and placing the result in the dictionary, place all prefixes of the concatenation in the dictionary. More specifically, if S and T are the last two matches, add St to the dictionary for every nonempty prefix t of T, including T itself.

Table 3.18 summarizes the principles of LZW, LZMW, and LZAP and shows how they naturally suggest another variant, LZY.

Increment string by	Add a string to the dictionary	
	per phrase	per input char.
One character:	LZW	LZY
Several chars:	LZMW	LZAP

Table 3.18: Four Variants of LZW.

LZW adds one dictionary string per phrase and increments strings by one symbol at a time. LZMW adds one dictionary string per phrase and increments strings by several symbols at a time. LZAP adds one dictionary string per input symbol and increments strings by several symbols at a time. LZY, Section 3.12, fits the fourth cell of 3.18. It is a method that adds one dictionary string per input symbol and increment strings by one symbol at a time.

3.10 LZMW

This LZW variant, developed by Miller and Wegman [Miller 85], is based on two principles:

1. When the dictionary gets full, the least recently used dictionary phrase is deleted. There are several ways to select this phrase, and the developers suggest that any reasonable way of doing so will work. One possibility is to identify all the dictionary phrases S for which there are no phrases Sa (nothing has been appended to S, meaning that S hasn't been used since it was placed in the dictionary) and delete the oldest of them. An auxiliary data structure has to be built and maintained in this case, pointing to dictionary phrases according to their age (the first pointer always points to the oldest phrase). The first 256 dictionary phrases should never be deleted.

2. Each phrase added to the dictionary is a concatenation of two strings, the previous match (S' in the algorithm below) and the current one (S). This is in contrast to LZW where each phrase added is the concatenation of the current match and the first symbol of the next match. The pseudo-code algorithm below shows how this is done.

```
Initialize Dict to all the symbols of alphabet A;
i:=1;
S':=null;
while i <= input size
 k:=longest match of Input[i] to Dict;
 Output(k);
 S:=Phrase k of Dict;
 i:=i+length(S);
 If phrase S'S is not in Dict, append it to Dict;
 S':=S;
endwhile;
```

By adding the concatenation S'S to the LZMW dictionary, dictionary phrases can grow by more than one symbol at a time. This means that LZMW dictionary phrases are more "natural" units of the input (e.g., if the input is text in a natural language, dictionary phrases will tend to be complete words or even several words in that language). This in turn implies that the LZMW dictionary generally adapts to the input faster than the LZW dictionary.

Table 3.19 illustrates the LZMW method by applying it to the string

"sir␣sid␣eastman␣easily␣teases␣sea␣sick␣seals".

LZMW adapts to its input faster than LZW but has the following disadvantages:

The dictionary data structure cannot be the simple LZW trie since not every prefix of a dictionary phrase is included in the dictionary. This means that the one-symbol-at-a-time search method used in LZW will not work. Instead, when a phrase S is added to the LZMW dictionary, every prefix of S must be added to the

Step	Input	Output	S	Add to dict.	S'
	sir⊔sid⊔eastman⊔easily⊔teases⊔sea⊔sick⊔seals				
1	s	115	s	—	s
2	i	105	i	256-si	i
3	r	114	r	257-ir	r
4	–	32	⊔	258-r⊔	⊔
5	si	256	si	259-⊔si	si
6	d	100	d	260-sid	d
7	–	32	⊔	261-d⊔	⊔
8	e	101	e	262-⊔e	e
9	a	97	a	263-ea	a
10	s	115	s	264-as	s
11	t	117	t	265-st	t
12	m	109	m	266-tm	m
13	a	97	a	267-ma	a
14	n	110	n	268-an	n
15	–e	262	⊔e	269-n⊔e	⊔e
16	as	264	as	270-⊔eas	as
17	i	105	i	271-asi	i
18	l	108	l	272-il	l
19	y	121	y	273-ly	y
20	–	32	⊔	274-y⊔	⊔
21	t	117	t	275-⊔t	t
22	ea	263	ea	276-tea	ea
23	s	115	s	277-eas	s
24	e	101	e	278-se	e
25	s	115	s	279-es	s
26	–	32	⊔	280-s⊔	⊔
27	se	278	se	281-⊔se	se
28	a	97	a	282-sea	a
29	–si	259	⊔si	283-a⊔si	⊔si
30	c	99	c	284-⊔sic	c
31	k	107	k	285-ck	k
32	–se	281	⊔se	286-k⊔se	⊔se
33	a	97	a	287-⊔sea	a
34	l	108	l	288-al	l
35	s	115	s	289-ls	s

Table 3.19: LZMW Example.

data structure, and every node in the data structure must have a tag indicating whether the node is in the dictionary or not.

Finding the longest string may require backtracking. If the dictionary contains "aaaa" and "aaaaaaaa", we have to reach the eighth symbol of phrase "aaaaaaab" to realize that we have to choose the shorter phrase. This implies that dictionary searches in LZMW are slower than in LZW. This problem does not apply to the LZMW decoder.

A phrase may be added to the dictionary twice. This again complicates the choice of data structure for the dictionary.

▶ **Exercise 3.12:** Use the LZMW method to compress the string "swiss⌴miss".

▶ **Exercise 3.13:** Compress the string "yabbadabbadabbadoo" by using LZMW.

Bibliography

Miller, V. S., and M. N. Wegman (1985) "Variations On a Theme by Ziv and Lempel," in A. Apostolico and Z. Galil, eds., NATO ASI series Vol. F12, *Combinatorial Algorithms on Words*, Springer, Berlin, pp. 131–140.

3.11 LZAP

This is an extension of LZMW. The "AP" stands for "All Prefixes" [Storer 88]. LZAP adapts to its input fast, like LZMW, but eliminates the need for backtracking, a feature that makes it faster than LZMW. The principle is: instead of adding the concatenation S'S of the last two phrases to the dictionary, add all the strings S't where t is a prefix of S (including S itself). Thus if S'="a" and S="bcd", add phrases "ab","abc", and "abcd" to the LZAP dictionary. Table 3.20 shows the matches and the phrases added to the dictionary for "yabbadabbadabbadoo".

Step	Input	Match	Add to dictionary
	yabbadabbadabbadoo		
1	y	y	—
2	a	a	256-ya
3	b	b	257-ab
4	b	b	258-bb
5	a	a	259-ba
6	d	d	260-ad
7	ab	ab	261-da, 262-dab
8	ba	ba	263-abb, 264-abba
9	dab	dab	265-bad, 266-bada, 267-badab
10	ba	ba	268-dabb, 269-dabba
11	d	d	270-bad
12	o	o	271-do
13	o	o	272-oo

Table 3.20: LZAP Example.

In step 7 the encoder concatenates "d" to the two prefixes of "ab" and adds the two phrases "da" and "dab" to the dictionary. In step 9 it concatenates "ba" to the three prefixes of "dab" and adds the resulting three phrases "bad", "bada", and "badab" to the dictionary.

LZAP adds more phrases to its dictionary than does LZMW, so it takes more bits to represent the position of a phrase. At the same time LZAP provides a bigger selection of dictionary phrases as matches for the input string, so it ends up compressing slightly better than LZMW while being faster (because of the simpler dictionary data structure, which eliminates the need for backtracking). This kind of tradeoff is common in computer algorithms.

3.12 LZY

This method is due to Dan Bernstein. The Y stands for Yabba, which came from the input string originally used to test the algorithm. The LZY dictionary is initialized to all the single symbols of the alphabet. For every symbol C in the input stream, the decoder looks for the longest string P that precedes C and is already included in the dictionary. If the string PC is not in the dictionary, it is added to it as a new phrase.

As an example, the input "yabbadabbadabbadoo" causes the phrases "ya", "ab", "bb", "ba", "ad", "da", "abb", "bba", "ada", "dab", "abba", "bbad", "bado", "ado", and "oo" to be added to the dictionary.

While encoding the input, the encoder keeps track of the list of "matches-so-far" L. Initially L is empty. If C is the current input symbol, the encoder (before adding anything to the dictionary) checks, for every string M in L, whether string MC is in the dictionary. If it is, then MC becomes a new match-so-far and is added to L. Otherwise, the encoder outputs the number of L (its position in the dictionary) and adds C, as a new match-so-far, to L.

Here is a pseudo-code algorithm for constructing the LZY dictionary. The author's personal experience suggests that implementing such an algorithm in a "real" programming language results in a deeper understanding of its operation.

```
Start with a dictionary containing all the symbols of the
 alphabet, each mapped to a unique integer.
M:=empty string.
Repeat
 Append the next symbol C of the input stream to M.
 If M is not in the dictionary, add it to the dictionary,
  delete the first character of M, and repeat this step.
Until end-of-input.
```

The output of LZY is not synchronized with the dictionary additions. Also the encoder must be careful not to have the longest output match overlap itself. Because of this, the dictionary should consist of two parts, S and T, where only the former is used for the output. The algorithm is

```
Start with S mapping each single character to a unique integer;
set T empty; M empty; and O empty.
Repeat
```

```
Input the next symbol C. If OC is in S, set O:=OC;
otherwise output S(O), set O:=C, add T to S,
  and remove everything from T.
While MC is not in S or T, add MC to T (mapping to the next
    available integer), and chop off the first character of M.
After M is short enough so that MC is in the dict., set M:=MC.
Until end-of-input.
Output S(O) and quit.
```

The decoder reads the compressed stream. It uses each code to find a phrase in the dictionary, it outputs the phrase as a string, then uses each symbol of the string to add a new phrase to the dictionary in the same way the encoder does. Here are the decoding steps:

```
Start with a dictionary containing all the symbols of the
  alphabet, each mapped to a unique integer.
M:=empty string.
Repeat
  Read D(O) from the input and take the inverse under D to find O.
  As long as O is not the empty string, find the first character C
    of O, and update (D,M) as above.
  Also output C and chop it off from the front of O.
Until end-of-input.
```

Notice that encoding requires two fast operations on strings in the dictionary: (1) testing whether string SC is in the dictionary if S's position is known and (2) finding S's position given CS's position. Decoding requires the same operations plus fast searching to find the first character of a string when its position in the dictionary is given.

Table 3.21 illustrates LZY for the input string "abcabcabcabcabcabcabcx". It shows the phrases added to the dictionary at each step, as well as the list of current matches.

The encoder starts with no matches. When it inputs a symbol, it appends it to each match-so-far; any results that are already in the dictionary become the new matches-so-far (the symbol itself becomes another match). Any results that are not in the dictionary are deleted from the list and added to the dictionary.

Before reading the fifth "c", for example, the matches-so-far are "bcab", "cab", "ab", and "b". The encoder appends "c" to each match. "bcabc" doesn't match, so the encoder adds it to the dictionary. The rest are still in the dictionary, so the new list of matches-so-far is "cabc", "abc", "bc", and "c".

When the "x" is input, the current list of matches-so-far is "abcabc", "bcabc", "cabc", "abc", "bc", and "c". None of "abcabcx", "bcabcx", "cabcx", "abcx", "bcx", or "cx" are in the dictionary, so they are all added to it, and the list of matches-so-far is reduced to just a single "x".

Step	Input	Add to dict.	Current matches
	abcabcabcabcabcabcabcx		
1	a	—	a
2	b	256-ab	b
3	c	257-bc	c
4	a	258-ca	a
5	b	—	ab, b
6	c	259-abc	bc, c
7	a	260-bca	ca, a
8	b	261-cab	ab, b
9	c	—	abc, bc, c
10	a	262-abca	bca, ca, a
11	b	263-bcab	cab, ab, b
12	c	264-cabc	abc, bc, c
13	a	—	abca, bca, ca, a
14	b	265-abcab	bcab, cab, ab, b
15	c	266-bcabc	cabc, abc, bc, c
16	a	267-cabca	abca, bca, ca, a
17	b	—	abcab, bcab, cab, ab, b
18	c	268-abcabc	bcabc, cabc, abc, bc, c
19	a	269-bcabca	cabca, abca, bca, ca, a
20	b	270-cabcab	abcab, bcab, cab, ab, b
21	c	—	abcabc, bcabc, cabc, abc, bc, c
22	x	271-abcabcx	x
23		272-bcabcx	
24		273-cabcx	
25		274-abcx	
26		275-bcx	
27		276-cx	

Table 3.21: LZY Example.

3.13 LZP

This LZ77 variant is due to C. Bloom [Bloom 96] (the P stands for "prediction"). It is based on the principle of context prediction, which says "if a certain string 'abcde' has appeared in the input stream in the past and was followed by 'fg...', then when 'abcde' appears again in the input stream, there is a good chance that it will be followed by the same 'fg...'." Section 3.23.1 should be consulted for the relation between dictionary-based and prediction algorithms.

Figure 3.22 shows an LZ77 sliding buffer with "fgh..." as the current symbols (this string is denoted S) in the look-ahead buffer, immediately preceded by "abcde" in the search buffer. The string "abcde" is called the *context* of "fgh..." and is denoted C. In general, the context of a string S is the N-symbol string C immediately to the left of S. A context can be of any length N, and variants of LZP, discussed in Sections 3.13.3 and 3.13.4, use different values of N. The algorithm passes the

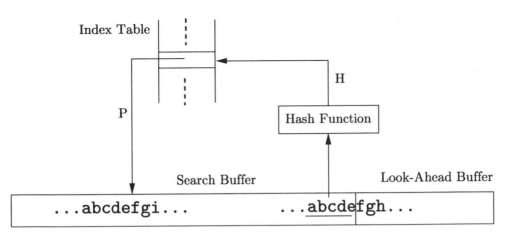

Figure 3.22: The Principle of LZP: Part I.

context through a hash function and uses the result H as an index to a table of pointers called the *index table*. The index table contains pointers to various symbols in the search buffer. H is used to select a pointer P. In a typical case, P points to a previously seen string whose context is also "abcde" (see below for atypical cases). The algorithm then performs the following steps:

Step 1. It saves P and replaces it in the index table with a fresh pointer Q pointing to "fgh..." in the look-ahead buffer (Figure 3.22II). An integer variable L is set to zero. It is used later to indicate the match length.

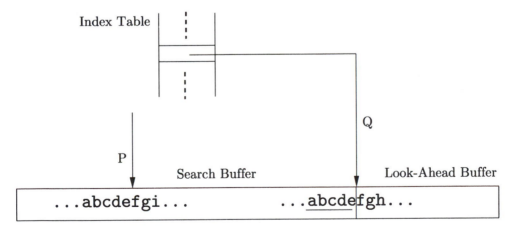

Figure 3.22: (Continued) The Principle of LZP: Part II.

Step 2. If P is not a null pointer, the algorithm follows it and compares the string pointed at by P (string "fgi..." in the search buffer) to the string "fgh..." in the look-ahead buffer. Only two symbols match in our example, so the match length, L, is set to 2.

Step 3. If L = 0 (no symbols have been matched), the buffer is slid to the right (or, equivalently, the input is shifted to the left) **one position** and the first symbol of string S (the "f") is written on the compressed stream as a raw ASCII code (a literal).

Step 4. If L > 0 (L symbols have been matched), the buffer is slid to the right **L positions** and the value of L is written on the compressed stream (after being suitably encoded).

In our example the single, encoded value L = 2 is written on the compressed stream instead of the two symbols "fg", and it is this step that produces compression. Clearly, the larger the value of L, the better the compression. Large values of L result when an N-symbol context C in the input stream is followed by the same long string S as a previous occurrence of C. This may happen when the input stream features high redundancy. In a random input stream each occurrence of the same context C is likely to be followed by another S, leading to L = 0 and thus to no compression. An "average" input stream results in more literals than L values being written on the output stream (see also exercise 3.15).

The decoder inputs the compressed stream item by item and creates the decompressed output in a buffer B. The steps are:

Step 1. Input the next item I from the compressed stream.

Step 2. If I is a raw ASCII code (a literal), it is appended to buffer B, and the data in B is shifted to the left one position.

Step 3. If I is an encoded match length, it is decoded, to obtain L. The present context C (the rightmost N symbols in B) is hashed to an index H, which is used to select a pointer P from the index table. The decoder copies the string of L symbols starting at B[P] and appends it to the right end of B. It also shifts the data in B to the left L positions and replaces P in the index table with a fresh pointer, to keep in lockstep with the encoder.

Two points remain to be discussed before we are ready to look at a detailed example.

1. When the encoder starts, it places the first N symbols of the input stream in the search buffer, to become the first context. It then writes these symbols, as literals, on the compressed stream. This is the only special step needed to start the compression. The decoder starts by reading the first N items off the compressed stream (they should be literals), and placing them at the rightmost end of buffer B, to serve as the first context.

2. It has been mentioned before that in the typical case, P points to a previously seen string whose context is identical to the present context C. In an atypical case, P may be pointing to a string whose context is different. The algorithm, however, does not check the context and always behaves in the same way. It simply tries to match as many symbols as possible. At worst, zero symbols will match, leading to one literal written on the compressed stream.

3.13.1 Example

The input stream "xyabcabcabxy" is used to illustrate the operation of the LZP encoder. To simplify the example, we use N=2.

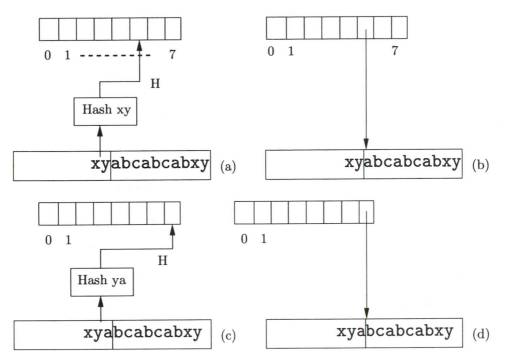

Figure 3.23: LZP Compression of "xyabcabcabxy": Part I.

1. To start the operation, the encoder shifts the first 2 symbols "xy" to the search buffer and outputs them as literals. It also initializes all locations of the index table to the null pointer.

2. The current symbol is "a" (the first "a") and the context is "xy". It is hashed to, say, 5, but location 5 of the index table contains a null pointer, so P is null (Figure 3.23a). Location 5 is set to point to the first "a" (Figure 3.23b), which is then output as a literal. The data in the encoder's buffer is shifted to the left.

3. The current symbol is the first "b" and the context is "ya". It is hashed to, say, 7, but location 7 of the index table contains a null pointer, so P is null (Figure 3.23c). Location 7 is set to point to the first "b" (Figure 3.23d), which is then output as a literal. The data in the encoder's buffer is shifted to the left.

4. The current symbol is the first "c" and the context is "ab". It is hashed to, say, 2, but location 2 of the index table contains a null pointer, so P is null (Figure 3.23e). Location 2 is set to point to the first "c" (Figure 3.23f), which is then output as a literal. The data in the encoder's buffer is shifted to the left.

5. The same thing happens two more times, writing the literals "a" and "b" on the compressed stream. The current symbol is now (the second) "c" and the context is "ab". This context is hashed, as in step 4, to 2, so P points to "cabc...". Location 2 is set to point to the current symbol (Figure 3.23g), and the encoder tries to match strings "cabcabxy" and "cabxy". The resulting match length is L=3. The number 3 is written, encoded, on the compressed stream, and the data

is shifted three positions to the left.

6. The current symbol is the second "x" and the context is "ab". It is hashed to 2, but location 2 of the index table points to the second "c" (Figure 3.23h). Location 2 is set to point to the current symbol, and the encoder tries to match strings "cabxy" and "xy". The resulting match length is, of course, L=0, so the encoder writes "x" on the compressed stream as a literal and shifts the data one position.

7. The current symbol is the second "y" and the context is "bx". It is hashed to, say, 7. This is a hash collision since context "ya" was hashed to 7 in step 3, but the algorithm does not check for collisions. It continues as usual. Location 7 of the index table points to the first "b" (or rather to the string "bcabcabxy"). It is set to point to the current symbol, and the encoder tries to match strings "bcabcabxy" and "y", resulting in L=0. The encoder writes "y" on the compressed stream as a literal and shifts the data one position.

8. The current symbol is the end-of-data, so the algorithm stops.

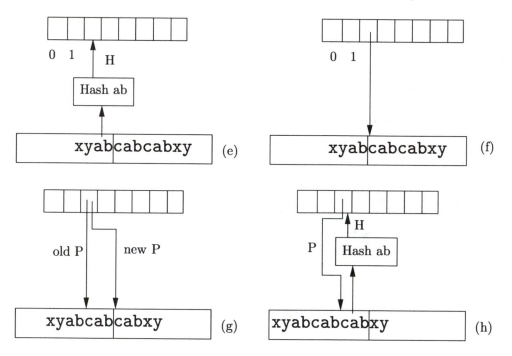

Figure 3.23 (Continued). LZP Compression of "xyabcabcabxy": Part II.

▶ **Exercise 3.14:** Write the LZP encoding steps for the input string "xyaaaa...".

3.13.2 Practical Considerations

Shifting the data in the buffer would require updating all the pointers in the index table. An efficient implementation should therefore adopt a better solution. Two approaches are described below, but other ones may also work.

1. Reserve a buffer as large as possible and compress the input stream in blocks. Each block is input into the buffer and is never shifted. Instead, a pointer is moved from left to right, to point at any time to the current symbol in the buffer. When the entire buffer has been encoded, the buffer is filled up again with fresh input. This approach simplifies the program but has the disadvantage that the data at the end of a block cannot be used to predict anything for the next block. Each block is encoded independently of the other ones, leading to poorer compression.

2. Reserve a large buffer and use it as a circular queue (Section 3.2.1). The data itself does not have to be shifted but after encoding the current symbol the data is *effectively* shifted by updating the start and end pointers, and a new symbol is input and stored in the buffer. The algorithm is somewhat more complicated but this approach has the advantage that the entire input is encoded as one stream. Every symbol benefits from the D symbols preceding it (where D is the total length of the buffer).

Imagine a pointer P in the index table pointing to some symbol X in the buffer. When the movement of the two pointers in the circular queue leaves X outside the queue, some new symbol Y will be input into the position occupied by X, and P will now be pointing to Y. When P is next selected by the hashing function and is used to match strings, the match will likely result in L=0. However, the algorithm always replaces the pointer that it uses, so such a case should not degrade the algorithm's performance significantly.

3.13.3 LZP1 and LZP2

There are currently four versions of LZP, denoted LZP1 through LZP4. This section discusses the details of the first two. The context used by LZP1 is order-3, i.e., it is the 3 bytes preceding the current one. The hash function produces a 12-bit index H and is best described by the following C code:

$$H=((C>>11)^{\wedge}C)\&0xFFF.$$

Since H is 12 bits, the index table should be $2^{12} = 4,096$ entries long. Each entry is 2 bytes (16 bits) but only 14 of the 16 bits are used. A pointer P selected in the index table thus points to a buffer of size $2^{14} = 16K$.

The LZP1 encoder creates a compressed stream with literals and L values mixed together. Each item must therefore be preceded by a flag indicating its nature. Since only two flags are needed, the simplest choice would be 1-bit flags. However, we have already mentioned that an "average" input stream results in more literals than L values, so it makes sense to assign a short flag (less than one bit) to indicate a literal, and a long flag (a wee bit longer than one bit) to indicate a length. The scheme used by LZP1 uses 1 to indicate two literals, 01 to indicate a literal followed by a match length, and 00 to indicate a match length.

▶ **Exercise 3.15:** Let T indicate the probability of a literal in the compressed stream. For what value of T does the above scheme produce flags that are 1-bit long on average?

A literal is written on the compressed stream as an 8-bit ASCII code. Match lengths are encoded according to Table 3.24. Initially the codes are 2-bits. When these are all used up, 3 bits are added, for a total of 5 bits, where the first 2 bits are

1s. When these are also all used, 5 bits are added, to produce 10-bit codes where the first 5 bits are 1s. From then on another group of 8 bits is added to the code whenever all the old codes have been used up. Notice how the pattern of all 1s is never used as a code and is reserved to indicate longer and longer codes. Notice also that a unary code or a general unary code (Section 2.3.1) might have been a better choice.

Length	Code	Length	Code
1	00	11	11|111|00000
2	01	12	11|111|00001
3	10	⋮	
4	11|000	41	11|111|11110
5	11|001	42	11|111|11111|00000000
6	11|010	⋮	
⋮		296	11|111|11111|11111110
10	11|110	297	11|111|11111|11111111|00000000

Table 3.24: Codes Used by LZP1 and LZP2 for Match Lengths.

The compressed stream consists of a mixture of literals (bytes with ASCII codes) and control bytes containing flags and encoded lengths. This is illustrated by the output of the example of Section 3.13.1. The input of this example is the string "xyabcabcabxy", and the output items are "x", "y", "a", "b", "c", "a", "b", 3, "x", and "y". The actual output stream consists of the single control byte "111 01|10 1" followed by 9 bytes with the ASCII codes of "x", "y", "a", "b", "c", "a", "b", "x", and "y".

▶ **Exercise 3.16:** Explain the contents of the control byte "111 01|10 1".

Another example of a compressed stream is the three literals "x", "y", and "a" followed by the four match lengths 12, 12, 12, and 10. We first prepare the flags

$$1 \ (\text{``x''}, \text{``y''}) \ 01 \ (\text{``a''}, 12) \ 00 \ (12) \ 00 \ (12) \ 00 \ (12) \ 00 \ (10)$$

then substitute the codes of 12 and 10,

$$1xy01a11|111|0000100|11|111|0000100|11|111|0000100|11|111|0000100|11|110,$$

and finally group together the bits that make up the control bytes. The result is 10111111 "x", "y", "a", 00001001 11110000 10011111 00001001 11110000 10011110. Notice that the first control byte is followed by the three literals.

The last point to be mentioned is the case: ...0 1yyyyyyy zzzzzzzz. The first control byte ends with the 0, and the second byte starts with the 1, of a pair 01. This indicates a literal followed by a match length. The match length is the yyy bits (at least some of them) in the second control byte. If the code of the match length is long, then the zzz bits or some of them may be part of the code. The literal is either the zzz byte or the byte following it.

LZP2 is identical to LZP1 except that literals are coded using non-adaptive Huffman codes. Ideally, two passes should be used: the first one counting the frequency of occurrence of the symbols in the input stream and the second doing the actual compression. In between the passes, the Huffman code table can be constructed.

3.13.4 LZP3 and LZP4

LZP3 is similar to both LZP1 and LZP2. It uses order-4 contexts and more sophisticated Huffman codes to encode both the match lengths and the literals. The LZP3 hash function is

$$H=((C>>15)\,\hat{}\,C)\&0xFFFF),$$

so H is a 16-bit index, to be used with an index table of size $2^{16} = 64K$. The index table contains, in addition to the pointers P, also the contexts C. Thus if a context C is hashed to an index H, the encoder expects to find the same context C in location H of the index table. This is called *context confirmation*. If the encoder finds something else, or if it finds a null pointer, it sets P to null and hashes an order-3 context. If the order-3 context confirmation also fails, the algorithm hashes the order-2 context and, if that also fails, the algorithm sets P to null and writes a literal on the compressed stream. This method thus attempts to find the highest order context seen so far.

LZP4 uses order-5 contexts and a multi-step lookup process. In step 1, the rightmost 4 bytes I of the context are hashed to create a 16-bit index H according to the following:

$$H=((I>>15)\,\hat{}\,I)\&0xFFFF).$$

Then H is used as an index to the index table that has 64K entries, each corresponding to one value of H. Each entry points to the start of a list linking nodes that have the same hash value. Suppose that the contexts "abcde", "xbcde", and "mnopq" hash to the same index H=13 (i.e., the hash function computes the same index 13 when applied to "bcde" and "nopq") and we are looking for context "xbcde". Location 13 of the index table would point to a list with nodes for these contexts (and perhaps others that have also been hashed to 13). The list is traversed until a node is found with "bcde". This node points to a second list linking "a", "x" and perhaps other symbols that precede "bcde". The second list is traversed until a node with "x" is found. That node contains a pointer to the most recent occurrence of context "xbcde" in the search buffer. If a node with "x" is not found, a literal is written to the compressed stream.

This complex lookup procedure is used by LZP4 because a 5-byte context does not fit comfortably in a single word in most present computers.

Bibliography

Bloom, C. R. (1996), "LZP: A New Data Compression Algorithm," in *Proceedings of Data Compression Conference*, J. Storer, editor, Los Alamitos, CA, IEEE Computer Society Press, p. 425.

3.14 Repetition Finder

All the dictionary-based methods described so far have one thing in common: they use a large memory buffer as a dictionary that holds fragments of text found so far. The dictionary is used to locate strings of symbols that repeat. The method described here is different. Instead of a dictionary it uses a fixed-size array of integers to find previous occurrences of strings of text. The array size equals the square of the alphabet size, so it is not very large. The method is due to Hidetoshi Yokko [Yokko 91], who elected not to call it LZHY but left it nameless. The reason a name of the form LZxx was not used is that the method does not employ a traditional Ziv-Lempel dictionary. The reason it was left nameless is that it does not compress very well and should thus be considered the first step in a new field of research rather than a mature, practical method.

The method alternates between two modes, normal and repeat. It starts in the normal mode, where it inputs symbols and encodes them using adaptive Huffman. When it identifies a repeated string it switches to the "repeat" mode where it outputs an escape symbol, followed by the length of the repeated string.

Assume that the input stream consists of symbols $x_1 x_2 \ldots$ from an alphabet A. Both encoder and decoder maintain an array REP of dimensions $|A| \times |A|$ that is initialized to all zeros. For each input symbol x_i, the encoder (and decoder) compute a value y_i according to $y_i = i - \text{REP}[x_{i-1}, x_i]$, and then update $\text{REP}[x_{i-1}, x_i] := i$. The following 13-symbol string:

$$x_i: \text{ X A B C D E Y A B C D E Z}$$
$$i\ :\ 1 \quad 3 \quad 5 \quad 7 \quad 9 \quad 11 \quad 13$$

results in the following y values

$$
\begin{array}{lccccccccccccc}
i = & 1 & 2 & 3 & 4 & 5 & 6 & 7 & 8 & 9 & 10 & 11 & 12 & 13 \\
y_i = & 1 & 2 & 3 & 4 & 5 & 6 & 7 & 8 & 6 & 6 & 6 & 6 & 13 \\
x_{i-1}x_i: & \text{XA} & \text{AB} & \text{BC} & \text{CD} & \text{DE} & \text{EY} & \text{YA} & \text{AB} & \text{BC} & \text{CD} & \text{DE} & \text{EZ}
\end{array}
$$

Table 3.25a shows the state of array REP after the eighth symbol has been input and encoded. Table 3.25b shows the state of REP after all 13 symbols have been input and encoded.

	A	B	C	D	E	...	X	Y	Z
A	3								
B		4							
C			5						
D				6					
E							7		
⋮									
X	2								
Y	8								
Z									

	A	B	C	D	E	...	X	Y	Z
A	9								
B		10							
C			11						
D				12					
E									13
⋮									
X	2								
Y	8								
Z									

Table 3.25: (a) REP at $i = 8$. (b) REP at $i = 13$.

Perhaps a better way to explain the way y is calculated is by means of

$$y_i = \begin{cases} 1, & \text{for } i = 1; \\ i, & \text{for } i > 1 \text{ and first occurrence of } x_{i-1}x_i; \\ \min(k), & \text{for } i > 1 \text{ and } x_{i-1}x_i \text{ identical to } x_{i-k-1}x_{i-k}. \end{cases}$$

This shows that y is either i or is the distance k between the current string $x_{i-1}x_i$ and its most recent copy $x_{i-k-1}x_{i-k}$. However, recognizing a repetition of a string is done by means of array REP and without using any dictionary (which is the main point of this method).

When a string of length l repeats itself in the input, l consecutive identical values of y are generated, and this is the signal for the encoder to switch to the "repeat" mode. As long as consecutive different values of y are generated, the encoder stays in the "normal" mode, where it encodes x_i in adaptive Huffman and outputs it. When the encoder senses $y_{i+1} = y_i$, it outputs x_i in the normal mode, and then enters the "repeat" mode. In the example above, this happens for $i = 9$, so the string "XABCDEYAB" is output in the normal mode.

Once in the "repeat" mode, the encoder inputs more symbols and calculates y values until it finds the first value that differs from y_i. In our example this happens at $i = 13$, when the Z is input. The encoder compresses the string "CDE" (corresponding to $i = 10, 11, 12$) in the "repeat" mode by outputting an (encoded) escape symbol, followed by the (encoded) length of the repeated string (3 in our example). The encoder then switches back to the normal mode, where it saves the y value for Z as y_i and inputs the next symbol.

The escape symbol must be an extra symbol, one that's not included in the alphabet A. Notice that only two y values, y_{i-1} and y_i, need be saved at any time. Notice also that the method is not very efficient since it senses the repeating string "too late" and encodes the first two repeating symbols in the normal mode. In our example only three of the five repeating symbols are encoded in the "repeat" mode.

The decoder inputs and decodes the first nine symbols, decoding them into the string "XABCDEYAB" while updating array REP and calculating y values. When the escape symbol is input, i has the value 9 and y_i has the value 6. The decoder inputs and decodes the length, 3, and now it has to figure out the repeated string of length 3 using just the data in array REP, not any of the previously decoded input. Since $i = 9$ and y_i is the distance between this string and its copy, the decoder knows that the copy started at position $i - y_i = 9 - 6 = 3$ of the input. It scans REP, looking for a 3. It finds it at position REP[A,B], so it starts looking for a 4 in row B of REP. It finds it in REP[B,C], so the first symbol of the required string is "C". Looking for a 5 in row C, the decoder finds it in REP[C,D], so the second symbol is "D". Looking now for a 6 in row D, the decoder finds it in REP[D,E].

This is how a repeated string can be decoded without maintaining a dictionary.

Both encoder and decoder store values of i in REP, so an entry of REP should be at least 2 bytes long. This way i can have values of up to $64K - 1 \approx 65,500$, so the input has to be encoded in blocks of size 64K. For an alphabet of 256 symbols, the size of REP should thus be $256 \times 256 \times 2 = 128$Kbytes, not very large. For larger alphabets REP may have to be uncomfortably large.

In the normal mode, symbols (including the escape) are encoded using adaptive Huffman (Section 2.9). In the repeat mode, lengths are encoded in a recursive prefix code denoted $Q_k(i)$, where k is a positive integer (see Section 2.3 for prefix codes). Assuming that i is an integer whose binary representation is 1α, the prefix code of i is defined by

$$Q_0(i) = 1^{|\alpha|}0\alpha; \qquad Q_k(i) = \begin{cases} 0, & i = 1; \\ 1Q_{k-1}(i-1), & i > 1. \end{cases}$$

Where $|\alpha|$ is the length of α and $1^{|\alpha|}$ is a string of $|\alpha|$ ones. Table 3.26 shows some of the proposed codes.

i	α	$Q_0(i)$	$Q_1(i)$	$Q_2(i)$
1	null	0	0	0
2	0	100	10	10
3	1	101	1100	110
4	00	11000	1101	11100
5	01	11001	111000	11101
6	10	11010	111001	1111000
7	11	11011	111010	1111001
8	000	1110000	111011	1111010
9	001	1110001	11110000	1111011

Table 3.26: Proposed Prefix Code.

A careful study of this table suggests that there is something wrong with the definition of this code. It is easy to see that $Q_k(i)$ depends on i but not on k since

$$Q_k(i) = 1Q_{k-1}(i-1) = 11Q_{k-2}(i-2) = \underbrace{11\ldots1}_{i-1}Q_{k-(i-1)}(1) = \underbrace{11\ldots1}_{i-1}0.$$

However, any of the prefix codes of Section 2.3 can be used instead of the one proposed here.

The developer of this method indicates that compression performance is not very sensitive to the precise value of k, and he proposes $k = 2$ for best overall performance.

As mentioned earlier, the method is not very efficient, which is why it should be considered the beginning of a new field of research where repeated strings are identified without the need for a large dictionary.

Bibliography

Yokko, Hidetoshi (1991) "An Improvement of Dynamic Huffman Coding with a Simple Repetition Finder," *IEEE Transactions on Communications* **39**(1):8–10, January.

3.15 UNIX Compression

In the large UNIX world, `compress` is used virtually exclusively to compress data. This utility (also called LZC) uses LZW with a growing dictionary. It starts with a small dictionary of just $2^9 = 512$ entries (with the first 256 of them already filled up). While this dictionary is being used, 9-bit pointers are written onto the output stream. When the original dictionary fills up, its size is doubled, to 1024 entries, and 10-bit pointers are used from this point. This process continues until the pointer size reaches a maximum set by the user (it can be set to between 9 and 16 bits, with 16 as the default value). When the largest allowed dictionary fills up, the program continues without changing the dictionary (which then becomes static), but with monitoring the compression ratio. If the ratio falls below a predefined threshold, the dictionary is deleted, and a new, 512-entry dictionary is started. This way, the dictionary never gets "too out of date."

Decoding is done by the `uncompress` command, which implements the LZC decoder. Its main task is to maintain the dictionary in the same way as the encoder.

Two improvements to LZC, proposed by [Horspool 91], are listed below:

1. Encode the dictionary pointers with the phased-in binary codes of Section 2.9.1. Thus if the dictionary size is $2^9 = 512$ entries, pointers can be encoded in either 8 or 9 bits.

2. Find out all the impossible strings at any point. Suppose that the current string in the look-ahead buffer is "abcd..." and the dictionary contains strings "abc" and "abca" but not "abcd". The encoder will output, in this case, the pointer to "abc" and will start encoding a new string starting with "d". The point is that after decoding "abc", the decoder knows that the next string cannot start with an "a" (if it did, an "abca" would have been encoded, instead of "abc"). In general, if S is the current string then the next string cannot start with any symbol x that satisfies "Sx is in the dictionary." This knowledge can be used by both the encoder and decoder to reduce redundancy even further. When a pointer to a string should be output, it should be coded, and the method of assigning the code should eliminate all the strings that are known to be impossible at that point. This may result in a somewhat shorter code but is probably too complex to justify its use in practice.

Bibliography

Horspool, N. R. (1991) "Improving LZW," in *Proceedings of the 1991 Data Compression Conference*, J. Storer Ed., Los Alamitos, CA, IEEE Computer Society Press, pp .332–341.

3.16 GIF Images

GIF—the graphics interchange format—was developed by Compuserve Information Services in 1987 as an efficient, compressed graphics file format, which allows for images to be sent between different computers. The original version of GIF is known as GIF 87a. The current standard is GIF 89a and, at the time of writing, can be freely obtained as file "`http://delcano.mit.edu/info/gif.txt`". GIF is not a data compression method; it is a graphics file format that uses a variant of LZW to compress the graphics data. This section reviews only the data compression aspects of GIF.

In compressing data, GIF is very similar to `compress` and uses a dynamic, growing dictionary. It starts with the number of bits per pixel b, as a parameter. For a monochromatic image, $b = 2$; for an image with 256 colors or shades of gray, $b = 8$. The dictionary starts with 2^{b+1} entries and is doubled in size each time it fills up, until it reaches a size of $2^{12} = 4,096$ entries, where it remains static. At such a point, the encoder monitors the compression ratio and may decide to discard the dictionary at any point and start with a new, empty one. When making this decision, the encoder emits the value 2^b as the *clear code*, which is the sign for the decoder to discard its dictionary.

The pointers, which get longer by 1 bit from one dictionary to the next, are accumulated and are output in blocks of 8-bit bytes. Each block is preceded by a header that contains the block size (255 bytes maximum) and is terminated by a byte of eight zeros. The last block contains, just before the terminator, the eof value, which is $2^b + 1$. An interesting feature is that the pointers are stored with their least significant bit on the left. Consider, for example, the following 3-bit pointers 3, 7, 4, 1, 6, 2, and 5. Their binary values are 011, 111, 100, 001, 110, 010, and 101, so they are packed in 3 bytes |10101001|11000011|11110...|.

Most graphics file formats use some kind of compression. For more information on those files, see [Murray 94].

Bibliography

Blackstock, Steve (1987) "LZW and GIF Explained," public domain, available from URL "http://www.ece.uiuc.edu/~ece291/class-resources/gpe/gif.txt.html".

Murray, James D. and William vanRyper, (1994) *Encyclopedia of Graphics File Formats*, O'Reilly and Assoc.

> Time is the image of eternity
> —Diogenes Laertius.

3.17 The V.42bis Protocol

This is a set of rules, or a standard, published by the ITU-T (page 62) for use in fast modems. It is based on the existing V.32bis protocol [Thomborson 92] and is supposed to be used for fast transmission rates, up to 57.6K baud. The ITU-T standards are recommendations, but they are normally followed by all major modem manufacturers. The standard contains specifications for data compression and error-correction, but only the former is discussed here.

V.42bis specifies two modes: a *transparent* mode, where no compression is used, and a *compressed* mode using an LZW variant. The former is used for data streams that don't compress well and may even cause expansion. A good example is an already-compressed file. Such a file looks like random data; it does not have any repetitive patterns, and trying to compress it with LZW will fill up the dictionary with short, two-symbol phrases.

The compressed mode uses a growing dictionary, whose initial size is negotiated between the modems when they initially connect. V.42bis recommends a dictionary size of 2,048 entries. The minimum size is 512 entries. The first three entries, corresponding to pointers 0, 1, and 2, do not contain any phrases and serve as special codes. Code 0 (enter transparent mode—ETM) is sent when the encoder notices low compression ratio, and it decides to start sending uncompressed data. (Unfortunately, V.42bis does not say how the encoder should test for low compression.) Code 1 is FLUSH, to flush data. Code 2 (STEPUP) is sent when the dictionary is almost full and the encoder decides to double its size. A dictionary is considered almost full when its size exceeds that of a special threshold (which is also negotiated by the modems).

When the dictionary is already at its maximum size and it becomes full, V.42bis recommends a *reuse* procedure. The least recently used phrase is located and deleted, to make room for a new phrase. This is done by searching the dictionary from entry 256 for the first phrase that is not a prefix to any other phrase. Suppose that the phrase "abcd" is found, and there are no phrases of the form "abcdx" for any x. This means that "abcd" has not been used since it was created, and that it is the oldest such phrase. It therefore makes sense to delete it, since it reflects an old pattern in the input stream. This way, the dictionary always reflects recent patterns in the input.

Bibliography

Thomborson, Clark (1992) "The V.42bis Standard for Data-Compressing Modems," *IEEE Micro* pp. 41–53, October.

3.18 Zip and Gzip

These popular programs implement the so-called "deflation" algorithm which uses a variation of LZ77 combined with static Huffman. It uses a 32Kbyte-long sliding dictionary, and a look-ahead buffer of 258 bytes. When a string is not found in the dictionary it is emitted as a sequence of literal bytes.

The input stream is divided by the encoder into blocks. Block sizes are arbitrary, except that non-compressible blocks are limited to 64Kbytes. A block is terminated when the "deflate" encoder determines that it would be useful to start another block with fresh Huffman trees. (This is somewhat similar to UNIX compress.) Literals or match lengths are compressed with one Huffman tree, and match distances are compressed with another tree. The trees are stored in a compact form at the start of each block. The Huffman trees for each block are independent of those for previous or subsequent blocks.

Duplicated strings are found using a hash table. All input strings of length 3 are inserted in the hash table. A hash index is computed for the next 3 bytes. If the hash chain for this index is not empty, all strings in the chain are compared with the current input string, and the longest match is selected.

The hash chains are searched starting with the most recent strings, to favor small distances and thus take advantage of the Huffman encoding. The hash chains are singly linked. There are no deletions from the hash chains; the algorithm simply discards matches that are too old.

To avoid a worst-case situation, very long hash chains are arbitrarily truncated at a certain length, determined by a runtime option. As a result, Deflate does not always find the longest possible match, but it generally finds a match that's long enough.

Deflate also defers the selection of matches with a greedy evaluation mechanism. After a match of length N has been found, Deflate searches for a longer match at the next input byte. If a longer match is found, the previous match is truncated to a length of one (thus producing a single literal byte) and the longer match is emitted afterwards. Otherwise, the original match is kept, and the next match search is attempted only N steps later.

The greedy match evaluation is also controlled by a runtime parameter. If the current match is long enough, Deflate reduces the search for a longer match, thus speeding up the entire process. If compression ratio is more important than speed, Deflate attempts a complete second search even if the first match is already long enough.

The greedy match evaluation is not executed for the fastest compression modes. For these fast modes, new strings are inserted in the hash table only when no match was found, or when the match is not too long. This degrades the compression ratio but saves time since there are both fewer insertions and fewer searches.

3.19 ARC and PKZip

ARC is a compression/archival/cataloging program developed by Robert A. Freed of System Enhancement Associates in the mid 1980s. It immediately became very popular among PC users since it offered good compression and the ability to combine several files into one file, called an *archive*. Here are two situations where archiving is useful:

1. A group of files has to be up- or down-loaded by modem. Archiving them into one large file can save transmission time since the modems on both sides have to go through a protocol for each file.

2. Storing hundreds of small files on a large hard disk can be space consuming since the bigger the disk, the larger the minimum block size. A typical 500Mbyte disk may have a minimum file size of 5Kbytes, so 100 small block of, say, 500 bytes each, will occupy 500Kbyte. When combined into an archive, the same information may occupy just 50Kbyte.

Most modern archivers are self extracting. Such an archiver includes a small decompressor in the compressed file, so the file becomes a bit longer, but can decompress itself. In the PC world such archives have a suffix of ".SFX". On the Macintosh computer they are known as ".sea" files (for "self extracting application").

ARC offers several compression methods, and the user can select any method for compressing a file. The general format of an ARC file is:
[[archive-mark + header-version + file header + file data]...] + archive-mark + end-of-arc-mark.

The archive-mark is the byte "1A". The file header is 27 bytes long and is defined by the following C structure:

```
typedef struct archive_file_header
  { char name[13]; /* file name */
    unsigned long size; /* size of compressed file */
    unsigned short date; /* file date */
    unsigned short time; /* file time */
```

```
    unsigned short crc; /* cyclic redundancy check */
    unsigned long length; /* true file length */
};
```

The "name" field is the null-terminated file name.

The "size" is the number of bytes in the file data area following the header.

The "date" and "time" are stored in the same packed format as a DOS directory entry.

The "CRC" is a 16-bit code computed from the file data (Section 3.22).

The "length" is the actual uncompressed size of the file.

Arc uses the following compression methods:

1. No compression (obsolete).

2. Stored—The file is simply copied on the output stream with no compression.

3. Packed—(non-repeat packing of text characters).

4. Squeezed (Huffman squeezing, after packing).

5. Crunched (Obsolete—12-bit static LZW without non-repeat pack).

6. Crunched (Obsolete—12-bit static LZW with non-repeat packing).

7. Crunched (Obsolete—after packing, using faster hash algorithm).

8. Crunched (Using dynamic LZW variations, after packing. The initial LZW code size is 9 bits with a maximum code size of 12 bits. Adaptive resets of the dictionary are implemented in this mode.)

9. Squashed (The file was compressed with Dynamic LZW compression without non-repeat packing. The initial LZW code size is 9 bits with a maximum maximum code size of 13 bits. Adaptive resets of the dictionary are implemented in this mode.)

PKArc is an improved version of ARC. It was developed by Phil Katz who has founded the PKWare company ("`http://www.pkware.com`"), which markets the PKzip, PKunzip, PKlite, and PKarc software. The PK programs are faster and more general than ARC and also provide for more user control. As a result, ARC is no longer very popular. Several more PC compression programs are mentioned in Sections 3.20 and 3.21.

PKarc uses the same compression methods and file format as ARC. The other PK programs have several compression methods implemented, and the user can select any method to compress a file. Here is a short description of some of these methods:

1. *Shrinking.* This uses a version of dynamic LZW with partial clearing of the dictionary. The initial code size is 9 bits, with a maximum of 13 bits. Shrinking differs from other dynamic LZW implementations in two respects:

a. The code size is determined by the compressor and is increased by it from time to time. When the compressor decides to increment the code size, it emits the sequence 256,1. This is a signal to the decompressor to do the same thing.

b. When the dictionary fills up it is not erased. Instead, the compresser clears all the leaves of the dictionary tree and emits the sequence 256,2 as a signal for the decompressor. The code size is not increased. The cleared dictionary nodes are then reused

2. *Reducing.* This is a two-step method. It uses RLE followed by a statistical method. The statistical method prepares an array of "follower sets" S(j), for j=0 to 255, corresponding to the 256 possible bytes. Each set contains between 0 and 32 characters, to be denoted S(j)[0],...,S(j)[m], where $m < 32$. The sets are stored at the beginning of the output stream in reverse order, with S(255) first, and S(0) last.

The sets are written on the output stream as {N(j),S(j)[0],...,S(j)[N(j)-1]}, where N(j) is the size of set S(j). N(j)=0 indicates an empty follower set S(j). Each N(j) is stored in 6 bits, followed by N(j) 8-bit characters corresponding to S(j)[0] through S(j)[N(j)-1]. If N(j)=0, then nothing is stored for S(j), and the value of N(j-1) immediately follows. Right after the follower sets, the output stream contains the compressed data stream, which is created by the compressor according to the pseudo-code below:

```
Last-Character:=0;
repeat
  if the follower set S(Last-Character) is empty then
    read 8 bits from the input stream, and
              write it on the output stream;
  else (the follower set S(Last-Character) is non-empty) then
    read 1 bit from the input stream;
    if this bit is not zero then
      read 8 bits from the input stream, and
                write it on the output stream;
    else (this bit is zero) then
      read B(N(Last-Character)) bits from the input stream,
                                    and assign it to i;
    Write value of S(Last-Character)[i] on output stream;
    endif;
  endif;
Last-Character:=last value written on the output stream;
until end-of-input
```

where B(N(j)) is defined as the minimal number of bits required to encode the value N(j)-1.

The decompressor works as follows:

```
State:=0;
repeat
  read 8 bits from the input stream to C.
  case State of
0: if C is not equal DLE (ASCII 144) then write C on output stream;
  else if C is equal to DLE then let State <- 1; endif;
    endif;

1: if C is non-zero then
  V:=C;
  Len:=L(V);
```

```
    State:=F(Len);
    else if C is zero then
      copy the value 144 (decimal) to the output stream;
    State:=0;
     endif;

2:  Len:=Len+C;
    State:=3;


3:   Move backwards D(V,C) bytes in the output stream
     (if this position is before the start of the output
     stream, then assume that all the data before the
     start of the output stream is filled with zeros).
     Write Len+3 bytes from this position to the output stream;
     State:=0;
   end case;
until end-of-input
```

The functions F, L, and D depend on the "compression factor," 1 through 4, and are defined as follows:

- For compression factor 1:
  L(X) equals the lower 7 bits of X.
  F(X)=2 if X equals 127; otherwise F(X) equals 3.
  D(X,Y) equals the (upper 1 bit of X) * 256 + Y + 1.

- For compression factor 2:
  L(X) equals the lower 6 bits of X.
  F(X)=2 if X equals 63; otherwise F(X)=3.
  D(X,Y) equals the (upper 2 bits of X) * 256 + Y + 1.

- For compression factor 3:
  L(X) equals the lower 5 bits of X.
  F(X)=2 if X equals 31; otherwise F(X)=3.
  D(X,Y) equals the (upper 3 bits of X) * 256 + Y + 1.

- For compression factor 4:
  L(X) equals the lower 4 bits of X.
  F(X)=2 if X equals 15; otherwise F(X)=3.
  D(X,Y) equals the (upper 4 bits of X) * 256 + Y + 1.

3. *Imploding.* This again is a combination of two methods. The first step compresses repeated byte sequences using a sliding dictionary (which is either 4K or 8Kbytes long). The second step uses multiple Shannon-Fano tree to compress the output of the first step.

The Shannon-Fano trees are stored at the start of the output stream. Either two or three trees are stored. If three trees are stored, the first of them represents the encoding of the Literal characters, the second tree represents the encoding of the Length information, and the third represents the encoding of the Distance information. When two Shannon-Fano trees are stored, the Length tree is stored first, followed by the Distance tree.

If the "Literal" Shannon-Fano tree is present, it is used to represent every possible 8-bit byte, and it contains 256 values. This tree is used to compress any data not compressed by the sliding dictionary algorithm. When this tree is present, the Minimum Match Length for the sliding dictionary is 3. If this tree is absent, the Minimum Match Length is 2.

The "Length" Shannon-Fano tree is used to compress the "Length" part of the (length, distance) pairs from the sliding dictionary output. The "Length" tree contains 64 values, ranging from the Minimum Match Length, to 63+Minimum Match Length.

The "Distance" Shannon-Fano tree is used to compress the "Distance" part of the (length, distance) pairs from the sliding dictionary output. This tree contains 64 values, ranging from 0 to 63, representing the upper 6 bits of the distance value. The distance values themselves will be between 0 and the sliding dictionary size, which is either 4K or 8K.

The Shannon-Fano trees themselves are stored in a compressed format. The first byte of the tree data contains the number of bytes of data representing the (compressed) Shannon-Fano tree minus 1. The remaining bytes contain the Shannon-Fano tree data encoded as:

High 4 bits: Number of values at this bit length +1. (1–16)

Low 4 bits: Bit Length needed to represent value +1. (1–16)

The Shannon-Fano codes can be constructed from the bit lengths using the following algorithm:

a. Sort the Bit Lengths in ascending order, while retaining the order of the original lengths stored in the file.

b. Generate the Shannon-Fano trees:

```
Code:=0;
CodeIncrement:=0;
LastBitLength:=0;
i:=number of Shannon-Fano codes -1 (either 255 or 63);

loop while i>=0
Code:=Code + CodeIncrement;
if BitLength(i) <> LastBitLength then
  LastBitLength=BitLength(i);
  CodeIncrement = 1 shifted left (16-LastBitLength);
 endif;
ShannonCode(i):=Code;
i:=i-1;
end loop;
```

c. Reverse the order of the bits in the above ShannonCode() array, so that the most significant bit becomes the least significant one.

d. Restore the order of Shannon-Fano codes as originally stored within the file.

The compressed data stream begins immediately after the compressed Shannon Fano data. It is created as follows:

```
repeat
  read 1 bit from input stream;
    if this bit is non-zero then (encoded data is literal data)
     if Literal Shannon-Fano tree is present
        read and decode symbol using Literal Shannon-Fano tree;
     else
       read 8 bits from input stream and write them on
        the output stream;
      endif;
    else                  (encoded data is sliding dictionary match)
      if 8K dictionary size
       read 7 bits for offset Distance (lower 7 bits of offset);
      else
       read 6 bits for offset Distance (lower 6 bits of offset);
      endif;
    endif;
Using the Distance Shannon-Fano tree, read and decode the
upper 6 bits of the Distance value;

Using the Length Shannon-Fano tree, read and decode the Length;

Length:=Length + Minimum Match Length;

if Length = 63 + Minimum Match Length
  then read 8 bits from the input stream, and
   add this value to Length;
endif;

Move backwards Distance+1 bytes in the output stream, and copy
Length characters from this position to the output stream.
(if this position is before the start of the output stream,
then assume that all the data before the start of  the output
stream is filled with zeros).

until end-of-input;
```

> I do not know it—it is without name—it is a word unsaid, It is not in any dictionary, utterance, symbol.
>
> —Walt Whitman, *Leaves of Grass*

3.20 ARJ and LHArc

ARJ is a compression/archiving utility written by Robert K. Jung to compete with ARC and the various PK utilities. Here are some of its more powerful features:

1. It can search archives for any text without the user having to extract the archives.

2. It can save drive letter and pathname information.

3. It can sort the individual files within an archive.

4. It can merge two or more archives without decompressing and re-compressing their files.

5. It can extract files directly to DOS devices.

6. It can synchronize an archive and a directory of files with just a few commands.

7. It can compare the contents of an archive and a directory of files byte for byte without extracting and decompressing the archive.

8. It allows duplicates of a file to be archived, producing several versions of a file within an archive.

9. It can display an archive's creation and modification dates and times.

ICE, LHArc, and LHA are all from Haruyasu Yoshizaki. They use adaptive Huffman coding with features drawn from LZSS.

3.21 EXE Compressors

The LZEXE program is freeware originally written in the late 1980s by Fabrice Bellard as a special-purpose utility to compress EXE files (PC executable files). The idea is that an EXE file compressed by LZEXE can be decompressed **and** executed with one command. The decompressor does not write the decompressed file on the disk but loads it in memory, relocates addresses, and executes it! The decompressor uses memory that's eventually used by the program being decompressed, so it does not require any extra RAM. In addition, the decompressor is very small compared to decompressors in self extracting archives.

The algorithm is based on LZ. It uses a circular queue and a dictionary tree for finding string matches. The position and size of the match are encoded by an auxiliary algorithm based on the Huffman method. Uncompressed bytes are kept unchanged since trying to compress them any further would have entailed a much more complex and larger decompressor. The decompressor is located at the end of the compressed EXE file and is 330 bytes long (in version 0.91). The main steps of the decoder are:

1. Check the CRC (Section 3.22) to ensure data reliability.

2. Locate itself in high RAM; then move the compressed code in order to leave sufficient room for the EXE file.

3. Decompress the code, check that it is correct, and adjust the segments if bigger than 64K.

4. Decompress the relocation table and update the relocatable addresses of the EXE file.

5. Run the program, updating the CS, IP, SS, and SP registers.

The idea of EXE compressors, introduced by LZEXE, was attractive to both users and software developers, so a few more have been developed:

PKlite, from PKWare, is a similar EXE compressor that can also compress .COM files.

DIET, by Teddy Matsumoto, is a more general EXE compressor that can compress data files. DIET can act as a monitor, permanently residing in RAM, watching for applications trying to read files from the disk. When an application tries to read a DIET-compressed data file, DIET senses it, and does the reading and decompressing in a process that's transparent to the application.

3.22 CRC

The idea of a parity bit is simple, old, and familiar to most computer practitioners. A parity bit is the simplest type of error detecting code. It adds reliability to a group of bits by making it possible for hardware to detect certain errors that occur when the group is stored in memory, is written on a disk, or is sent over communication lines between modems. A single parity bit does not make the group completely reliable. There are certain errors that cannot be detected with a parity bit, but experience shows that even a single parity bit can make data transmission reliable in most practical cases.

The parity bit is computed from a group of $n-1$ bits, then added to the group, making it n bits long. A common example is a 7-bit ASCII code that becomes 8 bits long after a parity bit is added. The parity bit "p" is computed by counting the number of "1" bits in the original group, and setting "p" to complete that number to either odd or even. The former is called odd parity and the latter, even parity.

Examples: Given the group of 7 bits 1010111, the number of "1" bits is 5, which is odd. Assuming odd parity, the value of "p" should be 0, leaving the total number of 1s odd. Similarly, the group 1010101 has 4 bits of "1," so its odd parity bit should also be a "1," bringing the total number of 1s to 5.

Imagine a block of data where the most significant bit (MSB) of each byte is an odd parity bit, and the bytes are written vertically (Table 3.27a).

1 01101001	1 01101001	1 01101001	1 01101001
0 00001011	0 00001011	0 00001011	0 00001011
0 11110010	0 11010010	0 11010110	0 11010110
0 01101110	0 01101110	0 01101110	0 01101110
1 11101101	1 11101101	1 11101101	1 11101101
1 01001110	1 01001110	1 01001110	1 01001110
0 11101001	0 11101001	0 11101001	0 11101001
1 11010111	1 11010111	1 11010111	1 11010111
			0 00011100
(a)	(b)	(c)	(d)

Table 3.27: Horizontal and Vertical Parities.

When this block is read from a disk or is received by a modem, it may contain transmission errors. Errors caused by imperfect hardware or by electrical interference along the way. We can think of the parity bits as *horizontal reliability*. When the block is read, the hardware can check every byte, verifying the parity. This is done by simply counting the number of "1" bits in the byte. If this number is odd, the hardware assumes that the byte is good. This assumption is not always correct, since two bits may get corrupted during transmission (Table 3.27c). A single parity bit is thus useful (Table 3.27b) but does not provide complete protection from errors.

A simple way to add more reliability to a block of data is to compute vertical parities. The block is considered eight vertical columns, and an odd parity bit is computed for each column (Table 3.27d). If 2 bits in 1 byte go bad, the horizontal parity will not catch it, but 2 of the vertical ones will. Even the vertical bits do not provide complete error detection capabilities, but they are a simple way to improve data reliability.

A CRC is a glorified vertical parity. CRC stands for Cyclical Redundancy Check (or Cyclical Redundancy Code) and it is a rule that shows how to obtain the vertical check bits (they are now called check bits, not just simple parity bits) from all the bits of the data. Here is how CRC-32 is computed (this is one of the many standards developed by the CCITT). The block of data is written as one, long binary number. In our example this will be the 64-bit number:

101101001|000001011|011110010|001101110|111101101|101001110|011101001|111010111.

The individual bits are considered the coefficients of a *polynomial* (see below for definition). In our example, this will be the degree-63 polynomial

$$P(x) = 1 \times x^{63} + 0 \times x^{62} + 1 \times x^{61} + 1 \times x^{60} + \cdots + 1 \times x^2 + 1 \times x^1 + 1 \times x^0$$
$$= x^{63} + x^{61} + x^{60} + \cdots + x^2 + x + 1.$$

This polynomial is then divided by the standard CRC-32 *generating polynomial*

$$CRC_{32}(x) = x^{32} + x^{26} + x^{23} + x^{22} + x^{16} + x^{12} + x^{11} + x^{10} + x^8 + x^7 + x^5 + x^4 + x^2 + x^1 + 1.$$

When an integer M is divided by an integer N, the result is a quotient Q (which we will ignore), and a remainder R which is in the range $[0, N-1]$. Similarly, when a polynomial $P(x)$ is divided by a degree-32 polynomial, the result is two polynomials, a quotient and a remainder. The remainder is a degree-31 polynomial, which means it has 32 coefficients, each a single bit. Those 32 bits are the CRC-32 code, which is appended to the block of data as 4 bytes.

The CRC is sometimes called "the fingerprint" of the file. Of course, since it is a 32-bit number, there may only be 2^{32} different CRCs. This number equals approximately 4.3 billion, so, in theory, there may be different files with the same CRC, but in practice this is rare. The CRC is useful as an error detecting code because it has the following properties:

1. Every bit in the data block is used to compute the CRC. This means that changing even one bit may produce a different CRC.

2. Even small changes in the data normally produce very different CRCs. Experience with CRC-32 shows that it is very rare that introducing errors in the data would not change the CRC.

3. Any histogram of CRC-32 values for different data blocks is flat (or very close to flat). For a given data block, the probability of any of the 2^{32} possible CRCs being produced is practically the same.

Other common generating polynomials are $CRC_{12}(x) = x^{12} + x^3 + x + 1$ and $CRC_{16}(x) = x^{16} + x^{15} + x^2 + 1$. They generate the common CRC-12 and CRC-16 codes, which are 12 and 16 bits long, respectively.

Definition: A polynomial of degree n in x is the function

$$P_n(x) = \sum_{i=0}^{n} a_i x^i = a_0 + a_1 x + a_2 x^2 + \cdots + a_n x^n;$$

where a_i are the $n+1$ coefficients (in our case, real numbers). Appendix I discusses the parametric representation of polynomials.

Bibliography

Ramabadran, Tenkasi V., and Sunil S. Gaitonde (1988) "A Tutorial on CRC Computations," *IEEE Micro* pp. 62–75, August.

3.23 Summary

The dictionary-based methods presented here are different but are based on the same principle. They read the input stream symbol by symbol and add phrases to the dictionary. The phrases are symbols or strings of symbols from the input. The main difference between the methods is in deciding what phrases to add to the dictionary. When a string in the input stream matches a dictionary phrase, the encoder outputs the position of the match in the dictionary. If that position requires fewer bits than the matched string, compression results.

In general, dictionary-based methods, when carefully implemented, give better compression than statistical methods. This is why many popular compression programs are dictionary based or involve a dictionary as one of several compression steps.

3.23.1 A Unification

Dictionary-based methods and methods based on prediction approach the problem of data compression from two different directions. Any method based on prediction predicts (i.e., assigns probability to) the current symbol based on its order-N context (the N symbols preceding it). Such a method normaly stores many contexts of different sizes in a data structure and has to deal with frequency counts, probabilities, and probability ranges. It then uses arithmetic coding to encode the entire input stream as one large number. A dictionary-based method, on the other hand, works differently. It identifies the next phrase in the input stream, stores it in its dictionary, assigns it a code, and continues with the next phrase. Both approaches can be used to compress data because each obeys the general law of data compression, namely, to assign short codes to common events (symbols or phrases) and long codes, to rare events.

On the surface, the two approaches are completely different. A predictor deals with probabilities, so it can be highly efficient. At the same time, it can be expected to be slow, since it deals with individual symbols. A dictionary-based method deals with strings of symbols (phrases), so it gobbles up the input stream faster, but it ignores correlations between phrases, typically resulting in poorer compression.

The two approaches are similar because a dictionary-based method *does use* contexts and probabilities (although implicitly) just by storing phrases in its dictionary and searching it. The following discussion uses the LZW trie to illustrate this concept, but the argument is true for every dictionary-based method, no matter what the details of its algorithm and its dictionary data structure.

Imagine the phrase "abcdef..." stored in an LZW trie (Figure 3.28a). We can think of the substring "abcd" as the order-4 context of "e". When the encoder finds another occurrence of "abcde.." in the input stream, it will locate our phrase in the dictionary, will parse it symbol by symbol starting at the root, will get to node "e", and will continue from there, trying to match more symbols. Eventually the encoder will get to a leaf, where it will add another symbol and allocate another code. We can think of this process as adding a new leaf to the subtree whose root is the "e" of "abcde...". Every time the string "abcde" becomes the prefix of a parse, both its subtree and its code space (the number of codes associated with it) get bigger by 1. It therefore makes sense to assign node "e" a probability depending on the size of its code space, and the above discussion shows that the size of the code space of node "e" (or, equivalently, string "abcde") can be measured by counting the number of nodes of the subtree whose root is "e". This is how probabilities can be assigned to nodes in any dictionary tree.

The ideas of Glen Langdon in the early 1980s (see [Langdon 83] but notice that his equation (8) is wrong; it should read $P(y|s) = c(s)/c(s \cdot y)$; [Langdon 84] is perhaps more useful) led to a simple way of associating probabilities not just to nodes but also to arcs in a dictionary tree. This is more useful since the arc from node "e" to node "f", e.g., signifies an "f" whose context is "abcde". The probability of this arc is thus the probability that an "f" will follow "abcde" in the input stream. The fact that these probabilities can be calculated in a dictionary tree shows that every dictionary-based data compression algorithm can be "simulated" by a prediction algorithm (although the converse is not true). Algorithms based on prediction are, in this sense, more general, but the important fact is that these two seemingly different classes of compression methods can be united by the observations above.

The process whereby a dictionary encoder slides down from the root of its dictionary tree, parsing a string of symbols, can now be given a different interpretation. We can visualize it as a sequence of making predictions for individual symbols, computing codes for them, and combining the codes into one longer code, which is eventually written on the compressed stream. It is as if the code generated by a dictionary encoder for a phrase is actually made up of small chunks, each a code for one symbol.

The rule for calculating the probability of the arc $e \rightarrow f$ is: count the number of nodes in the subtree whose root is "f" (including node "f" itself) and divide by the number of nodes in the subtree of "e". Figure 3.28b shows a typical dictionary tree

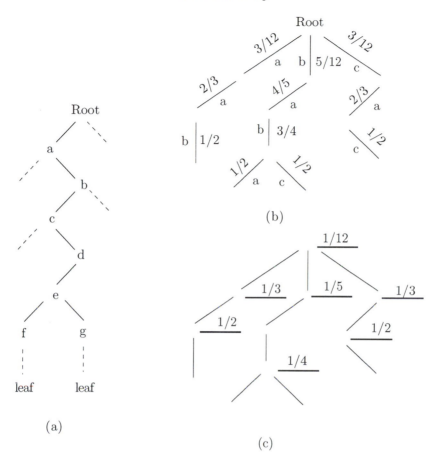

Figure 3.28: Defining Probabilities in a Dictionary Tree.

with the strings "aab", "baba", "babc", and "cac". The probabilities associated with every arc are also shown and should be easy for the reader to verify. Note that the probabilities of sibling subtrees don't add up to 1. The probabilities of the three subtrees of the root, e.g., add up to 11/12. The remaining 1/12 is assigned to the root itself and represents the probability that a fourth string will eventually start at the root. These "missing probabilities" are shown as horizontal lines in Figure 3.28c.

The two approaches, dictionary and prediction, can be combined in a single compression method. The LZP method of Section 3.13 is one example; the LZRW4 method (Section 3.8) is another. These methods work by considering the context of a symbol before searching the dictionary.

> REASON = To weight probabilities in the scales of desire.
> —Ambrose Bierce, *The Devil's Dictionary*

Bibliography

Langdon, Glen G. (1983) "A Note on the Ziv-Lempel Model for Compressing Individual Sequences," *IEEE Transactions on Information Theory* IT-29(2):284–287, March.

Langdon, Glen G. (1984) *On Parsing vs. Mixed-Order Model Structures for Data Compression*, IBM research report RJ-4163 (46091), Jan 18, 1984, San Jose.

> The nymph (her fingers in her ears): "And
> words. They are not in my dictionary."
>
> James Joyce, *Ulysses*

> Words fascinate me. They always have. For me, browsing
> in a dictionary is like being turned loose in a bank.
>
> Eddie Cantor

4
Image Compression

Modern computers employ graphics extensively. Window-based operating systems display the disk's file directory graphically. The progress of many system operations, such as downloading a file, may also be displayed graphically. Many applications provide a graphical user interface (GUI), which makes it easier to use the program and to interpret displayed results. Computer graphics is used in many areas in everyday life to convert many types of complex information to images. Images are thus important, but they tend to be big! Since modern hardware can display many colors, it is common to have a pixel represented internally as a 24-bit number, where the precentages of red, green and blue occupy 8 bits each. Such a 24-bit pixel can specify one of $2^{24} \approx 16.78$ million colors. An image at a resolution of 512×512 that consists of such pixels thus occupies 786,432 bytes. At a resolution of 1024×1024 it gets four times as big, requiring 3,145,728 bytes. Movies are also commonly used with computers, making for even bigger images. This is why image compression is so important. An important feature of image compression is that it can be lossy. An image, after all, exists for people to look at, so, when it is compressed, it is okay to lose image features for which the human eye is not sensitive. This is one of the main ideas behind JPEG and other lossy image compression methods described in this chapter.

The idea of losing image information becomes more palatable when we consider how digital images are created. Here are three examples: (1) A real-life image may be scanned from a photograph or a painting and digitized (converted to pixels). (2) An image may be recorded by a video camera that creates pixels and stores them directly in memory. (3) An image may be painted on the screen by means of a paint program. In all these cases, the image loses some information when it is digitized. The fact that the viewer is willing to put up with this loss suggests that further loss of information might be tolerable if done carefully.

4.1 Introduction

How should an image be compressed? So far we have discussed three principles: RLE, statistical methods, and dictionary-based methods. None is very satisfactory for color or grayscale images. Here is why:

Section 1.4.1 shows how RLE can be used to (lossless or lossy) compress an image. This is simple and it is used by certain parts of JPEG, especially by its lossless mode. In general, however, the other principles used by JPEG produce much better compression than using just RLE.

Statistical methods work best when the symbols being compressed have different probabilities. An input stream where all symbols have the same probability will not compress, even though it may not necessarily be random. It turns out that, in a continuous-tone color or grayscale image, the different colors or shades of gray have roughly the same probabilities. This is why statistical methods are not a good choice for compressing such images, and why new approaches are necessary. Images with color discontinuities, where adjacent pixels have widely different colors, compress better with statistical methods.

Dictionary-based compression methods also tend to be unsuccessful in dealing with continuous-tone images. Such an image typically contains adjacent pixels with similar colors, but does not contain repeating patterns. Even an image that contains repeated patterns such as vertical lines may lose them when digitized. A vertical line in the original image may become slightly slanted when the image is digitized (Figure 4.1), so the pixels in a scan row may end up having slightly different colors from those in the preceding and following rows, resulting in a dictionary with short strings.

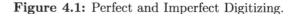

An ideal vertical rule is shown in (a). In (b), the rule is assumed to be perfectly digitized into ten pixels, laid vertically. However, if the image is placed in the digitizer slightly slanted, the digitizing process may be imperfect, and the resulting pixels might look as in (c).

(a)   (b)   (c)

Figure 4.1: Perfect and Imperfect Digitizing.

Traditional methods are thus unsatisfactory for image compression (lossy or lossless), so novel approaches to image compression are discussed here. Among them are JPEG, quadtrees, weighted finite automata (WFA), wavelets, and iterated function systems (IFS).

4.2 JPEG

JPEG is a sophisticated lossy compression method for color or grayscale still images (not movies). It does not handle bi-level (black and white) images very well. It also works best on continuous-tone images, where adjacent pixels have similar colors. One advantage of JPEG is the use of many parameters, allowing the user to adjust the amount of the data lost (and thus also the compression ratio) over a very wide range. Many times the eye cannot see any image degradation even at compression ratios of 10:1 or 20:1. There are two main modes: lossy (also called baseline) and lossless (which typically gives a 2:1 compression ratio). Most implementations support just the lossy mode. This mode includes progressive and hierarchical coding.

➥ JPEG is a compression method, not a complete standard for image representation. This is why it does not specify image features such as pixel aspect ratio, color space, or interleaving of bitmap rows.

JPEG has been designed as a compression method for continuous-tone images. The main goals in JPEG compression were the following:

1. High compression ratios, especially in cases where image quality is judged as very good to excellent.

2. The use of many parameters, allowing sophisticated users to experiment and achieve the desired compression/quality tradeoff.

3. Obtaining good results with any kind of continuous-tone image, regardless of image dimensions, color spaces, pixel aspect ratios, or other image features.

4. A sophisticated, but not too complex compression method, allowing software and hardware implementations on many platforms.

5. Several modes of operation: (a) Sequential mode: each image component (color) is compressed in a single left-to-right, top-to-bottom scan; (b) Progressive mode: the image is compressed in multiple blocks (known as "scans") to be viewed from coarse- to fine-detail; (c) Lossless mode: important for cases where the user decides that no pixels should be lost (the tradeoff is low compression ratio compared to the lossy modes); and (d) Hierarchical mode: the image is compressed at multiple resolutions allowing lower-resolution blocks to be viewed without first having to decompress the following higher-resolution blocks.

The word JPEG is an acronym that stands for Joint Photographic Experts Group. This was a joint effort by the CCITT and the ISO (the International Standards Organization) that started in June 1987 and produced the first JPEG draft proposal in 1991. The JPEG standard has proved successful and has become widely used for image compression, especially in Web pages.

The main JPEG compression steps are outlined below, and each step is then described in detail later.

1. Color images are transformed from RGB into a luminance/chrominance color space (Section 4.2.1; this step is skipped for grayscale images). The eye is sensitive to small changes in luminance but not in chrominance, so the chrominance part can later lose a lot of data, and thus be highly compressed, without visually affecting the overall image quality much. This step is optional but important since the remainder of the algorithm works on each color component separately. Without

transforming the color space, none of the three color components will tolerate much loss, leading to worse compression.

2. Color images are downsampled by creating low-resolution pixels from the original ones (this step is only used when hierarchical compression is needed; it is always skipped for grayscale images). The downsampling is not done for the luminance component. Downsampling is done either at a ratio of 2:1 both horizontally and vertically (the so-called 2h2v or "4:1:1" sampling) or at ratios of 2:1 horizontally and 1:1 vertically (2h1v or "4:2:2" sampling). Since this is done on two of the three color components, 2h2v reduces the image to $1/3 + (2/3) \times (1/4) = 1/2$ its original size, while 2h1v reduces it to $1/3 + (2/3) \times (1/2) = 2/3$ its original size. Since the luminance component is not touched, there is no noticeable loss of image quality. Grayscale images don't go through this step.

3. The pixels of each color component are organized in groups of 8×8 pixels called *data units*. If the number of image rows or columns is not a multiple of 8, the bottom row and the rightmost column are duplicated as many times as necessary. The *discrete cosine transform* (DCT) is then applied to each data unit to create an 8×8 map of frequency components (Section 4.2.2). They represent the average pixel value, and successive higher-frequency changes within the group. This prepares the image data for the crucial step of losing information. Since DCT involves the transcendental function cosine, it must involve some loss of information due to the limited precision of computer arithmetic. This means that, even without the main lossy step (step 4 below), there will be some loss of image quality, but it is normally small.

4. Each of the 64 frequency components in a data unit is divided by a separate number called its "quantization coefficient" (QC), and then rounded to an integer (Section 4.2.5). This is where information is irretrievably lost. Large QCs cause more loss, so the high-frequency components typically have larger QCs. Each of the 64 QCs is a JPEG parameter and can, in principle, be specified by the user. In practice most JPEG implementations use the QC tables recommended by the JPEG standard (see, e.g., Table 4.10).

5. The 64 quantized frequency coefficients (which are now integers) of each data unit are encoded using a combination of RLE and Huffman coding (Section 4.2.6). An extension to JPEG uses the same arithmetic coding variant used in JBIG at this stage.

6. The last step adds headers and all the JPEG parameters used, and outputs the result. In specialized applications, where the same parameters are always used, the parameters don't have to go on the output stream, which saves a few hundred bytes.

The JPEG decoder performs the reverse steps.

The progressive mode is a JPEG option. In this mode, higher-frequency DCT coefficients are written on the compressed stream in blocks called "scans." Each scan read and processed by the decoder results in a sharper image. The idea is to use the first few scans to quickly create a low-quality, blurred preview of the image, and then either input the remaining scans or stop the process and reject the image. The tradeoff is that the encoder has to go through all the steps for each scan, making the progressive mode slow.

In the hierarchical mode, the encoder stores the image several times in the output stream, at several resolutions. However, each high-resolution part uses information from the low-resolution parts of the output stream, so the total amount of information is less than that required to store the different resolutions separately. Each hierarchical part may use the progressive mode.

The hierarchical mode is useful in cases where a high-resolution image needs to be output in low resolution. Older dot-matrix printers may be a good example of a low-resolution output device still in use.

The lossless mode of JPEG (Section 4.2.7) calculates a "predicted" value for each pixel, generates the difference between the pixel and its predicted value (see Section 1.3.1 for relative encoding), and encodes the difference using the same method (Huffman or arithmetic coding) used by step 5 above. The predicted value is calculated using values of pixels above and to the left of the current pixel (pixels that have already been input and encoded). Here are the steps in more detail:

4.2.1 Luminance

The main international organization devoted to light and color is the International Committee on Illumination (Commission Internationale de l'Éclairage), abbreviated CIE. It is responsible for developing standards and definitions in this area. One of the early achievements of the CIE was its *chromaticity diagram*, developed in 1931. It shows how no fewer than three parameters are required to define color. Expressing a certain color by the triplet (x, y, z) is similar to denoting a point in three-dimensional space, hence the term *color space*. The most common color space is RGB, where the three parameters are the intensities of Red, Green, and Blue in a color. When used in computers, these parameters are normally in the range 0–255 (8 bits).

The CIE defines color as the perceptual result of light in the visible region of the spectrum, having wavelengths in the region of 400 nm to 700 nm, incident upon the retina (a nanometer, nm, equals 10^{-9} meter). Physical power (or radiance) is expressed in a spectral power distribution (SPD), often in 31 components each representing a 10 nm band.

The CIE defines brightness as the attribute of a visual sensation according to which an area appears to emit more or less light. The brain's perception of brightness is impossible to define, so the CIE defines a more practical quantity called *luminance*. It is defined as radiant power weighted by a spectral sensitivity function that's characteristic of vision. The luminous efficiency of the Standard Observer is defined by the CIE as a positive function of the wavelength, which has a maximum at about 555 nm. When an SPD is integrated using this function as a weighting function, the result is CIE luminance, which is denoted Y.

Luminance is proportional to the power of the light source. It is similar to intensity but the spectral composition of luminance is related to the brightness sensitivity of human vision.

The eye is very sensitive to small changes in luminance, which is why it is useful to have color spaces that use Y as one of their three parameters. A simple way to do this is to subtract Y from the Blue and Red parameters of RGB, and use the three parameters Y, B–Y, and R–Y as a new color space. The last two parameters are called chroma.

Various number ranges are used in B–Y and R–Y for different applications. The YPbPr ranges are optimized for component analog video. The YCbCr ranges are appropriate for component digital video such as studio video, JPEG, and MPEG.

The YCbCr color space was developed as part of Recommendation ITU-R BT.601 (formerly CCIR 601) during the development of a worldwide digital component video standard. Y is defined to have a range of 16 to 235; Cb and Cr are defined to have a range of 16 to 240, with 128 equal to zero. There are several YCbCr sampling formats, such as 4:4:4, 4:2:2, 4:1:1, and 4:2:0, which are also described in the recommendation.

Conversions between RGB with a 16–235 range and YCbCr are straightforward:

$$Y = (77/256)R + (150/256)G + (29/256)B,$$
$$Cb = -(44/256)R - (87/256)G + (131/256)B + 128,$$
$$Cr = (131/256)R - (110/256)G - (21/256)B + 128;$$

$$R = Y + 1.371(Cr - 128),$$
$$G = Y - 0.698(Cr - 128) - 0.336(Cb - 128),$$
$$B = Y + 1.732(Cb - 128).$$

When performing YCbCr to RGB conversion, the resulting RGB values have a nominal range of 16–235, with possible occasional values in the 0–15 and 236–255 ranges.

4.2.2 DCT

Readers not familiar with Fourier transforms and their use in computer graphics should read Appendix F before attempting this section.

A *function* is a rule of calculation that tells how to obtain a result y given some input x. A *transform* is a similar rule that tells how to obtain a function $G(f)$ from another function $g(t)$. The Fourier transform is one way of doing this but it produces complex numbers. JPEG uses the *discrete cosine transform* (DCT), a variant of the discrete Fourier transform (DFT) that produces just real numbers. Our first goal in this section is to understand the results the two transforms generate, and why the DCT is better than the DFT for lossy image compression. We start with one-dimensional versions of these transforms, and apply them to eight points. Given a set of 8 numbers p_t (e.g., eight points on a curve, eight samples from a sound wave, or eight pixel values), their DFT is the eight complex numbers

$$G_f = \sum_{t=0}^{7} p_t \cos\left(\frac{2\pi ft}{8}\right) - i \sum_{t=0}^{7} p_t \sin\left(\frac{2\pi ft}{8}\right); \quad \text{for } f = 0, 1, \ldots, 7.$$

Their DCT looks similar but produces real numbers since it lacks the part with the sine function

$$G_f = \frac{1}{2} C_f \sum_{t=0}^{7} p_t \cos\left(\frac{(2t+1)f\pi}{16}\right), \tag{4.1}$$

$$\text{where } C_f = \begin{cases} \frac{1}{\sqrt{2}}, & f = 0; \\ 1, & f > 0; \end{cases} \quad \text{for } f = 0, 1, \ldots, 7;$$

In both cases the results have similar meanings. The eight numbers G_f tell what sinusoidal (harmonic) functions should be combined to approximate the function described by the eight original numbers p_t. In the case of the DFT, each sinusoidal function is a complex sum of a sine and a cosine. In the case of the DCT, each sinusoidal is a real cosine function.

The inverse DCT (or IDCT) performs the reverse transformation

$$p_t = \frac{1}{2} \sum_{j=0}^{7} C_j G_j \cos\left(\frac{(2t+1)j\pi}{16}\right); \quad \text{for } t = 0, 1, \ldots, 7. \tag{4.2}$$

To better understand the meaning of "sinusoidal... functions... combined to approximate," let's write one of the DCT coefficients, say G_3, explicitly.

$$
\begin{aligned}
G_3 &= \frac{1}{2} C_3 \sum_{t=0}^{7} p_t \cos\left(\frac{(2t+1)3\pi}{16}\right) \\
&= \frac{1}{2}\left(p_0 \cos\left(\frac{3\pi}{16}\right) + p_1 \cos\left(\frac{3 \times 3\pi}{16}\right) + p_2 \cos\left(\frac{5 \times 3\pi}{16}\right) + p_3 \cos\left(\frac{7 \times 3\pi}{16}\right) \right. \\
&\quad + p_4 \cos\left(\frac{9 \times 3\pi}{16}\right) + p_5 \cos\left(\frac{11 \times 3\pi}{16}\right) + p_6 \cos\left(\frac{13 \times 3\pi}{16}\right) \\
&\quad \left. + p_7 \cos\left(\frac{15 \times 3\pi}{16}\right) \right).
\end{aligned}
$$

This expression makes it clear that G_3 represents the contributions of the sinusoidals with frequencies $3t\pi/16$ (multiples of $3\pi/16$) to the eight numbers p_t. If G_3 turns out to be a large number, then these particular sinusoidals contribute much to the eight numbers. Similarly, coefficient G_7 represents the contributions of the sinusoidals with frequencies $7t\pi/16$ (multiples of $7\pi/16$) to the eight numbers p_t. Each of the eight DCT coefficients thus represents the contributions of sinusoidals of higher and higher frequencies. Exercise 4.1 shows the explicit representation of G_0 and why it is called the "DC coefficient."

There are three main differences between the DFT and the DCT:

1. The DFT produces results that are complex numbers (they contain the quantity $i = \sqrt{-1}$). The DCT, in contrast, involves just real numbers.

2. The DFT assumes that the function described by the eight original numbers p_t is *periodic*. The DCT makes no such assumption.

3. The DCT is more complex computationally, involving more arithmetic operations than the DFT.

The JPEG committee elected to use DCT instead of DFT because of point 2, and in spite of point 3 (point 1 does not make much difference since it is possible to use just the real parts of the DFT). The DCT is applied to the pixels of an image, and experience shows that image pixels don't correspond to any periodic function. Figure 4.2 shows what this means. In (a) eight pixels are shown along a straight line.

They approximate a ramp function. When these pixels are DFT transformed, the DFT assumes that they are part of the periodic function of 4.2c. When the results of the DFT are used to reproduce the function, the result is something similar to Figure 4.2b. In contrast, when the eight pixels are DCT transformed, the results can be used to recreate the original function to a high degree of accuracy.

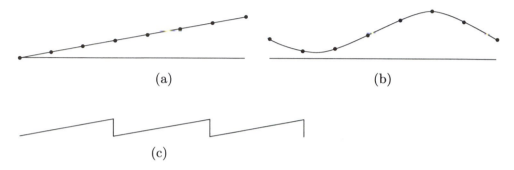

(a)   (b)

(c)

Figure 4.2: A DCT and DFT Example.

Here are the details of the DCT of Figure 4.2. Let's assume that the eight pixels are 11,22,33,44,55,66,77, and 88. Using *Mathematica*™ to calculate the one-dimensional DCT,

`DCT[i_]:={(1/2)Cr[i]Sum[Pixl[[x+1]]Cos[(2x+1)i Pi/16], {x,0,7,1}]};`

creates the eight coefficients $140, -71, 0, -7, 0, -2, 0$, and 0. Deleting the last two nonzero coefficients and applying the one-dimensional IDCT (Equation(4.2)),

`IDCT[x_]:={(1/2)Sum[Cr[i]G[[i+1]]Cos[(2x+1)i Pi/16], {i,0,7,1}]};`

on the sequence $140, -71, 0, 0, 0, 0, 0$, and 0 yields $15, 20, 30, 43, 56, 69, 79$, and 84. These are not identical to the original pixels, but the maximum difference is only 4.

▸ **Exercise 4.1:** Using Equation (4.1), write the explicit expression for G_0 using the eight pixels above and show that it equals approximately 140.

▸ **Exercise 4.2:** Using Equation (4.1), write the explicit expression for the AC coefficient G_5. What does it mean to say that this coefficient has the small value -2?

So far we have discussed the one-dimensional DFT and DCT. We next describe the two-dimensional DCT. The mathematical expression is a double-sum, similar to Equation (4.1). Given an image consisting of the $n \times n$ pixels p_{xy}, its two-dimensional DCT produces the $n \times n$ array of numbers G_{ij} given by

$$G_{ij} = \frac{1}{\sqrt{2n}} C_i C_j \sum_{x=0}^{n-1} \sum_{y=0}^{n-1} p_{xy} \cos\left(\frac{(2x+1)i\pi}{2n}\right) \cos\left(\frac{(2y+1)j\pi}{2n}\right). \qquad (4.3)$$

Where i and j vary from 0 to $n-1$ (JPEG uses $n = 8$, see below). The conventional interpretation is that each pixel p_{xy} can be considered a point in three-dimensional space. The indexes xy of the pixel are its xy coordinates and its value (color component or shade of gray) is its z coordinate. The $n \times n$ pixels (in JPEG, 8×8 or 64) can thus be viewed as points on a surface. The result of the DCT is the square $n \times n$ array G_{ij} of real numbers, which can be thought of as describing the two-dimensional sinusoidal functions needed to reconstruct this surface (mathematically, G_{ij} are called "spatial frequencies"). For a surface close to flat, most of G_{ij} will be zero. For a surface that oscillates much, many G_{ij} coefficients will be nonzero. The numbers at the top left of array G_{ij} describe the contributions of low-frequency sinusoidals to the surface. The ones at the bottom right describe the contributions of high-frequency sinusoidals. This interpretation considers the DCT a "harmonic analyzer" and its inverse, the IDCT, a "harmonic synthesizer."

The array of numbers G_{ij} can also be regarded as the relative amount of the two-dimensional spatial frequencies contained in the surface defined by the 64 pixels. The coefficient G_{00} with zero frequency in both dimensions is called the "DC coefficient," (exercise 4.1) and the remaining 63 coefficients are called the "AC coefficients." Because pixel values in an image normally vary slowly from point to point, the surface described by 64 pixels is close to flat, resulting in a large DC and small AC coefficients. the DCT makes it possible to compress the image by concentrating most of the image information in the lower spatial frequencies.

Given this interpretation of the DCT, the way to lose the unimportant image information is to reduce the size of the 64 numbers G_{ij}, especially the ones at the right bottom. There is a chance that this won't degrade the image quality much. This does not always work, so, in general, each of the 64 numbers G_{ij} is divided by a different quantization coefficient (QC) in order to reduce its size, and all 64 QCs are parameters that can be controlled, in principle, by the user (Section 4.2.5).

Another interpretation of G_{ij} is offered below but first here is a practical point. The JPEG standard calls for applying the DCT not to the entire image but to data units of 8×8 pixels. The reasons for this are: (1) Applying DCT to all $n \times n$ pixels of an image produces better compression but also involves many arithmetic operations and is thus slow. Applying DCT to data units reduces the overall compression ratio but is faster (Section 4.2.3). (2) Experience shows that, in a continuous-tone image, correlations between pixels are short range. A pixel in such an image has a value (color component or shade of gray) that's close to those of its near neighbors, but has nothing to do with the values of far neighbors. Equation (4.3) above thus reduces to

$$G_{ij} = \frac{1}{4} C_i C_j \sum_{x=0}^{7} \sum_{y=0}^{7} p_{xy} \cos\left(\frac{(2x+1)i\pi}{16}\right) \cos\left(\frac{(2y+1)j\pi}{16}\right),$$

$$\text{where } C_f = \begin{cases} \frac{1}{\sqrt{2}}, & f = 0; \\ 1, & f > 0; \end{cases} \text{ and } 0 \leq i, j \leq 7.$$

(4.4)

Here is another way to interpret the results of Equation (4.4). Imagine a large group of points in three dimensions. If the group is large, we can think of it as a cloud. If the points are not randomly distributed in space, the cloud will not be spherical, but will have some complex shape. As we move around the cloud and look at it from various directions, we may find some directions where it looks flat. We select one such direction and rotate the cloud and the direction such that the direction will end up in the xy plane. Most of our points are now either in the xy plane or very close to it. Their z coordinates are either zero or very small. We can consider those points as two-dimensional (or very close to it). By rotating the points, we have effectively reduced the entire group from three to two dimensions.

We now interpret the 64 pixels p_{ij} of a data unit as eight vectors of eight numbers each. Each vector can be considered a point in eight-dimensional space. We interpret the DCT as a *rotation* in eight-dimensional space, which reduces the points to a lower dimension. After the rotation, many of the coordinates will be zero, or very small numbers.

The decoder works by computing the inverse DCT (IDCT).

$$p_{xy} = \frac{1}{4} \sum_{i=0}^{7} \sum_{j=0}^{7} C_i C_j G_{ij} \cos\left(\frac{(2x+1)i\pi}{16}\right) \cos\left(\frac{(2y+1)j\pi}{16}\right),$$

$$\text{where } C_f = \begin{cases} \frac{1}{\sqrt{2}}, & f = 0; \\ 1, & f > 0. \end{cases}$$

(4.5)

It takes the 64 quantized DCT results and calculates 64 pixels p_{xy}. If the QCs are the right ones, the new 64 pixels will be very similar to the original ones. Mathematically, the DCT is a one-to-one mapping of 64-point vectors from the image domain to the frequency domain. The IDCT is the reverse mapping. If the DCT and IDCT could be calculated with infinite precision and if the DCT coefficients were not quantized, the original 64 pixels could be exactly reconstructed.

4.2.3 Practical DCT

Equation (4.4) can be coded directly in any higher-level language. However, several improvements are possible, which speed it up considerably. Since this equation is the "heart" of JPEG, its fast calculation is essential. Here are some ideas.

1. Regardless of the image size, only 64 cosine functions are involved. They can be precomputed once and used repeatedly to calculate all the 8×8 data units. Calculating the expression

$$p_{xy} \cos\left(\frac{(2x+1)i\pi}{16}\right) \cos\left(\frac{(2y+1)j\pi}{16}\right)$$

now amounts to performing two multiplications. The double sum of (4.4) thus requires $64 \times 2 = 128$ multiplications and 63 additions.

2. A little algebraic tinkering shows that the double sum of (4.4) can be written as the matrix product $\mathbf{CPC}^T$, where $\mathbf{P}$ is the 8×8 matrix of the pixels, $\mathbf{C}$ is the matrix defined by

$$C_{ij} = \begin{cases} \frac{1}{\sqrt{8}}, & i = 0, \\ \frac{1}{2} \cos\left(\frac{(2j+1)i\pi}{16}\right), & i > 0, \end{cases}$$

and $\mathbf{C}^T$ is the transpose of $\mathbf{C}$.

(The product of two matrices $\mathbf{A}_{mp}$ and $\mathbf{B}_{pn}$ is a matrix $\mathbf{C}_{mn}$ defined by

$$C_{ij} = \sum_{k=1}^{p} a_{ik} b_{kj}.$$

For other properties of matrices, see Appendix D or any text on linear algebra.)

Calculating one matrix element of the product $\mathbf{CP}$ thus requires eight multiplications and seven (but for simplicity let's say eight) additions. Multiplying the two 8×8 matrices $\mathbf{C}$ and $\mathbf{P}$ requires $64 \times 8 = 8^3$ multiplications and the same number of additions. Multiplying the product $\mathbf{CP}$ by $\mathbf{C}^T$ requires the same number of operations, so the DCT of one 8×8 data unit requires 2×8^3 multiplications (and the same number of additions). Assuming that the entire image consists of $n \times n$ pixels, and that $n = 8q$, there are $q \times q$ data units, so the DCT of all the data units requires $2q^2 8^3$ multiplications (and the same number of additions). In comparison, performing one DCT for the entire image would require $2n^3 = 2q^3 8^3 = (2q^2 8^3)q$ operations. By dividing the image into data units we reduce the number of multiplications (and also of additions) by a factor of q. Unfortunately, q cannot be too large since that would mean very small data units.

We should remember that a color image consists of three components (normally RGB, but usually converted to YCbCr or YPbPr). Each is DC-transformed separately, bringing the total number of arithmetic operations to $3 \times 2q^2 8^3 = 3,072q^2$. For a 512×512-pixel image, this would be $3,072 \times 64^2 = 12,582,912$ multiplications (and the same number of additions).

3. Another way to speed up the DCT is to perform all the arithmetic operations on fixed-point (scaled integer), rather than floating-point, numbers. Operations on fixed-point numbers require (somewhat) sophisticated programming techniques but are considerably faster than floating-point operations.

4.2.4 Examples

Here are some examples of the results of applying the DCT to several data units. All the computations were done by the *Mathematica*™ code below (with different pixel values and different accuracies).

```
Clear[Pixl, G];
Cr[i_]:=If[i==0, 1/Sqrt[2], 1];
DCT[i_,j_]:={(1/4)Cr[i]Cr[j]Sum[Pixl[[x+1,y+1]]
          Cos[(2x+1)i Pi/16]Cos[(2y+1)j Pi/16],
  {x,0,7,1}, {y,0,7,1}]};
Pixl={{128,10,10,10,10,10,10,10},{10,128,10,10,10,10,10,10},
{10,10,128,10,10,10,10,10},{10,10,10,128,10,10,10,10},
 {10,10,10,10,128,10,10,10},{10,10,10,10,10,128,10,10},
 {10,10,10,10,10,10,128,10},{10,10,10,10,10,10,10,128}};
G=Table[N[DCT[m,n]], {m,0,7} ,{n,0,7}];
TableForm[SetAccuracy[G,2]]
```

1. A data unit with all 64 pixels set to 128 (corresponding to a flat surface) produces a DCT matrix with a DC coefficient of 1,024 and 63 AC coefficients of zero.

2. A data unit with vertical stripes (corresponding to a periodic surface) is transformed into a matrix with an upper nonzero row (Table 4.3).

3. A data unit with horizontal stripes is transformed into a matrix with a left nonzero column (Table 4.4).

4. Pixels with values 128 along the main diagonal produce a diagonal DCT matrix (Table 4.5).

5. Random pixels in the range 0–128, generated by

$$\texttt{Pixl-Tablo[128Random[],\{8\},\{8\}]}$$

(pixels shown in Table 4.6) produce a DCT matrix with all nonzero elements (Table 4.7), showing that it is harder to reconstruct such an irregular surface, but even here it is easy to see how they generally get smaller toward the bottom right corner.

6. Random pixels in the range 130–150, (corresponding to a flat, crinkled surface) generated by

$$\texttt{Pixl=Table[SetAccuracy[130+20Random[],0],\{8\},\{8\}]}$$

again produce a DCT matrix with all nonzero elements (Table 4.8), but here it is easy to see how very few coefficients dominate.

4.2.5 Quantization

After each 8×8 matrix of DCT coefficients G_{ij} is calculated, it is quantized. This is the step where the information loss (except for some unavoidable loss because of finite precision calculations in other steps) occurs. Each number in the DCT coefficients matrix is divided by the corresponding number from the particular "quantization table" used, and the result is rounded to the nearest integer. As has already been mentioned, three such tables are needed, for the three color components. The JPEG standard allows for up to four tables, and the user can select any of the four for quantizing each color component. The 64 numbers comprising each quantization table are all JPEG parameters. In principle they can all be specified and fine-tuned by the user for maximum compression. In practice few users have the time or expertise to experiment with so many parameters, so JPEG software normally uses the two approaches below:

1. Default quantization tables. One such table, for the luminance (grayscale) component, is the result of many experiments performed by the JPEG committee. It has been included in the draft JPEG standard part 1 and is reproduced here as Table 4.10. It is easy to see how the QCs in the table generally grow as we move from the upper left corner to the bottom right one. This is how JPEG reduces the DCT coefficients with high spatial frequencies.

2. A simple quantization table Q is computed, based on one parameter R supplied by the user. A simple expression such as $Q_{ij} = 1 + (i + j) \times R$ guarantees that QCs start small at the upper left corner and get bigger toward the bottom right corner.

Example: After dividing the 64 DCT coefficients of Table 4.7 by the quantization factors of Table 4.10 and rounding to the nearest integer, most AC coefficients are zeros (this is Table 4.11a, but remember that this is a contrived example of random pixels). An even more drastic behavior is shown in Table 4.11b, which displays the results of quantizing the 64 DCT coefficients of Table 4.8 by the QCs

10	128	10	10	128	10	10	128
10	128	10	10	128	10	10	128
10	128	10	10	128	10	10	128
10	128	10	10	128	10	10	128
10	128	10	10	128	10	10	128
10	128	10	10	128	10	10	128
10	128	10	10	128	10	10	128
10	128	10	10	128	10	10	128

434.	−57.47	63.86	−78.6	118.	−395.14	−154.17	38.4
0.	0.	0.	0.	0.	0.	0.	0.
0.	0.	0.	0.	0.	0.	0.	0.
0.	0.	0.	0.	0.	0.	0.	0.
0.	0.	0.	0.	0.	0.	0.	0.
0.	0.	0.	0.	0.	0.	0.	0.
0.	0.	0.	0.	0.	0.	0.	0.
0.	0.	0.	0.	0.	0.	0.	0.

Table 4.3: Vertical Stripes of Pixels.

10	10	10	10	10	10	10	10		434.	0.	0.	0.	0.	0.	0.	0.
128	128	128	128	128	128	128	128		−57.47	0.	0.	0.	0.	0.	0.	0.
10	10	10	10	10	10	10	10		63.86	0.	0.	0.	0.	0.	0.	0.
10	10	10	10	10	10	10	10		−78.6	0.	0.	0.	0.	0.	0.	0.
128	128	128	128	128	128	128	128		118.	0.	0.	0.	0.	0.	0.	0.
10	10	10	10	10	10	10	10		−395.14	0.	0.	0.	0.	0.	0.	0.
10	10	10	10	10	10	10	10		−154.17	0.	0.	0.	0.	0.	0.	0.
128	128	128	128	128	128	128	128		38.4	0.	0.	0.	0.	0.	0.	0.

Table 4.4: Horizontal Stripes of Pixels.

128	10	10	10	10	10	10	10		198.	0.	0.	0.	0.	0.	0.	0.
10	128	10	10	10	10	10	10		0.	118.	0.	0.	0.	0.	0.	0.
10	10	128	10	10	10	10	10		0.	0.	118.	0.	0.	0.	0.	0.
10	10	10	128	10	10	10	10		0.	0.	0.	118.	0.	0.	0.	0.
10	10	10	10	128	10	10	10		0.	0.	0.	0.	118.	0.	0.	0.
10	10	10	10	10	128	10	10		0.	0.	0.	0.	0.	118.	0.	0.
10	10	10	10	10	10	128	10		0.	0.	0.	0.	0.	0.	118.	0.
10	10	10	10	10	10	10	128		0.	0.	0.	0.	0.	0.	0.	118.

Table 4.5: A Diagonal Data Unit.

87.0786	64.4845	116.92	32.5291	51.4957	69.0415	116.617	71.904
84.4433	22.6334	71.2894	120.229	22.9243	53.2736	2.883	3.93644
72.4648	50.0736	103.744	0.103997	92.8995	124.246	59.1829	65.916
37.1069	125.542	113.893	73.1882	112.976	125.698	72.9573	97.6729
103.228	61.6884	84.5332	102.735	66.4958	109.423	32.2806	124.653
28.5424	118.875	25.5255	6.89471	78.9631	118.793	34.8613	4.75396
9.35065	22.1543	65.8646	103.447	1.18117	8.22679	31.2366	1.22152
121.952	37.2349	7.53621	99.5506	26.9121	26.4397	18.6029	45.1664

Table 4.6: A Highly Random Data Unit.

505.96	40.49	−29.3	13.94	−17.98	0.31	55.43	−30.16
77.14	−18.92	8.47	−0.92	−43.69	−1.03	44.39	57.22
−98.05	45.46	24.19	−14.92	38.26	104.08	−28.42	7.68
−4.99	−6.39	4.98	−0.71	−41.85	−10.51	−21.22	−3.35
103.43	−20.83	52.65	−21.53	35.92	−0.96	1.72	1.68
14.27	−39.92	−12.99	−35.13	−79.2	−21.92	−28.64	51.13
28.56	−29.91	46.51	82.37	−51.87	−74.69	0.29	44.55
3.6	−20.38	28.19	−25.66	29.47	40.77	45.77	23.52

Table 4.7: The DCT of Table 4.6.

136	131	135	139	135	138	139	145	1118	6	5	−6	7	4	−1	−5
139	146	132	146	135	133	138	134	−2	0	4	5	7	−5	−7	2
148	145	140	144	148	132	134	149	−10	−7	−5	−12	−2	6	2	−7
149	145	142	132	137	137	139	143	−4	−8	−3	3	−4	6	2	−3
149	140	132	139	150	146	145	130	−3	−4	4	11	0	0	4	6
141	137	144	145	131	133	134	149	3	−4	3	−6	−7	−2	7	2
132	143	146	146	133	146	144	135	0	−2	6	−11	15	−3	8	4
139	135	143	144	132	134	135	143	7	−3	−10	12	0	−1	−4	3

Table 4.8: A Slightly Random Data Unit and Its DCT Coefficient Matrix.

of Table 4.10. Of the 64 coefficients, only the first one is nonzero. It's hard to believe that anything resembling the original data unit could be reconstructed from a single DCT coefficient!

▶ **Exercise 4.3:** What is the result of applying the inverse DCT to the quantized coefficients of Table 4.11b?

The answer to exercise 4.3 shows that the quantization matrix of Table 4.10 is not always the right one. To get a better reconstruction of the original data unit, Table 4.8, we tried a quantization table based on the expression $Quant(i, j) = 1 + (i + j) \times R$. Selecting $R = 2$ has produced the quantization coefficients of Table 4.12a and the quantized data unit of Table 4.12b. This table has only four nonzero coefficients, but these are enough to reconstruct the original data unit to a high precision (Table 4.9).

137	139	141	140	136	135	137	139
139	140	141	140	138	137	138	139
142	141	140	140	141	141	140	139
145	142	139	140	143	143	141	138
145	142	139	140	143	143	141	138
142	141	140	140	141	141	140	139
139	140	141	140	138	137	138	139
137	139	141	140	136	135	137	139

Table 4.9: Restored Data Unit of Table 4.8.

Comparing the restored data unit in Table 4.9 to the original pixels of Table 4.8 shows that the maximum difference between an original pixel and a restored one is 10. Selecting $R < 2$ can improve the reconstruction significantly while adding just a few nonzero AC coefficients to the quantized data unit.

▶ **Exercise 4.4:** Repeat this example for the case R=1.

If the quantization is done right, very few nonzero numbers will be left in the DCT coefficients matrix, and they will typically be concentrated at the upper left corner. These numbers are the output of JPEG but they are further compressed before being written on the output stream. In the JPEG literature this compression is called "entropy coding" and Section 4.2.6 shows in detail how it is done. Three techniques are used by entropy coding to compress the 8×8 matrix of integers:

1. The 64 numbers are collected by scanning the matrix in zig-zags (Figure 1.8b). This produces a string of 64 numbers that starts with some nonzeros and typically ends with many consecutive zeros. Only the nonzero numbers are output (after further compressing them) and are followed by a special end-of block (EOB) code. This way there is no need to output the trailing zeros (we can say that the EOB is the run-length encoding of all the trailing zeros). The interested reader should also see Section 5.4 for other methods to compress binary strings with many consecutive zeros.

▶ **Exercise 4.5:** What is the zig-zag sequence of the 64 coefficients of Table 4.12b?

16	11	10	16	24	40	51	61
12	12	14	19	26	58	60	55
14	13	16	24	40	57	69	56
14	17	22	29	51	87	80	62
18	22	37	56	68	109	103	77
24	35	55	64	81	104	113	92
49	64	78	87	103	121	120	101
72	92	95	98	112	100	103	99

Table 4.10: Sample Quantization Table.

32	4	−3	0	0	0	1	0
6	−2	0	0	−2	0	0	1
−7	3	2	0	0	2	0	0
0	0	0	0	0	0	0	0
6	0	1	0	0	0	0	0
0	−1	0	0	0	0	0	0
0	0	0	0	0	0	0	0
0	0	0	0	0	0	0	0

(a)

70	0	0	0	0	0	0	0
0	0	0	0	0	0	0	0
0	0	0	0	0	0	0	0
0	0	0	0	0	0	0	0
0	0	0	0	0	0	0	0
0	0	0	0	0	0	0	0
0	0	0	0	0	0	0	0
0	0	0	0	0	0	0	0

(b)

Table 4.11: (a): The Quantized Coefficients of Table 4.7. (b): Those of Table 4.8.

1	3	5	7	9	11	13	15
3	5	7	9	11	13	15	17
5	7	9	11	13	15	17	19
7	9	11	13	15	17	19	21
9	11	13	15	17	19	21	23
11	13	15	17	19	21	23	25
13	15	17	19	21	23	25	27
15	17	19	21	23	25	27	29

(a)

1118	2	0	0	0	0	0	0
0	0	0	0	0	0	0	0
-2	0	0	-1	0	0	0	0
0	0	0	0	0	0	0	0
0	0	0	0	0	0	0	0
0	0	0	0	0	0	0	0
0	0	0	0	0	0	0	0
0	0	0	0	0	0	0	0

(b)

Table 4.12: (a): The Quantization Table $1 + (i + j) \times 2$. (b): Quantized Coefficients Produced by (a).

▶ **Exercise 4.6:** Suggest a practical way of writing a loop that traverses an 8×8 matrix in zig-zag.

    2. The nonzero numbers are compressed using Huffman coding (Section 4.2.6).

    3. The first of those numbers (the DC coefficient, page 171) is treated differently from the others (the AC coefficients).

4.2.6 Coding

We first discuss point 3 above. Each 8×8 matrix of quantized DCT coefficients contains one DC coefficient [at position $(0,0)$, the top left corner] and 63 AC co-efficients. The DC coefficient is a measure of the average value of the 64 original pixels, comprising the data unit. Experience shows that in a continuous-tone image, adjacent data units of pixels are normally correlated in the sense that the average values of the pixels in adjacent data units are close. We already know that the DC coefficient of a data unit is a multiple of the average of the 64 pixels constituting the unit. This implies that the DC coefficients of adjacent data units don't differ much. JPEG outputs the first one (encoded), followed by *differences* (also encoded) of the DC coefficients of consecutive data units. The concept of differencing is discussed in Section 1.3.1.

    Example: If the first three 8×8 data units of an image have quantized DC coefficients of 1118, 1114, and 1119, then the JPEG output for the first data unit is 1118 (Huffman encoded, see below) followed by the 63 (encoded) AC coefficients of that data unit. The output for the second data unit will be $1114 - 1118 = -4$ (also Huffman encoded), followed by the 63 (encoded) AC coefficients of that data unit, and the output for the third data unit will be $1119 - 1114 = 5$ (also Huffman encoded), again followed by the 63 (encoded) AC coefficients of that data unit. This complex handling of the DC coefficients is worth the extra trouble since the differences are small.

    Coding the DC differences is done by using Table 4.13, so first here are a few words about this table. Each row has a row number (on the left), the unary code for the row (on the right), and several columns in between. Each row contains greater numbers (and also more numbers) than its predecessor but not the numbers contained in previous rows. Row i contains the range of integers $[-(2^i-1), +(2^i-1)]$ but is missing the middle range $[-(2^{i-1}-1), +(2^{i-1}-1)]$. The rows thus get very long, which means that a simple two-dimensional array is not a good data structure for this table. In fact, there is no need to store all these integers in any data structure since the program can figure out where in the table any given integer x is supposed to reside by analyzing the bits of x.

    The first DC coefficient to be encoded in our example is 1118. It resides in row 11 column 930 of the table (column numbering starts at zero), so it is encoded as 111111111110|01110100010 (the unary code for row 11, followed by the 11-bit binary value of 930). The second DC difference is -4. It resides in row 3 column 3 of Table 4.13, so it is encoded as 1110|011 (the unary code for row 3, followed by the 3-bit binary value of 3).

▶ **Exercise 4.7:** How is the third DC difference, 5, encoded?

    Point 2 above has to do with the precise way the 63 AC coefficients of a data unit are compressed. It uses a combination of RLE and either Huffman or arithmetic coding. The idea is that the sequence of AC coefficients normally contains just a few nonzero numbers, with runs of zeros between them, and with a long run of trailing zeros. For each nonzero number x, the encoder: (1) finds the number Z of consecutive zeros preceding x; (2) finds x in Table 4.13 and prepares its row and column numbers (R and C); (3) the pair (R, Z) [that's (R,Z), not (R,C)] is used as row and column numbers for Table 4.14; and (4) the Huffman code found in that position in the table is concatenated to C (where C is written as an R-bit number) and the result is (finally) the code emitted by the JPEG encoder for the AC coefficient x and all the consecutive zeros preceding it.

0:	0										0
1:	-1	1									10
2:	-3	-2	2	3							110
3:	-7	-6	-5	-4	4	5	6	7			1110
4:	-15	-14	...	-9	-8	8	9	10 ...	15		11110
5:	-31	-30	-29	...	-17	-16	16	17 ...	31		111110
6:	-63	-62	-61	...	-33	-32	32	33 ...	63		1111110
7:	-127	-126	-125	...	-65	-64	64	65 ...	127		11111110
⋮				⋮						
14:	-16383	-16382	-16381	...	-8193	-8192	8192	8193 ...	16383	111111111111110
15:	-32767	-32766	-32765	...	-16385	-16384	16384	16385 ...	32767	1111111111111110
16:	32768									1111111111111111

Table 4.13: Coding the Differences of DC Coefficients.

The Huffman codes in Table 4.14 are not specified by the JPEG standard, and each codec has to decide what codes to use. The standard just says that up to four such tables can be used by the codec, except that the baseline mode can only use two such tables. The actual codes in Table 4.14 are thus hypothetical but the code at position (0,0) is the EOB, and the code at position (0,15) is ZRL, the code emitted for 15 consecutive zeros when the number of consecutive zeros exceeds 15.

As an example consider the sequence

$$1118, 2, 0, -2, \underbrace{0, \ldots, 0}_{12}, -1, 0, \ldots$$

of exercise 4.5. The first AC coefficient 2 has no zeros preceding it, so Z = 0. It is found in Table 4.13 in row 2, column 2, so R = 2 and C = 2. The Huffman code in position (R, Z) = (2, 0) of Table 4.14 is 01, so the final code emitted for 2 is 01|10. The next nonzero coefficient, -2, has one zero preceding it, so Z = 1. It is found in Table 4.13 in row 2, column 1, so R = 2 and C = 1. The Huffman code in position (R, Z) = (2, 1) of Table 4.14 is 11011, so the final code emitted for 2 is 11011|01.

▶ **Exercise 4.8:** What code is emitted for the last nonzero AC coefficient, -1?

Finally, the sequence of trailing zeros is encoded as 1010 (EOB), so the output for the above sequence of AC coefficients is 0110110111011101011010. We saw earlier that the DC coefficient is encoded as 111111111110|1110100010, so the final output for the entire 64-pixel data unit is the 45-bit number

$$111111111110011101000100110110111011101011010.$$

These 45 bits encode one color component of the 64 pixels of a data unit. Let's assume that the other two color components are also encoded into 45-bit numbers. If each pixel originally consists of 24 bits then this corresponds to a compression factor of $64 \times 24/(45 \times 3) \approx 11.38$; very impressive!

(Notice that the DC coefficient of 1118 has contributed 23 of the 45 bits. Subsequent data units code differences of their DC coefficient, which may take less than 10 bits instead of 23. They may feature much higher compression factors as a result.)

The same tables 4.13 and 4.14 used by the encoder should, of course, be used by the decoder. The tables may be predefined and used by a JPEG codec as defaults, or they may be specifically calculated for a given image in a special pass preceding the actual compression. The JPEG standard does not specify any code tables, so any JPEG codec must use its own.

R Z:	0	1	...	15
0:	1010			11111111001(ZRL)
1:	00	1100	...	1111111111110101
2:	01	11011	...	1111111111110110
3:	100	1111001	...	1111111111110111
4:	1011	111110110	...	1111111111111000
5:	11010	11111110110	...	1111111111111001
⋮	⋮			

Table 4.14: Coding AC Coefficients.

Some JPEG variants use a particular version of arithmetic coding, which is specified in the JPEG standard. This version of arithmetic coding is adaptive, so it does not need Tables 4.13 and 4.14. It adapts its behavior to the image statistics as it goes along. Using arithmetic coding may produce 5–10% better compression than Huffman for a typical continuous-tone image. However, it is more complex to implement than Huffman coding, so in practice it is rare to find a JPEG codec that uses it.

4.2.7 Lossless Mode

The lossless mode of JPEG uses differencing (Section 1.3.1) to reduce the values of pixels before they are compressed. This particular form of differencing is called *predicting*. The values of some near-neighbors of a pixel are subtracted from the pixel to get a small number, which is then compressed further using Huffman or arithmetic coding. Figure 4.15a shows a pixel X and three neighbor pixels A, B and C. Figure 4.15b shows eight possible ways (predictions) to combine the values of the three neighbors. In the lossless mode, the user can select one of these predictions, and the encoder then uses it to combine the three neighbor pixels and subtract the combination from the value of X. The result is normally a small number, which is then entropy-coded in a way very similar to that described for the DC coefficient in Section 4.2.6.

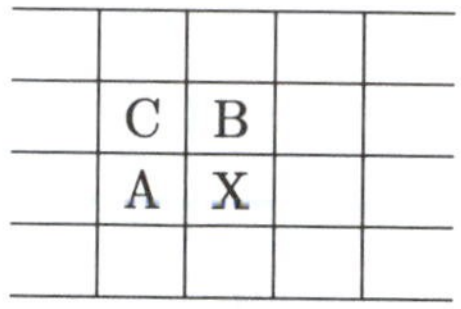

	Selection value	Prediction
	0	no prediction
	1	A
	2	B
	3	C
	4	$A + B - C$
	5	$A + ((B - C)/2)$
	6	$B + ((A - C)/2)$
	7	$(A + B)/2$

$$\begin{array}{|c|c|c|c|}\hline & & & \\ \hline C & B & & \\ \hline A & X & & \\ \hline & & & \\ \hline \end{array}$$

(a)   (b)

Figure 4.15: Pixel Prediction in the Lossless Mode.

Predictor 0 is used only in the hierarchical mode of JPEG. Predictors 1, 2 and 3 are called "one-dimensional." Predictors 4, 5, 6 and 7 are "two-dimensional."

4.2.8 JFIF

It has been mentioned earlier that JPEG is a compression method, not a graphics file format, which is why it does not specify image features such as pixel aspect ratio, color space, or interleaving of bitmap rows. This is where JFIF comes in.

JFIF (JPEG File Interchange Format) is a graphics file format that makes it possible to exchange JPEG-compressed images between different computers. The main features of JFIF are the use of the YCbCr triple-component color space for color images (only one component for gray scale images) and the use of a *marker* to specify features missing from JPEG, such as image resolution, aspect ratio, and features that are application-specific.

The JFIF marker (called the APP0 marker) starts with the zero-terminated string "JFIF". Following this, there is pixel information and other specifications (see below). Following this, there may be additional segments specifying JFIF extensions. A JFIF extension contains more platform-specific information about the image.

Each extension starts with the zero-terminated string "JFXX", followed by a 1-byte code identifying the extension. An extension may contain application-specific information, in which case it starts with a different string, not "JFIF" or "JFXX" but something that identifies the specific application or its maker.

The format of the first segment of an APP0 marker is as follows:

1. APP0 marker (4 bytes): "FFD8FFE0".

2. Length (2 bytes): Total length of marker, including the 2 bytes of the "length" field but excluding the APP0 marker itself (field 1).

3. Identifier (5 bytes): $4A46494600_{16}$. This is the "JFIF" string that identifies the APP0 marker.

4. Version (2 bytes): Example: 0102_{16} specifies version 1.02.

5. Units (1 byte): Units for the X and Y densities. 0, no units; the Xdensity and Ydensity fields specify the pixel aspect ratio. 1, Xdensity and Ydensity are dots per inch. 2, they are dots per cm.

6. Xdensity (2 bytes), Ydensity (2 bytes): Horizontal and vertical pixel densities (both should be nonzero).

7. Xthumbnail (1 byte), Ythumbnail (1 byte): Thumbnail horizontal and vertical pixel counts.

8. (RGB)n (3n bytes): Packed (24-bit) RGB values for the thumbnail pixels. n = Xthumbnail × Ythumbnail.

The syntax of the JFIF extension APP0 marker segment is:

1. APP0 marker.

2. Length (2 bytes): Total length of marker, including the 2 bytes of the "length" field but excluding the APP0 marker itself (field 1).

3. Identifier (5 bytes): $4A46585800_{16}$ This is the "JFXX" string identifying an extension.

4. Extension code (1 byte): 10_{16} = Thumbnail coded using JPEG. 11_{16} = Thumbnail coded using 1 byte/pixel (monochromatic). 13_{16} = Thumbnail coded using 3 bytes/pixel (eight colors).

5. Extension data (variable): This field depends on the particular extension.

Bibliography

Blinn, J. F. (1993) "What's the Deal with the DCT," *IEEE Computer Graphics and Applications* pp. 78–83, July.

Pennebaker, William B., and Joan L. Mitchell (1992) *JPEG Still Image Data Compression Standard*, Van Nostrand Reinhold.

Rao, K. R., and P. Yip (1990) *Discrete Cosine Transform—Algorithms, Advantages, Applications*, London, Academic Press.

Wallace, Gregory K. (1991) "The JPEG Still Image Compression Standard," *Communications of the ACM* **34**(4):30–44, April.

Zhang, Manyun (1990) *The JPEG and Image Data Compression Algorithms* (Dissertation).

> She had just succeeded in curving it down into a graceful zigzag, and was going to dive in among the leaves, which she found to be nothing but the tops of the trees under which she had been wandering, when a sharp hiss made her draw back in a hurry.
> —Lewis Carroll, *Alice in Wonderland*

4.3 Progressive Image Compression

Most modern image compression methods are either progressive or optionally so. Progressive compression is an attractive choice when compressed images are transmitted over a communications line and are decompressed and viewed in real time. When such an image is received and decompressed, the decoder can very quickly display the entire image in a low-quality format, and then improve the display quality as more and more of the image is being received and decompressed. A user watching the image develop on the screen can normally recognize most of the image features after only 5–10% of it have been decompressed.

This should be compared to raster-scan image compression. When an image is raster scanned and compressed, a user normally cannot tell much about the image when only 5–10% of it has been decompressed and displayed. Since images are supposed to be viewed by humans, progressive compression makes sense even in cases where it is slower or less efficient than non-progressive.

Perhaps a good way to think of progressive image compression is to imagine that the encoder compresses the most important image information first, then compresses less important information and appends it to the compressed stream, and so on. This explains why all progressive image compression methods have a natural lossy option. Simply stop compressing at a certain point. The user can control the amount of loss by means of a parameter that tells the encoder how soon to stop the progressive encoding process. The sooner encoding is stopped, the better the compression ratio and the higher the data loss.

Progressive image compression has already been mentioned, in connection with JPEG (page 166). JPEG uses DCT to break the image up into its spatial frequency components, and it compresses the low-frequency components first. The decoder can therefore display these parts quickly, and it is these low-frequency parts that contain the general image information. The high-frequency parts contain image details. JPEG thus encodes spatial frequency data progressively.

It is useful to think of progressive decoding as the process of improving image features with time, and this can be done in three ways:

1. Encode spatial frequency data progressively. An observer watching such an image being decoded sees the image changing from blurred to sharp. Methods that work this way typically feature medium speed encoding and slow decoding.

2. Start with a gray image and add colors or shades of gray to it. An observer watching such an image being decoded will see all the image details from the beginning, and will see them improve as more color is continuously added to them. Vector quantization methods use this kind of progressive compression. Such a method normally features slow encoding and fast decoding.

3. Encode the image in layers, where early layers consist of a few large, low-resolution pixels, followed by later layers with smaller, higher-resolution pixels. When a person watches such an image being decoded, they will see more details added to the image with time. Such a method thus adds details (or resolution) to the image as it is being decompressed. This way of progressively encoding an image is called *pyramid coding*. Most progressive methods use this principle, so this section discusses general ideas for implementing pyramid coding.

Assume that the image size is $2^n \times 2^n = 4^n$ pixels. The simplest method that comes to mind, when trying to do progressive compression, is to calculate each pixel of layer $i-1$ as the average of a group of 2×2 pixels of layer i. Thus layer n is the entire image, layer $n-1$ contains $2^{n-1} \times 2^{n-1} = 4^{n-1}$ large pixels of size 2×2, and so on, down to layer 1, with $4^{n-n} = 1$ large pixel, representing the entire image. If the image isn't too large, all the layers can be saved in memory. The pixels are then written on the compressed stream in reverse order, starting with layer 1. The single pixel of layer 1 is the "parent" of the four pixels of layer 2, each of which is the parent of four pixels in layer 3, and so on. The total number of pixels in the pyramid is

$$4^0 + 4^1 + \cdots + 4^{n-1} + 4^n = (4^{n+1} - 1)/3 \approx 4^n(4/3) \approx 1.33 \times 4^n = 1.33(2^n \times 2^n),$$

which is 33% more than the original number!

A simple way to bring the total number of pixels in the pyramid down to 4^n is to include only three of the four pixels of a group in layer i, and to compute the value of the 4th pixel using the parent of the group (from the preceding layer, $i-1$) and its three siblings. A small complication with this method is the pixel size. Assume that pixels are represented by 8 bits. Adding four 8-bit pixels produces a 10-bit number. Dividing it by four, to create the average, reduces the sum back to an 8-bit number but, if we want to use the average to calculate one of the pixels of layer i, we should keep it at full precision (10 bits in our example).

▶ **Exercise 4.9:** Show that the sum of four n-bit numbers is an $n+2$-bit number.

A better method is to let the parent of a group help in calculating the values of its four children. This can be done by calculating the differences between the parent and its children, and writing the differences (suitably coded) in layer i of the compressed stream. The decoder decodes the differences, then uses the parent from layer $i-1$ to compute the values of the four pixels. Either Huffman or arithmetic coding can be used to encode the differences. If all the layers are calculated and saved in memory, then the distribution of difference values can be found and used to achieve the best statistical compression.

If there is no room in memory for all the layers, a simple adaptive model can be implemented. It starts by assigning a count of 1 to every difference value (to avoid the zero-probability problem). When a particular difference is calculated, it is assigned a probability and is encoded according to its count, and its count is then updated. It is a good idea to update the counts by incrementing them by a value > 1, since this way the original counts of 1 become insignificant very quickly.

Some improvement can be achieved if the parent is used to help calculate the values of three child pixels, and then these three plus the parent are used to calculate the value of the fourth pixel of the group. If the four pixels of a group are a, b, c, and d, then their average is $v = (a + b + c + d)/4$. The average becomes part of layer $i-1$, and layer i need only contain the three differences $k = a - b$, $l = b - c$, and $m = c - d$. Once the decoder has read and decoded the three differences, it can use their values, together with the value of v from the previous layer to compute the values of the four pixels of the group. Dividing v by 4 still causes the loss of 2 bits, but this 2-bit quantity can be isolated before the division, and retained by encoding it separately, following the three differences.

The improvements mentioned above are based on the well-known fact that small numbers are easy to compress (page 16).

The parent pixel of a group does not have to be its average. One alternative is to select the maximum (or the minimum) pixel of a group as the parent. This has the advantage that the parent is identical to one of the pixels in the group. The encoder has to encode just three pixels in each group, and the decoder decodes three pixels (or differences) and uses the parent as the fourth pixel, to complete the group. When encoding consecutive groups in a layer, the encoder should alternate between selecting the maximum and the minimum as parents, since always selecting the same creates progressive layers that are either too dark or too bright.

Selecting the median of a group is a little slower than selecting the maximum or the minimum, but it improves the appearance of the layers during progressive decompression. In general, the median of a sequence $(a_1, a_2, \ldots, a_n)$ is an element a_i such that half the elements (or very close to half) are smaller than a_i and the other half, bigger. If the four pixels of a group satisfy $a < b < c < d$, then either b or c can be considered the median pixel of the group. The main advantage of selecting the median as the group's parent is that it tends to smooth large differences in pixel values because of one, extreme pixel. In the group 1, 2, 3, 100, e.g., selecting 2 or 3 as the parent is much more representative than selecting the average. Finding the median of four pixels requires a few comparisons, but calculating the average requires a division by 4 (or, alternatively, a right shift).

Once the median has been selected and encoded as part of layer $i - 1$, the remaining three pixels can be encoded in layer i by encoding their (three) differences, preceded by a 2-bit code telling which of the four is the parent. Another, small advantage of using the median is that, once the decoder reads this 2-bit code, it knows how many of the three pixels are smaller, and how many are bigger than the median. If the code says, e.g., that one pixel is smaller, and the other two are bigger than the median, and the decoder reads a pixel that's smaller than the median, it knows that the next two pixels decoded will be bigger than the median. This knowledge changes the distribution of the differences, and it can be taken advantage of by using three count tables to estimate probabilities when the differences are encoded. One table is used when a pixel is encoded that the decoder will know is bigger than the median. Another table is used to encode pixels that the decoder will know are smaller than the median, and the third table is used for pixels where the decoder will not know in advance their relations to the median. This improves compression by a few percent and is another example of how adding more features to a compression method brings diminishing returns.

Some of the important progressive image compression methods used in practice are described in the rest of this chapter.

4.4 JBIG

No single compression method can efficiently compress every type of data. This is why new, special-purpose methods are being developed all the time. JBIG is one of them. It has been developed specifically for progressive compression of bi-level images. Such images, also called monochromatic or black and white, are common in applications where drawings (technical or artistic), with or without text, need to be saved in a data base and retrieved. The term "progressive compression" means the image is saved in several "layers" in the compressed stream, at higher and higher resolutions. When such an image is decompressed and viewed, the viewer first sees an imprecise, rough image (the first layer) and then better versions of it (later layers). This way, if the image is the wrong one, it can be rejected at an early stage, without having to retrieve and decompress all of it. It should be noted that each high-resolution version uses information from the preceding lower-resolution versions, so there is no duplication of data.

The name JBIG stands for Joint Bi-Level Image Processing Group. This is a group of experts from several international organizations, formed in 1988 to recommend such a standard. The official name of the JBIG method is "ITU-T recommendation T.82." ITU is the International Telecommunications Union (part of the United Nations). JBIG uses multiple arithmetic coding to compress the image, and this part of JBIG, which is discussed below, is separate from the progressive compression part discussed in Section 4.4.1.

One feature of arithmetic coding is that it is easy to separate the statistical model (the table with frequencies and probabilities) from the encoding and decoding operations. It is easy to encode, e.g., the first half of a data stream using one model, and the second half, using another model. This is called multiple arithmetic coding, and it is especially useful in encoding images, since it takes advantage of any local structures that might exist in the image. JBIG uses multiple arithmetic coding with many models, each a two-entry table that gives the probabilities of a white and a black pixel. There are between 1,024 and 4,096 such models, depending on the image resolution used.

A bi-level image is made up of black and white dots called *pixels*. The simplest way to compress such an image using arithmetic coding is to count the frequency of black and white pixels, and compute their probabilities. In practice, however, the probabilities change from region to region in the image, and this fact can be used to achieve better compression. Certain regions, such as the margins of a page, may be completely white, while other regions, such as the center of a complex diagram, or a large, thick rule, may be dominantly or completely black.

Consider an image with 25% black pixels. Its entropy is $-0.25 \log_2 0.25 - 0.75 \log_2 0.75 \approx 0.8113$. The best that we can hope for is to represent each pixel with 0.81 bits instead of the original 1 bit: an 81% compression ratio (or 0.81 bpp). Now assume that we discover that 80% of the image is predominantly white, with just 10% black pixels, and the remaining 20% have 85% black pixels. The entropies of these parts are $-0.1 \log_2 0.1 - 0.9 \log_2 0.9 \approx 0.47$ and $-0.85 \log_2 0.85 - 0.15 \log_2 0.15 \approx 0.61$ so, if we encode each part separately, we can have 0.47 bpp 80% of the time and 0.61 bpp the remaining 20%. On the average this results in 0.498 bpp or a compression ratio of about 50%; much better than 81%!

Let's assume that a white pixel is represented by a 0 and a black one by a 1. In practice we don't know in advance how many black and white pixels exist in each part of the image, so the JBIG encoder stops at every pixel X and examines the ten neighboring pixels above and to the left of X (those that have already been input; the ones below and to the right are still unknown). It interprets the values of those ten pixels as a 10-bit number and uses this number as a pointer to a statistical model, which is then used to encode pixel X. There are $2^{10} = 1,024$ 10-bit numbers, so there should be 1,024 models. Each model is a small table consisting of the probabilities of black and white pixels (just one probability needs be saved in the table, since the probabilities add up to 1).

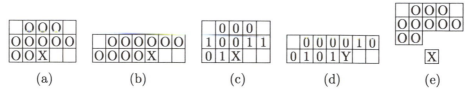

(a)   (b)   (c)   (d)   (e)

Figure 4.16: Three-Line and Two-Line Neighborhoods.

The ten pixels may be taken from a 3-line or from a 2-line neighborhood of pixel X (Figure 4.16a, b). Figure 4.16c shows the 10-bit neighborhood 0001001101, which becomes the pointer 77. The pointer shown in Figure 4.16d for pixel Y is 0000100101 or 37. The ten pixels do not even have to be in the immediate neighborhood of pixel X (Figure 4.16e) but can be located anywhere in the image. This option is useful if the user wants to take advantage of regular or repeating graphical features in the image, such as vertical or horizontal lines, or halftone patterns that repeat throughout the image. The compressed stream should, in such a case, contain extra information that tells the decoder where to place the ten-pixel neighborhood.

When higher-resolution layers are generated later, they use 11- or even 12-bit neighborhoods, so the number of models has to be increased to 2^{11} or 2^{12}.

4.4.1 Progressive Compression

One advantage of the JBIG method is its ability to generate low-resolution versions (layers) of the same image in one compressed stream. The basic idea is to group four high-resolution pixels into one low-resolution pixel, a process called *downsampling*. The only problem is to determine the value (black or white) of that pixel. If all four original pixels have the same value, or even if three are identical, the solution is obvious. When two pixels are black and two are white, we can try one of the following solutions:

1. Create a low-resolution pixel that's always black (or always white). This is a bad solution since it may eliminate important details of the image, making it impossible for an observer to evaluate the image by viewing the low-resolution layer.

2. Assign a random value to the new low-resolution pixel. This solution is also bad since it may add too much noise to the image.

3. Assign a value to the low-resolution pixel that depends on the four high-resolution pixels **and** on some of their nearest neighbors. This solution is used by JBIG. If most neighbors are white, a white low-resolution pixel is created; otherwise a black one is created. Figure 4.17a shows the 12 high-resolution neighboring pixels and the 3 low-resolution ones that are used in making this decision. A, B, and C are three low-resolution pixels whose values have already been determined. Pixels

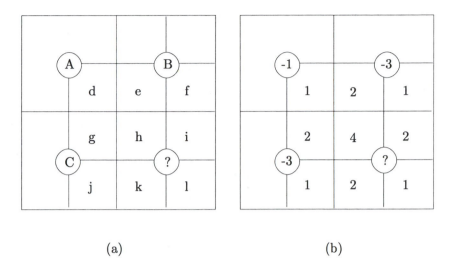

(a)   (b)

Figure 4.17: HiRes and LoRes Pixels.

d, e, f, g, and, j are on top or to the left of the current group of four pixels. Pixel "?" is the low-resolution pixel whose value needs to be determined.

Figure 4.17b shows the weights assigned to the various pixels involved in the determination of pixel "?". The weighted sum of the pixels can also be written as

$$4h + 2(e + g + i + k) + (d + f + j + l) - 3(B + C) - A =$$
$$4h + 2(i + k) + l + (d - A) + 2(g - C) + (j - C) + 2(e - B) + (f - B). \tag{4.6}$$

The second line of Equation (4.6) shows how the value of pixel "?" depends on differences such as $d - A$ (a difference of a high-resolution pixel and the adjacent low-resolution one). Assuming equal probabilities for black and white pixels, the first line of Equation (4.6) can have values between zero (when all 12 pixels are white) and 9 (when all are black), so the rule is to assign pixel "?" the value 1 (black) if expression (4.6) is greater than 4.5 (if it is 5 or more), and the value 0 (white) otherwise (if it is 4 or less). This expression thus acts as a filter that preserves the density of the high-resolution pixels in the low-resolution image.

JBIG also includes exceptions to the above rule in order to preserve edges (132 exceptions), preserve vertical and horizontal lines (420 exceptions), periodic patterns in the image (10 exceptions, for better performance in regions of transition to and from periodic patterns), and dither patterns in the image (12 exceptions which help preserve very low density or very high density dithering, i.e., isolated background or foreground pixels). The last two groups are used to preserve certain shading patterns and also patterns generated by halftoning. Each exception is a 12-bit number. Table 4.18 lists some of the exception patterns.

The pattern of Figure 4.19b was developed in order to preserve thick horizontal, or near-horizontal, lines. A two-pixel wide high-resolution horizontal line, e.g., will result in a low-resolution line whose width alternates between one and two low-resolution pixels. When the upper row of the high-resolution line is scanned, it will

The 10 periodic pattern preservation exceptions are (in hex):

5c7 36d d55 b55 caa aaa c92 692 a38 638.

The 12 dither pattern preservation exceptions are:

fef fd7 f7d f7a 145 142 ebd eba 085 082 028 010.

The 132 edge-preservation exception patterns are:

a0f 60f 40f 20f e07 c07 a07 807 607 407 207 007 a27 627 427 227 e1f 61f e17 c17 a17
617 e0f c0f 847 647 447 247 e37 637 e2f c2f a2f 62f e27 c27 24b e49 c49 a49 849 649
449 249 049 e47 c47 a47 e4d c4d a4d 84d 64d 44d 24d e4b c4b a4b 64b 44b e69 c69
a69 669 469 269 e5b 65b e59 c59 a59 659 ac9 6c9 4c9 2c9 ab6 8b6 e87 c87 a87 687
487 287 507 307 cf8 8f8 ed9 6d9 ecb ccb acb 6cb ec9 cc9 949 749 549 349 b36 336
334 f07 d07 b07 907 707 3b6 bb4 3b4 bb2 3a6 b96 396 d78 578 f49 d49 b49 ff8 df8
5f8 df0 5f0 5e8 dd8 5d8 5d0 db8 fb6 bb6.

Where the 12 bits of each pattern are numbered as in the diagram.

Table 4.18: Some JBIG Exception Patterns.

Figure 4.19 shows three typical exception patterns. A pattern of six zeros and
three ones, as in 4.19a is an example exception, introduced to preserve horizontal
lines. It means that the low-resolution pixel marked "C" should be complemented
(assigned the opposite of its normal value). The normal value of this pixel depends,
of course, on the three low-resolution pixels above it and to the left. Since these
three pixels can have 8 different values, this pattern covers eight exceptions. Reflecting 4.19a about its main diagonal produces a pattern (actually, eight patterns)
that's natural to use as an exception to preserve vertical lines in the original image.
Figure 4.19a thus corresponds to 16 of the 420 line-preservation exceptions.

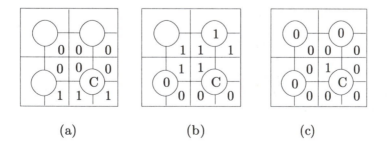

(a)   (b)   (c)

Figure 4.19: Some JBIG Exception Patterns.

result in a row of low-resolution pixels because of Figure 4.19a. When the next high-resolution row is scanned, the two rows of the thick line will generate alternating low-resolution pixels because pattern 4.19b requires a zero in the bottom-left low-resolution pixel in order to complement the bottom-right low-resolution pixel.

Pattern 4.19b leaves two pixels unspecified, so it counts for four patterns. Its reflection is also used, to preserve thick vertical lines, so it counts for 8 of the 420 line-preservation exceptions.

Figure 4.19c complements a low-resolution pixel in cases where there is 1 black high-resolution pixel among 11 white ones. This is common when a grayscale image is converted to black and white by halftoning. This pattern is 1 of the 12 dither preservation exceptions.

The JBIG method for reducing resolution seems complicated—especially since it includes so many exceptions—but is actually simple to implement, and also executes very fast. The decision whether to paint the current low-resolution pixel black or white depends on 12 of its neighboring pixels, 9 high-resolution pixels, and 3 low-resolution ones. Their values are combined into a 12-bit number, which is used as a pointer to a 4,096-entry table. Each entry in the table is one bit, which becomes the value of the current low-resolution pixel. This way, all the exceptions are already lncluded in the table and don't require any special treatment by the program.

Bibliography

Pennebaker, W. B., and J. L. Mitchell (1988) "Probability Estimation for the Q-coder," *IBM Journal of Research and Development* **32**(6):717–726.

Pennebaker, W. B., et al. (1988) "An Overview of the Basic Principles of the Q-coder Adaptive Binary Arithmetic Coder," *IBM J. of Research and Development* **32**(6):737–752.

4.5 Context-Based Image Compression

Most image-compression methods are based on the observation that, for any randomly selected pixel in the image, its near-neighbors tend to have the same value as the pixel. A context-based image compression method generalizes this observation. It is based on the idea that the context of a pixel can be used to predict (estimate the probability of) the pixel.

Such a method compresses an image by scanning it pixel by pixel, examining the context of every pixel, and assigning it a probability depending on how many times the same context was seen in the past. The pixel and its assigned probability are then sent to an arithmetic encoder that does the actual encoding. The methods described here are due to [Langdon 81] and [Moffat 91], and apply to monochromatic (bi-level) images.

The context of a pixel consists of some of its neighbor pixels that have already been seen. The diagram below shows a possible seven-pixel context (the pixels marked P) made up of five pixels above and two on the left of the current pixel X. The pixels marked "?" haven't been input yet, so they cannot be included in the context.

.	.	P	P	P	P	P	.	.
.	.	P	P	X	?	?	?	?

The main idea is to use the values of the seven context pixels as a 7-bit index to a frequency table, and find the number of times a 0 pixel and a 1 pixel were seen in the past with the same context. Here is an example:

·	·	1	0	0	1	1	·	·
·	·	0	1	X	?	?	?	?

Since $1001101_2 = 77$, location 77 of the frequency table is examined. It contains a count of 15 for a 0 pixel and a count of 11, for a 1 pixel. The current pixel is thus assigned probability $15/(15 + 11) \approx 0.58$ if it is 0 and $11/26 \approx 0.42$ if it is 1.

$$
\begin{array}{c}
77 \\
\hline
\cdots\ |\ 15\ |\ \cdots \\
\hline
\cdots\ |\ 11\ |\ \cdots
\end{array}
$$

One of the counts at location 77 is then incremented, depending on what the current pixel is. Figure 4.20 shows ten possible ways to select contexts. They range from a 1-bit, to a 22-bit context. In the latter case, there may be $2^{22} \approx 4.2$ million contexts, most of which will rarely, if ever, occur in the image. Instead of maintaining a huge, mostly empty array, the frequency table can be implemented as a binary search tree or a hash table (Appendix H). For short, 7-bit contexts, the frequency table can be an array, resulting in fast search.

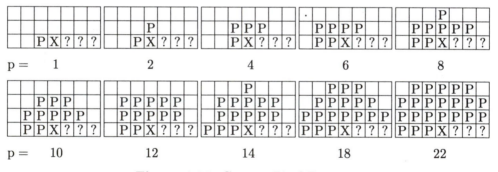

Figure 4.20: Context Pixel Patterns.

Experience shows that longer contexts result in better compression, up to about 12–14 bits. Contexts longer than that result in worse compression, indicating that a pixel in a typical image does not "relate" to distant pixels (correlations between pixels are typically limited to a distance of 1–2).

As usual for a context-based compression method, care should be taken to avoid zero probabilities. The frequency table should thus be initialized to nonzero values, and experience shows that the precise way of doing this does not affect the compression performance significantly. It seems best to initialize every table entry to 1.

When the process starts, the first pixels to be scanned don't have any neighbors above them or to the left. A simple way to handle this is to assume that any non-existent neighbors are zeros. It is as if the image was extended by adding as many rows of zero pixels as neccesary on top and as many zero columns on the left.

The 2-bit context of Figure 4.20 is now used, as an example, to encode the first row of the 4 × 4 image

$$
\begin{array}{c|cccc}
 & 0\,0\,0\,0 \\
\hline
0 & 1\,0\,1\,1 \\
0 & 0\,1\,0\,1 \\
0 & 1\,0\,0\,1 \\
0 & 0\,0\,1\,0 \\
\end{array}
$$

The results are summarized in Table 4.21.

Number	Pixel	Context	Counts	Probability	New counts
1	1	00=0	1,1	$1/(1+1) = 1/2$	1,2
2	0	01=1	1,1	1/2	2,1
3	1	00=0	1,2	2/3	1,3
4	1	01=1	2,1	1/3	2,2

Table 4.21: Counts and Probabilities for First Four Pixels.

▶ **Exercise 4.10:** Continue Table 4.21 for the next row of four pixels 0101.

The contexts of Figure 4.20 are not symmetric about the current pixel, since they must use pixels that have already been input ("past" pixels). If the algorithm scans the image by rows, those will be the pixels above and to the left of the current pixel. In practical work it is impossible to include "future" pixels in the context, but for experiments it is possible to store the entire image in memory so that the encoder can examine any pixel at any time. Experiments performed with symmetric contexts have shown that compression performance can improve by as much as 30%. (The MLP method, Section 4.8, provides an interesting twist to the question of a symmetric context.)

▶ **Exercise 4.11:** Why is it possible to use "future" pixels in an experiment but not in practice? It would seem that the image, or part of it, could be stored in memory and the encoder could use any pixel as part of a context?

One disadvantage of a large context is that it takes the algorithm longer to "learn" it. A 20-bit context, e.g., allows for about a million different contexts. It takes many millions of pixels to collect enough counts for all those contexts, which is one reason large contexts do not result in better compression. One way to improve our method is to implement a *two-level* algorithm that uses a long context only if that context has already been seen Q times or more (where Q is a parameter, typically set to a small value such as 2 or 3). If a context has been seen fewer than Q times, it is deemed unreliable, and only a small subset of it is used to predict the current pixel. Figure 4.22 shows four such contexts, where the pixels of the subset are labeled S. The notation p, q means a two-level context of p bits with a subset of q bits.

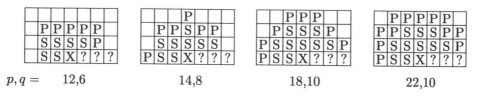

$$p, q = \quad 12,6 \qquad\qquad 14,8 \qquad\qquad 18,10 \qquad\qquad 22,10$$

Figure 4.22: Two-Level Context Pixel Patterns.

Experience shows that the 18,10 and 22,10 contexts result in better, although not revolutionary, compression.

Bibliography

Langdon, G., and J. Rissanen (1981) "Compression of Black White Images with Arithmetic Coding," *IEEE Transactions on Communications* COM-29(6):858–867, June.

Moffat, A. (1991) "Two-Level Context Based Compression of Binary Images," in *Proceedings of the 1991 Data Compression Conference*, J. Storer Ed., Los Alamitos, CA, IEEE Computer Society Press, pp. 382–391.

4.6 FELICS

FELICS is an acronym for Fast, Efficient, Lossless Image Compression System [Howard 93]. It is a special-purpose compression method designed for grayscale images and it competes with the lossless mode of JPEG (Section 4.2.7). It is fast and it generally produces good compression. However, it cannot compress an image to below one bit per pixel, so it is not a good choice for highly redundant images.

The principle of FELICS is to code each pixel with a variable-size code based on the values of two of its previously seen neighbor pixels. Figure 4.23a shows the two known neighbors A and B of some pixels P. For a general pixel, these are the neighbors above it and to its left. For a pixel in the top row, these are its two left neighbors (except for the first two pixels of the image). For a pixel in the leftmost column, these are the first two pixels of the line above it. Notice that the first two pixels of the image don't have any previously seen neighbors but, since there are only two of them, they can be output without any encoding, causing just a slight degradation in the overall compression.

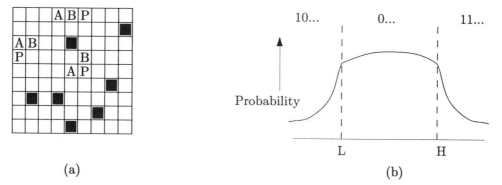

(a)   (b)

Figure 4.23: (a) The Two Neighbors; (b) The Three Regions.

Consider the two neighbors A and B of a pixel P. We use A, B, and P to denote both the three pixels and their intensities (grayscale values). We denote by L and H the neighbors with the smaller and the larger intensities, respectively. Pixel P should be assigned a variable-size code depending on where the intensity P is located relative to L and H. There are three cases:

1. The intensity of pixel P is between L and H (it is located in the central region of Figure 4.23b). This case is known experimentally to occur in about half the pixels, and P is assigned, in this case, a code that starts with 0. (A special case occurs when L=H. In such a case, the range [L,H] consists of one value only and the chance that P will have that value is small.) The probability that P will be in this central region is almost, but not completely, flat so P should be assigned a binary code that has about the same size in the entire region but is slightly shorter at the center of the region.

2. The intensity of P is lower than L (P is in the left region). The code assigned to P in this case starts with 10.

3. P's intensity is greater than H. P is assigned a code that starts with 11.

When pixel P is in one of the outer regions, the probability that its intensity will differ from L or H by much is small, so P can be assigned a long code in these cases.

The code assigned to P should thus depend heavily on whether P is in the central region or in one of the outer regions. Here is how the code is assigned when P is in the central region. We need H–L+1 variable-size codes that will not differ much in size and will, of course, satisfy the prefix property. We denote $k = \lfloor \log_2(H - L + 1) \rfloor$ and compute integers a and b by

$$a = 2^{k+1} - (H - L + 1); \quad b = 2(H - L + 1 - 2^k).$$

[*Example:* if H–L=9, then $k = 3$, $a = 2^{3+1} - (9 + 1) = 6$ and $b = 2(9 + 1 - 2^3) = 4$.] We now select the a codes $2^k - 1$, $2^k - 2,\ldots$ expressed as k-bit numbers, and the b codes 0, 1, 2,... expressed as $k + 1$-bit numbers. In the example above, the a codes are $8 - 1 = 111$, $8 - 2 = 110$ through $8 - 6 = 010$, and the b codes, 0000, 0001, 0010, and 0011. The a short codes are assigned to values of P in the middle of the central region and the b long codes are assigned to values of P closer to L or H. Notice that b is even, so the b codes can always be divided evenly. Table 4.24 shows how ten such codes can be assigned in the case L=15, H=24.

When P is in one of the outer regions, say the upper one, the value P–H should be assigned a variable-size code whose size can grow quickly as P–H gets bigger. One way to do this is to select a small non-negative integer m (typically 0, 1, 2, or 3) and to assign the integer n a 2-part code. The second part is the lower m bits of n and the first part, the unary code of [n without its lower m bits] (see exercise 2.5 for the unary code). Example: If $m = 2$, then $n = 1101_2$ is assigned the code 110|01 since 110 is the unary code of 11. This code is a special case of the Golomb code (Section 2.4), where the parameter b is a power of 2 (2^m). Table 4.25 shows some examples of this code for $m = 0, 1, 2, 3$ and $n = 1, 2, \ldots, 9$. The value of m used in any particular compression job can be selected, as a parameter, by the user.

Pixel P	Region code	Pixel code
L=15	0	0000
16	0	0010
17	0	010
18	0	011
19	0	100
20	0	101
21	0	110
22	0	111
23	0	0001
H=24	0	0011

Table 4.24: The Codes for the Central Region.

Pixel P	P–H	Region code	m = 0	1	2	3
H+1=25	1	11	0	00	000	0000
26	2	11	10	01	001	0001
27	3	11	110	100	010	0010
28	4	11	1110	101	011	0011
29	5	11	11110	1100	1000	0100
30	6	11	111110	1101	1001	0101
31	7	11	1111110	11100	1010	0110
32	8	11	11111110	11101	1011	0111
33	9	11	111111110	111100	11000	10000
...	...	...	...		...	

Table 4.25: The Codes for an Outer Region.

$$
\begin{matrix}
2 & 5 & 7 & 12 \\
3 & 0 & 11 & 10 \\
2 & 1 & 8 & 15 \\
4 & 13 & 11 & 9
\end{matrix}
$$

Figure 4.26: A 4×4 Bitmap.

▸ **Exercise 4.12:** Given the 4×4 bitmap of Figure 4.26, calculate the FELICS codes for the three pixels with values 8, 7, and 0.

Bibliography

Howard, P. G. and J. S. Vitter, (1993) "Fast and Efficient Lossless Image Compression," in *Proceedings of the 1993 Data Compression Conference*, J. Storer Ed., Los Alamitos, CA, IEEE Computer Society Press, pp. 351–360.

4.7 Progressive FELICS

The original FELICS method can easily be generalized to progressive compression of images because of its main principle. FELICS scans the image row by row (raster scan) and encodes a pixel based on the values of 2 of its (previously seen and encoded) neighbors. Progressive FELICS works similarly, but it scans the pixels in levels. Each level uses the k pixels encoded in all previous levels to encode k more pixels, so the number of encoded pixels doubles after each level. Assuming that the image consists of $n \times n$ pixels, and the first level starts with just four pixels, consecutive levels result in

$$4, 8, \ldots, \frac{n^2}{8}, \frac{n^2}{4}, \frac{n^2}{2}, n^2$$

pixels. The number of levels is thus the number of terms, $2 \log_2 n - 1$ in this sequence.

▸ **Exercise 4.13:** Prove this!

Figure 4.27 shows the pixels encoded in most of the levels of a 16×16-pixel image. Figure 4.28 shows how the pixels of each level are selected. In 4.28(a) there are $8 \times 8 = 64$ pixels, one quarter of the final number, arranged in a square grid. Each group of four pixels is used to encode a new pixel, so 4.28(b) has 128 pixels, half the final number. The image of 4.28(b) is then rotated 45° and scaled by factors of $\sqrt{2} \approx 1.414$ in both directions, to produce Figure 4.28(c), which is a square grid that looks exactly like 4.28(a). The next step (not shown in the figure) is to use every group of 4×4 pixels in 4.28(c) to encode a pixel, thereby encoding the remaining 128 pixels. In practice there is no need to actually rotate and scale the image; the program simply alternates between xy- and diagonal coordinates.

Each group of four pixels is used to encode the pixel at its center. Notice that in early levels the four pixels of a group are far from each other and are thus not correlated, resulting in poor compression. However, the last two levels encode 3/4 of the total number of pixels, and these levels contain compact groups. Two of the four pixels of a group are selected to encode the center pixel, and are designated L and H. Experience shows that the best choice for L and H is the two median pixels (page 186), the ones with the middle values (i.e., not the maximum or the minimum pixels of the group). Ties can be resolved in any way, but it should be consistent. If the two medians in a group are the same, then the median and the minimum (or the median and the maximum) pixels can be selected. The two selected pixels, L and H, are used to encode the center pixel in the same way FELICS uses two neighbors to encode a pixel. The only difference is that a new prefix code (Section 4.7.1) is used, instead of the Golomb code.

▸ **Exercise 4.14:** Why is it important to resolve ties in a consistent way?

4.7.1 Subexponential Code

In early levels, the four pixels used to encode a pixel are far from each other. As more levels are progressively encoded the groups get more compact, so their pixels get closer. The encoder uses the absolute difference between the L and H pixels in a group (the *context* of the group) to encode the pixel at the center of the group, but a

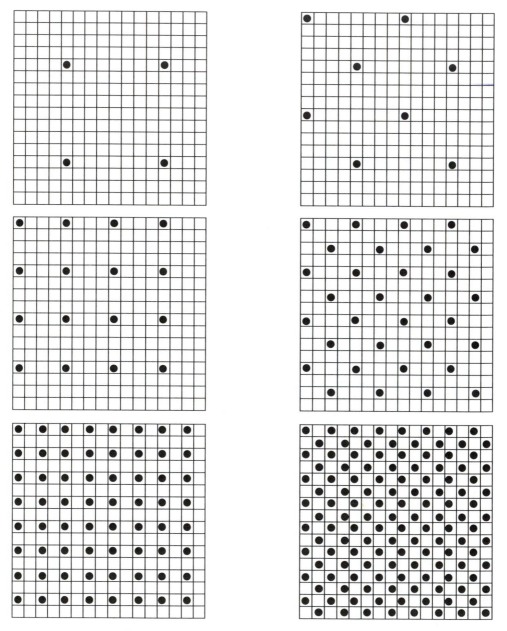

Figure 4.27: Some Levels of a 16×16 Image.

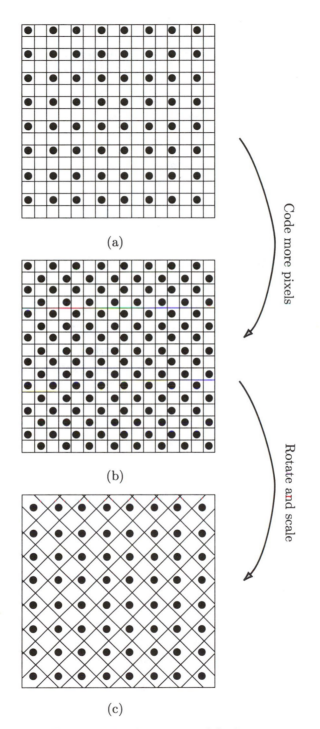

(a)

Code more pixels

(b)

Rotate and scale

(c)

Figure 4.28: Rotation and Scaling.

given absolute difference means more for late levels than for early ones, because the groups of late levels are smaller, so their pixels are more correlated. The encoder should thus scale the difference by a weight parameter s that gets heavier from level to level. The specific value of s is not critical and experiments recommend the value 12.

The prefix code used by progressive FELICS is called *subexponential*. Like the Golomb code (Section 2.4), this new code depends on a parameter $k \geq 0$. The main feature of the subexponential code is its length. For integers $n < 2^{k+1}$ the code length increases linearly with n but, for larger n, it increases logarithmically. The subexponential code of the non-negative integer n is computed in two steps. In the first step, values b and u are calculated by

$$b = \begin{cases} k & \text{if } n < 2^k; \\ \lfloor \log_2 n \rfloor & \text{if } n \geq 2^k; \end{cases} \quad \text{and} \quad u = \begin{cases} 0 & \text{if } n < 2^k; \\ b - k + 1 & \text{if } n \geq 2^k. \end{cases}$$

In the second step, the unary code of u (in $u + 1$ bits), followed by the b least significant bits of n, becomes the subexponential code of n. The total size of the code is thus

$$u + 1 + b = \begin{cases} k + 1 & \text{if } n < 2^k, \\ 2\lfloor \log_2 n \rfloor - k + 2 & \text{if } n \geq 2^k. \end{cases}$$

Table 4.29 shows examples of the subexponential code for various values of n and k. It can be shown that for a given n, the code lengths for consecutive values of k differ by at most 1.

n	$k = 0$	$k = 1$	$k = 2$	$k = 3$	$k = 4$	$k = 5$
0	0|	0|0	0|00	0|000	0|0000	0|00000
1	10|	0|1	0|01	0|001	0|0001	0|00001
2	110|0	10|0	0|10	0|010	0|0010	0|00010
3	110|1	10|1	0|11	0|011	0|0011	0|00011
4	1110|00	110|00	10|00	0|100	0|0100	0|00100
5	1110|01	110|01	10|01	0|101	0|0101	0|00101
6	1110|10	110|10	10|10	0|110	0|0110	0|00110
7	1110|11	110|11	10|11	0|111	0|0111	0|00111
8	11110|000	1110|000	110|000	10|000	0|1000	0|01000
9	11110|001	1110|001	110|001	10|001	0|1001	0|01001
10	11110|010	1110|010	110|010	10|010	0|1010	0|01010
11	11110|011	1110|011	110|011	10|011	0|1011	0|01011
12	11110|100	1110|100	110|100	10|100	0|1100	0|01100
13	11110|101	1110|101	110|101	10|101	0|1101	0|01101
14	11110|110	1110|110	110|110	10|110	0|1110	0|01110
15	11110|111	1110|111	110|111	10|111	0|1111	0|01111
16	111110|0000	11110|0000	1110|0000	110|0000	10|0000	0|10000

Table 4.29: Some Subexponential Codes.

If the value of the pixel to be encoded lies between those of L and H, the pixel is encoded as in FELICS. If it lies outside the range [L, H], the pixel is encoded by using the subexponential code where the value of k selected by the following rule.

Suppose that the current pixel P to be encoded has context C. The encoder maintains a cumulative total, for some reasonable values of k, of the code length the encoder would have if it had used that value of k to encode all pixels encountered so far in context C. The encoder then uses the k value with the smallest cumulative code length to encode P.

4.8 MLP

Text compression methods can use context to predict (i.e., to estimate the probability of) the next character of text. Using context to predict the intensity of the next pixel in image compression is more complex for two reasons: (1) An image is two-dimensional, allowing for many possible contexts; and (2) a digital image is normally the result of digitizing an analog image. The intensity of any individual pixel is thus determined by the details of digitization and may differ from the "ideal" intensity.

The multi-level progressive method (MLP) described here [Howard and Vitter 92a], is a computationally intensive, lossless method for compressing grayscale images. It uses context to predict the intensities of pixels, and arithmetic coding to encode the difference between the prediction and the actual value of a pixel (the error). The Laplace distribution is used to estimate the probability of the error. The method combines four separate steps: (1) pixel sequencing, (2) prediction (image modeling), (3) error modeling (by means of the Laplace distribution), and (4) arithmetically encoding the errors.

MLP is also progressive, encoding the image in levels, where the pixels of each level are selected as in progressive FELICS. When the image is decoded, each level adds details to the entire image, not just to certain parts, so a user can view the image as it is being decoded and decide in real time whether to accept or reject it. This feature is useful when an image has to selected from a large archive of compressed images. The user can browse through images very fast, without having to wait for any image to be completely decoded. Another advantage of progressive compression is that it provides a natural lossy option. The encoder may be told to stop encoding before it reaches the last level (thereby encoding only half the total number of pixels) or before it reaches the next to last level (encoding only a quarter of the total number of pixels). Such an option results in excellent compression ratio but a loss of image data. The decoder may be told to use interpolation to determine the intensities of any missing pixels.

Like any compression method for grayscale images, MLP can be used to compress color images. The original color image should be separated into three color components, and each component compressed individually as a grayscale image. Following is a detailed description of the individual MLP encoding steps.

Pixel sequencing: Pixels are selected in levels, as in progressive FELICS, where each level encodes the same number of pixels as all the preceding levels combined, thereby doubling the number of encoded pixels. This means that the last level encodes half the number of pixels, the level preceding it encodes a quarter of the total number, and so on. The first level should start with at least four pixels, but may also start with 8, 16, or any desired power of 2.

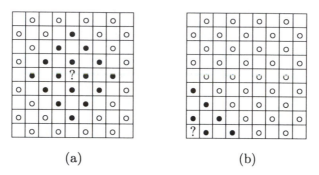

(a)   (b)

Figure 4.30: (a) 16 Neighbors. (b) 6 Neighbors.

Prediction: A pixel is predicted by calculating a weighted average of 16 of its known neighbors. Keep in mind that pixels are not raster scanned but are encoded (and thus also decoded) in levels. When decoding the pixels of a level L, the MLP decoder has already decoded all the pixels of all the preceding levels and it can use their values (gray levels) to predict values of pixels of L. Figure 4.30a shows the situation when the MLP encoder processes the last level. Half the pixels have already been encoded in previous levels, so they will be known to the decoder when the last level is decoded. The encoder can thus use a diamond-shaped group of 4×4 pixels (shown in black) from previous levels to predict the pixel at the center of the group. This group is the context of the pixel. Compression methods that scan the image row by row (raster scan) can use only pixels above and to the left of pixel P to predict P. Because of the progressive nature of MLP, it can use a symmetric context, which produces more accurate predictions. On the other hand, the pixels of the context are not near neighbors and may even be (in early levels) far from the predicted pixel.

Table 4.31 shows the 16 weights used for a group. They are calculated by polynomial interpolation (Appendix I) and are normalized such that they add up to 1. (Notice that in Table 4.31a the weights are not normalized; they add up to 256. When these integer weights are used, the weighted sum should be divided by 256.) To predict a pixel near an edge, where some of the 16 neighbors are missing (as in Figure 4.30b), only those neighbors that exist are used, and their weights are renormalized, to bring their sum to 1.

▸ **Exercise 4.15:** Why do the weights have to add up to 1?

▸ **Exercise 4.16:** Show how to renormalize the six weights needed to predict the pixel at the bottom right corner of Figure 4.30b.

The encoder predicts all the pixels of a level by using the diamond-shaped group of 4×4 (or fewer) "older" pixels around each pixel of the level. This is the *image model* used by MLP.

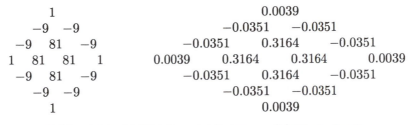

$$
\begin{array}{ccccc}
 & 1 & & & \\
-9 & -9 & & & \\
-9 & 81 & -9 & & \\
1 & 81 & 81 & 1 & \\
-9 & 81 & -9 & & \\
-9 & -9 & & & \\
 & 1 & & &
\end{array}
\qquad
\begin{array}{cccc}
 & 0.0039 & & \\
-0.0351 & & -0.0351 & \\
-0.0351 & 0.3164 & & -0.0351 \\
0.0039 & 0.3164 & 0.3164 & 0.0039 \\
-0.0351 & 0.3164 & & -0.0351 \\
-0.0351 & & -0.0351 & \\
 & 0.0039 & &
\end{array}
$$

Table 4.31: 16 Weights. (a) Integers. (b) Normalized.

4.8.1 MLP Error Modeling

Assume that the weighted sum of the 16 near-neighbors of pixel P is R. R is thus the value predicted for P. The prediction error, E, is simply the difference R–P. Assuming an image with 16 gray levels (4 bits per pixel) the largest value of E is 15 (when R=15 and P=0) and the smallest is −15. Depending on the image, we can expect most errors to be small integers, either zero or close to it. Few errors should be ±15 or close to that. Experiments with a large number of images have produced the error distribution shown in Figure 4.33a. This is a symmetric, narrow curve, with a sharp peak, indicating that most errors are small and are thus concentrated at the top. Such a curve has the shape of the well-known Laplace distribution with mean 0. This is a statistical distribution, similar to the normal (Gaussian) distribution, but narrower and sharply peaked. The general Laplace distribution with variance V and mean m is given by

$$
L(V, x) = \frac{1}{\sqrt{2V}} \exp\left(-\sqrt{\frac{2}{V}} |x - m| \right).
$$

Table 4.32 shows some values for the Laplace distributions with m=0 and V=3, 4, 5, and 1,000. Figure 4.33b shows the graphs of the first three of those. It is clear that, as V grows, the graph becomes lower and wider, with a less-pronounced peak.

			x			
V	0	2	4	6	8	10
3:	0.408248	0.0797489	0.015578	0.00304316	0.00059446	0.000116125
4:	0.353553	0.0859547	0.020897	0.00508042	0.00123513	0.000300282
5:	0.316228	0.0892598	0.025194	0.00711162	0.00200736	0.000566605
1,000:	0.022360	0.0204475	0.018698	0.0170982	0.0156353	0.0142976

Table 4.32: Some Values of the Laplace Distribution with V=3, 4, 5, and 1,000.

The reason for the factor $1/\sqrt{2V}$ in the definition of the Laplace distribution is to scale the area under the curve of the distribution to 1. Because of this, it is easy to use the curve of the distribution to calculate the probability of any error value. Figure 4.33c shows a gray strip 1 unit wide, under the curve of the distribution,

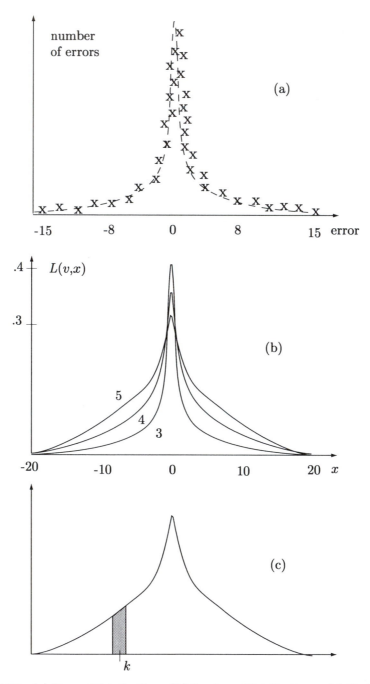

Figure 4.33: (a) Error Distribution. (b) Laplace Distributions. (c) Probability of k.

centered about an error value of k. The area of this strip equals the probability of any error E having the value k. Mathematically, the area is the integral

$$P_V(k) = \int_{k-.5}^{k+.5} \frac{1}{\sqrt{2V}} \exp\left(-\sqrt{\frac{2}{V}}|x|\right) dx, \qquad (4.7)$$

▮▮▶ and this is the key to encoding the errors. With 4-bit pixels, error values are in the range $[-15, +15]$. When an error k is obtained, the MLP encoder encodes it arithmetically with a probability computed by Equation (4.7). In practice, both encoder and decoder should have a table with all the possible probabilities precomputed.

▸ **Exercise 4.17:** What is the indefinite integral of the Laplace distribution?

The only remaining point to discuss is what value of the variance V should be used in Equation (4.7). Both encoder and decoder need to know this value. It is clear, from Figure 4.33b, that using a large variance (which corresponds to a low, flat distribution) results in too low a probability estimate for small error values k. The arithmetic encoder would produce an unnecessarily long code in such a case. On the other hand, using a small variance (which corresponds to a high, narrow distribution) would allocate too low probabilities to large error values k. The choice of variance is thus important. An ideal method to estimate the variance should assign the best variance value to each error and should involve no overhead (i.e., no extra data should be written on the compressed stream to help the decoder estimate the variances). Here are some approaches to variance selection:

1. The Laplace distribution was adopted as the MLP error distribution after many experiments with real images. The distribution obtained by all those images has a certain value of V, and this value should be used by MLP. This is a simple approach, which can be used in fast versions of MLP. However, it is not adaptive (since it always uses the same variance), and thus does not result in best compression performance for all images.

2. (A two-pass compression job.) Each compression should start with a pass where all the error values are computed and their variance calculated. This variance should be used, after the first pass, to calculate a table of probabilities from Equation (4.7). The table should be used in the second pass where the error values are encoded and written on the compressed stream. Compression performance would be excellent but any two-pass job is slow. Notice that the entire table can be written at the start of the compressed stream, thereby greatly simplifying the task of the decoder.

▸ **Exercise 4.18:** Show an example where this approach is practical (i.e., when slow encoding is unimportant but a fast decoder and excellent compression are important).

3. Every time an error is obtained and is about to be arithmetically coded, use some method to estimate the variance associated with that error. Quantize the estimate and use a number of precomputed probability tables, one for each quantized variance value, to compute the probability of the error. This is computationally intensive but may be a good compromise between approaches 1 and 2 above.

We now need to discuss how the variance of an error can be estimated, and we start with an explanation of the concept of variance. Variance is a statistical concept defined for a sequence of values $a_1, a_2, \ldots, a_n$. It measures how elements a_i vary by calculating the differences between them and the average A of the sequence, which is given, of course, by $A = (1/n)\sum a_i$. This is why the curves of Figure 4.33b that correspond to smaller variances are narrower; their values are concentrated near the average, which in this case is zero. The sequence $(5, 5, 5)$, e.g., has average 5 and variance 0, since every element of the sequence equals the average. The sequence $(0, 5, 10)$ also has average 5 but should have a nonzero variance since 2 of its elements differ from the average. In general, the variance of the sequence a_i is defined as the non-negative quantity

$$V = \sum_{1}^{n}(a_i - A)^2,$$

so the variance of $(0, 5, 10)$ is $(0 - 5)^2 + (5 - 5)^2 + (10 - 5)^2 = 50$. Statisticians also use a quantity called *standard deviation* (denoted σ) which is defined as the square root of the variance.

We now discuss several ways to estimate the variance of a prediction error E.

3.1. Equation (4.7) gives the probability of an error E with value k, but this probability depends on V. We can consider $P_V(k)$ a function of the two variables V and k, and find the optimal value of V by solving the equation $\partial P_V(k)/\partial V = 0$. The solution is $V = 2k^2$ but this method is not practical since the decoder does not know k (it is trying to decode k so it can find the value of pixel P), and thus cannot mirror the operations of the encoder. It is possible to write the values of all the variances on the compressed stream but this would significantly reduce the compression ratio. This method can be used to encode a particular image in order to find the best compression ratio of the image and compare it to what is achieved in practice.

3.2. While the pixels of a level are being encoded, consider their errors E a sequence of numbers, and find its variance V. Use V to encode the pixels of the next level. The number of levels is never very large, so all the variance values can be written (arithmetically encoded) on the compressed stream, resulting in fast decoding. The variance used to encode the first level should be a user-controlled parameter whose value is not critical since that level contains just a few pixels. Since MLP quantizes a variance to one of 37 values (see below), each variance written on the compressed stream is encoded in just $\log_2 37 \approx 5.21$ bits, a negligible overhead. The obvious disadvantage of this method is that it disregards local concentrations of identical or very similar pixels in the same level.

3.3. (Similar to 3.2.) While the pixels of a level are being encoded, collect the prediction errors of each block of $b \times b$ pixels and use them to calculate a variance that will be used to encode the pixels inside this block in the next level. The variance values for a level can also be written on the compressed stream following all the encoded errors for that level, so the decoder could use them without having to compute them. Parameter b should be adjusted by experiments, and the authors recommend the value $b = 16$. This method entails significant overhead and thus may degrade compression performance.

3.4. (This is a later addition to MLP; see [Howard and Vitter 92b].) A *variability index* is computed, by both the encoder and decoder, for each pixel. This index should depend on the amount by which the pixel differs from its near neighbors. The variability indexes of all the pixels in a level are then used to adaptively estimate the variances for the pixels, based on the assumption that pixels with similar variability index should use Laplace distributions with similar variances. The method proceeds in the following steps:

1. Variability indexes are calculated for all the pixels of the current level, based on values of pixels in the preceding levels. This is done by the encoder and is later mirrored by the decoder. After several tries, the developers of MLP have settled on a simple way to calculate the variability index. It is calculated as the variance of the four nearest neighbors of the current pixel (the neighbors are from preceding levels, so the decoder can mirror this operation).

2. The variance estimate V is set to some initial value. The choice of this value is not critical, as V is going to be updated later many times. The decoder chooses this value in the same way.

3. The pixels of the current level are sorted in variability index order. The decoder can mirror this even though it still does not have the values of these pixels (the decoder has already calculated the values of the variability index in step 1, since they depend on pixels of previous levels).

4. The encoder loops over the sorted pixels in decreasing order (from large variability indexes to small ones). For each pixel:

4.1. The encoder calculates the error E of the pixel and sends E and V to the arithmetic encoder. The decoder mirrors this step. It knows V, so it can decode E.

4.2. The encoder updates V by

$$V \leftarrow f \times V + (1 - f)E^2,$$

where f is a smoothing parameter (experience suggests a large value, such as 0.99, for f). This is how V is adapted from pixel to pixel, using the errors E. Because of the large value of f, V is decreased in small steps. This means that latter pixels (those with small variability indexes) will get small variances assigned. The idea is that compressing pixels with large variability indexes is less sensitive to accurate values of V.

As the loop progresses, V gets more accurate values and these are used to compress pixels with small variability indexes, which are more sensitive to variance values. Notice that the decoder can mirror this step since it has already decoded E in step 4.1. Notice also that the arithmetic encoder writes the encoded error values on the compressed stream in decreasing variability index order, not row by row. The decoder can mirror this too since it has already sorted the pixels in this order in step 3.

This method gives excellent results but is even more computationally intensive than the original MLP (end of method 3.4).

Using one of the four methods above, variance V is estimated. Before using V to encode error E, V is quantized to one of 37 values as shown in Table 4.34. For example, if the estimated variance value is 0.31, it is quantized to 7. The quantized value is then used to select one of 37 precomputed probability tables (in our example Table 7, precomputed for variance value 0.290, is selected) prepared using Equation (4.7), and the value of error E is used to index that table. The value retrieved from the table is the probability that's sent to the arithmetic encoder, together with the error value, to arithmetically encode error E.

Variance range	Var. used	Variance range	Var. used	Variance range	Var. used
0.005–0.023	0.016	2.882–4.053	3.422	165.814–232.441	195.569
0.023–0.043	0.033	4.053–5.693	4.809	232.441–326.578	273.929
0.043–0.070	0.056	5.693–7.973	6.747	326.578–459.143	384.722
0.070–0.108	0.088	7.973–11.170	9.443	459.143–645.989	540.225
0.108–0.162	0.133	11.170–15.627	13.219	645.989–910.442	759.147
0.162–0.239	0.198	15.627–21.874	18.488	910.442–1285.348	1068.752
0.239–0.348	0.290	21.874–30.635	25.875	1285.348–1816.634	1506.524
0.348–0.502	0.419	30.635–42.911	36.235	1816.634–2574.021	2125.419
0.502–0.718	0.602	42.911–60.123	50.715	2574.021–3663.589	3007.133
0.718–1.023	0.859	60.123–84.237	71.021	3663.589–5224.801	4267.734
1.023–1.450	1.221	84.237–118.157	99.506	5224.801–7247.452	6070.918
1.450–2.046	1.726	118.157–165.814	139.489	7247.452–10195.990	8550.934
2.046–2.882	2.433				

Table 4.34: Thirty-Seven Quantized Variance Values.

MLP is thus one of the many compression methods that implement a model to estimate probabilities and use arithmetic coding to do the actual compression.

Table 4.35 is a pseudo-code summary of MLP encoding.

```
for each level L do
 for every pixel P in level L do
  Compute a prediction R for P using a group from level L-1;
  Compute E=R-P;
  Estimate the variance V to be used in encoding E;
  Quantize V and use it as an index to select a Laplace table LV;
  Use E as an index to table LV and retrieve LV[E];
  Use LV[E] as the probability to arithmetically encode E;
 endfor;
 Determine the pixels of the next level (rotate & scale);
endfor;
```

Table 4.35: MLP Encoding.

Bibliography

Howard, Paul G., and J. S. Vitter (1992a), "New Methods for Lossless Image Compression Using Arithmetic Coding," *Information Processing and Management*, **28**(6):765–779.

Howard, Paul G., and J. S. Vitter (1992b), "Error Modeling for Hierarchical Lossless Image Compression," in *Proceedings of the 1992 Data Compression Conference*, J. Storer ed., Los Alamitos, CA, IEEE Computer Society Press, pp. 269–278.

4.9 PPPM

The reader should review the PPM method, Section 2.17, before reading this section. The PPPM method described here uses the ideas of MLP (Section 4.8). It is also (remotely) related to the context-based image compression method of Section 4.5.

PPM encodes a symbol by comparing its present context to other, similar contexts and selecting the longest match. The context selected is then used to estimate the symbol's probability in the present context. This way of context matching works well for text, where we can expect strings of symbols to repeat exactly, but it does not work well for images since a digital image is normally the result of digitizing an analog image. Assume that the current pixel has intensity 118 and its context is the two neighboring pixels with values 118 and 120. It is possible that 118 was never seen in the past with the context 118, 120 but was seen with contexts 119, 120 and 118, 121. Clearly these contexts are close enough to the current one, to justify using one of them. Once a closely matching context has been found, it is used to estimate the variance (not the probability) of the current prediction error. This idea serves as one principle of the Prediction by Partial Precision Matching (PPPM) method [Howard and Vitter 92a]. The other principle is to use the Laplace distribution to estimate the probability of the prediction error, as done in MLP.

Figure 4.36: Prediction and Variance-
Estimation Contexts for PPPM.

Figure 4.36 shows how prediction is done in PPPM. Pixels are raster-scanned, row by row. The two pixels labeled C are used to predict the one labeled P. The prediction R is simply the rounded average of the two C pixels. Pixels in the top or left edges are predicted by one neighbor only. The top-left pixel of the image is encoded without prediction. After predicting the value of P, the encoder calculates the error E=R–P and uses the Laplace distribution to estimate the probability of the error, as in MLP.

The only remaining point to discuss is how PPPM estimates the variance of the particular Laplace distribution that should be used to obtain the probability of E. PPPM uses the four neighbors labeled C and S in Figure 4.36. These pixels have already been encoded, so their values are known. They are used as the variance-estimation context of P. Assume that the 4 values are 3, 0, 7, and 5, expressed as 4-bit numbers. They are combined to form the 16-bit key 0011|0000|0111|0101, and the encoder uses a hash table to find all the previous occurrences of this context. If this context occurred enough times in the past (more than the value of a threshold parameter), the statistics of these occurrences are used to obtain a mean m and a variance V. if the context did not occur enough times in the past, the least-significant bit of each of the four values is dropped to obtain the 12-bit key 001|000|011|010, and the encoder hashes this value. The encoder thus iterates in a loop until it finds m and V. (It turns out that using the errors of the C and S pixels as a key, instead of their values, produces slightly better compression, so this is what PPPM does.)

Once m and V are obtained, the encoder quantizes V and uses it to select one of 37 Laplace probability tables, as in MLP. The encoder then adds $E+m$ and sends this value to be arithmetically encoded with the probability obtained from the Laplace table. To update the statistics, the PPPM encoder uses a lazy approach. It updates the statistics of the context actually used plus, if applicable, the context with 1 additional bit of precision.

One critical point is the number of times a context had to be seen in the past to be considered meaningful and not random. The PPMB method, Section 2.17.4, "trusts" a context if it had been seen twice. For an image, a threshold of 10–15 is more reasonable.

4.10 CALIC

Sections 4.5 through 4.9 describe context-based image compression methods that have one feature in common: they determine the context of a pixel using some of its neighbor pixels that have already been seen. Normally these are the pixels above and to the left of the current pixel, leading to asymmetric context. It seems intuitive that a symmetric context, one that predicts the current pixel using pixels all around it, would produce better compression, so attempts have been made to develop image compression methods that use such contexts.

The MLP method, Section 4.8, provides an interesting twist to the problem of symmetric context. The CALIC method described here uses a different approach. The name CALIC ([Wu 95] and [Wu 96]) stands for Context-based, Adaptive, Lossless Image Compression. It uses three passes to create a symmetric context around the current pixel, and it uses quantization to reduce the number of possible contexts to something manageable. The method has been developed for compressing grayscale images (where each pixel is a c-bit number representing a shade of gray) but, like any other method for grayscale images, it can handle a color image by separating it into three color components and treating each component as a grayscale image.

4.10.1 Three Passes

Assume an image $I[i,j]$ consisting of H rows and W columns of pixels. Both encoder and decoder perform three passes over the image. The first pass calculates averages of pairs of pixels. It only looks at pixels $I[i,j]$ where i and j have the same parity (i.e., both are even or both are odd). The second pass uses these averages to actually encode the same pixels. The third pass uses the same averages plus the pixels of the second pass to encode all pixels $I[i,j]$ where i and j have different parities (one is odd and the other even).

The first pass calculates the $W/2 \times H/2$ values $\mu[i,j]$ defined by

$$\mu[i,j] = (I[2i,2j] + I[2i+1,2j+1])/2, \text{ for } 0 \le i < H/2, \ 0 \le j < W/2. \quad (4.8)$$

(In the original CALIC papers i and j denote the columns and rows, respectively. We use the standard notation where the first index denotes the rows.) Each $\mu[i,j]$ is thus the average of two diagonally adjacent pixels. Table 4.37 shows the pixels (in boldface) involved in this calculation for an 8×8-pixel image. Each pair that's used to calculate a value $\mu[i,j]$ is connected with an arrow. Notice that the two original pixels cannot be fully reconstructed from the average because 1 bit may be lost by the division by 2 in Equation (4.8).

```
0,0  0,1  0,2  0,3  0,4  0,5  0,6  0,7
1,0  1,1  1,2  1,3  1,4  1,5  1,6  1,7
2,0  2,1  2,2  2,3  2,4  2,5  2,6  2,7
3,0  3,1  3,2  3,3  3,4  3,5  3,6  3,7
4,0  4,1  4,2  4,3  4,4  4,5  4,6  4,7
5,0  5,1  5,2  5,3  5,4  5,5  5,6  5,7
6,0  6,1  6,2  6,3  6,4  6,5  6,6  6,7
7,0  7,1  7,2  7,3  7,4  7,5  7,6  7,7
```

Table 4.37: The 4×4 Values $\mu[i,j]$ for an 8×8-Pixel Image.

The newly calculated values $\mu[i,j]$ are now considered the pixels of a new, small, $W/2 \times H/2$-pixel image (a quarter of the size of the original image). This image is raster-scanned and each of its pixels is predicted by four of its neighbors, three centered above it and one on its left. If $x = \mu[i,j]$ is the current pixel, it is predicted by the quantity

$$\hat{x} = \frac{1}{2}\mu[i-1,j] + \frac{1}{2}\mu[i,j-1] + \frac{1}{4}\mu[i-1,j+1] - \frac{1}{4}\mu[i-1,j-1]. \qquad (4.9)$$

(The coefficients $1/2$, $1/4$, and $-1/4$, as well as the coefficients used in the other passes, were determined by linear regression, using a set of "training" images. The idea is to find the set of coefficients a_k that gives the best compression for those images, then round them to integer powers of 2, and build them into the algorithm.) The error value $x - \hat{x}$ is then encoded.

The second pass involves the same pixels as the first pass (half the pixels of the original image) but this time each of them is individually predicted. They are raster scanned and, assuming that $x = I[2i, 2j]$ denotes the current pixel, it is predicted using five known neighbor pixels above it and to its left, and three averages μ, known from the first pass, below it and to its right:

$$\hat{x} = 0.9\mu[i,j] + \frac{1}{6}(I[2i+1, 2j-1] + I[2i-1, 2j-1] + I[2i-1, 2j+1])$$
$$- 0.05(I[2i, 2j-2] + I[2i-2, 2j]) - 0.15(\mu[i, j+1] + \mu[i+1, j]). \qquad (4.10)$$

Figure 4.38a shows the five pixels (gray dots) and three averages (slanted lines) involved. The task of the encoder is again to encode the error value $x - \hat{x}$ for each pixel x.

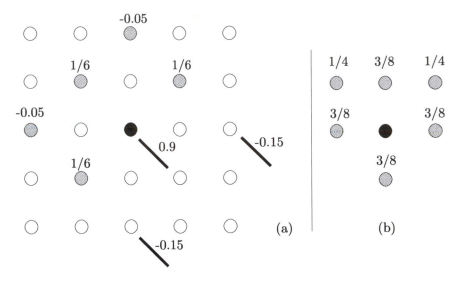

Figure 4.38: Weighted Sums for 360° Contexts.

▶ **Exercise 4.19:** Pixel $I[2i - 1, 2j + 1]$ is located below $x = I[2i, 2j]$, so how does the decoder know its value when x is decoded?

The third pass involves the remaining pixels:

$$I[2i, 2j + 1] \text{ and } I[2i + 1, 2j]; \quad \text{for } 0 \le i < H/2, \quad 0 \le j < W/2. \tag{4.11}$$

Each is predicted by an almost symmetric context of six pixels (Figure 4.38b) consisting of all of its four-connected neighbors and two of its eight-connected beighbors. If $x = I[i, j]$ is the current pixel, it is predicted by

$$\hat{x} = \frac{3}{8} \left(I[i, j - 1] + I[i - 1, j] + I[i, j + 1] + I[i + 1, j] \right)$$
$$- \frac{1}{4} \left(I[i - 1, j - 1] + I[i - 1, j + 1] \right). \tag{4.12}$$

The decoder can mimic this operation since the pixels below and to the right of x are known to it from the second pass.

Notice that each of the last two passes of the decoder creates half of the image pixels. CALIC can thus be considered a progressive method where the two progressive steps increase the resolution of the image.

4.10.2 Context Quantization

In each of the three passes, the error values $x - \hat{x}$ are arithmetically encoded, which means that they have to be assigned probabilities. Assume that pixel x is predicted by the n pixel neighbors $x_1, x_2, \ldots, x_n$. The values of n for the three passes are 4, 8, and 6, respectively. In order to assign a probability to x the encoder has to count the number of times x was found in the past with every possible n-pixel context. If a pixel is stored as a c-bit number (representing a shade of gray) then the number of possible contexts for a pixel is $2^{n \cdot c}$. Even for $c = 4$ (just 16 shades of gray) this number is $2^{8 \cdot 4} \approx 4.3$ billion, too large for a practical implementation. CALIC reduces the number of contexts in several steps. It first creates the single n-bit number $t = t_n \ldots t_1$ by

$$t_k = \begin{cases} 0, & \text{if } x_k \geq \hat{x}, \\ 1, & \text{if } x_k < \hat{x}. \end{cases}$$

Next it calculates the quantity

$$\Delta = \sum_{k=1}^{n} w_k |x_k - \hat{x}|,$$

where the coefficients w_k were calculated in advance, by using the same set of training images, and are built into the algorithm. The quantity Δ is called the *error strength discriminant* and is quantized to one of L integer values d, where L is typically set to 8. Once $\hat{x}$ and the n neighbors $x_1, x_2, \ldots, x_n$ are known, both t and the quantized value d of Δ can be calculated, and they become the indexes of the context. This reduces the number of contexts to $L \cdot 2^n$, which is at most $8 \cdot 2^8 = 2,048$. The encoder maintains an array S of d rows and t columns where context counts are kept. The following is a summary of the steps performed by the CALIC encoder.

```
For all passes
INITIALIZATION: N(d,t):=1; S(d,t):=0; d=0,1,...,L, t=0,1,...,2^n;
PARAMETERS: a_k and w_k are assigned their values;
for all pixels x in the current pass do
  0: x̂ = ∑_{k=1}^{n} a_k x_k;
  1: Δ = ∑_{k=1}^{n} w_k(x_k − x̂);
  2: d = Quantize(Δ);
  3: Compute t = t_n ... t_2 t_1;
  4: ε̄ = S(d,t)/N(d,t);
  5: ẋ = x̂ + ε̄;
  6: ε = x − ẋ;
  7: S(d,t) := S(d,t) + ε;  N(d,t) := N(d,t) + 1;
  8: if N(d,t) ≥ 128 then
        S(d,t) := S(d,t)/2;  N(d,t) := N(d,t)/2;
  9: if S(d,t) < 0 encode(−ε,d) else encode(ε,d);
endfor;
end.
```

Bibliography

Wu, Xiaolin (1995), "Context Selection and Quantization for Lossless Image Coding," in Storer, James A., and Martin Cohn (eds.), *DCC '95, Data Compression Conference*, Los Alamitos, CA, IEEE Computer Society Press, p. 453.

Wu, Xiaolin (1996), "An Algorithmic Study on Lossless Image Compression," in Storer, James A. (ed.), *DCC '96, Data Compression Conference*, Los Alamitos, CA, IEEE Computer Society Press.

4.11 Differential Lossless Image Compression

There is always a tradeoff between speed and preformance, so there is always a demand for fast compression methods as well as for methods that are slow but very efficient. The differential method of this section, due to Sayood and Anderson [Sayood 92], belongs to the former class. It is fast and simple to implement, while offering good, albeit not spectacular, performance.

The principle is to compare each pixel p to a *reference pixel*, which is one of its immediate neighbors, and encode p in two parts—a prefix, which is the number of most significant bits of p that are identical to those of the reference pixel—and a suffix, which is the remaining least significant bits of p. For example, if the reference pixel is 10110010 and p is 10110100 then the prefix is 5, since the 5 most significant bits of p are identical to those of the reference pixel, and the suffix is 00. Notice that the remaining three least significant bits are 100 but the suffix does not have to include the 1 since the decoder can easily deduce its value.

▶ **Exercise 4.20:** How can the decoder do this?

The prefix is thus an integer in the range $[0, 8]$ and compression can be improved by encoding the prefix further. Huffman coding is a good choice for this purpose, with either a fixed set of nine Huffman codes or with adaptive codes. The suffix can be any number of between 0 and 8 bits, so there are 256 possible suffixes. Since this number is relatively large, and since we expect most suffixes to be small, it makes sense to write the suffix on the output stream unencoded.

This method encodes each pixel using a different number of bits. The encoder generates bits until it has 8 or more of them, then outputs a byte. The decoder can easily mimic this. All that it has to know is the location of the reference pixel and the Huffman codes. In the example above, if the Huffman code of 6 is, say, 010, the code of p will be the 5 bits 010|00.

The only point to be discussed is the selection of the reference pixel. It should be near the current pixel p, and it should be known to the decoder when p is decoded. The rules for selecting the reference pixel are thus simple. The very first pixel of an image is written on the output stream unencoded. For every other pixel in the first scan line, the reference pixel is its immediate left neighbor. For the first pixel on subsequent scan lines, the reference pixel is the one above it. For every other pixel, it is possible to select the reference pixel in one of three ways: (1) the pixel immediately to its left; (2) the pixel above it; and (3) the pixel on the left but, if the resulting prefix is less than a predetermined threshold, the pixel above it.

An example of case 3 is a threshold value of 3. Initially, the reference pixel for p is its left neighbor but, if this results in a prefix value of 0, 1, or 2, the reference pixel is changed to the one above p, regardless of the prefix value which is then produced.

This method assumes 1 byte per pixel (256 colors or grayscale values). If a pixel is defined by 3 bytes, the image should be separated into three parts, and the method applied individually to each part.

▶ **Exercise 4.21:** Can this method be used for images with 16 grayscale values (where each pixel is 4 bits, and a byte contains two pixels)?

Bibliography

Sayood, K., and K. Robinson (1992) "A Differential Lossless Image Compression Scheme," *IEEE Transactions on Signal Processing* **40**(1):236–241, January.

4.12 Quadtrees

This is a data compression method for bitmap images. A quadtree compression of an image is based on the observation that, if we select a pixel in the image at random, there is a good chance that its neighbors will have the same color. The quadtree method thus scans the bitmap, area by area, looking for areas full of identical pixels (uniform areas). This should be compared to RLE image compression (Section 1.4).

The input consists of bitmap pixels, and the output is a tree (a quadtree, where a node is either a leaf or has exactly four children). The size of the quadtree depends on the complexity of the image. For complex images the tree may be bigger than the original bitmap (expansion). The method starts by building a single node, the root of the final quadtree. It divides the bitmap into four quadrants, each to become a child of the root. A uniform quadrant (one where all the pixels are the same color) is saved as a leaf child of the root. A non-uniform quadrant is saved as an (interior node) child of the root. Any non-uniform quadrants are then recursively divided into four smaller subquadrants that are saved as four sibling nodes of the quadtree. Figure 4.39 shows a simple example:

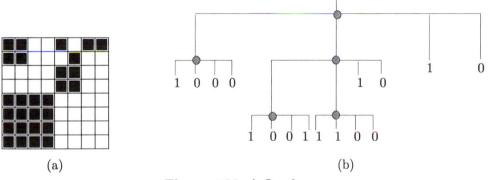

(a)   (b)

Figure 4.39: A Quadtree.

The 8×8 bitmap in 4.39a produces the 21-node quadtree of 4.39b. Sixteen nodes are leaves (each containing the color of one quadrant, 0 for white, 1 for black) and the other five (the gray circles) interior nodes containing only pointers. The quadrant numbering used is $\binom{0\,1}{2\,3}$.

The size of a quadtree depends on the complexity of the image. Assuming a bitmap size of $2^N \times 2^N$, one extreme case is where all the pixels are identical. The quadtree in this case consists of just one node, the root. The other extreme case is where each quadrant, even the smallest one, is non-uniform. The lowest level of the quadtree has, in such a case, $2^N \times 2^N = 4^N$ nodes. The level directly above it has a quarter of that number (4^{N-1}), and the level above that one has 4^{N-2} nodes. The total number of nodes in this case is $4^0 + 4^1 + \cdots + 4^{N-1} + 4^N = (4^{N+1} - 1)/3 \approx$

$4^N(4/3) \approx 1.33 \times 4^N = 1.33(2^N \times 2^N)$. In this worst case the quadtree has thus $\approx 33\%$ more nodes than the number of pixels (the bitmap size). Such an image therefore generates considerable expansion when converted to a quadtree.

A procedure for generating a quadtree from a bitmap is outlined in Figure 4.40 in a Pascal-like notation. It is straightforward, recursive, easy to understand, but not efficient.

The leaves of the quadtree have data fields with values B and W. All interior nodes have data fields with a Gray value. The procedure makes four recursive calls for the four quadrants of the bitmap. Each call returns a root for a subtree. If the root is B or W, then it is a single leaf. If it is G, then it is more than a leaf. The procedure then checks the four roots (see below).

The last recursive calls get a quadrant of size 2×2 (the case L=2). Such a call generates four nodes with the colors (B or W) of the four pixels.

Each call then checks the four nodes. If all four have the same color (but not gray), they are replaced by one node T with that color. If they are different (or if they are all gray) they become the children of a single node T, and the color of T is set to Gray.

Even though the procedure is recursive, the maximum depth of the recursion is N (where the bitmap size is $2^N \times 2^N$), which is typically in the range 8 to 12 (for image resolution range of 256×256 to $4K \times 4K$).

An advantage of this method is that it tests each pixel only once. Some unnecessary nodes are generated but are disposed of very quickly. The running time is the total number of the recursive calls. Originally there is one call (for the full bitmap of size $2^N \times 2^N$), which generates four recursive ones (for size $2^{N-1} \times 2^{N-1}$), each generating four more. Thus in the second level of recursion there are $16 = 4^2$ calls, each handling a part of size $2^{N-2} \times 2^{N-2}$. The lowest recursion level makes 4^{N-1} recursive calls, each for a 2×2 part of the bitmap. The total number of calls is thus $(1/3) \times 4^N$, which is a quarter of the size of a complete quadtree.

Another, non-recursive, approach starts by building the complete quadtree assuming that all quadrants are non-uniform and then checking the assumption. Every time a quadrant is tested and found to be uniform, the four nodes corresponding to its four quarters are deleted from the quadtree. This process proceeds from the bottom (the leaves) up towards the root. The main steps are the following:

I. A complete quadtree of height N is built. It contains levels $0, 1, \ldots, N$ where level k has 4^k nodes.

II. All $2^N \times 2^N$ pixels are copied from the bitmap into the leaves (the lowest level) of the quadtree.

III. The tree is scanned level by level, from the bottom (level N) to the root (level 0). When level k is scanned, its 4^k nodes are examined in groups of four, the four nodes in each group having a common parent. If the four nodes in a group are leaves and have the same color (i.e., if they represent a uniform quadrant), they are deleted and their parent is changed from an interior node to a leaf having the same color.

Here is a simple analysis of the time complexity. A complete quadtree has $\approx 1.33 \times 4^N$ nodes and, since each is tested once, the number of operations (in step III) is 1.33×4^N. Step I also requires 1.33×4^N operations and step II requires 4^N

```
type color=(W,B,G); noderecord {White, Black,Gray}
parent :↑node;
data :color;
s1,s2,s3,s4 :↑node
end;
var Bitmap: array[0..63, 0..63] of (B,W);  Root: ↑node;
Procedure QuadTree(i,j,L: integer; T: ↑node);
var M :integer; n1, n2, n3, n4: ↑node;
begin
new(n1); new(n2); new(n3); new(n4);
if L>2 {the quadrant size is >2x2 and should be
            subdivided recursively}
then begin
M:=L div 2;
QuadTree(i,j,M,n1); QuadTree(i+1,j,M,n2);
QuadTree(i+1,j+1,M,n3); QuadTree(i,j+1,M,n4);
     end
else begin {quadrant size is 2x2 so deal with each of the 4 pixels
                  individually}
n1↑.data:=Bitmap[i,j];      n2↑.data:=Bitmap[i+1,j];
n3↑.data:=Bitmap[i+1,j+1]; n4↑.data:=Bitmap[i,j+1];
     end;
if n1↑.data ↑G and n1↑.data =...=n4↑.data
then begin   {all 4 quadrants have the same non-Gray color}
T↑.data:=n1↑.data; T↑.s1:=nil; T↑.s2:=nil;  T↑.s3:=nil; T↑.s4:=nil;
dispose(n1); dispose(n2); dispose(n3); dispose(n4);
     end
else begin  {quadrants have either different colors or are all Gray}
T↑.data:=G; T↑.s1:=n1; T↑.s2:=n2;  T↑.s3:=n3; T↑.s4:=n4;
n1↑.parent:=T; n2↑.parent:=T; n3↑.parent:=T; n4↑.parent:=T;
     end;
end {QuadTree};
 .
 .          {main program}
 .
New(Root); Root↑.parent:=nil;
QuadTree(0,0,64,Root); {original call, starts at pixel (0,0), for a
                  64x64 bitmap}
SaveTree(Root, Filename); {traverse the tree and save all nodes on
                          file}
 .
 .
end.
```

Figure 4.40: Generating a Quadtree.

operations. The total number of operations is thus $(1.33+1.33+1)\times 4^N = 3.66\times 4^N$. We are faced with comparing the first method, which requires $1/3 \times 4^N$ steps, with the second method, which needs 3.66×4^N operations. Since N usually varies in the narrow range 8–12, the difference is not very significant. Similarly, an analysis of storage requirements shows that the first method uses just the amount of memory required by the final quadtree, whereas the second one uses all the storage needed for a complete quadtree.

It should also be noted that quadtrees are a special case of the Hilbert curve discussed in Section 4.13.

4.13 Space-Filling Curves

A space-filling curve is a parametric function $\mathbf{P}(t)$ that goes through every point in a given two-dimensional area, normally the unit square, when its parameter t varies in the range $[0, 1]$. For any value t_0, the value of $\mathbf{P}(t_0)$ is a point $[x_0, y_0]$ in the unit square. Mathematically such a curve is a mapping from the interval $[0, 1]$ to the two-dimensional interval $[0, 1] \times [0, 1]$. To understand how such a curve is constructed it is best to think of it as the limit of an infinite sequence of curves $\mathbf{P}_1(t)$, $\mathbf{P}_2(t),\ldots$, which are drawn inside the unit square, where each curve is derived from its predecessor by a process of *refinement*. The details of the refinement depend on the specific curve. Appendix C discusses two well-known space-filling curves, the Hilbert curve and the Sierpinski curve. Since the sequence of curves is infinite, it is impossible to compute all its components. Fortunately, we are interested in a curve that goes through every pixel in a bitmap, not through every mathematical point in the unit square. Since the number of pixels is finite, it is possible to construct such a curve in practice.

To understand why such curves are useful for image compression, the reader should recall the principle that has been mentioned several times in the past, namely, if we select a pixel in an image at random, there is a good chance that its neighbors will have the same color. Both RLE image compression and the quadtree method are based on this principle, but they are not always efficient as Figure 4.41 shows. This 8×8 bitmap has two concentrations of pixels but neither RLE nor the quadtree method compress it very well since there are no long runs and since the pixel concentrations happen to cross quadrant boundaries.

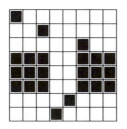

Figure 4.41: An 8×8 Bitmap.

Better compression may be produced by a method that scans the bitmap area by area instead of line by line or quadrant by quadrant. This is why space-filling curves provide a new approach to image compression. Such a curve visits every point in a given area, and does that by visiting all the points in a subarea, then moves to the next subarea and traverses it, and so on. We use the Hilbert curve (Figures C.1 through C.7) as an example. Each curve H_i is constructed by making four copies of the previous curve H_{i-1}, shrinking them, rotating them, and connecting them. The new curve ends up covering the same area as its predecessor. This is the refinement process for the Hilbert curve.

Scanning an 8×8 bitmap in a Hilbert curve results in the sequence of pixels

$$(0,0), (0,1), (1,1), (1,0), (2,0), (3,0), (3,1), (2,1),$$
$$(2,2), (3,2), (3,3), (2,3), (1,3), (1,2), (0,2), (0,3),$$
$$(0,4), (1,4), (1,5), (0,5), (0,6), (0,7), (1,7), (1,6),$$
$$(2,6), (2,7), (3,7), (3,6), (3,5), (2,5), (2,4), (3,4),$$
$$(4,4), (5,4), (5,5), (4,5), (4,6), (4,7), (5,7), (5,6),$$
$$(6,6), (6,7), (7,7), (7,6), (7,5), (6,5), (6,4), (7,4),$$
$$(7,3), (7,2), (6,2), (6,3), (5,3), (4,3), (4,2), (5,2),$$
$$(5,1), (4,1), (4,0), (5,0), (6,0), (6,1), (7,1), (7,0).$$

Appendix C discusses space-filling curves in general and shows methods for fast traversal of some curves. Here we would like to point out that quadtrees (Section 4.12) are a special case of the Hilbert curve, a fact illustrated by Figures C.1 through C.7.

▶ **Exercise 4.22:** Scan the 8×8 bitmap of Figure 4.41 using a Hilbert curve. Calculate the runs of identical pixels and compare them to the runs produced by RLE.

Bibliography

Prusinkiewicz, P., and A. Lindenmayer (1990) *The Algorithmic Beauty of Plants*, New York, Springer Verlag.

Prusinkiewicz, P., A. Lindenmayer, and F. D. Fracchia (1991) "Synthesis of Space-Filling Curves on the Square Grid," in *Fractals in the Fundamental and Applied Sciences*, edited by Peitgen, H.-O. et al., Amsterdam, Elsevier Science Publishers, pp. 341–366.

Sagan, Hans (1994) *Space-Filling Curves*, New York, Springer Verlag.

4.14 Weighted Finite Automata

Finite-state automata (or finite-state machines) will be introduced in Section 5.7, in connection with dynamic Markov coding. The method discussed here, due to K. Culik [Culik 96], starts with a bi-level (monochromatic) image and creates a finite-state automaton that completely describes the image. The automaton is then written on the compressed stream and it becomes the compressed image. The method is lossless but it is easy to add a lossy option where a user-controlled parameter indicates the amount of loss permitted. (We later show how this method can be extended to grayscale images, where it is normally used as a lossy compression method.) The method is based on two principles:

1. Any quadrant, subquadrant, and pixel in the image can be represented by a string of the digits 0, 1, 2, and 3. The longer the string, the smaller the image area it represents.

2. Images used in practice have a certain amount of self-similarity, i.e., it is possible many times to find part of the image that looks the same as another part, except for size, or is at least very similar to it. Sometimes part of an image has to be rotated, reflected, or video-reversed in order for it to look like another part, and this feature is also used by the method.

Quadtrees were introduced in Section 4.12. We assume that the quadrant numbering of Figure 4.42a is extended recursively to subquadrants. Figure 4.42b shows how each of the 16 subquadrants produced from the 4 original ones are identified by a 2-digit string of the digits 0, 1, 2, and 3. After another subdivision, each of the resulting subsubquadrants is identified by a 3-digit string, and so on. The black area in Figure 4.42c is identified by the string 1032.

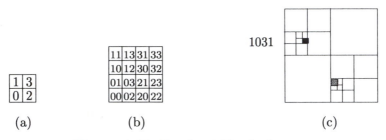

(a)   (b)   (c)

Figure 4.42: Quadrant Numbering.

▶ **Exercise 4.23:** What string identifies the gray area of Figure 4.42c?

If the image size is $2^n \times 2^n$ then a single pixel is represented by a string of n digits, and a string of k digits represents a subquadrant of size $2^{n-k} \times 2^{n-k}$ pixels. Once this is grasped, it is easy to see how an image can be represented by a finite-state automaton. This is based on three rules:

1. Each state of the automaton represents part of the image. State 0 is the entire image; other states represent quadrants or subquadrants of various sizes.

2. Given a state i that represents part of the image, it is divided into four quadrants. If, e.g., quadrant 2 of i is identical to the image part represented by state j, then an arc is drawn from state i to state j, and is labeled 2 (the label is the "weight" of the arc, hence the name "weighted finite automata" or WFA).

3. There is no need to worry about parts that are totally white. If quadrant 1 of state i, e.g., is completely white, there is no need to find an identical state and to have an arc with weight 1 coming out of i. When the automaton is used to reconstruct the image (i.e., when the compressed stream is decoded) any missing arcs are assumed to point to white subquadrants of the image.

Figure 4.43a shows a 2×2 chessboard. This is a simple, symmetric, and highly self-similar image, so its WFA is especially simple. The entire image becomes state 0 of the WFA. Quadrant 0 is all-white, so there is no need for an arc labeled 0 out of state 0. Quadrant 1 is black, so we add a new state, state 1, that's all black, and construct an arc labeled 1 from state 0 to state 1 (Figure 4.43b). We denote it 0(1)1. Quadrant 2 is also black, so we construct another arc, labeled 2, from state

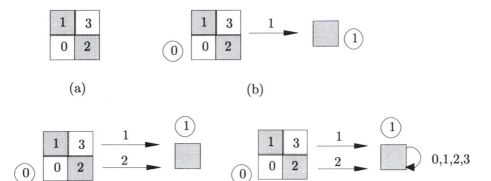

(a)   (b)

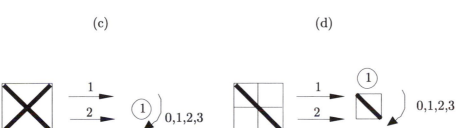

(c)   (d)

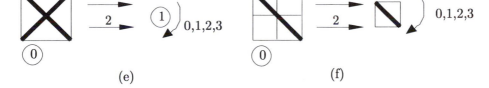

(e)   (f)

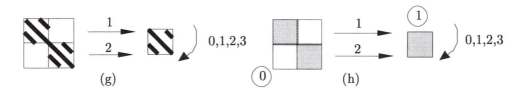

(g)   (h)

Figure 4.43: Encoding and Decoding a 2×2 Chessboard.

0 to state 1 (Figure 4.43c). It is denoted $0(2)1$. There is no need to worry about quadrant 3 since it is white.

We next move to state 1. We divide it into four quadrants and notice that every one is identical to the entire state. We thus construct four arcs, labeled 0, 1, 2, and 3, all going from state 1 to itself (Figure 4.43d). The WFA is now complete since there are no more states to be considered.

Notice that nothing has been said about the resolution of this chessboard. The process of constructing the automaton does not depend on the resolution, which is why this compression method can be applied to *multiresolution images*, i.e., images that may exist in several different resolutions.

▶ **Exercise 4.24:** Construct the WFA representing an 8×8 chessboard.

Constructing a WFA for a given image is somewhat similar to building a quadtree. We start by declaring the entire image state 0. It becomes the first state in the list of states of the WFA (a state is represented in this list as just a number, not any pixels) and is also pushed into a stack where states that are still "to be examined" will be kept. The main loop is then started, which repeats until the stack is empty. In each iteration a state i "to be examined" is popped off the stack and is partitioned into 4 quadrants. Each quadrant q_k of i is examined to see if it is identical to a (smaller version of) an existing state j. If yes, an arc labeled k is constructed from i to j [i.e., the item $i(k)j$ is added to the list of arcs]. If not, quadrant q_k is added to the list of states, as a new state q_k, it is also pushed into the stack, as another state "to be examined" in the future, and an arc $i(k)q_k$ is added to the list of arcs.

Figure 4.44 is a pseudo-code algorithm of this process.

```
states:=φ;    [list of states]
stack:=φ;     [empty stack]
arcs:=φ;      [set of arcs]
append(states,0); [add entire image as state 0]
push(0);
repeat
 i:=pop();
 for each quadrant q_k in i do
  if q_k ≠white then
    search states for state j such that j = q_k;
    if successful then append(arcs,i(k)j);
     else append(states,q_k); push(q_k); append(arcs,i(k)q_k)
    endif
   endif
  endfor
until stack is empty;
```

Figure 4.44: Building the WFA of an Image.

When the WFA is complete, the list of arcs is written (after being arithmetically encoded) on the compressed stream. It becomes the compressed image. Decoding is done by reading the arcs, by using them to reconstruct the WFA, and following the arcs from state to state. However, decoding is very different from encoding (the WFA method is highly asymmetric) because the WFA does not have a "final" state. This makes it hard to decide when to stop the decoding loop. Figures 4.43e–h show the initial steps in decoding the 2×2 chessboard. The decoder does not know the images associated with the individual states, so it starts by setting state 0 (the entire image) to an arbitrary image (except that this cannot be all white) and all the other states to empty images. Figure 4.43e shows how state 0 is set to an arbitrary criss-cross image.

The arcs for quadrants 0 and 3 are missing, so these quadrants must be all white. The arcs for quadrants 1 and 2 lead to state 1, indicating that this state must be identical to the two quadrants (and implying that the two quadrants must also be identical). Figure 4.43f shows how state 1 is now set to a diagonal line. All arcs from state 1 end up in state 1, indicating that all four quadrants of state 1 are identical (up to a scale factor) to the entire state. Figure 4.43g shows the result of making the four quadrants of state 1 identical to the entire state. The new image of state 1 is then copied back into quadrants 1 and 3 of state 0. The decoding loop then continues, improving the shape of state 1 and, as a result, that of state 0, until a satisfactory result is obtained (Figure 4.43h). If the resolution of the image is $2^n \times 2^n$, then at most n iterations are needed to completely reconstruct the image but the user, watching the decoding process in real time, may decide to stop the loop earlier if the result is satisfactory.

Figure 4.45: Image for Exercise 4.25.

The compression performance depends on the number of arcs in the WFA which, in turn, depends on the number of states. To decrease the number of states, a new parameter t (transformation) is added. If quadrant k of state i is not identical to state j, the WFA-building algorithm checks to see whether a transformation of k will make it identical to j. Figure 4.46 shows seven basic transformations, 1–7, of an image 0. Three of them (1–3) are 90° rotations and the other four (4–7) are rotations of a reflection of 0. In addition there are eight more transformations, with numbers 8–15, which are the reverse videos of 0–7, respectively. Each transformation t is thus a 4-bit number, which is included in all the arcs. An arc now looks like $i(k, t)j$, where $t = 0$ if no transformation is needed.

Figure 4.47 shows another example of an image and its WFA. The 11 resulting arcs are shown in the table with their transformations.

▶ **Exercise 4.25:** Construct the WFA of the image of Figure 4.45 using transformations, and list all the resulting arcs in a table.

Another "trick" to improve performance is to express small images explicitly. Experience shows that small images do not compress well by this method; the

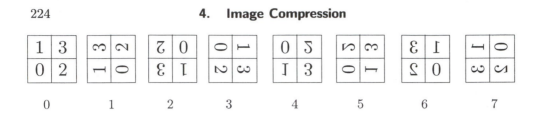

Figure 4.46: Rotations and Reflections of an Image.

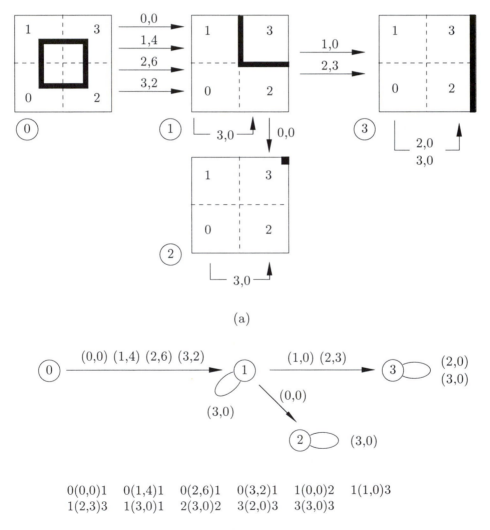

(a)

0(0,0)1   0(1,4)1   0(2,6)1   0(3,2)1   1(0,0)2   1(1,0)3
1(2,3)3   1(3,0)1   2(3,0)2   3(2,0)3   3(3,0)3

(b)

Figure 4.47: An Example WFA.

size of the WFA is about the same as that of the image (small input streams rarely compress well, regardless of the compression method used). The improved algorithm thus uses an extra step. If the size of quadrant k of state i is 8×8 pixels, an arc of the form $i(k, 0)r$ is created, where r is a code identifying one of the 256 possible patterns of the quadrant. When the decoder encounters such an arc, it can immediately generate the 8×8 image of the quadrant. We can consider code r as a special "final" state of the WFA. When the decoder reaches such a state, it can fully recreate a subquadrant and that subquadrant will not have to be included in any further iterations of the decoder.

The lossy option considers quadrant k of state i identical to an existing state j if they differ by at most p pixels, where p is a user-controlled parameter. This parameter lets the user control the tradeoff between compression performance and image quality. Compression ratios of 0.015 to 0.025 bpp are common, with a loss of less than 1% of the original pixels. WFA is therefore an excellent compression method for bi-level images.

4.14.1 WFA for Grayscale Images

It is possible to extend the WFA method from bi-level to grayscale images and thus also to color images. This section outlines the main ideas but not all the details of this extension. The main problem is that such an image is richer than a bi-level (monochromatic) one since a pixel can have one of many values. (We assume that a white pixel is represented by a 0 and a black one by a 1. The value of a pixel is thus a real number in the range $[0, 1]$.) Given a quadrant q_k, this problem makes it harder to find a state j identical to q_k. The solution is to express q_k as a linear combination of several states. We may thus end up with the arcs $i(k, 1/2)j$ and $i(k, 1/4)l$, which mean that quadrant q_k of state i equals (up to a scale factor) the weighted sum of states j and l, where $1/2$ and $1/4$ are the weights rather than any transformations.

A simple example is the image of Figure 4.48c. Assuming that the origin of coordinates for this image is at its bottom-left corner, a pixel at position (i, j) has intensity (or gray value) proportional to the sum $i + j$. Pixels located around the bottom-left corner have small values (they are close to white), while those near to the top-right corner are close to black. Figure 4.48d is the WFA of 4.48c. It contains just two states. State 0 is the entire image and state 1 is black. Quadrant 0 of the image, e.g., equals the entire image with a weight of $1/2$. Quadrant 1 is the sum of states 0 and 1 with weights $1/2$ and $1/4$, respectively. We can say that this quadrant equals a light version of the entire image, plus a little darkening of all its pixels. State 1 is uniform black, so each of its four quadrants is identical to the entire state.

Once the WFA is obtained, it is written on the compressed stream and it becomes the compressed image. Decoding is especially easy. It is done by means of four matrices W_k and two vectors I and F. An element $W_k(i, j)$ of matrices W_k is the weight w of arc $i(k, w)j$. Each of the four matrices W_k thus has dimensions $s \times s$ where s is the number of states of the WFA. In our example there are two states, so $s = 2$ and the four matrices have dimensions 2×2. The matrices therefore are

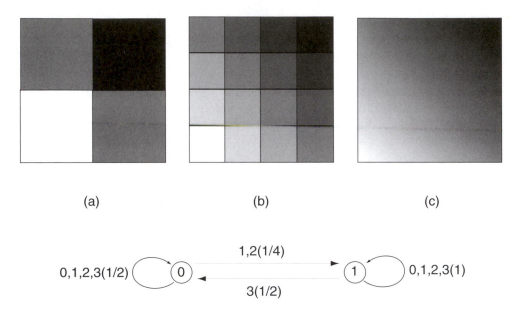

(a)   (b)   (c)

1,2(1/4)

0,1,2,3(1/2) $\quad$ 0 $\quad$ $\xrightarrow{\hspace{2cm}}$ $\quad$ 1 $\quad$ 0,1,2,3(1)

3(1/2)

(d)

Figure 4.48: A Simple, Self-Similar Image and Its WFA.

$$W_0 = \begin{pmatrix} 1/2 & 0 \\ 0 & 1 \end{pmatrix}; \; W_1 = \begin{pmatrix} 1/2 & 1/4 \\ 0 & 1 \end{pmatrix}; \; W_2 = \begin{pmatrix} 1/2 & 1/4 \\ 0 & 1 \end{pmatrix}; \; W_3 = \begin{pmatrix} 1/2 & 1/2 \\ 0 & 1 \end{pmatrix}.$$

Vectors I and F are also of size s. Vector I contains a single 1 followed by zeros. Each element of vector F is the average pixel values of one state of the WFA. In our example, state 0 has the same number of light and dark pixels (it is balanced) so its average pixel value is $1/2$. State 1 is made of black pixels, so its average value is 1. We thus have $I = (1, 0)$ and $F = (1/2, 1)$.

The encoder prepares I, F, and the four matrices W_k, and writes them on the compressed tream. Once they are read by the decoder, it is easy to decode the image at any resolution. The key to decoding is to compute the value

$$f(k_1 k_2 \cdots k_n) = I W_{k_1} W_{k_2} \cdots W_{k_n} F \tag{4.13}$$

for each subquadrant (or "fat" pixel) $k_1 k_2 \cdots k_n$ of the decoded image. Notice that n determines the resolution, $2^n \times 2^n$, of the decoded image.

For $n = 1$ (a resolution of 2×2), we get $f(k_1) = I W_{k_1} F$, so the 2×2 decoded image becomes

$$f(0) = IW_0F = (1,0)\begin{pmatrix} 1/2 & 0 \\ 0 & 1 \end{pmatrix}\begin{pmatrix} 1/2 \\ 1 \end{pmatrix} = (1/2,0)\begin{pmatrix} 1/2 \\ 1 \end{pmatrix} = 1/4,$$

$$f(1) = IW_1F = (1,0)\begin{pmatrix} 1/2 & 1/4 \\ 0 & 1 \end{pmatrix}\begin{pmatrix} 1/2 \\ 1 \end{pmatrix} = (1/2,1/4)\begin{pmatrix} 1/2 \\ 1 \end{pmatrix} = 1/2,$$

$$f(2) = IW_2F = (1,0)\begin{pmatrix} 1/2 & 1/4 \\ 0 & 1 \end{pmatrix}\begin{pmatrix} 1/2 \\ 1 \end{pmatrix} = (1/2,1/4)\begin{pmatrix} 1/2 \\ 1 \end{pmatrix} = 1/2,$$

$$f(3) = IW_3F = (1,0)\begin{pmatrix} 1/2 & 1/2 \\ 0 & 1 \end{pmatrix}\begin{pmatrix} 1/2 \\ 1 \end{pmatrix} = (1/2,1/2)\begin{pmatrix} 1/2 \\ 1 \end{pmatrix} = 3/4.$$

The 4 "fat" pixels are shown in Figure 4.48a. Note that the average of the four pixels $(1/4 + 1/2 + 1/2 + 3/4)/4 = 1/2$ equals the average pixel value of the entire image.

For $n = 2$ the image is decoded at a resolution of $2^2 \times 2^2$. The 16 pixels are shown in Figure 4.48b. Each is given by the expression $f(k_1k_2) = IW_{k_1}W_{k_2}F$. Pixel $f(03)$, e.g., has value

$$
\begin{aligned}
f(03) &= IW_0W_3F \\
&= (1,0)\begin{pmatrix} 1/2 & 0 \\ 0 & 1 \end{pmatrix}\begin{pmatrix} 1/2 & 1/2 \\ 0 & 1 \end{pmatrix}\begin{pmatrix} 1/2 \\ 1 \end{pmatrix} \\
&= (1,0)\begin{pmatrix} 1/4 & 1/4 \\ 0 & 1 \end{pmatrix}\begin{pmatrix} 1/2 \\ 1 \end{pmatrix} \\
&= (1/4,1/4)\begin{pmatrix} 1/2 \\ 1 \end{pmatrix} = 1/8 + 1/4 = 3/8.
\end{aligned}
$$

▸ **Exercise 4.26:** Compute the values of pixels $f(00)$, $f(01)$, and $f(02)$,

Notice that the average of the four pixels $f(ij)$, which is $(1/8 + 2/8 + 2/8 + 3/8)/4 = 1/4$, equals the value of the "fat" pixel $f(0)$. Equation (4.13) is thus average-preserving, an important property for decoding multiresolution images.

▸ **Exercise 4.27:** Show that, for a large value of n, the bottom-left pixel of the high-resolution decoded image approaches 0 and the top-right one approaches 1.

The compressed stream consists of the arcs and of vector F. As has been mentioned before, there is no need to write the images associated with the states on the compressed stream. However, it is easy to figure out the actual image represented by state i at resolution n. It is given by

$$\psi_i(k_1k_2\cdots k_n) = (W_{k_1}W_{k_2}\cdots W_{k_n}F)_i. \tag{4.14}$$

As an example

$$\psi_i(0) = (W_0F)_i = \begin{pmatrix} 1/2 & 0 \\ 0 & 1 \end{pmatrix}\begin{pmatrix} 1/2 \\ 1 \end{pmatrix}_i = \begin{pmatrix} 1/4 \\ 1 \end{pmatrix}_i ;$$

so $\psi_0(0) = 1/4$ and $\psi_1(0) = 1$. The image associated with quadrant 0 of state 0 consists of pixels set to 1/4. That of quadrant 0 of state 1 is all 1s (black).

▶ **Exercise 4.28:** Compute images $\psi_0(00)$ and $\psi_0(01)$.

The grayscale version of WFA can be easily extended to cartoon-like color images (images where large areas have uniform color). Such an image is first separated into three grayscale images, one for each color component. Since the original color image has large uniform areas, each of the three grayscale images has some degree of self-similarity, which contributes to compression efficiency. The encoder builds a WFA for one of the three grayscale images and then adds states and arcs to this WFA to encode the other two images.

Bibliography

Culik, Karel II, and V. Valenta (1996), "Finite Automata Based Compression of Bi-Level Images," in Storer, James A. (ed.), *DCC '96, Data Compression Conference,* Los Alamitos, CA, IEEE Computer Society Press, pp. 280–289.

4.15 Iterated Function Systems (IFS)

Fractals have been popular since the 1970s, and have many applications. One such application, relatively underused, is data compression. Applying fractals to data compression is called *iterated function systems* or IFS. Two good references to IFS are [Barnsley 88] and [Fisher 95]. IFS compression can be very efficient, achieving excellent compression factors (32 is not uncommon) but it is lossy and also computationally intensive. The IFS encoder partitions the image into parts called ranges, matches each range to some other part called a domain, and produces an *affine transformation* from the domain to the range. The transformations are written on the compressed stream and they become the compressed image. We start with an introduction to two-dimensional affine transformations.

4.15.1 Affine Transformations

In computer graphics, a complete two-dimensional image is built part by part and is normally edited before it is considered satisfactory. Editing is done by selecting a figure (part of the drawing) and applying a transformation to it. Typical transformations (Figure 4.49) are moving or sliding (translation), reflecting or flipping (mirror image), zooming (scaling), rotating, and shearing.

The transformation can be applied to every pixel of the figure. Alternatively, it can be applied to a few key points that completely define the figure (such as the four corners of a rectangle), following which, the figure is reconstructed from the transformed key points.

We use the notation $\mathbf{P} = (x, y)$ for a two-dimensional point, and $\mathbf{P}^* = (x^*, y^*)$ for the transformed point. The simplest linear transformation is $x^* = ax + cy$; $y^* = bx + dy$, in which each of the new coordinates is a *linear combination* of the two old ones. This transformation can be written $\mathbf{P}^* = \mathbf{P}\mathbf{T}$, where $\mathbf{T}$ is the 2×2 matrix $\left(\begin{smallmatrix} a & b \\ c & d \end{smallmatrix}\right)$ (see Appendix D for matrices).

To understand the functions of the four matrix elements, we start by setting $b = c = 0$. The transformation becomes $x^* = ax$, $y^* = dy$. Such a transformation is called *scaling*. If applied to all the points of an object, all the x dimensions are scaled by a factor a, and all the y dimensions, by a factor d. Note that a and d can also be < 1, causing shrinking of the object. If any of a or d equals -1, the

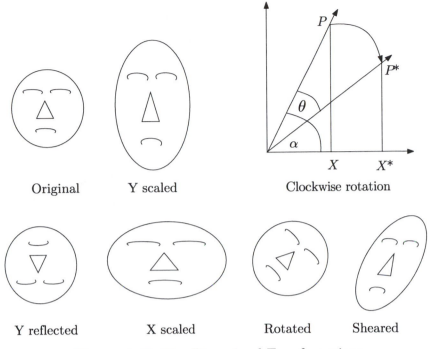

Figure 4.49: Two-Dimensional Transformations.

transformation is a *reflection*. Any other negative values cause both scaling and reflection.

Note that scaling an object by factors of a and d changes its area by a factor of $a \times d$, and that this factor is also the value of the determinant (Appendix D) of the scaling matrix $\begin{pmatrix} a & 0 \\ 0 & d \end{pmatrix}$.

Below are examples of matrices for scaling and reflection. In a, the y-coordinates are scaled by a factor of 2. In b, the x-coordinates are reflected. In c, the x dimensions are shrunk to 0.001 their original values. In d, the figure is shrunk to a vertical line:

$$ a = \begin{pmatrix} 1 & 0 \\ 0 & 2 \end{pmatrix}; \quad b = \begin{pmatrix} -1 & 0 \\ 0 & 1 \end{pmatrix}; \quad c = \begin{pmatrix} .001 & 0 \\ 0 & 1 \end{pmatrix}; \quad d = \begin{pmatrix} 0 & 0 \\ 0 & 1 \end{pmatrix}. $$

The next step is to set $a = 1$, $d = 1$ (no scaling or reflection), and explore the effect of b and c on the transformations. The transformation becomes $x^* = x + cy$, $y^* = bx + y$. We first select matrix $\begin{pmatrix} 1 & 1 \\ 0 & 1 \end{pmatrix}$ and use it to transform the rectangle whose four corners are $(1,0)$, $(3,0)$, $(1,1)$ and $(3,1)$. The corners are transformed to $(1,1)$, $(3,3)$, $(1,2)$, $(3,4)$. The original rectangle has been *sheared* vertically, and transformed into a parallelogram. A similar effect occurs when we try the matrix $\begin{pmatrix} 1 & 0 \\ 1 & 1 \end{pmatrix}$. The quantities b and c are thus responsible for *shearing*. Figure 4.50 shows the connection between shearing and the operation of scissors, which is the reason for the word shearing.

Figure 4.50: Scissors and Shearing.

▶ **Exercise 4.29:** Apply the shearing transformation $\left(\begin{smallmatrix}1 & -1\\ 0 & 1\end{smallmatrix}\right)$ to the four points $(1,0)$, $(3,0)$, $(1,1)$, and $(3,1)$. What are the transformed points? What geometrical figure do they represent?

The next important transformation is *rotation*. Figure 4.49 illustrates rotation. It shows a point $\mathbf{P}$ rotated clockwise through an angle θ to become $\mathbf{P}^*$. Simple trigonometry yields $x = R\cos\alpha$ and $y = R\sin\alpha$. From this we get the expressions for x^* and y^*:

$$x^* = R\cos(\alpha - \theta) = R\cos\alpha\cos\theta + R\sin\alpha\sin\theta = x\cos\theta + y\sin\theta,$$
$$y^* = R\sin(\alpha - \theta) = -R\cos\alpha\sin\theta + R\sin\alpha\cos\theta = -x\sin\theta + y\cos\theta.$$

Thus the rotation matrix in two dimensions is:

$$\begin{pmatrix} \cos\theta & -\sin\theta \\ \sin\theta & \cos\theta \end{pmatrix}, \quad \text{which also equals} \quad \begin{pmatrix} \cos\theta & 0 \\ 0 & \cos\theta \end{pmatrix} \begin{pmatrix} 1 & -\tan\theta \\ \tan\theta & 1 \end{pmatrix}.$$

Which proves that any rotation in 2D is a combination of scaling (and, perhaps, reflection) and shearing, an unexpected result that's true for all angles satisfying $\tan\theta \neq \infty$.

Matrix $\mathbf{T}_1$ below rotates anticlockwise. Matrix $\mathbf{T}_2$ reflects about the line $y = x$, and matrix $\mathbf{T}_3$ reflects about the line $y = -x$. Note the determinants of these matrices. In general, a determinant of $+1$ indicates pure rotation, whereas a determinant of -1 indicates pure reflection. (As a reminder, $\det\left(\begin{smallmatrix}a & b\\ c & d\end{smallmatrix}\right) = ad - bc$. See also Appendix D.)

$$\mathbf{T}_1 = \begin{pmatrix} \cos\theta & \sin\theta \\ -\sin\theta & \cos\theta \end{pmatrix} \qquad \mathbf{T}_2 = \begin{pmatrix} 0 & 1 \\ 1 & 0 \end{pmatrix} \qquad \mathbf{T}_3 = \begin{pmatrix} 0 & -1 \\ -1 & 0 \end{pmatrix}.$$

4.15.2 A 90° Rotation

In the case of a 90° clockwise rotation, the rotation matrix is

$$\begin{pmatrix} \cos(90) & -\sin(90) \\ \sin(90) & \cos(90) \end{pmatrix} = \begin{pmatrix} 0 & -1 \\ 1 & 0 \end{pmatrix}. \tag{4.15}$$

A point $\mathbf{P} = (x, y)$ is thus transformed to the point $(y, -x)$. For a counterclockwise 90° rotation, (x, y) is transformed to $(-y, x)$. This is called the *negate and exchange* rule.

The Golden Ratio

Imagine a straight segment of length l. We divide it into two parts a and b such that $a + b = l$ and $l/a = a/b$.

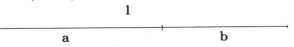

The ratio a/b is a constant called the *Golden Ratio* and denoted ϕ. It is one of the important mathematical constants, such as π and e, and has already been known to the ancient Greeks. It is believed that geometric figures can be made more pleasing to the human eye if they involve this ratio. One example is the golden rectangle, with sides of dimensions x and $x\phi$. Many classical buildings and paintings involve this ratio. [Huntley 70] is a lively introduction to the golden ratio. It illustrates properties such as

$$\phi = \sqrt{1 + \sqrt{1 + \sqrt{1 + \sqrt{1 + \cdots}}}} \quad \text{and} \quad \phi = 1 + \cfrac{1}{1 + \cfrac{1}{1 + \cfrac{1}{\cdots}}}.$$

The value of ϕ is easy to calculate: $l/a = a/b = \phi \Rightarrow (a + b)/a = a/b = \phi \Rightarrow 1 + b/a = \phi \Rightarrow 1 + 1/\phi = \phi \Rightarrow \phi^2 - \phi - 1 = 0$. The last equation is easy to solve, yielding $\phi = (1 + \sqrt{5})/2 \approx 1.618\ldots$

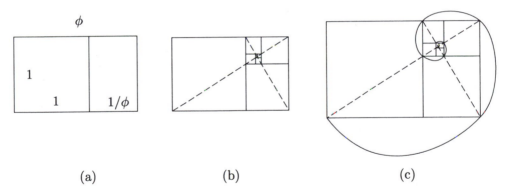

| (a) | (b) | (c) |

Figure 4.51: The Golden Ratio.

The equation $\phi = 1 + 1/\phi$ illustrates another unusual property of ϕ. Imagine the golden rectangle with sides $1 \times \phi$ (Figure 4.51a). Such a rectangle can be divided into a 1×1 square and a smaller golden rectangle of dimensions $1 \times 1/\phi$. The smaller rectangle can now be divided into a $1/\phi \times 1/\phi$ square, and an even smaller golden rectangle (Figure 4.51b). When this process continues, the rectangles converge to a point. Figure 4.51c shows how a logarithmic spiral can be drawn through corresponding corners of the rectangles.

4.15.3 Translations

Unfortunately, our simple 2×2 matrix cannot generate all the necessary transformations! Specifically, it cannot generate *translation*. This is proved by realizing that
any object containing the origin will, after any of the transformations above, still
contain the origin (the result of $(0,0) \times \mathbf{T}$ is $(0,0)$ for any matrix $\mathbf{T}$).

One way to implement translation (which can be expressed by $x^* = x + m$,
$y^* = y + n$), is to generalize our transformations to $\mathbf{P}^* = \mathbf{PT} + (m, n)$, where $\mathbf{T}$ is
the familiar 2×2 transformation matrix $\begin{pmatrix} a & b \\ c & d \end{pmatrix}$. A more elegant approach, however,
is to stay with $\mathbf{P}^* = \mathbf{PT}$ and to generalize $\mathbf{T}$ to the 3×3 matrix

$$\mathbf{T} = \begin{pmatrix} a & b & 0 \\ c & d & 0 \\ m & n & 1 \end{pmatrix}.$$

This approach is called *homogeneous coordinates* and is commonly used in projective
geometry. It makes it possible to unify all the two-dimensional transformations
within one matrix. Notice that only six of the nine elements of matrix $\mathbf{T}$ above are
variables. Our points should now be the triplets $\mathbf{P} = (x, y, 1)$.

It is easy to see that the transformations discussed above can change lengths
and angles. Scaling changes the lengths of objects. Rotation and shearing change
angles. One thing that's preserved, though, is parallel lines. A pair of parallel lines
will remain parallel after any scaling, reflection, rotation, shearing, and translation.
A transformation that preserves parallelism is called *affine*.

The final conclusion of this section is: any affine two-dimensional transformation can be fully specified by only six numbers!

Affine transformations can be defined in different ways. One important definition is: a transformation of points in space is affine if it preserves *barycentric
sums* of the points. A barycentric sum of points $\mathbf{P}_i$ has the form $\sum w_i \mathbf{P}_i$ where w_i
are numbers and $\sum w_i = 1$, so if $\mathbf{P} = \sum w_i \mathbf{P}_i$ and if $\sum w_i = 1$, then any affine
transformation $\mathbf{T}$ satisfies

$$\mathbf{TP} = \sum_{1}^{n} w_i \mathbf{TP}_i.$$

4.15.4 IFS Definition

A simple example of IFS is the set of three transformations

$$\mathbf{T}_1 = \begin{pmatrix} .5 & 0 & 0 \\ 0 & .5 & 0 \\ 8 & 8 & 1 \end{pmatrix}; \quad \mathbf{T}_2 = \begin{pmatrix} .5 & 0 & 0 \\ 0 & .5 & 0 \\ 96 & 16 & 1 \end{pmatrix}; \quad \mathbf{T}_3 = \begin{pmatrix} .5 & 0 & 0 \\ 0 & .5 & 0 \\ 120 & 60 & 1 \end{pmatrix}. \quad (4.16)$$

We first discuss the concept of the *fixed point*. Imagine the sequence $\mathbf{P}_1 = \mathbf{P}_0 \mathbf{T}_1$,
$\mathbf{P}_2 = \mathbf{P}_1 \mathbf{T}_1 \cdots$, where transformation $\mathbf{T}_1$ is applied repeatedly to create a sequence
of points $\mathbf{P}_1, \mathbf{P}_2 \ldots$. It is easy to prove that $\lim_{n \to \infty} \mathbf{P}_n = (2m, 2n) = (16, 16)$.
This point is called the *fixed point* of $\mathbf{T}_1$, and *it does not depend* on the particular
starting point $\mathbf{P}_0$ selected.

Proof: $\mathbf{P}_1 = \mathbf{P}_0\mathbf{T}_1 = (.5x_0 + 8, .5y_0 + 8)$, $\mathbf{P}_2 = \mathbf{P}_1\mathbf{T}_1 = (.5(.5x_0 + 8) + 8, .5(.5y_0 + 8) + 8)$. It is easy to see (and to prove by induction) that $x_n = .5^n x_0 + .5^{n-1}8 + .5^{n-2}8 + \cdots + .5^1 8 + 8$. In the limit $x_n = .5^n x_0 + 8\sum_{i=0}^{\infty} 0.5^i = .5^n x_0 + 8 \times 2$, which approaches the limit $8 \times 2 = 16$ for large n regardless of x_0. ◄

Now it is easy to show that, for the transformations above, with scale factors of 0.5 and no shearing, each new point in the sequence moves half the remaining distance toward the fixed point. Given a point $\mathbf{P}_i = (x_i, y_i)$, the point midway between $\mathbf{P}_i$ and the fixed point $(16, 16)$ is

$$\left(\frac{x_i + 16}{2}, \frac{y_i + 16}{2}\right) = (.5x_i + 8, .5y_i + 8) = (x_{i+1}, y_{i+1}) = \mathbf{P}_{i+1}.$$

Consequently, for the particular transformations above there is no need to use the transformation matrix. At each step of the iteration, point $\mathbf{P}_{i+1}$ is obtained by $(\mathbf{P}_i + (2m, 2n))/2$. For other transformations, matrix multiplication is necessary to compute point $\mathbf{P}_{i+1}$.

In general, every affine transformation where the scale and shear factors are < 1 has a fixed point, but it may not be easy to find it.

The principle of IFS is now easy to describe. A set of transformations (an IFS code) is selected. A sequence of points is calculated and plotted by starting with an arbitrary point $\mathbf{P}_0$, selecting a transformation from the set at random, and applying it to $\mathbf{P}_0$, transforming it into a point $\mathbf{P}_1$, and then randomly selecting another transformation and applying it to $\mathbf{P}_1$, thereby generating point $\mathbf{P}_2$, and so on.

Every point is plotted on the screen as it is calculated, and gradually the object begins to take shape before the viewer's eyes. The shape of the object is called the IFS *attractor*, and it depends on the IFS code (the transformations) selected. The shape also depends slightly on the particular selection of $\mathbf{P}_0$. It is best to choose $\mathbf{P}_0$ as one of the fixed points of the IFS code (if they are known in advance). In such a case, all the points in the sequence will lie inside the attractor. For any other choice of $\mathbf{P}_0$, a finite number of points will lie outside the attractor, but eventually they will move into the attractor and stay there.

It is surprising that the attractor does not depend on the precise order of the transformations used. This result has been proved ,by the mathematician John Elton.

Another surprising property of IFS is that the random numbers used don't have to be uniformly distributed; they can be weighted. Transformation $\mathbf{T}_1$, e.g., may be selected at random 50% of the time, transformation $\mathbf{T}_2$, 30%, and $\mathbf{T}_3$, 20%. The shape being generated does not depend on the probabilities, but the computation time does. The weights should add up to one (a normal requirement for a set of mathematical weights), and none can be zero.

The three transformations of Equation (4.16) above create an attractor in the form of a Sierpinski triangle (Figure 4.52a). The translation factors determine the coordinates of the three triangle corners. The six transformations of Table 4.53 create an attractor in the form of a fern (Figure 4.52b). The notation used in Table 4.53 is $\begin{pmatrix} ab \\ cd \end{pmatrix} + \begin{pmatrix} m \\ n \end{pmatrix}$.

The Sierpinski triangle, also known as the Sierpinski gasket (Figure 4.52a) is defined recursively. Start with any triangle, find the midpoint of each edge, connect the three midpoints to obtain a new triangle, fully contained in the original one, and cut the new triangle out. The newly created hole now divides the original triangle into three smaller ones. Repeat the process on each of the smaller triangles. At the limit, there is no area left in the triangle. It resembles Swiss cheese without any cheese, just holes.

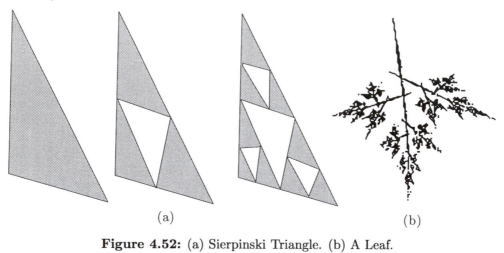

(a)   (b)

Figure 4.52: (a) Sierpinski Triangle. (b) A Leaf.

The program of Figure 4.54 calculates and displays IFS attractors for any given set of transformations. It runs on the Macintosh computer under the Metrowerks™ Pascal compiler.

The following sets of numbers create especially interesting patterns.

1. A frond.

5

0	-28	0	29	151	92
64	0	0	64	82	6
-2	37	-31	29	85	103
17	-51	-22	3	183	148
-1	18	-18	-1	88	147

2. A coastline

4

-17	-26	34	-12	84	53
25	-20	29	17	192	57
35	0	0	35	49	3
25	-6	6	25	128	28

3. A leaf (Figure 4.52b)

4

2	-7	-2	48	141	83
40	0	-4	65	88	10
-2	45	-37	10	82	132
-11	-60	-34	22	237	125

4. A Sierpinski Triangle

3

50	0	0	50	0	0
50	0	0	50	127	79
50	0	0	50	127	0

▶ **Exercise 4.30:** The three affine transformations of example 4 above (the Sierpinski triangle) are different from those of Equation (4.16). What's the explanation?

	a	b	c	d	m	n		a	b	c	d	m	n
1:	0	-28	0	29	151	92	4:	64	0	0	64	82	6
2:	-2	37	-31	29	85	103	5:	0	-80	-22	1	243	151
3:	-1	18	-18	-1	88	147	6:	2	-48	0	50	160	80

Table 4.53: All numbers are shown as integers, but a, b, c, and d should be divided by 100, to make them < 1. The values m and n are the translation factors.

```
PROGRAM IFS;
USES ScreenIO, Graphics, MathLib;
CONST LB = 5; Width = 490; Height = 285;
(* LB=left bottom corner of window *)
VAR i,k,x0,y0,x1,y1,NumTransf: INTEGER;
Transf: ARRAY[1..6,1..10] OF INTEGER;
Params:TEXT;
filename:STRING;
BEGIN (* main *)
Write('params file='); Readln(filename);
Assign(Params,filename); Reset(Params);
Readln(Params,NumTransf);
FOR i:=1 TO NumTransf DO
Readln(Params,Transf[1,i],Transf[2,i],Transf[3,i],
 Transf[4,i],Transf[5,i],Transf[6,i]);
 OpenGraphicWindow(LB,LB,Width,Height,'IFS shape');
 SetMode(paint);
 x0:=100; y0:=100;
 REPEAT
 k:=RandomInt(1,NumTransf+1);
 x1:=Round((x0*Transf[1,k]+y0*Transf[2,k])/100)+Transf[5,k];
 y1:=Round((x0*Transf[3,k]+y0*Transf[4,k])/100)+Transf[6,k];
 Dot(x1,y1); x0:=x1; y0:=y1;
 UNTIL Button()=TRUE;
  ScBOL; ScWriteStr('Hit a key & close this window to quit');
  ScFreeze;
END.
```

Figure 4.54: Calculate and Display IFS Attractors.

4.15.5 Another Look at IFS

Before we describe how IFS is used to compress real-life images, let's look at IFS
from a different point of view. Figure 4.55 shows three images, a person, the letter
"T," and the Sierpinski gasket (or triangle). The first two images are transformed
in a special way. Each image is shrunk to half its size, is copied three times, and
the three copies are arranged in the shape of a triangle. When this transformation
is applied a few times to an image, it is still possible to discern the individual
copies of the original image. However, when it is applied many times, the result
is the Sierpinski gasket (or something very close to it, depending on the number
of iterations and on the resolution of the output device). The point is that each
transformation shrinks the image (the transformations are *contractive*), so the final
result does not depend on the shape of the original image. The shape can be
that of a person, a letter, or anything else; the final result depends only on the
particular transformation applied to the image. A different transformation will
create a different result which again will not depend on the particular image being
transformed. Figure 4.55d, e.g., shows the results of transforming the letter "T" by
reducing it, making three copies, arranging them in a triangle, and flipping the top
copy. The final image obtained at the limit, after applying a certain transformation
infinitely many times, is called the *attractor* of the transformation.

The result of each transformation is an image containing all the images of all
previous transformations. If we apply the same transformation many times, it is
possible to zoom on the result, to magnify it many times, and still see details of the
original images. In principle, if we apply the transformation an infinite number of
times, the final result will show details at *any* magnification. It will be a fractal.

The case of Figure 4.55c is especially interesting. It seems that the original
image is simply shown four times, without any transformations. A little thinking,
however, shows that our particular transformation transforms this image to itself.
The original image is already the Sierpinski gasket and it gets transformed to itself
because it is self-similar.

▸ **Exercise 4.31:** Explain the geometrical meaning of the combined three affine
transformations below and show the attractor they converge to.

$$
w_1 \begin{pmatrix} x \\ y \end{pmatrix} = \begin{pmatrix} 1/2 & 0 \\ 0 & 1/2 \end{pmatrix} \begin{pmatrix} x \\ y \end{pmatrix},
$$

$$
w_2 \begin{pmatrix} x \\ y \end{pmatrix} = \begin{pmatrix} 1/2 & 0 \\ 0 & 1/2 \end{pmatrix} \begin{pmatrix} x \\ y \end{pmatrix} + \begin{pmatrix} 0 \\ 1/2 \end{pmatrix},
$$

$$
w_3 \begin{pmatrix} x \\ y \end{pmatrix} = \begin{pmatrix} 1/2 & 0 \\ 0 & 1/2 \end{pmatrix} \begin{pmatrix} x \\ y \end{pmatrix} + \begin{pmatrix} 1/2 \\ 0 \end{pmatrix}.
$$

The Sierpinski gasket is thus easy to compress because it is self-similar; it is
easy to find parts of it that are identical to the entire image. In fact, every part of
it is identical to the entire image. Figure 4.56 shows the bottom-right part of the
gasket surrounded by dashed lines. It is easy to see the relation between this part
and the entire image. Their shapes are identical, up to a scale factor. The size of
this part is half the size of the image, and we know where it is positioned relative to

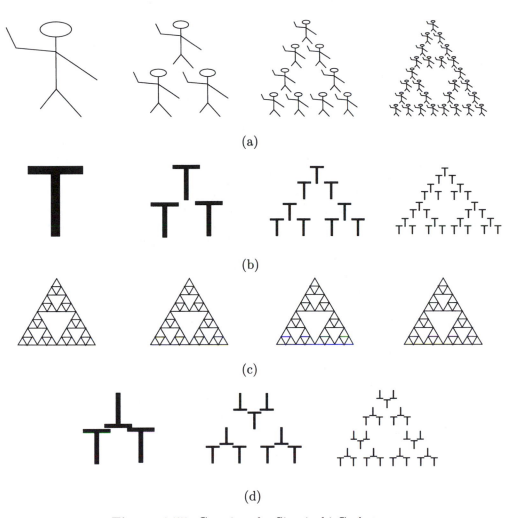

(a)

(b)

(c)

(d)

Figure 4.55: Creating the Sierpinski Gasket.

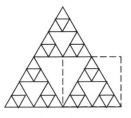

Figure 4.56: A Self-Similar Image.

the entire image (we can measure the displacement of its bottom-left corner from the bottom-left corner of the entire image).

This points to a possible way to compress real images. If we can divide an image into parts such that each part is identical (or at least very close) to the entire image up to a scale factor, then we can highly compress the image by IFS. All that we need is the scale factor (actually two scale factors, in the x and y directions) and the displacement of each part relative to the entire image [the (x, y) distances between one corner of the part and the same corner of the image]. Sometimes we may find a part of the image that has to be reflected in order to become identical to the entire image. In such a case we also need the reflection coefficients. We can thus compress an image by figuring out the transformations that transform each part (called "range") into the entire image. The transformation for each part is expressed by a few numbers, and these numbers become the compressed stream.

It is easy to see that this simple approach will not work on real-life images. Such images are complex and it is generally impossible to divide such an image into parts that will all be identical (or even very close) to the entire image. A different approach is needed to make IFS practical. The approach used by any practical IFS algorithm is to partition the image into non-overlapping parts called *ranges*. They can be of any size and shape but in practice it is easiest to work with squares, rectangles, or triangles. For each range R_i, the encoder has to find a *domain* D_i that's very similar, or even identical in shape, to the range but is bigger. Once such a domain is found, it is easy to figure out the transformation w_i that will transform the domain into the range $R_i = w_i(D_i)$. Two scale factors have to be determined (the scaling is shrinking since the domain is bigger than the range) as well as the displacement of the domain relative to the range [the (x, y) distances between one corner of the domain and the same corner of the range]. Sometimes the domain has to be rotated and/or reflected to make it identical to the range, and the transformation should, of course, include these factors as well. This approach to IFS image compression is called PIFS (for partitioned IFS).

4.15.6 IFS Decoding

Before looking into the details of PIFS encoding, let's try to understand how the PIFS decoder works. All that the decoder has is the set of transformations, one per range. It does not know the shapes of any ranges or domains. In spite of this, decoding is very simple. It is based on the fact, mentioned earlier, that a contractive transformation creates a result that does not depend on the shape of the initial image used. We can thus create any range R_i by applying transformation w_i many times on *any* shape D_i (except an all-white shape).

The decoder thus starts by setting all the domains to arbitrary shapes (e.g., it can initially set the entire image to black). It then goes into a loop where, in each iteration, it applies every transformation w_i once. The first iteration applies the transformations to domains D_i that are all black. This creates ranges R_i that may already, after this single iteration, slightly resemble the original ranges. This iteration changes the image from the initial all black to something resembling the original image. In the second iteration the decoder applies again all the w_i transformations but this time they are applied to domains that are no longer all black.

The domains already somewhat resemble the original ones, so the second iteration results in better-looking ranges, and thus in a better image. Experience shows that only 8–10 iterations are normally needed to get a result closely resembling the original image.

It is important to realize that this decoding process is resolution independent! Normally the decoder starts with an initial image whose size is identical to that of the original image. It can, however, start with an all-black image of any size. The affine transformations used to encode the original image do not depend on the resolution of the image or on the resolutions of the ranges. Decoding an image at, say, twice its original size will create a large, smooth image, with details not seen in the original and without pixelization (without jagged edges or "fat" pixels). The extra details will, of course, be artificial. They may not be what one would see when looking at the original image through a magnifying glass, but the point is that PIFS decoding is resolution independent; it creates a natural-looking image at any size, and it does not involve pixelization.

The resolution-independent nature of PIFS decoding also means that we have to be careful when measuring the compression performance. After compressing a 64Kbytes image into, say, 2Kbytes, the compression factor is 32. Decoding the 2Kbyte compressed file into a large, 2Mbyte image (with a lot of artificial detail) does not mean that we have changed the compression factor to 2M/2K=1,024. The compression factor is still the same 32.

4.15.7 IFS Encoding

PIFS decoding is thus easy, if somewhat magical, but we still need to see the details of PIFS encoding. The first point to consider is how to select the ranges and find the domains. Here are some possibilities:

1. Suppose that the original image has resolution of 512×512. We can select as ranges the non-overlapping groups of 16×16 pixels. There are $32 \times 32 = 1,024$ such groups. The domains should be bigger than the ranges, so we may select as domains all the 32×32 groups of pixels in the image (they may, of course, overlap). There are $(512 - 31) \times (512 - 31) = 231,361$ such groups. The encoder should compare each range to all 231,361 domains. Each comparison involves eight steps, since a range may be identical to a rotation or a reflection of a domain (Figure 4.46). The total number of steps in comparing ranges and domains is thus $1,024 \times 231,361 \times 8 = 1,895,309,312$, perhaps too big for some computers.

▶ **Exercise 4.32:** Repeat the computation above for a 256×256 image with ranges of size 8×8 and domains of size 16×16.

If the encoder is looking for a domain to match range R_i and it is lucky to find one that's identical to R_i, it can proceed to the next range. In practice, however, domains identical to a given range are very rare, so the encoder has to compare all $231,361 \times 8$ domains to each range R_i and select the one that's closest to R_i (PIFS is, in general, a lossy compression method). We thus have to answer two questions: When is a domain identical to a range (remember: they have different sizes) and how to measure the "distance" between a domain and a range?

To compare a 32×32 pixel domain to a 16×16 pixel range, we can either choose one pixel from each 2×2 square of pixels in the domain (this is called subsampling) or average each 2×2 square of pixels in the domain and compare it to one pixel of the range (averaging).

To decide how close a range R_i is to a domain D_j, we have to use one of several *metrics*. A metric is a function that measures "distance" between, or "closeness" of, two mathematical quantities. Experience recommends the use of the *rms* (root mean square) metric

$$M_{\text{rms}}(R_i, D_j) = \sqrt{\sum_{x,y} \left[R_i(x,y) - D_j(x,y) \right]^2}. \qquad (4.17)$$

This involves a square root calculation, so a simpler metric may be

$$M_{\text{max}}(R_i, D_j) = \max |R_i(x,y) - D_j(x,y)|$$

(the largest difference between a pixel of R_i and one of D_j). Whatever metric is used, a comparison of a range and a domain involves subsampling (or averaging) followed by a metric calculation.

After comparing range R_i to all the (rotated and reflected) domains, the encoder selects the domain with the smallest metric and calculates the transformation that will bring the domain to the range. This process is repeated for all ranges.

Even this simple way of matching parts of the image produces excellent results. Compression factors are typically in the 15–32 range and data loss is minimal.

▷ **Exercise 4.33:** What's a reasonable way to estimate the amount of image information lost in PIFS compression?

The main disadvantage of this method of determining ranges and domains is the fixed size of the ranges. A method where ranges can have different sizes may lead to better compression ratios and less loss. Imagine an image of a hand with a ring on one finger. If the ring happens to be inside a large range R_i, it may be impossible to find any domain that will even come close to R_i. Too much data may be lost in such a case. On the other hand, if part of an image is fairly uniform, it may become a large range, since there is a better chance that it will match some domain. Clearly large ranges are preferable since the compressed stream contains one transformation per range. Quadtrees, discussed below, therefore offer a good solution.

2. Quadtrees. We start with a few large ranges, each a subquadrant. If a range does not match well any domain (the metric between it and any domain is greater than a user-controlled tolerance parameter), it is divided into four subranges, and each is matched separately. As an example, consider a 256×256-pixel image. We can choose for domains all the image squares of size 8, 12, 16, 24, 32, 48, and 64. We start with ranges that are subquadrants of size 32×32. Each range is compared with domains that are larger than itself (48 or 64). If a range does not match well, it is divided into four quadrants of size 16×16 each, and each is compared, as a new range, with all domains of sizes 24, 32, 48, and 64. This process continues until all ranges have been matched to domains. Large ranges result in better compression but small ranges are easier to match since they contain a few adjacent pixels, and we know from experience that adjacent pixels tend to be highly correlated in real-life images.

4.15.8 IFS for Grayscale Images

Up until now we have assumed that our transformations have to be affine. The truth is that any contractive transformations, even non-linear ones, can be used for IFS. Affine transformations are used simply because they are linear and thus computationally simple. Also, up to now we have assumed a monochromatic image, where the only problem is to determine which pixels should be black. IFS can easily be extended to compress grayscale images (and therefore also color images; see below). The problem here is to determine which pixels to paint, and what gray level to paint each.

Matching a domain to a range now involves the intensities of the pixels in both. Whatever metric is used, it should only use those intensities to determine the "closeness" of the domain and the range. Assume that a certain domain D contains n pixels with gray levels $a_1 \cdots a_n$, and the IFS encoder tries to match D to a range R containing n pixels with gray levels $b_1 \ldots b_n$. The rms metric, mentioned earlier, works by finding two numbers, r and g (called the contrast and brightness controls), that will minimize the expression

$$Q = \sum_1^n \left((r \cdot a_i + g) - b_i \right)^2. \tag{4.18}$$

This is done by solving the two equations $\partial Q / \partial r = 0$ and $\partial Q / \partial g = 0$ for the unknowns r and g (see details below). Minimizing Q minimizes the difference in contrast and brightness between the domain and the range. The value of the rms metric is $\sqrt{Q}$ [compare with Equation (4.17)].

When the IFS encoder finally decides what domain to associate with the current range, it has to figure out the transformation w between them. The point is that r and g should be included in the transformation, so that the decoder will know what gray level to paint the pixels when the domain is recreated in successive decoding iterations. It is common to use transformations of the form

$$w \begin{pmatrix} x \\ y \\ z \end{pmatrix} = \begin{pmatrix} a & b & 0 \\ c & d & 0 \\ 0 & 0 & r \end{pmatrix} \begin{pmatrix} x \\ y \\ z \end{pmatrix} + \begin{pmatrix} l \\ m \\ g \end{pmatrix}. \tag{4.19}$$

A pixel (x, y) in the domain D is now given a third coordinate z (its gray level) and is transformed into a pixel (x^*, y^*, z^*) in the range R, where $z^* = z \cdot r + g$. Transformation (4.19) has another property. It is contractive if $r < 1$, regardless of the scale factors.

Any compression method for grayscale images can be extended to color images. It is only necessary to separate the image into three color components (preferably YIQ) and compress each individually as a grayscale image. This is how IFS can be applied to compression of color images.

The next point to consider is how to write the coefficients of a transformation w on the compressed stream. There are three groups of coefficients, the scale factors a, d, the reflection/rotation factors a, b, c, d, the displacement l, m, and the contrast/brightness controls r, g. If a domain is twice as large as a range, then the scale factors are always 0.5 and thus do not have to be written on the compressed stream. If the domains and ranges can have several sizes, then only certain scale factors are possible and they can be encoded either arithmetically or by some prefix code. The particular rotation or reflection of the domain relative to the range can be coded in 3 bits since there are only eight rotations/reflections possible. The displacement can be encoded by encoding the positions and sizes of the domain and range.

The quantities r and g are not distributed in any uniform way, and they are also real (floating-point) numbers that can have many different values. They should thus be quantized, i.e., converted to an integer in a certain range. Experience shows that the contrast r can be quantized into a 4- or 5-bit integer (i.e., 16 or 32 contrast values are enough in practice), whereas the brightness g should become a 6- or 7-bit integer (resulting in 64 or 128 brightness values).

Here are the details of calculating r and g that minimize Q and then calculating the (minimized) Q and the rms metric.

From Equation (4.18), we get

$$\frac{\partial Q}{\partial g} = 0 \rightarrow \sum 2(r \cdot a_i + g - b_i) = 0 \rightarrow ng + \sum(r \cdot a_i - b_i) = 0$$

$$g = \frac{1}{n}\left[\sum b_i - r \sum a_i\right]. \tag{4.20}$$

$$\frac{\partial Q}{\partial r} = 0 \rightarrow \sum 2(r \cdot a_i + g - b_i)a_i = 0 \rightarrow \sum(r \cdot a_i^2 + g \cdot a_i - a_i b_i) = 0$$

$$r \sum a_i^2 + \frac{1}{n}\left[\sum b_i - r \sum a_i\right]\sum a_i - \sum a_i b_i) = 0$$

$$r\left[\sum a_i - \frac{1}{n}\left(\sum a_i\right)^2\right] = \sum a_i b_i - \frac{1}{n}\sum a_i \sum b_i$$

$$r = \frac{\sum a_i b_i - \frac{1}{n}\sum a_i \sum b_i}{\sum a_i - \frac{1}{n}\left(\sum a_i\right)^2} = \frac{n\sum a_i b_i - \sum a_i \sum b_i}{n\sum a_i - \left(\sum a_i\right)^2}. \tag{4.21}$$

From the same (4.18), we also get the minimized Q

$$Q = \sum_1^n (r \cdot a_i + g - b_i)^2 = \sum r^2 a_i^2 + g^2 + b_i^2 + 2rga_i - 2ra_i b_i - 2gb_i)$$

$$= r^2 \sum a_i^2 + ng^2 + \sum b_i^2 + 2rg \sum a_i - 2r \sum a_i b_i - 2g \sum b_i. \tag{4.22}$$

The following steps are needed to calculate the rms metric:

1. Compute the sums $\sum a_i$ and $\sum a_i^2$ for all domains.
2. Compute the sums $\sum b_i$ and $\sum b_i^2$ for all ranges.
3. Every time a range R and a domain D are compared, compute:
3.1. The sum $\sum a_i b_i$.
3.2. The quantities r and g from Equations (4.20) and (4.21) using the five sums above. Quantize r and g.

3.3. Compute Q from Equation (4.22) using the quantized r, g and the five sums. The value of the rms metric for these particular R and D is $\sqrt{Q}$.

Finally, figures 4.57 and 4.58 are pseudo-code algorithms outlining two approaches to IFS encoding. The former is more intuitive. For each range R it selects the domain that's closest to R. The latter tries to reduce data loss by sacrificing compression ratio. This is done by letting the user specify the minimum number T of transformations to be generated. (Each transformation w is written on the compressed stream using roughly the same number of bits, so the size of that stream is proportional to the number of transformations.) If every range has been matched, and the number of transformations is still $< T$, the algorithm continues by taking ranges that have already been matched, and partitioning them into smaller ones. This increases the number of transformations but reduces the data loss since smaller ranges are easier to match with domains.

> He gathered himself together and then banged his fist on the table. "To hell with art, I say."
>
> "You not only say it, but you say it with tiresome iteration," said Clutton severely.
>
> —W. Somerset Maugham, *Of Human Bondage*

Bibliography

Barnsley, F., and Sloan, A. D. (1988) "A Better Way to Compress Images," *Byte magazine* pp. 215–222 January.

Barnsley, M. (1988) *Fractals Everywhere*, New York, Academic Press.

Demko, S., L. Hodges, and B. Naylor (1985) "Construction of Fractal Objects with Iterated Function Systems," *Computer Graphics* **19**(3):271–278, July.

Feder, Jens (1988) *Fractals*, New York, Plenum Press.

Fisher, Yuval (ed.), (1995) *Fractal Image Compression: Theory and Application*, New York, Springer-Verlag.

Mandelbrot, B., (1982) *The Fractal Geometry of Nature*, San Francisco, CA, W. H. Freeman.

Peitgen, H. -O., et al. (eds.) (1982) *The Beauty of Fractals*, Berlin, Springer-Verlag.

Peitgen, H. -O., and Dietmar Saupe (1985) *The Science of Fractal Images*, Berlin, Springer-Verlag.

Reghbati, H. K. (1981) "An Overview of Data Compression Techniques," *IEEE Computer* **14**(4):71–76.

```
t:=some default value; [t is the tolerance]
push(entire image); [stack contains ranges to be matched]
repeat
 R:=pop();
 match all domains to R, find the one (D) that's closest to R,
  pop(R);
 if metric(R,D)<t then
   compute transformation w from D to R and output it;
 else partition R into smaller rnages and push them
       into the stack;
 endif;
until stack is empty;
```

Figure 4.57: IFS Encoding: Version I.

```
input T from user;
push(entire image); [stack contains ranges to be matched]
repeat
 for every unmatched R in the stack find the best matching domain D,
  compute the transformation w, and push D and w into the stack;
 if the number of ranges in the stack is <T then
   find range R with largest metric (worst match)
   pop R, D and w from the stack
   partition R into smaller ranges and push them, as unmatched,
    into the stack;
 endif
until all ranges in the stack are matched;
output all transformations w from the stack;
```

Figure 4.58: IFS Encoding: Version II.

4.16 Wavelets

Wavelets have been developed, in the 1980s, as an alternative to the windowed Fourier transform for digital signal processing. They have since found many applications in signal processing and computer graphics, in addition to their use in data compression. This section presents a simplified approach to the use of wavelets for image compression. We first discuss the wavelet compression of grayscale images and then show how it can be generalized to color images.

An image is a two-dimensional array of pixel values. To illustrate the main concept of wavelet compression, we start with a single row of pixel values, i.e., a one-dimensional array of n values. For simplicity we assume that n is a power of 2. Consider the array of eight values $(1, 2, 3, 4, 5, 6, 7, 8)$. We first compute the four averages $(1 + 2)/2 = 3/2$, $(3 + 4)/2 = 7/2$, $(5 + 6)/2 = 11/2$, and $(7 + 8)/2 = 15/2$. It is impossible to reconstruct the original eight values from these four averages, so we also compute the four differences $(1 - 2)/2 = -1/2$, $(3 - 4)/2 = -1/2$, $(5 - 6)/2 = -1/2$ and $(7 - 8)/2 = -1/2$. These differences are also called *detail coefficients*.

It is easy to see that the array $(3/2, 7/2, 11/2, 15/2, -1/2, -1/2, -1/2, -1/2)$ that's made of the four averages and four differences can be used to reconstruct the original eight values. This array has eight values but its last four components, the differences, tend to be small numbers, which helps in compression. Encouraged by this, we repeat the process on the four averages, the large components of our array. They are transformed into two averages and two differences, yielding the array $(10/4, 26/4, -4/4, -4/4, -1/2, -1/2, -1/2, -1/2)$. The next, and last, iteration of this process transforms the first two components of the new array into one average (the average of all eight components of the original array) and one difference $(36/8, -16/8, -4/4, -4/4, -1/2, -1/2, -1/2, -1/2)$. The last array is called the *wavelet transform* of the original array.

Because of the differences, the wavelet transform tends to have numbers smaller than the original pixel values, so it is easier to compress using RLE, perhaps combined with move-to-front and Huffman coding. Lossy compression can be obtained if some of the smaller differences are changed to zero.

It is useful to associate with each iteration a quantity called *resolution*, which is defined as the number of remaining averages at the end of the iteration. The resolutions after each of the three iterations above are $4(= 2^2)$, $2(= 2^1)$, and $1(= 2^0)$. Theory shows that it is better to normalize each component of the wavelet transform by dividing it by the square root of the resolution. (This has to do with representing the components of the wavelet transform by means of the *orthonormal Haar transform* [Stollnitz 96] and will not be discussed here.) Our example wavelet transform thus becomes

$$\left(\frac{36/8}{\sqrt{2^0}}, \frac{-16/8}{\sqrt{2^0}}, \frac{-4/4}{\sqrt{2^1}}, \frac{-4/4}{\sqrt{2^1}}, \frac{-1/2}{\sqrt{2^2}}, \frac{-1/2}{\sqrt{2^2}}, \frac{-1/2}{\sqrt{2^2}}, \frac{-1/2}{\sqrt{2^2}} \right).$$

If the normalized wavelet transform is used, it can be formally proved that ignoring the smallest differences is the best choice for lossy wavelet compression since it creates the smallest loss of image information.

The two procedures of Figure 4.59 illustrate how the normalized wavelet transform of an array of n components (where n is a power of 2) can be computed. Reconstructing the original array from the normalized wavelet transform is illustrated by the pair of procedures of Figure 4.60.

These procedures seem at first to be different from the averages and differences discussed earlier. They don't compute averages since they divide by $\sqrt{2}$ instead of by 2; the first one starts by dividing the entire array by $\sqrt{n}$, and the second one ends by doing the reverse. The final result, however, is the same as that shown above. Starting with array $(1, 2, 3, 4, 5, 6, 7, 8)$, the three iterations of procedure NWTcalc result in

$$
\left(\frac{3}{\sqrt{2^4}}, \frac{7}{\sqrt{2^4}}, \frac{11}{\sqrt{2^4}}, \frac{15}{\sqrt{2^4}}, \frac{-1}{\sqrt{2^4}}, \frac{-1}{\sqrt{2^4}}, \frac{-1}{\sqrt{2^4}}, \frac{-1}{\sqrt{2^4}} \right),
$$
$$
= \left(\frac{10}{\sqrt{2^5}}, \frac{26}{\sqrt{2^5}}, \frac{-4}{\sqrt{2^5}}, \frac{-4}{\sqrt{2^5}}, \frac{-1}{\sqrt{2^4}}, \frac{-1}{\sqrt{2^4}}, \frac{-1}{\sqrt{2^4}}, \frac{-1}{\sqrt{2^4}} \right),
$$
$$
= \left(\frac{36}{\sqrt{2^6}}, \frac{-16}{\sqrt{2^6}}, \frac{-4}{\sqrt{2^5}}, \frac{-4}{\sqrt{2^5}}, \frac{-1}{\sqrt{2^4}}, \frac{-1}{\sqrt{2^4}}, \frac{-1}{\sqrt{2^4}}, \frac{-1}{\sqrt{2^4}} \right),
$$
$$
= \left(\frac{36/8}{\sqrt{2^0}}, \frac{-16/8}{\sqrt{2^0}}, \frac{-4/4}{\sqrt{2^1}}, \frac{-4/4}{\sqrt{2^1}}, \frac{-1/2}{\sqrt{2^2}}, \frac{-1/2}{\sqrt{2^2}}, \frac{-1/2}{\sqrt{2^2}}, \frac{-1/2}{\sqrt{2^2}} \right).
$$

4.16.1 The Wavelet Transform

Once the concept of a wavelet transform is grasped, it's easy to generalize it to a complete, two-dimensional image. This can be done in two ways, called the *standard decomposition* and the *nonstandard decomposition*.

The former (Figure 4.61) starts by computing the wavelet transform of every row of the image. This results in a transformed image where the first column contains averages and all the other columns contain differences. The standard algorithm then computes the wavelet transform of every column. This results in one average value at the top-left corner, with the rest of the top row containing averages of differences, and with all other pixel values transformed into differences.

The latter method computes the wavelet transform of the image by alternating between rows and columns. The first step is to calculate averages and differences for all the rows (just one iteration, not the entire wavelet transform). This creates averages in the left half of the image and differences in the right half. The second step is to calculate averages and differences for all the columns, which results in averages in the top-left quadrant of the image and differences elsewhere. Steps 3 and 4 operate on the rows and columns of that quadrant, resulting in averages concentrated in the top-left octant. Pairs of steps continue recursively on smaller and smaller quadrants, until only one average is left, at the top-left corner of the image, and all other pixel values have been reduced to differences. This process is summarized in Figure 4.62.

Either method, standard and nonstandard, results in a transformed—although not yet compressed—image that has one average at the top-left corner and smaller numbers, differences, or averages of differences, everywhere else. This can now be compressed using a combination of methods, such as RLE, move-to-front and

```
procedure NWTcalc(a:array of real, n:int);
 comment n is the array size (a power of 2)
 a:=a/√n comment divide entire array
 j:=n;
 while j≥ 2 do
  NWTstep(a, j);
  j:=j/2;
 endwhile;
end;

procedure NWTstep(a:array of real, j:int);
 for i=1 to j/2 do
  b[i]:=(a[2i-1]+a[2i])/√2;
  b[j/2+i]:=(a[2i-1]-a[2i])/√2;
 endfor;
 a:=b; comment move entire array
end;
```

Figure 4.59: Computing the Normalized Wavelet Transform.

```
procedure NWTreconst(a:array of real, n:int);
 j:=2;
 while j≤n do
  NWTRstep(a, j);
  j:=2j;
 endwhile
 a:=a√n; comment multiply entire array
end;

procedure NWTRstep(a:array of real, j:int);
 for i=1 to j/2 do
  b[2i-1]:=(a[i]+a[j/2+i])/√2;
  b[2i]:=(a[i]-a[j/2+i])/√2;
 endfor;
 a:=b; comment move entire array
end;
```

Figure 4.60: Restoring From a Normalized Wavelet Transform.

```
procedure StdCalc(a:array of real, n:int);
 comment array size is nxn (n = power of 2)
 for r=1 to n do NWTcalc(row r of a, n);
 endfor;
 for c=n to 1 do comment loop backwards
  NWTcalc(col c of a, n);
 endfor;
end;
procedure StdReconst(a:array of real, n:int);
 for c=n to 1 do comment loop backwards
  NWTreconst(col c of a, n);
 endfor;
 for r=1 to n do
  NWTreconst(row r of a, n);
 endfor;
end;
```

Figure 4.61: The Standard Image Wavelet Transform.

```
procedure NStdCalc(a:array of real, n:int);
 a:=a/√n comment divide entire array
 j:=n;
 while j≥ 2 do
  for r=1 to j do NWTstep(row r of a, j);
  endfor;
  for c=j to 1 do comment loop backwards
   NWTstep(col c of a, j);
  endfor;
  j:=j/2;
 endwhile;
end;
procedure NStdReconst(a:array of real, n:int);
 j:=2;
 while j≤n do
  for c=j to 1 do comment loop backwards
   NWTRstep(col c of a, j);
  endfor;
  for r=1 to j do
   NWTRstep(row r of a, j);
  endfor;
  j:=2j;
 endwhile
 a:=a√n; comment multiply entire array
end;
```

Figure 4.62: The Nonstandard Image Wavelet Transform.

Huffman coding. If lossy compression is acceptable, some of the smallest differences should be replaced by zeros, which may create run-lengths of zeros, making the use of RLE more desirable.

Color Images: So far we have assumed that each pixel is a single number (a single-component image, in which all pixels are shades of the same color, normally gray). Any compression method for single-component images can be extended to color (three-component) images by separating the three components and compressing each individually. If the compression method is lossy, it makes sense to convert the three image components from their original color representation, which is normally *RGB*, to the *YIQ* color representation. The *Y* component of this representation is called *luminance*, and the *I* and *Q* (the chrominance) components are responsible for the color information. The advantage of this color representation is that the human eye is most sensitive to *Y* and least sensitive to *Q*. A lossy method should thus leave the *Y* component alone and delete some data from the *I*, and more data from the *Q* components, resulting in good compression and in loss for which the eye is not that sensitive.

It is interesting to note that U.S. color television transmission also takes advantage of the *YIQ* representation. Signals are broadcast with bandwidths of 4 MHz for *Y*, 1.5 Mhz for *I*, and only 0.6 MHz for *Q*.

Bibliography

DeVore R. et al. (1992) "Image Compression Through Wavelet Transform Coding," *IEEE Transactions on Information Theory* **38**(2):719–746, March.

Stollnitz, E. J., T. D. DeRose, and D. H. Salesin (1996) *Wavelets for Computer Graphics*, San Francisco, CA, Morgan Kaufmann.

> As soon as we use words like "image," we are already thinking of how one shape corresponds to the other—of how you might move one shape to bring it into coincidence with the other. Bilateral symmetry means that if you reflect the left half in a mirror, then you obtain the right half. Reflection is a mathematical concept, but it is not a shape, a number, or a formula. It is a *transformation*—that is, a rule for moving things around.
>
> Ian Stewart, *Nature's Numbers*

5
Other Methods

Previous chapters discuss the main classes of compression methods: RLE, statistical methods, and dictionary-based methods. There are data compression methods that are not easy to classify and do not clearly belong in any of the classes discussed so far. A few such methods are described here.

■ The Burrows-Wheeler method (Section 5.1) starts with a string S of n symbols and scrambles (i.e., permutes) them into another string L that satisfies two conditions: (1) Any area of L will tend to have a concentration of just a few symbols. (2) It is possible to reconstruct the original string S from L.

■ The technique of symbol ranking (Section 5.2) uses context to rank symbols rather than assign them probabilities.

■ ACB is a new method, based on an associative dictionary (Section 5.3). It has features that relate it to the traditional dictionary-based methods as well as to the symbol ranking method.

■ The special case of sparse binary strings is discussed in Section 5.4. Such strings can be compressed very efficiently due to the large number of consecutive zeros they contain.

■ Compression methods that are based on words rather than individual symbols are described in Section 5.5.

■ Textual image compression is the topic of Section 5.6. When a printed document has to be saved in the computer, it has to be scanned first, a process that converts it into an image typically containing millions of pixels. The complex method described here has been developed for this kind of data, which forms a special type of image, a *textual image*. Such an image is made of pixels, but most of the pixels are grouped to form characters, and the number of different groups is not large.

• Dynamic Markov Coding uses finite-state machines to estimate the probability of symbols, and arithmetic coding to actually encode them. This is a compression method for two-symbol (binary) alphabets.

• The chapter concludes with a short discussion of sound compression. Section 5.8 describes how sound is digitized, how conventional compression methods perform on sound files, and how special, lossy methods can be developed to compress digitized sound.

5.1 The Burrows-Wheeler Method

Most compression methods operate in the *streaming mode*, where the codec inputs a byte or several bytes, processes them and continues until an end-of-file is sensed. The Burrows-Wheeler (BW) method, described in this section, works in a *block mode*, where the input stream is read block by block and each block is encoded separately as one string. The method is thus also referred to as *block sorting*. The BW method is general purpose, it works well on images, sound, and text, and can achieve very high compression ratios (1 bit per byte or even better).

The main idea of the BW method is to start with a string S of n symbols and to scramble them into another string L that satisfies two conditions:

1. Any region of L will tend to have a concentration of just a few symbols. Another way of saying this is: if a symbol s is found at a certain position in L, then other occurrences of s are likely to be found nearby. This property means that L can easily and efficiently be compressed using the move-to-front method (Section 1.5), perhaps in combination with RLE. This also means that the BW method will work well only if n is large (at least several thousand symbols per string).

2. It is possible to reconstruct the original string S from L (a little more data may be needed for the reconstruction, in addition to L, but not much).

The mathematical term for scrambling symbols is *permutation*, and it is easy to show that a string of n symbols has $n!$ (pronounced "n factorial") permutations. This is a large number even for relatively small values of n, so the particular permutation used by BW has to be carefully selected. The BW codec proceeds in the following steps:

1. String L is created, by the encoder, as a permutation of S. Some more information, denoted I, is also created, to be used later by the decoder in step 3.

2. The encoder compresses L and I and writes the results on the output stream. This step typically starts with RLE, continues with move-to-front coding, and finally applies Huffman coding.

3. The decoder reads the output stream and decodes it by applying the same methods as in 2 above but in reverse order. The result is string L and variable I.

4. Both L and I are used by the decoder to reconstruct the original string S.

The first step is to understand how string L is created from S, and what information needs to be stored in I for later reconstruction. We use the familiar string "swiss␣miss" to illustrate this process.

The encoder constructs an $n \times n$ matrix where it stores string S in the top row, followed by $n-1$ copies of S, each cyclically shifted (rotated) one symbol to the left (Figure 5.1a). The matrix is then sorted lexicographically by rows (see Section 3.3

> I do hate sums. There is no greater mistake than to call arithmetic an exact science. There are permutations and aberrations discernible to minds entirely noble like mine; subtle variations which ordinary accountants fail to discover; hidden laws of number which it requires a mind like mine to perceive. For instance, if you add a sum from the bottom up, and then from the top down, the result is always different.
>
> — Mrs. La Touche, *Mathematical Gazette*, v. 12

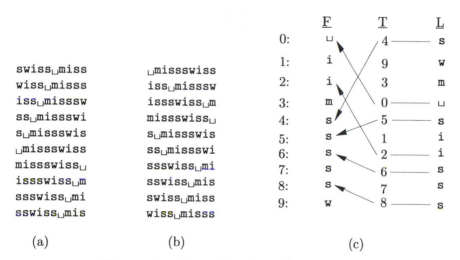

| (a) | (b) | (c) |

Figure 5.1: Principles of BW Compression.

for lexicographic order), producing the sorted matrix of Figure 5.1b. Notice that every row and every column of each of the two matrices is a permutation of S and thus contains all n symbols of S. The permutation L selected by the decoder is the **last column** of the sorted matrix. In our example this is the string "swm␣siisss". The only other information needed to eventually reconstruct S from L is the row number of the original string in the sorted matrix, which in our example is 8 (row and column numbering starts from 0). This number is stored in I.

It is easy to see why L contains concentrations of identical symbols. Assume that the words "bail", "fail", "hail", "jail", "mail", "nail", "pail", "rail", "sail", "tail", and "wail" appear somewhere in S. After the sort, all the permutations that start with "il" will appear together. All of them will contribute an "a" to L, so L will have a concentration of a's. Also, all the permutations starting with "ail" will end up together, contributing to a concentration of the letters "bfhjmnprstw" in one region of L.

We can now characterize the BW method by saying that it uses sorting to group together symbols based on their contexts. However, the method considers context on only one side of each symbol.

▸ **Exercise 5.1:** (Easy.) The last column, L, of the sorted matrix contains concentrations of identical characters, which is why L is easy to compress. However, the first column, F, of the same matrix is even easier to compress since it contains runs, not just concentrations, of identical characters. Why select column L and not column F?

Notice also that the encoder does not really have to construct the two $n \times n$ matrices (or even one of them) in memory. The practical details are discussed in Section 5.1.2, as well as the compression of L and I, but let's first see how the decoder works.

The decoder reads a compressed stream, decompresses it using Huffman, move-to-front (and perhaps also RLE), and then reconstructs string S from the decompressed L in three steps:

1. The first column of the sorted matrix (column F in Figure 5.1c) is constructed from L. This is a straightforward process since F and L contain the same symbols (both are permutations of S) and F is sorted. The decoder simply sorts string L to obtain F.

2. While sorting L, the decoder prepares an auxiliary array T that shows the relations between elements of L and F (Figure 5.1c). The first element of T is 4, implying that the first symbol of L (the letter "s") is located in position 4 of F. The second element of T is 9, implying that the second symbol of L (the letter "w") is located in position 9 of F, and so on. The contents of T in our example is $(4, 9, 3, 0, 5, 1, 2, 6, 7, 8)$.

3. String F is no longer needed. The decoder uses L, I, and T to reconstruct S according to,

$$S[n - 1 - i] \leftarrow L[T^i[I]]; \quad \text{for } i = 0, 1, \dots, n - 1;$$
$$\text{where } T^0[j] = j, \text{ and } T^{i+1}[j] = T[T^i[j]]. \tag{5.1}$$

Here are the first two steps in this reconstruction:

```
S[10-1-0]=L[T⁰[I]]=L[T⁰[8]]=L[8]=s;
S[10-1-1]=L[T¹[I]]=L[T[T⁰[I]]]=L[T[8]]=L[7]=s;
```

▸ **Exercise 5.2:** Complete this reconstruction.

Before getting to the details of the compression, it may be interesting to understand why equation (5.1) reconstructs S from L. The following arguments explain why this process works:

1. T is constructed such that F[T[i]]=L[i].

2. A look at the sorted matrix of Figure 5.1b shows that, in each row i, symbol L[i] precedes symbol F[i] in the original string S (the word *precedes* has to understood as *precedes cyclically*). Specifically, in row I (8 in our example), L[I] cyclically precedes F[I], but F[I] is the first symbol of S, so L[I] is the *last* symbol of S. The reconstruction starts with L[I] and reconstructs S from right to left.

3. L[i] precedes F[i] in S for $i = 0, \ldots, n-1$. Therefore L[T[i]] precedes F[T[i]], but F[T[i]]=L[i]. The conclusion is that L[T[i]] precedes L[i] in S.

4. The reconstruction thus starts with L[I]=L[8]="**s**" (the last symbol of S) and proceeds with L[T[I]]=L[T[8]]=L[7]="**s**" (the next-to-last symbol of S). This is why equation (5.1) correctly describes the reconstruction.

5.1.1 Compressing L

Compressing L is based on its main attribute, namely, it contains concentrations (although not necessarily runs) of identical symbols. Using RLE makes sense, but only as a first step in a multi-step compression process. The main step in compressing L should use the move-to-front method (Section 1.5). This method is applied to our example L="**swm⊔siisss**" as follows:

1. Initialize A to a list containing our alphabet A=("⊔", "i", "m", "s", "w").

2. For $i := 0, \ldots, n-1$, encode symbol L_i as the number of symbols preceding it in A, and then move symbol L_i to the beginning of A.

3. Combine the codes of step 2 in a list C, which will be further compressed using Huffman or arithmetic coding.

The results are summarized in Figure 5.2a. The final list of codes is C=(3,4,4,3,3,4,0,1,0,0), illustrating how any concentration of identical symbols produces small codes. The first occurrence of "i" is assigned code 4 but the second one, code 0. The first two occurrences of "s" get code 3 but the next one, code 1.

L	A	Code	L	A	Code
s	⊔imsw	3	3	⊔imsw	s
w	s⊔imw	4	4	s⊔imw	w
m	ws⊔im	4	4	ws⊔im	m
⊔	mws⊔i	3	3	mws⊔i	⊔
s	⊔mwsi	3	3	⊔mwsi	s
i	s⊔mwi	4	4	s⊔mwi	i
i	is⊔mw	0	0	is⊔mw	i
s	is⊔mw	1	1	is⊔mw	s
s	si⊔mw	0	0	si⊔mw	s
s	si⊔mw	0	0	si⊔mw	s
	(a)			(b)	

Figure 5.2: Encoding/Decoding L by Move-to-Front.

It is interesting to compare the codes in C, which are integers in the range $[0, n-1]$, to the codes obtained without the extra step of "moving to front." It is easy to encode L using the three steps above but without moving symbol L_i to the beginning of A. The result is C'=(3,4,2,0,3,1,1,3,3,3), a list of integers *in the same range* $[0, n-1]$. This is why applying move-to-front is not enough. Lists C and C' contain elements in the same range, but the elements of C are smaller on the average. They should therefore be further encoded using Huffman coding or some other statistical method. Huffman codes for C can be assigned assuming that code 0 has the highest probability and code $n-1$, the smallest.

In our example a possible set of Huffman codes is
0—0, 1—10, 2—110, 3—1110, 4—1111. Applying this set to C yields the 29-bit
string "1110|1111|1111|1110|1110|1111|0|10|0|0". (Applying it to C' yields the 32-
bit string "1110|1111|110|0|1110|10|10|1110|1110|1110".) Our original 10-character
string "swiss␣miss" has thus been coded using 2.9 bits/character, a very good result. It should be noted that the Burrows-Wheeler method can easily achieve better
compression than that when applied to longer strings (thousands of symbols).

▶ **Exercise 5.3:** Given the string S="sssssssssh" calculate string L and its move-
to-front compression.

Decoding C is done with the inverse of move-to-front. We assume that the
alphabet list A is available to the decoder (it is either the list of all possible bytes
or it is written by the encoder on the output stream). Figure 5.2b shows the details
of decoding C=(3,4,4,3,3,4,0,1,0,0). The first code is 3, so the first symbol in the
newly constructed L is the *fourth* one in A, or "s". This symbol is then moved to
the front of A, and the process continues.

5.1.2 Implementation Hints

Since the Burrows-Wheeler method is efficient only for long strings (at least thousands of symbols) any practical implementation should allow for large values of n.
The maximum value of n should be so large that two $n \times n$ matrices would not fit
in the available memory (at least not comfortably), and all the encoder operations
(preparing the permutations and sorting them) should be done with one-dimensional
arrays of size n. In principle it is enough to have just the original string S and the
auxiliary array T in memory.

String S contains the original data and also all the necessary permutations.
Since the only permutations we need to generate are rotations, we can generate
permutation i of matrix 5.1a by scanning S from position i to the end, and then
continuing cyclically from the start of S to position $i - 1$. Permutation 5, for
example, can be generated by scanning substring (5,9) of S ("␣miss"), followed by
substring (0,4) "swiss". The result is "␣missswiss". The first step in a practical
implementation would thus be to write a procedure that takes a parameter i and
scans the corresponding permutation.

Sorting the permutations is done by comparing them, regardless of the specific
sorting method used. We therefore need a procedure to compare two permutations,
and again this can be done by scanning them in S, without having to move symbols
or to create new arrays in memory.

Once the sorting algorithm determines that permutation i should be in position
j in the sorted matrix (Figure 5.1b), it sets T[i] to j. In our example, the sort ends
up with T=(5, 2, 7, 6, 4, 3, 8, 9, 0, 1).

▶ **Exercise 5.4:** Show how T is used to create the encoder's main output, L and I.

Implementing the decoder is straightforward since it does not need to create
$n \times n$ matrices. The decoder inputs bits which are Huffman codes. It uses them
to create the codes of C, decompressing each as it is created, using inverse move-
to-front, into the next symbol of L. When L is ready, the decoder sorts it into F,
generating array T in the process. Following that, it reconstructs S from L and T.

The decoder thus needs at most three structures at one time, the two strings L and F (having typically one byte per symbol), and the array T (with at least 2 bytes per pointer, to allow large values of n).

Bibliography

Burrows, Michael and D. J. Wheeler (1994) *A Block-Sorting Lossless Data Compression Algorithm*, Digital, Systems Research Center report 124, Palo Alto, Calif, May 10.

Manber, U., and E. W. Myers (1993) "Suffix Arrays: A New Method for On-Line String Searches," *SIAM Journal on Computing* **22**(5):935–948, October.

McCreight, E. M. (1976) "A Space Economical Suffix Tree Construction Algorithm," *Journal of the ACM* **32**(2):262–272, April.

5.2 Symbol Ranking

Like so many other ideas, the idea of text compression by symbol ranking is due to Claude Shannon, the founder of information theory. In his classic paper on the information content of English text [Shannon 51] he describes a method for experimentally determining the entropy of such texts. In a typical experiment a passage of text has to be predicted, character by character, by a person (the examinee). In one version of the method the examinee predicts the next character and is then told by the examiner if the prediction was correct or, if it was not, what the next character is. In another version, the examinee has to continue predicting until he obtains the right answer. The examiner then uses the number of wrong answers to estimate the entropy of the text.

As it turned out, in the latter version of the test, the human examinees were able to predict the next character in one guess about 79% of the time and rarely needed more than 3–4 guesses. Table 5.3 shows the distribution of guesses as published by Shannon.

# of guesses:	1	2	3	4	5	> 5
Probability:	79%	8%	3%	2%	2%	5%

Table 5.3: Probabilities of Guesses of English Text.

The fact that this probability is so skewed implies low entropy (Shannon's conclusion was an entropy of English text in the range of 0.6–1.3 bits per letter), which in turn implies the possibility of very good compression.

The symbol ranking method of this section [Fenwick 96] is based on the latter version of the Shannon test. The method uses the context C of the current symbol S (the N symbols preceding S) to prepare a list of symbols that are likely to follow C. The list is arranged from most likely to least likely. The position of S in this list (position numbering starts from 0) is then written by the encoder, after being suitably encoded, on the output stream. If the program performs as well as a human examinee, we can expect 79% of the symbols being encoded to result in 0 (first position in the ranking list), creating runs of zeros, which can easily be compressed by RLE.

The various context-based methods described elsewhere in this book, most notably PPM, use context to estimate symbol probabilities. They have to generate and output escape symbols when switching contexts. In contrast, symbol ranking does not estimate probabilities and does not use escape symbols. The absence of escapes seems to be the main feature contributing to the excellent performance of the method. Following is an outline of the main steps of the encoding algorithm.

Step 0. The *ranking index* (an integer counting the position of S in the ranked list) is set to zero.

Step 1. An LZ77-type dictionary is used, with a search buffer containing text that has already been input and encoded, and with a look-ahead buffer containing new, unprocessed text. The most recent text in the search buffer becomes the *current context* C. The leftmost symbol, R, in the look-ahead buffer (immediately to the right of C) is the *current symbol*. The search buffer is scanned from right to left (from recent to older text) for strings matching C. This process is very similar to the one described in Section 3.13 (LZP compression). The longest match is selected (if there are several longest matches, the most recent one is selected). The match length, N, becomes the *current order*. The symbol P following the matched string (i.e., immediately to the right of it) is examined. This is the symbol ranked first by the algorithm. If P is identical to R, the search is over and the algorithm outputs the ranking index (which is currently zero).

Step 2. If P is different from R, the ranking index is incremented by 1, P is declared *excluded*, and the other order-N matches, if any, are examined in the same way. Assume that Q is the symbol following such a match. If Q is in the list of excluded symbols then it is pointless to examine it, and the search continues with the next match. If Q has not been excluded, it is compared with R. If they are identical, the search is over, and the encoding algorithm outputs the ranking index. Otherwise the ranking index is incremented by 1, and Q is excluded.

Step 3. If none of the order-N matches is followed by a symbol identical to R, the order is decremented by 1, and the search buffer is again scanned from right to left (from recent to older text) for strings of size $N-1$ matching C. For each failure the ranking index is incremented by 1, and Q is excluded.

Step 4. When the match order gets all the way down to zero, symbol R is compared to symbols in a list containing the entire alphabet, again using exclusions and incrementing the ranking index. If the algorithm gets to this step it will find R in this list, and will output the current value of the ranking index (which will then normally be a large number).

Some implementation details are discussed below.

1. Implementing exclusion. When a string S that matches C is found, the symbol P immediately to the right of S is compared with R. If P and R are different, P should be declared excluded. This means that any future occurrences of P should be ignored. The first implementation of exclusion that comes to mind is a list to which excluded symbols are appended. Searching such a list, however, is time consuming, and it is possible to do much better.

The method described here uses an array **excl** indexed by the alphabet symbols. If the alphabet consists, e.g., of just the 26 letters, the array will have 26 locations indexed "a" through "z". Figure 5.4 shows a simple implementation that requires just one step to determine whether a given symbol is excluded. Assume that the current context C is the string "...abc". We know that the "c" will remain in the context even if the algorithm has to go down all the way to order-1. The algorithm therefore prepares a pointer to "c" (to be called the *context index*). Assume that the scan finds another string "abc", followed by a "y", and compares it to the current context. They match, but they are followed by different symbols. The decision is to exclude "y" and this is done by setting array element excl[y] to the context index (i.e., to point to "c"). As long as the algorithm scans for matches to the same context C, the context index will stay the same. If another matching string "abc" is later found, also followed by "y", the algorithm compares excl[y] to the context index, finds that they are equal, so it knows that "y" has already been excluded. When switching to the next current context there is no need to initialize or modify the pointers in array excl.

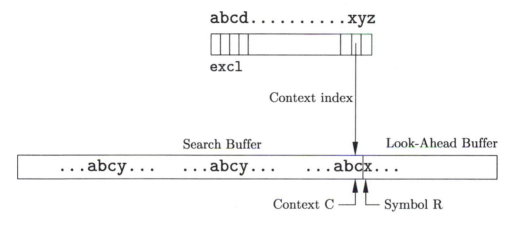

Figure 5.4: Exclusion Mechanism.

2. It has been mentioned earlier that scanning and finding matches to the current context C is done by a method similar to the one used by LZP. The reader should review Section 3.13 before reading ahead. Recall that initially the order N is unknown. The algorithm has to scan the search buffer and find the longest match to the current context. Once this is done, the length, N of the match becomes the current order. The process therefore starts by hashing the two rightmost symbols of the current context C and using them to locate a possible match.

Figure 5.5 shows the current context "...amcde". We assume that it has already been matched to some string of length 3 (i.e., a string "...cde") and we try to match it to a longer string. The two symbols "de" are hashed and produce a pointer to string "lmcde". The problem is to compare the current context to "lmcde" and find if and by how much they match. This is done by the following three rules.

Rule 1: Compare the symbols preceding (i.e., to the left of) "cde" in the two strings. In our example they are both "m", so the match is now of size 4. Repeat this rule until it fails. It determines the order N of the match. Once the order is known

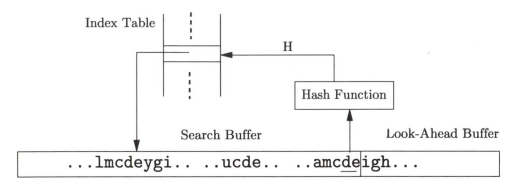

Figure 5.5: String Search and Comparison Method.

the algorithm may have to decrement it later and compare shorter strings. In such a case this rule has to be modified. Instead of comparing the symbols *preceding* the strings, it should compare the leftmost symbols of the two strings.

Rule 2: (We are still not sure if the two strings are identical.) Compare the middle symbols of the two strings. In our case, since the strings have a length of 4, this would be either the "c" or the "d". If the comparison fails, the strings are different. Otherwise rule 3 is used.

Rule 3: Compare the strings symbol by symbol to finally determine if they are identical.

It seems unnecessarily cumbersome to go through three rules when only the third one is really necessary. However, the first two rules are simple and they identify 90% of the cases where the two strings are different. Rule 3, which is slow, has to be applied only if the first two rules have not identified the strings as different.

3. If the encoding algorithm has to decrement the order all the way down to 1, it faces a special problem. It can no longer hash two symbols. Searching for order-1 matching strings (i.e., single symbols) therefore requires a different method that is illustrated by Figure 5.6. Two linked lists are shown, one linking occurrences of "s" and the other, of "i". Notice how only certain occurrences of "s" are linked while others are skipped. The rule is to skip an occurrence of "s" that is followed by a symbol that's already been seen. Thus the first occurrences of "si", "ss", "s␣", and "sw" are linked, whereas other occurrences of "s" are skipped.

The list linking these occurrences of "s" starts empty and is built gradually, as more text is input and is moved into the search buffer. When a new context is created with "s" as its rightmost symbol, the list is updated. This is done by finding the symbol to the right of the new "s", say, "a", scanning the list for a link "sa", deleting it if found (not more than one may exist), and linking the current "s" to the list.

This list makes it easy to search and find all occurrences of the order-1 context "s" that are followed by different symbols (i.e., with exclusions).

Such a list should be built and updated for each symbol in the alphabet. If the algorithm is implemented to handle 8-bit symbols, then 256 such lists are needed

Figure 5.6: Context Searching for Order-1.

and have to be updated.

The implementation details above show how complex this method is. It is slow but it produces excellent compression.

Bibliography

Fenwick, P. (1996) *Symbol Ranking Text Compression*, Tech. Rep. 132, Dept. of Computer Science, University of Auckland, New Zealand, June.

Shannon, C. (1951) "Prediction and Entropy of Printed English," *Bell System Technical Journal* **30**(1):50–64, January.

5.3 ACB

Not many details are available of the actual implementation of ACB, a new, highly efficient text compression method by G. Buyanovsky. The only documentation currently available is in Russian [Buyanovsky 94] and is already outdated. (An informal interpretation in English, by Leonid Broukhis, is available on the web at URL "http://wwwvms.utexas.edu/~cbloom" as file "/news/leoacb.html".) The name ACB stands for "Associative Coder (of) Buyanovsky." We start with an example and follow with some features and a variant. The precise details of the ACB algorithm, however, are still unknown.

Assume that the text "...swiss␣miss␣is␣missing..." is part of the input stream. The method uses an LZ77-type sliding buffer where we assume that the first seven symbols have already been input and are now in the search buffer. The look-ahead buffer starts with the string "iss␣is...".

> | ...swiss␣m | iss␣is␣missing... | ...← text to be read

While text is input and encoded, all contexts are placed in a dictionary, each with the text following it. This text is called the *content* string of the context. The six entries that correspond to the seven symbols are shown in Table 5.7a. The dictionary is then sorted by contexts, *from right to left*, as shown in Table 5.7b. Both the contexts and contents are unbounded. They are assumed to be as long as possible but may include only symbols from the search buffer since the look-ahead buffer is unknown to the decoder. This way both encoder and decoder can create and update their dictionaries in lockstep.

5.3.1 The Encoder

The current context "...swiss␣m" is matched by the encoder to the dictionary entries. The best match is between entries 2 and 3 (matching is from right to left). We arbitrarily assume that the match algorithm selects entry 2 (the algorithm does

```
...s|wiss␣m        1   ...swiss␣|m
...sw|iss␣m        2    ...swi|ss␣m
...swi|ss␣m        3    ...s|wiss␣m
...swis|s␣m        4   ...swis|s␣m
...swiss|␣m        5   ...swiss|␣m
...swiss␣|m        6    ...sw|iss␣m
```

(a)   (b)

Table 5.7: Six Contexts and Contents.

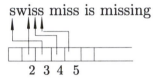

Figure 5.8: Dictionary Organization.

```
...s|wiss␣miss␣i        1   ...swiss␣miss␣|i
...sw|iss␣miss␣i        2     ...swiss␣|miss␣i
...swi|ss␣miss␣i        3    ...swiss␣mi|ss␣i
...swis|s␣miss␣i        4       ...swi|ss␣miss␣i
...swiss|␣miss␣i        5    ...swiss␣m|iss␣i
...swiss␣|miss␣i        6        ...s|wiss␣miss␣i
...swiss␣m|iss␣i        7   ...swiss␣mis|s␣i
...swiss␣mi|ss␣i        8      ...swis|s␣miss␣i
...swiss␣mis|s␣i        9   ...swiss␣miss|␣i
...swiss␣miss|␣i       10      ...swiss|␣miss␣i
...swiss␣miss␣|i       11       ...sw|iss␣miss␣i
```

(a)   (b)

Table 5.9: Eleven Contexts and Their Contents.

not, of course, make arbitrary decisions and is the same for encoder and decoder). The current content "iss..." is also matched to the dictionary. The best content match is to entry 6. The four symbols "iss␣" match, so the output is $(6 - 2, 4, \text{"i"})$, a triplet that compresses the *five* symbols "iss␣i". The first element of the tripet is the distance d between the best content and best context matches (it can be negative). The second element is the number 1 of symbols matched (hopefully large, but could also be zero). The third element is the first unmatched symbol in the look-ahead buffer (in the spirit of LZ77). The five compressed symbols are appended to the "content" fields of *all* the dictionary entries (Table 5.9a) and are also shifted into the search buffer. These symbols also cause five entries to be added to the dictionary which is shown, resorted, in Table 5.9b.

The new sliding buffer is

> ...swiss␣miss␣i|s␣missing...|...← text to be read.

The best context match is between entries 2 and 3 (we arbitrarily assume that the match algorithm selects entry 3). The best content match is entry 8. The six symbols "s␣miss" match, so the output is (8 − 3,6,"i"), a triplet that compresses seven symbols. The seven symbols are appended to the "content" field of every dictionary entry and are also shifted into the search buffer. Seven new entries are added to the dictionary, which is shown in Table 5.10a (unsorted) and 5.10b (sorted).

...s|wiss␣miss␣is␣missi 1	...swiss␣miss␣is␣|missi
...sw|iss␣miss␣is␣missi 2	...swiss␣miss␣|is␣missi
...swi|ss␣miss␣is␣missi 3	...swiss␣|miss␣is␣missi
...swis|s␣miss␣is␣missi 4	...swiss␣miss␣i|s␣missi
...swiss|␣miss␣is␣missi 5	...swiss␣miss␣is␣mi|ssi
...swiss␣|miss␣is␣missi 6	...swiss␣mi|ss␣is␣missi
...swiss␣m|iss␣is␣missi 7	...swi|ss␣miss␣is␣missi
...swiss␣mi|ss␣is␣missi 8	...swiss␣miss␣is␣m|issi
...swiss␣mis|s␣is␣missi 9	...swiss␣m|iss␣is␣missi
...swiss␣miss|␣is␣missi 10	...s|wiss␣miss␣is␣missi
...swiss␣miss␣|is␣missi 11	...swiss␣miss␣is|␣missi
...swiss␣miss␣i|s␣missi 12	...swiss␣miss␣is␣mis|si
...swiss␣miss␣is|␣missi 13	...swiss␣mis|s␣is␣missi
...swiss␣miss␣is␣|missi 14	...swis|s␣miss␣is␣missi
...swiss␣miss␣is␣m|issi 15	..swiss␣miss␣is␣miss|i
...swiss␣miss␣is␣mi|ssi 16	...swiss␣miss|␣is␣missi
...swiss␣miss␣is␣mis|si 17	...swiss␣|miss␣is␣missi
..swiss␣miss␣is␣miss|i 18	...sw|iss␣miss␣is␣missi

(a) (b)

Table 5.10: Eighteen Contexts and Their Contents.

The new sliding buffer is

> ...swiss␣miss␣is␣missi|ng...|...← text to be read.

(Notice that each sorted dictionary is a permutation of the text symbols in the search buffer. This feature of ACB resembles the Burrows-Wheeler method, Section 5.1.)

The best context match is now entries 6 or 7 (we assume that 6 is selected), but there is no content match since no content starts with an "n". No symbols match, so the output is (0,0,"n"), a triplet that compresses the single symbol "n" (it actually generates expansion). This symbol should now be added to the dictionary and also shifted into the search buffer. (End of example.)

▶ **Exercise 5.5:** Why does this triplet have a first element of zero?

5.3.2 The Decoder

The ACB decoder builds and updates the dictionary in lockstep with the encoder. At each step the encoder and decoder have the same dictionary (same contexts and contents). The difference between them is that the decoder does not have the data in the look-ahead buffer. The decoder does have the data in the search buffer, though, and uses it to find the best context match at, say, dictionary entry t. This is done before the decoder inputs anything. It then inputs a triplet (d,l,x) and adds the distance d to t to find the best content match c. The decoder then simply copies l symbols from the content part of entry c, appends symbol x, and outputs the resulting string to the decompressed stream. This string is also used to update the dictionary.

A modified version of ACB writes pairs (distance, match length) on the compressed stream instead of triplets. When the match length l is zero, the raw symbol code (typically ASCII or 8 bits) is written, instead of a pair. Each output, a pair or raw code, must now be preceded by a flag indicating its type.

The dictionary may be organized as a list of pointers to the search buffer. Figure 5.8 shows how dictionary entry 4 points to the second "s" of "swiss". Following this pointer, it is easy to locate both the context of entry 4 (the search buffer to the left of the pointer, the past text) and its content (that part of the search buffer to the right of the pointer, the future text).

Part of the excellent performance of ACB is attributed to the way it encodes the distances d and match lengths l, which are its main output. Unfortunately, the details of this are still unknown.

It is clear that ACB is somewhat related to both LZ77 and LZ78. What is not immediately obvious is that ACB is also related to the symbol ranking method (Section 5.2). The distance d between the best-content and best-context entries can be regarded a measure of ranking. In this sense ACB is a *phrase-ranking* compression method.

5.3.3 A Variation

Here is a variation of the basic ACB method that's slower, requiring an extra sort for each match, but is more efficient. We assume the string

$$\boxed{\text{...your}_\sqcup\text{swiss}_\sqcup\text{mis}\,|\,\text{s}_\sqcup\text{is}_\sqcup\text{mistress...}}\text{...}\leftarrow \text{ text to be read.}$$

in the search- and look-ahead buffers. We denote this string S. Part of the current dictionary (sorted by context, as usual) is shown in Table 5.11a, where the first eight and the last five entries are from the current search buffer "your$_\sqcup$swiss$_\sqcup$mis", and the middle ten entries are assumed to be from older data.

All dictionary entries whose context fields agree with the search buffer by at least k symbols—where k is a parameter, set to 9 in our example—are selected and become the *associative list*, shown in Table 5.11b. Notice that these entries agree with the search buffer by ten symbols, but we assume that k has been set to 9. All the entries in the associative list have identical, k-symbol contexts and represent dictionary entries with contexts similar to the search buffer (hence the name "associative").

```
           ...your␣|swiss␣mis
        ...your␣swiss␣|mis
     ...your␣swiss␣mi|s
          ...your␣swi|ss␣mis
     ...your␣swiss␣m|is
              ...yo|ur␣swiss␣mis
            ...your|␣swiss␣mis
          ...your␣s|wiss␣mis
        ...young␣mis|creant...
     ...unusual␣mis|fortune...
      ...plain␣mis|ery...
   ...no␣swiss␣mis|spelled␣it␣so..
   ...no␣swiss␣mis|s␣is␣mistaken..
   ...or␣swiss␣mis|read␣it␣to...
 ..your␣swiss␣mis|s␣is␣missing...
 ...his␣swiss␣mis|s␣is␣here...
 ...my␣swiss␣mis|s␣is␣trouble...
    ...always␣mis|placed␣it...
      ...your␣swis|s␣mis
    ...your␣swiss|␣mis
           ...you|r␣swiss␣mis
        ...your␣sw|iss␣mis
             ...y|our␣swiss␣mis
```

```
swiss␣mis|spelled␣it␣so.
swiss␣mis|s␣is␣mistaken.
swiss␣mis|read␣it␣to...
swiss␣mis|s␣is␣missing..
swiss␣mis|s␣is␣here...
swiss␣mis|s␣is␣trouble..
```

| (a) | (b) |

Table 5.11: (a) Sorted Dictionary. (b) Associative List.

```
1  swiss␣mis|read␣it␣to...
2  swiss␣mis|s␣is␣here...
3  swiss␣mis|s␣is␣missing...
4  swiss␣mis|s␣is␣mistaken..
5  swiss␣mis|s␣is␣trouble...
6  swiss␣mis|spelled␣it␣so..
```

```
4. swiss mis|s is mistaken..
S. swiss mis|s is mistress..
5. swiss mis|s is trouble...
```

| (a) | (b) |

Table 5.12: (a) Sorted Associative List. (b) Three Lines.

```
4. xx...x0zz...z0A        4. xx...x0CC...          4. xx...x0CC...
S. xx...x0zz...z1B        S. xx...x1zz...z0B        S. xx...x1zz...z1B
5. xx...x1CC...           5. xx...x1zz...z1A        5. xx...x1zz...z0A
```

| (a) | (b) | (c) |

Table 5.13: Two Possibilities (a, b), and One Impossibility (c), of Three Lines.

The associative list is now sorted in ascending order by the **contents**, producing Table 5.12a. It is now obvious that S can be placed between entries 4 and 5 of the sorted list (Table 5.12b).

Since each of these three lines is sorted, we can temporarily forget that they consist of characters, and simply consider them three sorted bit-strings that can be written as in Table 5.13a. The "xx...x" bits are the part were all three lines agree (the string "swiss␣mis|s␣is␣"), and the "zz...z" bits are a further match between entry 4 and the look-ahead buffer (the string "mist"). All that the encoder has to output is the index 4, the underlined bit (which we denote b and that may, of course, be a zero), and the length 1 of the "zz...z" string. The encoder's output is thus the triplet (4,b,1).

In our example S agrees best with the entry preceding it. In some cases it may best agree with the entry following it, as in Table 5.13b (where bit b is shown as zero).

▶ **Exercise 5.6:** Why is the configuration of Table 5.13c impossible?

The decoder maintains the dictionary in lockstep with the encoder, so it can create the same associative list, sort it, and use the identical parts (the intersection) of entries 4 and 5 to identify the "xx...x" string. It then uses 1 to identify the "zz...z" part in entry 4 and generates the bit-string "xx...x$\bar{b}$zz...zb" (where $\bar{b}$ is the complement of b) as the decompressed output of the triplet (4,b,1).

This variant can be further improved (producing better but slower compression) if instead of 1, the encoder generates the number q of $\bar{b}$ bits in the "zz...z" part. This improves compression since q≤1. The decoder then starts copying bits from the "zz...z" part of entry 4 until it finds the q+1st occurrence of $\bar{b}$, which it ignores. Example: if b=1 and the "zz...z" part is "01011110001011" (preceded by $\bar{b}$=0 and followed by b=1) then q=6. The three lines are shown in Table 5.14. It is easy to see how the decoder can create the 14-bit "zz...z" part by copying bits from entry 4 until it finds the seventh 0, which it ignores. The encoder's output is thus the (encoded) triplet (4,1,6) instead of (4,1,14). Writing 6 (encoded) instead of 14 on the compressed stream improves the overall compression somewhat.

```
                      zz..........z
4.  xx...x0|01011110001011|0A
S.  xx...x0|01011110001011|1B
5.  xx...x1 CC...
```

Table 5.14: An Example.

Another possible improvement is to delete any identical entries in the sorted associative list. This technique may be called *phrase exclusion*, in analogy with the exclusion techniques of PPM and the symbol ranking method. In our example, Table 5.12a, there are no identical entries but had there been any, exclusion would have reduced the number of entries to fewer than 6.

▶ **Exercise 5.7:** How would this improve compression?

The main strength of ACB stems from the way it operates. It selects dictionary entries with contexts that are similar to the current context (the search buffer), and then sorts the selected entries by content and selects the best content match. This is slow and also requires a huge dictionary (a small dictionary would not provide good matches) but results in excellent context-based compression without the need for escape symbols or any other "artificial" device.

5.3.4 Context Files

An interesting feature of ACB is its ability to create and use *context files*. When a file "abc.ext" is compressed, the user may specify the creation of a context file called, e.g., "abc.ctx". This file contains the final dictionary generated during the compression of "abc.ext". The user may later compress another file "lmn.xyz" asking ACB to use "abc.ctx" as a context file. File "lmn.xyz" will thus be compressed by using the dictionary of "abc.ext". Following this, ACB will replace the contents of "abc.ctx". Instead of the original dictionary, it will now contain the dictionary of "lmn.xyz" (which was not used for the actual compression of "lmn.xyz"). If the user wants to keep the original contents of "abc.ctx", they can set its attributes to "read only." Context files can be very useful, as the following examples illustrate.

1. A writer emails a large manuscript to an editor. Because of its size, the manuscript file should be sent compressed. The first time this is done, the writer asks ACB to create a context file, then emails both the compressed manuscript and the context file to the editor. Two files need be emailed, so compression doesn't do much good this first time.

The editor decompresses the manuscript using the context file, reads it, and responds with proposed modifications to the manuscript. The writer modifies the manuscript, compresses it again with the same context file, and emails it, this time without the context file. The writer's context file has now been updated, so the writer cannot use it to decompress what he has just emailed (but then he doesn't need to). The editor still has the original context file, so he can decompress the second manuscript version, during which process ACB creates a new context file for the editor's use next time.

2. The complete collection of detective stories by a famous author should be compressed and saved as an archive. Since all the files are detective stories and are all by the same author, it makes sense to assume that they feature similar writing styles and therefore similar contexts. One story is selected to serve as a "training" file. It is compressed and a context file created. This context file is permanently saved and is used to compress and decompress all the other files in the archive.

3. A shareware author writes an application abc.exe that is used (and paid for) by many people. The author decides to make version 2 available. He starts by compressing the old version while creating a context file abc.ctx. The resulting compressed file is not needed and is immediately deleted. The author then uses abc.ctx as a context file to compress his version 2, and then deletes abc.ctx. The result is a compressed (i.e., small) file, containing version 2, that's placed on the internet, to be downloaded by users of version 1. Anyone who has version 1 can download the result and decompress it. All they need is to compress their version 1

in order to obtain a context file, and then use that context file to decompress what has been downloaded.

Bibliography

Buyanovsky, G. (1994), "Associative Coding," (in Russian), *Monitor*, Moscow, #8, 10–19, August. (Hard copies of the Russian source and English translation are available from the author of this book. Send requests to "dxs@ecs.csun.edu".)

Fenwick, P. (1996), "Symbol Ranking Text Compression," *Tech. Rep. 132*, Dept. of Computer Science, University of Auckland, New Zealand, June.

5.4 Sparse Strings

Regardless of what the input data represents, text, binary, images, or anything else, we can think of the input stream as a string of bits. If most of the bits are zeros, the string is *sparse*. Sparse strings can be compressed very efficiently, and this section describes methods developed specifically for this task. Before getting to the individual methods it may be useful to convince the reader that sparse strings are not a theoretical concept but occur commonly in practice. Here are some examples.

1. A drawing. Imagine a drawing, technical or artistic, done with a black pen on white paper. If the drawing is not very complex, most of it remains white. When such a drawing is scanned and digitized, most of the resulting pixels are white, and the percentage of black ones is small. The resulting bitmap is an example of a sparse string, an example that occurs many times in certain computer applications.

2. A *bitmap* index for a large data base. Imagine a large data base of text documents. A bitmap for such a data base is a set of bit-strings (or bitvectors) that makes it easy to identify all the documents where a given word w appears. To implement a bitmap, we first have to prepare a list of all the distinct words w_j in all the documents. Suppose that there are W such words. The next step is to go over each document d_i and prepare a bit-string D_i that's W bits long, containing a 1 in position j if word w_j appears in document d_i. The bitmap is the set of all those bit-strings. Depending on the contents of the data base, such bit-strings may be sparse.

(Indexing large data bases is an important operation since a computerized data base should be easy to search. The traditional method of indexing is to prepare a *concordance*. Originally, the word concordance referred to any comprehensive index of the Bible, but today there are concordances for the collected works of Shakespeare, Wordsworth, and many others. A computerized concordance is called an *inverted file*. Such a file includes one entry for each term in the documents constituting the data base. An entry is a list of pointers to all the occurrences of the term, similar to an index of a book. A pointer may be the number of a chapter, of a section, a page, a page-line pair, of a sentence, or even of a word. An inverted file where pointers point to individual words is considered *fine grained*. One where they point to, say, a chapter is considered *coarse grained*. A fine-grained inverted file may seem preferable but it must use large pointers and, as a result, it may turn out to be so large it may have to be stored in compressed form.)

3. Sparse strings have also been mentioned in Section 4.2.5, in connection with JPEG.

The methods described here are due to [Fraenkel 85].

5.4.1 Oring Bits

This method starts with a sparse string L_1 of size n_1 bits. In the first step, L_1 is divided into k substrings of equal size. In each substring all bits are logically ORed, and the results (one bit per substring) become string L_2, which will be compressed in step 2. All zero substrings of L_1 are now deleted. Here is an example of a sparse, 64-bit string L_1, that we divide into 16 substrings of size 4 each.

$$L_1 = 0000|0000|0000|0100|0000|0000|0000|1000|0000$$
$$|0000|0000|0000|0010|0000|0000|0000.$$

After Oring each 4-bit substring we get the 16-bit string $L_2 = 0001|0001|0000|1000$.

In step 2, the same process is applied to L_2, and the result is the 4-bit string $L_3 = 1101$, which is short enough so no more compression steps are needed. After deleting all zero substrings in L_1 and L_2, we end up with the three short strings

$$L_1 = 0100|1000|0010, \qquad L_2 = 0001|0001|1000, \qquad L_3 = 1101.$$

The output stream consists of seven 4-bit substrings instead of the original 16! (A few more numbers are needed, to indicate how long each substring is.)

The decoder works differently (this is an asymmetric compression method). It starts with L_3 and considers each of its 1 bits a pointer to a substring of L_2 and each of its 0 bits a pointer to a substring of all zeros that's not stored in L_2. This way string L_2 can be reconstructed from L_3, and string L_1, in turn, from L_2. Figure 5.15 illustrates this process. The substrings shown in square brackets are the ones not contained in the compressed stream.

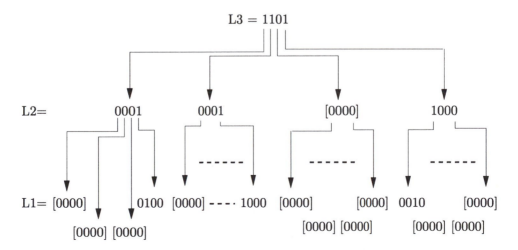

Figure 5.15: Reconstructing L_1 from L_3.

▶ **Exercise 5.8:** This method becomes highly inefficient for strings that are not sparse, and may easily result in expansion. Analyse the worst case, where every group of L_1 is nonzero.

5.4.2 Variable-Size Codes

We start with an input stream that's a sparse string L of n bits. We divide it into groups of l bits each, and assign each group a variable-size code. Since a group of l bits can have one of 2^l values, we need 2^l codes. Since L is sparse, most groups will consist of l zeros, implying that the variable-size code assigned to the group of l zeros (the zero group) should be the shortest (perhaps just one bit). The other $2^l - 1$ variable-size codes can be assigned arbitrarily, or according to the frequencies of occurrence of the groups. The latter choice requires an extra pass over the input stream to compute the frequencies. In the ideal case, where all the groups are zeros, and each is coded as one bit, the output stream will consist of n/l bits, yielding a compression ratio of $1/l$. This shows that, in principle, the compression ratio can be improved by increasing l but, in practice, large l means many codes which, in turn, increases the code size, and decreases the compression ratio for an "average" string L.

A better approach can be developed once we realize that a sparse input stream must contain **runs** of zero groups. A run of zero groups may consist of 1, 2, or up to n/l such groups. It is possible to assign variable-size codes to the runs of zero groups, as well as to the nonzero groups, and Table 5.16 illustrates this approach for the case of 16 groups. Trouble is, there are $2^l - 1$ non-zero groups and n/l possible run lengths of zero groups. Normally n is large and l is small, so n/l is large. If we increase l, then n/l gets smaller but $2^l - 1$ gets bigger. We thus always end up with many codes, which implies long codes.

Size of run length	Run of zeros	Nonzero group
1	0000 1	0001
2	0000 0000	2 0010
3	0000 0000 0000	3 0011
⋮	⋮ ⋮	⋮
16	0000 0000 … 0000	15 1111
(a)		(b)

Table 5.16: (a) n/l Run-lengths. (b) $2^l - 1$ Nonzero Groups.

A more promising approach is to divide the run lengths (which are integers between 1 and n/l) into classes, assign one variable-size code C_i to each class i, and assign a two-part code to each run length. Imagine a run of r zero groups, where r happens to be in class i, and happens to be the third one in this class. When a run of r zero groups is found in the input stream, the code of r is written to the output stream. Such a code consists of two parts, the first is the class code C_i, and the second is 2, the position of r in its class (positions are numbered from zero). Experience with algorithm design and binary numbers suggests the following definition of classes: A run length of r zero groups is in class i if $2^{i-1} \le r < 2^i$ where $i = 1, 2, \ldots, \lfloor \log_2(n/l) \rfloor$. This definition implies that the position of r in its class is $m = r - 2^{i-1}$, a number that can be written in $i - 1$ bits. Table 5.17 shows the four classes for the case $n/l = 16$ (16 groups). Notice how the numbers m are written as $i - 1$-bit numbers, so for $i = 1$ (the first class), no m is necessary. The variable-size Huffman codes C_i shown in the table are for illustration purposes only and are based on the (arbitrary) assumption that the most common run lengths are 5, 6, and 7.

Run length	Code	$r - 2^{i-1}$	$i - 1$	Huffman code|m
1	C_1	$1 - 2^{1-1} = 0$	0	00010
2	C_2	$2 - 2^{2-1} = 0$	1	00011|0
3	C_2	$3 - 2^{2-1} = 1$	1	0010|1
4	C_3	$4 - 2^{3-1} = 0$	2	0011|00
5	C_3	$5 - 2^{3-1} = 1$	2	010|01
6	C_3	$6 - 2^{3-1} = 2$	2	011|10
7	C_3	$7 - 2^{3-1} = 3$	2	1|11
8	C_4	$8 - 2^{4-1} = 0$	3	00001|000
9	C_4	$9 - 2^{4-1} = 1$	3	000001|001
$\vdots$				$\vdots$
15	C_4	$15 - 2^{4-1} = 7$	3	000000000001|111

Table 5.17: $\log_2(n/l)$ Classes of Run-Lengths.

It is easy to see from the table that a run of 16 zero groups (which corresponds to an input stream of all zeros) does not belong in any of the classes. It should thus be assigned a special variable-size code. The total number of variable-size codes required in this approach is therefore $2^l - 1$ (for the nonzero groups) plus $\lfloor \log_2(n/l) \rfloor$ (for the run lengths of zero groups) plus 1 for the special case where all the groups are zero. A typical example is a 1-megabit input stream ($n = 2^{20}$). Assuming $l = 8$, the number of codes is $2^8 - 1 + \log_2(2^{20}/8) + 1 = 256 - 1 + 17 + 1 = 273$. With $l = 4$ the number of codes is $2^4 - 1 + \log_2(2^{20}/4) + 1 = 16 - 1 + 18 + 1 = 34$: much smaller, but more codes are required to encode the same input stream.

The operation of the decoder is straightforward. It reads the next variable-size code, which represents either a non-zero group of l bits, or a run of r zero groups, or an input stream of all zeros. In the first case, the decoder creates the nonzero group. In the second case, the code tells the decoder the class number i. The decoder then reads the next $i - 1$ bits to get the value of m, and computes $r = m + 2^{i-1}$ as the size of the run length of zero groups. The decoder then creates a run of r zero groups. In the third case the decoder creates a stream of n zero bits.

Example: An input stream of size $n = 64$ divided into 16 groups of $l = 4$ bits each. The number of codes needed is $2^4 - 1 + \log_2(64/4) + 1 = 16 - 1 + 4 + 1 = 20$. We assume that each of the 15 nonzero groups occurs with probability $1/40$, and that the probability of occurrence of runs in the four classes are $6/40$, $8/40$, $6/40$, and $4/40$, respectively. The probability of occurrence of a run of 16 groups is assumed to be $1/40$. Table 5.18 shows possible codes for each non-zero group and for each class of runs of zero groups. The code for 16 zero groups is 00000 (corresponds to the 16 in italics).

Nonzero groups				Classes	
1 111111	5 01111	9 00111	13 00011	C_1	110
2 111110	6 01110	10 00110	14 00010	C_2	10
3 111101	7 01101	11 00101	15 00001	C_3	010
4 111100	8 01100	12 00100	*16* 00000	C_4	1110

Table 5.18: Twenty Codes.

▶ **Exercise 5.9:** Encode the input stream

0000|0000|0000|0100|0000|0000|0000|1000|0000|0000|0000|0000|0010|0000|0000|0000

using the codes of Table 5.18.

5.4.3 Variable-Size Codes for Base 2

Classes defined as in the preceding section require a set of $(2^l - 1) + \lfloor \log_2(n/l) \rfloor + 1$ codes. The method is efficient but slow since the code for a run of zero groups involves both a class code C_i and the quantity m. In this section we look at a way to handle runs of zero groups by defining codes R_1, R_2, R_4, R_8... for run lengths of $1, 2, 4, 8, \ldots, 2^i$ zero groups. The binary representation of the number 17, e.g., is 10001, so a run of 17 zero groups would be coded as R_{16} followed by R_1. Since run lengths can be from 1 to n/l, the number of codes R_i required is $1 + (n/l)$, more than before. Experience shows, however, that long runs are rare, so the Huffman codes assigned to R_i should be short for small values of i, and long for large i's. In addition to the R_i codes, we still need $2^l - 1$ codes for the nonzero groups. In the case $n = 64$, $l = 4$ we need 15 codes for the nonzero groups and 7 codes for R_1 through R_{64}. An example is illustrated in Table 5.19 where all the codes for nonzero groups are 5 bits long and start with 0, while the seven R_i codes start with 1 and are variable-size.

The R_i codes don't have to correspond to powers of 2. They may be based on 3, 4, or even larger integers. Let's take a quick look at octal R_i codes (8-based). They are denoted R_1, R_8, R_{64}.... To encode a run length of 17 zero groups ($= 21_8$) we need **two** copies of the code for R_8, followed by the code for R_1. The number of R_i codes is smaller, but some may have to appear several times.

The general rule is: Suppose that the R_i codes are based on the number B. If we identify a run of R zero groups, we first have to express R in base B, and then create copies of the R_i codes according to the digits of that number. If $R = d_3 d_2 d_1$ in base B, then the coded output for run length R should consist of d_1 copies of R_1, followed by d_2 copies of R_2 and by d_3 copies of R_3.

Nonzero groups		Run lengths	
1 0 0001	9 0 1001	R_1	1 1
2 0 0010	10 0 1010	R_2	1 01
3 0 0011	11 0 1011	R_4	1 001
4 0 0100	12 0 1100	R_8	1 00011
5 0 0101	13 0 1101	R_{16}	1 00010
6 0 0110	14 0 1110	R_{32}	1 00001
7 0 0111	15 0 1111	R_{64}	1 00000
8 0 1000			

Table 5.19: Codes for Base-2 R_i.

▶ **Exercise 5.10:** Encode the 64-bit input stream of exercise 5.9 by using the codes of Table 5.19.

5.4.4 Fibonacci-Based Variable-Size Codes

The codes R_i used in the previous section are based on powers of 2, since any positive integer can be expressed in this base using just the digits 0 and 1. It turns out that the well-known Fibonacci numbers also have this property. Any positive integer R can be expressed as $R = b_1F_1 + b_2F_2 + b_3F_3 + b_4F_5 + \cdots$ (that's b_4F_5, not b_4F_4) where the F_i are the Fibonacci numbers $1, 2, 3, 5, 8, 13, \ldots$ and the b_i are binary digits. The Fibonacci numbers grow slower than the powers of 2, meaning that more of them are needed to express a given run length R of zero groups. However, this representation has the interesting property that the string $b_1b_2\ldots$ does not contain any adjacent 1's ([Knuth 73], ex. 34, p. 85). If the representation of R in this base consists of d digits, at most $\lceil d/2 \rceil$ codes F_i would actually be needed to code a run length of R zero groups. As an example, the integer 33 equals the sum $1 + 3 + 8 + 21$, so it is expressed in the Fibonacci base as the 7-bit number 1010101. A run length of 33 zero groups is therefore coded, in this method, as the four codes F_1, F_3, F_8, and F_{21}.

Table 5.20 is an example of Fibonacci codes for the run length of zero groups. Notice that with seven Fibonacci codes we can only express runs of up to $1 + 2 + 3 + 5 + 8 + 13 + 21 = 53$ groups. Since we want up to 64 groups, we need one more code. Table 5.20 thus has eight codes, compared to seven in Table 5.19.

Nonzero groups		Run lengths	
1 0 0001	9 0 1001	F_1	1 1
2 0 0010	10 0 1010	F_2	1 01
3 0 0011	11 0 1011	F_3	1 001
4 0 0100	12 0 1100	F_5	1 00011
5 0 0101	13 0 1101	F_8	1 00010
6 0 0110	14 0 1110	F_{13}	1 00001
7 0 0111	15 0 1111	F_{21}	1 00000
8 0 1000		F_{34}	1 000000

Table 5.20: Codes for Fibonacci-Based F_i.

▶ **Exercise 5.11:** Encode the 64-bit input stream of exercise 5.9 using the codes of Table 5.20.

This section and the previous one suggest that any number system can be used to construct codes for the run lengths of zero groups. However, number systems based on binary digits are preferable, since certain codes can be omitted in such a case, and no code has to be duplicated. Another possibility is to use number systems where certain combinations of digits are impossible. Here is an example, also based on Fibonacci numbers.

The well-known recurrence relation these numbers satisfy is $F_i = F_{i-1} + F_{i-2}$. It can be written

$$F_{i+2} = F_{i+1} + F_i = (F_i + F_{i-1}) + F_i = 2F_i + F_{i-1}.$$

The numbers produced by this relation can also serve as the basis for a number system that has two interesting properties: (1) Any positive integer can be expressed using just the digits 0, 1, and 2. (2) Any digit of 2 is followed by a 0.

The first few numbers produced by this relation are 1, 3, 7, 17, 41, 99, 239, 577, 1,393 and 3,363. It is easy to verify the following examples:

1. $7000_{10} = 2001002001$ (since $7000_{10} = 2 \times 3363 + 239 + 2 \times 17 + 1$.
2. $168_{10} = 111111$.
3. $230_{10} = 201201$.
4. $271_{10} = 1001201$.

Thus a run of 230 zero groups can be compressed by generating two copies of the Huffman code of 99, followed by the Huffman code of 17, by two copies of the code of 7, and by the code of 1. Another possibility is to assign each of the base numbers 1, 3, 7, etc., two Huffman codes, one for two copies and the other one, for a single copy.

Bibliography

Fraenkel, A. S., and S. T. Klein (1985), "Novel Compression of Sparse Bit-Strings—Preliminary Report," in A. Apostolico and Z. Galil, eds., *Combinatorial Algorithms on Words*, Vol. 12, NATO ASI Series F:169–183, New York, Springer-Verlag.

Knuth, D. E. (1973), *The Art of Computer Programming*, Vol. 1, 2nd Ed., Reading, MA, Addison-Wesley.

5.5 Word-Based Text Compression

All the data compression methods considered in this book operate on small alphabets. A typical alphabet may consist of the two binary digits, the sixteen 4-bit pixels, the 7-bit ASCII codes, or the 8-bit bytes. In this section we consider the application of known methods to large alphabets that consist of *words*.

It is not clear how to define a word in cases where the input stream consists of the pixels of an image, so we limit our discussion to text streams. In such a stream a word is defined as a maximal string of either alphanumeric characters (letters and digits) or other characters (punctuations and spaces). We denote by **A** the alphabet of all the alphanumeric words and by **P**, that of all the other words. One consequence of this definition is that, in any text stream—whether the source code of a computer program, a work of fiction, or a restaurant menu—words from A and P strictly *alternate*. A simple example is the C source line

"␣␣for␣(␣short␣i=0;␣i␣<␣npoints;␣i++␣)•"

where • indicates the end-of-line character (CR, LF, or both). This line can easily be broken up into the 15-word alternating sequence

"␣␣" "for" "␣(␣" "short" "␣" "i" "=" "0" ";␣" "i" "␣<␣" "npoints" ";␣" "i" "++␣)•"

Clearly, the size of a word alphabet can be very large and may for all practical purposes be considered infinite. This implies that a method that requires storing the entire alphabet in memory cannot be modified to deal with words as the basic units (symbols) of compression.

▶ **Exercise 5.12:** What is an example of such a method?

A minor point to keep in mind is that short input streams tend to have a small number of distinct words so, when an existing compression method is modified to operate on words, care should be taken to make sure it still operates efficiently on small quantities of data.

Any compression method based on symbol frequencies can be modified to compress words if an extra pass is added, where the frequency of occurrence of all the words in the input is counted. This is impractical because:

1. A two-pass method is inherently slow.

2. The information gathered by the first pass has to be included in the compressed stream, since the decoder needs it. This decreases the compression efficiency even if that information is included in compressed form.

It therefore makes more sense to come up with *adaptive* versions of existing methods. Such a version should start with an empty data base (dictionary or frequency counts) and should add words to it as they are found in the input stream. When a new word is input, the raw, uncompressed ASCII codes of the individual characters in the word should be output, preceded by an escape code. In fact, it is even better to use some simple compression scheme to compress the ASCII codes. Such a version should also take advantage of the alternating nature of the words in the input stream.

5.5.1 Word-Based Adaptive Huffman Coding

This is a modification of the character-based adaptive Huffman coding (Section 2.9). Two Huffman trees are maintained, for the two alphabets A and P, and the algorithm alternates between them. Table 5.21 lists the main steps of the algorithm.

The main problems with this method are the following:

1. In what format to output new words. A new word can be written on the output stream, following the escape code, using the ASCII codes of its characters. However, since a word normally consists of several characters, a better idea is to code it by using the original, character-based adaptive Huffman method. The word-based adaptive Huffman algorithm thus "contains" a character-based adaptive Huffman algorithm that's used from time to time. This point is critical since a short input stream normally contains a high percentage of new words. Writing their

```
repeat
 input an alphanumeric word W;
 if W is in the A-tree then
  output code of W;
  increment count of W;
 else
  output an A-escape;
  output W (perhaps coded);
  add W to the A-tree with a count of 1;
  Increment the escape count
 endif;
 rearrange the A-tree if necessary;
 input an ''other'' word P;
 if P is in the P-tree then
 ...
 ...  code similar to the above
 ...
until end-of-file.
```

Table 5.21: Word-Based Adaptive Huffman Algorithm.

raw codes on the output stream may degrade the overall compression performance considerably.

2. What to do when the encoder runs out of memory because of large Huffman trees. A good solution is to delete nodes from the tree (and to rearrange the tree after such deletions, so that it remains a Huffman tree) instead of deleting the entire tree. The best nodes to delete are those whose counts are so low that their Huffman codes are longer than the codes they would be assigned if they were seen for the first time. If there are just a few such nodes (or none at all), then nodes with low frequency counts should be deleted.

Experience shows that word-based adaptive Huffman coding produces better compression than the character-based version but is slower since the Huffman trees tend to get big, slowing down the search and update operations.

3. The first word in the input stream may be alphanumeric or other. The compressed stream should therefore start with a flag indicating the type of the first word.

5.5.2 Word-Based LZW

This is a modification of the character-based LZW method (Section 3.9). The number of words in the input stream is not known beforehand and may also be very large. As a result, the LZW dictionary cannot be initialized to all the possible words, as is done in the character-based, original LZW method. The main idea is to start with an empty dictionary (actually two dictionaries, an A-dictionary and a P-dictionary) and use escape codes.

Each phrase added to a dictionary consists of two strings, one from A and the other from P. All phrases where the first string is from A are added to the P-dictionary. All those where the first string is from P are added to the P-dictionary. The advantage of having 2 dictionaries is that phrases can be numbered starting from 1 in each dictionary, which keeps the phrase numbers small. Notice that two different phrases in the two dictionaries can have the same number since the decoder knows whether the next phrase to be decoded comes from the A- or the P-dictionary. Table 5.22 is a general algorithm where the notation "S,W" stands for string "W" appended to string "S".

```
S:=empty string;
repeat
if currentIsAlph then input alphanumeric word W
                 else input non-alphanumeric word W;
endif;
if W is a new word then
  if S is not the empty string then output string # of S; endif;
  output an escape followed by the text of W;
  S:=empty string;
else
  if startIsAlph then search A-dictionary for string S,W
                 else search P-dictionary for string S,W;
  endif;
  if S,W was found then S:=S,W
  else
    output string numer of S;
    add S to either the A- or the P-dictionary;
    startIsAlph:=currentIsAlph;
    S:=W;
  endif;
endif;
currentIsAlph:=not currentIsAlph;
until end-of-file.
```

Table 5.22: Word-Based LZW.

Notice the line "output an escape followed by the text of W;". Instead of writing the raw code of W on the output stream it is again possible to use (character-based) LZW to code it.

5.5.3 Word-Based Order-1 Prediction

English grammar imposes obvious correlations between consecutive words. It is common, e.g., to find the pairs of words "the boy" or "the beauty" in English text, but rarely a pair such as "the went". This reflects the basic syntax rules governing the structure of a sentence and should exist in other languages as well. A compression algorithm using order-1 prediction can thus be very successful when applied to an input stream that obeys strict syntax rules. Such an algorithm should maintain an appropriate data structure for the frequencies of all the pairs of alphanumeric words seen so far. Assume that the text "...$P_i\, A_i\, P_j$" has recently been input, and the next word is A_j. The algorithm should get the frequency of the pair (A_i, A_j) from the data structure, compute its probability, send it to an arithmetic encoder together with A_j, and update the count of (A_i, A_j). Notice that there are no obvious correlations between consecutive punctuation words, but there may be some correlations between a pair (P_i, A_i) or (A_i, P_j). An example is a punctuation word that contains a period, which usually indicates the end of a sentence, suggesting that the next alphanumeric word is likely to start with an upper-case letter, and to be an article. Table 5.23 is a basic algorithm in pseudo-code, implementing these ideas. It tries to discover correlations only between alphanumeric words.

Since this method uses an arithmetic encoder to encode words, it is natural to extend it to use the same arithmetic encoder, applied to individual characters, to encode the raw text of new words.

Bibliography

Horspool, N. R. and G. V. Cormack (1992) "Constructing Word-Based Text Compression Algorithms," in *Proceedings of the 1992 Data Compression Conference*, J. Storer Ed., Los Alamitos, CA, IEEE Computer Society Press, pp. 62–71, April.

```
prevW:=escape;
repeat
 input next puntuation word WP and output its text;
 input next alphanumeric word WA;
 if WA is new then
  output an escape;
  output WA arithmetically encoded by characters;
  add AW to list of words;
  set frequency of pair (prevW,WA) to 1;
  increment frequency of the pair (prevW,escape) by 1;
 else
  output WA arithmetically encoded;
  increment frequency of the pair (prevW,WA);
 endif;
prevW:=WA;
until end-of-file.
```

Table 5.23: Word-Based Order-1 Predictor.

When I use a word it means just what I choose it to mean—neither more nor less.

—Humpty Dumpty.

5.6 Textual Image Compression

All of the methods described so far assume that the input stream is either a computer file or resides in memory. Life, however, isn't always so simple and sometimes the data to be compressed consists of a printed document that includes text, perhaps in several columns, and rules (horizontal and vertical). The method described here cannot deal with images very well, so we assume that the input documents do not include any images. The document may be in several languages and fonts, and may contain music notes or other notations instead of plain text. It may also be handwritten, but the method described here works best with printed material, since handwriting normally has too much variation. Examples are: (1) rare books and important original historical documents that are deteriorating because of old age or mishandling, (2) old library catalog cards about to be discarded because of automation, and (3) typed manuscripts that are of interest to scholars. In many of these cases it is important to preserve *all* the information on the document, not just the text. This includes the original fonts, margin notes, and various smudges, fingerprints, and other stains.

Before any processing by computer, the document has, of course, to be scanned and converted into black and white pixels. Such a scanned document is called a *textual image* since it is text described by pixels. In the discussion below, this collection of pixels is called *the input* or the *original image*. The scanning resolution should be as high as possible, but this raises the question of compression. Even at the low resolution of 300 dpi, an 8.5×11" page with 1-inch margins on all sides has a printed area of $6.5 \times 9 = 58.5$ square inch, which translates to $58.5 \times 300^2 = 5.265$ million pixels. At 600 dpi (medium resolution) such a page is converted to about 21 billion pixels. Compression makes even more sense if the document contains lots of blank space since in such a case most of the pixels would be white.

One approach to this problem is OCR (optical character recognition). Existing OCR software uses sophisticated algorithms to recognize the shape of printed characters and output their ASCII codes. If OCR is used, the compressed file should include the ASCII codes, each with a pair of (x, y) coordinates specifying its position on the page.

▶ **Exercise 5.13:** The (x, y) coordinates may specify the position of a character with respect to an origin, perhaps at the top-left or the bottom-left corner of the page. What may be a better choice for the coordinates?

OCR may be a good solution in cases where the entire text is in one font, and there is no need to preserve stains, smudges, and the precise shape of badly printed characters. This makes sense for documents such as old technical manuals that are not quite obsolete and might be needed in the future. However, if the document contains several fonts, OCR software normally does a poor job. It also cannot handle accents, images, stains, music notes, hieroglyphs, or anything other than text.

Facsimile compression (Section 2.13) can be used but does not produce the best results since it is based on RLE and does not pay any attention to the text itself. A document where letters repeat all the time and another one where no character appears twice may end up being compressed by the same amount.

The method described here [Witten 92] is complex and requires several steps, but is general, it preserves the entire document, and results in excellent compression. Compression factors of 25 are not uncommon. The method can also be easily modified to include lossy compression as an option, in which case it may produce compression factors of 100 [Witten 94].

The principle of the method is to separate the pixels representing text from the rest of the document. The text is then compressed with a method that counts symbol frequencies and assigns them probabilities, while the rest of the document—which typically consists of random pixels and may be considered "noise"—is compressed by another, more appropriate method. Here is a summary of the method (the reader is referred to [Witten 94] for the full details).

The encoder starts by identifying the lines of text. It then scans each line, identifying the boundaries of individual characters. The encoder does not attempt to actually recognize the characters. It treats each connected set of pixels as a character, called a *mark*. Many times a mark is a character of text, but it may also be part of a character. The letter "i", e.g., is made up of two, unconnected parts, the stem and the dot, so each becomes a mark. Something like "ö" becomes three marks. This way the algorithm does not need to know anything about the languages, fonts, or accents used in the text. The method works even if the "text" is made up of "exotic" characters, music notes, or hieroglyphs. Figure 5.24 shows examples of three marks and some specks. A human can easily recognize the marks as the letters "PQR", but software would have a hard time at this, especially since some pixels are missing.

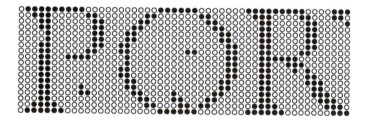

Figure 5.24: Marks and Specks.

Very small marks (less than the size of a period) are left in the input and are not further processed. Each mark above a certain size is compared to a library of previously found marks (called symbols). If the mark is identical to one of the symbols, its pixels are removed from the original textual image (the input). If the mark is "close enough" to one of the library symbols, then the difference between the mark and the symbol is left in the input (it becomes part of what is called the *residue*) and the rest is removed. If the mark is sufficiently different from all the library symbols, it is added to the library as a new symbol and all its pixels are removed from the input. In each of these cases the encoder generates the triplet

(# of symbol in the library, x, y),

which is later compressed. The quantities x and y are the horizontal and vertical distances (measured in pixels) between the bottom-left corner of the mark and the bottom-right corner of its predecessor; they are thus *offsets*. The first mark on a print line normally has a large negative offset since it is located way to the left of its predecessor.

The case where a mark is "sufficiently close" to a library symbol is important. In practice this usually means that the mark and the symbol describe the same character but there are small differences between them due to poor printing or bad alignment of the document during scanning. The pixels that constitute the difference are therefore normally in the form of a *halo* around the mark. The residue is thus made up of halos (that are recognizable or almost recognizable as "ghost" characters) and specks and stains that are too small to be included in the library. Considered as an image, the residue is thus fairly random (and therefore poorly compressible) since it does not satisfy the condition "the near neighbors of a pixel should have the same value as the pixel itself."

When the entire input (the scanned document) has been scanned in this way, the encoder selects all the library symbols that matched just one mark and returns their pixels to the input. They become part of the residue. (This step is omitted when the lossy compression option is used.) The encoder is then left with the symbol library, the string of symbol triplets, and the residue. Each of these is compressed separately.

The decoder first decompresses the library and the list of triplets. This is fast and normally results in text that can immediately be displayed and interpreted by the user. The residue is then decompressed, adding pixels to the display and bringing it to its original form. This process suggests a way to implement lossy compression. Just ignore the residue (and omit the step above of returning once-used symbols to the residue). This speeds up both compression and decompression, and significantly improves the compression performance. Experiments show that the residue, even though made up of relatively few pixels, may occupy up to 75% of the compressed stream since it is random in nature and thus compresses poorly.

The actual algorithm is very complex since it has to identify the marks and decide if a mark is close enough to any library symbol. Here, however, we will discuss just the way the library, triplets, and residue are compressed.

The number of symbols in the library is encoded first, by using one of the prefix codes of Section 2.3.1. Each symbol is then encoded in two parts. The first encodes the height and depth of the symbol (using the same code as for the number of symbols); the second encodes the pixels of the symbol using the two-level context-based image compression method of Section 4.5.

The triplets are encoded in three parts. The first part is the list of symbol numbers, which is encoded in a modified version of PPM (Section 2.17). The original PPM method was designed for an alphabet whose size is known in advance, but the number of marks in a document is unknown in advance and can be very large (especially if the document consists of more than one page). The second part is the list of x offsets and the third part, the list of y offsets. They are encoded with adaptive arithmetic coding,

The x and y offsets are the horizontal and vertical distances (measured in pixels) between the bottom-right corner of one mark and the bottom-left corner of the next. In a neatly printed page, such as this one, all characters on a line, except those with descenders, are vertically aligned at their bottoms, which means that most y offsets will be either zero or small numbers. If a proportional font is used, then the horizontal gaps between characters in a word are also identical, resulting in x offsets that are also small numbers. The first character in a word has an x offset whose size is the interword space. In a neatly printed page all interword spaces on a line should be the same, although those on other lines may be different.

All this means that many values of x will appear several times in the list of x values, and the same for y values. What's more, if an x value of, say, 3 is found to be associated with symbol s, there is a good chance that other occurrences of the same s will have an x offset of 3. This argument suggests the use of an adaptive compression method for compressing the lists of x and y offsets.

The actual method inputs the next triplet (s, x, y) and checks to see if symbol s was seen in the past followed by the same offset x. If yes, then offset x is encoded with a probability

$$\frac{\text{the number of times this x was seen associated with this s}}{\text{the number of times this s was seen}},$$

and the count (s,x) incremented by 1. If x hasn't been seen associated with this s, then the algorithm outputs an escape code, and assigns x the probability

$$\frac{\text{the number of times this x was seen}}{\text{the total number of x offsets seen so far}},$$

(disregarding any associated symbols). If this particular value of x has never been seen in the past, the algorithm outputs a second escape code and encodes x using the same prefix code used for the number of library symbols (and for the height and width of a symbol). The y value of the triplet is then encoded in the same way.

Compressing the residue presents a special problem since, viewed as an image, the residue is random and thus incompressible. However, viewed as text, the residue consists mostly of halos around characters (in fact, most of it may be legible, or close to legible), which suggests the following approach.

The encoder compresses the library and triplets, and writes them on the compressed stream, followed by the compressed residue. The decoder reads the library and triplets, and uses them to decode the *reconstructed text*. Only then does it read and decompress the residue. Both encoder and decoder thus have access to the reconstructed text when they encode and decode the residue, and this fact is used to compress the residue! The two-level context-based image compression method of Section 4.5 is used, but with a twist.

A table of size 2^{17} is used to accumulate frequency counts of 17-bit contexts (in practice it is organized as a binary search tree or a hash table). The residue pixels are scanned row by row. The first step in encoding a pixel at residue position (r,c) is to go to the same position (r,c) *in the reconstructed text* (which is, of course, an image made of pixels) and use the 13-pixel context shown in Figure 5.25a to generate a 13-bit index. The second step is to use the four-pixel context of Figure 5.25b *on the pixels of the residue* to add 4 more bits to this index. The final 17-bit index is then used to compute a probability for the current pixel based on the pixel's value

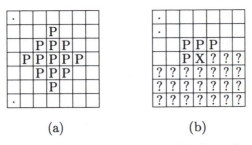

Figure 5.25: (a) Clairvoyant Context. (b) Secondary Context.

(0 or 1) and on the counts found in the table for this 17-bit index. The point is that the 14-bit part of the index is based on pixels that *follow* the current pixel in the reconstructed text. Such a context is normally impossible (it is called *clairvoyant*) but can be used in this case since the reconstructed text is known to the decoder. This is an interesting variation on the theme of compressing random data.

Even with this clever method, the residue still takes up a large part (up to 75%) of the compressed stream. After some experimentation the developers realized that it is not necessary to compress the residue at all! Instead, the original image (the input) can be compressed and decompressed using the method above, and this gives better results, even though the original image is less sparse than the residue, because it (the original image) is not as random as the residue.

This approach, of compressing the original image instead of the residue also means that the residue isn't necessary at all. The encoder does not need to reserve memory space for it and actually create the pixels, which speeds up encoding.

The compressed stream thus contains two parts, the symbol library and triplets (which are decoded to form the reconstructed text), followed by the entire input in compressed form. The decoder decompresses the first part, displays it so the user could read it immediately, then uses it to decompress the second part. Another advantage of this method is that as pixels of the original image are decompressed and become known, they can be displayed, replacing the pixels of the reconstructed text and thus improving the decompressed image seen by the user in *real time*. The decoder is therefore able to display an approximate image very quickly, and then clean it up row by row, while the user is watching, until the final image is displayed.

As has been mentioned, the details of this method are complex since they involve a pattern recognition process in addition to the encoding and decoding algorithms. Here are some of the complexities involved.

Identifying and extracting a mark from the document is done by scanning the input from left to right and top to bottom. The first non-white pixel found is thus the top-left pixel of a mark. This pixel is used to trace the entire boundary of the mark, a complex process involving an algorithm similar to those used in computer graphics to fill an area. The main point is that the mark may have an inside boundary as well as an outside one (think of the letters "O," "P," "Q," and "Φ") and there may be other marks nested inside it.

▶ **Exercise 5.14:** It seems that no letter of the alphabet is made of two nested parts.

What are examples of marks that contain other, smaller marks nested within them?

Tracing the boundary of a mark also involves the question of connectivity. When are pixels considered connected? Figure 5.26 illustrates the concepts of 4- and 8-connectivity and makes it clear that the latter method should be used because the former may miss letter segments that we normally consider connected.

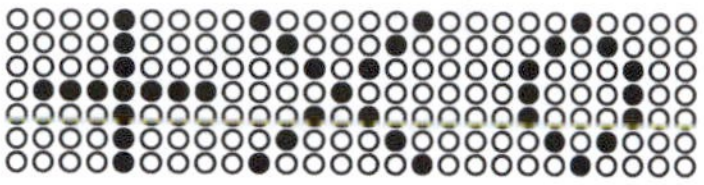

Figure 5.26: 4- and 8-Connectivity.

Comparing a mark to library symbols is the next complex problem. When is a mark considered "sufficiently close" to a library symbol? It is not enough to simply ignore small areas of pixels where the two differ, as this may lead to identifying, e.g., an "e" with a "c". A more complex method is needed, based on pattern-recognition techniques. It is also important to speed up the process of comparing a mark to a symbol, since a mark has to be compared to all the library symbols before it is considered a new one. An algorithm is needed that will find out quickly if the mark and the symbol are too different. This algorithm may use clues such as large differences in the height and width of the two, or in their total areas or perimeters, or in the number of black pixels of each.

When a mark is determined to be sufficiently different from all the existing library symbols, it is added to the library and becomes a symbol. Other marks may be found in the future that are close enough to this symbol and end up being associated with it. They should be "remembered" by the encoder. The encoder therefore maintains a list attached to each library symbol, containing the marks associated with the symbol. When the entire input has been scanned, the library contains the first version of each symbol, along with a list of marks that are similar. To achieve better compression, each symbol is now replaced with an average of all the marks in its list. A pixel in this average is set to black if it is black in more than half the marks in the list. The averaged symbols not only result in better compression but also look better in the reconstructed text, making it possible to use lossy compression more often. In principle, any change in a symbol should result in modifications to the residue, but we already know that in practice the residue does not have to be maintained at all.

All these complexities make textual images a hard, interesting example of a special-purpose data compression method and shows how much can be gained from a systematic approach in which every idea is implemented and experimented with before it is rejected, accepted, or improved upon.

Bibliography

Witten, I. H., T. C. Bell, M. E. Harrison, M. L. James, and A. Moffat (1992) "Textual Image Compression," in *Proceedings of the 1992 Data Compression Conference*, J. Storer ed., Los Alamitos, CA, IEEE Computer Society Press, pp. 42–51.

Witten, I. H., et al. (1994) *Managing Gigabytes: Compressing and Indexing Documents and Images*, New York, Van Nostrand Reinhold.

5.7 Dynamic Markov Coding

This is an adaptive, two-stage statistical compression method due to G. V. Cormack and R. N. Horspool [Cormack 87] (see also [Yu 96] for an implementation). Stage 1 uses a finite-state machine to estimate the probability of the next symbol. Stage 2 is an arithmetic encoder that performs the actual compression. Recall that the PPM method (Section 2.17) works similarly. Before describing the DMC algorithm, here is a short discussion of finite-state machines and their relation to estimating probabilities.

5.7.1 Finite-State Machines

Such a machine (also called a finite-state automaton) is a mathematical tool used to describe processes involving inputs and outputs. A finite-state machine can be in one of several states and can switch between states depending on input that it reads. Once it settles in a state, it reads the next input symbol, performs some computational task associated with the new input, outputs a symbol, and switches to a new state depending on the input. Notice that the new state may be identical to the current state. Figure 5.28a shows an example of such a machine with four states labeled 1 through 4. The input consists of a string of symbols from the alphabet "abc" and the output is a string of symbols from "mnpq". The machine starts in state 1. If it inputs an "a" it stays in state 1 and outputs an "m". If it inputs a "b", it switches to state 2 and outputs a "p". Notice that this particular machine can get "stuck" if it happens to be in a state that does not tell it what to do with a certain input. This will happen, e.g., with the input string "abbc..." since the "c" will be input while the machine is in state 4, where it expects an "a".

Figure 5.28b shows an example of a two-state machine that can be used to add binary numbers. The machine starts in state 1 (no carry) and inputs a pair of bits. If the pair is 11, the machine outputs a 0 and switches to state 2 (carry), where the next pair of bits is input and is added to a carry bit of 1. Table 5.27 shows the individual steps in adding the two 6-bit numbers 19 and 23 (these are actually 5-bit numbers but the simple design of this machine requires that an extra 0 bit be appended to the left end of every number). Since adding numbers is done from right to left, the six columns of the table should also be read in this direction.

Step:	6	5	4	3	2	1
19:	0	0	1	1	1	0
23:	0	1	0	1	1	1
Input:	00	01	10	11	11	01
Initial state:	2	2	2	2	1	1
Output:	1	0	0	1	0	1
Final state:	1	2	2	2	2	1

Table 5.27: Adding 19 and 23.

Figure 5.28c shows an example of a three-state machine where each edge is labeled by an input symbol and a probability, but no output. The diagram illustrates

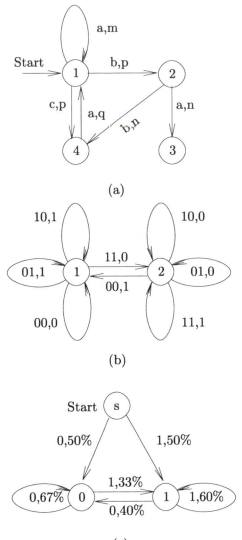

(a)

(b)

(c)

Figure 5.28: Examples of Finite-State Machines.

a machine that inputs a stream of bits where the first bit has probability 50% of being a 0 or a 1, and each consecutive bit is likely to be identical to its predecessor. A zero follows another zero with a probability of 2/3, and a one follows a one with a probability of 3/5. This machine does not produce any outputs but any practical finite-state machine should, of course, do something (meaning, produce some output).

In general, a finite-state machine is fully defined by specifying the following:

1. The set of states S.

2. The alphabet A of the input and output symbols.

3. A function $f : S \times A \to S \times A$. An example is $f(X, j) = (Y, i)$ meaning, if the current state is X and the next input is j, switch to state Y and output i.

4. The start state S_0.

Mathematically, a finite-state machine is a quartet (S, A, f, S_0).

A finite-state machine can be used in data compression as a model, to compute probabilities of input symbols. Figure 5.29a shows the simplest model, a one-state machine. The alphabet consists of the three symbols "a", "b", and "c". Assume that the input stream is the 600-symbol string "aaabbcaaabbc...". Each time a symbol is input, the machine outputs its estimated probability, updates its count, and stays in its only state. Each of the three probabilities is initially set to 1/3 and gets very quickly updated to its correct value (300/600 for "a", 200/600 for "b", and 100/600 for "c") because of the regularity of this particular input. Assuming that the machine always uses the correct probabilities, the entropy (number of bits per input symbol) of this first example is

$$-\frac{300}{600} \log_2 \left(\frac{300}{600}\right) - \frac{200}{600} \log_2 \left(\frac{200}{600}\right) - \frac{100}{600} \log_2 \left(\frac{100}{600}\right) \approx 1.46.$$

The purpose of models is not to fit the data but to sharpen the questions.
—Samuel Karlin, 11th R. A. Fisher Memorial Lecture, 1983

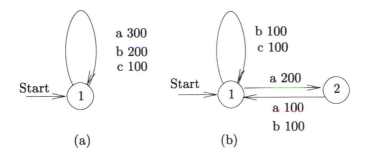

(a)   (b)

Figure 5.29: Finite-State Models for Data Compression.

Figure 5.29b illustrates a two-state model. When an "a" is input by state 1, it gets counted, and the machine switches to state 2. When state 2 inputs an "a" or a "b" it counts them and switches back to state 1 (this model will stop prematurely if state 2 inputs a "c"). Each sextet of symbols read from the input stream switches between the two states four times as follows:

$$a \xrightarrow{2} a \xrightarrow{1} a \xrightarrow{2} b \xrightarrow{1} b \xrightarrow{1} c \xrightarrow{1} .$$

State 1 accumulates 100 counts for "a", 200 counts for "b" and 100 counts for "c". State 2 accumulates 200 counts for "a". State 1 thus handles 400 of the 600 symbols and state 2, the remaining 200. The probability of the machine being in state 1 is therefore $400/600 = 4/6$, and that of its being in state 2 is $2/6$.

The entropy of this model is calculated separately for each state, and the total entropy is the sum of the individual entropies of the two states, weighted by the probabilities of the states. State 1 has "a", "b", and "c" coming out of it with probabilities $2/6$, $1/6$, and $1/6$, respectively. State 2 has "a", "b" and "c" coming out of it, each with probability $1/6$. The entropies of the two states are thus

$$-\frac{100}{600} \log_2 \left(\frac{100}{600}\right) - \frac{200}{600} \log_2 \left(\frac{200}{600}\right) - \frac{100}{600} \log_2 \left(\frac{100}{600}\right) \approx 1.3899 \quad \text{(state 1)}$$

$$-\frac{100}{600} \log_2 \left(\frac{100}{600}\right) - \frac{100}{600} \log_2 \left(\frac{100}{600}\right) \approx 0.8616 \quad \text{(state 1)}.$$

The total entropy is thus $1.3899 \times 4/6 + 0.8616 \times 2/6 = 1.21$.

Assuming that the arithmetic encoder works at or close to the entropy, this two-state model encodes a symbol in 1.21 bits, compared to 1.46 bits/symbol for the previous, one-state model. This is how a finite-state machine with the right states can be used to produce good probability estimates (good predictions) for compressing data.

The natural question at this point is: given a particular input stream, how do we find the particular finite-state machine that will feature the smallest entropy for that stream. A simple, brute force approach is to try all the possible finite-state machines, pass the input stream through each of them, and measure the results. This approach is impractical since there are n^{na} n-state machines for an alphabet of size a. Even for the smallest alphabet, with two symbols, this number grows exponentially. One 1-state machine, 16 2-state machines, 729 3-state machines, and so on.

Clearly, a clever approach is needed, where the algorithm can start with a simple, one-state machine, and adapt it to the particular input data by adding states as it goes along, based on the counts accumulated at any step. This is the approach adopted by the DMC algorithm.

5.7.2 The DMC Algorithm

This algorithm was originally developed for binary data (i.e., a two-symbol alphabet). Common examples of binary data are machine code (executable) files, images (both monochromatic and color), and sound. Each state of the finite-state DMC machine (or DMC model; in this section the words "machine" and "model" are used interchangeably) reads a bit from the input stream, assigns it a probability based on what it has counted in the past, and switches to one of two other states depending on whether the input bit was 1 or 0. The algorithm starts with a small machine (perhaps as simple as just one state) and adds states to it based on the input. It is thus adaptive. As soon as a new state is added to the machine, it starts counting bits and using them to calculate probabilities for 0 and 1. Even in this simple form, the machine can grow very large and quickly fill up the entire available memory. One advantage of dealing with binary data is that the arithmetic encoder can be made very efficient if it has to deal with just two symbols.

In its original form, the DMC algorithm does not compress text very well. Recall that compression is done by reducing redundancy, and that the redundancy of a text file is featured in the text characters, not in the individual bits. It is possible to extend DMC to handle the 128 ASCII characters by implementing a finite-state machine with more complex states. A state in such a machine should input an ASCII character, assign it a probability based on what characters were counted in the past, and switch to one of 128 other states depending on what the input character was. Such a machine would grow to consume even more memory space than the binary version.

The DMC algorithm has two parts; the first is concerned with calculating probabilities and the second is concerned with adding new states to the existing machine. The first part calculates probabilities by counting, for each state S, how many zeros and ones were input in that state. Assume that in the past the machine was in state S several times, and it input a zero s_0 times and a one, s_1 times while in this state (i.e., it switched out of state S s_0 times on the 0 output, and s_1 times on the 1 output; Figure 5.30a). The simplest way to assign probabilities to the 2 bits is by defining the following:

The probability that a zero will be input while in state S $= \dfrac{s_0}{s_0 + s_1}$;

The probability that a one will be input while in state S $= \dfrac{s_1}{s_0 + s_1}$.

But this, of course, raises the *zero-probability problem* since either s_0 or s_1 may be zero. The solution adopted by DMC is to assign probabilities that are always nonzero and that depend on a positive integer parameter c. The definitions are the following:

The probability that a zero will be input while in state S $= \dfrac{s_0 + c}{s_0 + s_1 + 2c}$;

The probability that a one will be input while in state S $= \dfrac{s_1 + c}{s_0 + s_1 + 2c}$.

Assigning small values to c implies that small values of s_0 and s_1 will affect the probabilities significantly. This is done when the user feels that the distributions of the 2 bits in the data can be "learned" fast by the model. If the data is such that it takes longer to adapt to the correct bit distributions, larger values of c can lead to better compression. Experience shows that for very large input streams, the precise value of c does not make much difference.

▶ **Exercise 5.15:** Why is there c in the numerator but $2c$ in the denominator of the two probabilities?

The second part of the DMC algorithm is concerned with how to add a new state to the machine. Consider the five states shown in Figure 5.30b, which may be part of a large finite-state DMC model. When a 0 is input while in state A, or when a 1 is input while in state B, the machine switches to state C. The next input bit switches it to either D or E. When switching to D, e.g., some information is lost since the machine does not "remember" whether it got there from A or from

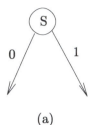

(a)

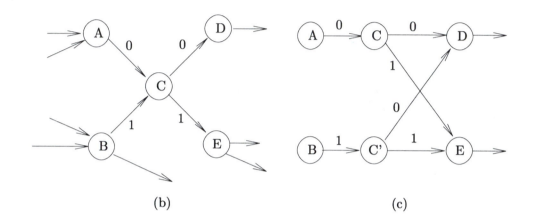

(b)   (c)

Figure 5.30: The Principles of DMC.

B. This information may be important if the input bits are correlated (i.e., if the probabilities of certain bit patterns are much different from those of other patterns). If the machine is currently in state A, it will get to D if it inputs 00. If it is currently in state B, it will get to D if it inputs 10. If the probabilities of the input patterns 00 and 10 are very different, the model may compute better probabilities (may produce better predictions) if it knew whether it came to D from A or from B.

☞ The central idea of DMC is to compare the counts of the transitions A → C and B → C, and if they are significantly different, to create a copy of state C, call it C', and place the copy such that A → C → (D, E) but B → C' → (D, E) (Figure 5.30c). This copying process is called *cloning*. The machine becomes more complex but can now keep better counts (counts that depend on the specific correlations between A and D, A and E, B and D, and B and E) and, as a result, compute better probabilities. Even adding one state may improve the probability estimates significantly since it may "bring to light" correlations between a state preceding A and one following D. In general, the more states are added by cloning, the easier it is for the model to "learn" about correlations (even long ones) between the input bits.

Once the new state C' is created, the original counts of state C should be divided between C and C'. Ideally they should be divided in proportion to the counts of the transitions A → C → (D, E) and B → C → (D, E), but these counts are not available (in fact, the cloning is done precisely in order to have these counts in the future). The next best thing is to divide the new counts in proportion to the counts of the transitions A → C and B → C.

An interesting point is that unnecessary cloning does not do much harm. It increases the size of the finite-state machine by one state, but the computed probabilities will not get worse. (Since the machine now has one more state, each state will be visited less often, which will lead to smaller counts and will therefore amplify small fluctuations in the distribution of the input bits, but this is a minor disadvantage.)

All this suggests that cloning be performed as early as possible, so we need to decide on the exact rule(s) for cloning. A look at Figure 5.30b shows that cloning should only be done when both transitions A → C and B → C have high counts. If both have low counts, then there is "not enough statistics" to justify cloning. If A has a high count, and B a low count, not much will be gained by cloning C since B is not very active. This suggests that cloning should be done when both A and B have high counts and one of them has a much higher count than the other. The DMC algorithm thus uses two parameters C1 and C2, and the following rule:

> If the current state is A and the next one is C, then C is a candidate for cloning, and should be cloned if the count for the transition A → C is greater than C1 **and** the total counts for all the other transitions X → C are greater than C2 (X stands for all the states feeding C, except the current state A).

The choice of values for C1 and C2 is critical. Small values mean fast cloning of states. This implies better compression, since the model "learns" the correlations in the data faster, but also more memory usage, increasing the chance of running out of memory while there is still a lot of data to be compressed. Large values have the opposite effect. Any practical implementation should thus let the user specify the values of the two parameters. It also makes sense to start with small values and increase them gradually as compression goes along. This enables the model to "learn" fast initially, and also delays the moment when the algorithm runs out of memory.

▸ **Exercise 5.16:** Figure 5.31 shows part of a finite-state DMC model. State A switches to D when it inputs a 1, so D is a candidate for cloning when A is the current state. Assuming that the algorithm has decided to clone D, show the states after the cloning.

Figure 5.32 is a simple example that shows six steps of adding states to a hypothetical DMC model. The model starts with the single state 0 whose two outputs loop back and become its inputs (they are *reflexive*). In 5.32b a new state, state 1, is added to the 1-output of state 0. We use the notation 0, 1 → 1 (read: state 0 output 1 goes to new state 1) to indicate this operation. In 5.32c the operation 0, 0 → 2 adds a new state 2. In 5.32d,e,f states 3, 4, and 5 are added by the operations 1, 1 → 3; 2, 1 → 4 and 0, 0 → 5. Figure 5.32f, e.g., was constructed by adding state 5 to output 0 of state 0. The two outputs of state 5 are determined by examining the 0-output of state 0. Since this output used to go to state 2, the new 0-output of state 5 goes to state 2. Also, since this output used to go to state

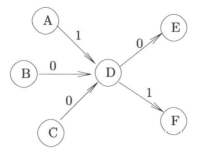

Figure 5.31: State D is a Candidate.

2, the new 1-output of state 5 becomes a copy of the 1-output of state 2, which is why it goes to state 4.

▶ **Exercise 5.17:** Draw the DMC model after the operation $1, 1 \rightarrow 6$.

5.7.3 DMC Start and Stop

When the DMC algorithm starts, it needs only have one state that switches to itself when either 0 or 1 are input, as shown in Figure 5.33a. This state is cloned many times and may grow very fast to become a complex finite-state machine with many thousands of states. This way to start the DMC algorithm works well for binary input. However, if the input consists of non-binary symbols, an appropriate initial machine, one that takes advantage of possible correlations between the individual bits of a symbol, may lead to much better compression. The tree of Figure 5.33b is a good choice for 4-bit symbols since each level corresponds to one of the 4 bits. If there is, e.g., a large probability that a second bit of 1 in the input symbols will be followed by a third bit of 1, the model will discover it very quickly and will clone the state marked in the figure. A similar complete binary tree, but with 255 states instead of 15, may be appropriate as an initial model in cases where the data consists of 8-bit symbols. More complex initial machines may even take advantage of correlations between the last bit of an input symbol and the first bit of the next symbol. One such model, a *braid* designed for 3-bit input symbols, is shown in Figure 5.33c.

  Any practical implementation of DMC should address the question of memory use. The number of states can grow very rapidly and fill up any amount of available memory. The simplest solution is to continue, once memory is full, without cloning. A better solution is to discard the existing model and start afresh. This has the advantage that new states being cloned will be based on new correlations discovered in the data, and old correlations will be forgotten. An even better solution is to always keep the k most recent input symbols in a circular queue and use them to build a small initial model when the old one is discarded. When the algorithm resumes, this small initial model will let it take advantage of the recently discovered correlations, so the algorithm will not have to "relearn" the data from scratch. This method minimizes the loss of compression associated with discarding the old model.

▶ **Exercise 5.18:** How does the loss of compression depend on the value of k?

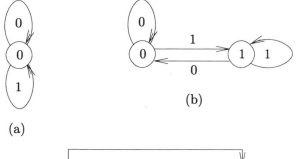

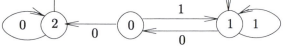

(a)

(b)

(c)

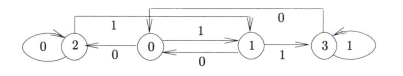

(d)

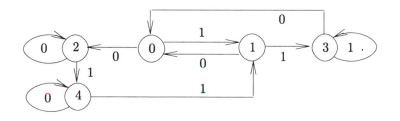

(e)

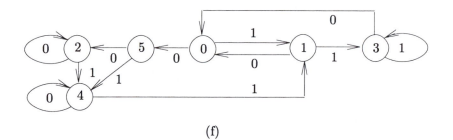

(f)

Figure 5.32: First Six States.

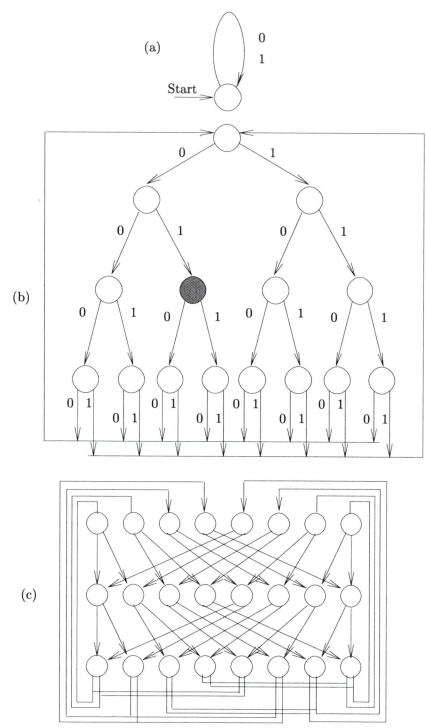

Figure 5.33: Initial DMC Models.

The main principle of DMC, the rule of cloning, is based on intuition and not on any theoretical principles. Consequently, the main justification of DMC is that it works! It produces very good compression, equivalent to that achieved by PPM, while also being faster.

Bibliography

Cormack G. V. and R. N. S. Horspool (1987) "Data Compression Using Dynamic Markov Modelling," *The Computer Journal* **30**(6):541–550.

Yu, Tong Lai. (1996) "Dynamic Markov Compression," *Dr Dobb's Journal* pp. 30–31, January.

5.8 Sound Compression

Text does not occupy much space in the computer. A large book, consisting of a million words, can be stored uncompressed in about 1Mbyte, since each character of text occupies 1 byte. In contrast, images take much more space, lending another meaning to the phrase "a picture is worth a thousand words." Depending on the number of colors used in an image, a single pixel occupies between 1 bit and 3 bytes. A 512×512-pixel image can thus occupy between 32Kbytes and 768Kbytes. With the advent of powerful, inexpensive personal computers, came multimedia applications, where text, images, and *sound* are stored in the computer, and can be displayed, played, and edited. This section starts with a short introduction to sound files, continues with a look at how conventional compression methods perform on sound files, and concludes with some ideas for special methods to compress sound.

5.8.1 Sampling

Much as an image can be digitized and broken up into pixels, where each pixel is a number, sound can also be digitized and broken up into numbers. When sound is played into a microphone, it becomes a voltage that changes continuously with time. Figure 5.34 shows a typical example of sound that starts at zero and oscillates several times. Such voltage is the *analog* representation of the sound. Digitizing sound is done by measuring the voltage at many points, translating each measurement into a number, and writing the numbers on a file. This process is called *sampling*. The sound wave is sampled, and the samples become the digitized sound. The device used for sampling is called an analog-to-digital converter (ADC).

Since the sound samples are numbers, they are easy to edit. However, the main use of a sound file is to play it back. This is done by converting the numeric samples back into voltages that are continuously fed into a speaker. The device that does that is called a digital-to-analog converter (DAC). Intuitively it is clear that a high sampling rate would result in better sound reproduction, but also in many more samples and thus larger files. The main problem in sound sampling is thus how often to sample a given sound.

Figure 5.34a shows what may happen if the sampling rate is too low. The sound wave in the figure is sampled eight times, and all eight samples happen to be identical. When these samples are used to play back the sound, the result is a uniform sound, resembling a buzz. Figure 5.34b shows 32 samples, and it is clear that they "follow" the original wave fairly close. Even 32 samples are not enough

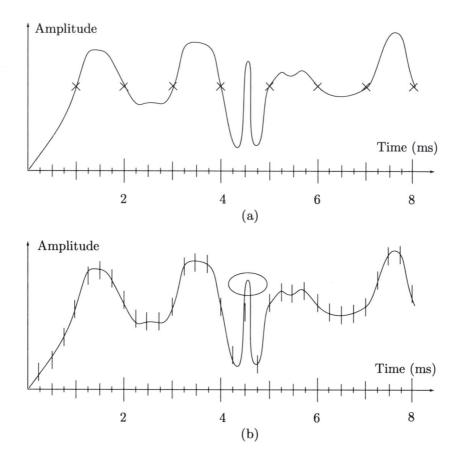

Figure 5.34: Sampling a Sound Wave.

to truly reproduce this sound, since one region of the wave (the region around the small circle) has higher frequency and is not sampled enough. The wave part inside a circle is not sampled and will not participate in any playback.

The solution to the sampling problem is to sample sound at the *Nyquist rate* (page 353), which is twice the maximum frequency included in the sound. Such sampling rate guarantees true reproduction of the sound.

The range of human hearing is typically between 16 Hz and 22,000 Hz, depending on the person and on age. When sound is digitized at high-fidelity, it should therefore be sampled at the Nyquist rate of 44,000 Hz (or higher). Anything lower than that results in distortions. Many low-fidelity applications sample sound at 11,000 Hz, and the telehone system, originally designed for conversations, not digital communications, samples sound at only 8 KHz. Any frequency higher than 4000 Hz gets distorted when sent over the phone, which is why it is hard to distinguish, on the phone, between "f" and "s." This is also why, when someone gives you an address over the phone you should ask is it H street, as in EFGH? Many times the answer is No, this is Eighth street, as in sixth, seventh, eighth.

> The meeting was in Mr. Rogers' law office, at 1415 *H* Street. My
> slip of paper said 1415 *8th* Street. (The address had been given over the
> telephone.)
> —Richard P. Feynman, *What Do YOU Care What Other People Think?*

A frequency of 500 Hz is common in speech and music. The period that corresponds to this frequency is 0.002 sec, or 2 ms (2 milliseconds). Assuming that
the first half of the sound wave of Figure 5.34 is at this frequency, it is easy to
see that the entire sample lasts only 8 ms. In 5.34a the wave is sampled once per
millisecond, and in 5.34b, four times each ms.

The second problem of sound sampling is the sample size. Each sample becomes
a number, but how large should this number be? In practice, samples are normally
either 8 or 16 bits, although some high-quality sound cards may optionally use 32-
bit samples. Assuming that the highest voltage in a sound wave is 1 volt, an 8-bit
sample can distinguish voltages as low as $1/256 \approx 0.004$ volt, or 4 millivolts. A
quiet sound, generating a wave lower than 2 mv, would be sampled as zero and
played back as silence. In contrast, a 16-bit sample can distinguish sounds as low
as $1/65,536 \approx 15$ microvolt.

▶ **Exercise 5.19:** Suppose that the sample size is 1 bit. Each sample has a value of
either 0 or 1. What would we hear when these samples are played back?

5.8.2 Conventional Methods

Conventional methods, such as RLE, statistical, and dictionary-based, can be used
to losslessly compress sound files, but the results depend heavily on the specific
sound. Some sounds may compress well under RLE but not under a statistical
method. Other sounds may lend themselves to statistical compression but may
expand when processed by a dictionary method. Here is how sounds respond to
each of the three classes of compression methods.

RLE may work well when the sound contains long runs of identical samples.
With 8-bit samples this may be common. Recall that the difference between the two
8-bit samples n and $n+1$ is about 4 mv. A few seconds of uniform music, where the
wave does not oscillate more than 4 mv, may produce a run of hundreds of identical
samples. With 16-bit samples, long runs may be rare and RLE, consequently,
ineffective.

Statistical methods assign variable-size codes to the samples according to their
frequency of occurrence. With 8-bit samples, there are only 256 different samples so,
in a large sound file, we can typically expect the samples to have a flat distribution.
Such a file may therefore respond well to Huffman coding. With 16-bit samples
there are more than 65,000 possible samples, so they may sometimes feature skewed
probabilities (i.e., some samples may occur very often while others may be rare).
Such a file may therefore compress better with arithmetic coding, which works well
even for skewed probabilities.

Dictionary-based methods expect to find the same phrases again and again in the data. This happens with text, where certain strings may repeat exactly many times. Sound, however, is an analog signal and the particular samples generated depend on the precise way the ADC works. With 8-bit samples, e.g., a wave of 8 mv becomes a sample of size 2 but waves very close to that, say, 7.6 mv or 8.5 mv, may become samples of different sizes. This is why parts of speech that sound the same to us, and should therefore have become identical phrases, end up being digitized slightly differently, and go into the dictionary as different phrases, thereby reducing the compression performance. Dictionary-based methods are thus not very well suited to sound compression.

5.8.3 Lossy Sound Compression

It is possible to get better sound compression by developing lossy methods that take advantage of the way we hear, and delete data to which the human ear is not sensitive. This is similar to lossy image compression, where data is deleted, to which the human eye is not sensitive. In both cases we use the fact that the original information (image or sound) is analog and has already lost some information when digitized. Losing some more data, if done carefully, may not significantly affect the played-back sound, and may therefore be acceptable. We briefly describe two approaches, *silence compression* and *companding*.

The principle of silence compression is to treat small samples as if they were silence (i.e., as samples of zero). This generates run lengths of zero, so silence compression is actually a variant of RLE, suitable for sound compression. This method uses the fact that some people have less sensitive hearing than others, and will tolerate the loss of sound that's so quiet they may not hear it anyway. Sound files containing long periods of low-volume sound will respond to silence compression better than other files with high-volume sound. This method requires a user-controlled parameter that specifies the largest sample that should be suppressed. Two other parameters are also necessary, although they may not have to be user-controlled. One specifies the shortest run-length of small samples, typically 2 or 3. The other specifies the minimum number of consecutive large samples that should terminate a run of silence. For example, a run of 15 small samples, followed by 2 large samples, followed by 13 small samples may be considered one silence run of 30 samples, whereas a situation of 15, 3, 13 may become two distinct silence runs of 15 and 13 samples, with non-silence in between.

Companding (short for "compressing/expanding") uses the fact that the ear requires more precise samples at low amplitudes (soft sounds), but is more forgiving at higher amplitudes. A typical ADC used in sound cards for personal computers converts voltages to numbers linearly. If an amplitude a is converted to the number n, then amplitude $2a$ will be converted to the number $2n$. A compression method using companding examines every sample in the sound file, and uses a non-linear formula to reduce the number of bits devoted to it. For 16-bit samples, e.g., a companding encoder may use a formula as simple as

$$32767 \left(2^{\frac{\text{sample}}{65536}} - 1 \right), \tag{5.2}$$

to reduce each sample. This formula maps the 16-bit samples non-linearly to 15-bit numbers (i.e., numbers in the range [0, 32767]) such that small samples are less affected than large ones. Table 5.35 illustrates the non-linearity of this mapping. It shows eight pairs of samples where the two samples in each pair differ by 100. The two samples of the first pair get mapped to numbers that differ by 34, whereas the two samples of the last pair are mapped to numbers that differ by 65. The mapped 15-bit numbers can be decoded back into the original 16-bit samples by the inverse formula

$$\text{Sample} = 65536 \log_2 \left(1 + \frac{\text{mapped}}{32767} \right). \tag{5.3}$$

Sample	To	Diff	Sample	To	Diff
100→	35		30000→	12236	
200→	69	34	30100→	12283	47
1000→	348		40000→	17256	
1100→	383	35	40100→	17309	53
10000→	3656		50000→	22837	
10100→	3694	38	50100→	22896	59
20000→	7719		60000→	29040	
20100→	7762	43	60100→	29105	65

Table 5.35: 16-Bit Samples Mapped to 15-Bit Numbers.

Reducing 16-bit numbers to 15-bits doesn't produce much compression. Better compression can be achieved by substituting a smaller number for 32,767 in equations (5.2) and (5.3). A value of 127, e.g., would map each 16-bit sample into an 8-bit one, producing a compression ratio of 0.5. However, decoding would be less accurate. A 16-bit sample of 60,100, e.g., would be mapped into the 8-bit number 113, but this number would produce 60,172 when decoded by equation (5.3). Even worse, the small 16-bit sample 1000 would be mapped into 1.35, which has to be rounded to 1. When equation (5.3) is used to decode a 1, it produces 742, significantly different from the original sample. The amount of compression should thus be a user-controlled parameter, and this is an interesting example of a compression method where the compression ratio is *known in advance*!

In practice there is no need to go through equations (5.2) and (5.3) since the mapping of all the samples can be prepared in advance in a table. Both encoding and decoding are thus fast.

Other, more sophisticated, sound compression methods exist, and as sound becomes more common in computer applications, more will no doubt be developed.

Thou hast damnable iteration, and art indeed able to corrupt a saint.
— William Shakespeare, *King Henry IV (Part I)*

A

The ASCII Code

Table A.1 shows the 128 ASCII codes. Each code is shown in octal (leftmost column and top row) and hexadecimal (rightmost column and either the top or bottom rows). Octal numbers are typeset in italics, preceded by a quote ('). Hex numbers are typeset in a fixed-width font, preceded by a double-quote ("). To find the code of a character, substitute the code from the top or bottom row for the x. The octal code of "A," e.g., is found by substituting the *'1* from the top row for the x in the *'10x* from the left column, i.e., it is octal 101 or binary 1000001. Similarly, the hex code of "A" is a combination of "4x and *'1*, i.e., it is "41.

▶ **Exercise A.1:** What is the hex code of "I"?

The first 32 codes (0–31) as well as the last one (DEL) are control characters. SP (code 32) stands for a blank space. The other codes are for the letters, digits, and punctuation marks.

A.1 ASCII Features

1. The first 32 codes, and also the last code, are the control characters. Those are characters used in input/output and computer communications, and have no corresponding graphics, i.e., they cannot be printed out. They are described in Table A.2.

2. The ASCII codes are arbitrary. The code of "A" is 41_{16} but there is no special reason for assigning that particular value, and almost any other value would have served as well. About the only rule for assigning codes is that the code of "B" should follow, numerically, the code of "A." Thus "B" has the code 42_{16}, "C" has 43_{16}, and so on. The same thing is true for the lower-case letters and for the ten digits.

There is also a simple relationship between the codes of the upper- and lower-case letters. The code of "a" is obtained from the code of "A" by setting the 7th bit to 1.

3. The parity bit in Table A.1 is always 0. The ASCII code does not specify the value of the parity bit and any value can be used. Different computers use the ASCII code with even parity, odd parity, no parity, or even a fixed parity of 1.

4. The code of the control character DEL is all ones (except the parity that is, as usual, unspecified). This is a tradition from the old days of computing (and also from telegraphy), when punched paper tape was an important medium for input/output. When punching information on a paper tape, whenever the user noticed an error, they would delete the bad character by pressing the DEL key on the keyboard. This worked by backspacing the tape and punching a frame of all 1's on top of the holes of the bad character. When reading the tape, the tape reader would simply skip any frame of all 1's.

	′0	′1	′2	′3	′4	′5	′6	′7	
′00x	NUL	SOH	STX	ETX	EOT	ENQ	ACK	BEL	″0x
′01x	BS	HT	LF	VT	FF	CR	SO	SI	
′02x	DLE	DC1	DC2	DC3	DC4	NAK	SYN	ETB	″1x
′03x	CAN	EM	SUB	ESC	FS	GS	RS	US	
′04x	SP	!	"	#	$	%	&	'	″2x
′05x	(	)	*	+	,	-	.	/	
′06x	0	1	2	3	4	5	6	7	″3x
′07x	8	9	:	;	<	=	>	?	
′10x	@	A	B	C	D	E	F	G	″4x
′11x	H	I	J	K	L	M	N	O	
′12x	P	Q	R	S	T	U	V	W	″5x
′13x	X	Y	Z	[	\	]	ˆ	_	
′14x	'	a	b	c	d	e	f	g	″6x
′15x	h	i	j	k	l	m	n	o	
′16x	p	q	r	s	t	u	v	w	″7x
′17x	x	y	z	{	|	}	~	DEL	
	″8	″9	″A	″B	″C	″D	″E	″F	

Table A.1: The ASCII Code.

NUL (Null): No character, Used for filling in space in an I/O device when there are no characters.

SOH (Start of heading): Indicates the start of a heading on an I/O device. The heading may include information pertaining to the entire record that follows it.

STX (Start of text): Indicates the start of the text block in serial I/O.

ETX (End of text): Indicates the end of a block in serial I/O. Matches a STX.

EOT (End of transmission): Indicates the end of the entire transmission in serial I/O.

ENQ (Enquiry): An enquiry signal typically sent from a computer to an I/O device before the start of an I/O transfer, to verify that the device is there and is ready to accept or to send data.

ACK (Acknowledge): An affirmative response to an ENQ.

BEL (Bell): Causes the I/O device to ring a bell or to sound a buzzer or an alarm in order to call the operator's attention.

BS (Backspace): A command to the I/O device to backspace one character. Not every I/O device can respond to BS. A keyboard is a simple example of an input device that cannot go back to the previous character. Once a new key is pressed, the keyboard loses the previous one.

HT (Horizontal tab): Sent to an output device to indicate a horizontal movement to the next tab stop.

LF (Line feed): An important control code. Indicates to the output device to move vertically, to the beginning of the next line.

VT (Vertical tab): Commands an output device to move vertically to the next vertical tab stop.

FF (Form feed): Commands the output device to move the output medium vertically to the start of the next page. some output devices, such as a tape or a plotter, do not have any pages and for them the FF character is meaningless.

CR (Carriage return): Commands an output device to move horizontally, to the start of the line.

SO (Shift out): Indicates that the character codes that follow (until an SI is sensed), are not in the standard character set.

SI (Shift in): Terminates a non-standard string of text.

DLE (Data link escape): Changes the meaning of the character immediately following it.

DC1–DC4 (Device controls): Special characters for sending commands to I/O devices. Their meaning is not predefined.

NAK (Negative acknowledge): A negative response to an enquiry.

SYN (Synchronous idle): Sent by a synchronous serial transmitter when there is no data to send.

ETB (End transmission block): Indicates the end of a block of data in serial transmission. Is used to divide the data into blocks.

CAN (Cancel): Tells the receiving device to cancel (disregard) the previously received block because of a transmission error.

EM (End of medium): Sent by an I/O device when it has sensed the end of its medium. The medium can be a tape, paper, card, or anything else used to record and store information.

SUB (Substitute): This character is substituted by the receiving device, under certain conditions, for a character that has been received incorrectly (had a bad parity bit).

ESC (Escape): Alters the meaning of the immediately following character. This is used to extend the character set. Thus ESC followed by an "X" may mean something special to a certain program.

FS (File separator):
GS (Group separator):
RS (Record separator):
US (Unit separator): The four separators on the left have no predefined meaning in ASCII, except that FS is the most general separator (separates large groups) and US, the least general.

SP (Space): This is the familiar blank or space between words. It is non-printing and is therefore considered a control character rather than a punctuation mark.

DEL (Delete): This is sent immediately after a bad character has been sent. DEL Indicates deleting the preceding character (see note 4 earlier).

Table A.2: The ASCII Control Characters.

ASCII stupid question, get a stupid ANSI.

Anonymous

B
Bibliography

B.1 General Works

Abut, Huseyin (ed.), *Vector Quantization*, IEEE Press, NY, 1990.

Barnsley, M. F., and Lyman P. Hurd, *Fractal Image Compression*, Wellesley, MA, AK Peters, 1993.

Bell, T. C., I. H. Witten, and J. G. Cleary, *Text Compression*, Englewood Cliffs, NJ, Prentice-Hall, 1990.

Bryan, Marvin, *Diskdoubler and Autodoubler: An Illustrated Tutorial*, New York, Windcrest/McGraw-Hill,1994.

Cappellini, V. (ed.), *Data Compression and Error Control Techniques with Applications*, New York, Academic Press, 1985.

Clarke, R. J., *Digital Compression of Still Images and Video*, New York, Academic Press, 1995.

Cushing, John Aikin and Yukio Rikiso, *Data Compression Algorithms for English Text Based on Word Frequency*, Kobe, Japan, Institute of Economic Research, Kobe University of Commerce, 1990.

Dasarathy, Belur V. (ed.), *Image Data Compression: Block Truncation Coding (BTC) Techniques*, Los Alamitos, CA, IEEE Computer Society Press, 1995.

Farrelle, Paul Michael, *Recursive Block Coding for Image Data Compression*, New York, Springer-Verlag, 1990.

Fisher, Yuval (ed.), *Fractal Image Compression: Theory and Application*, New York, Springer Verlag, 1995.

Gersho, Allen and Robert M. Gray, *Vector Quantization and Signal Compression*, Boston, Kluwer Academic Publishers, 1992.

Harris, Matthew, *The Disk Compression Book*, Que, Indianapolis, IN, 1993.

Held, Gilbert and Thomas R. Marshall, *Data and Image Compression: Tools and Techniques*, 4th Ed., New York, John Wiley, 1996.

Held, Gilbert, *Personal Computer File Compression: A Guide to Shareware, DOS, and Commercial Compression Programs*, New York, Van Nostrand, 1994.

Hubbard, Barbara Burke, *The World According to Wavelets*, Wellesley, MA, AK Peters, 1996.

Krichevskii, R. E., *Universal Compression and Retrieval*, Boston, Kluwer Academic Publishers, 1994.

Kou, Weidong, *Digital Image Compression: Algorithms and Standards*, Boston, Kluwer Academic Publishers, 1995.

Lynch, Thomas J., *Data Compression Techniques and Applications*, Belmont, CA, Lifetime Learning Publications,1985.

Nelson, Mark, and Jean-Loup Gailly, *The Data Compression Book*, 2nd Ed., New York, M&T Books, 1996.

Pennebaker, William B., and Joan L. Mitchell, *JPEG Still Image Data Compression Standard*, New York, Van Nostrand Reinhold, 1992.

Rabbani, Majid, and Paul W. Jones, *Digital Image Compression Techniques*, Bellingham, WA, Spie Optical Engineering Press, 1991.

Ramapriyan, H. K. (ed.), *Scientific Data Compression Workshop (1988: Snowbird, Utah) Proceedings of the Scientific Data Compression Workshop*, NASA conference publication 3025.

Ramstad, T. A. et al., *Subband Compression of Images: Principles and Examples*, New York, Elsevier, 1995.

Rao, K.R. and P. Yip, *Discrete Cosine Transform—Algorithms, Advantages, Applications*, London, Academic Press, 1990.

Sayood, Khalid.*Introduction to Data Compression*, San Francisco, Morgan Kaufmann, 1996.

Storer, James A., John H. Reif (eds.), *DCC '91: Data Compression Conference*, Los Alamitos, CA, IEEE Computer Society Press, 1991.

Storer, James A., and Martin Cohn (eds.), *DCC '92: Data Compression Conference*, Los Alamitos, CA, IEEE Computer Society Press, 1992.

Storer, James A., and Martin Cohn (eds.), *DCC '93: Data Compression Conference*, Los Alamitos, CA, IEEE Computer Society Press, 1993.

Storer, James A., and Martin Cohn (eds.), *DCC '94: Data Compression Conference*, Los Alamitos, CA, IEEE Computer Society Press, 1994.

Storer, James A., and Martin Cohn (eds.), *DCC '95: Data Compression Conference*, Los Alamitos, CA, IEEE Computer Society Press, 1995.

Storer, James A. (ed.), *DCC '96: Data Compression Conference*, Los Alamitos, CA, IEEE Computer Society Press, 1996.

Storer, James A., (ed.), *Image and Text Compression*, Boston, Kluwer Academic Publishers, 1992.

Storer, James A., *Data Compression: Methods and Theory*, Rockville, MD, Computer Science Press, 1988.

Tseng, Nai-yu, and W.D. Burnside, *A Very Efficient RCS Data Compression and Reconstruction Technique*, NASA contractor report; NASA CR-191378. 1992.

Vasudev, Bhaskaran, and Konstantinos Konstantinides, *Image and Video Compression Standards: Algorithms and Architectures*, Boston, Kluwer Academic Publishers.

Williams, Ross N., *Adaptive Data Compression*, Boston, Kluwer Academic Publishers, 1991.

Witten, Ian H., Alistair Moffat, and Timothy C. Bell, *Managing Gigabytes: Compressing and Indexing Documents and Images*, New York, Van Nostrand Reinhold, 1994.

B.2 References

Abelson, H. and A. A. diSessa (1982) *Turtle Geometry*, Cambridge, MA, MIT Press.

Anderson, K. L., et al., (1987) "Binary-Image-Manipulation Algorithm in the Image View Facility," *IBM J. of Research and Development* **31**(1):16–31, January.

Backus, J. W. (1959) "The Syntax and Semantics of the Proposed International Algebraic Language," in *Proceedings of the International Conference on Information processing*, pp. 125–132, UNESCO.

Barnsley, F., and Sloan, A. D. (1988) "A Better Way to Compress Images," *Byte Magazine* pp. 215–222 January.

Barnsley, M. (1988) *Fractals Everywhere*, New York, Academic Press.

Bell, T. C., I. H. Witten, and J. G. Cleary (1990) *Text Compression*, Prentice-Hall.

Bell, T. C. (1986) "Better OPM/L Text Compression," *IEEE Transactions on Communications* COM-34(12):1176–1182, December.

Bentley, J. L. et al. (1986) "A Locally Adaptive Data Compression Algorithm," *Communications of the ACM* **29**(4):320–330, April.

Blackstock, Steve (1987) "LZW and GIF Explained," available from URL "http://www.ece.uiuc.edu/~ece291/class-resources/gpe/gif.txt.html".

Blinn, J. F. (1993) "What's the Deal with the DCT," *IEEE Computer Graphics and Applications* pp. 78–83, July.

Bloom, C. R., (1996) "LZP: A New Data Compression Algorithm," in *Proceedings of Data Compression Conference*, J. Storer, editor, Los Alamitos, CA, IEEE Computer Society Press, p. 425.

Burrows, Michael, et al. (1992) *On-line Data Compression in a Log-Structured File System*, Digital, Systems Research Center, Palo Alto, CA.

Burrows, Michael and D. J. Wheeler (1994) *A Block-Sorting Lossless Data Compression Algorithm*, Digital, Systems Research Center report 124, Palo Alto, Calif, May 10.

Cappellini, V. (ed.) (1985) *Data Compression and Error Control Techniques with Applications*, New York, Academic Press.

Chomsky, N. (1956) "Three Models for the Description of Language," *IRE Transactions on Information Theory* $\mathbf{2}$(3):113–124.

Cleary, J. G. and I. H. Witten (1984) "Data Compression Using Adaptive Coding and Partial String Matching," *IEEE Transactions on Communications* COM-32(4):396–402, April.

Cole, A. J. (1985) "A Note on Peano Polygons and Gray Codes," *International Journal of Computer Mathemathics* $\mathbf{18}$:3–13.

Cole, A. J. (1986) "Direct Transformations Between Sets of Integers and Hilbert Polygons," *International Journal of Computer Mathemathics* $\mathbf{20}$:115–122.

Cormack G. V. and R. N. S. Horspool (1987) "Data Compression Using Dynamic Markov Modelling," *The Computer Journal* $\mathbf{30}$(6):541–550.

Culik, Karel II, and V. Valenta (1996), "Finite Automata Based Compression of Bi-Level Images," in Storer, James A. (ed.), *DCC '96, Data Compression Conference*, Los Alamitos, CA, IEEE Computer Society Press, pp. 280–289.

Cushing, John Aikin and Yukio Rikiso (1990) *Data Compression Algorithms for English Text Based on Word Frequency*, Institute of Economic Research, Kobe University of Commerce, Kobe, Japan.

Czech, Z. J., et al (1992) "An Optimal Algorithm for Generating Minimal Perfect Hash Functions," *Information Processing Letters* $\mathbf{43}$:257–264.

Dasarathy, Belur V. (ed.) (1995) *Image Data Compression: Block Truncation Coding (BTC) Techniques*, Los Alamitos, CA, IEEE Computer Society Press.

Demko, S., L. Hodges, and B. Naylor (1985) "Construction of Fractal Objects with Iterated Function Systems," *Computer Graphics* $\mathbf{19}$(3):271–278, July.

DeVore R. et al. (1992) "Image Compression Through Wavelet Transform Coding," *IEEE Transactions on Information Theory* $\mathbf{38}$(2):719–746, March.

Elias, P. (1975) "Universal Codeword Sets and Representations of the Integers," *IEEE Transactions on Information Theory* IT-21(2):194–203, March.

Fang I. (1966) "It Isn't ETAOIN SHRDLU; It's ETAONI RSHDLC," *Journalism Quarterly* **43**:761–762.

Feder, Jens (1988) *Fractals*, New York, Plenum Press.

Fenwick, P. (1996) *Symbol Ranking Text Compression*, Tech. Rep. 132, Dept. of Computer Science, University of Auckland, New Zealand, June.

Fiala, E. R., and D. H. Greene (1989), "Data Compression with Finite Windows," *Communications of the ACM* **32**(4):490–505.

Fisher, Yuval (ed.), (1995) *Fractal Image Compression: Theory and Application*, New York, Springer-Verlag.

Floyd, Sally, and Manfred Warmuth (1993) *Sample Compression, Learnability, and the Vapnik-Chervonenskis Dimension*, Tec. report UCSC-CRL-93-13. Univ. of California, Santa Cruz.

Fox, E. A. et al. (1991) "Order Preserving Minimal Perfect Hash Functions and Information Retrieval," *ACM Transactions on Information Systems* **9**(2):281–308.

Fraenkel, A. S., and S. T. Klein (1985) "Novel Compression of Sparse Bit-Strings—Preliminary Report," in A. Apostolico and Z. Galil, eds. *Combinatorial Algorithms on Words*, Vol. 12, NATO ASI Series F:169–183, New York, Springer-Verlag.

Gabor, G., and Z. Gyorfi (1986) *Recursive Source Coding: A Theory for the Practice of Waveform Coding*, New York, Springer-Verlag.

Gersho, Allen, and Robert M. Gray (1992) *Vector Quantization and Signal Compression*, Boston, MA, Kluwer Academic Publishers.

Gilliam, Laurence Bradley (1988) *Raster Cartographic Data Compression* (Dissertation).

Glover, Daniel, and S. C. Kwatra, *Compressing Subbanded Image Data with Lempel-Ziv-based Coders*, NASA technical memo 105998.

Glover, Daniel (19930 *Transform Coding for Space Applications*, NASA technical memorandum; 106362.

Golomb, S. W. (1966) "Run-Length Encodings," *IEEE Transactions on Information Theory* IT-12(3):399–401.

Gottlieb, D., et al (1975) *A Classification of Compression Methods and their Usefulness for a Large Data Processing Center*, Procedings of National Computer Conference **44**:453–458.

Gray, Robert T. (1983) *Multispectral Data Compression using Staggered Detector Arrays*, (Dissertation)

Gray, F. (1953) U. S. Patent 2632058, March.

Gulati, Amit (1993) *Tessellated Image Compression* (Dissertation).

Hamming, Richard (1950) "Error Detecting and Error Correcting Codes," *Bell Systems Technical Journal* **29**:147–160, April.

Hamming, Richard (1986) *Coding and Information Theory*, 2nd Ed., Englewood Cliffs, NJ, Prentice-Hall.

Harris, Matthew (1993) *The Disk Compression Book*, Indianapolis, IN, Que.

Hartz, William G. (1989) *Data Compression Techniques Applied to High-Resolution High Frame Rate Video Technology*, NASA contractor report; NASA CR-4263.

Hassner, Martin (1981) *A Nonprobabilistic Source and Channel Coding Theory* (Dissertation).

Havas, G. et al. (1993) *Graphs, Hypergraphs and Hashing* in Proceedings of the International Workshop on Graph-Theoretic Concepts in Computer Science (WG'93), Berlin, Springer-Verlag.

Held, Gilbert, and Thomas R. Marshall (1991) *Data Compression: Techniques and Applications: Hardware and Software Considerations*, 3rd Ed., New York, John Wiley.

Held, Gilbert, and Thomas R. Marshall (1996) *Data and Image Compression: Tools and Techniques*, 4th Ed., New York, John Wiley.

Held, Gilbert (1994) *Personal Computer File Compression: A Guide to Shareware, DOS, and Commercial Compression Programs*, New York, Van Nostrand.

Hilbert, D. (1891) "Ueber Stetige Abbildung Einer Linie auf ein Flachenstuck," *Math. Annalen* **38**:459–460.

Hirschberg, D., and D. Lelewer (1990) "Efficient Decoding of Prefix Codes," *Communications of the ACM* **33**(4):449–459.

Horspool, N. R. (1991) "Improving LZW," in *Proceedings of the 1991 Data Compression Conference*, J. Storer Ed., Los Alamitos, CA, IEEE Computer Society Press, pp .332–341.

Horspool, N. R. and G. V. Cormack (1992) "Constructing Word-Based Text Compression Algorithms," in *Proceedings of the 1992 Data Compression Conference*, J. Storer Ed., Los Alamitos, CA, IEEE Computer Society Press, pp. 62–71, April.

Howard, Paul G., and J. S. Vitter (1992a), "New Methods for Lossless Image Compression Using Arithmetic Coding," *Information Processing and Management*, **28**(6):765–779.

Howard, Paul G., and J. S. Vitter (1992b), "Error Modeling for Hierarchical Lossless Image Compression," in *Proceedings of the 1992 Data Compression Conference*, J. Storer ed., Los Alamitos, CA, IEEE Computer Society Press, pp. 269–278.

Howard, P. G. and J. S. Vitter, (1993) "Fast and Efficient Lossless Image Compression," In *Proceedings of the 1993 Data Compression Conference*, J. Storer Ed., Los Alamitos, CA, IEEE Computer Society Press, pp. 351–360.

Huffman, David (1952) "A Method for the Construction of Minimum Redundancy Codes," *Proceedings of the IRE* **40**(9):1098–1101.

Hunter, R., and A. H. Robinson (1980) "International Digital Facsimile Coding Standards," *Proceedings of the IEEE* **68**(7):854–867, July.

Huntley, H. E. (1970) *The Divine Proportion: A Study in Mathematical Beauty*, New York, Dover Publications.

Kespret, Irene (1993) *PKZIP, LHarc and Co.: The Ultimate Data Compression Book*, Grand Rapids, MI, Abacus.

Kespret, Istok (1996) *ZIP Bible*, Grand Rapids, MI, Abacus.

Kespret, Istok (1994) *PKZIP, LHARC and Co.: The Ultimate Data Compression Book*, Grand Rapids, MI, Abacus.

Knuth, D. E. (1973) *The Art of Computer Programming*, Vol. 1, 2nd Ed., Reading, MA, Addison-Wesley.

Knuth, D. E. (1985) "Dynamic Huffman Coding," *Journal of Algorithms* **6**:163–180.

Kossentini, Faouzi et al., *Necessary Conditions for the Optimality of Variable Rate Residual Vector Quantizers*, NASA contractor report; NASA CR-193730.

Krichevskii, R. E. (1994) *Universal Compression and Retrieval*, Kluwer Academic.

Langdon, G., and J. Rissanen (1981) "Compression of Black White Images with Arithmetic Coding," *IEEE Transactions on Communications* COM-29(6):858–867, June.

Langdon, Glen G. (1983) "A Note on the Ziv-Lempel Model for Compressing Individual Sequences," *IEEE Transactions on Information Theory* IT-29(2):284–287, March.

Langdon, Glen G. (1984) *On Parsing vs. Mixed-Order Model Structures for Data Compression*, IBM research report RJ-4163 (46091), Jan 18, 1984, San Jose.

Lin, Shu (1970) *An Introduction to Error Correcting Codes*, Englewood Cliffs, NJ, Prentice-Hall.

Lindenmayer, A. (1968) "Mathematical Models for Cellular Interaction in Development," *Journal of Theoretical Biology* **18**:280–315.

Lowe, Doug (1994) *Microsoft Press Guide to DOUBLESPACE: Understanding Data Compression with MS-DOS 6.0 and 6.2*, Redmond, WA, Microsoft Press.

Lynch, Thomas J. (1985) *Data Compression Techniques and Applications*, Belmont, CA, Lifetime Learning Publications.

Manber, U., and E. W. Myers (1993) "Suffix Arrays: A New Method for On-Line String Searches," *SIAM Journal on Computing* **22**(5):935–948, October.

Mandelbrot, Benoit (1982) *The Fractal Geometry of Nature*, San Francisco, CA, W. H. Freeman.

Marking, Michael P. (1990) "Decoding Group 3 Images," *The C Users Journal* pp. 45–54, June.

McConnell, Kenneth R. (1992) *FAX: Digital Facsimile Technology and Applications*, Norwood, MA, Artech House.

McCreight, E. M (1976) "A Space Economical Suffix Tree Construction Algorithm," *Journal of the ACM* **32**(2):262–272, April.

Miller, V. S., and M. N. Wegman (1985) "Variations On a Theme by Ziv and Lempel," in A. Apostolico and Z. Galil, eds., NATO ASI series Vol. F12, *Combinatorial Algorithms on Words*, Springer, Berlin, pp. 131–140.

Moffat, A. (1990) "Implementing the PPM Data Compression Scheme," *IEEE Transactions on Communications* COM-38(11):1917–1921, November.

Moffat, A. (1991) "Two-Level Context Based Compression of Binary Images," in *Proceedings of the 1991 Data Compression Conference*, J. Storer Ed., Los Alamitos, CA, IEEE Computer Society Press, pp. 382–391.

Murray, James D. (1994) and William vanRyper, *Encyclopedia of Graphics File Formats*, Sebastopol, CA, O'Reilly and Assoc.

Naur, P. et al. (1960) "Report on the Algorithmic Language ALGOL 60," *Communications of the ACM* **3**(5):299–314, revised in *Communications of the ACM* **6**(1):1–17.

Nelson, Mark and Jean-Loup Gailly (1996) *The Data Compression Book*, 2nd Ed., New York, M&T Books.

Nesenbergs, M., *Image Data Compression Overview: Issues and Partial Solutions*, NTIA report; 89-252.

Nix, R. (1981) "Experience With a Space Efficient Way to Store a Dictionary," *Communications of the ACM* **24**(5):297–298.

Nussbaum, Howard Steven (1977) *Source Coding and Adaptive Data Compression for Communication Networks* (Dissertation).

Paola, Justin D., and Robert A. Schowengerdt (1995) *The Effect of Lossy Image Compression on Image Classification*, NASA contractor report; NASA CR-199550.

Paola, Justin D., and Robert A. Schowengerdt (1995) *Searching for Patterns in Remote Sensing Image Databases Using Neural Networks*, NASA contractor report; NASA CR-199549.

Peano, G. (1890) "Sur Une Courbe Qui Remplit Toute Une Aire Plaine," *Math. Annalen* **36**:157–160.

Peitgen, H. -O., et al. (eds.) (1982) *The Beauty of Fractals*, Berlin, Springer-Verlag.

Peitgen, H. -O., and Dietmar Saupe (1985) *The Science of Fractal Images*, Berlin, Springer-Verlag.

Pennebaker, W. B., and J. L. Mitchell (1988) "Probability Estimation for the Q-coder," *IBM Journal of Research and Development* **32**(6):717–726.

Pennebaker, W. B., J. L. Mitchell, et al. (1988) "An Overview of the Basic Principles of the Q-coder Adaptive Binary Arithmetic Coder," *IBM Journal of Research and Development* **32**(6):737–752.

Pennebaker, William B., and Joan L. Mitchell (1992) *JPEG Still Image Data Compression Standard*, Van Nostrand Reinhold.

Phillips, Dwayne (1992) "LZW Data Compression," *The Computer Application Journal* Circuit Cellar Inc., **27**:36–48, June/July.

Press, W. H., B. P. Flannery, et al. (1988) *Numerical Recipes in C: The Art of Scientific Computing*, Cambridge University Press. (Also available on-line from `http://nr.harvard.edu/nr/bookc.html`.)

Prusinkiewicz, Przemyslav (1986) *Graphical Applications oi L-systems*, in Proc. of Graphics Interface '86 — Vision Interface '86, pp .247–253.

Prusinkiewicz, P., and A. Lindenmayer (1990) *The Algorithmic Beauty of Plants*, New York, Springer Verlag.

Prusinkiewicz, P., A. Lindenmayer, and F. D. Fracchia (1991) "Synthesis of Space-Filling Curves on the Square Grid," in *Fractals in the Fundamental and Applied Sciences*, edited by Peitgen, H.-O. et al., Amsterdam, Elsevier Science Publishers, pp. 341–366.

Rabbani, Majid, and Paul W. Jones (1991) *Digital Image Compression Techniques*, Bellingham, WA, Spie Optical Engineering Press.

Ramabadran, Tenkasi V., and Sunil S. Gaitonde (1988) "A Tutorial on CRC Computations," *IEEE Micro* pp. 62–75, August.

Ramapriyan, H. K. (ed.) (1988) *Scientific Data Compression Workshop (1988: Snowbird, Utah) Proceedings of the Scientific Data Compression Workshop*, NASA conference publication 3025.

Ramstad, T. A. et al (1995) *Subband Compression of Images: Principles and Examples*, Amsterdam, Elsevier Science Publishers.

Rao, K. R., and P. Yip (1990) *Discrete Cosine Transform—Algorithms, Advantages, Applications*, London, Academic Press.

Reghbati, H. K. (1981) "An Overview of Data Compression Techniques," *IEEE Computer* **14**(4):71–76.

Rice, Robert F. et al., *Algorithms for a Very High Speed Universal Noiseless Coding Module*, NASA contractor report; NASA CR-187974.

Robinson, P., and D. Singer (1981) "Another Spelling Correction Program," *Communications of the ACM* **24**(5):296–297.

Rost, Martin C. (1988) *Data Compression Using Adaptive Transform Coding*, NASA contractor report; NASA CR-189956.

Sacco, William et al. (1988) *Information Theory, Saving Bits*, Janson Publications, Providence, R.I.

Sagan, Hans (1994) *Space-Filling Curves*, New York, Springer Verlag.

Sauer, Ken et al. (1992) *Sub-band/Transform Compression of Video Sequences: Final Report*, NASA contractor report; NASA CR-189786.

Sayood, K., and K. Robinson (1992) "A Differential Lossless Image Compression Scheme," *IEEE Transactions on Signal Processing* **40**(1):236–241, January.

Sayood, Khalid (1996) *Introduction to Data Compression*, San Francisco, CA, Morgan Kaufmann.

Shannon, C. (1951) "Prediction and Entropy of Printed English," *Bell System Technical Journal* **30**(1):50–64, January.

Sieminski, A. (1988) "Fast Decoding of the Huffman Codes," *Information Processing Letters* **26**(5):237–241.

Sierpinski, W. (1912) "Sur Une Nouvelle Courbe Qui Remplit Toute Une Aire Plaine," *Bull. Acad. Sci. Cracovie* Serie A:462–478.

Smith, Alvy Ray (1984) "Plants, Fractals and Formal Languages," *Computer Graphics* **18**(3):1–10.

Stollnitz, E. J., T. D. DeRose, and D. H. Salesin (1996) *Wavelets for Computer Graphics*, San Francisco, CA, Morgan Kaufmann.

Storer, J. A. and T. G. Szymanski (1982) "Data Compression via Textual Substitution," *Journal of the ACM* **29**:928–951.

Storer, James A. (1988) *Data Compression: Methods and Theory*, Rockville, MD, Computer Science Press.

Storer, James A., (ed.) (1992) *Image and Text Compression*, Boston, MA, Kluwer Academic Publishers.

Storer, James A., and John H. Reif (eds.) (1991) *DCC '91: Data Compression Conference*, Los Alamitos, CA, IEEE Computer Society Press.

Storer, James A., and Martin Cohn (eds.) (1992) *DCC '92: Data Compression Conference*, Los Alamitos, CA, IEEE Computer Society Press.

Storer, James A., and Martin Cohn (eds.) (1993) *DCC '93: Data Compression Conference*, Los Alamitos, CA, IEEE Computer Society Press.

Storer, James A., and Martin Cohn (eds.) (1994) *DCC '94: Data Compression Conference*, Los Alamitos, CA, IEEE Computer Society Press.

Storer, James A., and Martin Cohn (eds.) (1995) *DCC '95: Data Compression Conference*, Los Alamitos, CA, IEEE Computer Society Press.

Storer, James A., (ed.) (1996) *DCC '96: Data Compression Conference*, Los Alamitos, CA, IEEE Computer Society Press.

Sutardja, Budi (1991) *LZWBSWRT—A Technique for High Performance Universal Delta Data Compression* (Dissertation).

Szilard, A. L. and R. E. Quinton (1979) "An Interpretation for D0L Systems by Computer Graphics," *The Science Terrapin* 4:8–13.

Tabatabai, Y. M. A., (1981) *Edge Location and Data Compression for Digital Imagery* (Dissertation).

Thomborson, Clark, (1992) "The V.42bis Standard for Data-Compressing Modems," *IEEE Micro* pp. 41–53, October.

Tilton, James C., (ed.) (1991) *Space and Earth Science Data Compression Workshop (1991: Snowbird, Utah)*, NASA conference publication 3130.

Tilton, James C., (ed.) (1992) *Space and Earth Science Data Compression Workshop (1992: Snowbird, Utah)*, NASA conference publication 3183.

Tilton, James C., (ed.) (1994) *Space and Earth Science Data Compression Workshop (4th: 1994: Salt Lake City, Utah)*, NASA conference publication 3255.

Tseng, Nai-yu and W. D. Burnside (1992) *A Very Efficient RCS Data Compression and Reconstruction Technique*, NASA contractor report; NASA CR-191378.

Vasudev, Bhaskaran, and Konstantinos Konstantinides, *Image and Video Compression Standards : Algorithms and Architectures*, Boston, MA, Kluwer Academic Publishers.

Vitter, Jeffrey S. (1987) "Design and Analysis of Dynamic Huffman Codes," *Journal of the ACM* **34**(4):825-845, October.

Wallace, Gregory K. (1991) "The JPEG Still Image Compression Standard," *Communications of the ACM* **34**(4):30–44, April.

Welch, T. A. (1984) "A Technique for High-Performance Data Compression," *IEEE Computer* **17**(6):8–19, June.

Williams, Ross N. (1991) *Adaptive Data Compression*, Boston, MA, Kluwer Academic Publishers.

Williams, Ross (1991),"An Extremely Fast Ziv-Lempel Data Compression Algorithm," in *Proceedings of the 1991 Data Compression Conference*, J. Storer ed., Los Alamitos, CA, IEEE Computer Society Press, pp. 362–371.

Wirth, N. (1976) *Algorithms + Data Structures = Programs*, Englewood Cliffs, NJ, Prentice-Hall, 2nd Ed.

Witten, I. H., T. C. Bell, M. E. Harrison, M. L. James, and A. Moffat (1992) "Textual Image Compression," in *Proceedings of the 1992 Data Compression Conference*, J. Storer ed., Los Alamitos, CA, IEEE Computer Society Press, pp. 42–51.

Witten, I. H., et al. (1994) *Managing Gigabytes: Compressing and Indexing Documents and Images*, New York, Van Nostrand Reinhold.

Wright, E. V. (1939) *Gadsby*, Los Angeles, Wetzel. Reprinted by University Microfilms, Ann Arbor, 1991.

Wu, Xiaolin (1995), "Context Selection and Quantization for Lossless Image Coding," in Storer, James A., and Martin Cohn (eds.), *DCC '95, Data Compression Conference*, Los Alamitos, CA, IEEE Computer Society Press, p. 453.

Wu, Xiaolin (1996), "An Algorithmic Study on Lossless Image Compression," in Storer, James A. (ed.), *DCC '96, Data Compression Conference*, Los Alamitos, CA, IEEE Computer Society Press.

Yokko, Hidetoshi (1991) "An Improvement of Dynamic Huffman Coding with a Simple Repetition Finder," *IEEE Transactions on Communications* **39**(1):8–10, January.

Young, D. M. (1985) "MacWrite File Format," *Wheels for the Mind* **1**:34, Fall.

Yu, Tong Lai. (1996) "Dynamic Markov Compression," *Dr Dobb's Journal* pp. 30–31, January.

Zandi, Ahmad (1992) *Adaptation to Nonstationary Binary Sources for Data Compression* (Dissertation).

Zhang, Manyun (1990) *The JPEG and Image Data Compression Algorithms* (Dissertation).

Ziv, Jacob and A. Lempel (1977) "A Universal Algorithm for Sequential Data Compression," *IEEE Transactions on Information Theory* IT-23(3):337–343.

Ziv, Jacob and A. Lempel (1978) "Compression of Individual Sequences via Variable-Rate Coding," *IEEE Transactions on Information Theory* IT-24(5):530–536.

> Bibliography still helps us with a further glimpse of our characters. I have here before me a small volume (printed for private circulation: no printer's name; n.d.), 'Poesies par Frederic et Amelie.' Mine is a presentation copy, obtained for me by Mr. Bain in the Haymarket; and the name of the first owner is written on the fly leaf in the hand of Prince Otto himself.
>
> — Robert Louis Stevenson, *Prince Otto*

C
Curves That Fill Space

A space-filling curve completely fills up part of space by passing through every point in that part. It does that by changing direction repeatedly. We will only discuss curves that fill up part of the two-dimensional plane, but the concept of a space-filling curve exists for any number of dimensions.

Several such curves are known and all are defined recursively. A typical definition starts with a simple curve C_0 shows how to use it to construct another, more complex curve C_1, and defines the final, space-filling curve as the limit of the sequence of curves $C_0, C_1, \ldots$.

C.1 The Hilbert Curve

(This discussion is based on the approach of [Wirth 76].) Perhaps the most familiar of these curves is the Hilbert curve, discovered by the great mathematician David Hilbert in 1891. The Hilbert curve [Hilbert 91] is the limit of a sequence $H_0, H_1, H_2 \ldots$ of curves, some of which are shown in Figure C.1. They are defined by the following:

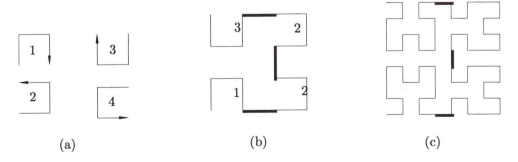

(a) (b) (c)

Figure C.1: Hilbert Curves of Orders 1, 2, and 3.

0. H_0 is a single point.

1. H_1 consists of four copies of (the point) H_0, connected with three straight segments of length h at right angles to each other. Four orientations of this curve, labeled 1, 2, 3, and 4, are shown in Figure C.1a.

2. The next curve, H_2, in the sequence is constructed by connecting four copies of different orientations of H_1 with three straight segments of length $h/2$ (shown in bold in Figure C.1b). Again there are four possible orientations of H_2, and the one shown is #2. It is constructed of orientations 1223 of H_1, connected by segments that go to the right, up, and to the left. The construction of the four orientations of H_2 is summarized in Table C.2.

Drawing this curve is thus done recursively. A procedure to draw orientation #4 of H_i is shown in Figure C.3. It makes four recursive calls to draw the four curves of order $i - 1$, and draws straight segments between the calls, to connect them (the names A, B, C, and D are used instead of 1, 2, 3, and 4).

Figure C.4 is a complete Pascal program for H_n, compiled by the Metrowerks™ Macintosh Pascal compiler. Notice how the main program determines the initial values of the starting point (x, y) of the curve, and the segment size h. Variable $h0$ defines the size, in pixels, of the square containing the curve, and should be a power of 2.

Figures C.5, C.6 and C.7 show the Hilbert curves of orders 4, 5 and 6. It is easy to see how fast these curves become extremely complex.

C.2 The Sierpinski Curve

Another well-known space-filling curve is the Sierpinski curve. Figure C.8 shows curves S_1 and S_2, and Sierpinski has proved [Sierpinski 12] that the limit of the sequence $S_1, S_2, \ldots$ is a curve that passes through every point of the unit square $[0, 1] \times [0, 1]$.

To construct this curve, we need to figure out how S_2 is constructed out of four copies of S_1. The first thing that comes to mind is to follow the construction method used for the Hilbert curve, i.e., to take four copies of S_1, eliminate one edge in each, and connect them. This, unfortunately, does not work, since the Sierpinski curve is very different from the Hilbert curve. It is closed, and it has one orientation only. A better approach is to start with four parts that constitute four orientations of one open curve, and connect them with straight segments. The segments are the ones shown in bold in Figure C.8. Notice how Figure C.8a is constructed of four orientations of a basic, three-part curve connected by four short, bold segments. Figure C.8b is similarly constructed of four orientations of a complex, 15-part curve, connected by the same short, bold segments. If we denote the four basic curves A, B, C, and D, then the basic construction rule of the Sierpinski curve is S: A$\searrow$B$\swarrow$C$\searrow$D$\nearrow$, and the recursion rules are:

$$
\begin{array}{ll}
\text{A:} & \text{A}\searrow\text{B}\rightarrow\rightarrow\text{D}\nearrow\text{A} \\
\text{B:} & \text{B}\swarrow\text{C}\downarrow\downarrow\text{A}\searrow\text{B} \\
\text{C:} & \text{C}\searrow\text{D}\leftarrow\leftarrow\text{B}\swarrow\text{C} \\
\text{D:} & \text{D}\nearrow\text{A}\uparrow\uparrow\text{C}\searrow\text{D}
\end{array} \qquad (C.1)
$$

$$1: 2 \uparrow \quad 1 \rightarrow 1 \downarrow \quad 4$$
$$2: 1 \rightarrow 2 \uparrow \quad 2 \leftarrow 3$$
$$3: 4 \downarrow \quad 3 \leftarrow 3 \uparrow \quad 2$$
$$4: 3 \leftarrow 4 \downarrow \quad 4 \rightarrow 1$$

Table C.2: The Four Orientations of H_2.

```
PROCEDURE D(i: INTEGER);
BEGIN
IF i>0 THEN BEGIN
  A(i-1); x:=x-h; MoveTo(x,y);
  D(i-1); y:=y-h; MoveTo(x,y);
  D(i-1); x:=x+h; MoveTo(x,y);
  C(i-1);
  END;
END (*A*);
```

Figure C.3: A Recursive Procedure.

```
PROGRAM Hilbert; (* A Hilbert curve *)
USES ScreenIO, Graphics;

CONST LB = 5; Width = 630; Height = 430;
(* LB=left bottom corner of window *)
n=6; (* n is the order of the curve*)
h0=8; (* h0 should be a power of 2 *)

VAR h,x,y,x0,y0: INTEGER;

PROCEDURE B (i: INTEGER); FORWARD;
PROCEDURE C (i: INTEGER); FORWARD;
PROCEDURE D (i: INTEGER); FORWARD;

PROCEDURE A(i: INTEGER);
BEGIN
IF i>0 THEN BEGIN
  D(i-1); x:=x-h; MoveTo(x,y);
  A(i-1); y:=y-h; MoveTo(x,y);
  A(i-1); x:=x+h; MoveTo(x,y);
  B(i-1);
  END;
END (*A*);

PROCEDURE B(i: INTEGER);
BEGIN
IF i>0 THEN BEGIN
  C(i-1); y:=y+h; MoveTo(x,y);
  B(i-1); x:=x+h; MoveTo(x,y);
  B(i-1); y:=y-h; MoveTo(x,y);
  A(i-1);
  END;
END (*B*);
```

```
PROCEDURE C(i: INTEGER);
BEGIN
IF i>0 THEN BEGIN
  B(i-1); x:=x+h; MoveTo(x,y);
  C(i-1); y:=y+h; MoveTo(x,y);
  C(i-1); x:=x-h; MoveTo(x,y);
  D(i-1);
  END;
END (*C*);

PROCEDURE D(i: INTEGER);
BEGIN
IF i>0 THEN BEGIN
  A(i-1); y:=y-h; MoveTo(x,y);
  D(i-1); x:=x-h; MoveTo(x,y);
  D(i-1); y:=y+h; MoveTo(x,y);
  C(i-1);
  END;
END (*D*);

BEGIN (* Main *)
  OpenGraphicWindow
    (LB,LB,Width,Height,'Hilbert curve');
  SetMode(paint);
  h:=h0; x0:=h DIV 2; y0:=x0; h:=h DIV 2;
  x0:=x0+(h DIV 2); y0:=y0+(h DIV 2);
  x:=x0+400; y:=y0+350; SetPen(x,y);
  A(n);

  ScBOL;
  ScWriteStr
    ('Hit a key & close window to quit');
  ScFreeze;
END.
```

Figure C.4: Pascal Program for a Hilbert Curve of Order i.

Figure C.5: Hilbert Curve of Order 4.

Figure C.6: Hilbert Curve of Order 5.

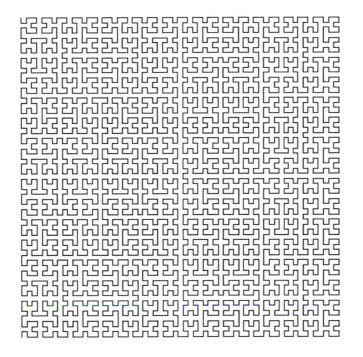

Figure C.7: Hilbert Curve of Order 6.

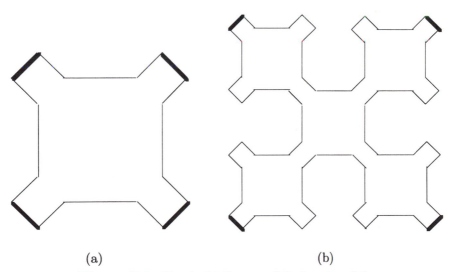

(a)   (b)

Figure C.8: Sierpinski Curves of Orders 1 and 2.

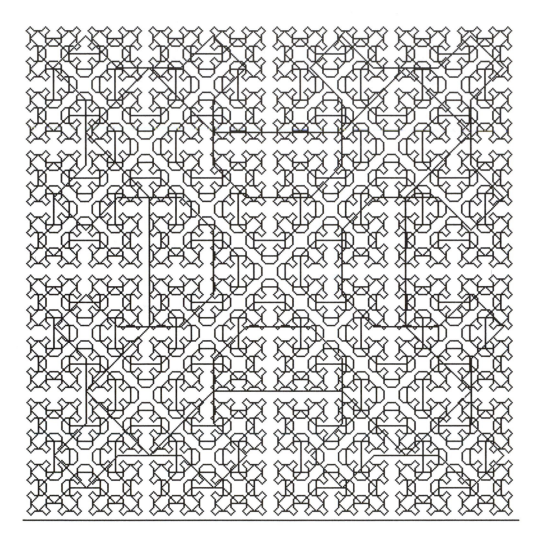

Figure C.9: Sierpinski Curves of Orders 1–5.

Figure C.9 shows the five Sierpinski curves of orders 1 through 5 superimposed on each other. They were drawn by the Pascal program of Figure C.10.

▶ **Exercise C.1:** Figure C.17 shows three iterations of the Peano space-filling curve, discovered in 1890. Use the techniques developed earlier for the Hilbert and Sierpinski curves, to describe how the Peano curve is constructed. (Hint: The curves shown are P_1, P_2, and P_3. The first curve, P_0 in this sequence is not shown.)

```
program Sierpinski;

USES ScreenIO, QuickDraw;

PROCEDURE SierpinskiP(size,number:word);
(* Adapted from Wirth, 2nd ed, p.115 *)

VAR
H, x, y:   INTEGER;

PROCEDURE B (level: word); FORWARD;
PROCEDURE C (level: word); FORWARD;
PROCEDURE D (level: word); FORWARD;

PROCEDURE A (level: word);
BEGIN
IF level > 0 THEN
BEGIN
A(level-1); Line(H,-H);
IF ScTellInput()>0 THEN BEGIN END;
B(level-1); Line(2*H,0);
IF ScTellInput()>0 THEN BEGIN END;
D(level-1); Line(H,H);
IF ScTellInput()>0 THEN BEGIN END;
A(level-1)
END
END {A};

PROCEDURE B (level: word);
BEGIN
IF level > 0 THEN
BEGIN
B(level-1); Line(-H,-H);
IF ScTellInput()>0 THEN BEGIN END;
C(level-1); Line(0,-2*H);
IF ScTellInput()>0 THEN BEGIN END;
A(level-1); Line(H,-H);
IF ScTellInput()>0 THEN BEGIN END;
B(level-1)
END
END {B};

PROCEDURE C (level: word);
BEGIN
IF level > 0 THEN
BEGIN
C(level-1); Line(-H,H);
IF ScTellInput()>0 THEN BEGIN END;
D(level-1); Line(-2*H,0);
IF ScTellInput()>0 THEN BEGIN END;
B(level-1); Line(-H,-H);
IF ScTellInput()>0 THEN BEGIN END;
C(level-1)
END
END {C};
```

```
PROCEDURE D (level: word);
BEGIN
IF level > 0 THEN
BEGIN
D(level-1); Line(H,H);
IF ScTellInput()>0 THEN BEGIN END;
A(level-1); Line(0,2*H);
IF ScTellInput()>0 THEN BEGIN END;
C(level-1); Line(-H,H);
IF ScTellInput()>0 THEN BEGIN END;
D(level-1)
END
END {D};

VAR
level: WORD;
BEXIT : BOOLEAN;

BEGIN (* SierpinskiP *)

level := 0;
H := size DIV 4;
x := 2 * H;
y := 3 * H;
    BEXIT := FALSE;
REPEAT
level := level + 1;; x := x - H;;
H := H DIV 2; y := y + H;;
MoveTo (x, y);
A (level); Line (H, -H);
IF ScTellInput()>0 THEN BEXIT:=TRUE;
B (level); Line (-H, -H);
IF ScTellInput()>0 THEN BEXIT:=TRUE;
C (level); Line (-H, H);
IF ScTellInput()>0 THEN BEXIT:=TRUE;
D (level); Line (H, H);
IF ScTellInput()>0 THEN BEXIT:=TRUE;
IF level = number THEN BEXIT:=TRUE;
 UNTIL BEXIT;
END {SierpinskiP};

VAR
ch: CHAR;
prop: termProp;

BEGIN
ScOpenWindow( 10, 10, 400, 400 );
ScGetProp (prop);
prop. showCurs := FALSE;
ScSetProp(prop); (*Hide alpha cursor*)
ScClear;
SierpinskiP(400,1);ScBeep (1);ScFreeze;
SierpinskiP(400,2);ScBeep (1);ScFreeze;
SierpinskiP(400,3);ScBeep (1);ScFreeze;
SierpinskiP(400,4);ScBeep (1);ScFreeze;
SierpinskiP(400,5);ScBeep (1);ScFreeze;
ScClose;
END {Sierpinski}.
```

Figure C.10: A Pascal Program for Sierpinski Curves of Orders 1–5.

C.3 Traversing the Hilbert Curve

Space-filling curves are used in image compression (Section 4.13), which is why it is important to develop methods for a fast traversal of such a curve. Two approaches, both table-driven, are illustrated here for traversing the Hilbert curve.

The first approach [Cole 86] is based on the observation that the Hilbert curve H_i is constructed of four copies of its predecessor H_{i-1} placed at different orientations. A look at Figures C.1, C.5, C.6, and C.7 should convince the reader that H_i consists of 2^{2i} nodes connected with straight segments. The node numbers thus go from 0 to $2^{2i} - 1$ and require $2i$ bits each. The (x, y) coordinates of a node in H_i are i-bit numbers.

A look at Figure C.5 shows how successive nodes are initially located at the bottom left quadrant, and then move to the bottom right quadrant, the top right quadrant, and finally the top left one. This figure shows orientation #2 of the curve, so we can say that this orientation of H_i traverses quadrants 0, 1, 2, and 3, where quadrants are numbered $\left(\begin{smallmatrix} 3 & 2 \\ 0 & 1 \end{smallmatrix}\right)$. It is now clear that the two leftmost bits of a node number determine its quadrant. Similarly, the next pair of bits in the node number determine its subquadrant within the quadrant, but here we run into the added complication that each subquadrant is placed at a different orientation in its quadrant. This approach thus uses Tables C.11 to determine the coordinates of a node from its number.

Bit pair	x	y	Next table	Bit pair	x	y	Next table	Bit pair	x	y	Next table	Bit pair	x	y	Next table
00	0	0	2	00	0	0	1	00	1	1	4	00	1	1	3
01	1	0	1	01	0	1	2	01	0	1	3	01	1	0	4
10	1	1	1	10	1	1	2	10	0	0	3	10	0	0	4
11	0	1	4	11	1	0	3	11	1	0	2	11	0	1	1
	(1)				(2)				(3)				(4)		

Table C.11: Coordinates of nodes in H_i.

As an example, we compute the xy coordinates of node 109 (the 110th node) of orientation #2 of H_4. The H_4 curve has $2^{2 \cdot 4} = 256$ nodes, so node numbers are 8 bits each, and $109 = 01101101_2$. We start with Table C.11(1). The 2 leftmost bits of the node number are 01, and table (1) tells us that the x coordinate start with 1, the y coordinate, with 0, and we should continue with table (1). The next pair of bits is 10, and table (1) tells us that the next bit of x is 1, the next bit of y is 1, and we should stay with table (1). The third pair of bits is 11, so table (1) tells us that the next bit of x is 0, the next bit of y is 1, and we should move to table (4). The last pair of bits is 01, and table (4) tells us to append 1 and 0 to the coordinates of x and y, respectively. The coordinates are thus $x = 1101 = 13$, $y = 0110 = 6$, as can be verified directly from Figure C.5 (the small circle).

It is also possible to transform a pair of coordinates (x, y), each in the range $[0, 2^i - 1]$, to a node number in H_i by means of Table C.12.

xy pair	Int. pair	Next table		xy pair	Int. pair	Next table		xy pair	Int. pair	Next table		xy pair	Int. pair	Next table
00	00	2		00	00	1		00	10	3		00	10	4
01	11	4		01	01	2		01	01	3		01	11	1
10	01	1		10	11	3		10	11	2		10	01	4
11	10	1		11	10	2		11	00	4		11	00	3
	(1)				(2)				(3)				(4)	

Table C.12: Node Numbers in H_i.

▸ **Exercise C.2:** Use Table C.12 to compute the node number of the H_4 node whose coordinates are $(13, 6)$.

The second approach to Hilbert curve traversal uses Table C.2. Orientation #2 of the H_2 curve shown in Figure C.1(b) is traversed in order 1223. The same orientation of the H_3 curve of Figure C.1(c) is traversed in 2114 1223 1223 4332 but Table C.2 tells us that 2114 is the traversal order for orientation #1 of H_2, 1223 is the traversal for orientation #2 of H_2, and 4332 is for orientation #3. The traversal of orientation #2 of H_3 is thus also based on the sequence 1223. Similarly orientation #2 of H_4 is traversed (Figure C.5) in the order

$$1223\ 2114\ 2114\ 3441\ \ 2114\ 1223\ 1223\ 4332$$
$$2114\ 1223\ 1223\ 4332\ \ 3441\ 4332\ 4332\ 1223,$$

which is reduced to 2114 1223 1223 4332, which in turn is reduced to the same sequence 1223.

The idea is therefore to create the traversal order for orientation #2 of H_i by starting with the sequence 1223 and recursively expanding it $i - 1$ times, using Table C.2.

▸ **Exercise C.3:** (Easy.) Show how to apply this method to traversing orientation #1 of H_i.

C.4 Traversing the Peano Curve

The Peano curves P_0, P_1, and P_2 of Figure Ans.30 have 1, 3^2 and 3^4 nodes, respectively. In general P_n has 3^{2n} nodes, numbered $0, 1, 2, \ldots, 3^{2n} - 1$. This suggests that the Peano curve [Peano 90] is somehow based on the number 3, in contrast to the Hilbert curve, which is based on 2. The coordinates of the nodes vary from $(0,0)$ to $(n-1, n-1)$. It turns out that there is a correspondence between the node numbers and their coordinates [Cole 85], which uses base-3 reflected Gray codes (RGC).

A reflected Gray code [Gray 53] is a permutation of the i-digit integers such that consecutive integers differ by one digit only. Here is one way to develop these codes for binary numbers. Start with $i = 1$. There are only two 1-bit digits, namely, 0 and 1, and they differ by 1 bit only. To get the RGC for $i = 2$ follow the following steps:

1. Copy the sequence $(0, 1)$.

2. Append a 0 bit to the original sequence and a bit of 1 to the copy. The result is $(00, 01)$, $(10, 11)$.

3. Reflect (reverse) the second sequence. The result is $(11, 10)$.

4. Concatenate the two sequences to get $(00, 01, 11, 10)$.

It is easy to see that consecutive numbers differ by one bit only.

▶ **Exercise C.4:** Follow the rules above to get the binary RGC for $i = 3$.

Notice that the first and last numbers in an RGC also differ by one bit. RGCs can be created for any number system using the following notation and rules: Let $a = a_1 a_2 \cdots a_m$ be a non-negative, base-n integer (i.e., $0 \le a_i < n$). Define the quantity $p_j = \left(\sum_{i=1}^{j} a_i \right) \bmod 2$, and denote the base-$n$ RGC of a by $a' = b_1 b_2 \cdots b_m$. The digits b_i of a' can be computed by

$$b_1 = a_1; \quad b_i = \begin{cases} \begin{array}{ll} a_i & \text{if } p_{i-1} = 0; \\ n - 1 - a_i & \text{if } p_{i-1} = 1. \end{array} & \text{Odd } n \\ \hline \begin{array}{ll} a_i & \text{if } a_{i-1} \text{ is even}; \\ n - 1 - a_i & \text{if } a_{i-1} \text{ is odd.} \end{array} & \text{Even } n \end{cases} \quad i = 2, 3, \ldots, m.$$

[Note that $(a')' = a$ for both even and odd n.] For example, the RGC of the sequence of base-3 numbers (trits) 000, 001, 002, 010, 011, 012, 020, 021, 022, 100, 101... is 000, 001, 002, 012, 011, 010, 020, 021, 022, 122, 121... .

The connection between Peano curves and RGCs is: Let a be a node in the peano curve P_m. Write a as a ternary (base-3) number with $2m$ trits $a = a_1 a_2 \cdots a_{2m}$. Let $a' = b_1 b_2 \cdots b_{2m}$ be the RGC equivalent of a. Compute the two numbers $x' = b_2 b_4 b_6 \cdots b_{2m}$ and $y' = b_1 b_3 b_5 \cdots b_{2m-1}$. The number x' is the RGC of a number x, and similarly for y'. The two numbers (x, y) are the coordinates of node a in P_m.

C.5 L Systems

Lindenmayer Systems (or L-systems for short) were developed by the biologist Aristid Lindenmayer in 1968 as a tool [Lindenmayer 68] to describe the morphology of plants. They were initially used in computer science, in the 1970s, as a tool to define formal languages, but have become really popular only after 1984, when Alvy Ray Smith pointed out [Smith 84] that L-systems can be used to draw many types of fractals, in addition to their use in botany. Today L-systems are also used to generate tilings, geometric art, and even musical scores.

The main idea of L-systems is to define a complex object by (1) defining an initial simple object, called the *axiom*; and (2) giving rules that show how to replace parts of the axiom.

> ✎ The following true story is an example of Aristid's modesty. At one of the American conferences somebody asked him what the L in "L-systems" stands for. Aristid's answer was "Languages."
>
> —Grzegorz Rozenberg.

work on formal grammars, and also of the BNF notation. N. Chomsky showed, in the 1950s, how to describe the syntax of a natural language by means of production rules. At about the same time Backus and Naur developed the BNF notation, which is based on rewriting rules, specifically to provide a formal definition [Naur 60] of the syntax of ALGOL 60.

Figure C.13 shows how a fractal, the Koch snowflake curve, is constructed, in several steps, out of an axiom that's a simple triangle (C.13a) and a rewriting rule that says: Replace each straight segment with the curve of C.13b. Figure C.13c is the result of applying the rule on **all** three triangle sides. Figure C.13d is the result of applying the same rule on all 12 sides of C.13c, and so on.

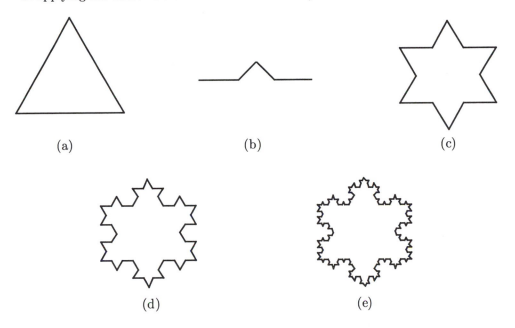

(a) (b) (c)

(d) (e)

Figure C.13: Successive Generations of the Koch Snowflake.

Notice that in order to construct iteration $i + 1$ of an object, the rule has to be applied to **all** parts of iteration i of the object. This is the main difference between L-systems and Chomsky grammars, and this is also one reason why L-systems are so powerful. Another reason is the notation used in modern L-systems, a notation introduced in 1979 by A. Szilard and R. E. Quinton and improved by P. Prusinkiewicz in 1986. It is based on the LOGO language [Abelson 82] and the concept of turtle moves. These two differences are illustrated below.

Example: An L-system dealing with the two letters x and y. The axiom is y and the two rewriting rules are: $x \rightarrow xy$ (every occurrence of x should be replaced by xy) and $y \rightarrow x$ (every occurrence of y should be replaced by x). The first iteration starts with the axiom y, and applies **both** rules to it. The first rule does not apply, and the second yields x. The result of the first iteration is thus x. Iteration 2 applies both rules to x. The first rule replaces x by xy and the second first iteration starts with the axiom y, and applies **both** rules to it. The first rule does not apply, and the second yields x. The result of the first iteration is thus x. Iteration 2 applies both rules to x. The first rule replaces x by xy and the second rule does not apply since the original string x did not have any y in it. Iteration 3 replaces the x of xy by xy and the y of xy by x. The result is xyx. Successive iterations produce the strings

$$y \to x \to xy \to xyx \to xyxxy \to xyxxyxyx.$$

(This does not seem useful, but wait until this method is applied to geometric shapes.) The two parts on the left and right of a production rule are called its *predecessor* and *successor*, respectively. An L-system such as the one above is called a D0L-system. (D0L stands for Deterministic, Context-Free L-system. Notice that most texts on L-systems corrupt this name and spell it "DOL" instead of "D0L.")

Turtle Moves: It is possibe to define geometric shapes by imagining a turtle moving on the two-dimensional plane, sometimes leaving marks behind. The LOGO programming language supports drawing commands that "move" the turtle from point to point and cause it to turn at an angle when it reaches a point. The production rules of L-systems also use this notation. Mathematically, the state of the turtle is represented by a triplet (x, y, α) where (x, y) are the present coordinates of the turtle and α is its heading. The basic notation used in such a rule employs the following characters:

F : The turtle moves forward a distance d, drawing a straight line of a given thickness W. The state of the turtle changes from (x, y, α) to $(x + d\cos\alpha, y + d\sin\alpha, \alpha)$.

f : The turtle moves forward as above, but without drawing anything.

+ : The turtle turns to the right (clockwise) by a given angle δ. Its new state is thus $(x, y, \alpha + \delta)$.

− : The turtle turns to the left (counterclockwise) by the same angle δ. Its new state is $(x, y, \alpha - \delta)$.

Table C.14 shows several more character commands that have traditionally been used in L-systems. As more research is done in this field, the number of turtle commands will grow, but the reader has to keep one important convention in mind: When a rewriting rule contains a command that the turtle (i.e., the computer implementation of L-systems) does not understand, *that command is ignored*; no error message is issued. This convention is useful and is commonly used in drawing complex shapes.

Table C.14 implies that several more parameters, such as C, sl, and Δ, are needed to completely specify the shape being drawn. These parameters should be supported by any computer implementation of L-systems; they should have default values, and should be easy for the user to modify. These parameters are listed in Table C.15.

The string F+F+F+F means to move forward one line length, turn right, and repeat three more times. If the turn angle is 90°, the result is a square of size d. If the initial turtle heading is $\alpha = 90°$, then the start/end point is the bottom left corner of the square (Figure C.16a). The string FFF+FF+F+F−F−F−FF+F+FFF draws the shape of Figure C.16b.

F	Move forward d units and draw a line.
f	Move forward d units without drawing.
+	Turn clockwise by an angle δ.
−	Turn counterclockwise by an angle δ.
|	Reverse direction (rotate by 180°).
[	Push current turtle state into the stack.
]	Pop current turtle state from the stack.
#	Increment the line width W by an amount w.
!	Decrement the line width W by an amount w.
@	Draw a dot with radius W.
{	Open a polygon.
}	Close a polygon and fill it with color C.
<	Divide line length d by scale factor sl.
>	Multiply line length d by scale factor sl.
&	Swap meaning of + and −.
(	Decrement turn angle δ by Δ.
)	Increment turn angle δ by Δ.
*	Match any character (used in context-sensitive L-systems only).
. . .	Ignore rule (used in context-sensitive L-systems only).

Table C.14: L-system Conventions for Turtle Commands.

d	The line length.
sl	Scale factor for line length d.
W	The line width.
w	The line width increment.
α	The initial turtle heading.
δ	Turn angle.
Δ	Increment/decrement the turn angle δ.
C	Default color for polygon fill.

Table C.15: Additional Turtle Parameters.

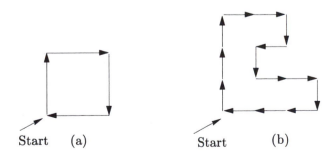

Figure C.16: Examples of Turtle Movements.

The Koch snowflake of Figure C.13 was generated by an L-system with an axiom F++F++F and the single production rule F->F-F++F-F. The initial heading was 0° and the turn angle 60°. Figure C.17 shows three iterations of the Peano space-filling curve drawn with an initial heading and a turn angle both of 90°.

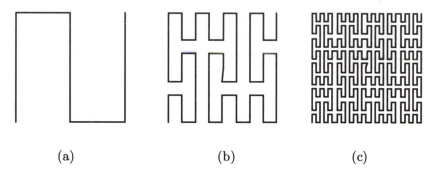

(a)   (b)   (c)

Figure C.17: Three Iterations of the Peano Curve.

The L-system for this curve consists of the axiom X and the two production rules

X->XFYFX+F+YFXFY-F-XFYFX and Y->YFXFY-F-XFYFX+F+YFXFY.

The key to understanding this L-system is the rule that any unknown turtle commands, in this case the characters X and Y, should be ignored. The first iteration draws the axiom X, which is unknown, causing nothing to be drawn. The next iteration executes the two rewriting rules. The first rule replaces the axiom X with XFYFX+F+YFXFY-F-XFYFX, which is plotted (since X and Y are unknown) as FF+F+FF-F-FF. The second rule looks for a Y in the axiom but finds none. The iteration thus draws FF+F+FF-F-FF, which results in Figure C.17a. The next iteration starts with XFYFX+F+YFXFY-F-XFYFX, replaces each X with the successor of rule 1, and replaces each Y with the successor of rule 2. The result is a very long string, which, when drawn, produces the curve of Figure C.17b.

The L-system for the Hilbert curve is similarly defined by the axiom X and the 2 production rules

X->-YF+XFX+FY- and Y->+XF-YFY-FX+.

▶ **Exercise C.5:** Show how to get the 4 orientations of the Hilbert curve out of the L-system above.

Bibliography

Abelson, H. and A. A. diSessa (1982) *Turtle Geometry*, Cambridge, MA, MIT Press.

Backus, J. W. (1959) "The Syntax and Semantics of the Proposed International Algebraic Language," in *Proceedings of the International Conference on Information processing*, pp. 125–132, UNESCO.

Chomsky, N. (1956) "Three Models for the Description of Language," *IRE Transactions on Information Theory* **2**(3):113–124.

Cole, A. J. (1985) "A Note on Peano Polygons and Gray Codes," *International Journal of Computer Mathemathics* **18**:3–13.

Cole, A. J. (1986) "Direct Transformations Between Sets of Integers and Hilbert Polygons," *International Journal of Computer Mathemathics* **20**:115–122.

Gray, F. (1953) U. S. patent 2632058, March.

Hilbert, D. (1891) "Ueber Stetige Abbildung Einer Linie auf ein Flachenstuck," *Math. Annalen* **38**:459–460.

Lindenmayer, A. (1968) "Mathematical Models for Cellular Interaction in Development," *Journal of Theoretical Biology* **18**:280–315.

Naur, P. et al. (1960) "Report on the Algorithmic Language ALGOL 60," *Communications of the ACM* **3**(5):299–314, revised in *Communications of the ACM* **6**(1):1–17.

Peano, G. (1890) "Sur Une Courbe Qui Remplit Toute Une Aire Plaine," *Math. Annalen* **36**:157–160.

Prusinkiewicz, Przemyslav (1986) *Graphical Applications of L-systems*, in Proc. of Graphics Interface '86 — Vision Interface '86, pp .247–253.

Prusinkiewicz, P., and A. Lindenmayer (1990) *The Algorithmic Beauty of Plants*, New York, Springer Verlag.

Prusinkiewicz, P., A. Lindenmayer, and F. D. Fracchia (1991) "Synthesis of Space-Filling Curves on the Square Grid," in *Fractals in the Fundamental and Applied Sciences*, edited by Peitgen, H.-O. et al., Amsterdam, Elsevier Science Publishers, pp. 341–366.

Sierpinski, W. (1912) "Sur Une Nouvelle Courbe Qui Remplit Toute Une Aire Plaine," *Bull. Acad. Sci. Cracovie* Serie A:462–478.

Sagan, Hans (1994) *Space-Filling Curves*, New York, Springer Verlag.

Smith, Alvy Ray (1984) "Plants, Fractals and Formal Languages," *Computer Graphics* **18**(3):1–10.

Szilard, A. L. and R. E. Quinton (1979) "An Interpretation for D0L Systems by Computer Graphics," *The Science Terrapin* **4**:8–13.

Wirth, N. (1976) *Algorithms + Data Structures = Programs*, Englewood Cliffs, NJ, Prentice-Hall, 2nd Ed.

All letters come and go—L is here to stay.

Grzegorz Rozenberg

D
Determinants and Matrices

A matrix $\mathbf{T}$ is a rectangular array of numbers, where each element a_{ij} is identified by its row and column. Matrix $\mathbf{T}_1$ below is "generic," with m rows and n columns. Notice how elements a_{ii} constitute the main diagonal of the matrix. Matrix $\mathbf{T}_2$ is diagonal ($a_{ij} = 0$ for $i \neq j$), and matrix $\mathbf{T}_3$, symmetric ($a_{ij} = a_{ji}$).

$$\mathbf{T}_1 = \begin{pmatrix} a_{11} & a_{12} & \cdots & a_{1n} \\ a_{21} & a_{22} & \cdots & a_{2n} \\ \vdots & \vdots & \ddots & \vdots \\ a_{m1} & a_{m2} & \cdots & a_{mn} \end{pmatrix}, \quad \mathbf{T}_2 = \begin{pmatrix} a_{11} & 0 & 0 & 0 \\ 0 & a_{22} & 0 & 0 \\ 0 & 0 & a_{33} & 0 \\ 0 & 0 & 0 & a_{44} \end{pmatrix},$$

$$\mathbf{T}_3 = \begin{pmatrix} 33 & -17 & 201 & -5 \\ -17 & 66 & 26 & -68 \\ 201 & 26 & 21 & -9 \\ -5 & -68 & -9 & 0 \end{pmatrix}.$$

The transpose of matrix $\mathbf{A}$ (denoted $\mathbf{A}^T$) is obtained from $\mathbf{A}$ by reflecting all the elements with respect to the main diagonal. A symmetric matrix equals its transpose.

D.1 Matrix Operations

The rule for matrix addition/subtraction is $c_{ij} = a_{ij} \pm b_{ij}$, where $\mathbf{C} = \mathbf{A} \pm \mathbf{B}$. The rule for matrix multiplication is slightly more complex: $c_{ij} = \sum_{k=1}^{n} a_{ik} b_{kj}$. Each element of $\mathbf{C}$ is the *dot product* of a row of $\mathbf{A}$ and a column of $\mathbf{B}$. In the dot product, corresponding elements from A and B are multiplied, and the products summed. In order for the multiplication to be well defined, each row of $\mathbf{A}$ must have the same size as a column of $\mathbf{B}$. Matrices $\mathbf{A}$ and $\mathbf{B}$ can therefore be multiplied only if the number of columns of **A** equals the number of rows of **B**. Note that matrix multiplication is not commutative, i.e., $\mathbf{AB} \neq \mathbf{BA}$ in general.

An example of matrix multiplication is the product of the 1×3 and 3×1 matrices

$$(1, -1, 5) \begin{pmatrix} 4 \\ -2 \\ 3 \end{pmatrix},$$

which yields the 1×1 matrix 21.

Tensor products. This is a special case of matrix multiplication. If **A** is a column vector and **B** is a row vector (each with n elements), then their tensor product **C** is defined by $\mathbf{C}_{ij} = \mathbf{A}_i \mathbf{B}_j$. Example:

$$\begin{pmatrix} 4 \\ -2 \\ 3 \end{pmatrix} (1, -1, 5) = \begin{pmatrix} 4 & -4 & 20 \\ -2 & 2 & -10 \\ 3 & -3 & 15 \end{pmatrix}.$$

A square matrix has a determinant, denoted either "det **A**" or $|\mathbf{A}|$, that is a number. The determinant of the 2×2 matrix $\begin{pmatrix} a & b \\ c & d \end{pmatrix}$ is defined as $ad - bc$. The determinant of a larger matrix can be calculated by the rule (note the alternating signs):

$$\begin{vmatrix} a_{11} & a_{12} & a_{13} \\ a_{21} & a_{22} & a_{23} \\ a_{31} & a_{32} & a_{33} \end{vmatrix} = a_{11} \begin{vmatrix} a_{22} & a_{23} \\ a_{32} & a_{33} \end{vmatrix} - a_{12} \begin{vmatrix} a_{21} & a_{23} \\ a_{31} & a_{33} \end{vmatrix} + a_{13} \begin{vmatrix} a_{21} & a_{22} \\ a_{31} & a_{32} \end{vmatrix}.$$

Matrix division is not defined, but certain matrices have an *inverse*. The inverse of **A** is denoted $\mathbf{A}^{-1}$, and has the property that $\mathbf{AA}^{-1} = \mathbf{A}^{-1}\mathbf{A} = \mathbf{I}$, where **I** is the *identity matrix* (with ones in the diagonal and zeros elsewhere). The inverse of a matrix is used, e.g., to solve systems of linear algebraic equations. Such a system can be denoted $\mathbf{Ax} = \mathbf{b}$ where **A** is the matrix of coefficients, **x** is the column of unknowns, and **b** is the column of the right-hand side coefficients. The solution is $\mathbf{x} = \mathbf{A}^{-1}\mathbf{b}$.

Example: The following system of three equations with three unknowns x, y, and z

$$x - y = 1,$$
$$-x + y = 2,$$
$$25x + 2y + z = 3, \tag{D.1}$$

can be written

$$\begin{pmatrix} 1 & -1 & 0 \\ -1 & 1 & 0 \\ 25 & 2 & 1 \end{pmatrix} \begin{pmatrix} x \\ y \\ z \end{pmatrix} = \begin{pmatrix} 1 \\ 2 \\ 3 \end{pmatrix}.$$

The inverse of the 3×3 transformation matrix

$$\mathbf{T} = \begin{pmatrix} a & b & 0 \\ c & d & 0 \\ m & n & 1 \end{pmatrix} \quad \text{is} \quad \mathbf{T}^{-1} = \frac{1}{ad - bc} \begin{pmatrix} d & -b & 0 \\ -c & a & 0 \\ cn - dm & bm - an & 1 \end{pmatrix}. \tag{D.2}$$

In general, however, the calculation of the inverse is not trivial and can be found in any text on Linear Algebra, and also in [Press 88].

Here is a summary of the properties of matrix operations:

$$\mathbf{A} + \mathbf{B} = \mathbf{B} + \mathbf{A}, \quad \mathbf{A} + (\mathbf{B} + \mathbf{C}) = (\mathbf{A} + \mathbf{B}) + \mathbf{C},$$
$$k(\mathbf{A} + \mathbf{B}) = k\mathbf{A} + k\mathbf{B}, \quad (k + m)\mathbf{A} = k\mathbf{A} + m\mathbf{A}, \quad k(m\mathbf{A}) = (km)\mathbf{A} = m(k\mathbf{A}),$$
$$\mathbf{A}(\mathbf{B}\mathbf{C}) = (\mathbf{A}\mathbf{B})\mathbf{C}, \quad \mathbf{A}(\mathbf{B} + \mathbf{C}) = \mathbf{A}\mathbf{B} + \mathbf{A}\mathbf{C},$$
$$(\mathbf{A} + \mathbf{B})\mathbf{C} = \mathbf{A}\mathbf{B} + \mathbf{A}\mathbf{C}, \quad \mathbf{A}(k\mathbf{B}) = k(\mathbf{A}\mathbf{B}) = (k\mathbf{A})\mathbf{B},$$
$$(\mathbf{A} + \mathbf{B})^T = \mathbf{A}^T + \mathbf{B}^T, \quad (k\mathbf{A})^T = k^T \mathbf{A}^T, \quad (\mathbf{A}\mathbf{B})^T = \mathbf{B}^T \mathbf{A}^T.$$

Information on the history of matrices and determinants can be found at URL "`http://www-groups.dcs.st-and.ac.uk/~history/HistTopics/`", file "`Matrices_and_determinants.html`".

▶ **Exercise D.1:** Add, subtract, and multiply the two matrices

$$\mathbf{A} = \begin{pmatrix} 1 & 2 & 3 \\ 4 & 5 & 6 \\ 7 & 8 & 9 \end{pmatrix}; \quad \mathbf{B} = \begin{pmatrix} 7 & 8 & 9 \\ 4 & 5 & 6 \\ 1 & 2 & 3 \end{pmatrix}.$$

▶ **Exercise D.2:** Calculate the inverse of

$$\mathbf{T} = \begin{pmatrix} 1 & -1 & 0 \\ -1 & 1 & 0 \\ 25 & 2 & 1 \end{pmatrix}.$$

Bibliography

Press, W. H., B. P. Flannery, et al. (1988) *Numerical Recipes in C: The Art of Scientific Computing*, Cambridge University Press.
(Also available on-line from `http://nr.harvard.edu/nr/bookc.html`.)

All problems in computer graphics can be solved with a matrix inversion.

James F. Blinn, 1993

We [he and Halmos] share a philosophy about linear algebra: we think basis-free, we write basis-free , but when the chips are down we close the office door and compute with matrices like fury.

Irving Kaplansky

E
Error Correcting Codes

The problem of adding reliability to data has already been mentioned in Section 2.12. This appendix discusses general methods for detecting and correcting errors. Reliability is, in a sense, the opposite of data compression since it is achieved by *increasing data redundancy*. Nevertheless, many practical situations call for reliable data, so a good data compression program should be able to use codes for increased reliability, if necessary.

Every time information is transmitted, on any channel, it may get corrupted by noise. In fact, even when information is stored in a storage device, it may become bad, because no hardware is absolutely reliable. This also applies to non-computer information. Speech sent on the air gets corrupted by noise, wind, high temperature, etc. Speech, in fact, is a good starting point for understanding the principles of error-detecting and -correcting codes. Imagine a noisy cocktail party where everybody talks simultaneously, on top of blaring music. We know that even in such a situation it is possible to carry a conversation, except that more attention than usual is needed.

E.1 First Principles

What makes our language so robust, so immune to errors? There are two properties, *redundancy* and *context*.

- Our language is redundant because only a very small fraction of all possible words are valid. A huge number of words can be constructed with the 26 letters of English. Just the number of seven-letter words, e.g., is $26^7 \approx 8.031$ billion. Yet only about 50,000 words are commonly used, and even the Oxford Dictionary lists "only" about 500,000 words. When we hear a garbled word our brain searches through many similar words, for the "closest" valid word. Computers are very good at such searches, which is why redundancy is the basis for error-detecting and error-correcting codes.

■ Our brain works by associations. This is why we humans excel in using the context of a message to repair errors in the message. In receiving a sentence with a garbled word or a word that doesn't belong, such as "pass the thustard please," we first use our memory to find words that are associated with "thustard." Then we use our accumulated life experience to select, among many possible candidates, the word that best fits in the present context. If we are on the freeway, we pass the bastard in front of us; if we are at dinner, we pass the mustard (or custard). Another example is the (corrupted) written sentence "a∗l n∗tu∗al l∗∗gua∗es a∗e red∗∗∗ant," which we can easily complete. Computers don't have much life experience and are notoriously bad at such tasks, which is why context is not used in computer codes. In extreme cases, where much of the sentence is bad, even we may not be able to correct it, and we may ask for a retransmission "say it again, Sam."

The idea of using redundancy to add reliability to information is due to Claude Shannon, the founder of information theory. It is not a trivial idea, since we are conditioned against it. Most of the time, we try to *eliminate* redundancy in computer data, in order to save space. In fact, all the data-compression methods discussed here do just that.

Figure E.1 shows the stages that a piece of computer data may go through when it is created, stored, transmitted, received, and used at the receiving end.

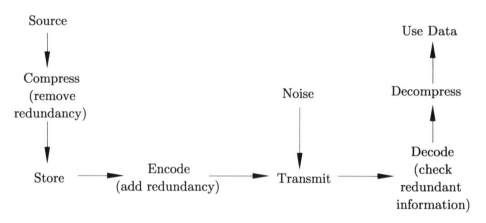

Figure E.1: Manipulating Information.

We discuss two approaches to reliable codes. The first approach is to *duplicate* the code, which leads to the idea of *voting codes*; the second one uses *check bits* and is based on the concept of *Hamming distance*.

E.2 Voting Codes

The first idea that usually occurs, when one thinks about redundancy, is to duplicate the message and send two copies. Thus if the code 110 has to be sent, one can send 110|110. A little thinking shows that this may, perhaps, be a good idea for error detection, but not for error correction. If the receiver receives two different copies, it cannot tell which one is good. What about triplicating the message? We can send 110|110|110 and tell the receiver to decide which of the three copies is good by comparing them. If all three are identical, the receiver assumes that they are correct. Moreover, if only two are identical and the third one different, the receiver assumes that the two identical copies are correct. This is the principle of *voting codes*. If all three copies are different, the receiver at least knows that an error has occurred, i.e., it can detect an error even though it cannot correct it.

To keep the analysis simple, let's limit ourselves to just 1-bit errors. When the three copies are received, the following cases are possible:

1. All three are identical. There are two subcases:
   1a: All three are good. This is the normal case.
   1b: All three have been corrupted in the same way. This is a rare case.
2. Two copies are identical, and the third one is different. Again, there are two subcases:
   2a: The two identical ones are good. This is the normal case.
   2b: They are bad. This is, we hope, a rare case.
3. All three copies are different.

Using the principle of voting, we assume that the three identical copies in case 1 are good. In case 1a our assumption is correct, and in case 1b, it isn't. Similarly, in case 2a the receiver makes the right decision, and in case 2b, the wrong one. In case 3, the receiver cannot correct the error but, at least, it can detect one, so it does not make a wrong decision.

The only cases where the receiver makes the wrong decision (where the principle of voting does not work) are therefore 1b and 2b. A little thinking shows that the probability of case 1b is much smaller than that of 2b. We will, therefore, try to estimate the probability of case 2b and, if it is small enough, there would be no need to worry about case 1b.

It is hard to calculate the probability of two copies being garbled *in the same way*. We will, therefore, calculate the probability that one bit gets changed in two of the three copies (either in the same or in different bit positions). If this probability is small enough, there is no need to worry about case 2b since its probability is even lower.

We denote by p the probability that one bit will get corrupted in our transmissions. The probability that one bit will go bad in two of the three copies is $\binom{3}{2}p^2 = 3p^2$. It is not simply p^2, since it is possible to select two objects out of three in $\binom{3}{2} =$ three ways.

[The notation $\binom{m}{n}$ is pronounced "m over n" and is defined as

$$\frac{m!}{n!(m-n)!}.$$

It is the number of ways n objects can be selected out of a set of m objects.]

Let's assume that $p = 10^{-6}$ (on average, one error in a million bits transmitted) and we want to send 10^8 bits. Without duplication we can expect $10^8 \times 10^{-6} = 100$ errors, an unacceptably high rate. With three copies sent, we have to send a total of 3×10^8 bits, and the probability that two out of the three copies will go wrong is 3×10^{-12}. The expected number of errors is thus $(3 \times 10^8) \times (3 \times 10^{-12}) = 9 \times 10^{-4} = 0.0009$ errors, a comfortably small number.

If higher reliability is needed, more copies can be sent. A code where each symbol is duplicated and sent nine times is extremely reliable. Voting codes are thus simple, reliable, and have only one disadvantage, they are too long. In practical situations, sending nine, or even three, copies of each message may be prohibitively expensive. This is why a lot of research has been done in the field of coding in the last 40 years and, today, many sophisticated codes are known that are more reliable and shorter than voting codes.

E.3 Check Bits

In practice, error-detection and correction is usually done by means of *check bits*, which are added to the original *information bits* of each word of the message. In general, k check bits are appended to the original m information bits, to produce a *codeword* of $n = m + k$ bits. Such a code is referred to as an (n, m) code. The codeword is then transmitted to the receiver. Only certain combinations of the information bits and check bits are valid, in analogy to a natural language. The receiver knows what the valid codewords are. If a non-valid codeword is received, the receiver considers it an error. In Section E.7 we show that, by adding more check bits, the receiver can also correct certain errors, not just detect them. The principle of error correction is that, on receiving a bad codeword, the receiver selects the valid codeword that is the "closest" to it.

Example: A set of 128 symbols needs to be coded. This implies $m = 7$. If we select $k = 4$, we end up with 128 valid codewords, each 11 bits long. This is therefore an $(11, 7)$ code. The valid codewords are selected from a total of $2^{11} = 2,048$ possible codewords, so there remain $2,048 - 128 = 1,920$ non-valid codewords. The big difference between the number of valid and non-valid codewords means that if a codeword gets corrupted, chances are it will change to a non-valid one.

It may, of course, happen that a valid codeword gets changed, during transmission, to another valid codeword. Our codes are thus not completely reliable, but can be made more and more reliable by adding more check bits and by selecting the valid codewords carefully. One of the basic theorems of information theory says that codes can be made as reliable as desired by adding check bits, as long as n (the size of a codeword) does not exceed the channel's capacity.

It is important to understand the meaning of the word "error" in data transmission. When a codeword is received, the receiver always receives n bits, but some of them may be bad. A bad bit does not disappear, nor does it change into something other than a bit. A bad bit simply changes its value, either from 0 to 1, or from 1 to 0. This makes it relatively easy to correct the bit. The code should tell the receiver which bits are bad, and the receiver can then easily correct those bits by inverting them.

In practice, bits may be sent on a wire as voltages. A binary 0 may, e.g., be represented by any voltage in the range 3–25 volts. A binary 1 may similarly be represented by the voltage range of $-25v$ to $-3v$. Such voltages tend to drop over long lines, and have to be amplified periodically. In the telephone network there is an amplifier (a *repeater*) every 20 miles or so. It looks at every bit received, decides whether it is a 0 or a 1 by measuring the voltage, and sends it to the next repeater as a clean, fresh pulse. If the voltage has deteriorated enough in passage, the repeater may make a wrong decision when sensing it, which introduces an error into the transmission. At present, typical transmission lines have error rates of about one in a billion but, under extreme conditions—such as in a lightning storm, or when the electric power suddenly fluctuates—the error rate may suddenly increase, creating a burst of errors.

E.4 Parity Bits

A parity bit can be added to a group of m information bits to complete the total number of 1 bits to an odd number. Thus the (odd) parity of the group 10110 is 0, since the original group plus the parity bit would have an odd number (3) of ones. Even parity can also be used, and the only difference between odd and even parity is that, in the case of even parity, a group of all zeros is valid, whereas, with odd parity, any group of bits with a parity bit added cannot be all zeros.

Parity bits can be used to design simple, but not very efficient, error-correcting codes. To correct 1-bit errors, the message can be organized as a *rectangle* of dimensions $(r-1) \times (s-1)$. A parity bit is added to each row of $s-1$ bits, and to each column of $r-1$ bits. The total size of the message (Table E.2a) becomes $s \times r$.

$$
\begin{array}{ccccc}
0 & 1 & 0 & 0 & \mathbf{1} \\
1 & 0 & 1 & 0 & \mathbf{0} \\
0 & 1 & 1 & 1 & \mathbf{1} \\
0 & 0 & 0 & 0 & \mathbf{0} \\
1 & 1 & 0 & 1 & \mathbf{1} \\
\mathbf{0} & \mathbf{1} & \mathbf{0} & \mathbf{0} & \mathbf{1}
\end{array}
\qquad
\begin{array}{ccccc}
0 & 1 & 0 & 0 & 1 \\
1 & 0 & 1 & 0 & \\
0 & 1 & 0 & & \\
0 & 0 & & & \\
1 & & & &
\end{array}
$$

(a)   (b)

Table E.2: Parity Bits.

If only one bit gets bad, a check of all $s-1+r-1$ parity bits will discover it, since only one of the $s-1$ parities and only one of the $r-1$ ones will be bad.

The overhead of a code is defined as the number of parity bits divided by the number of information bits. The overhead of the rectangular code is, therefore,

$$
\frac{(s-1+r-1)}{(s-1)(r-1)} \approx \frac{s+r}{s \times r - (s+r)}.
$$

A similar, slightly more efficient, code is a triangular configuration, where the information bits are arranged in a triangle, with the parity bits at the diagonal (Table E.2b). Each parity bit is the parity of all the bits in its row *and* column. If the top row contains r information bits, the entire triangle has $r(r+1)/2$ information bits and r parity bits. The overhead is thus

$$
\frac{r}{r(r+1)/2} = \frac{2}{r+1}.
$$

It is also possible to arrange the information bits in a number of two-dimensional planes, to obtain a three-dimensional cube, three of whose six outer surfaces are made up of parity bits.

It is not obvious how to generalize these methods to more than 1-bit error correction.

Symbol	$code_1$	$code_2$	$code_3$	$code_4$	$code_5$	$code_6$	$code_7$
A	0000	0000	001	001001	01011	110100	110
B	1111	1111	010	010010	10010	010011	0
C	0110	0110	100	100100	01100	001101	10
D	0111	1001	111	111111	10101	101010	111
k:	2	2	1	4	3	4	

Table E.3: Code Examples With $m = 2$.

E.5 Hamming Distance and Error Detecting

Richard Hamming developed the concept of distance, in the 1950s, as a general way to use check bits for error detection and correction.

To illustrate this concept, we start with a simple example involving just four symbols A, B, C, and D. Only 2 information bits are required, but the codes of Table E.3 add some check bits, for a total of 3–6 bits per symbol. $code_1$ is simple. Its four codewords were selected from the 16 possible 4-bit numbers, and are not the best possible ones. When the receiver receives one of them, say, 0111, it assumes that there is no error and the symbol received is D. When a non-valid codeword is received, the receiver signals an error. Since $code_1$ is not the best possible, not every error is detected. Even if we limit ourselves to single-bit errors, this code is not very good. There are 16 possible single-bit errors in our 4-bit codewords and, of those, the following 4 cannot be detected: A 0110 changed during transmission to 0111, a 0111 changed to 0110, a 1111 corrupted to 0111, and a 0111 changed to 1111. The error detection rate is thus 12 out of 16, or 75%. In comparison, $code_2$ does a much better job; it can detect every single-bit error.

▸ **Exercise E.1:** Prove the above statement.

We therefore say that the four codewords of $code_2$ are sufficiently *distant* from each other. The concept of distance of codewords is, fortunately, easy to define.

Definitions: (1) Two codewords are a Hamming distance d apart if they differ in exactly d of their n bits; and (2) a code has a Hamming distance of d if every pair of codewords in the code is, at least, a Hamming distance d apart.

These definitions have a simple geometric interpretation. Imagine a hypercube in n-dimensional space. Each of its 2^n corners can be numbered by an n-bit number (Figure E.4), such that each of the n bits corresponds to one of the n dimensions. In such a cube, points that are directly connected have a Hamming distance of 1, points with a common neighbor have a Hamming distance of 2, etc. If a code with

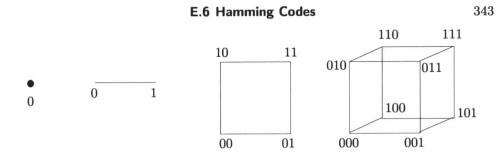

Figure E.4: Cubes of Various Dimensions and Corner Numbering.

a Hamming distance of 2 is desired, only points that are not directly connected should be selected as valid codewords.

The reason $code_2$ can detect all single-bit errors is that it has a Hamming distance of 2. The distance between valid codewords is 2, so a 1-bit error always changes a valid codeword into a non-valid one. When two bits go bad, a valid codeword is moved to another codeword at distance 2. If we want that other codeword to be non-valid, the code must have at least distance 3.

In general, a code with a Hamming distance of $d+1$ can detect all d-bit errors. $code_3$ has a Hamming distance of 2 and thus can detect all 1-bit errors even though it is short $(n = 3)$.

▸ **Exercise E.2:** Find the Hamming distance of $code_4$.

It is now obvious that we can increase the reliability of our transmissions to any desired level, but this feature does not come free. As always, there is a tradeoff, or a price to pay, in the form of the overhead. Our codes are much longer than m bits per symbol because of the added check bits. A measure of the price is $n/m = (m+k)/m = 1+k/m$, where the quantity k/m is called the *overhead* of the code. In the case of $code_1$ the overhead is 2 and, in the case of $code_3$, it is $3/2$.

Example: A code with a single check bit, which is a parity bit (even or odd). Any single-bit error can easily be detected since it creates a non-valid codeword. Such a code therefore has a Hamming distance of 2. $code_3$ above uses a single, odd, parity bit.

Example: A 2-bit error-detecting code for the same four symbols (see $code_4$). It must have a Hamming distance of 4, and one way of generating it is to duplicate $code_3$.

E.6 Hamming Codes

The principle of error-correcting codes is to separate the codes even farther by adding more redundancy (more check bits). When an invalid codeword is received, the receiver corrects the error by selecting the valid codeword that is closest to the one received. $code_5$ has a Hamming distance of 3. When one of its four codewords has a single bit changed, it is 1-bit distant from the original one, but is still 2 bits distant from any of the other codewords. Thus, if there is only one error, the receiver can always correct it. The receiver does that by comparing every codeword received to the list of valid codewords. If no match is found, the receiver assumes that a 1-bit error has occurred, and it corrects the error by selecting the codeword that's closest to the one received.

In general, when d bits go wrong in a codeword C_1, it turns into an invalid codeword C_2 at a distance d from C_1. If the distance between C_2 and the other valid codewords is at least $d+1$, then C_2 is closer to C_1 than it is to any other valid codeword. This is why a code with a Hamming distance of $d + (d + 1) = 2d + 1$ is needed to correct all d-bit errors.

How are the codewords selected? The problem is to select a good set of 2^m codewords out of the 2^n possible ones. The first approach uses brute force. It is easy to write a computer program that will examine all the possible sets of 2^m codewords, and select one that has the right distance. The problems with this approach are: (1) The time and storage required at the receiving end to verify and correct the codes received; and (2) the amount of time it takes to examine all the possible sets of codewords.

1. The receiver must have a list of all the 2^n possible codewords. For each codeword it must have a flag indicating whether it is valid and, if not, which valid codeword is the closest to it. Every codeword received has to be searched and located in this list in order to verify it.

2. In the case of four symbols, only four codewords need be selected. For $code_1$ and $code_2$, they had to be selected from among 16 possible numbers, which can be done in $\binom{16}{4} = 7,280$ ways. It is possible to write a simple program that will systematically select sets of four codewords until it finds a set with the required distance. In the case of $code_4$, the four codewords had to selected from a set of 64 numbers, which can be done in $\binom{64}{4} = 635,376$ ways. It is still possible to write a program that will systematically explore all the possible codeword selections for this case. In practical cases, however, where sets with hundreds of symbols are involved, the number of possibilities in selecting sets of codewords is too large even for the fastest computers to handle comfortably.

Clearly, a clever algorithm is needed, to select the best codewords, and to verify them on the fly, as they are being received. The transmitter should use the algorithm to generate the codewords when they have to be sent, and the receiver should use it to check them when they are received. The approach described here is due to Richard Hamming. In Hamming's codes [Hamming 86] the n bits of a codeword are indexed from 1 to n. The check bits are those with indexes that are powers of 2. Thus bits b_1, b_2, b_4, b_8, ... are check bits, and b_3, b_5, b_6, b_7, b_9, ... are information bits. The index of each information bit can be written as the sum of the indexes of certain check bits. Thus b_7 can be written as b_{1+2+4} and is, therefore, used in determining the values of check bits b_1, b_2, b_4. *The check bits are simply parity bits.* The value of b_2, e.g., is the parity (odd or even) of b_3, b_6, b_7, b_{10}, ... etc., since $3 = 2 + 1$, $6 = 2 + 4$, $7 = 2 + 1 + 4$, $10 = 2 + 8, \ldots$.

Example: A 1-bit error-correcting code for the set of symbols A, B, C, and D. It must have a Hamming distance of $2d + 1 = 3$. Two information bits are needed to code the four symbols, so they must be b_3 and b_5. The parity bits are therefore b_1, b_2, and b_4. Since $3 = 1 + 2$ and $5 = 1 + 4$, the 3 parity bits are defined as b_1 is the parity of bits b_3 and b_5, b_2 is the parity of b_3, and b_4 is the parity of b_5. This is how $code_5$ of Table E.3 was constructed.

Example: A 1-bit error-correcting code for a set of 256 symbols. It must have a Hamming distance of $2d + 1 = 3$. Eight information bits are required to code the 256 symbols, so they must be b_3, b_5, b_6, b_7, b_9, b_{10}, b_{11}, and b_{12}. The parity bits are, therefore, b_1, b_2, b_4, and b_8. The total size of the code is 12 bits. The following relations define the 4 parity bits:

$3 = 1+2$, $5 = 1+4$, $6 = 2+4$, $7 = 1+2+4$, $9 = 1+8$, $10 = 2+8$ $11 = 1+2+8$ and $12 = 4 + 8$.

They imply that b_1 is the parity of b_3, b_5, b_7, b_9, and b_{11}.

▸ **Exercise E.3:** What are the definitions of the other parity bits?

▸ **Exercise E.4:** Construct a 1-bit error-correcting Hamming code for 16-bit codes ($m = 16$).

A common question at this point is how the number of parity bits is determined. The answer is that it is determined implicitly. We know that m data bits are needed, and we also know that bits $b_1, b_2, b_4, b_8, \ldots$ should be the parity bits. We thus allocate the first m bits of the set $b_3, b_5, b_6, b_7, b_9, b_{10}, b_{11}, \ldots$ to the data, and this implicitly determines the number of parity bits needed.

What is the size of a general Hamming code? The case of a 1-bit error-correcting code is easy to analyse. Given a set of 2^m symbols, 2^m valid codewords are needed. We are looking for the smallest k required to construct codewords of size $m + k$ and Hamming distance 3. The 2^m valid codewords should be selected from a total of 2^n numbers (where $n = m + k$), such that each codeword consists of m information bits and k check bits.

Since we want any single-bit error in a codeword to be corrected, such an error should not take us too far from the original codeword. A single-bit error takes us to a codeword at distance 1 from the original one. As a result, all codewords at distance 1 from the original codeword should be non-valid. Each of the original 2^m codewords is n bits long and thus has n codewords at distance 1 from it. They should be declared non-valid. This means that the total number of codewords needed (valid plus non-valid) is $2^m + n2^m = (1 + n)2^m$. This number has to be selected from the 2^n available numbers, so we end up with the relation $(1 + n)2^m \leq 2^n$. Since $2^n = 2^{m+k}$, we get $1 + n \leq 2^k$ or $k \geq \log_2(1 + n)$. The following table illustrates the meaning of this relation for certain values of m.

n:	4	7	12	21	38	71
k:	2	3	4	5	6	7
$m = n - k$:	2	4	8	16	32	64
k/m:	1	.75	.5	.31	.19	.11

There is a geometric interpretation that provides another way of obtaining the same result. We imagine 2^m spheres of radius one tightly packed in our n-dimensional cube. Each sphere is centered around one of the corners and encompasses all its immediate corner neighbors. The *volume* of a sphere is defined as the number of corners it includes, which is $1 + n$. The spheres are tightly packed but they don't overlap, so their total volume is $(1 + n)2^m$, and this should not exceed the total volume of the cube, which is 2^n.

The case of a 2-bit error-correcting code is similarly analysed. Each valid codeword should define a set that includes itself, the n codewords at distance 1 from it, and the set of $\binom{n}{2}$ codewords at distance 2 from it, a total of $\binom{n}{0} + \binom{n}{1} + \binom{n}{2} = 1+n+n(n-1)/2$. Those sets should be non-overlapping, which implies the relation

$$\big(1+n+n(n-1)/2\big)2^m \leq 2^n \Rightarrow 1+n+n(n-1)/2 \leq 2^k \Rightarrow k \geq \log_2\big(1+n+n(n-1)/2\big).$$

In the geometric interpretation we again imagine 2^m spheres of radius 2 each. Each sphere centered around a corner and containing the corner, its n immediate neighbors, and its $\binom{n}{2}$ second place neighbors (corners differing from the center corner by 2 bits).

E.7 The SEC-DED Code

However, even though we can estimate the length of a 2-bit error-correcting Hamming code, we don't know how to construct it! The best that can be done today with Hamming codes is single-error-correction combined with double-error-detection. An example of such a SEC-DED code is code$_6$. It was created by simply adding a parity bit to code$_5$.

▶ **Exercise E.5:** Table E.3 contains one more code, code$_7$. What is it?

The receiver checks the SEC-DED code in two steps. In step 1, the single parity bit is checked. If it is bad, the receiver assumes that a 1-bit error occurred, and it uses the other parity bits, in step 2, to correct the error. It may happen, of course, that three or even five bits are bad, but the simple SEC-DED code cannot detect such errors.

If the single parity is good, then there are either no errors, or two bits are bad. The receiver goes to step 2, where it uses the other parity bits to distinguish between these two cases. Again, there could be four or six bad bits, but this code cannot handle these cases.

The SEC-DED code has a Hamming distance of 4. In general, a code for c-bit error correction and d-bit error detection should have a distance of $c + d + 1$.

> Hamming codes are the first class of linear codes devised for error correction. These codes and their variations have been widely used for error control in digital communication and data storage systems.
> —Shu Lin and Daniel J. Costello.

E.8 Generating Polynomials

There are many approaches to the problem of developing codes for more than 1-bit error correction. They are, however, more complicated than Hamming's method, and require a background in group theory and Galois fields. In this section we briefly sketch one such approach, using the concept of a *generating polynomial*.

We use the case $m = 4$ for illustration. Sixteen codewords are needed, which can be used to code any set of 16 symbols. We know from the discussion above that, for 1-bit error correction, 3 parity bits are needed, bringing the total size of the code to $n = 7$. Here is an example of such a code:

```
0000000  0001011  0010110  0011101  0100111  0101100  0110001  0111010
1000101  1001110  1010011  1011000  1100010  1101001  1110100  1111111
```

Note that it has the following properties:

▪ The sum (modulo 2) of any two codewords equals another codeword. This implies that the sum of any number of codewords is a codeword. The 16 codewords above thus form a *group* under this operation.

(Addition and subtraction modulo-2 is done by $0+0 = 1+1 = 0$, $0+1 = 1+0 = 1$, $1 - 0 = 0 - 1 = 1$. The definition of a group should be reviewed in any text on algebra.)

▪ Any circular shift of a codeword is another codeword. This code is thus *cyclic*.

▪ It has a Hamming distance of 3, as required for 1-bit error correction.

Interesting properties! The 16 codewords were selected from the 128 possible ones by means of a generator polynomial. The idea is to look at each codeword as a polynomial, where the bits are the coefficients. Here are some 7-bit codewords associated with polynomials of degree 6.

$$
\begin{array}{ccccccc}
1 & 0 & 0 & 1 & 1 & 1 & 1 \\
x^6 & & & +x^3 & +x^2 & +x & +1
\end{array}
$$

$$
\begin{array}{ccccccc}
0 & 1 & 1 & 0 & 0 & 1 & 0 \\
 & x^5 & +x^4 & & & +x &
\end{array}
$$

$$
\begin{array}{ccccccc}
0 & 1 & 0 & 0 & 1 & 1 & 1 \\
 & x^5 & & & +x^2 & +x & +1
\end{array}
$$

The 16 codewords in the table above were selected by finding the degree-6 polynomials which are evenly divisible (modulo 2) by the generating polynomial $x^3 + x + 1$. For example, the second codeword '0100111' in the table corresponds to the polynomial $x^5 + x^2 + x + 1$, which is divisible by $x^3 + x + 1$ because $x^5 + x^2 + x + 1 = (x^3 + x + 1)(x^2 + 1)$.

To understand how such polynomials can be calculated, let's consider similar operations on numbers. Suppose we want to know the largest multiple of 7 that's ≤ 30. We divide 30 by 7, obtaining a remainder of 2, and then subtract the 2 from the 30, getting 28. Similarly with polynomials. Let's start with the 4 information bits 0010, and calculate the remaining 3 parity bits. We write $0010ppp$, which gives us the polynomial x^4. We divide x^4 by the generating polynomial, obtaining a remainder of $x^2 + x$. Subtracting that remainder from x^4 gives us something that will be evenly divisible by the generating polynomial. The result of the subtraction is $x^4 + x^2 + x$, so the complete codeword is 0010110.

Any generating polynomial can get us the first two properties. To get the third property (the necessary Hamming distance), the right generating polynomial should be used, and it can be selected by examining its roots. This topic is outside the scope of this book, but it is discussed in any text on error-correcting codes. A common example of a generating polynomial is CRC (Section 3.22).

Bibliography

Hamming, Richard (1950) "Error Detecting and Error Correcting Codes," *Bell Systems Technical Journal* **29**:147–160, April.

Hamming, Richard (1986) *Coding and Information Theory*, 2nd Ed., Englewood Cliffs, NJ, Prentice-Hall.

Lin, Shu (1970) *An Introduction to Error Correcting Codes*, Englewood Cliffs, NJ, Prentice-Hall.

> Errors using inadequate data are much less than those using no data at all.
>
> Charles Babbage (1792–1871)

> Give me fruitful error any time, full of seeds, bursting with its own corrections. You can keep your sterile truth for yourself.
>
> Vilfredo Pareto (1848–1923)

F
Fourier Transform

The concept of a transform is familiar to mathematicians. It is a standard mathemtical tool used to solve problems in many areas. The idea is to change a mathematical quantity (a number, a vector, a function, or anything else) to another form, where it may look unfamiliar but may exhibit useful features. The transformed quantity is used to solve a problem or perform a calculation, and the reult is then transformed back to the original form.

A simple, illustrative example is Roman numerals. The ancient Romans presumably knew how to operate on such numbers but when we have to, say, multiply two Roman numerals, we may find it more convenient to transform them into modern (Arabic) notation, multiply, and then transform back. Here's a simple example.

$$XCVI \times XII \rightarrow 96 \times 12 = 1152 \rightarrow MCLII.$$

Functions used in science and engineering often use *time* as their parameter (or independent variable). We therefore say that a function $g(t)$ is represented in the *time domain*. Since a typical function oscillates, we can think of it as being similar to a wave, and we may try to represent it as a wave (or as a combination of waves). When this is done, we denote the resulting function $G(f)$, where f stands for the frequency of the wave, and we say that the function is represented in the *frequency domain*. This turns out to be a useful concept, since many operations on functions are easy to carry out in the frequency domain. Transforming a function between the time and frequency domains is easy when the function is *periodic*, but can also be done for certain nonperiodic functions.

Definition: A function $g(t)$ is periodic if there exists a constant P such that $g(t + P) = g(t)$ for all values of t. P is called the *period* of the function. If several such constants exist, only the smallest of them is considered the period.

A periodic function has four important attributes: its amplitude, period, frequency, and phase. The amplitude of the function is the maximum value it has in any period. The frequency f is the inverse of the period ($f = 1/P$). It is expressed

F. Fourier Transform

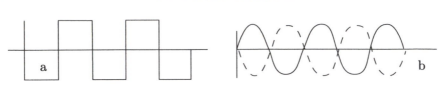

Figure F.1: Periodic Functions.

in cycles per second, or Hertz (Hz). The phase is the least understood of the four attributes. It measures the position of the function within a period, and it is easy to visualize when a function is compared to its own copy. Imagine the two sinusoids in Figure F.1b. They are identical but out of phase. One follows the other at a fixed interval called the *phase difference*. We can write them as $g_1(t) = A\sin(2\pi ft)$ and $g_2(t) = A\sin(2\pi ft + \theta)$. The phase difference between them is θ, but we can also say that the first one has no phase, while the second one has a phase of θ. (By the way, this example also shows that the cosine is a sine function with a phase θ of $\pi/2$.)

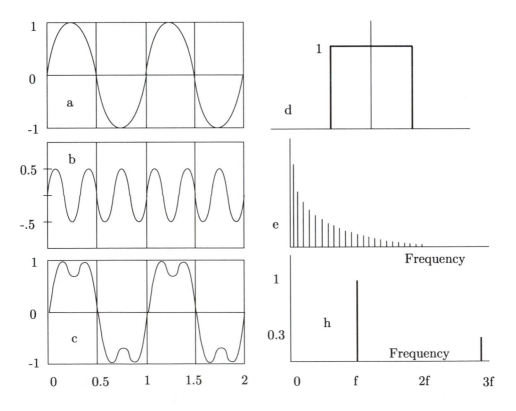

Figure F.2: Time and Frequency Domains.

F.1 The Frequency Domain

To understand the concept of frequency domain, let's look at two simple examples. The function $g(t) = \sin(2\pi ft) + (1/3)\sin(2\pi(3f)t)$ is a combination of two sine waves with amplitudes 1 and $1/3$, and frequencies f and $3f$, respectively. They are shown in Figure F.2ab. The sum (Figure F.2c) is also periodic, with frequency f (the smaller of the two frequencies). The frequency domain of $g(t)$ is a function consisting of just the two points $(f, 1)$ and $(3f, 1/3)$ (Figure F.2h). It indicates that the original (time domain) function is made up of frequency f with amplitude 1, and frequency $3f$ with amplitude $1/3$.

This example is extremely simple, since it involves just two frequencies. When a function involves several frequencies that are integer multiples of some lowest frequency, the latter is called the *fundamental frequency* of the function.

Not every function has a simple frequency domain representation. Consider the single square pulse in Figure F.2d. Its time domain is

$$g(t) = \begin{cases} 1, & -a/2 \le t \le a/2, \\ 0, & \text{elsewhere,} \end{cases}$$

but its frequency domain is Figure F.2e. It consists of all the frequencies from 0 to ∞, with amplitudes that drop continuously. This means that the time domain representation, even though simple, consists of all possible frequencies, with lower frequencies contributing more, and higher ones, less and less.

In general, a periodic function can be represented in the frequency domain as the sum of (phase shifted) sine waves with frequencies that are integer multiples (harmonics) of some fundamental frequency. However, the square pulse of Figure F.2d is not periodic. It turns out that frequency domain concepts can be applied to a nonperiodic function, but only if it is nonzero over a finite range (like our square pulse). Such a function is represented as the sum of (phase shifted) sine waves with all kinds of frequencies, not just harmonics.

The *spectrum* of the frequency domain is the range of frequencies it contains. For the function of Figure F.2h, the spectrum is the two frequencies f and $3f$. For the one of Figure F.2d, it is the entire range $[0, \infty]$. The *bandwidth* of the frequency domain is the width of the spectrum. It is $2f$ in our first example, and ∞, in the second one.

Another important concept to define is the *dc component* of the function. The time domain of a function may include a component of zero frequency. Engineers call this component the *direct current*, so the rest of us have adopted the term "dc component." Figure F.3a is identical to F.2c except that it goes from 0 to 2, instead of from -1 to $+1$. The frequency domain (Figure F.3b) now has an added point at $(0, 1)$, representing the dc component.

The entire concept of the two domains is due to the French mathematician Joseph Fourier. He proved a fundamental theorem that says that every periodic function can be represented as the sum of sine and cosine functions. He also showed how to transform a function between the time and frequency domains. If the shape of the function is far from a regular wave, its Fourier expansion will include an infinite number of frequencies. For a continuous function $g(t)$, the Fourier transform

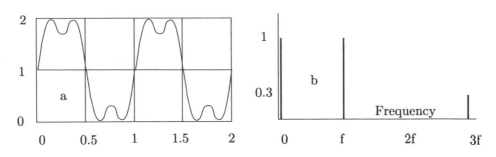

Figure F.3: Time and Frequency Domains With a dc Component.

and its inverse are given by:

$$G(f) = \int_{-\infty}^{\infty} g(t)[\cos(2\pi f t) - i\sin(2\pi f t)]\, dt;$$

$$g(t) = \int_{-\infty}^{\infty} G(f)[\cos(2\pi f t) + i\sin(2\pi f t)]\, df.$$

In computer applications, we normally have discrete functions that take just n (equally spaced) values. In such a case the discrete Fourier transform is

$$G(f) = \sum_{t=0}^{n-1} g(t)\left[\cos\left(\frac{2\pi f t}{n}\right) - i\sin\left(\frac{2\pi f t}{n}\right)\right], \qquad 0 \le f \le n-1$$

and its inverse

$$g(t) = \frac{1}{n}\sum_{f=0}^{n-1} G(f)\left[\cos\left(\frac{2\pi f t}{n}\right) + i\sin\left(\frac{2\pi f t}{n}\right)\right]; \qquad 0 \le t \le n-1.$$

Note that $G(f)$ is complex, so it can be written $G(f) = R(f) + iI(f)$. For any value of f, the amplitude (or magnitude) of G is given by $|G(f)| = \sqrt{R^2(f) + I^2(f)}$.

Note how the function in Figure F.2c, obtained by adding the simple functions in F.2a,b, starts resembling a square pulse. It turns out that we can bring it closer to a square pulse (like the one in Figure F.1a) by adding $(1/5)\sin(2\pi(5f)t)$, $(1/7)\sin(2\pi(7f)t)$, and so on. We say that the Fourier series of a square wave with amplitude A and frequency f is the infinite sum

$$A\sum_{k=1}^{\infty} \frac{1}{k}\sin(2\pi k f t),$$

where successive terms have smaller and smaller amplitudes.

We now apply these concepts to digitized images. Imagine a black and white photograph scanned line by line. For all practical purposes we can assume that the photograph has infinite resolution (its shades of gray can vary continuously). An ideal scan would thus result in an infinite sequence of numbers which can be considered the values of a (continuous) intensity function $i(t)$. In practice, we can only store a finite sequence in memory, so we have to select a finite number of values $i(1)$ through $i(n)$. This process is known as *sampling*.

Intuitively, sampling seems a tradeoff between quality and price. The bigger the sample, the better the quality of the final image, but more hardware (more memory and higher screen resolution) is required, resulting in higher costs. This intuitive conclusion, however, is not entirely true. Sampling theory tells us that we can sample an image and reconstruct it later in memory without loss of quality if we can do the following:

1. Transform the intensity function from the time domain $i(t)$ to the frequency domain $G(f)$.
2. Find the maximum frequency f_m.
3. Sample $i(t)$ at a rate $\geq 2f_m$ (e.g., if $f_m = 22,000$ Hz, generate samples at the rate of $44,000$ Hz or higher).
4. Store the sampled values in the bitmap. The resulting image would be equal in quality to the original one on the photograph.

There are two points to consider. The first is that f_m could be infinite. In such a case, a value f_m should be selected such that frequencies $> f_m$ do not contribute much (have low amplitudes). There is some loss of image quality in such a case. The second point is that the bitmap (and consequently, the resolution) may be too small for the sample generated in step 3. In such a case, a smaller sample has to be taken, again resulting in a loss of image quality.

The result above was proved by Harry Nyquist, and the quantity $2f_m$ is called the *Nyquist rate*. It is used in many practical situations. The range of human hearing, for instance, is between 16 Hz and 22,000 Hz. When sound is digitized, it is sampled at the Nyquist rate of 44,000 Hz (or higher). Anything lower than that results in distortions. This is why music recorded on a CD has such high quality.

Fourier is a mathematical poem.
William Thomson (Lord Kelvin) (1824-1907)

G
Group 4 Codes Summary

Table G.2 summarizes the codes emitted by the group 4 encoder. Figure G.1 is a tree with the same codes. Each horizontal branch corresponds to another zero and each vertical branch, to another 1.

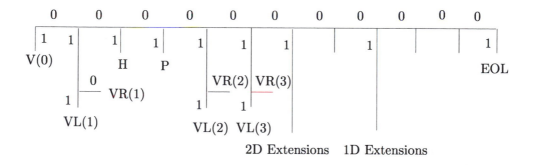

Figure G.1: Tree of Group 3 Codes.

G. Group 4 Codes Summary

Mode	Elements to Be Coded		Notation	Codeword
Pass	b_1, b_2		P	0001
Horizontal	$a_0 a_1, a_1 a_2$		H	$001 + M(a_0 a_1) + M(a_1 a_2)$
Vertical	a_1 just under b_1	$a_1 b_1 = 0$	V(0)	1
	a_1 to	$a_1 b_1 = 1$	VR(1)	011
	the right	$a_1 b_1 = 2$	VR(2)	000011
	of b_1	$a_1 b_1 = 3$	VR(3)	0000011
	a_1 to	$a_1 b_1 = 1$	VL(1)	010
	the left	$a_1 b_1 = 2$	VL(2)	000010
	of b_1	$a_1 b_1 = 3$	VL(3)	0000010
	2D Extensions			0000001xxx
	1D Extensions			000000001xxx
	EOL			000000000001
	1D Coding of Next Line			EOL+'1'
	2D Coding of Next Line			EOL+'0'

Table G.2: Group 4 Codes.

There are 8 groups from ICS-313 class participated in the experiment (G1::G8). Each group has 3 subjects, except for Group1 and Group4 who only have 2 subjects (1 subject dropped). Numbers in each cell represent the total number of faults in the corresponding artifacts founds by the group (EGSM) or by the individuals collectively (EIAM).

Danu Tjahjono, *ICS-TR-95-07 University of Hawaii, Jan, 1995*

H
Hashing

A hash table is a data structure allowing for fast insertions, searches, and deletions of data items. The table itself is just an array H, and the principle of hashing is to define a function h such that $h(k)$ produces an index to array H, where k is the key of a data item. The following examples illustrate the meaning of the terms "data item" and "key."

1. The LZRW1 method (Section 3.7), uses hashing to store pointers. The method uses the first three characters in the look-ahead buffer as a key which is hashed into a 12-bit number I used to index the hash table, an array of $2^{12} = 4,096$ pointers. The actual data stored in each location of the LZRW1 hash table is a pointer.

2. Virtually all computer languages use variables. A variable provides a name for a value that will be stored in memory, in a certain address A, when the program is eventually executed. When the program is compiled, each variable has two attributes, its name N (a string of characters assigned by the programmer) and its memory address A, assigned by the compiler. The compiler uses a hash table to store all the information about variables. The data item in this example is the address A of a variable; the key is the variable's name N. The compiler reads the name from the program source file, hashes it, finds it in the hash table, and retrieves the address in order to compile the current instruction. If the variable is not found in the hash table, it is assigned an address, and both the name and address are stored in the table (in principle only the address need be stored but the name is also stored because of collisions; see below).

The hash function h takes as argument a key, which may be a number or a string. It scrambles or hashes the bits of the key to produce an index to array H. In practice the array size is normally 2^n, so the result produced by h should be an n-bit number. Hashing is a good data structure since any operation on the hash table, adding, searching, or deleting, can be done in one step, regardless of

the table size. The only problem is *collisions*. In most applications it is possible
for two distinct keys k_1 and k_2 to get hashed to the same index, i.e., $h(k_1) = h(k_2)$
for $k_1 \neq k_2$. Example 2 above makes it easy to understand the reason for this.
Assuming variable names of five letters, there may be $26^5 = 11,881,376$ variable
names. Any program would use just a small percentage of this number, perhaps
a few hundred or a few thousand names. The size of the hash table thus doesn't
have to exceed a few thousand entries, and hashing 11.8 million names into a few
thousand index values must involve many collisions.

▶ **Exercise H.1:** How many names are possible if a name consists of exactly eight
letters and digits?

    Terminology: Two different keys that hash to the same index are called
synonyms. If a hash table contains m keys out of a set of M possible ones, then
m/M is the *density* of the table, and $\alpha = m/2^n$ is its *loading factor*.

H.1 Hash Functions

A hash function should be easy to compute and should minimize collisions. The
function should make use of all the bits of the key, such that changing even one
bit would typically (although not always) produce a different index. An ideal hash
function should also produce indexes that are uniformly distributed (calling the
function many times with random keys should produce each index the same number
of times). A function that produces, e.g., index 118 most of the time is obviously
biased and leads to collisions. The function should also assume that many keys
may be similar. In the case of variable names, e.g., programmers sometimes assign
names such as "A1", "A2", "A3" to variables. A hash function that uses just the
leftmost bits of a key would produce the same index for such names, leading to
many collisions. Following are some examples of hash functions used in practice.

    Mid-Square: The key k is considered an integer, it is squared and the middle
n bits of k^2 extracted to become the index. Squaring k has the advantage that the
middle bits of k^2 depend on *all* the bits of k. Thus two keys differing in one bit
would tend to produce different indexes. A variation, suitable for large keys, is to
divide the bits of the original key into several groups, add all the groups, square
the result, and extract its middle n bits.

    The keys "A1", "A2", and "A3", e.g., become the 16-bit numbers

$$01000001|00110001, \quad 01000001|00110010, \quad \text{and } 01000001|00110011.$$

After squaring and extracting the middle 8 bits, the resulting indexes are 158, 166,
and 175, respectively.

    Modulo: $h(k) = k \bmod m$. The result is the remainder of the integer division
k/m, so it is in the range $[0, m-1]$. In order for the result to be a valid index,
the hash table size should be m. The value of m is critical and should be selected
carefully. If m is a power of 2, say, 2^i, then the remainder of k/m is simply the i
rightmost bits of k. This would be a very biased hash function. If m is even, then
the remainder of k/m has the same parity as k (it is odd when k is odd and even
when k is even). This again is a bad choice for m, since it produces a biased hash
function that maps odd keys to odd location of H and even keys to even locations.

If p is a prime number evenly dividing m then keys that are permutations of each other (e.g., "ABC", "ACB", and "CBA") may many times be mapped to indexes that differ by p or by a multiple of p, again causing non-uniform distribution of the keys.

It can be shown that the modulo hash function achieves best results when m is a prime number that does not evenly divide $8^k \pm a$ where k and a are small numbers. In practice, good choices for m are prime numbers whose prime divisors are > 20.

Folding: This function is suitable for large keys. The bits comprising the key are divided into several groups, which are then added. The middle n bits of the sum are extracted to become the index. A variation is *reverse folding* where every other group of bits is reversed before being added.

H.2 Collision Handling

When an index i is produced by the hash function $h(k)$, the software using hashing should first check $H[i]$ for a collision. There must, therefore, be a way for the software to tell if entry $H[i]$ is empty or occupied. Initializing all entries of H to zero is normally not enough since zero may be a valid data item. A simple approach is to have an additional array F, of size $2^n/8$ bytes, where each bit is associated with an entry of H. Each bit of F acts as a flag indicating whether the corresponding entry of H is empty or not. The entire array F is initially set to zeros, indicating that all entries of H are empty. When the software decides to insert a data item in $H[i]$ it has to find the bit in F that corresponds to entry i and check it. The software should therefore calculate $j = \lfloor i/8 \rfloor$ and $k = i - 8j$ and check bit k of byte F[j]. If the bit is zero, entry H[i] is empty and can be used for a new data item. The bit then has to be set, which is done by using k to select one of the eight masks

00000001 00000010 00000100 00001000 00010000 00100000 01000000 10000000

and logically AND it with $F[j]$. If the bit is 1, entry $H[i]$ is already occupied, and this is a collision. The software should be able to check and tell whether entry $H[i]$ contains the data item d that corresponds to key k. This is why the keys have to be saved, together with the data items, in the hash table.

What should the software do in case of a collision? The simplest thing is to check entries $H[i+1]$, $H[i+2]$,...,$H[2^n - 1]$, $H[0]$, $H[1]$... until an empty entry is found or until the search reaches entry $H[i-1]$. In the latter case the software knows that the data item searched for is not in the table (if this was a search) or that the table is full (if this was an attempt to insert a new item in the table). This process is called *linear search*. Searching for a data item, which in principle should take one step, can now, because of collisions, take up to 2^n steps. Experience also shows that linear search causes occupied entries in the table to cluster, which is intuitively easy to understand. If the hash function is not ideal and hashes many keys to, say, index 54, then table entries 54, 55,... will quickly fill up, creating a cluster. Clusters also tend to grow and merge, creating even larger clusters and thereby increasing the search time. A theoretical analysis shows that the expected number of steps needed to locate an item when linear search is used is $(2 - \alpha)/(2 - 2\alpha)$, where α is the loading factor (percent full of the table). For $\alpha = 0.5$ we can expect 1.5 steps on the average but for $\alpha = 0.75$ the expected number of steps rises to 2.5, and for $\alpha = 0.9$ it become 5.5. It is clear that when linear search is used, the loading factor should be kept low (perhaps below 0.6–0.7). If more items need to be added to the table, a good solution is to declare a new table, twice as large as the original one, transfer all items from the old one to the new one (using a new hash function), and delete the old table.

A more sophisticated method of handling collisions is *quadratic search*. Assume that H is an array of size N. When entry $H[i]$ is found to be occupied, the software checks entries $H[(i \pm j^2) \bmod N]$ where $0 \le j \le (N-1)/2$. It can be shown that if N is a prime number of the form $4j + 3$ (where j is an integer) quadratic search will end up examining every entry of H.

A third way to treat collisions is to rehash. The software should have a choice of several hashing functions $h_1, h_2, \ldots$. If $i = h_1(k)$ and $H[i]$ is occupied, the software should calculate $i = h_2(k)$ then try the new $H[i]$. Still another way is to generate an array R of N pseudo-random numbers in the range $[0, N-1]$ where each number appears once. If entry $H[i]$ is occupied, the software should set $i = (i + R[i]) \bmod N$ and try the new $H[i]$.

It is possible to design a *perfect hash function* that, for a given set of data items, will not have any collisions. This makes sense for sets of data that never change. Examples are the Bible, the works of Shakespeare, or any data written on a CD-ROM. The size N of the hash table should, in such a case, be normally larger than the number of data items. It is also possible to design a *minimal perfect hash function* where the hash table size eqauls the size of the data (i.e., no entries remain empty after all data items have been inserted). See [Czech 92], [Fox 91], and [Havas 93] for details on these special hash functions.

Bibliography

Czech, Z. J., et al (1992) "An Optimal Algorithm for Generating Minimal Perfect Hash Functions," *Information Processing Letters* **43**:257–264.

Fox, E. A. et al. (1991) "Order Preserving Minimal Perfect Hash Functions and Information Retrieval," *ACM Transactions on Information Systems* **9**(2):281–308.

Havas, G. et al. (1993) *Graphs, Hypergraphs and Hashing* in Proceedings of the International Workshop on Graph-Theoretic Concepts in Computer Science (WG'93), Berlin, Springer-Verlag.

> "Why," said he, "a magician could call up a lot of genies, and they would hash you up like nothing before you could say Jack Robinson. They are as tall as a tree and as big around as a church."
>
> Mark Twain, *The Adventures Of Huckleberry Finn*

I
Interpolating Polynomials

This appendix shows how to predict the value of a pixel from those of 16 of its near neighbors by means of a two-dimensional interpolating polynomial. The results are used in Table 4.31. The main idea is to consider the 16 neighbor pixels as 4×4 equally spaced points on a surface (where the value of a pixel is interpreted as the height of the surface) and to use polynomials to find the mathematical expression of a surface $\mathbf{P}(u, w)$ that goes through all 16 points. The value of the pixel at the center of the 4×4 group can then be predicted by calculating the height of the center point $\mathbf{P}(.5, .5)$ of the surface. Mathematically, this surface is the two-dimensional polynomial interpolation of the 16 points.

I.1 One-Dimensional Interpolation

A surface can be viewed as a generalization of a curve, so we start by developing a one-dimensional polynomial (a curve) that interpolates four points, and then extend it to a two-dimensional polynomial (a surface) that interpolates a grid of 4×4 points.

We start with four given points $\mathbf{P}_1$, $\mathbf{P}_2$, $\mathbf{P}_3$, and $\mathbf{P}_4$ and we look for a polynomial that will go through them. In general a polynomial of degree n in x is defined (Section 3.22) as the function

$$P_n(x) = \sum_{i=0}^{n} a_i x^i = a_0 + a_1 x + a_2 x^2 + \cdots + a_n x^n,$$

where a_i are the $n + 1$ coefficients of the polynomial and the parameter x is a real number. The one-dimensional interpolating polynomial that's of interest to us here is special, and differs from the definition above in two respects

1. This polynomial goes from point $\mathbf{P}_1$ to point $\mathbf{P}_4$. Its length is finite, and it is therefore better to describe it as the function

$$P_n(t) = \sum_{i=0}^{n} a_i t^i = a_0 + a_1 t + a_2 t^2 + \cdots + a_n t^n; \quad \text{where } 0 \le t \le 1.$$

This is the *parametric representation* of a polynomial. We want this polynomial to go from $\mathbf{P}_1$ to $\mathbf{P}_4$ when the parameter t is varied from 0 to 1.

2. The only thing that's given are the four points and we have to use them to calculate all $n+1$ coefficients of the polynomial. This suggests the value $n = 3$ (a polynomial of degree 3, a cubic polynomial; one which has four coefficients). The idea is to set up and solve four equations, with the four coefficients as the unknowns, and with the four points as known quantities. We thus use the notation (T indicates transpose)

$$\mathbf{P}(t) = \mathbf{a}t^3 + \mathbf{b}t^2 + \mathbf{c}t + \mathbf{d} = (t^3, t^2, t, 1)(\mathbf{a}, \mathbf{b}, \mathbf{c}, \mathbf{d})^T = \mathbf{T}(t) \cdot \mathbf{A}. \qquad \text{(I.1)}$$

The four coefficients $\mathbf{a}, \mathbf{b}, \mathbf{c}, \mathbf{d}$ are shown in boldface because they are not numbers. Keep in mind that the polynomial has to go through the given points, so the value of $\mathbf{P}(t)$ for any t must be the three coordinates of a point. Each coefficient should thus be a triplet. $\mathbf{T}(t)$ is the row vector $(t^3, t^2, t, 1)$, and $\mathbf{A}$ is the column vector $(\mathbf{a}, \mathbf{b}, \mathbf{c}, \mathbf{d})^T$. Calculating the curve therefore involves finding the values of the four unknowns $\mathbf{a}, \mathbf{b}, \mathbf{c}, \mathbf{d}$. $\mathbf{P}(t)$ is called a *parametric cubic* (or PC) polynomial.

It turns out that degree 3 is the smallest one that's still useful for an interpolating polynomial. A polynomial of degree 1 has the form $\mathbf{P}_1(t) = \mathbf{A}t + \mathbf{B}$ and is, therefore, a straight line, so it can only be used in special cases. A polynomial of degree two (quadratic) has the form $\mathbf{P}_2(t) = \mathbf{A}t^2 + \mathbf{B}t + \mathbf{C}$ and is a conic section, so it can only take a few different shapes. A polynomial of degree 3 (cubic) is thus the simplest one that can take on complex shapes, and can also be a space curve.

▶ **Exercise I.1:** Prove that a quadratic polynomial must be a plane curve.

Our ultimate problem is to interpolate equally spaced pixels. We therefore assume that the two interior points $\mathbf{P}_2$ and $\mathbf{P}_3$ are equally spaced between $\mathbf{P}_1$ and $\mathbf{P}_4$. The first point $\mathbf{P}_1$ is the start point $\mathbf{P}(0)$ of the polynomial, the last point, $\mathbf{P}_4$ is the endpoint $\mathbf{P}(1)$, and the two interior points $\mathbf{P}_2$ and $\mathbf{P}_3$ are the two equally spaced interior points $\mathbf{P}(1/3)$ and $\mathbf{P}(2/3)$ of the polynomial.

We thus write $\mathbf{P}(0) = \mathbf{P}_1$, $\mathbf{P}(1/3) = \mathbf{P}_2$, $\mathbf{P}(2/3) = \mathbf{P}_3$, $\mathbf{P}(1) = \mathbf{P}_4$, or

$$\mathbf{a}(0)^3 + \mathbf{b}(0)^2 + \mathbf{c}(0) + \mathbf{d} = \mathbf{P}_1.$$
$$\mathbf{a}(1/3)^3 + \mathbf{b}(1/3)^2 + \mathbf{c}(1/3) + \mathbf{d} = \mathbf{P}_2.$$
$$\mathbf{a}(2/3)^3 + \mathbf{b}(2/3)^2 + \mathbf{c}(2/3) + \mathbf{d} = \mathbf{P}_3.$$
$$\mathbf{a}(1)^3 + \mathbf{b}(1)^2 + \mathbf{c}(1) + \mathbf{d} = \mathbf{P}_4.$$

These equations are easy to solve and the solutions are:

$$\mathbf{a} = -9/2\mathbf{P}_1 + 27/2\mathbf{P}_2 - 27/2\mathbf{P}_3 + 9/2\mathbf{P}_4.$$
$$\mathbf{b} = 9\mathbf{P}_1 - 45/2\mathbf{P}_2 + 18\mathbf{P}_3 - 9/2\mathbf{P}_4.$$
$$\mathbf{c} = -11/2\mathbf{P}_1 + 9\mathbf{P}_2 - 9/2\mathbf{P}_3 + \mathbf{P}_4.$$
$$\mathbf{d} = \mathbf{P}_1.$$

Substituting into Equation (I.1) gives

$$\mathbf{P}(t) = (-9/2\mathbf{P}_1 + 27/2\mathbf{P}_2 - 27/2\mathbf{P}_3 + 9/2\mathbf{P}_4)t^3$$
$$+ (9\mathbf{P}_1 - 45/2\mathbf{P}_2 + 18\mathbf{P}_3 - 9/2\mathbf{P}_4)t^2$$
$$+ (-11/2\mathbf{P}_1 + 9\mathbf{P}_2 - 9/2\mathbf{P}_3 + \mathbf{P}_4)t + \mathbf{P}_1.$$

Which, after rearranging, becomes

$$\begin{aligned}
\mathbf{P}(t) &= (-4.5t^3 + 9t^2 - 5.5t + 1)\mathbf{P}_1 + (13.5t^3 - 22.5t^2 + 9t)\mathbf{P}_2 \\
&\quad + (-13.5t^3 + 18t^2 - 4.5t)\mathbf{P}_3 + (4.5t^3 - 4.5t^2 + t)\mathbf{P}_4 \\
&= G_1(t)\mathbf{P}_1 + G_2(t)\mathbf{P}_2 + G_3(t)\mathbf{P}_3 + G_4(t)\mathbf{P}_4 \\
&= \mathbf{G}(t) \cdot \mathbf{P},
\end{aligned}$$ (I.2)

where

$$\begin{array}{ll}
G_1(t) = (-4.5t^3 + 9t^2 - 5.5t + 1), & G_2(t) = (13.5t^3 - 22.5t^2 + 9t), \\
G_3(t) = (-13.5t^3 + 18t^2 - 4.5t), & G_4(t) = (4.5t^3 - 4.5t^2 + t);
\end{array}$$ (I.3)

$\mathbf{P}$ is the column $(\mathbf{P}_1, \mathbf{P}_2, \mathbf{P}_3, \mathbf{P}_4)^T$, and $\mathbf{G}(t)$ is the row vector

$$\big(G_1(t), G_2(t), G_3(t), G_4(t)\big).$$

The functions $G_i(t)$ are called *blending functions* since they create any point on the curve as a blend of the four given points. Note that they add up to 1 for any value of t. This property must be satisfied by any set of blending functions, and such functions are called *barycentric*. We can also write

$$G_1(t) = (t^3, t^2, t, 1)(-4.5, 9, -5.5, 1)^T$$

and, similarly, for $G_2(t)$, $G_3(t)$, and $G_4(t)$. In matrix notation this becomes

$$\mathbf{G}(t) = (t^3, t^2, t, 1) \begin{pmatrix} -4.5 & 13.5 & -13.5 & 4.5 \\ 9.0 & -22.5 & 18 & -4.5 \\ -5.5 & 9.0 & -4.5 & 1.0 \\ 1.0 & 0 & 0 & 0 \end{pmatrix} = \mathbf{T}(t) \cdot \mathbf{N}.$$ (I.4)

The curve can now be written $\mathbf{P}(t) = \mathbf{G}(t) \cdot \mathbf{P} = \mathbf{T}(t) \cdot \mathbf{N} \cdot \mathbf{P}$. $\mathbf{N}$ is the Hermite basis matrix and $\mathbf{P}$ is the geometry vector. From Equation (I.1) we know that $\mathbf{P}(t) = \mathbf{T}(t) \cdot \mathbf{A}$, so we can write $\mathbf{A} = \mathbf{N} \cdot \mathbf{P}$.

> The word *barycentric* is derived from *barycenter*, meaning "center of gravity," because such weights are used to calculate the center of gravity of an object. Barycentric weights have many uses in geometry in general, and in curve and surface design in particular.

Given the four points, the interpolating polynomial can be calculated in two steps:
1. Set-up the equation $\mathbf{A} = \mathbf{N} \cdot \mathbf{P}$ and solve it for $\mathbf{A} = (\mathbf{a}, \mathbf{b}, \mathbf{c}, \mathbf{d})^T$.
2. The polynomial is $\mathbf{P}(t) = \mathbf{T}(t) \cdot \mathbf{A}$.

I.1.1 Example

(This example is in two dimensions, each of the four points $\mathbf{P}_i$ and each of the four coefficients $\mathbf{a}$, $\mathbf{b}$, $\mathbf{c}$, and $\mathbf{d}$ is a pair. For three-dimensional curves, the method is the same, except that triplets should be used, instead of pairs.) Given the four two-dimensional points $\mathbf{P}_1 = (0,0)$, $\mathbf{P}_2 = (1,0)$, $\mathbf{P}_3 = (1,1)$, and $\mathbf{P}_4 = (0,1)$, we set up the equation

$$\begin{pmatrix} \mathbf{a} \\ \mathbf{b} \\ \mathbf{c} \\ \mathbf{d} \end{pmatrix} = \mathbf{A} = \mathbf{N} \cdot \mathbf{P} = \begin{pmatrix} -4.5 & 13.5 & -13.5 & 4.5 \\ 9.0 & -22.5 & 18 & -4.5 \\ -5.5 & 9.0 & -4.5 & 1.0 \\ 1.0 & 0 & 0 & 0 \end{pmatrix} \begin{pmatrix} (0,0) \\ (1,0) \\ (1,1) \\ (0,1) \end{pmatrix},$$

which is easy to solve

$$\mathbf{a} = -4.5(0,0) + 13.5(1,0) - 13.5(1,1) + 4.5(0,1) = (0,-9);$$
$$\mathbf{b} = 19(0,0) - 22.5(1,0) + 18(1,1) - 4.5(0,1) = (-4.5, 13.5);$$
$$\mathbf{c} = -5.5(0,0) + 9(1,0) - 4.5(1,1) + 1(0,1) = (4.5, -3.5);$$
$$\mathbf{d} = 1(0,0) - 0(1,0) + 0(1,1) - 0(0,1) = (0,0).$$

Thus $\mathbf{P}(t) = \mathbf{T} \cdot \mathbf{A} = (0,-9)t^3 + (-4.5, 13.5)t^2 + (4.5, -3.5)t.$

It is now easy to calculate and verify that $\mathbf{P}(0) = (0,0) = \mathbf{P}_1$, and

$$\mathbf{P}(1/3) = (0,-9)1/27 + (-4.5, 13.5)1/9 + (4.5, -3.5)1/3 = (1,0) = \mathbf{P}_2;$$

$$\mathbf{P}(1) = (0,-9)1^3 + (-4.5, 13.5)1^2 + (4.5, -3.5)1 = (0,1) = \mathbf{P}_4.$$

▶ **Exercise I.2:** Calculate $\mathbf{P}(2/3)$ and verify that it is equal to $\mathbf{P}_3$.

▶ **Exercise I.3:** Imagine the circular arc of radius one in the first quadrant (a quarter circle). Write the coordinates of the four points that are equally spaced on this arc. Use the coordinates to calculate a PC interpolating polynomial approximating this arc. Calculate point $\mathbf{P}(1/2)$. How far does it deviate from the midpoint of the true quarter circle?

The main advantage of this method is its simplicity. Given the four points, it is easy to calculate the PC polynomial that passes through them.

▶ **Exercise I.4:** This method makes sense if the four points are (at least approximately) equally spaced along the curve. If they are not, the following may be done: Instead of using $1/3$ and $2/3$ as the intermediate values, the user may specify values α, β such that $\mathbf{P}_2 = \mathbf{P}(\alpha)$ and $\mathbf{P}_3 = \mathbf{P}(\beta)$. Generalize Equation (I.4) such that it depends on α and β.

I.2 Two-Dimensional Interpolation

The PC polynomial, Equation (I.1), can easily be extended to two dimensions by means of a technique called *cartesian product*. The polynomial is generalized from a curve to a *bicubic* surface.

A one-dimensional PC polynomial has the form $\mathbf{P}(t) = \sum_{i=0}^{3} \mathbf{a}_i t^i$. Two such curves, $\mathbf{P}(u)$ and $\mathbf{P}(w)$, can be combined by means of this technique to form the surface:

$$\mathbf{P}(u, w) = \sum_{i=0}^{3} \sum_{j=0}^{3} \mathbf{a}_{ij} u^i w^j$$

$$= \mathbf{a}_{33}u^3 w^3 + \mathbf{a}_{32}u^3 w^2 + \mathbf{a}_{31}u^3 w + \mathbf{a}_{30}u^3 + \mathbf{a}_{23}u^2 w^3 + \mathbf{a}_{22}u^2 w^2 + \mathbf{a}_{21}u^2 w + \mathbf{a}_{20}u^2$$

$$+ \mathbf{a}_{13}uw^3 + \mathbf{a}_{12}uw^2 + \mathbf{a}_{11}uw + \mathbf{a}_{10}u + \mathbf{a}_{03}w^3 + \mathbf{a}_{02}w^2 + \mathbf{a}_{01}w + \mathbf{a}_{00}$$

$$= (u^3, u^2, u, 1) \begin{pmatrix} \mathbf{a}_{33} & \mathbf{a}_{32} & \mathbf{a}_{31} & \mathbf{a}_{30} \\ \mathbf{a}_{23} & \mathbf{a}_{22} & \mathbf{a}_{21} & \mathbf{a}_{20} \\ \mathbf{a}_{13} & \mathbf{a}_{12} & \mathbf{a}_{11} & \mathbf{a}_{10} \\ \mathbf{a}_{03} & \mathbf{a}_{02} & \mathbf{a}_{01} & \mathbf{a}_{00} \end{pmatrix} \begin{pmatrix} w^3 \\ w^2 \\ w \\ 1 \end{pmatrix}; \quad \text{where } 0 \le u, w \le 1. \quad (I.5)$$

This is a double cubic polynomial (hence the name *bicubic*) with 16 terms, where each of the 16 coefficients $\mathbf{a}_{ij}$ is a triplet. Note that the surface depends on all 16 coefficients. Any change in any of them produces a different surface. Equation (I.5) is the *algebraic representation* of a bicubic surface. In order to use it in practice, the 16 unknown coefficients have to be expressed in terms of the 16 known, equally spaced points. We denote these points

$$\begin{matrix} \mathbf{P}_{03} & \mathbf{P}_{13} & \mathbf{P}_{23} & \mathbf{P}_{33} \\ \mathbf{P}_{02} & \mathbf{P}_{12} & \mathbf{P}_{22} & \mathbf{P}_{32} \\ \mathbf{P}_{01} & \mathbf{P}_{11} & \mathbf{P}_{21} & \mathbf{P}_{31} \\ \mathbf{P}_{00} & \mathbf{P}_{10} & \mathbf{P}_{20} & \mathbf{P}_{30}. \end{matrix}$$

To calculate the 16 unknown coefficients, we write 16 equations, each based on one of the given points:

$$\begin{matrix} \mathbf{P}(0,0) = \mathbf{P}_{00} & \mathbf{P}(0,1/3) = \mathbf{P}_{01} & \mathbf{P}(0,2/3) = \mathbf{P}_{02} & \mathbf{P}(0,1) = \mathbf{P}_{03} \\ \mathbf{P}(1/3,0) = \mathbf{P}_{10} & \mathbf{P}(1/3,1/3) = \mathbf{P}_{11} & \mathbf{P}(1/3,2/3) = \mathbf{P}_{12} & \mathbf{P}(1/3,1) = \mathbf{P}_{13} \\ \mathbf{P}(2/3,0) = \mathbf{P}_{20} & \mathbf{P}(2/3,1/3) = \mathbf{P}_{21} & \mathbf{P}(2/3,2/3) = \mathbf{P}_{22} & \mathbf{P}(2/3,1) = \mathbf{P}_{23} \\ \mathbf{P}(1,0) = \mathbf{P}_{30} & \mathbf{P}(1,1/3) = \mathbf{P}_{31} & \mathbf{P}(1,2/3) = \mathbf{P}_{32} & \mathbf{P}(1,1) = \mathbf{P}_{33}. \end{matrix}$$

Solving, substituting the solutions in Equation (I.5), and simplifying produces the *geometric representation* of the bicubic surface

$$\mathbf{P}(u, w) = (u^3, u^2, u, 1)\mathbf{N} \begin{pmatrix} \mathbf{P}_{33} & \mathbf{P}_{32} & \mathbf{P}_{31} & \mathbf{P}_{30} \\ \mathbf{P}_{23} & \mathbf{P}_{22} & \mathbf{P}_{21} & \mathbf{P}_{20} \\ \mathbf{P}_{13} & \mathbf{P}_{12} & \mathbf{P}_{11} & \mathbf{P}_{10} \\ \mathbf{P}_{03} & \mathbf{P}_{02} & \mathbf{P}_{01} & \mathbf{P}_{00} \end{pmatrix} \mathbf{N}^T \begin{pmatrix} w^3 \\ w^2 \\ w \\ 1 \end{pmatrix}, \quad (I.6)$$

where $\mathbf{N}$ is the Hermite matrix of Equation (I.4).

The surface of Equation (I.6) can now be used to predict the value of a pixel as a polynomial interpolation of 16 of its near neighbors. All that's necessary is to substitute $u = 0.5$ and $w = 0.5$. The following *Mathematica*™ code

```
Clear[Nh,P,U,W];
Nh={{-4.5,13.5,-13.5,4.5},{9,-22.5,18,-4.5},
  {-5.5,9,-4.5,1},{1,0,0,0}};
P={{p33,p32,p31,p30},{p23,p22,p21,p20},
  {p13,p12,p11,p10},{p03,p02,p01,p00}};
U={u^3,u^2,u,1};
W={w^3,w^2,w,1};
u:=0.5;
w:=0.5;
Expand[U.Nh.P.Transpose[Nh].Transpose[W]]
```

does that and produces

$$\mathbf{P}(.5, .5)$$
$$= 0.00390625\mathbf{P}_{00} - 0.0351563\mathbf{P}_{01} - 0.0351563\mathbf{P}_{02} + 0.00390625\mathbf{P}_{03}$$
$$- 0.0351563\mathbf{P}_{10} + 0.316406\mathbf{P}_{11} + 0.316406\mathbf{P}_{12} - 0.0351563\mathbf{P}_{13}$$
$$- 0.0351563\mathbf{P}_{20} + 0.316406\mathbf{P}_{21} + 0.316406\mathbf{P}_{22} - 0.0351563\mathbf{P}_{23}$$
$$+ 0.00390625\mathbf{P}_{30} - 0.0351563\mathbf{P}_{31} - 0.0351563\mathbf{P}_{32} + 0.00390625\mathbf{P}_{33}.$$

Where the 16 coefficients are the ones used in Table 4.31.

▸ **Exercise I.5:** How can this method be used in cases where not all 16 points are known?

Readers who find it hard to follow the details above should compare the way two-dimensional polynomial interpolation is presented here to the way it is discussed by [Press 88]. The following quotation is from page 125: "...The formulas that obtain the c's from the function and derivative values are just a complicated linear transformation, with coefficients which, having been determined once, in the mists of numerical history, can be tabulated and forgotten."

> A precisian professor had the habit of saying: "...quartic polynomial $ax^4 + bx^3 + cx^2 + dx + e$, where e need not be the base of the natural logarithms."
> J. E. Littlewood (1885–1977), *A Mathematician's Miscellany*

> Seated at his disorderly desk, caressed by a counterpane of drifting tobacco haze, he would pore over the manuscript, crossing out, interpolating, re-arguing, and then referring to volumes on his shelves.
> Christopher Morley, *The Haunted Bookshop*

Answers to Exercises

1: When a software house has a popular product they tend to come up with new versions. A user can update an old version to a new one, and the update usually comes as a compressed file on a floppy disk. Over time the updates get bigger and, at a certain point, an update may not fit on a single floppy. This is why good compression is important in the case of software updates. The time it takes to compress and decompress the update is unimportant since these operations are typically done just once.

1.1: An obvious way is to use them to code the five most common strings in the text. Since irreversible text compression is a special-purpose method, the user may know what strings are common in any particular text to be compressed. The user may specify five such strings to the encoder, and they should also be written at the start of the output stream, for the decoder's use.

1.2: 6,8,0,1,3,1,4,1,3,1,4,1,3,1,4,1,3,1,2,2,2,2,6,1,1. The first two numbers are the bitmap resolution (6×8). If each number occupies a byte on the output stream, then its size is 25 bytes, compared to a bitmap size of only 6×8 bits = 6 bytes. The method does not work for small images.

1.3: RLE of images is based on the idea that adjacent pixels tend to be identical. The last pixel of a row, however, has no reason to be identical to the first pixel of the next row.

1.4: Each of the first four rows yields the eight runs 1,1,1,2,1,1,1,eol. Rows 6 and 8 yield the four runs 0,7,1,eol each. Rows 5 and 7 yield the two runs 8,eol each. The total number of runs (including the eol's) is thus 44.

When compressing by columns, columns 1, 3, and 6 yield the five runs 5,1,1,1,eol each. Columns 2, 4, 5, and 7 yield the six runs 0,5,1,1,1,eol each. Column 8 gives 4,4,eol, so the total number of runs is 42. This image is thus "balanced" with respect to rows and columns.

1.5: As "11 22 90 00 00 33 44". The 00 following the 90 indicates no run, and the following 00 is interpreted as a regular character.

1.6: The six characters "123ABC" have ASCII codes 31, 32, 33, 41, 42 and 43. Translating these hexadecimal numbers to binary produces "00110001 00110010 00110011 01000001 01000010 01000011".
The next step is to divide this string of 48 bits into 6-bit blocks. They are 001100=12, 010011=19, 001000=8, 110011=51, 010000=16, 010100=20, 001001=9, 000011=3. The character at position 12 in the BinHex table is "-" (position numbering starts at zero). The one at position 19 is "6". The final result is the string "-6)c38*$".

1.7: Exercise 2.1 shows that the binary code of the integer i is $1 + \lfloor \log_2 i \rfloor$ bits long. We add $\lfloor \log_2 i \rfloor$ zeros, bringing the total size to $1 + 2\lfloor \log_2 i \rfloor$ bits.

1.8: Table Ans.1 summarizes the results. In (a), the first string is encoded with $k = 1$. In (b) it is encoded with $k = 2$. Columns (c) and (d) are the encodings of the second string with $k = 1$ and $k = 2$, respectively. The averages of the four columns are 3.4375, 3.25, 3.56 and 3.6875; very similar! The move-ahead-k method used with small values of k does not favor strings satisfying the concentration property.

a	abcdmnop	0	a	abcdmnop	0	a	abcdmnop	0	a	abcdmnop	0
b	abcdmnop	1	b	abcdmnop	1	b	abcdmnop	1	b	abcdmnop	1
c	bacdmnop	2	c	bacdmnop	2	c	bacdmnop	2	c	bacdmnop	2
d	bcadmnop	3	d	cbadmnop	3	d	bcadmnop	3	d	cbadmnop	3
d	bcdamnop	2	d	cdbamnop	1	m	bcdamnop	4	m	cdbamnop	4
c	bdcamnop	2	c	dcbamnop	1	n	bcdmanop	5	n	cdmbanop	5
b	bcdamnop	0	b	cdbamnop	2	o	bcdmnaop	6	o	cdmnbaop	6
a	bcdamnop	3	a	bcdamnop	3	p	bcdmnoap	7	p	cdmnobap	7
m	bcadmnop	4	m	bacdmnop	4	a	bcdmnopa	7	a	cdmnopba	7
n	bcamdnop	5	n	bamcdnop	5	b	bcdmnoap	0	b	cdmnoapb	7
o	bcamndop	6	o	bamncdop	6	c	bcdmnoap	1	c	cdmnobap	0
p	bcamnodp	7	p	bamnocdp	7	d	cbdmnoap	2	d	cdmnobap	1
p	bcamnopd	6	p	bamnopcd	5	m	cdbmnoap	3	m	dcmnobap	2
o	bcamnpod	6	o	bampnocd	5	n	cdmbnoap	4	n	mdcnobap	3
n	bcamnopd	4	n	bamopncd	5	o	cdmnboap	5	o	mndcobap	4
m	bcanmopd	4	m	bamnopcd	2	p	cdmnobap	7	p	mnodcbap	7
	bcamnopd			mbanopcd			cdmnobpa			mnodcpba	
	(a)			(b)			(c)			(d)	

Table Ans.1: Encoding with Move-Ahead-k.

1.9: Table Ans.2 summarizes the decoding steps. Notice how similar it is to Table 1.11, indicating that move-to-front is a symmetric data compression method.

Code input	A (before adding)	A (after adding)	Word
0the	()	(the)	the
1boy	(the)	(the, boy)	boy
2on	(boy, the)	(boy, the, on)	on
3my	(on, boy, the)	(on, boy, the, my)	my
4right	(my, on, boy, the)	(my, on, boy, the, right)	right
5is	(right, my, on, boy, the)	(right, my, on, boy, the, is)	is
5	(is, right, my, on, boy, the)	(is, right, my, on, boy, the)	the
2	(the, is, right, my, on, boy)	(the, is, right, my, on, boy)	right
5	(right, the, is, my, on, boy)	(right, the, is, my, on, boy)	boy
	(boy, right, the, is, my, on)		

Table Ans.2: Decoding Multiple-Letter Words.

2.1: It is $1 + \lfloor \log_2 i \rfloor$ as can be shown by simple experimenting.

2.2: Two is the smallest integer that can serve as the basis for a number system.

2.3: Replacing 10 by 3 we get $x = k \log_2 3 \approx 1.58k$. A trit is thus worth about 1.58 bits.

2.4: We assume an alphabet with two symbols a_1 and a_2, with probabilities P_1 and P_2, respectively. Since $P_1 + P_2 = 1$, the entropy of the alphabet is $-P_1 \log_2 P_1 - (1 - P_1) \log_2 (1 - P_1)$. Table Ans.3 shows the entropies for certain values of the probabilities. When $P_1 = P_2$, at least 1 bit is required to encode each symbol. However, when the probabilities are very different, the minimum number of bits required per symbol drops significantly. We may not be able to develop a compression method using 0.08 bits per symbol but we know that when $P_1 = 99\%$, this is the theoretical minimum.

P_1	P_2	Entropy
99	1	0.08
90	10	0.47
80	20	0.72
70	30	0.88
60	40	0.97
50	50	1.00

Table Ans.3: Probabilities and Entropies of Two Symbols.

2.5: It is easy to see that the unary code satisfies the prefix property, so it definitely can be used as a variable-size code. Since its length is approximately $\log_2 n$, it makes sense to use it in cases were the input data consists of integers n with probabilities $P(n) \approx 2^{-n}$. If the data lends itself to the use of the unary code, the entire Huffman algorithm can be skipped, and the codes of all the symbols can easily and quickly be constructed before compression or decompression starts.

2.6: The triplet $(n, 1, n)$ defines the standard n-bit binary codes, as can be verified by direct construction. The number of such codes is easily seen to be

$$\frac{2^{n+1} - 2^n}{2^1 - 1} = 2^n.$$

The triplet $(0, 0, \infty)$ defines the codes 0, 10, 110, 1110,... which are the unary codes but assigned to the integers 0, 1, 2,... instead of 1, 2, 3,... .

2.7: The number is $(2^{30} - 2^1)/(2^1 - 1) \approx$ A billion.

2.8: This is straightforward. Table Ans.4 shows the code. There are only three different codewords since "start" and "stop" are so close, but there are many codes since "start" is large.

n	$a =$ $10 + n \cdot 2$	nth codeword	Number of codewords	Range of integers
0	10	$0 \underbrace{x...x}_{10}$	$2^{10} = 1K$	0–1023
1	12	$10 \underbrace{xx...x}_{12}$	$2^{12} = 4K$	1024–5119
2	14	$11 \underbrace{xx...xx}_{14}$	$2^{14} = 16K$	5120–21503
		Total	21504	

Table Ans.4: The General Unary Code (10,2,14).

2.9: Each part of C_4 is the standard binary code of some integer, so it starts with a 1. A part that starts with a 0 thus signals to the decoder that this is the last bit of the code.

2.10: Subsequent splits can be done in different ways, but Table Ans.5 shows one way of assigning Shannon-Fano codes to the 7 symbols.

	Prob.	Steps				Final
1.	0.25	1	1			:11
2.	0.20	1	0			:101
3.	0.15	1	0			:100
4.	0.15	0	1			:01
5.	0.10	0	0	1		:001
6.	0.10	0	0	0	0	:0001
7.	0.05	0	0	0	0	:0000

Table Ans.5: Shannon-Fano Example.

The average size in this case is $0.25 \times 2 + 0.20 \times 3 + 0.15 \times 3 + 0.15 \times 2 + 0.10 \times 3 + 0.10 \times 4 + 0.05 \times 4 = 2.75$ bits/symbols.

2.11: This is immediate $-2(0.25 \times \log_2 0.25) - 4(0.125 \times \log_2 0.125) = 2.5$.

2.12: Imagine a large alphabet where all the symbols have (about) the same probability. Since the alphabet is large, that probability will be small, resulting in long codes. Imagine the other extreme case, where certain symbols have high probabilities (and, therefore, short codes). Since the probabilities have to add up to 1, the rest of the symbols will have low probabilities (and, therefore, long codes). We thus see that the size of a code depends on the probability, but is indirectly affected by the size of the alphabet.

2.13: Answer not provided.

2.14: Figure Ans.6 shows Huffman codes for 5, 6, 7, and 8 symbols with equal probabilities. In the case where n is a power of 2, the codes are simply the fixed-sized ones. In other cases the codes are very close to fixed-size. This shows that symbols with equal probabilities do not benefit from variable-size codes. (This is another way of saying that random text cannot be compressed.) Table Ans.7 shows the codes, their average sizes and variances.

2.15: The number of groups increases exponentially from 2^s to $2^{s+n} = 2^s \times 2^n$.

2.16: Figure Ans.8 shows how the loop continues until the heap shrinks to just one node that is the single pointer 2. Thus the total frequency (which happens to be 100 in our example) is stored in A[2]. All other frequencies have been replaced by pointers. Figure Ans.9a shows the heaps generated during the loop.

2.17: The code lengths for the seven symbols are 2, 2, 3, 3, 4, 3, and 4 bits. This can also be verified from the Huffman code-tree of Figure Ans.9b. A set of codes derived from this tree is shown in the following table:

Count:	25	20	13	17	9	11	5
Code:	01	11	101	000	0011	100	0010
Length:	2	2	3	3	4	3	4

2.18: A symbol with high frequency of occurrence should be assigned a shorter code. Therefore it has to appear high in the tree. The requirement that at each level the frequencies be sorted from left to right is artificial. In principle it is not necessary but it simplifies the process of updating the tree.

2.19: Figure Ans.10 shows the initial tree and how it is updated in the 11 steps (a) through (k). Notice how the *eof* symbol gets assigned different codes all the time, and how the differnt symbols move about in the tree and change their codes. Code 10, e.g., is the code of symbol "i" in steps (f) and (i), but is the code of "s" in steps (e) and (j). The code of a blank space is 011 in step (h), but 00 in step (k).

The final output is: "'s'0'i'00'r'100'␣'1010000'd'011101000". A total of 62 bits. The compression ratio is thus $62/88 \approx 0.7$.

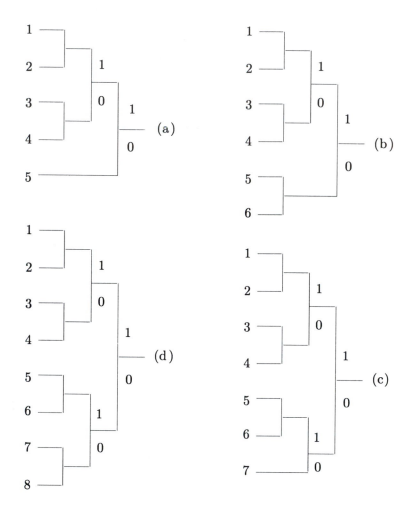

Figure Ans.6: Huffman Codes for Equal Probabilities.

										Avg.	
n	p	a_1	a_2	a_3	a_4	a_5	a_6	a_7	a_8	size	Var.
5	0.200	111	110	101	100	0				2.6	0.64
6	0.167	111	110	101	100	01	00			2.672	0.2227
7	0.143	111	110	101	100	011	010	00		2.86	0.1226
8	0.125	111	110	101	100	011	010	001	000	3	0

Table Ans.7: Huffman Codes for 5–8 Symbols.

1	2	3	4	5	6	7	8	9	10	11	12	13	14
[7	11	6	8	9]	24	14	25	20	6	17	7	6	7

1	2	3	4	5	6	7	8	9	10	11	12	13	14
[11	9	8	6]		24	14	25	20	6	17	7	6	7

1	2	3	4		5	6	7	8	9	10	11	12	13	14
[11	9	8	6]	17+14	24	14	25	20	6	17	7	6	7

1	2	3	4	5	6	7	8	9	10	11	12	13	14
[5	9	8	6]	31	24	5	25	20	6	5	7	6	7

1	2	3	4	5	6	7	8	9	10	11	12	13	14
[9	6	8	5]	31	24	5	25	20	6	5	7	6	7

1	2	3	4	5	6	7	8	9	10	11	12	13	14
[6	8	5]		31	24	5	25	20	6	5	7	6	7

1	2	3		4	5	6	7	8	9	10	11	12	13	14
[6	8	5]	20+24	31	24	5	25	20	6	5	7	6	7

1	2	3	4	5	6	7	8	9	10	11	12	13	14
[4	8	5]	44	31	4	5	25	4	6	5	7	6	7

1	2	3	4	5	6	7	8	9	10	11	12	13	14
[8	5	4]	44	31	4	5	25	4	6	5	7	6	7

1	2	3	4	5	6	7	8	9	10	11	12	13	14
[5	4]		44	31	4	5	25	4	6	5	7	6	7

1	2		3	4	5	6	7	8	9	10	11	12	13	14
[5	4]	25+31	44	31	4	5	25	4	6	5	7	6	7

1	2	3	4	5	6	7	8	9	10	11	12	13	14
[3	4]	56	44	3	4	5	3	4	6	5	7	6	7

1	2	3	4	5	6	7	8	9	10	11	12	13	14
[4	3]	56	44	3	4	5	3	4	6	5	7	6	7

1	2	3	4	5	6	7	8	9	10	11	12	13	14
[3]		56	44	3	4	5	3	4	6	5	7	6	7

1		2	3	4	5	6	7	8	9	10	11	12	13	14
[3]	56+44	56	44	3	4	5	3	4	6	5	7	6	7

1	2	3	4	5	6	7	8	9	10	11	12	13	14
[2]	100	2	2	3	4	5	3	4	6	5	7	6	7

Figure Ans.8: Sifting the Heap.

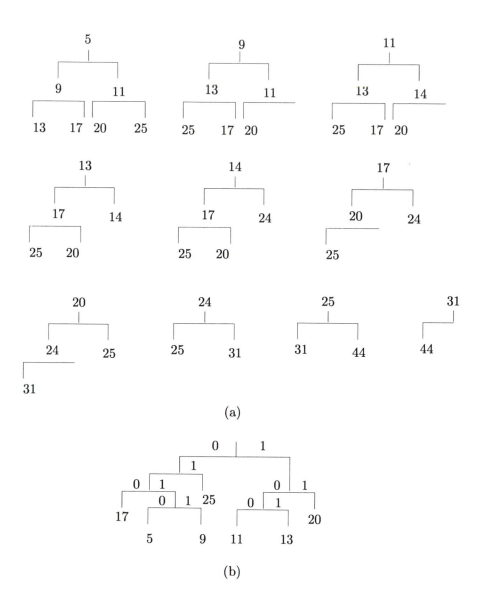

(a)

(b)

Figure Ans.9: (a) Heaps. (b) Huffman Code-Tree.

Initial tree

(a). Input: s. Output: 's'.
$eof\ s_1$

(b). Input: i. Output: 0'i'.
$eof\ i_1\ 1\ s_1$

(c). Input: r. Output: 00'r'.
$eof\ r_1\ 1\ i_1\ 2\ s_1 \rightarrow$
$eof\ r_1\ 1\ i_1\ s_1\ 2$

(d). Input: ␣. Output: 100'␣'.
$eof\ ␣_1\ 1\ r_1\ 2\ i_1\ s_1\ 3 \rightarrow$
$eof\ ␣_1\ 1\ r_1\ s_1\ i_1\ 2\ 2$

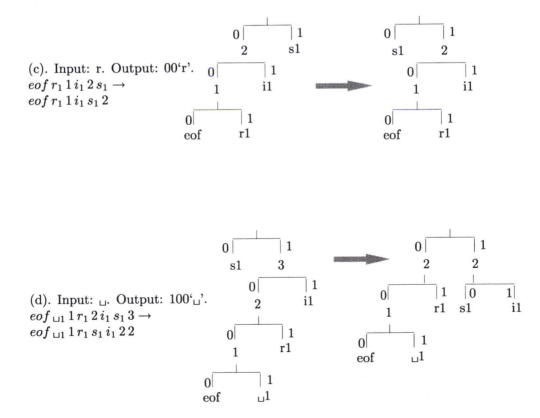

Figure Ans.10: Exercise 2.19. Part I.

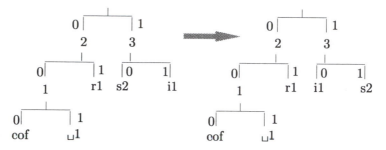

(e). Input: s. Output: 10.

$eof_{\sqcup 1} 1\, r_1\, s_2\, i_1\, 2\, 3 \rightarrow$

$eof_{\sqcup 1} 1\, r_1\, i_1\, s_2\, 2\, 3$

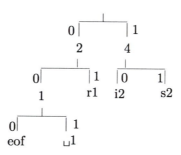

(f). Input: i. Output: 10.

$eof_{\sqcup 1} 1\, r_1\, i_2\, s_2\, 2\, 4$

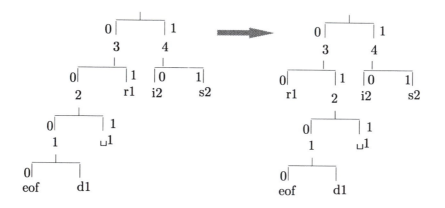

(g). Input: d. Output: 000'd'.

$eof\, d_1\, 1_{\sqcup 1} 2\, r_1\, i_2\, s_2\, 3\, 4 \rightarrow$

$eof\, d_1\, 1_{\sqcup 1} r_1\, 2\, i_2\, s_2\, 3\, 4$

Figure Ans.10: Exercise 2.19. Part II.

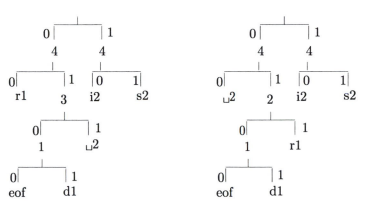

(h). Input: ␣. Output: 011.
$eof\, d_1\, 1\, {}_{␣2}\, r_1\, 3\, i_2\, s_2\, 4\, 4 \to$
$eof\, d_1\, 1\, r_1\, {}_{␣2}\, 2\, i_2\, s_2\, 4\, 4$

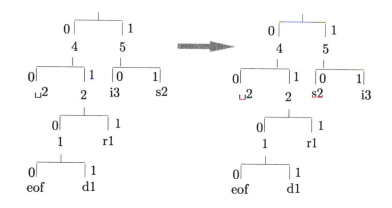

(i). Input: i. Output: 10.
$eof\, d_1\, 1\, r_1\, {}_{␣2}\, 2\, i_3\, s_2\, 4\, 5 \to$
$eof\, d_1\, 1\, r_1\, {}_{␣2}\, 2\, s_2\, i_3\, 4\, 5$

Figure Ans.10: Exercise 2.19. Part III.

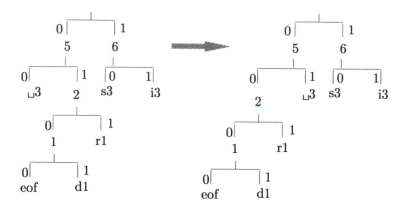

(k). Input: ⊔. Output: 00.

$eof\ d_1\ 1\ r_1\ {}_{⊔3}\ 2\ s_3\ i_3\ 5\ 6 →$

$eof\ d_1\ 1\ r_1\ 2\ {}_{⊔3}\ s_3\ i_3\ 5\ 6$

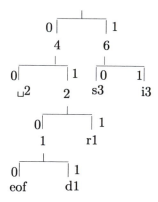

(j). Input: s. Output: 10.

$eof\ d_1\ 1\ r_1\ {}_{⊔2}\ 2\ s_3\ i_3\ 4\ 6$

Figure Ans.10: Exercise 2.19. Part IV.

2.20: A simple calculation shows that the average size of a token in Table 2.25 is about 9 bits. In stage 2, each 8-bit byte will be replaced, on the average, by a 9-bit token, resulting in an expansion factor of $9/8 = 1.125$ or 12.5%.

2.21: The decompressor will interpret the input data as "111110 0110 11000 0...", which is the string "XRP...".

2.22: A typical fax machine scans lines that are about 8.2 inches wide (≈ 208 mm). A blank scan line thus produces 1,664 consecutive white pels.

2.23: There may be fax machines (now or in the future) built for wider paper, so the Group 3 code was designed to accomodate them.

2.24: The code of a run length of one white pel is 000111, and that of one black pel is 010. Two consecutive pels of different colors are thus coded into 9 bits. Since the uncoded data requires just two bits (01 or 10), the compression factor is $9/2=4.5$ (the compressed stream is 4.5 times longer than the uncompressed one).

2.25: Figure Ans.11 shows the modes and the actual code generated from the two lines.

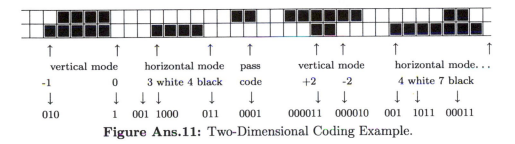

Figure Ans.11: Two-Dimensional Coding Example.

2.26: Table Ans.12 shows the steps in encoding the string $a_2a_2a_2a_2$. Because of the high probability of a_2 the low and high variables start at very different values and approach each other slowly.

a_2	$0.0 + (1.0 - 0.0) \times 0.023162=0.023162$
	$0.0 + (1.0 - 0.0) \times 0.998162=0.998162$
a_2	$0.023162 + .975 \times 0.023162=0.04574495$
	$0.023162 + .975 \times 0.998162=0.99636995$
a_2	$0.04574495 + 0.950625 \times 0.023162=0.06776322625$
	$0.04574495 + 0.950625 \times 0.998162=0.99462270125$
a_2	$0.06776322625 + 0.926859375 \times 0.023162=0.08923124309375$
	$0.06776322625 + 0.926859375 \times 0.998162=0.99291913371875$

Table Ans.12: Encoding the String $a_2a_2a_2a_2$.

2.27: If $0.999\ldots < 1$ then their average $a = (1 + 0.999\ldots)/2$ would be a number between $0.999\ldots$ and 1, but there is no way to write a. It is impossible to give it more digits than to $0.999\ldots$ since the latter already has an infinite number of digits. It is impossible to make the digits any bigger since they are already 9s. This is why the infinite fraction $0.999\ldots$ must be equal to 1.

2.28: An argument similar to the one in the previous exercise shows that there are two ways of writing this number. It can be written either as $0.1000\ldots$ or $0.0111\ldots$.

2.29: In practice, the eof symbol has to be included in the original table of frequencies and probabilities. This symbol is the last to be encoded and the decoder stops when it detects an eof.

2.30: The encoding steps are simple (see first example on page 69). We start with the interval $[0, 1)$. The first symbol a_2 reduces the interval to $[0.4, 0.9)$. The second one, to $[0.6, 0.85)$, the third one to $[0.7, 0.825)$ and the eof symbol, to $[0.8125, 0.8250)$. The approximate binary values of the last interval are 0.1101000000 and 0.1101001100, so we select the 7-bit number 1101000 as our code.

The probability of the string "$a_2 a_2 a_2 \text{eof}$" is $(0.5)^3 \times 0.1 = 0.0125$, but since $-\log_2 0.125 \approx 6.322$ it follows that the practical minimum code size is 7 bits.

2.31: In practice, an encoder may encode texts other than English, such as a foreign language or the source code of a computer program. Even in English there are some examples of a "q" not followed by a "u", such as in this sentence. (The author has noticed that science-fiction writers tend to use non-English sounding words, such as "Qaal," to name characters in their works.)

2.32: $256^2 = 65,536$, a manageable number, but $256^3 = 16,777,216$, perhaps too big for a practical implementation, unless a sophisticated data structure is used, or unless the encoder gets rid of older data from time to time.

2.33: A color or gray-scale image with 4-bit pixels. Each symbol is a pixel, and there are 16 different ones.

2.34: An object file generated by a compiler or an assembler normally has several distinct parts including the machine instructions, symbol table, relocation bits, and constants. Such parts may have different bit distributions.

2.35: The alphabet has to be extended, in such a case, to include one more symbol. If the original alphabet consisted of all the possible 256 8-bit bytes, it should be extended to 9-bit symbols, and should include 257 values.

2.36: Table Ans.13 shows the groups generated in both cases and makes it clear why these particular probabilities were assigned.

Context	f	p
abc→ a_1	1	1/20
→ a_2	1	1/20
→ a_3	1	1/20
→ a_4	1	1/20
→ a_5	1	1/20
→ a_6	1	1/20
→ a_7	1	1/20
→ a_8	1	1/20
→ a_9	1	1/20
→ a_{10}	1	1/20
Esc	10	10/20
Total	20	

Context	f	p
abc→x	10	10/11
Esc	1	1/11

Table Ans.13: Stable vs. Variable Data.

2.37: The "d" is added to the order-0 contexts with frequency 1. The escape frequency should be incremented from 5 to 6, bringing the total frequencies from 19 up to 21. The probability assigned to the new "d" is therefore 1/21, and that assigned to the escape is 6/21. All other probabilities are reduced from $x/19$ to $x/21$.

2.38: The new "d" would require switching from order-2 to order-0, sending two escapes that take 1 and 1.32 bits. The "d" is now found in order-0 with probability 1/21, so it is encoded in 4.39 bits. The total number of bits required to encode the second "d" is thus $1 + 1.32 + 4.39 = 6.71$, still greater than 5.

2.39: The first three cases don't change. They still code a symbol with 1, 1.32, and 6.57 bits, which is less than the 8 bits required for a 256-symbol alphabet without compression. Case 4 is different since the "d" is now encoded with a probability of 1/256, producing 8 instead of 4.8 bits. The total number of bits required to encode the "d" in case 4 is now $1 + 1.32 + 1.93 + 8 = 12.25$.

2.40: The final trie is shown in Figure Ans.14.

3.1: The size of the output stream is $N[48 - 28P] = N[48 - 25.2] = 22.8N$. The size of the input stream is, as before, $40N$. The compression factor is thus $40/22.8 \approx 1.75$.

3.2: The next step matches the space and encodes the string "␣e".

sir␣sid|␣eastman␣easily␣	⇒	(4,1,"e")
sir␣sid␣e|astman␣easily␣te	⇒	(0,0,"a")

and the next one matches nothing and encodes the "a".

3.3: The first two characters "CA" at positions 17–18 are a repeat of the "CA" at positions 9–10, so they will be encoded as a string of length 2 at offset $18 - 10 = 8$. The next two characters "AC" at positions 19–20 are a repeat of the string at positions 8–9, so they will be encoded as a string of length 2 at offset $20 - 9 = 11$.

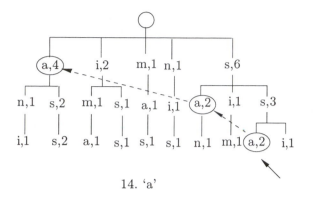

14. 'a'

Figure Ans.14: Final Trie of "assanissimassa".

3.4: The decoder interprets the first 1 of the end marker as the start of a token. The second 1 is interpreted as the prefix of a 7-bit offset. The next 7 bits are 0 and they identify the end-marker as such, since a "normal" offset cannot be zero.

3.5: This is straightforward. The remaining steps are shown in Table Ans.15

Dictionary		Token		Dictionary		Token
15	"ᵘt"	(4, "t")		21	"ᵘsi"	(19,"i")
16	"e"	(0, "e")		22	"c"	(0, "c")
17	"as"	(8, "s")		23	"k"	(0, "k")
18	"es"	(16,"s")		24	"ᵘse"	(19,"e")
19	"ᵘs"	(4, "s")		25	"al"	(8, "l")
20	"ea"	(4, "a")		26	"s(eof)"	(1, "(eof)")

Table Ans.15: Next 12 Encoding Steps in LZ78.

3.6: Table Ans.16 shows the last three steps.

p_src	3 chars	Hash index	P	Output	Binary output
11	"hᵘt"	7	any→7	h	01101000
12	"ᵘth"	5	5→5	4,7	0000|0011|00000111
16	"ws"			ws	01110111|01110011

Table Ans.16: Last Steps of Encoding "that thatch thaws".

The final compressed stream consists of 1 control word followed by 11 items (9 literals and 2 copy items)
0000010010000000|01110100|01101000|01100001|01110100|00100000|0000|0011
|00000101|01100011|01101000|0000|0011|00000111|01110111|01110011.

3.7: Following the steps in the text, the output emitted by the encoder is

97 (a), 108 (1), 102 (f), 32 (␣), 101 (e), 97 (a), 116 (t), 115 (s), 32 (␣), 256 (al), 102 (f), 265 (alf), 97 (a),

and the following new entries are added to the dictionary

(256: al), (257: lf), (258: f␣), (259: ␣e), (260: ea), (261: at), (262: ts), (263: s␣), (264: ␣a), (265: alf), (266: alfa).

3.8: The encoder inputs the first "a" into I, searches and finds "a" in the dictionary. It inputs the next "a" but finds that Ix, which is now "aa", is not in the dictionary. The encoder thus adds string "aa" to the dictionary as entry 256 and outputs the token 97 (a). Variable I is initialized to the second "a". The third "a" is input, so Ix is the string "aa", which is now in the dictionary. I becomes this string, and the fourth "a" is input. Ix is now "aaa" which is not in the dictionary. The encoder thus adds string "aaa" to the dictionary as entry 257 and outputs 256 (aa). I is initialized to the fourth "a". Continuing this process is straightforward.

The result is that strings "aa", "aaa", "aaaa",... are added to the dictionary as entries 256, 257, 258,..., and the output is

$$97 \text{ (a)}, 256 \text{ (aa)}, 257 \text{ (aaa)}, 258 \text{ (aaaa)},\dots$$

The output consists of pointers pointing to longer and longer strings of as. The first k pointers thus point at strings whose total length is $1 + 2 + \cdots + k = (k + k^2)/2$.

Assuming an input stream that consists of one million as, we can find the size of the compressed output stream by solving the quadratic equation $(k + k^2)/2 = 1000000$ for the unknown k. The solution is $k \approx 1414$. The original, 8-million bit input is thus compressed into 1414 pointers, each at least 9-bit (and in practice, probably 16-bit) long. The compression factor is thus either $8M/(1414 \times 9) \approx 628.6$ or $8M/(1414 \times 16) \approx 353.6$.

This is an impressive result but such input streams are rare (notice that this particular input can best be compressed by generating an output stream containing just "1000000 a", and without using LZW).

3.9: We simply follow the decoding steps described in the text. The results are:

1. Input 97. This is in the dictionary so set I="a" and output "a". String "ax" needs to be saved in the dictionary but x is still unknown..

2. Input 108. This is in the dictionary so set J="l" and output "l". Save "al" in entry 256. Set I="l".

3. Input 102. This is in the dictionary so set J="f" and output "f". Save "lf" in entry 257. Set I="f".

4. Input 32. This is in the dictionary so set J="␣" and output "␣". Save "f␣" in entry 258. Set I="␣".

5. Input 101. This is in the dictionary so set J="e" and output "e". Save "␣e" in entry 259. Set I="e".

6. Input 97. This is in the dictionary so set J="a" and output "a". Save "ea" in entry 260. Set I="a".

7. Input 116. This is in the dictionary so set J="t" and output "t". Save "at" in entry 261. Set I="t".

8. Input 115. This is in the dictionary so set J="s" and output "s". Save "ts" in entry 262. Set I="t".

9. Input 32. This is in the dictionary so set J="␣" and output "␣". Save "s␣" in entry 263. Set I="␣".

10. Input 256. This is in the dictionary so set J="al" and output "al". Save "␣a" in entry 264. Set I="al".

11. Input 102. This is in the dictionary so set J="f" and output "f". Save "alf" in entry 265. Set I="f".

12. Input 265. This has just been saved in the dictionary so set J="alf" and output "alf". Save "fa" in dictionary entry 266. Set I="alf".

13. Input 97. This is in the dictionary so set J="a" and output "a". Save "alfa" in entry 267 (even though it will never be used). Set I="a".

14. Read eof. Stop.

3.10: Assuming that the dictionary is initialized to just the two entries (1: **a**) and (2: **b**). The encoder outputs

1 (a), 2 (b), 3 (ab), 5(aba), 4(ba), 7 (bab), 6 (abab), 9 (ababa), 8 (baba),...

and adds the new entries (3: **ab**), (4: **ba**), (5: **aba**), (6: **abab**), (7: **bab**), (8: **baba**), (9: **ababa**), (10: **ababab**), (11: **babab**),... to the dictionary. This regular behavior can be analyzed and the kth output pointer and dictionary entry predicted, but the effort is probably not worth it.

3.11: The answer to exercise 3.8 shows the relation between the size of the compressed file and the size of the largest dictionary string for the "worst case" situation (input that creates the longest strings). For a 1Mbyte input stream, there will be 1,414 strings in the dictionary, the largest of which is 1,414 symbols long.

3.12: This is straightforward (Table Ans.17) but not very efficient since only one two-symbol dictionary phrase is used.

Step	Input	Output	S	Add to dict.	S'
	swiss␣miss				
1	s	115	s	—	s
2	w	119	w	256-sw	w
3	i	105	i	257-wi	i
4	s	115	s	258-is	s
5	s	115	s	259-ss	s
6	␣	32	␣	260-s␣	␣
7	m	109	m	261-␣m	m
8	is	258	is	262-mis	is
9	s	115	s	263-iss	s

Table Ans.17: LZMW Compression of "swiss miss".

Step	Input	Output	S	Add to dict.	S'
	yabbadabbadabbadoo				
1	y	121	y	—	y
2	a	97	a	256-ya	a
3	b	98	b	257-ab	b
4	b	98	b	258-bb	b
5	a	97	a	259-ba	a
6	d	100	a	260-ad	a
7	ab	257	ab	261-dab	ab
8	ba	259	ba	262-abba	ba
9	dab	261	dab	263-badab	dab
10	ba	259	ba	264-dabba	ba
11	d	100	d	265-bad	d
12	o	111	o	266-do	o
13	o	111	o	267-o	o

Table Ans.18: LZMW Compression of "yabbadabbadabbadoo".

3.13: Table Ans.18 shows all the steps. In spite of the short input, the result is quite good (13 codes to compress 18-symbols) because the input contains concentrations of as and bs.

3.14: 1. The encoder starts by shifting the first two symbols "xy" to the search buffer, outputting them as literals and initializing all locations of the index table to the null pointer.

2. The current symbol is "a" (the first "a") and the context is "xy". It is hashed to, say, 5, but location 5 of the index table contains a null pointer, so P is null. Location 5 is set to point to the first "a", which is then output as a literal. The data in the encoder's buffer is shifted to the left.

3. The current symbol is the second "a" and the context is "ya". It is hashed to, say, 1, but location 1 of the index table contains a null pointer, so P is null. Location 1 is set to point to the second "a", which is then output as a literal. The data in the encoder's buffer is shifted to the left.

4. The current symbol is the third "a" and the context is "aa". It is hashed to, say, 2, but location 2 of the index table contains a null pointer, so P is null. Location 2 is set to point to the third "a", which is then output as a literal. The data in the encoder's buffer is shifted to the left.

5. The current symbol is the fourth "a" and the context is "aa". We know from step 4 that it is hashed to 2, and location 2 of the index table points to the third "a". Location 2 is set to point to the fourth "a", and the encoder tries to match the string starting with the third "a" to the string starting with the fourth "a". Assuming that the look-ahead buffer is full of as, the match length L will be the size of that buffer. The encoded value of L will be written to the compressed stream, and the data in the buffer shifted L positions to the left.

6. If the original input stream is long, more a's will be shifted into the look-ahead buffer, and this step will also result in a match of length L. If only n as remain in the input stream, they will be matched, and the encoded value of n output.

The compressed stream will consist of the three literals "**x**", "**y**", and "**a**", followed by (perhaps several values of) L, and possibly ending with a smaller value.

3.15: T percent of the compressed stream is made up of literals, some appearing consecutively (and thus getting the flag "1" for two literals, half a bit per literal) and others with a match length following them (and thus getting the flag "01", one bit for the literal). We assume that two thirds of the literals appear consecutively and one third are followed by match lengths. The total number of flag bits created for literals is thus

$$\frac{2}{3}T \times 0.5 + \frac{1}{3}T \times 1.$$

A similar argument for the match lengths yields

$$\frac{2}{3}(1 - T) \times 2 + \frac{1}{3}(1 - T) \times 1$$

for the total number of the flag bits. We now write the equation

$$\frac{2}{3}T \times 0.5 + \frac{1}{3}T \times 1 + \frac{2}{3}(1 - T) \times 2 + \frac{1}{3}(1 - T) \times 1 = 1,$$

which is solved to yield $T = 2/3$. This means that if two thirds of the items in the compressed stream are literals, there would be 1 flag bit per item on the average. More literals would result in fewer flag bits.

3.16: The first three ones indicate six literals. The following 01 indicates a literal (b) followed by a match length (of 3). The 10 is the code of match length 3, and the last 1 indicates two more literals ("**x**" and "**y**").

4.1: Substituting $f = 0$ in Equation (4.1), we get the simple expression

$$G_0 = \frac{1}{2}C_0 \sum_{t=0}^{7} p_t \cos\left(\frac{(2t + 1)0\pi}{16}\right) = \frac{1}{2}\frac{1}{\sqrt{2}} \sum_{t=0}^{7} p_t$$

$$= \frac{1}{\sqrt{8}}(11 + 22 + 33 + 44 + 55 + 66 + 77 + 88) \approx 140.$$

The reason for the name "DC coefficient" is that G_0 does not contain any sinusoidals. It simply equals some multiple of the eight pixels (rather, some multiple of their average).

4.2: The explicit expression is

$$G_5 = \frac{1}{2}C_5 \sum_{t=0}^{7} p_t \cos\left(\frac{(2t+1)5\pi}{16}\right)$$

$$= \frac{1}{2}\left(11\cos\left(\frac{5\pi}{16}\right) + 22\cos\left(\frac{3\times5\pi}{16}\right) + 33\cos\left(\frac{5\times5\pi}{16}\right) + 44\cos\left(\frac{7\times5\pi}{16}\right) + \right.$$

$$\left.55\cos\left(\frac{9\times5\pi}{16}\right) + 66\cos\left(\frac{11\times5\pi}{16}\right) + 77\cos\left(\frac{13\times5\pi}{16}\right) + 88\cos\left(\frac{15\times5\pi}{16}\right)\right)$$

$$= -2,$$

from which it is clear that this coefficient represents the contributions of the sinusoidals with frequencies $5t\pi/16$ (multiples of $5\pi/16$). The fact that it equals -2 means that these sinusoidals do not contribute much to our eight pixels.

4.3: When the following *Mathematica*[TM] code is applied to Table 4.11b it creates a data unit with 64 pixels, all having the value 140, which is the average value of the pixels in the original data unit 4.8.

```
Cr[i_]:=If[i==0, 1/Sqrt[2], 1];
IDCT[x_,y_]:={(1/4)Sum[Cr[i]Cr[j]G[[i+1,j+1]]Quant[[i+1,j+1]]*
  Cos[(2x+1)i Pi/16]Cos[(2y+1)j Pi/16], {i,0,7,1}, {j,0,7,1}]};
```

4.4: Selecting $R = 1$ has produced the quantization coefficients of Table Ans.19a and the quantized data unit of Table Ans.19b. This table has 18 nonzero coefficients which, when used to reconstruct the original data unit, produce Table Ans.20, only a small improvement over Table 4.9.

4.5: The zig-zag sequence is $1118, 2, 0, -2, \underbrace{0, \ldots, 0}_{12}, -1, 0, \ldots$ (there are only four nonzero coefficients).

4.6: Perhaps the simplest way is to manually figure out the zig-zag path and to record it in an array **zz** of structures, where each structure contains a pair of coordinates for the path as shown, e.g., in Figure Ans.21.

 If the two components of a structure are **zz.r** and **zz.c**, then the zig-zag traversal can be done by a loop of the form :

```
for (i=0; i<64; i++){
row:=zz[i].r; col:=zz[i].c
...data_unit[row][col]...}
```

4.7: It is located in row 3 column 5, so it is encoded as 1110|101.

1	2	3	4	5	6	7	8
2	3	4	5	6	7	8	9
3	4	5	6	7	8	9	10
4	5	6	7	8	9	10	11
5	6	7	8	9	10	11	12
6	7	8	9	10	11	12	13
7	8	9	10	11	12	13	14
8	9	10	11	12	13	14	15

1118.	3	2	-1	1	0	0	0
-1	0	1	1	1	0	0	0
-3	-2	0	-2	0	0	0	0
-1	-2	0	0	0	0	0	0
0	0	0	1	0	0	0	0
0	0	0	0	0	0	0	0
0	0	0	-1	1	0	0	0
0	0	0	1	0	0	0	0

(a)   (b)

Table Ans.19: (a): The Quantization table $1 + (i + j) \times 1$. (b): Quantized Coefficients Produced by (a).

139	139	138	139	139	138	139	140
140	140	140	139	139	139	139	140
142	141	140	140	140	139	139	140
142	141	140	140	140	140	139	139
142	141	140	140	140	140	140	139
140	140	140	140	139	139	139	141
140	140	140	140	139	139	140	140
139	140	141	140	139	138	139	140

Table Ans.20: Restored data unit of Table 4.8.

(0,0)	(0,1)	(1,0)	(2,0)	(1,1)	(0,2)	(0,3)	(1,2)
(2,1)	(3,0)	(4,0)	(3,1)	(2,2)	(1,3)	(0,4)	(0,5)
(1,4)	(2,3)	(3,2)	(4,1)	(5,0)	(6,0)	(5,1)	(4,2)
(3,3)	(2,4)	(1,5)	(0,6)	(0,7)	(1,6)	(2,5)	(3,4)
(4,3)	(5,2)	(6,1)	(7,0)	(7,1)	(6,2)	(5,3)	(4,4)
(3,5)	(2,6)	(1,7)	(2,7)	(3,6)	(4,5)	(5,4)	(6,3)
(7,2)	(7,3)	(6,4)	(5,5)	(4,6)	(3,7)	(4,7)	(5,6)
(6,5)	(7,4)	(7,5)	(6,6)	(5,7)	(6,7)	(7,6)	(7,7)

Figure Ans.21: Coordinates for the Zig-Zag Path.

4.8: Twelve consecutive zeros precede this coefficient, so $Z = 12$. The coefficient itself is found in Table 4.13 in row 1, column 0, so $R = 1$ and $C = 0$. Assuming that the Huffman code in position $(R, Z) = (1, 12)$ of Table 4.14 is 1110101, the final code emitted for 1 is 1110101|.

4.9: This is shown by adding the largest four n-bit numbers, $\underbrace{11\ldots1}_{n}$. Adding two such numbers produces the $n+1$-bit number $1\underbrace{1\ldots1}_{n}0$. Adding two of these $n+1$-bit numbers produces $1\underbrace{1\ldots10}_{n}0$, an $n + 2$-bit number.

4.10: Table Ans.22 summarizes the results. Notice how a 1-pixel with a context of 00 is assigned high probability after being seen 3 times.

#	Pixel	Context	Counts	Probability	New counts
5	0	10=2	1,1	1/2	2,1
6	1	00=0	1,3	3/4	1,4
7	0	11=3	1,1	1/2	2,1
8	1	10=2	2,1	1/3	2,2

Table Ans.22: Counts and Probabilities for Next four Pixels.

4.11: Such a thing is possible for the encoder but not for the decoder. A compression method using "future" pixels in the context is useless because its output would be impossible to decompress.

4.12: The two previously seen neighbors of P=8 are A=1 and B=11. P is thus in the central region, where all codes start with a zero, and L=1, H=11. The computations are straightforward:

$$k = \lfloor \log_2(11 - 1 + 1) \rfloor = 3; \qquad a = 2^{3+1} - 11 = 5; \qquad b = 2(11 - 2^3) = 6.$$

Table Ans.23 lists the five 3-bit codes and six 4-bit codes for the central region. The code for 8 is thus 0|111.

The two previously seen neighbors of P=7 are A=2 and B=5. P is thus in the right outer region, where all codes start with 11, and L=2, H=7. We are looking for the code of $7 - 5 = 2$. Choosing $m = 1$ yields, from Table 4.25, the code 11|01.

The two previously seen neighbors of P=0 are A=3 and B=5. P is thus in the left outer region, where all codes start with 10, and L=3, H=5. We are looking for the code of $3 - 0 = 3$. Choosing $m = 1$ yields, from Table 4.25, the code 10|100.

Pixel P	Region code	Pixel code
1	0	0000
2	0	0010
3	0	0100
4	0	011
5	0	100
6	0	101
7	0	110
8	0	111
9	0	0001
10	0	0011
11	0	0101

Table Ans.23: The Codes for a Central Region.

4.13: The first term can be written

$$4 = \frac{n^2}{2^{-2}n^2} = \frac{n^2}{2^{2\log n - 2}}.$$

Terms in the sequence thus contain powers of 2 that go from 0 to $2\log_2 n - 2$, showing that there are $2\log_2 n - 1$ terms.

4.14: Because the decoder has to resolve ties in the same way as the encoder.

4.15: Because this will result in a weighted sum whose value is in the same range as the values of the pixels. If pixel values are, e.g., in the range $[0, 15]$ and the weights add up to 2, a prediction may result in values of up to 31.

4.16: Each of the three weights 0.0039, -0.0351, and 0.3164 are used twice. The sum of the weights is thus 0.5704 and the result of dividing each weight by this sum is 0.0068, -0.0615, and 0.5547. It is easy to verify that the sum of the renormalized weights $2(0.0068 - 0.0615 + 0.5547)$ equals 1.

4.17: Using Mathematica^{TM} it is easy to obtain this integral separately for negative and non-negative values of x.

$$\int L(V, x)\, dx = \begin{cases} \frac{-1}{V \exp\left(\sqrt{\frac{2}{V}}x\right)}, & x \geq 0; \\ \frac{1}{\sqrt{2V}} \exp\left(\sqrt{\frac{2}{V}}x\right), & x < 0. \end{cases}$$

4.18: An archive of static images. NASA has a large archive of images taken by various satellites. They should be kept highly compressed, but they never change so each image has to be compressed only once. A slow encoder is therefore acceptable but a fast decoder is certainly handy. Another example is an art collection. Many museums have digitized their collection of paintings, and those are also static.

4.19: The decoder knows this pixel since it knows the value of average $\mu[i-1, j] = 0.5(I[2i-2, 2j] + I[2i-1, 2j+1])$ and since it has already decoded pixel $I[2i-2, 2j]$

4.20: When the decoder inputs the 5, it knows that the difference between p (the pixel being decoded) and the reference pixel starts at position 6 (counting from left). Since bit 6 of the reference pixel is 0, that of p must be 1.

4.21: Yes, but compression would suffer. One way to apply this method is to separate each byte into two 4-bit pixels and encode each pixel separately. This approach is bad since the prefix and suffix of a 4-bit pixel may many times require more than 4 bits. Another approach is to ignore the fact that a byte contains two pixels, and use the method as originally described. This may still compress the image, but is not very efficient, as the following example illustrates.

Example: The two bytes 1100|1101 and 1110|1111 represent four pixels, each differing from its two immediate neighbors by its least significant bit. The four pixels thus have similar colors (or grayscales). Comparing consecutive pixels results in prefixes of 3 or 2, but comparing the 2 bytes produces the prefix 2.

4.22: Using a Hilbert curve produces the 21 runs 5, 1, 2, 1, 2, 7, 3, 1, 2, 1, 5, 1, 2, 2, 11, 7, 2, 1, 1, 1, 6. RLE produces the 27 runs 0, 1, 7, eol, 2, 1, 5, eol, 5, 1, 2, eol, 0, 3, 2, 3, eol, 0, 3, 2, 3, eol, 0, 3, 2, 3, eol, 4, 1, 3, eol, 3, 1, 4, eol.

4.23: The string 2011.

4.24: The four-state WFA is shown in Figure Ans.24. The 14 arcs constructed are 0(0)1, 0(1)1, 0(2)1, 0(3)1, 1(0)2, 1(1)2, 1(2)2, 1(3)2, 2(1)3, 2(2)3, 3(0)3, 3(1)3, 3(2)3 and 3(3)3.

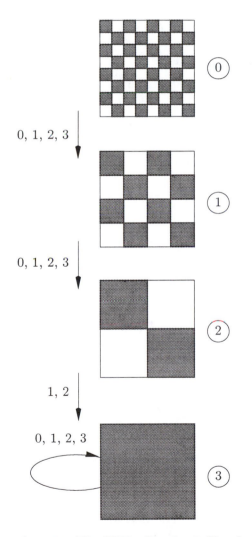

Figure Ans.24: The WFA of an 8 × 8 Chessboard.

4.25: Figure Ans.25 shows the six states and all 21 arcs. The WFA is more complex than pervious ones since this image is less self-similar.

4.26: This is a direct application of Equation (4.13).

$$f(00) = IW_0W_0F$$

$$= (1,0) \begin{pmatrix} 1/2 & 0 \\ 0 & 1 \end{pmatrix} \begin{pmatrix} 1/2 & 0 \\ 0 & 1 \end{pmatrix} \begin{pmatrix} 1/2 \\ 1 \end{pmatrix}$$

$$= (1,0) \begin{pmatrix} 1/4 & 0 \\ 0 & 1 \end{pmatrix} \begin{pmatrix} 1/2 \\ 1 \end{pmatrix}$$

$$= (1/4,0) \begin{pmatrix} 1/2 \\ 1 \end{pmatrix} = 1/8.$$

$$f(01) = IW_0W_1F$$

$$= (1,0) \begin{pmatrix} 1/2 & 0 \\ 0 & 1 \end{pmatrix} \begin{pmatrix} 1/2 & 1/4 \\ 0 & 1 \end{pmatrix} \begin{pmatrix} 1/2 \\ 1 \end{pmatrix}$$

$$= (1,0) \begin{pmatrix} 1/4 & 1/8 \\ 0 & 1 \end{pmatrix} \begin{pmatrix} 1/2 \\ 1 \end{pmatrix}$$

$$= (1/4,1/8) \begin{pmatrix} 1/2 \\ 1 \end{pmatrix} = 1/8 + 1/8 = 2/8.$$

$$f(02) = f(01).$$

4.27: This is again a direct application of Equation (4.13).

$$f(\underbrace{00\ldots0}_{n}) = IW_0W_0\ldots W_0F$$

$$= (1,0) \begin{pmatrix} 1/2 & 0 \\ 0 & 1 \end{pmatrix} \begin{pmatrix} 1/2 & 0 \\ 0 & 1 \end{pmatrix} \cdots \begin{pmatrix} 1/2 \\ 1 \end{pmatrix}$$

$$= (1,0) \begin{pmatrix} (1/2)^n & 0 \\ 0 & 1 \end{pmatrix} \begin{pmatrix} 1/2 \\ 1 \end{pmatrix} = ((1/2)^n,0) \begin{pmatrix} 1/2 \\ 1 \end{pmatrix}$$

$$= (1/2)^{n+1} \to 0.$$

$$f(\underbrace{33\ldots3}_{n}) = IW_3W_3\ldots W_0F$$

$$= (1,0) \begin{pmatrix} 1/2 & 1/2 \\ 0 & 1 \end{pmatrix} \begin{pmatrix} 1/2 & 1/2 \\ 0 & 1 \end{pmatrix} \cdots \begin{pmatrix} 1/2 \\ 1 \end{pmatrix}$$

$$= (1,0) \begin{pmatrix} (1/2)^n & (1/2)^n + (1/2)^{n-1} + \cdots + 1 \\ 0 & 1 \end{pmatrix} \begin{pmatrix} 1/2 \\ 1 \end{pmatrix}$$

$$= ((1/2)^n, (1/2)^n + (1/2)^{n-1} + \cdots + 1) \begin{pmatrix} 1/2 \\ 1 \end{pmatrix}$$

$$= (1/2)^{n+1} + (1/2)^n + (1/2)^{n-1} + \cdots + 1 \to 1.$$

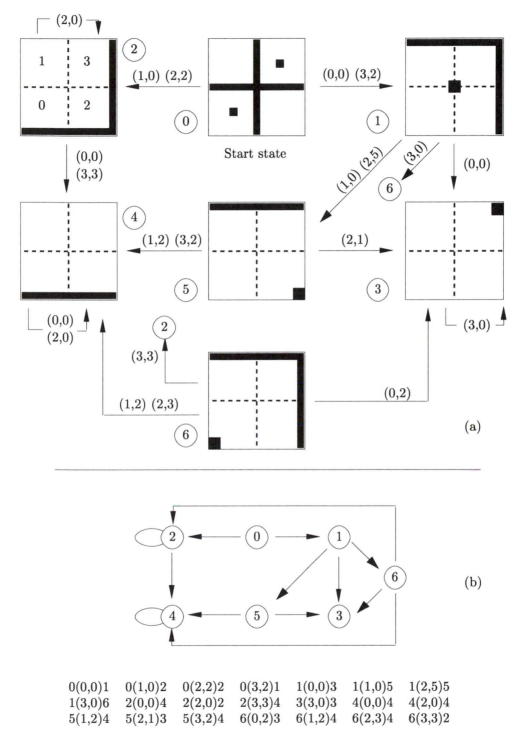

$$
\begin{array}{lllllll}
0(0,0)1 & 0(1,0)2 & 0(2,2)2 & 0(3,2)1 & 1(0,0)3 & 1(1,0)5 & 1(2,5)5 \\
1(3,0)6 & 2(0,0)4 & 2(2,0)2 & 2(3,3)4 & 3(3,0)3 & 4(0,0)4 & 4(2,0)4 \\
5(1,2)4 & 5(2,1)3 & 5(3,2)4 & 6(0,2)3 & 6(1,2)4 & 6(2,3)4 & 6(3,3)2
\end{array}
$$

Figure Ans.25: A WFA for Exercise 4.25.

4.28: Using Equation (4.14) we get

$$\psi_i(00) = (W_0 W_0 F)_i = \begin{pmatrix} 1/2 & 0 \\ 0 & 1 \end{pmatrix} \begin{pmatrix} 1/2 & 0 \\ 0 & 1 \end{pmatrix} \begin{pmatrix} 1/2 \\ 1 \end{pmatrix}_i = \begin{pmatrix} 1/8 \\ 1 \end{pmatrix}_i,$$

so $\psi_0(00) = 1/8$. Also

$$\psi_i(01) = (W_0 W_1 F)_i = \begin{pmatrix} 1/2 & 0 \\ 0 & 1 \end{pmatrix} \begin{pmatrix} 1/2 & 1/4 \\ 0 & 1 \end{pmatrix} \begin{pmatrix} 1/2 \\ 1 \end{pmatrix}_i = \begin{pmatrix} 1/4 \\ 1 \end{pmatrix}_i,$$

so $\psi_0(01) = 1/4$.

4.29: The transformation can be written $(x, y) \to (x, -x + y)$, so $(1, 0) \to (1, -1)$, $(3, 0) \to (3, -3)$, $(1, 1) \to (1, 0)$ and $(3, 1) \to (3, -2)$. The original rectangle is thus transformed into a parallelogram.

4.30: The two sets of transformations produce the same Sierpinski triangle but at different sizes and orientations.

4.31: All three transformations shrink an image to half its original size. In addition, w_2 and w_3 place two copies of the shrunken image at relative displacements of $(0, 1/2)$ and $(1/2, 0)$, as shown in Figure Ans.26. The result is the familiar Sierpinski gasket but in a different orientation.

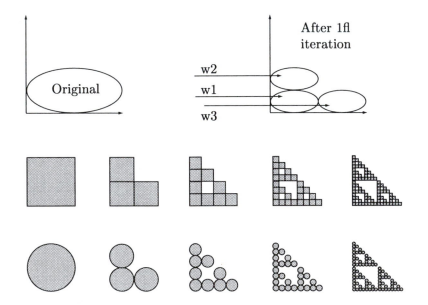

Figure Ans.26: Another Sierpinski Gasket.

4.32: There are $32 \times 32 = 1,024$ ranges and $(256 - 15) \times (256 - 15) = 58,081$ domains. The total number of steps is thus $1,024 \times 58,081 \times 8 = 475,799,552$, still a large number. PIFS is thus computationally intensive.

4.33: Suppose that the image has G levels of gray. A good measure of data loss is the difference between the value of an average decompressed pixel and its correct value, expressed in number of gray levels. For large values of G (hundreds of gray levels) an average difference of $\log_2 G$ gray levels (or fewer) is considered satisfactory.

5.1: Because the original string S can be reconstructed from L but not from F.

5.2: A direct application of equation (5.1) eight more times produces:

```
S[10-1-2]=L[T²[I]]=L[T[T¹[I]]]=L[T[7]]=L[6]=i;
S[10-1-3]=L[T³[I]]=L[T[T²[I]]]=L[T[6]]=L[2]=m;
S[10-1-4]=L[T⁴[I]]=L[T[T³[I]]]=L[T[2]]=L[3]=⊔;
S[10-1-5]=L[T⁵[I]]=L[T[T⁴[I]]]=L[T[3]]=L[0]=s;
S[10-1-6]=L[T⁶[I]]=L[T[T⁵[I]]]=L[T[0]]=L[4]=s;
S[10-1-7]=L[T⁷[I]]=L[T[T⁶[I]]]=L[T[4]]=L[5]=i;
S[10-1-8]=L[T⁸[I]]=L[T[T⁷[I]]]=L[T[5]]=L[1]=w;
S[10-1-9]=L[T⁹[I]]=L[T[T⁸[I]]]=L[T[1]]=L[9]=s;
```

The original string "swiss⊔miss" is indeed reproduced in S from right to left.

5.3: Figure Ans.27 shows the rotations of S and the sorted matrix. The last column, L of Ans.27b happens to be identical to S, so S=L="sssssssssh". Since A=(s,h), a move-to-front compression of L yields C=(1,0,0,0,0,0,0,0,0,1). Since C contains just the two values 0 and 1, they can serve as their own Huffman codes, so the final result is 1000000001, 1 bit per character!

sssssssssh	hssssssss
ssssssshs	shsssssss
sssssshss	sshssssss
ssssshsss	ssshsssss
sssshssss	sssshssss
ssshsssss	ssssshsss
sshssssss	sssssshss
shsssssss	ssssssshs
hssssssss	sssssssssh
(a)	(b)

Figure Ans.27: Permutations of "sssssssssh".

5.4: The encoder starts at T[0], which contains 5. The first element of L is thus the last symbol of permutation 5. This permutation starts at position 5 of S, so its last element is in position 4. The encoder thus has to go through symbols S[T[i-1]] for $i = 0, \ldots, n - 1$, where the notation $i - 1$ should be interpreted cyclically (i.e., $0 - 1$ should be $n - 1$). As each symbol S[T[i-1]] is found, it is compressed using move-to-front. The value of I is the position where T contains 0. In our example, T[8]=0, so I=8.

5.5: The first element of a triplet is the distance between two dictionary entries, the one best matching the content and the one best matching the context. In this case there is no content match, no distance, so any number could serve as the first element, 0 being the best (smallest) choice.

5.6: Because the three lines are sorted in ascending order. The bottom two lines of Table 5.13c are not in sorted order. This is why the "zz...z" part of string S must be preceded and followed by complementary bits.

5.7: The encoder places S between two entries of the sorted associative list and writes the (encoded) index of the entry above or below S on the compressed stream. The fewer the number of entries, the smaller this index, and the better the compression.

5.8: All n_1 bits of string L_1 need be written on the output stream. This already shows that there is going to be no compression. String L_2 consists of n_1/k 1's, so all of it has to be written on the output stream. String L_3 similarly consists of n_1/k^2 1's, and so on. The size of the output stream is thus

$$n_1 + \frac{n_1}{k} + \frac{n_1}{k^2} + \frac{n_1}{k^3} + \cdots + \frac{n_1}{k^m} = n_1 \frac{k^{m+1} - 1}{k^m (k - 1)},$$

for some value of m. The limit of this expression, when $m \to \infty$, is $n_1 k/(k - 1)$. For $k = 2$ this equals $2n_1$. For larger values of k this limit is always between n_1 and $2n_1$.

For the curious reader, here is how the sum above is calculated. Given the series

$$S = \sum_{i=0}^{m} \frac{1}{k^i} = 1 + \frac{1}{k} + \frac{1}{k^2} + \frac{1}{k^3} + \cdots + \frac{1}{k^{m-1}} + \frac{1}{k^m},$$

we multiply both sides by $1/k$

$$\frac{S}{k} = \frac{1}{k} + \frac{1}{k^2} + \frac{1}{k^3} + \cdots + \frac{1}{k^m} + \frac{1}{k^{m+1}},$$

and subtract

$$\frac{S}{k}(k - 1) = \frac{k^{m+1} - 1}{k^{m+1}} \to S = \frac{k^{m+1} - 1}{k^m (k - 1)}.$$

5.9: The input stream consists of:

1. A run of three zero groups, coded as 10|1 since 3 is in second position in class 2.

2. The nonzero group 0100, coded as 111100.

3. Another run of three zero groups, again coded as 10|1.

4. The nonzero group 1000, coded as 01100.

5. A run of four zero groups, coded as 010|0 since 4 is in first position in class 3.

6. 0010, coded as 111110.

7. A run of two zero groups, coded as 10|0.

The output stream is thus the 30-bit string 101111100101011000100111110100.

5.10: The input stream consists of:

1. A run of three zero groups, coded as R_2R_1 or 101|11.

2. The nonzero group 0100, coded as 00100.

3. Another run of three zero groups, again coded as 101|11.

4. The nonzero group 1000, coded as 01000.

5. A run of four zero groups, coded as $R_4 = 1001$.

6. 0010, coded as 00010.

7. A run of two zero groups, coded as $R_2 = 101$.

The output stream is thus the 32-bit string
10111001001011101000100100010101.

5.11: The input stream consists of:

1. A run of three zero groups, coded as F_3 or 1001.

2. The nonzero group 0100, coded as 00100.

3. Another run of three zero groups, again coded as 1001.

4. The nonzero group 1000, coded as 01000.

5. A run of four zero groups, coded as $F_3F_1 = 1001|11$.

6. 0010, coded as 00010.

7. A run of two zero groups, coded as $F_2 = 101$.

The output stream is thus the 32-bit string
10010010010010100010011100010101.

5.12: The LZW method, which starts with the entire alphabet stored at the beginning of its dictionary. However, an adaptive version of LZW can be designed to compress words instead of individual characters.

5.13: Relative values (or *offsets*). Each (x, y) pair may specify the position of a character relative to its predecessor. This results in smaller numbers for the coordinates, and smaller numbers are easier to compress.

5.14: There may be such letters in other, "exotic" alphabets, but a more common example is a rectangular box enclosing text. The four rules comprising such a box should be considered a mark, but the text characters inside the box should be identified as separate marks.

5.15: Because this guarantees that the two probabilities will add up to 1.

5.16: Figure Ans.28 shows how state A feeds into the new state D' which, in turn, feeds into states E and F. Notice how states B and C haven't changed. Since the new state D' is identical to D, it is possible to feed A into either D or D' (cloning can be done in two different but identical ways). The original counts of state D should now be divided between D and D' in proportion to the counts of the transitions A → D and B, C → D.

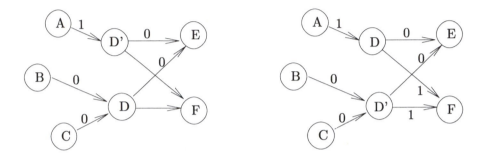

Figure Ans.28: New State D' Cloned.

5.17: Figure Ans.29 shows the new state 6. Its 1-ouptut is identical to that of state 1, and its 0-output is a copy of the 0-ouput of state 3.

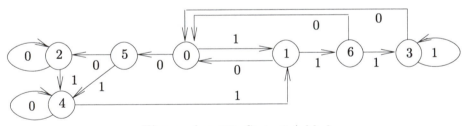

Figure Ans.29: State 6 Added.

5.18: A precise answer requires many experiments with various data files. A little thinking, though, shows that the larger k, the better the initial model that's created when the old one is discarded. Larger values of k thus minimize the loss of compression. However, very large values may produce an initial model that's already large and cannot grow much. The best value for k is therefore one that produces an initial model large enough to provide information about recent correlations in the data, but small enough so it has room to grow before it too has to be discarded.

5.19: Each 0 would result in silence and each sample of 1, in the same tone. The result would be a non-uniform buzz. Such sounds were common on early personal computers.

A.1: It is a combination of "4x and "9, or "49.

C.1: The key is to realize that P_0 is a single point, and P_1 is constructed by connecting nine copies of P_0 with straight segments. Similarly, P_2 consists of nine copies of P_1, in different orientations, connected by segments (the bold segments in Figure Ans.30).

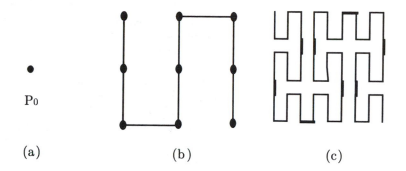

P_0

(a)   (b)   (c)

Figure Ans.30: The First Three Iterations of the Peano Curve.

C.2: Written in binary, the coordinates are $(1101, 0110)$. We repeat four times, each time taking 1 bit from the x coordinate and 1 bit from the y coordinate to form an (x, y) pair. The pairs are 10, 11, 01, 10. The first one yields [from Table C.12(1)] 01. The second pair yields [also from Table C.12(1)] 10. The third pair [from Table C.12(1)] 11, and the last pair [from Table C.12(4)] 01. The result is thus $01|10|11|01 = 109$.

C.3: Table C.2 shows that this traversal is based on the sequence 2114.

C.4: This is straightforward

$$(00, 01, 11, 10) \rightarrow (000, 001, 011, 010)(100, 101, 111, 110)$$
$$\rightarrow (000, 001, 011, 010)(110, 111, 101, 100)$$
$$\rightarrow (000, 001, 011, 010, 110, 111, 101, 100).$$

C.5: The axiom and the production rules stay the same. Only the initial heading and the turn angle change. The initial heading can be either 0 or 90°, and the turn angle either 90° or 270°.

D.1: This is straightforward

$$\mathbf{A + B} = \begin{pmatrix} 8 & 10 & 12 \\ 8 & 10 & 12 \\ 8 & 10 & 12 \end{pmatrix}; \mathbf{A - B} = \begin{pmatrix} -6 & -6 & -6 \\ 0 & 0 & 0 \\ 6 & 6 & 6 \end{pmatrix}; \mathbf{A \times B} = \begin{pmatrix} 18 & 24 & 30 \\ 54 & 69 & 84 \\ 90 & 114 & 138 \end{pmatrix}.$$

D.2: Equation (D.2) gives

$$\mathbf{T}^{-1} = \frac{1}{1 \cdot 1 - 1 \cdot 1} (\cdots),$$

which is undefined. Matrix $\mathbf{T}$ is thus *singular*, it does not have an inverse! This becomes easy to understand when we think of $\mathbf{T}$ as the coefficients matrix of the system of equations (D.1) above. This is a system of three equations in the three unknowns x, y, and z, but its first two equations are contradictory. The first one says that $x - y$ equals 1, while the second one says that the same $x - y$ equals -2. Mathematically, such a system has a singular coefficients matrix.

E.1: A direct check shows that when only a single bit is changed in any of the codewords of $code_2$, the result is not any of the other codewords.

E.2: A direct check shows that $code_4$ has a Hamming distance of 4, which is more than enough to detect all 2-bit errors.

E.3: b_2 is the parity of b_3, b_6, b_7, b_{10}, and b_{11}. b_4 is the parity of b_5, b_6, and b_7. b_8 is the parity of b_9, b_{10}, and b_{11}.

E.4: Table Ans.31 summarizes the definitions of the five parity bits required for this case.

Parity	Data bits																
bits	3	5	6	7	9	10	11	12	13	14	15	17	18	19	20	21
1	x	x		x	x		x		x		x	x		x		x
2	x		x	x		x	x			x	x		x	x		
4		x	x	x				x	x	x	x				x	x
8					x	x	x	x	x	x	x					
16												x	x	x	x	x

Table Ans.31: Hamming Code for $m = 16$.

E.5: It is a variable-size code (Chapter 2). It's easy to see that it satisfies the prefix property.

H.1: Each of the 8 characters of a name can be one of the 26 letters or the ten digits, so the total number of names is $36^8 = 2,821,109,907,456$; close to 3 trillion.

I.1: Such a polynomial depends on three coefficients $\mathbf{A}$, $\mathbf{B}$, and $\mathbf{C}$ that can be considered three-dimensional points, and any three points are on the same plane.

I.2:

$$\begin{aligned}
\mathbf{P}(2/3) &= (0, -9)(2/3)^3 + (-4.5, 13.5)(2/3)^2 + (4.5, -3.5)(2/3) \\
&= (0, -8/3) + (-2, 6) + (3, -7/3) \\
&= (1, 1) = \mathbf{P}_3
\end{aligned}$$

I.3: We use the relations $\sin 30° = \cos 60° = .5$ and the approximation $\cos 30° = \sin 60° \approx .866$. The four points are $\mathbf{P}_1 = (1, 0)$, $\mathbf{P}_2 = (\cos 30°, \sin 30°) = (.866, .5)$, $\mathbf{P}_3 = (.5, .866)$, and $\mathbf{P}_4 = (0, 1)$. The relation $\mathbf{A} = \mathbf{N} \cdot \mathbf{P}$ becomes

$$\begin{pmatrix} \mathbf{a} \\ \mathbf{b} \\ \mathbf{c} \\ \mathbf{d} \end{pmatrix} = \mathbf{A} = \mathbf{N} \cdot \mathbf{P} = \begin{pmatrix} -4.5 & 13.5 & -13.5 & 4.5 \\ 9.0 & -22.5 & 18 & -4.5 \\ -5.5 & 9.0 & -4.5 & 1.0 \\ 1.0 & 0 & 0 & 0 \end{pmatrix} \begin{pmatrix} (1, 0) \\ (.866, .5) \\ (.5, .866) \\ (0, 1) \end{pmatrix}$$

and the solutions are

$$\mathbf{a} = -4.5(1, 0) + 13.5(.866, .5) - 13.5(.5, .866) + 4.5(0, 1) = (.441, -.441),$$
$$\mathbf{b} = 19(1, 0) - 22.5(.866, .5) + 18(.5, .866) - 4.5(0, 1) = (-1.485, -0.162),$$
$$\mathbf{c} = -5.5(1, 0) + 9(.866, .5) - 4.5(.5, .866) + 1(0, 1) = (0.044, 1.603),$$
$$\mathbf{d} = 1(1, 0) - 0(.866, .5) + 0(.5, .866) - 0(0, 1) = (1, 0).$$

The PC is thus $\mathbf{P}(t) = (.441, -.441)t^3 + (-1.485, -0.162)t^2 + (0.044, 1.603)t + (1, 0)$. The midpoint is $\mathbf{P}(.5) = (.7058, .7058)$, only 0.2% away from the midpoint of the arc, which is at $(\cos 45°, \sin 45°) \approx (.7071, .7071)$.

I.4: The new equations are easy enough to set up. Using *Mathematica*™, they are also easy to solve. The following code

```
Solve[{d==p1,
a al^3+b al^2+c al+d==p2,
a be^3+b be^2+c be+d==p3,
a+b+c+d==p4},{a,b,c,d}];
ExpandAll[Simplify[%]]
```

(where al and be stand for α and β, respectively) produces the (messy) solutions

$$\mathbf{a} = -\frac{\mathbf{P}_1}{\alpha\beta} + \frac{\mathbf{P}_2}{-\alpha^2 + \alpha^3 + \alpha\beta - \alpha^2\beta} + \frac{\mathbf{P}_3}{\alpha\beta - \beta^2 - \alpha\beta^2 + \beta^3} + \frac{\mathbf{P}_4}{1 - \alpha - \beta + \alpha\beta}$$

$$\mathbf{b} = \mathbf{P}_1\left(-\alpha + \alpha^3 + \beta - \alpha^3\beta - \beta^3 + \alpha\beta^3\right)/\gamma + \mathbf{P}_2\left(-\beta + \beta^3\right)/\gamma$$
$$\quad + \mathbf{P}_3\left(\alpha - \alpha^3\right)/\gamma + \mathbf{P}_4\left(\alpha^3\beta - \alpha\beta^3\right)/\gamma$$

$$\mathbf{c} = -\mathbf{P}_1\left(1 + \frac{1}{\alpha} + \frac{1}{\beta}\right) + \frac{\beta\mathbf{P}_2}{-\alpha^2 + \alpha^3 + \alpha\beta - \alpha^2\beta}$$

$$\quad + \frac{\alpha\mathbf{P}_3}{\alpha\beta - \beta^2 - \alpha\beta^2 + \beta^3} + \frac{\alpha\beta\mathbf{P}_4}{1 - \alpha - \beta + \alpha\beta}$$

$$\mathbf{d} = \mathbf{P}_1.$$

where $\gamma = (-1 + \alpha)\alpha(-1 + \beta)\beta(-\alpha + \beta)$.

From here, the basis matrix immediately follows

$$\begin{pmatrix} -\frac{1}{\alpha\beta} & \frac{1}{-\alpha^2 + \alpha^3\alpha\beta - \alpha^2\beta} & \frac{1}{\alpha\beta - \beta^2 - \alpha\beta^2 + \beta^3} & \frac{1}{1 - \alpha - \beta + \alpha\beta} \\ \frac{-\alpha + \alpha^3 + \beta - \alpha^3\beta - \beta^3 + \alpha\beta^3}{\gamma} & \frac{-\beta + \beta^3}{\gamma} & \frac{\alpha - \alpha^3}{\gamma} & \frac{\alpha^3\beta - \alpha\beta^3}{\gamma} \\ -\left(1 + \frac{1}{\alpha} + \frac{1}{\beta}\right) & \frac{\beta}{-\alpha^2 + \alpha^3 + \alpha\beta - \alpha^2\beta} & \frac{\alpha}{\alpha\beta - \beta^2 - \alpha\beta^2 + \beta^3} & \frac{\alpha\beta}{1 - \alpha - \beta + \alpha\beta} \\ 1 & 0 & 0 & 0 \end{pmatrix}$$

A direct check, again using *Mathematica*, for $\alpha = 1/3$ and $\beta = 2/3$, produces matrix **N** of Equation (I.4).

I.5:   The missing points will have to be estimated by interpolation or extrapolation from the known points before our method can be applied. Obviously, the fewer points are known, the worse the final interpolation. Note that 16 points are necessary since a bicubic polynomial has 16 coefficients.

> Kneading is difficult to describe in words, but many cookbooks have pictures. The idea is to exercise the dough and work some more flour into it.
>
> Harry S. Delugach

Glossary

ACB

A new, very efficient text compression method by G. Buyanovsky (Section 5.3). It uses a dictionary with unbounded contexts and contents to select the context that best matches the search buffer and the content that best matches the look-ahead buffer.

Adaptive Compression

A compression method that modifies its operations and/or its parameters according to the new data read from the input stream. Examples are the adaptive Huffman method of Section 2.9 and the dictionary-based methods of Chapter 3. (See also Semi-adaptive compression and Locally adaptive compression.)

Affine Transformations

Two-dimensional or three-dimensional geometric transformations, such as scaling, reflection, rotation, and translation, that preserve parallel lines (Section 4.15.1).

Alphabet

The set of all possible symbols in the input stream. In text compression the alphabet is normally the set of 128 ASCII codes. In image compression it is the set of values a pixel can take (2, 16, 256, or anything else). (See also Symbol.)

Archive

A set of one or more files combined into one file (Section 3.19). The individual members of an archive may be compressed. An archive provides a convenient way of transferring or storing groups of related files. (See also ARC, ARJ.)

ARC

A compression/archival/cataloging program written by Robert A. Freed in the mid 1980s (Section 3.19). It offers good compression and the ability to combine several files into an archive. (See also Archive, ARJ.)

Arithmetic Coding

A statistical compression method (Section 2.14) that assigns one (normally long) code to the entire input stream, instead of assigning codes to the individual symbols. The method reads the input stream symbol by symbol and appends more bits to the code each time a symbol is input and processed. Arithmetic coding is slow but it compresses at or close to the entropy, even when the symbol probabilities are skewed. (See also Model of compression, Statistical methods.)

ARJ

A free compression/archiving utility for MS/DOS (Section 3.20), written by Robert K. Jung to compete with ARC and the various PK utilities. (See also Archive, ARC.)

ASCII Code

The standard character code on all modern computers. ASCII stands for American Standard Code for Information Interchange. It is a $1 + 7$-bit code, meaning 1 parity bit and 7 data bits per symbol. As a result, 128 symbols can be coded (Appendix A). They include the upper- and lower-case letters, the ten digits, some punctuation marks, and control characters.

BinHex

A file format for safe file transfers, designed by Yves Lempereur for use on the Macintosh computer (Section 1.4.2).

Bits/char

Bits per character. A measure of the performance in text compression. Also a measure of entropy.

Bits/symbol

Bits per symbol. A general measure of compression performance.

Block Coding

A general term for image compression methods that work by breaking the image into small blocks of pixels, and encoding each block separately. JPEG (Chapter 4) is a good example, since it processes blocks of 8×8 pixels.

Burrows-Wheeler Method

This method (Section 5.1) prepares a string of data for later compression. The compression itself is done using move-to-front method (Section 1.5), perhaps in combination with RLE. The BW method converts a string S to another string L that satisfies two conditions:

1. Any region of L will tend to have a concentration of just a few symbols.

2. It is possible to reconstruct the original string S from L (a little more data may be needed for the reconstruction, in addition to L, but not much).

CALIC

A context-based, lossless image compression method (Section 4.10) whose two main features are (1) the use of three passes in order to achieve symmetric contexts and (2) context quantization, to significantly reduce the number of possible contexts without degrading compression performance.

CCITT

The International Telegraph and Telephone Consultative Committee (Comité Consultatif International de télégraphie et Téléphonie). The old name of the ITU, the International Telecommunications Union. A United Nations organization responsible for developing and recommending standards for data communications (not just compression). (See also ITU.)

CIE

CIE is an abbreviation for Commission Internationale de l'Éclairage (The International Committee on Illumination). This is the main international organization devoted to light and color. It is responsible for developing standards and definitions in this area. (See Luminance.)

Circular Queue

A basic data structure (Section 3.2.1) that moves data along an array in circular fashion, updating two pointers to point to the start and end of the data in the array.

Codes

A code is a symbol that stands for another symbol. In computer and telecommunications applications, codes are virtually always binary numbers. The ASCII code is the de-facto standard, but the older EBCDIC is still used on some old IBM computers. (See also ASCII.)

Compress

In the large UNIX world, `compress` is used virtually exclusively to compress data. This utility uses LZW with a growing dictionary. It starts with a small dictionary of just 512 entries and doubles its size each time it fills up, until it reaches 64K bytes (Section 3.15).

Compression Factor

The inverse of compression ratio. It is defined as

$$\text{Compression factor} = \frac{\text{size of the input stream}}{\text{size of the output stream}}.$$

Values > 1 mean compression and values < 1, expansion. (See also Compression ratio.)

Compression Gain

This measure is defined by

$$100 \log_e \frac{\text{reference size}}{\text{compressed size}}.$$

Where the reference size is either the size of the input stream or the size of the compressed stream produced by some standard lossless compression method.

Compression Ratio

One of several quantities that are commonly used to express the efficiency of a compression method. It is the ratio

$$\text{Compression ratio} = \frac{\text{size of the output stream}}{\text{size of the input stream}}.$$

A value of 0.6 means that the data occupies 60% of its original size after compression. Values > 1 mean an output stream bigger than the input stream (negative compression).

Sometimes the quantity $100 \times (1 - \text{compression ratio})$ is used to express the quality of compression. A value of 60 means that the output stream occupies 40% of its original size (or that the compression has resulted in a savings of 60%). (See also Compression factor.)

Context

The N symbols preceding the next symbol. A context-based model uses context to assign probabilities to symbols.

CRC

CRC stands for *Cyclical Redundancy Check* (or *Cyclical Redundancy Code*). It is a rule that shows how to obtain vertical check bits from all the bits of a data stream (Section 3.22). The idea is to generate a code that depends on all the bits of the data stream, and use it to detect errors (bad bits) when the data is transmitted (or when it is strored and then retrieved).

Decoder

A decompression program (or algorithm).

Dictionary-Based Compression

Compression methods (Chapter 3) that save pieces of the data in a "dictionary" data structure (normally a tree). If a string of new data is identical to a piece already saved in the dictionary, a pointer to that piece is output to the compressed stream. (See also LZ methods.)

Differential Image Compression

A lossless image compression method where each pixel p is compared to a *reference pixel*, which is one of its immediate neighbors, and is then encoded in two parts—a prefix, which is the number of most significant bits of p that are identical to those of the reference pixel—and a suffix, which is (almost all) the remaining least significant bits of p.

Digram

A pair of consecutive symbols.

Discrete Cosine Transform

A variant of the discrete Fourier transform (DFT) that produces just real numbers. The DCT (Section 4.2.2) transforms a set of data points from their normal spatial representation (as points in two or three dimensions) to their frequency domain. The DCT and its inverse, the IDCT, are used in JPEG (Section 4.2) to reduce the image size without distorting it much, by deleting the high-frequency parts of an image. (See also Fourier transform.)

Encoder

A compression program (or algorithm).

Entropy

The entropy of a single symbol a_i is defined (in Section 2.1) as $-P_i \log_2 P_i$ where P_i is the probability of occurrence of a_i in the data. The entropy of a_i is the smallest number of bits needed, on the average, to represent symbol a_i. Claude Shannon, the creator of information theory, coined the term *entropy* in 1948 since this term is used in thermodynamics to indicate the amount of disorder in a physical system. (See also Information theory.)

Error-Correcting Codes

The opposite of data compression, these codes (Appendix E) detect and correct errors in digital data by increasing the redundancy of the data. They use check bits or parity bits, and are sometimes designed with the help of generating polynomials.

EXE Compressor

A compression program for compressing EXE files on the PC. Such a compressed file can be decompressed and executed with one command. The original EXE compressor is LZEXE, by Fabrice Bellard (Section 3.21).

Facsimile Compression

Transferring a typical page between two fax machines can take up to 10–11 minutes without compression, This is why the ITU has developed several standards for compression of facsimile data. The current standards (Section 2.13) are T4 (Group 3) and T6 (Group 4).

FELICS

A Fast, Efficient, Lossless Image Compression method designed for grayscale images that competes with the lossless mode of JPEG. The principle is to code each pixel with a variable-size code based on the values of two of its previously seen neighbor pixels. Both the unary code and the Golomb code are used. There is also a progressive version of FELICS (Section 4.7). (See also Progressive FELICS.)

Fourier Transform

A mathematical transformation that produces the frequency components of a function (Appendix F). The Fourier transform shows how a periodic function can be written as the sum of sines and cosines, thereby showing explicitly the frequencies "hidden" in the original representation of the function. (See also Discrete cosine transform.)

GIF

The name stands for Graphics Interchange Format. This format (Section 3.16) was developed by Compuserve Information Services in 1987 as an efficient, compressed graphics file format that allows for images to be sent between different computers. The original version of GIF is known as GIF 87a. The current standard is GIF 89a.

Golomb Code

A way to generate a variable-size code for integers n (Section 2.4). It depends on the choice of a parameter b and is created in two steps.

1. Compute the two quantities

$$q = \left\lfloor \frac{n-1}{b} \right\rfloor ; \qquad r = n - qb - 1;$$

2. Construct the Golomb code of n in two parts; the first is the value of $q+1$, coded in unary (exercise 2.5), and the second, the binary value of r coded in either $\lfloor \log_2 b \rfloor$ bits (for the small remainders) or in $\lceil \log_2 b \rceil$ bits (for the large ones). (See also Unary code.)

GZip

A popular program that implements the so-called "deflation" algorithm (Section 3.18) that uses a variation of LZ77 combined with static Huffman coding. It uses a 32Kbyte-long sliding dictionary, and a look-ahead buffer of 258 bytes. When a string is not found in the dictionary it is emitted as a sequence of literal bytes. (See also Zip.)

Hamming codes

A type of error-correcting code for 1-bit errors, where it is easy to generate the required parity bits.

Huffman Coding

A commonly used method for data compression (Section 2.8). It assigns a set of "best" variable-size codes to a set of symbols based on their probabilities. It serves as the basis for several popular programs used on personal computers. Some of them use just the Huffman method while others use it as one step in a multi-step compression process. The Huffman method is somewhat similar to the Shannon-Fano method. It generally produces better codes and, like the Shannon-Fano method, it produces best code when the probabilities of the symbols are negative powers of 2. The main difference between the two methods is that Shannon-Fano constructs its codes top to bottom (from the leftmost to the rightmost bits), while Huffman constructs a code tree from the bottom up (builds the codes from right to left). (See also Shannon-Fano coding, Statistical methods.)

Information Theory

A mathematical theory that quantifies information. It shows how to measure information, so that one can answer the question: How much information is included in this piece of data? with a precise number! Information theory is the creation, in 1948, of Claude Shannon of Bell labs. (See also Entropy.)

ISO

The International Standards Organization. This is one of the organizations responsible for developing standards. Among other things it is responsible (together with the ITU) for the JPEG and MPEG compression standards. (See also ITU, CCITT and MPEG.)

Iterated Function Systems (IFS)

An image compressed by IFS is uniquely defined by a few affine transformations (Section 4.15.1). The only rule is that the scale factors of these transformations must be < 1 (shrinking). The image is saved in the output stream by writing the sets of six numbers that define each transformation. (See also Affine transformations, Resolution Independent Compression.)

ITU

The International Telecommunications Union; the new name of the CCITT. A United Nations organization responsible for developing and recommending standards for data communications (not just compression). (See also CCITT.)

JBIG

A special-purpose compression method (Section 4.4) developed specifically for progressive compression of bi-level images. The name JBIG stands for Joint Bi-Level Image Processing Group. This is a group of experts from several international organizations, formed in 1988 to recommend such a standard. JBIG uses multiple arithmetic coding and a resolution-reduction technique to achieve its goals.

JFIF

The full name of this method is JPEG File Interchange Format. It is a graphics file format (Section 4.2.8) that makes it possible to exchange JPEG-compressed images between different computers. The main features of JFIF are the use of the YCbCr triple-component color space for color images (only one component for gray scale images) and the use of a *marker* to specify features missing from JPEG, such as image resolution, aspect ratio, and features that are application-specific.

JPEG

A sophisticated lossy compression method (Section 4.2) for color or gray-scale still images (not movies). It also works best on continuous-tone images, where adjacent pixels have similar colors. One advantage of JPEG is the use of many parameters, allowing the user to adjust the amount of the data lost (and thus also the compression ratio) over a very wide range. There are two main modes: lossy (also called baseline) and lossless (which typically gives a 2:1 compression ratio). Most implementations support just the lossy mode. This mode includes progressive and hierarchical coding.

The main idea behind JPEG is that an image exists for people to look at, so when the image is compressed, it is okay to lose image features for which the human eye is not sensitive.

The name JPEG is an acronym that stands for Joint Photographic Experts Group. This was a joint effort by the CCITT and the ISO that started in June 1987. The JPEG standard has proved successful and has become widely used for image presentation, especially in Web pages. (See also MPEG.)

Kraft-MacMillan Inequality

A relation (Section 2.5) that says something about unambiguous variable-size codes. Its first part states: given an unambiguous variable-size code, with n codes of sizes L_i, then

$$\sum_{i=1}^{n} 2^{-L_i} \leq 1.$$

The second part states the opposite, namely, given a set of n positive integers $(L_1, L_2, \ldots, L_n)$ that satisfy Equation (2.1), there exists an unambiguous variable-size code such that L_i are the sizes of its individual codes. Together, both parts say that a code is unambiguous if and only if it satisfies relation (2.1).

L Systems

Lindenmayer Systems (or L-systems for short) were developed by the biologist Aristid Lindenmayer in 1968 as a tool [Lindenmayer 68] to describe the morphology of plants. They were initially used in computer science, in the 1970s, as a tool to define formal languages, but have become really popular only after 1984, when it became apparent that they can be used to draw many types of fractals, in addition to their use in botany (Section C.5).

LHArc

This method, as well as with ICE and LHA (Section 3.20), is by Haruyasu Yoshizaki. These methods use adaptive Huffman coding with features drawn from LZSS.

Locally Adaptive Compression

A compression method that adapts itself to local conditions in the input stream, and changes this adaptation as it moves from area to area in the input. An example is the move-to-front method method of Section 1.5. (See also Adaptive compression, Semi-adaptive compression.)

Luminance

This quantity is defined by the CIE (Section 4.2.1) as radiant power weighted by a spectral sensitivity function that's characteristic of vision. (See also CIE.)

LZ Methods

All dictionary-based compression methods are based on the work of J. Ziv and A. Lempel, published in 1977 and 1978. Today, these are called LZ77 and LZ78 methods, respectively. Their ideas have been a source of inspiration to many researchers who generalized, improved, and combined them with RLE and statistical methods to form many commonly used, adaptive compression methods, for text, images, and sound. (See also Dictionary-based compression, Sliding-window compression.)

LZAP

The LZAP method (Section 3.11) is an LZW variant based on the idea: instead of just concatenating the last two phrases and placing the result in the dictionary, place all prefixes of the concatenation in the dictionary. The AP stands for All Prefixes.

LZFG

This is the name of several related methods (Section 3.6) that are hybrids of LZ77 and LZ78. They were developed by Edward Fiala and Daniel Greene. All these methods are based on the following scheme. The encoder produces a compressed file with tokens and literals (raw ASCII codes) intermixed. There are two types of tokens, a *literal* and a *copy*. A literal token indicates that a string of literals follow; a copy token points to a string previously seen in the data. (See also LZ methods.)

LZMW

A variant of LZW, the LZMW method (Section 3.10) works by: instead of adding I plus one character of the next phrase to the dictionary, add I plus the entire next phrase to the dictionary. (See also LZW.)

LZP

An LZ77 variant developed by C. Bloom (Section 3.13). It is based on the principle of context prediction that says "if a certain string 'abcde' has appeared in the input stream in the past and was followed by 'fg...', then when 'abcde' appears again in the input stream, there is a good chance that it will be followed by the same 'fg...'." (See also Context.)

LZSS

This version of LZ77 (Section 3.3) was developed by Storer and Szymanski in 1982 [Storer 82]. It improves on the basic LZ77 in three ways: (1) it holds the look-ahead buffer in a circular queue, (2) it holds the search buffer (the dictionary) in a binary search tree, and (3) it creates tokens with two fields instead of three.

LZW

This is a popular variant of LZ78, developed by T. Welch in 1984 (Section 3.9). Its main feature is eliminating the second field of a token. An LZW token consists of just a pointer to the dictionary. As a result, such a token always encodes a string of more than one symbol.

LZY

LZY (Section 3.12) is an LZW variant that adds one dictionary string per input character and increments strings by one character at a time.

MLP

A progressive compression method for grayscale images. An image is compressed in levels. A pixel is predicted by a symmetric pattern of its neighbors from preceding levels, and the prediction error is arithmetically encoded. The Laplace distribution is used to estimate the probability of the error. (See also Progressive FELICS.)

MNP5, MNP7

These have been developed by Microcom, Inc., a maker of modems, for use in its modems. MNP5 (Section 2.10) is a two-stage process that starts with run-length encoding, followed by adaptive frequency encoding. MNP7 (Section 2.11) combines run-length encoding with a two-dimensional variant of adaptive Huffman coding.

Model of Compression

A model is a method to "predict" (to assign probabilities to) the data to be compressed. This concept is important in statistical data compression. When a statistical method is used, a model for the data has to be constructed before compression can begin. A simple model can be built by reading the entire input stream, counting the number of times each symbol appears (its frequency of occurrence), and computing the probability of occurrence of each symbol. The data stream is then input again, symbol by symbol, and is compressed using the information in the probability model. (See also Statistical methods.)

One feature of arithmetic coding is that it is easy to separate the statistical model (the table with frequencies and probabilities) from the encoding and decoding operations. It is easy to encode, e.g., the first half of a data stream using one model, and the second half using another model.

Move-to-Front Coding

The basic idea behind this method (Section 1.5) is to maintain the alphabet A of symbols as a list where frequently occurring symbols are located near the front. A symbol s is encoded as the number of symbols that precede it in this list. After symbol s is encoded, it is moved to the front of list A.

MPEG

A standard for representing movies in compressed form. The name MPEG stands for Moving Pictures Experts Group, a working group of the ISO still at work on this standard. (See also ISO, JPEG.)

Multiresolution Image

A compressed image that may be decompressed at any resolutions. (See also Resolution Independent Compression, Iterated Function Systems, WFA.)

Phrase

A piece of data placed in a dictionary to be used in compressing future data. The concept of phrase is central in dictionary-based data compression methods since the success of such a method depends a lot on how it selects phrases to be saved in its dictionary. (See also Dictionary-based compression, LZ methods.)

PKZip

A compression program for MS/DOS (Section 3.19), written by Phil Katz who has founded the PKWare company ("http://www.pkware.com"), which also markets the PKunzip, PKlite, and PKArc software.

Prediction

Assigning probabilities to symbols. (See also PPM.)

Prefix Property

One of the principles of variable-size codes. It states: once a certain bit pattern has been assigned as the code of a symbol, no other codes should start with that pattern (the pattern cannot be the *prefix* of any other code). Once the string 1, e.g., is assigned as the code of a_1, no other codes should start with 1 (i.e., they all have to start with 0). Once 01, e.g., is assigned as the code of a_2, no other codes can start with 01 (they all should start with 00). (See also Variable-size codes, Statistical methods.)

Progressive FELICS

A progressive version of FELICS where pixels are encoded in levels. Each level doubles the number of pixels encoded. To decide what pixels are included in a certain level, the preceding level can conceptually be rotated 45° and scaled by $\sqrt{2}$ in both dimensions. (See also FELICS, MLP, Progressive image compression.)

Progressive Image Compression

An image compression method where compressed stream is made up of "layers," such that each layer contains more detail of the image. The decoder can very quickly display the entire image in a low-quality format and then improve the display quality as more and more layers are being read and decompressed. A user watching the decompressed image develop on the screen can normally recognize most of the image features after only 5–10% of it have been decompressed. Improving image quality over time can be done by: (1) sharpening it, (2) adding colors, or (3) adding resolution. (See also Progressive FELICS, MLP, JBIG.)

PPM

A compression method that assigns probabilities to symbols based on the context (long or short) in which they appear. (See also Prediction, PPPM.)

PPPM

A lossless compression method for grayscale (and color) images that assigns probabilities to symbols based on the Laplace distribution, like MLP. Different contexts of a pixel are examined and their statistics used to select the mean and variance for a particular Laplace distribution. (See also Prediction, PPM, MLP.)

QIC-122 Compression

An LZ77 variant that has been developed by QIC for text compression on 1/4-inch data cartridge tape drives.

Quadtrees

This is a data compression method for bitmap images. A quadtree (Section 4.12) is a tree where each leaf corresponds to a uniform part of the image (a quadrant, subquadrant or a single pixel) and each interior node has exactly four children.

Relative Encoding

A variant of RLE, sometimes called *differencing* (Section 1.3.1). It is used in cases where the data to be compressed consists of a string of numbers that don't differ by much, or in cases where it consists of strings that are similar to each other. The principle of relative encoding is to send the first data item a_1 followed by the differences $a_{i+1} - a_i$. (See also RLE.)

Reliability

Variable-size codes and other codes are vulnerable to errors. In cases where reliable transmission of codes is important, the codes can be made more reliable by adding check bits, parity bits, or CRC (Section 2.12 and Appendix E). Notice that reliability is, in a sense, the opposite of data compression since it is done by increasing redundancy. (See also CRC.)

Resolution Independent Compression

An image compression method that does not depend on the resolution of the specific image being compressed. The image can be decompresed at any resolution. (See also Multiresolution, Iterated Function Systems, WFA.)

RLE

A general name for methods that compress data by replacing a run length of identical symbols with one code, or token, containing the symbol and the length of the run. RLE sometimes serves as one step in a multi-step statistical or dictionary-based method. (See also Relative encoding.)

Semi-Adaptive Compression

A compression method that uses a two-pass algorithm, where the first pass reads the input stream to collect statistics on the data to be compressed, and the second pass does the actual compressing. The statistics (model) is included in the compressed stream. (See also Adaptive compression, Locally Adaptive compression.)

Shannon-Fano Coding

An early algorithm for finding a minimum-length variable-size code given the probabilities of all the symbols in the data (Section 2.6). This method was later superseded by the Huffman method. (See also Statistical methods, Huffman coding.)

Sliding Window Compression

The LZ77 method (Section 3.2) uses part of the previously seen input stream as the dictionary. The encoder maintains a window to the input stream, and shifts the input in that window from right to left as strings of symbols are being encoded. The method is thus based on a *sliding window*. (See also LZ methods.)

Space-Filling Curves

A space-filling curve (Section 4.13) is a function $\mathbf{P}(t)$ that goes through every point in a given two-dimensional area, normally the unit square. Such curves are defined recursively and are used in image compression.

Sparse Strings

Regardless of what the input data represents, text, binary, images, or anything else, we can think of the input stream as a string of bits. If most of the bits are zeros, the string is called *sparse*. Sparse strings can be compressed very efficiently by specially designed methods (Section 5.4).

Statistical Methods

These methods (Chapter 2) work by assigning variable-size codes to symbols in the data, with the shorter codes assigned to symbols or groups of symbols that appear more often in the data (have a higher probability of occurrence). (See also Variable-size codes, Prefix property, Shannon-Fano coding, Huffman coding, and Arithmetic coding.)

String Compression

In general, compression methods based on strings of symbols can be more efficient than methods that compress individual symbols (Section 3.1).

Symbol

The smallest unit of the data to be compressed. A symbol is normally a byte but may also be one bit, a trit $\{0, 1, 2\}$, or anything else. (See also Alphabet.)

Symbol Ranking

A context-based method (Section 5.2) where the context C of the current symbol S (the N symbols preceding S) is used to prepare a list of symbols that are likely to follow C. The list is arranged from most likely to least likely. The position of S in this list (position numbering starts from 0) is then written by the encoder, after being suitably encoded, on the output stream.

TAR

The standard UNIX archiver. The name TAR stands for Tape ARchive. It groups a number of files into one file without compression. After being compressed by the UNIX `compress` program, a TAR file gets an extension name of TAR.Z.

Textual Image Compression

A compression method for hard copy documents containing printed or typed (but not handwritten) text. The text can be in many fonts and may consist of music notes, hieroglyphs, or any symbols. Pattern recognition techniques are used to recognize text characters that are identical or at least similar. One copy of each group of identical characters is kept in a library. Any leftover material is considered residue. The method uses different compression techniques for the symbols and the residue. It includes a lossy option where the residue is ignored.

Token

A unit of data written on the compressed stream by some compression algorithms. A token is made of several fields that may have either fixed or variable sizes.

Unary Code

A way to generate variable-size codes in one step. The unary code of the non-negative integer n is defined (Section 2.3.1) as $n - 1$ ones followed by one zero (Table 2.3). There is also a general unary code. (See also Golomb code.)

V.42bis Protocol

This is a standard, published by the ITU-T (page 62) for use in fast modems. It is based on the existing V.32bis protocol and is supposed to be used for fast transmission rates, up to 57.6K baud. The standard contains specifications for data compression and error-correction, but only the former is discussed, in Section 3.17.

V.42bis specifies two modes: a *transparent* mode, where no compression is used, and a *compressed* mode using an LZW variant. The former is used for data streams that don't compress well, and may even cause expansion. A good example is an already-compressed file. Such a file looks like random data, it does not have any repetitive patterns, and trying to compress it with LZW will fill up the dictionary with short, two-symbol phrases.

Variable-Size Codes

These are used by statistical methods. Such codes should satisfy the prefix property (Section 2.2) and should be assigned to symbols based on their probabilities. (See also Prefix property, Statistical methods.)

WFA

A weighted finite automaton (WFA) is constructed from a bi-level image in a process similar to constructing a quadtree. The WFA becomes the compressed image. This method uses the fact that most images of interest have a certain amount of self-similarity (i.e., parts of the image are similar, up to size, to the entire image or to other parts). The method is lossless but can have a lossy option where a user-controlled parameter indicates the amount of loss permitted. This is a very efficient method that can be extended to grayscale images. (See also Quadtrees, Resolution Independent Compression.)

Zero-Probability Problem

When samples of data are read and analysed in order to generate a statistical model of the data, certain contexts may not appear, leaving entries with zero counts and thus zero probability in the frequency table. Any compression method requires that such entries be somehow assigned non-zero probabilities.

Zip

A popular program that implements the so-called "deflation" algorithm (Section 3.18) that uses a variation of LZ77 combined with static Huffman coding. It uses a 32Kbyte-long sliding dictionary, and a look-ahead buffer of 258 bytes. When a string is not found in the dictionary it is emitted as a sequence of literal bytes. (See also Gzip.)

> Lossy rag.
> Anagram of "glossary"

Index

How did he bank it up, swank it up,
the whaler in the punt, a guinea by a
groat, his index on the balance and such
wealth into the bargain, with the boguey
which he snatched in the baggage coach
ahead?

    —James Joyce, *Finnegans Wake* (1920)

Colophon

This book was designed by the author and was typeset by him with the TEX typesetting system developed by D. Knuth. The text and tables were done with Textures, a commercial TEX implementation for the Macintosh. The diagrams were done with Superpaint and Adobe Illustrator, also on the Macintosh computer. The following features illustrate the amount of work that went into it:

- The book contains about 215,600 words, consisting of about 1,226,800 characters. However, the size of the auxiliary material collected in the author's computer while working on the book is about 10 times bigger than the entire book. This material includes articles and source codes available on the internet, as well as many pages of information collected from various sources and scanned into image files.

- The text is typeset mainly in font cmr10, but 30 other fonts were used.

- The raw index file contained 1650 items.

- There are about 430 cross-references in the book.

- The following table shows some results of compressing a file containing the entire text of the book. The original file size is 1,227,187 bytes.

Computer	Program	Compressed	Ratio
Macintosh	Compactor	445,174	.36
	Stuffit Light	400,536	.33
	UNIX Compress	527,671	.43
	Disk Doubler	748,360	.61
	Zip (deflate)	390,787	.32
	GnuZip	392,432	.32
UNIX	compress	527,295	.43
PC	Winzip (Packed mode)	390,028	.32
	Winzip (Normal mode)	395,756	.32

Necessity is the mother of compression.

Aesop (paraphrased)